The Sundance Reader

The Sundance Reader

SIXTH EDITION

MARK CONNELLY

MILWAUKEE AREA TECHNICAL COLLEGE

Australia • Brazil • Japan • Korea • Mexico • Singapore • Spain • United Kingdom • United States

WADSWORTH
CENGAGE Learning™

The Sundance Reader,
Sixth Edition
Mark Connelly

Senior Publisher: Lyn Uhl

Acquiring Sponsoring Editor:
Kate Derrick

Development Editor: Kathy
Sands-Boehmer

Editorial Assistant: Elizabeth
Reny

Media Editor: Janine Tangney

Marketing Manager: Stacey
Purviance

Marketing Coordinator: Ryan
Ahern

Content Project Manager:
Aimee Chevrette Bear

Art Director: Jill Ort

Print Buyer: Betsy Donaghey

Rights Acquisition Specialist,
Text: Katie Huha

Rights Acquisition Specialist,
Images: Jennifer Meyer Dare

Production Service: MPS Limited, a Macmillan Company

Cover Designer: Sarah Bishins

Compositor: MPS Limited, a
Macmillan Company

© 2012 Wadsworth, Cengage Learning

For product information and technology assistance, contact us at **Cengage Learning Academic Resource Center,**
1-800-423-0563

For permission to use material from this text or product, submit all requests online at **www.cengage.com/permissions.**
Further permissions questions can be e-mailed to
permissionrequest@cengage.com.

Library of Congress Control Number: 2010935206

ISBN-13: 978-0-4959-1294-1

ISBN-10: 0-4959-1294-8

Wadsworth Cengage Learning
25 Thomson Place
Boston, MA 02210-1202
USA

Cengage Learning products are represented in Canada by Nelson Education, Ltd.

For your course and learning solutions, visit
academic.cengage.com.

Purchase any of our products at your local college store or at our preferred online store **www.ichapters.com.**

Printed in the U.S.A.

1 2 3 4 5 6 7 12 11 10

To Stanley Felber

CONTENTS

Thematic Contents   xxv

Preface   xxxiii

1   The Writing Context   **1**

How We Write   1

The Writer   3
    The Writer's Purpose   3
    A Note About Modes   5
    The Writer's Role   6

The Reader   7
    Individual Readers   8
    Extended Readerships   8
    The Perceptual World   9

The Discipline   11
    Writing Contexts   13

2   The Writing Process   **15**

Critical Thinking   15
    Avoiding Errors in Critical Thinking   18

Strategies for Enhancing Critical Thinking   21
    Prewriting   23
    Moving from Topic to Thesis   27
    Elements of a Thesis Statement   28
    Supporting the Thesis   29
    Developing Outlines   30

How to Write an Essay   33

Strategies for Creating a Composing Style   34

Writing the Whole Composition   35
   Prewriting   35
   Planning   36
   First Draft with Revision Notes   36
   Revised Draft with Instructor's Annotations   37
   Final Draft   39

Writing on a Computer   41

Strategies for Writing on a Computer   41

Collaborative Writing   42
   Strategies for Collaborative Writing   43

Writer's Block   44
   Strategies for Overcoming Writer's Block   44
   Avoid Plagiarism   46
   Strategies for Avoiding Plagiarism   47

3   Critical Reading   49

Reading Critically   49

Strategies for Critical Reading   49
   First Reading   50
   Second Reading   50
   Before Class Discussion   52
   Above All, Read to Learn   52

Cornel West   *Black Political Leadership* (annotated)   53

   Using *The Sundance Reader*   55

Analyzing Visual Images   56
   Photographs, Film, and Video   57
   Perspective and Contrast   57
   Context   59
   Visual Connotations   60
   Timing and Duplication   61
   Manipulating Images   61
   Gender and Cultural Issues   62
   Perception and Analysis   64

Strategies for Analyzing Visual Images   64

4   Narration: Relating Events   **65**

What Is Narration?   65
  The Writer's Purpose   65
  Focus   66
  Chronology   67

Strategies for Reading Narration   68
  Understanding Meaning   68
  Evaluating Strategy   68
  Appreciating Language   68

Samuel Scudder   *Take This Fish and Look at It* (annotated)   69
  Instead of lecturing, a famous scientist repeats a simple command to his new
  student—"look again, look again!"

James Dillard   *A Doctor's Dilemma*   74
  A young doctor learns that to avoid the threat of a lawsuit, the next time he
  sees an accident victim, he should "drive on."

Andrew Braaksma   *Some Lessons From the Assembly Line*   78
  A student recounts lessons learned working in a factory.

Maya Angelou   *Champion of the World*   82
  For African Americans in the segregated South, Joe Louis was more than a
  prizefighter. He was a symbol of hope and change.

Ramon "Tianguis" Pérez   *The Fender-Bender*   87
  A minor traffic incident reveals the tenuous existence of undocumented
  aliens in America.

Martin Gansberg   *Thirty-Eight Who Saw Murder and Didn't Call the Police*   91
  Gansberg recounts the 1964 murder of a young woman whose neighbors
  ignored her cries for help because they "did not want to get involved."

BLENDING THE MODES   96

George Orwell   *Shooting an Elephant*   96
  Orwell recounts how a crowd pressured him to act against his will although
  he was an armed officer.

WRITING BEYOND THE CLASSROOM   103

Walter Lord   *The Reconstructed Logbook of the* Titanic   103
  Lord provides a minute-by-minute account of the famed luxury liner's
  doomed maiden voyage.

RESPONDING TO IMAGES   106

New Orleans Following Hurricane Katrina, September, 2005   106

Strategies for Writing Narration   107

Suggested Topics for Writing Narration   108

Student Paper   *Spare Change*   110
A trip across the Mexican border leads a student to alter his views
of poverty.

Narration Checklist   114

5   **Description: Presenting Impressions**   **115**

What Is Description?   115
    Objective and Subjective Description   116
    The Language of Description   118

Strategies for Reading Descriptions   122
    Understanding Meaning   122
    Evaluating Strategy   122
    Appreciating Language   122

Lansing Lamont   *The Bomb*   123
The world's first atomic bomb was a "bloated black squid girdled with cables
and leech-like detonators."

Truman Capote   *Out There*   126
The opening pages of *In Cold Blood* describe a remote Kansas town that
became the scene of an infamous mass murder.

Luis Alberto Urrea   *Border Story*   129
For Central Americans seeking a better life, the border between Mexico and
the United States is a war zone of poverty and violence.

José Antonio Burciaga   *My Ecumenical Father*   133
Burciaga recounts how his Mexican father, who worked as a custodian in an
El Paso synagogue, risked his life for the Jewish faith.

Carl T. Rowan   *Unforgettable Miss Bessie*   137
A noted columnist recalls the teacher who reminded him and other disadvantaged students that "what you put in your head…can never be pulled out
by the Ku Klux Klan [or] Congress.…"

Paul M. Barrett *American Islam* 142
Unlike the Muslims of Europe, American Muslims are mostly non-Arab, highly educated, and affluent.

BLENDING THE MODES 147

E. B. White *Once More to the Lake* 147
Describing a vacation trip, White compares past and present and realizes his sense of mortality.

WRITING BEYOND THE CLASSROOM 154

Bayou Printing *Job Announcement* 154
A want ad describes the ideal job candidate.

Monica Ramos *The Resume of Monica Ramos* 156
A job applicant details her skills and experience in response to a want ad.

RESPONDING TO IMAGES 159

Seattle Street Kids with Gun, 1983 159

Strategies for Writing Description 160

Suggested Topics for Descriptive Writing 161

Student Paper *My Bug* 163
A student considers his battered VW bug a "mobile family album."

Description Checklist 165

6 Definition: Establishing Meaning 167

What Is Definition? 167
  Methods of Definition 169
  The Purpose of Definition 170
  Definition in Context 170

Strategies for Reading Definitions 171
  Understanding Meaning 171
  Evaluating Strategy 171
  Appreciating Language 172

Eileen Simpson *Dyslexia* (annotated) 173
A psychotherapist defines a reading disability by detailing her own experiences as a person with dyslexia.

Janice Castro, Dan Cook, and Cristina Garcia   *Spanglish*   178
Castro offers a colorful definition of a new language emerging from the
blending of two cultures.

Ellen Goodman   *The Company Man*   181
Goodman defines the qualities of a classic workaholic.

Alissa Quart   *Listening to Madness*   184
Members of the "Mad Pride" movement embrace mental illness and reject
medication that will eliminate their inner voices.

Thomas Sowell   *Needs*   189
A noted economist examines what politicians and the public mean when
they use the word "need."

Joseph C. Phillips   *Who is Black?*   193
An actor and writer examines the definition of what it means to be black
in America.

BLENDING THE MODES   199

Marie Winn   *TV Addiction*   199
Television, like drugs and alcohol, can narrow and dehumanize those who
allow it to overwhelm their lives.

WRITING BEYOND THE CLASSROOM   207

The Encyclopedia of Psychology   *Depression*   207
An academic reference book defines the concept of depression for physicians
and psychologists.

Don D. Rosenberg   *What is Depression?*   209
A mental health clinic brochure defines depression for its clients
and the general public.

RESPONDING TO IMAGES   211

Anti-Gay Marriage Protest in Boston, 2004   211

Strategies for Writing Definitions   212

Suggested Topics for Writing Definitions   213

Student Paper   *Disneyland Dads*   215
The Disneyland Dad is the divorced father who offers his estranged children
material goods they want but not the parenting they need.

Definition Checklist   218

7   Comparison and Contrast: Indicating Similarities and Differences   221

What Is Comparison and Contrast?   221
   The Purposes of Comparison and Contrast   222
   Organizing Comparison and Contrast Papers   223
   Subject-by-Subject   224
   Point-by-Point   225

Strategies for Reading Comparison and Contrast   226
   Understanding Meaning   226
   Evaluating Strategy   227
   Appreciating Language   227

Yi-Fu Tuan   *Chinese Space, American Space* (annotated)   228
   Unlike the Chinese, "Americans have a sense of space, not place."

Rachel Carson   *A Fable for Tomorrow*   231
   An environmentalist offers a nightmarish depiction of how failure to protect
   the Earth can lead to disaster.

Suzanne Britt   *Neat People vs. Sloppy People*   234
   Britt observes that neat people are lazier than sloppy people.

Bruce Catton   *Grant and Lee*   237
   Meeting at Appomattox, the two most famous generals of the Civil War
   were studies in contrast who were "under everything else very much alike."

Sharon Begley   *East vs. West: One Sees the Big Picture, Other is Focused*   242
   Asians and Westerners see and remember different relationships.

Bharati Mukherjee   *Two Ways to Belong to America*   246
   Two sisters represent contrasting attitudes about the immigrant experience.

BLENDING THE MODES   251

Christopher Jencks   *Reinventing the American Dream*   251
   Jencks compares the Republican definition of the American Dream—a land
   of freedom and small government—with the Democratic vision of a country
   of shared prosperity and security.

WRITING BEYOND THE CLASSROOM   257

Peggy Kenna and Sondra Lacy   *Communication Styles:
United States and Taiwan*   257
   Two consultants offer business travelers a chart contrasting American
   and Taiwanese communication styles.

RESPONDING TO IMAGES   260

Henry Ford II Introduces the 1949 Ford   260
   Strategies for Writing Comparison and Contrast   261
   Suggested Topics for Comparison and Contrast Writing   262

Student Paper   *Parallel States: Israel and Ireland*   263
   Despite obvious differences, Israel and Ireland are both homelands to a great
   diaspora and share similar histories, social conflicts, and battles with terrorism.

Comparison and Contrast Checklist   267

Critical Issues: An Online Reader   **269**

   Confronting Issues   271

   • **Health Care**   274
   • **Immigration**   280
   • **Criminal Justice**   286
   • **Privacy in the Electronic Age**   292

8   Analysis: Making Evaluations   **299**

   What Is Analysis?   299
      Subjective and Objective Analysis   300
      Detailed Observation   301
      Critical Thinking for Writing Analysis   302

   Strategies for Reading Analysis   303
      Understanding Meaning   304
      Evaluating Strategy   304
      Appreciating Language   304

   Sharon Begley   *What's in a Word?*   305
      The German word for "bridge" is feminine, conjuring images of beauty and
      fragility; for the French it is a masculine word connoting strength and power.
      Words shape the way we perceive reality.

   Thomas Friedman   *What's Our Sputnik?*   309
      Russia's 1957 launch of the world's first satellite shocked Americans into fo-
      cusing on science and technology to catch up to the Soviets; Friedman won-
      ders what it will take to make today's Americans recognize the threat posed
      by China.

Fareed Zakaria   *Get Out the Wallets*   313
Americans are the world's great consumers, driving the global economy
and piling up debt.

Benjamin Radford   *How Television Distorts Reality*   317
Radford examines the impact of television which "distorts the reality
it claims to reflect and report on."

Scott Rosenberg   *Closing the Credibility Gap*   324
Journalists need to learn techniques used by bloggers to verify online
information.

Louis R. Mizell Jr.   *Who's Listening to Your Cell Phone Calls?*   328
Easily monitored, even the most innocent cellular phone messages can aid
criminals and stalkers.

BLENDING THE MODES   333

Jim Gemmell and Gordon Bell   *The E-Memory Revolution*   333
Digital records are revolutionizing library holdings and will change the way
the past is recalled.

WRITING BEYOND THE CLASSROOM   341

Alton Enterprises   *Preliminary Security Analysis*   341
A security consultant identifies security lapses.

RESPONDING TO IMAGES   343

Cell Phone Camera Image of Street Demonstration, Tehran, June 2009   343

Strategies for Writing Analysis   344

Suggested Topics for Writing Analysis   345

Student Paper   *Endless War*   346
No future president will declare a victory in the war on terrorism any more
than anyone will claim to have won the war against racism, organized crime,
or poverty.

Analysis Checklist   349

**9   Division and Classification:
Separating into Parts and Rating Categories   351**

What Are Division and Classification?   351
  Division   351

Critical Thinking for Writing Division   352
Classification   354
Critical Thinking for Writing Classification   355

Using Division and Classification   356

Strategies for Reading Division and Classification   356
Understanding Meaning   356
Evaluating Strategy   357
Appreciating Language   357

Judith Viorst   *Friends, Good Friends—and Such Good Friends*   358
Viorst outlines seven kinds of friends.

Martin Luther King Jr.   *Three Ways of Meeting Oppression*   364
Oppressed people can confront their situation in three ways: through
acquiescence, with violence, or by nonviolent resistance.

James Austin   *Four Kinds of Chance*   368
A scientist classifies the kinds of chance that occur in scientific research.

Bill Wasik   *Our Friend the Smear*   373
Political smears have four distinct stages as they unfold in the media.

Thomas H. Benton   *The Seven Deadly Sins of Students*   377
An experienced instructor details seven sins of today's students that threaten
their education and future success.

William Lutz   *Four Kinds of Doublespeak*   382
Lutz describes four ways language is used to minimize, distort, or spin events.

BLENDING THE MODES   388

Andrés Martin   *On Teenagers and Tattoos*   388
Teenagers get tattoos to shape their identity, establish control, and achieve a
sense of permanence.

WRITING BEYOND THE CLASSROOM   394

Motion Picture Association of America   *Parents: Stay Ahead of the Curve!*   394
The MPAA, which classifies movies from G to NC-17, e-mails parents ratings
of newly released films.

RESPONDING TO IMAGES   397

Symbols of Three Faiths, 2006   397

Strategies for Division and Classification Writing   398

Suggested Topics for Division and Classification Writing   399

Student Paper   *Hispanics on Campus*   401
Hispanic students do not form a homogenous group, but range from Spanish-speaking immigrants to highly assimilated "invisible" Hispanics.

Division and Classification Checklist   404

10 Process: Explaining How Things Work and Giving Directions   405

What Is Process?   405
Explaining How Things Work   405
Critical Thinking for Writing Explanations   406
Giving Directions   407
Critical Thinking for Writing Directions   408

Strategies for Reading Process   410
Understanding Meaning   410
Evaluating Strategy   410
Appreciating Language   410

Mortimer Adler   *How to Mark a Book* (annotated)   411
A good reader interacts with a book, making notes in the margins.

Armond D. Budish   *Fender Benders: Legal Do's and Don'ts*   417
A consumer reporter offers step-by-step advice to motorists involved in minor accidents.

Marvin Harris   *How Our Skins Got Their Color*   421
Sunlight, vitamin D, and skin cancer caused people to develop lighter and darker complexions.

Anne Weisbord   *Resumes That Rate a Second Look*   425
A career counselor offers eight tips for creating effective resumes.

Eugene Raudsepp   *Seeing Your Way Past Interview Jitters*   428
Job applicants can improve their interview performances by using a psychological technique called visualization.

Liz Grinslade   *Evaluating a Job Opportunity*   432
Accepting the wrong job can be worse than not being hired.

BLENDING THE MODES   436

Malcolm X   *My First Conk*   436
The noted Black Muslim leader recalls having his hair processed to make a
compelling argument about racial identity.

WRITING BEYOND THE CLASSROOM   441

Lucille Treganowan   *Cleaning Battery Terminals*   441
The author of Lucille's Car Care provides instructions on car repair.

RESPONDING TO IMAGES   444

Resume and Laptop   444

Strategies for Process Writing   445

Suggested Topics for Process Writing   445

Student Paper   *Securing Your Home*   448
Homeowners can deter robbers by following a few simple tips.

Process Checklist   453

**11   Cause and Effect: Determining Reasons
and Measuring or Predicting Results   455**

What Is Cause and Effect?   455
  Deduction and Induction   456
  Establishing Causes   458
  Measuring and Predicting Results   459

Critical Thinking for Cause-and-Effect Writing   460

Strategies for Reading Cause and Effect   462
  Understanding Meaning   462
  Evaluating Strategy   462
  Appreciating Language   462

John Brooks   *The Effects of the Telephone* (annotated)   463
The telephone, perhaps more than any other invention, revolutionized
human experience.

John Taylor Gatto   *Why Schools Don't Educate*   466
A former teacher-of-the-year lists reasons why schools fail to teach and
describes the effects faulty schools have on children.

Tanner Stransky   *Who Killed Miss America?*   470
Stransky examines the reasons why the Miss America pageant is
steadily losing viewers and ceasing to be an iconic feature of
American life.

Diana Bletter   *I Refuse to Live in Fear*   474
An American living in Israel asserts that by "resisting the temptation to
become paranoid and isolated" and "by sticking up for one another" people
can defeat terrorism.

BLENDING THE MODES   477

Brent Staples   *Black Men and Public Space*   477
An African American male relates the effects he causes by simply walking
down a public street.

OPPOSING VIEWPOINTS: LEGALIZING DRUGS   482

Peter Moskos   *Too Dangerous Not to Regulate*   482
Because the war on drugs has failed, Moskos argues America should legalize
drugs.

Lee P. Brown   *End the Demand, End the Supply*   485
A career law enforcement officer insists that because of their dangers, drugs
should never be legalized.

WRITING BEYOND THE CLASSROOM   488

Thomas Jefferson et al.   *The Declaration of Independence*   488
Jefferson details the reasons why the American colonies must sever ties with
Great Britain.

RESPONDING TO IMAGES   493

Foreclosure sign, Texas, 2008   493

Strategies for Cause-and-Effect Writing   494

Suggested Topics for Cause-and-Effect Writing   494

Student Paper   *Why They Hate Us*   496
The collapse of the Soviet Union left the world with one superpower, which
is no longer seen as the lesser of two evil empires.

Cause-and-Effect Checklist   499

12 Argument and Persuasion 501

What Is Argument and Persuasion?   501
  Persuasive Appeals   502
  Blending Appeals   504
  Appealing to Hostile Readers   505

Critical Thinking for Writing Argument and Persuasion   506

Strategies for Reading Argument and Persuasion   506
  Understanding Meaning   506
  Evaluating Strategy   506
  Appreciating Language   507

Anna Quindlen   *Stuff is Not Salvation*   508
Americans must realize that happiness does not lie solely in consumption.

Maggie Jackson   *Distracted: The New News World and the Fate of Attention*   512
The deluge of online information has given us more facts but stunted our ability to concentrate and analyze.

BLENDING THE MODES   518

Mary Sherry   *In Praise of the "F" Word*   518
A teacher argues that a failing grade can be a valuable learning experience.

OPPOSING VIEWPOINTS: CHINA IN THE 21ST CENTURY   522

Martin Jacques   *When China Rules the World*   522
Jacques argues that by midcentury China's economy will be the world's largest, leaving India and the United States battling for second place.

Minxin Pei   *Why China Won't Rule the World*   526
China, Pei argues, has grown quickly but has unresolved internal problems that will hinder its future growth and global influence.

OPPOSING VIEWPOINTS: ETHNIC IDENTITY   531

Armstrong Williams   *Hyphenated Americans*   531
A noted columnist argues that retaining an ethnic identity emphasizes separateness and erodes allegiance to a common civil society.

Julianne Malveaux   *Still Hyphenated Americans*   534
In celebrating Black History Month, African Americans, Malveaux insists, are only celebrating the hyphenated status history gave them.

WRITING BEYOND THE CLASSROOM   537

Covenant House   *Covenant House Needs Your Help*   537
Covenant House, the nation's largest shelter for homeless youth, seeks help
"to make cold lonely nights a little warmer for homeless kids who come to
our doorstep."

RESPONDING TO IMAGES   539

Sign Warning Drivers about Illegal Immigrants   539

Strategies for Writing Argument and Persuasion   540

Suggested Topics for Writing Argument and Persuasion   541

Student Paper   *Why a Black Student Union?*   543
Responding to critics, a student defends the existence of a black student
union on his campus.

Argument and Persuasion Checklist   548

Appendix A: A Writer's Guide to Documenting Sources   A-551

What Is Documentation?   A-551

Why Document Sources?   A-551

When to Document   A-552
   What *Not* to Document   A-552
   What to Document   A-553
   Evaluating Internet Sources Checklist   A-553

Using Quotations   A-555

Using Paraphrases   A-557

Using MLA Documentation   A-558
   Building a Works Cited List   A-558
   General Guidelines   A-558
   Print Sources   A-558
   Online Sources   A-559
   In-text Citations   A-560
   Sources and Sample Documented Essay   A-561
   Book Excerpt   A-561
   Magazine Article   A-562
   A Website   A-562

Student Essay   A-564

Using APA Documentation   A-566
  Building a Reference List   A-566

General Guidelines   A-567
  Print Sources   A-567

Online Sources   A-567
  In-text Citations   A-569

Strategies for Avoiding Common Documentation Problems   A-569

Informal Documentation   A-570

Appendix B: A Writer's Guide to Revising and Editing   B-571

What Are Revising and Editing?   B-571

Revising the Essay   B-571
  Review the Assignment and Your Goal   B-571
  Review the Whole Essay   B-571
  Examine the Thesis   B-572
  Review Topic Sentences and Controlling Ideas   B-572
  Review the Sequence of Paragraphs   B-572
  Revise the Introduction   B-572
  Introduction Checklist   B-573
  Revise Supporting Paragraphs   B-573
  Supporting Paragraphs Checklist   B-573
  Revise the Conclusion   B-573
  Conclusion Checklist   B-574

Revising Paragraphs   B-574
  First Draft   B-574
  Revision Notes   B-574
  Second Draft   B-574

Editing Sentences   B-575
  Common Grammar Errors   B-575
  Fragments   B-575
  Run-ons and Comma Splices   B-575
  Subject-Verb Agreement   B-576
  Pronoun Agreement   B-576
  Dangling and Misplaced Modifiers   B-576
  Faulty Parallelism   B-577

Awkward Shifts in Person   B-577
Avoid Awkward Shifts in Tense   B-577

Improving Sentences   B-578
Sentence Checklist   B-578
Be Brief   B-578
Delete Wordy Phrases   B-578
Eliminate Redundancy   B-579
Avoid Placing Minor Details in Separate Sentences   B-579
Vary Sentence Types   B-580

Editing Words   B-580
Diction Checklist   B-580
Use Words Precisely   B-581
Use Specific Words   B-581
Avoid Sexist Language   B-582
Avoid Clichés   B-582
Use Appropriate Levels of Diction   B-582
Appreciate the Impact of Connotations   B-583

Credits C-585

Index I-587

THEMATIC CONTENTS

Art and Entertainment

TV Addiction   Marie Winn (definition)   199

How Television Distorts Reality   Benjamin Radford (analysis)   317

Our Friend the Smear   Bill Wasik (division/classification)   373

Who Killed Miss America?   Tanner Stransky (cause and effect)   470

Distracted: The New News World and the Fate of Attention   Maggie Jackson
(argument/persuasion)   512

Autobiography

Take This Fish and Look at It   Samuel Scudder (narration)   69

A Doctor's Dilemma   James Dillard (narration)   74

Some Lessons From the Assembly Line   Andrew Braaksma (narration)   78

Champion of the World   Maya Angelou (narration)   82

The Fender-Bender   Ramon "Tianguis" Pérez (narration)   87

Shooting an Elephant   George Orwell (narration)   96

Once More to the Lake   E. B. White (description)   147

Who is Black?   Joseph C. Phillips (definition)   193

My First Conk   Malcolm X (process)   436

Biography

My Ecumenical Father   José Antonio Burciaga (description)   133

Unforgettable Miss Bessie   Carl T. Rowan (description)   137

Grant and Lee   Bruce Catton (comparison/contrast)   237

Business and Economics

The Company Man   Ellen Goodman (definition)   181

Needs   Thomas Sowell (definition)   189

Communication Styles: United States and Taiwan   Peggy Kenna and Sondra Lacy (comparison)   257

Get Out the Wallets   Fareed Zakaria (analysis)   313

Childhood

Champion of the World   Maya Angelou (narration)   82

My Ecumenical Father   José Antonio Burciaga (description)   133

Once More to the Lake   E. B. White (description)   147

Who is Black?   Joseph C. Phillips (definition)   193

The Seven Deadly Sins of Students
Thomas H. Benton (division/classification)   377

On Teenagers and Tattoos   Andres Martin (division/classification)   388

Why Schools Don't Educate   John Taylor Gatto (cause/effect)   466

In Praise of the "F" Word   Mary Sherry (argument/persuasion)   518

Civil Rights

Black Political Leadership   Cornel West (comparison/contrast)   53

Champion of the World   Maya Angelou (narration)   82

The Fender-Bender   Ramon "Tianguis" Pérez (narration)   87

Unforgettable Miss Bessie   Carl T. Rowan (description)   137

Who is Black?   Joseph C. Phillips (definition)   193

Two Ways to Belong to America   Bharati Mukherjee (comparison/contrast)   246

Three Ways of Meeting Oppression   Martin Luther King Jr.
(division/classification)   364

How Our Skins Got Their Color   Marvin Harris (process)   421

My First Conk   Malcolm X (process)   436

Black Men and Public Space   Brent Staples (cause/effect)   477

Hyphenated Americans   Armstrong Williams (argument/persuasion)   531

Still Hyphenated Americans   Julianne Malveaux (argument/persuasion)   534

Community and Culture

The Fender-Bender   Ramon "Tianguis" Pérez (narration)   87

Listening to Madness   Alissa Quart (definition)   184

Shooting an Elephant   George Orwell (narration)   96

My Ecumenical Father   José Antonio Burciaga (description)   133

American Islam   Paul M. Barrett (description)   142

Spanglish   Janice Castro, Dan Cook, and Cristina Garcia (definition)   178

Who is Black?   Joseph C. Phillips (definition)   193

Neat People vs. Sloppy People   Suzanne Britt (comparison/contrast)   234

East vs. West: One Sees the Big Picture, The Other is Focused   Sharon Begley
   (comparison/contrast)   242

Two Ways to Belong to America   Bharati Mukherjee (comparison/contrast)   246

On Teenagers and Tattoos   Andres Martin (division/classification)   388

My First Conk   Malcolm X (process)   436

Who Killed Miss America?   Tanner Stransky (cause/effect)   470

Black Men and Public Space   Brent Staples (cause/effect)   477

Hyphenated Americans   Armstrong Williams (argument/persuasion)   531

Still Hyphenated Americans   Julianne Malveaux (argument/persuasion)   534

Critical Thinking

Take This Fish and Look at It   Samuel Scudder (narration)   69

What's in a Word?   Sharon Begley (analysis)   305

How Television Distorts Reality   Benjamin Radford (analysis)   317

Closing the Credibility Gap   Scott Rosenberg (analysis)   324

Four Kinds of Chance   James Austin (division/classification)   368

Doublespeak   William Lutz (division/classification)   382

How to Mark a Book   Mortimer Adler (process)   411

Distracted: The New News World and the Fate of Attention   Maggie Jackson
   (argument/persuasion)   512

Diversity

Black Political Leadership   Cornel West (comparison/contrast)   53

Champion of the World   Maya Angelou (narration)   82

Border Story   Luis Alberto Urrea (description)   129

My Ecumenical Father   José Antonio Burciaga (description)   133

American Islam   Paul M. Barrett (description)   142

Spanglish   Janice Castro, Dan Cook, and Cristina Garcia (definition)   178

Chinese Space, American Space Yi-Fu Tuan (comparison/contrast)   228

East vs. West: One Sees the Big Picture, The Other is Focused   Sharon Begley
   (comparison/contrast)   242

Two Ways to Belong to America   Bharati Mukherjee (comparison/contrast)   246

My First Conk   Malcolm X (process)   436

Black Men and Public Space   Brent Staples (cause/effect)   477

Hyphenated Americans   Armstrong Williams (argument/persuasion)   531

Still Hyphenated Americans   Julianne Malveaux (argument/persuasion)   534

Education

Take This Fish and Look at It   Samuel Scudder (narration)   69

Unforgettable Miss Bessie   Carl T. Rowan (description)   137

Dyslexia   Eileen Simpson (definition)   173

The Seven Deadly Sins of Students   Thomas H. Benton
  (division/classification)   377

Why Schools Don't Educate   John Taylor Gatto (cause/effect)   466

In Praise of the "F" Word   Mary Sherry (argument/persuasion)   518

Environment

A Fable for Tomorrow   Rachel Carson (comparison/contrast)   231

Health and Medicine

A Doctor's Dilemma   James Dillard (narration)   74

Dyslexia   Eileen Simpson (definition)   173

Listening to Madness   Alissa Quart (definition)   184

Two Definitions of Depression   (definition)   207

History

Black Political Leadership   Cornel West (comparison/contrast)   53

The Reconstructed Logbook of the *Titanic*   Walter Lord
  (narration)   103

The Bomb   Lansing Lamont (description)   123

Grant and Lee   Bruce Catton (comparison/contrast)   237

The Effects of the Telephone   John Brooks (cause/effect)   466

The Declaration of Independence   Thomas Jefferson et al.
  (cause/effect)   488

Immigration

Ramon "Tianguis" Pérez   The Fender-Bender (narration)   87

American Islam   Paul M. Barrett (description)   142

Two Ways to Belong to America   Bharati Mukherjee (comparison/contrast)   246

Job Interviews

The Resume of Monica Ramos   Monica Ramos (description)   156

Resumes That Rate a Second Look   Anne Weisbord (process)   425

Seeing Your Way Past Interview Jitters   Eugene Raudsepp
  (process)   428

Language

Dyslexia   Eileen Simpson (definition)   173

Spanglish   Janice Castro, Dan Cook, and Cristina Garcia (definition)   178

Who is Black?   Joseph C. Phillips (definition)   193

What's in a Word?   Sharon Begley (analysis)   305

Doublespeak   William Lutz (division/classification)   382

Law and Crime

Thirty-Eight Who Saw Murder and Didn't Call the Police   Martin Gansberg (narration)   91

Who's Listening to Your Cell Phone Calls?   Louis R. Mizell Jr. (analysis)   328

Fender Benders: Legal Do's and Don'ts   Armond D. Budish (process)   417

Too Dangerous Not to Regulate   Peter Moskos (cause/effect)   482

End the Demand, End the Supply   Lee P. Brown (cause/effect)   485

Media and Image

TV Addiction   Marie Winn (definition)   199

How Television Distorts Reality   Benjamin Radford (analysis)   317

Who Killed Miss America?   Tanner Stranksy (cause/effect)   470

Minority Experience

Black Political Leadership   Cornel West (comparison/contrast)   53

Champion of the World   Maya Angelou (narration)   82

The Fender-Bender   Ramon "Tianguis" Pérez (narration)   87

Border Story   Luis Alberto Urrea (description)   129

Two Ways to Belong to America   Bharati Mukherjee (comparison/contrast)   246

My First Conk   Malcolm X (process)   436

Black Men and Public Space   Brent Staples (cause/effect)   477

Hyphenated Americans   Armstrong Williams (argument/persuasion)   531

Still Hyphenated Americans   Julianne Malveaux (argument/persuasion)   534

Nature

A Fable for Tomorrow   Rachel Carson (comparison/contrast)   231

Politics

Black Political Leadership   Cornel West (comparison/contrast)   53

Shooting an Elephant   George Orwell (narration)   96

Reinventing the American Dream Christopher Jencks (comparison) 251
What's Our Sputnik? Thomas Friedman (analysis) 309
Get Out the Wallets Fareed Zakaria (analysis) 313
Our Friend the Smear Bill Wasik (division/classification) 373
Why Schools Don't Educate John Taylor Gatto (cause/effect) 466
I Refuse to Live in Fear Diana Bletter (cause/effect) 474
Too Dangerous Not to Regulate Peter Moskos (cause/effect) 482
End the Demand, End the Supply Lee P. Borwn (cause/effect) 485
The Declaration of Independence Thomas Jefferson et al. (cause/effect) 488

Psychology and Human Behavior

Thirty-Eight Who Saw Murder and Didn't Call the Police
Martin Gansberg (narration) 91
Shooting an Elephant George Orwell (narration) 96
Dyslexia Eileen Simpson (definition) 173
Listening to Madness Alissa Quart (definition) 184
Needs Thomas Sowell (definition) 189
What is Depression? Don D. Rosenberg (definition) 209
Chinese Space, American Space Yi-Fu Tuan (comparison/contrast) 228
East vs. West: One Sees the Big Picture, The Other is Focused Sharon Begley
(comparison/contrast) 242
What's in a Word? Sharon Begley (analysis) 305
On Teenagers and Tattoos Andres Martin (division/classification) 388
Seeing Your Way Past Interview Jitters Eugene Raudsepp (process) 428
I Refuse to Live in Fear Diana Bletter (cause/effect) 474

Science and Technology

Take This Fish and Look at It Samuel Scudder (narration) 69
A Fable for Tomorrow Rachel Carson (comparison/contrast) 231
Who's Listening to Your Cell Phone Calls? Louis R. Mizell Jr. (analysis) 328
Four Kinds of Chance James Austin (division/classification) 368

Sociology

Black Political Leadership Cornel West (comparison/contrast) 53
Thirty-Eight Who Saw Murder and Didn't Call the Police Martin Gansberg
(narration) 91

The Company Man   Ellen Goodman (definition)   181

Needs   Thomas Sowell (definition)   189

On Teenagers and Tattoos   Andres Martin (division/classification)   388

Why Schools Don't Educate   John Taylor Gatto (cause/effect)   466

I Refuse to Live in Fear   Diana Bletter (cause/effect)   474

Black Men and Public Space   Brent Staples (cause/effect)   477

In Praise of the "F" Word   Mary Sherry (argument/persuasion)   518

Values

A Doctor's Dilemma   James Dillard (narration)   74

Some Lessons From the Assembly Line   Andrew Braaksma (narration)   78

Thirty-Eight Who Saw Murder and Didn't Call the Police
Martin Gansberg (narration)   91

My Ecumenical Father   José Antonio Burciaga (description)   133

The Company Man   Ellen Goodman (definition)   181

Reinventing the American Dream   Christopher Jencks (comparison)   251

What's Our Sputnik?   Thomas Friedman (analysis)   309

Get Out the Wallets   Fareed Zakaria (analysis)   313

On Teenagers and Tattoos   Andres Martin (division/classification)   388

Why Schools Don't Educate   John Taylor Gatto (cause/effect)   466

I Refuse to Live in Fear   Diana Bletter (cause/effect)   474

Too Dangerous Not to Regulate   Peter Moskos (cause/effect)   482

End the Demand, End the Supply   Lee P. Borwn (cause/effect)   485

The Declaration of Independence   Thomas Jefferson et al. (cause/effect)   488

Stuff is Not Salvation   Anna Quindlen (argument/persuasion)   508

In Praise of the "F" Word   Mary Sherry (argument/persuasion)   518

Women and Men

Black Men and Public Space   Brent Staples (cause/effect)   477

Work and Career

A Doctor's Dilemma   James Dillard (narration)   74

Some Lessons From the Assembly Line   Andrew Braaksma (narration)   78

The Company Man   Ellen Goodman (definition)   181

Resumes That Rate a Second Look   Anne Weisbord (process)   425

Seeing Your Way Past Interview Jitters   Eugene Raudsepp (process)   428

Writing

What's in a Word?   Sharon Begley (analysis)   305

Doublespeak   William Lutz (division/classification)   382

Resumes That Rate a Second Look   Anne Weisbord (process)   425

PREFACE

Why Write?

Few students plan to become writers. You may think of writers only as people who write for a living—journalists, novelists, and playwrights. But all professionals—all educated men and women, in fact—write to achieve their goals. Lawyers write motions and draft appeals. Doctors record a diagnosis and plan a course of treatment on a patient's chart. Police officers file reports about accidents and criminal investigations. Salespeople, administrators, and managers send streams of email to announce new products, respond to questions, and inform employees, customers, and investors. Men and women entering any profession soon realize that they depend on writing to share ideas, express opinions, and influence others.

Thinking about your future career, you probably imagine yourself in action—an engineer working in a test lab, a contractor walking through a construction site, or a restaurant owner supervising a banquet. But whether your goal is teaching children or owning your own business, writing will be critical to your success. In the information age nearly all jobs involve exchanging data. The ability to write not only will help you complete academic assignments but accomplish tasks and solve problems in any vocation you may enter.

Learning to write well sharpens your critical thinking skills, improving your ability to locate information, examine evidence, solve problems, and persuade others. The strategies you learn in a writing course can enhance your performance in oral presentations, job interviews, meetings, and conference calls. By learning to think more clearly, analyze your audience, and organize your ideas, you will be a more effective communicator in any situation.

The Sundance Reader

The Sundance Reader, Sixth Edition, contains over seventy readings drawn from a range of academic disciplines and professions. The collection of essays and articles, organized by rhetorical modes, includes both classic and contemporary authors such as George Orwell, E. B. White, Joseph C. Phillips,

Thomas Friedman, and Maya Angelou. In addition to writing from the disciplines of law, economics, and science by writers such as Thomas Sowell and Rachel Carson, *The Sundance Reader* offers students practical advice on resume writing and job interviews. Applied readings at the end of each chapter demonstrate how writers use the rhetorical modes beyond the classroom. Entries such as "The Reconstructed Logbook of the *Titanic*," and "Cleaning Battery Terminals" illustrate various writing tasks students will face in future courses and in their careers.

The Sundance Reader's wide variety of topics on the environment, culture, social issues, the media, and business make the textbook suitable for thematic courses. Individual chapters include self-contained units on current issues, and the thematic table of contents lists a number of topics that can be explored in depth.

With its wealth of readings and four-part questioning strategy following each entry, *The Sundance Reader* provides students a unique perspective on how writing is shaped in different contexts.

The Sundance Reader has several features that make it a useful teaching tool for college instructors:

- **A range of readings**   Each chapter opens with brief, readable entries that clearly demonstrate the rhetorical mode, followed by longer, more challenging essays. Each chapter highlights a model "blending" the modes showing how writers often use several methods of development to tell a story or explain a process. Samples of applied writing appear at the end, illustrating how writers use the mode in different professions. Instructors have flexibility in assigning readings best suited to their student populations.

- **Brief entries suitable for in-class reading**   Many of the essays are short enough to be read in class and used as writing prompts, reducing the need for handouts.

- **An emphasis on writing**   *The Sundance Reader* moves students from reading to *writing*. Chapters open with reading questions and conclude with writing strategies and lists of suggested topics. Each chapter ends with a checklist of common writing problems.

- **An emphasis on critical thinking**   *The Sundance Reader* stresses critical thinking by including essays such as James Austin's article about the role of chance in scientific research. Samuel Scudder's essay "Take This Fish and Look at It" dramatizes the importance of detailed observation. Benjamin Radford's "How Television Distorts Reality" and Maggie Jackson's "Distracted: The New News World and the Fate of Attention" demonstrate how the media shapes perceptions and influences public opinion.

- *Pro and con entries*   Instructors have found that presenting essays with opposing viewpoints can stimulate class discussions and prompt writing activities. *The Sundance Reader* presents pairs of pro and con articles on three critical issues: legalizing drugs, China in the twenty-first century, and ethnic identity.

- *Focus on diversity*   Over half the selections are written by women and minorities. African American, Hispanic, and Asian writers are represented. These essays cover diverse issues, including business and technology.

- *Writing across the curriculum*   *The Sundance Reader* demonstrates how each mode is developed by writers working in several disciplines, including law, medicine, psychology, history, law enforcement, and business.

- *Writing beyond the classroom*   Each chapter includes a section illustrating how writers use the modes in "the real world." Advertisements, brochures, government documents, and a resume introduce elements of business and technical writing to composition students.

- *Collaborative writing*   Writing suggestions following the readings include directions for collaborative writing activities. The introduction provides useful guidelines for successful group writing.

- *Advice on the job search*   *The Sundance Reader* contains articles offering students practical advice on writing resumes and succeeding in job interviews.

- *An annotated essay in each chapter*   The first essay used to introduce each mode is annotated to guide students through its construction.

- *Writer's Guide to Documenting Sources*   *The Sundance Reader* provides examples on how to apply both MLA and APA rules for documenting sources. The guide includes an MLA documented essay with its original sources, demonstrating the use of direct quotations and paraphrases.

Above all, *The Sundance Reader* has been designed to encourage students to read and develop confidence as writers.

NEW IN THIS EDITION

- *Nineteen new essays* New selections include "Some Lessons From the Assembly Line" by **Andrew Braaksma**, "Listening to Madness" by **Alissa Quart**, "East vs. West: One Sees the Big Picture, The Other is Focused" by **Sharon Begley**, "Reinventing the American Dream" by **Christopher Jencks**, "What's in a Word?" by **Sharon Begley**, "What's Our Sputnik?" by **Thomas Friedman**, "Get Out the Wallets" by **Fareed Zakaria**, "Closing the Credibility Gap" by **Scott Rosenberg**, "The E-Memory Revolution" by **Jim Gemmel and Gordon Bell**, "Our Friend the Smear" by **Bill Wasik**, "Doublespeak" by **William Lutz**, "On Teenagers and Tattoos" by **Andres Martin**, "Who Killed Miss America?" by **Tanner Stransky**, "Too Dangerous Not to Regulate" by **Peter Moskos**, "End the Demand, End the Supply" by **Lee P. Brown**, "Stuff is Not Salvation" by **Anna Quindlen**, "Distracted: The New News World and the Fate of Attention" by **Maggie Jackson**, "When China Rules the World" by **Martin Jacques**, and "Why China Won't Rule the World" by **Minxin Pei**.

- *Expanded commentary on the writing process* provides students with guidelines on developing outlines.

- *Revised MLA guidelines*

- *Critical Issues* offers students online readings and research guides for four issues: health care, immigration, criminal justice, and privacy in the electronic age.

- *A Writer's Guide to Revising and Editing* gives students strategies to improve their writing by overcoming common mistakes.

SUNDANCE CHOICE

Sundance Choice allows instructors to customize *The Sundance Reader* or create their own textbook by adding and deleting essays and entire chapters. In addition to providing supplemental choices in essays by mode, *Sundance Choice* offers instructors entries and apparatus that address fourteen themes in a variety of subject areas:

The War on Terrorism	Global Warming
Reparations for Slavery	Islam and the West
Medical Malpractice	Abortion: *Roe v. Wade* at Thirty
Fatherhood	Capital Punishment
Immigration	Gender Identity: Raising Boys and Girls

Welfare to Work	America's Role in the 21st Century: Public Schools
Empire or Republic?	American Identity: Melting Pot or Mosaic?

Sundance Choice includes rhetorical chapters to meet the unique needs of instructors and courses:

Critical Reading	Critical Thinking and Prewriting
Developing a Thesis	Supporting a Thesis
Choosing the Right Words	Improving Sentences and Paragraphs
Improving Introductions	Writing Essay Examinations and Conclusions
Conducting Research	Writing the Research Paper
Understanding Grammar	Handbook

 Info Write provides additional information on writing.
cengage.learning.infowrite.com

Acknowledgments

I would like to thank the following reviewers for their valuable suggestions to this edition of *The Sundance Reader*: Annie L. Burns, Meridian Community College; Sheryl Chisamore, SUNY, Ulster Community College; Eileen Curran-Kondrad, Plymouth State University; Sharifa Evans, Georgia Perimeter College; Rima S. Gulshan, Northern Virginia Community College, Annandale; Jeanine Horn, Houston Community College; and Joseph S. Horobetz, Northern Virginia Community College, Annandale. I'd also like to thank these reviewers of previous editions: Jeannette Adkins, Tarrant County College; Don Cunningham, University of Wisconsin; Francine DeFrance, Cerritos College; Jaime Herrera, Mesa Community College; Kathy Ivey, Lenoir-Rhyne College; Jill Jones, Southwestern Oklahoma State University; Lee Brewer Jones and Stuart Noel, Georgia Perimeter College; Richard Lee, SUNY College at Oneonta; Kathleen Monahan, St. Peter's College; Robin Nealy, Wharton County Junior College; Susanne Rauch and Bonita Startt, Tidewater Community College; Curt Riesberg, Imperial Valley College; Alfred Taylor, Valencia Community College; Renva Watterson, Georgia Highlands College; and Donna White, Arkansas Tech University.

All books are a collaborative effort. My special thanks go to Lyn Uhl, Publisher; Kate Derrick, Sponsoring Editor; Kathy Sands-Boehmer, Senior Development Editor; and Aimee Bear, Content Project Manager, for their continued support, vision, and enthusiasm for *The Sundance Reader*.

CHAPTER ONE

THE WRITING CONTEXT

HOW WE WRITE

In the summer of 1939, scientist Leo Szilard was worried. As Americans enjoyed the New York World's Fair, the exiled physicist followed events in Europe with growing anxiety. His experiments proved that a nuclear chain reaction could create an atomic bomb. German scientists had split the atom, and the Nazis had seized rich deposits of uranium in Czechoslovakia. As a Jew who had escaped on the last train out of Nazi Germany, Szilard was horrified at the prospect of Hitler obtaining nuclear weapons. Now living in New York, he tried to warn the American government, but officials in Washington were unwilling to fund atomic research. A refugee without resources or political contacts, Szilard sought help from his old friend Albert Einstein, a Nobel Prize winner with an international reputation. Szilard hoped the government would listen to Einstein. Although the idea of a nuclear chain reaction had never occurred to him, Einstein quickly grasped its implications and suggested writing to President Roosevelt. Einstein dictated a letter and asked Szilard to revise it. Szilard wrote a new version, then telephoned Einstein, who requested another meeting. Accompanied by fellow physicist Edward Teller, Szilard met Einstein at a summer cottage to discuss the letter. The scientists soon became frustrated. Einstein realized their abstract theories would be difficult to explain to a nonscientist. Equally frustrating was the fact that English was a second language to all three scientists. Einstein dictated a new draft to Edward Teller in German. Leo Szilard wrote two more letters in English and mailed them to Einstein. After reviewing them carefully, Einstein selected the longer version and signed it. Just eight paragraphs long, the letter was presented to President Roosevelt and helped launch the Manhattan Project and the nuclear age.

The story behind Einstein's letter demonstrates important elements about writing. Writing is a complex process and does not occur in a vacuum. It takes place in a *context* formed by three factors:

1. The writer's purpose and role

2. The knowledge base, attitudes, needs, expectations, and biases of the reader

3. The conventions, history, and culture of a particular discipline, profession, organization, publication, situation, or community

Writing, as the creation of Einstein's letter shows, is often *collaborative*, the product of a group activity. Writing may reflect the ideas of more than one person. Einstein's letter also illustrates a common dilemma writers face in a technological society. Experts frequently have to communicate with readers outside their discipline, people with little understanding or appreciation of the writers' subjects.

Context explains why a newspaper article about an airplane crash differs from a Federal Aviation Administration (FAA) report or the airline's condolence letter to the victims' families. Stated simply and printed in narrow columns for easy skimming, a newspaper account briefly describes current events for general readers. An FAA report detailing the causes of a plane crash runs to hundreds of pages and includes extensive data and testimony of witnesses and survivors. Directed to aviation safety experts, the report is stated in technical language largely incomprehensible to the average reader. The airline's letter to victims' families addresses people enduring confusion, grief, and anger. Carefully worded, it attempts to inform readers without appearing callous or falsely sympathetic.

You may have noticed how context affects your own writing. The notes you take in class for personal use look very different from the in-class essay you submit for a grade. The words you choose when adding a line to a birthday card for your seven-year-old cousin differ from those you use on a job application or in a note to your roommate. Almost unconsciously, you alter the way you write depending on your purpose, reader, and circumstances.

To be an effective writer in college and in your future career, it is important to increase your understanding of the three elements that form a writing context.

QUESTIONS

1. Can you recall writing situations where you had difficulty expressing your ideas because you were unsure how your reader would react? Did you have problems finding the right words or just "getting your thoughts on paper"?

2. Have you noticed that different teachers and professors have different attitudes about what constitutes "good writing"? How is writing a paper for an English literature class different from writing a report for a psychology or economics course?

3. Have you observed that magazines, websites, and blogs often have strikingly different writing styles? What do articles in *Cosmopolitan*, *Car and Driver*, or *The Wall Street Journal* reveal about their intended readers? What does the wording of a Facebook page suggest about its creator?

THE WRITER

All writing has a goal. A shopping list serves to refresh your memory. A company email informs employees of a policy change. Research papers demonstrate students' knowledge and skills. Resumes encourage employers to call applicants for job interviews. Even essays written for self-expression must contain more than random observations. To be effective, an essay must arouse interest, provide readers with information they can understand, and offer proof to support the writer's thesis.

The Writer's Purpose

Students and professionals in all fields face similar writing tasks. The way they present their ideas, the language they use, and even the physical appearance of their finished documents are determined in part by their purpose. Although every writing assignment forms a unique context, most writing tasks can be divided into basic modes or types:

narration *To relate a series of events, usually in chronological order.* Biographies, histories, and novels use narration. Business and government reports often include sections called *narratives* that provide a historical overview of a problem, organization, or situation. Emails to friends usually consist of narratives detailing recent events or experiences.

description *To create a picture or impression of a person, place, object, or condition.* Description is a basic element in all writing and usually serves to provide support for the writer's main goal. Descriptions may be wholly factual and objective, as in an accident report or parts catalog. Alternatively, they may contain personal impressions emphasizing what the writer saw, thought, or felt. A novelist describing a city is more likely to focus on his or her "feel" for the streets and people than on statistics and census figures.

definition *To explain a term, condition, topic, or issue.* In many instances, definitions are precise and standard, such as a state's definition of second-degree murder or a biology book's definition of a virus. Other definitions, such as that of a good parent or an ideal teacher, may be based on a writer's personal observation, experience, and opinion.

comparison and contrast *To examine the similarities and differences between two or more subjects.* Textbooks often employ comparison/contrast to discuss different scientific methods, theories, or subjects. Comparisons can serve to distinguish topics or to recommend one subject as superior to others. Consumer magazines frequently use comparison to highlight differences between competing products. Comparison can also provide a "before and after" description of a single subject, showing how a person, place, or condition has changed.

analysis *To evaluate a subject and identify its essential elements, impact, effectiveness, or qualities.* Writers of a formal analysis may follow a standard method. Stockbrokers, medical examiners, building inspectors, archaeologists, botanists, criminologists, and other professionals generally use uniform methods of studying subjects and presenting their conclusions. Essayists and newspaper columnists, on the other hand, often analyze issues from an entirely personal perspective, relying on anecdotal evidence and individual observation. A reviewer's column about a new movie, a sportswriter's opinion of a coach's performance, and a pollster's view on the president's popularity are examples of personal analysis.

division *To name subgroups or divisions in a broad class.* Writers seek to make a large or complex topic understandable or workable by dividing it into smaller units. Insurance can be divided into life, health, homeowner's, and auto policies. A zoology text divides animals into fish, birds, mammals, and reptiles.

classification *To place objects into different classes or ranks according to a single measurement.* Homicides are classified as first, second, or third degree according to circumstances and premeditation. Burns are classified as first, second, or third degree based on the severity of tissue damage. Like analysis, division and classification can be based on professional standards or personal evaluation. A financial adviser might rate mutual funds by risk and performance using commonly accepted criteria. A movie critic, however, could grade films on a one- to five-star scale based solely on his or her tastes.

process *To explain how something occurs or to demonstrate how to accomplish a specific task.* A nuclear power plant, the human heart, and inflation can be explained using process. By examining each stage, a writer can make a complex mechanism or event easier to understand. A recipe, the owner's manual of a computer, and a first-aid book offer step-by-step instructions to complete specific tasks.

cause and effect *To trace the reasons for or results of an occurrence.* A writer can list causes for an increase in crime, the return of an endangered species, or the success or failure of an advertising campaign. Similarly, he or she can list the effects crime has on a community, the response to rescued wildlife, or the impact of television commercials. Physicians refer to medical books that explain the causes of disease and the effects of drugs.

argument and persuasion *To influence reader opinion, attitudes, and actions.* Writers persuade with logical appeals based on factual evidence, with ethical appeals based on values or beliefs, or with emotional appeals that arouse feelings to support their views. A fund-raising letter persuades readers to donate money to a charity. An engineer's report presents an argument why a building should be condemned or an engine redesigned. Essayists and columnists try to influence readers to accept their opinions on topics ranging from globalization to immigration.

QUESTIONS

1. Consider how you have organized papers in the past. Did any assignments lend themselves to one of the modes? Could following one of these methods make it easier to present and organize your ideas?

2. Do you use modes such as *comparison, classification,* or *cause and effect* to organize your thoughts and solve problems? Do you *compare* apartments before deciding which one to rent, or *classify* courses you want to take next semester by difficulty or desirability?

The way writers achieve their goals depends greatly on the other two elements of context: their readers and the discipline. Each chapter of *The Sundance Reader* focuses on one of these modes, illustrating how writers use it in different contexts.

A Note about Modes

Modes refer to the writer's basic goal. Often writing cannot be neatly labeled. Few writing tasks call for the use of a single mode. A dictionary entry is pure definition, and a parts catalog offers simple product descriptions. But a movie review *analyzing* a new release will first *describe* the film and possibly *compare* it to the director's previous work. It might use *narration* to explain the plot and *classification* to rank it with other films in its genre. Some writing can easily fit two or more categories. The Declaration of Independence, for instance (page 488), is an example of both *cause and effect* and *persuasive writing*.

The Writer's Role

An important aspect of context is the writer's role. As a student, your role is much like that of a freelance writer. Your essays, reports, and research papers are expected to reflect only your own efforts. In general, each piece of your work is judged independently. A low grade on a first paper should not affect your chances of earning a higher grade later in the semester. What you write in psychology has no influence on your grades in English. Your comments on controversial issues are not likely to be raised at future job interviews.

Outside of academics, however, your role is more complicated. Often you act as an agent of a larger organization, corporation, or profession. Business letters, email, and reports are assumed to express the views of the employer, not a single employee. Expressing personal views that conflict with corporate practices or administrative policy can jeopardize your position. Frequently, you will have an ongoing relationship with your readers. Comments made in one letter or report affect how readers will respond to your ideas in the future.

Probably the most obvious aspect of a writer's role concerns *perspective*, or the writer's position. Writing in a newspaper's sports section, a columnist may be free to offer personal opinion: "Given poor ticket sales and the age of the stadium, I predict this town will lose its ball club within two years." A front-page article, however, would be weakened by the use of the first person. A reporter would express the same view in terms that are more objective: "The decline in ticket sales and the age of the stadium indicate the city is in danger of losing its baseball team."

When writing as a member of a group or as an agent of an organization, remember that the ideas you express will be considered the ideas of the group. Refrain from stating anything that would alienate other members or expose your organization to liability. If you state personal views, make sure you clearly identify them as being your opinions.

In many instances, your profession will dictate a role that will greatly shape what is expected in your writing. Police officers and nurses, for example, are required to provide objective and impersonal records of their observations. Fashion consultants, decorators, and advertising executives, who are esteemed for their creativity, are more likely to offer personal insights and make first-person statements.

QUESTIONS

1. Consider the jobs you have had and the businesses you have worked for. What writing style would be appropriate for professionals in these fields? Is objective reporting required, or are employees free to offer personal impressions and suggest innovations?

2. What type of writing do you expect to encounter in your career? How does writing in engineering and accounting differ from writing in public

relations, sales, or nonprofit charities? Does your future profession demand adherence to governmental regulations and industry standards, or does it encourage individual expression?

THE READER

Writing is more than self-expression; it is an act of communication. To be effective, your message must be understood. The content, form, and tone of your writing are largely shaped by the needs and expectations of your readers. A medical researcher announcing a new treatment for AIDS would word an article for *Immunology* very differently from one for *Newsweek* or *Redbook*.

Each magazine represents a different audience, a different knowledge base, and a different set of concerns. Fellow immunologists would be interested in the author's research methods and demand detailed proof of his or her claims. Readers of *Immunology* would expect to see extensive data and precise descriptions of experiments and testing methods. Most readers of nonmedical publications would require definitions of scientific terms and would expect brief summaries of data that they would be unable to evaluate on their own. Readers of *Newsweek* could be concerned with issues such as cost, government policy, and insurance coverage. Subscribers to a women's magazine such as *Redbook* might wonder if the treatment works equally well for both sexes or if it is safe for pregnant women.

Audiences often differ within a discipline. The medical researcher writing for the *New England Journal of Medicine* would be addressing practicing physicians, not laboratory researchers. Doctors would be interested in the practical aspects of the treatment. What drugs does it interact with? What are the side effects? Which patients should receive the drug and in what doses? An article in *Nursing* would focus on the concerns of nurses who closely monitor patients for reactions. What effect does the treatment have on a patient's physical and psychological well-being? Are there special considerations for patients with unrelated disorders, such as hypertension and diabetes?

As a writer, you have to determine how much knowledge your readers have about your subject. Do technical terms have to be defined? Does your writing include historical or biographical references requiring explanation? Do you use concepts that general readers might misunderstand or find confusing? In addition to your readers' level of understanding, you must consider your readers' needs and expectations in relation to your goal. What information do your readers want from you? Is your audience reading for general interest, curiosity, or entertainment, or do they demand specific information in order to make decisions or plan future actions?

It is also important to take into account how your readers will respond to your ideas. Is your audience likely to be favorable or hostile to you, your ideas, or the organization you might represent? Defense attorneys and prosecutors have different attitudes toward illegally obtained evidence. Environmentalists and real estate developers have conflicting philosophies of land use. Liberals and conservatives have opposing views of the role of government. When presenting ideas to audiences with undefined or differing attitudes, you will have to work hard to overcome their natural resistance, biases, and suspicions.

Individual Readers

The papers you write in high school and college are usually read by a single teacher or professor who is evaluating your work in the context of a particular course. Instructors form a special audience because they are expected to read your work objectively. Beyond the classroom, however, you may have to persuade someone to read your resume or proposal. Few of these readers will even attempt objectivity. Unlike the papers you write for instructors, your reports and email seek more than a grade. In many instances, you will ask an employer for a job or attempt to persuade a client to buy a product. In accepting your ideas, your reader may invest substantial resources on your behalf, conceivably placing his or her career in your hands. In writing to these individuals, you will have to analyze their needs and concerns very carefully.

Extended Readerships

Many contexts involve two audiences: the immediate person or persons who receive your document and a second, extended readership. When you write as a student, your work is returned to you. In most jobs, your email, reports, and publications are retained for future reference. The safety inspection report you write in April may be routinely skimmed by your supervisor, filed, and forgotten. But if a serious accident occurs in May, this report will be retrieved and closely examined by state inspectors, insurance investigators, and attorneys. If you have a dispute with a customer or another employee, your correspondence may be reviewed by a supervisor or, in the case of litigation, introduced into court as evidence. Many professionals practice "defensive writing," precisely wording their thoughts and observations, understanding that whatever they write may be examined by adversaries. In court, police officers and physicians are often asked to explain and defend comments they wrote months or years before.

When you write outside of academics, bear in mind who else may see your writing. This is a critical consideration whenever you are writing as an employee or agent of others. Think carefully before making remarks that might be misunderstood out of context.

The Perceptual World

To learn how readers respond to ideas, it is helpful to understand what communications researchers call the *perceptual world*—the context in which people perceive and react to new information and experiences. As individuals or groups, readers base their reactions on a number of factors that have varying significance and often operate simultaneously.

- **Social roles,** such as being a parent or a civic leader, influence how people evaluate ideas and respond to events. A thirty-year-old with two small children has different concerns from someone of the same age without children. Coaches, clergy members, shop stewards, and elected officials represent the interests of other people and often consider more than their personal opinions in making judgments.

- **Reference groups** include people or institutions readers respect and to whom they defer. A physician who is unsure about prescribing a new drug may base his or her decision on recommendations from the American Medical Association. A student thinking of changing his or her major might seek advice from parents and friends.

- **Past experiences** influence how people respond to new information and events. Readers who have lost money in the stock market will be more skeptical of an investment offer than those who have enjoyed substantial returns. A labor union with a harmonious relationship with management

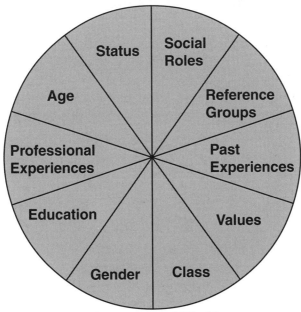

The Perceptual World

will view contract offers differently from a union with a history of stalled talks, bitter negotiations, and strikes.

- **Values,** whether religious, political, or cultural, shape readers' responses. Often these values are unspoken but deeply held. People's attitudes about money, sexual conduct, drug use, abortion, gun control, and many other issues affect how they react to new ideas.

- **Class** can shape the way people respond to political and economic issues. Those with wealth may have different attitudes about the role of government or taxes than working people or the poor.

- **Gender** influences the way people respond to many issues. Polls consistently show a "gender gap" between men and women about topics such as national defense, health care spending, divorce laws, and child support.

- **Education,** both formal and informal, affects people's reading ability, background knowledge, and understanding of terminology. Training in specific disciplines will also influence how readers evaluate the evidence writers present as support. Scientists and mathematicians may be more skeptical than the general public of advertising claims using statistics.

- **Professional experience,** along with training and job responsibilities, shapes people's attitudes. An economics professor with tenure may exhibit a greater ability to be objective about a new tax policy than a small business owner struggling to meet a weekly payroll. Police officers and emergency room doctors may be less sympathetic to drunken drivers than people who rarely see the harm these drivers cause.

- **Age** affects reader attitudes in two ways. People are products of the times they have lived through. Men and women who came of age during World War II have different views than those who grew up during the Vietnam War. In general, older readers have more invested in existing institutions than younger readers and may be more cautious about change.

- **Status** or amount of investment influences people's response to potential change. An entry-level employee is less likely to be concerned about a change in pension plans than someone nearing retirement. Homeowners have more invested in their neighborhoods than renters, and may show greater interest in crime or pollution.

Other aspects of the perceptual world include ethnicity and geography. In determining your readers' perceptual world, it is important to avoid basing assumptions on common stereotypes. Not all older people are conservative, and not all African Americans favor affirmative action. Many elements of the perceptual world are unconscious and cannot be easily ascertained. No doubt you have been surprised by the reactions of friends you believed you knew very well.

QUESTIONS

1. How would you describe the perceptual world of your parents, coworkers, or friends? How do their common experiences, values, roles, and education affect their attitudes? How would they respond to a letter urging them to donate money to the homeless, support a handgun ban, or picket an abortion clinic? Which issues would be difficult to present to them? Why?

2. Have you ever tried to understand someone you hoped to influence? In practicing a presentation, preparing for a job interview, or seeking the right words to discuss a difficult issue with a friend or family member, did you consider how that person might react? Is understanding people's perceptual worlds something we engage in every day?

THE DISCIPLINE

The communication between writer and reader occurs within a particular discipline, setting, culture, publication, or situation. Each academic discipline has a unique history. Some disciplines, such as literature and mathematics, have slowly evolved over thousands of years. Students still read *Oedipus* and study Euclid's principles of geometry. In contrast, the Internet and bioengineering are so new that many of their founders are still actively developing the nature of the discipline.

Every discipline has its own communications style and methods of measuring data, weighing results, and presenting conclusions. In the humanities, research is generally oriented to examining specific works. Whether the researcher is studying Bach, Shakespeare, or Georgia O'Keeffe, the artist's work is the central focus. Disciplines often contain several schools of thought or types of criticism. In literature, for example, some scholars interpret a novel in light of the author's life and thoughts. Other critics would analyze the book in terms of its historical position or political message. Some critics specialize in feminist or Marxist interpretations of literature. But no matter what their approach, literary critics aim to present an educated opinion based on interpretations of the text.

In the sciences, such as biology, chemistry, and physics, scholars base their evaluations on the principles of laboratory research and experiments. Scholars making new assertions in these fields must demonstrate where they obtained their data and prove that other scientists can repeat their experiments and obtain the same results. Although the sciences can seem exact, personal opinion can play a significant role in setting up experiments and interpreting data.

The social sciences of psychology, sociology, criminology, political science, and economics blend some of the features of the humanities and sciences. Although psychologists and criminologists can conduct experiments and often use scientific evidence, many of their conclusions are based on data that can be collected and interpreted in a number of ways.

As a college student, you can appreciate the nature of each discipline you study by examining your textbooks, particularly introductory chapters that often provide a history of the field.

Each profession forms its own context of historical experience, technical training, areas of concern, responsibilities, and political and social outlooks. Corporate executives charged with obtaining investor capital for expansion and research develop different attitudes toward capital gains taxes than social workers assisting low-income families. The medical profession has a strict tradition of relying on standardized treatment and research methods. Physicians tend to be skeptical of anyone claiming to have a cure for a disease unless the claims can be clearly supported by research, not simply anecdotal endorsements. Professions measure success differently, praising creativity, sales, or communications skills. Law enforcement officers approach a case of suspected child abuse with the goal of determining if evidence indicates that a crime has been committed. A mental health professional is more interested in the child's well-being, whether the situation meets the definitions of legal abuse or not. A therapist would treat even an imaginary incident seriously if it caused the child distress.

The discipline, profession, or situation creates different methods of using and looking at writing. David Ogilvy, a noted advertising executive, devoted his career to writing ad copy, coming up with snappy, creative, innovative ways of grabbing consumers' attention and boosting sales of his clients' products. For him, writing was a tool to project an image, gain attention, and, above all, sell:

> Always try to inject *news* into your headlines, because the consumer is always on the lookout for new products, or new ways to use an old product, or new improvements in an old product. The two most powerful words you can use in a headline are FREE and NEW. You can seldom use FREE, but you can almost always use NEW— if you try hard enough.

Fran Martin, a nurse who serves as an expert witness in medical malpractice trials, offers a very different kind of writing advice to nurses. Unlike ad writers, whose success depends on creativity or originality, nurses are expected to maintain precise records:

> You communicate with other health care providers through the chart and, obviously, incorrect data doesn't give an accurate

picture of your patient's condition. That could lead to life-threatening errors. It also raises the specter of fraud, which could make your actions appear not just negligent, but also criminal.

Writing Contexts

The contexts in which writers operate are limitless, but there are general patterns:

1. **Expert to general reader:** Most books and articles are written by experts to people reading for information or enjoyment. An attorney preparing a university brochure on drunk driving would have to anticipate that most students' understanding of the law has been shaped by movies and television. He or she might have to dispel common misconceptions and explain legal terms and procedures.

2. **Expert to expert within a discipline:** Law reviews, medical journals, and trade magazines are largely read by professionals within a specific field. Writers for these periodicals assume readers will understand basic concepts and terminology. Advanced textbooks in biology or criminal law rarely provide the introductory material found in first-year books. The email, reports, and documents generated within a corporation or government agency may adopt a unique style and format that almost become a code few outsiders can understand. But writers in these situations should always keep an extended readership in mind. An audit, budget review, or investigation could circulate as an email or be available online to a wider audience.

3. **Expert to expert in another discipline:** This is perhaps one of the most challenging contexts writers face. Einstein's letter to Roosevelt is a classic example of this context—a world-famous scientist attempting to explain a discovery to a powerful political leader with minimal knowledge of physics. How does an engineer explain the practical difficulties of construction to a designer interested in style and creativity? How does an economist persuade a governor facing reelection to raise taxes or cut benefits? In communicating with professionals in another discipline, it is important for writers to establish trust, address their readers' concerns, and explain unfamiliar concepts clearly.

Whenever you write, it is important to consider the context—your goals, your reader, the discipline, and the nature of the document. Context will determine how you should state your ideas, which supporting details to include, and which words you should choose.

Info Write provides additional information on the writing context.
cengage.learning.infowrite.com

CHAPTER TWO

THE WRITING PROCESS

Writing is a process as well as a product. Good writing respects each of the three elements of context. When you plan a writing project, determine your purpose, evaluate your readers, and follow the conventions of your discipline. Many college instructors provide requirements for writing assignments. In a professional situation, you can benefit from examining samples of the writing tasks you are undertaking.

CRITICAL THINKING

Good writing is never "about" a topic—it has a purpose and makes a point. An essay about your summer vacation can be simply a list of places you visited and things you did, or it can focus on something deeper, something more significant—how visiting Mount Rushmore made you contemplate American values, how traveling together helped you appreciate your family, how spending a weekend in a cabin without electricity led you to discover how lost you feel without the Internet. A good paper shares more than facts and dates, first impressions, or immediate reactions. Good writing seeks to get beyond the obvious to explore ideas and events, to analyze people and ideas.

For example, if you decide to write an essay about your first apartment, your initial thought might be to record every detail you can remember, trying to capture on paper what the apartment looked like:

```
On August 12, 2010, I moved into my first apartment. It was a
flat on Newhall Street on the top floor of a hundred-year-old
house. The living room was massive and had wood paneling and an-
tique brass chandeliers. The dining room had a huge built-in buf-
fet and china cabinets with glass doors I used as bookcases. The
kitchen was L-shaped and narrow, but there was a pantry with lots
of shelves. The battered refrigerator was old but spacious.
```

There were two big bedrooms. I planned to use the front bedroom for my study. The back bedroom was a bit smaller, but it had a great advantage. It was away from the street and shielded from the noise of traffic. In addition, there were awnings that blocked the morning sun, so I could sleep late on weekends. The bedrooms did not have any closets. Instead, there were large two-door wardrobes with built-in drawers. There was a spacious balcony off the front bedroom. It was covered by a redwood deck and had new patio furniture and an outdoor grill.

I had little money and had to get furniture from Goodwill and the Salvation Army. The floors were bare, but I covered them with old carpeting from my parents' house.

This approach will probably create an essay that lists physical details of minimal interest to anyone else. Before beginning to write, you might think about the topic and ask yourself some questions:

Why did you choose this topic? Of all the possible subjects, why did you decide to write about your first apartment? What made you think of that, rather than your first car, your last boss, a trip to Mexico, or a recent job interview? Clearly, something about that apartment made it significant. What did it represent to you? What events took place there that changed your life? Are your memories of this place happy or sad? Why? What did you learn there? What is the most important thing you want your readers to know?

What are the most significant details? Instead of listing everything you can remember about your subject, select the most memorable details. Is the date you moved or the number of bedrooms really important? What do you want readers to remember about your topic?

How can you share your thoughts and feelings with readers? Readers may not be interested in a room-by-room description of an apartment, but they may be able to identify with more universal experiences, thoughts, or emotions. How did you feel about moving? What change did it make in your life? What are the larger issues that other people can relate to?

What is the dominant impression you want to give readers? Focusing on a single impression or message can help you select details. If you concentrate on describing your excitement about getting your first apartment, you can ignore irrelevant details such as dates, furnishings, and parking.

Considering these questions can help create an essay that has greater meaning for both you and your reader:

> In August I moved into my first apartment, a great flat on Newhall Street. Although I could only afford to furnish it with battered items from Goodwill and the Salvation Army, I was excited. I was finally going to be on my own, free of my parents, my cramped room, my sisters' fighting, my brother's stereo. I spent two weeks cleaning, painting, and organizing the old flat into my home. I hung up posters of my favorite bands, stocked the kitchen with my favorite foods, and set the radio to my favorite stations. I was finally on my own, free at last.
>
> But coming home from class, I was struck by the silence. Instead of hearing the drone of my brother's stereo, my sisters' laughing and fighting, I heard the hum of the refrigerator and the nervous tick-tick of an electric clock. I always hated that my mother watched soap operas but found myself turning the television on in the afternoon to hear the hated but familiar voices while I labored over algebra or ironed clothes.
>
> On weekends I went home—but not to raid the kitchen or borrow money. I had been an adult. I had been responsible. I saved money over the summer and budgeted it carefully. I could easily afford my new apartment. I had hungered for a place of my own all through high school. But I never imagined what it would feel like to go to bed and to wake up in an empty house.

By thinking in more detail about a subject, you can probe its depth, developing writing that does more than simply report facts and record observations.

Critical thinking involves moving beyond first impressions by carefully analyzing subjects, people, and ideas. Too often we rush to judgment, making instant assumptions based on what we think we know rather than what we can prove. We confuse opinions with facts, accept statistics without question, and let stereotypes color our evaluations. We allow what we "feel" to short-circuit how we think:

> Pete Wilson was a great quarterback—he'll make a great coach.
>
> Nancy's driving a BMW—her new travel agency must be a success.
>
> Alabama improved reading scores 12 percent using this program—our schools should use it, too.
>
> Jersey Lube ruined my car—two days after I went there for an oil change my transmission went out.

All these statements make a kind of sense at first glance. But further analysis will lead you to question their validity:

> Does a skilled quarterback necessarily know how to coach—how to inspire, manage, and teach other players, especially those on defense?

> Does Nancy even own the BMW she was seen driving? Did she get it as a gift, pay for it with existing savings, borrow it from a friend, or lease it at a low rate? Does the car really prove anything about the success or failure of her travel agency?

> Alabama may have improved reading scores with a particular program, but does that really prove the program will work in Nevada or Minnesota? Could children in other states have low reading scores caused by other reasons than those in Alabama?

> Did Jersey Lube ruin your transmission? The mechanics may have only changed the oil and never touched the transmission, which was due to fail in two days. Had you driven through a car wash the day before, could you just as easily blame them?

Errors like these are easy to make. Unless you develop critical thinking skills, you can be impressed by evidence that at first glance seems reliable and convincing.

Avoiding Errors in Critical Thinking

Lapses in critical thinking are called logical fallacies. In reading the works of others and developing your own ideas, try to avoid these common mistakes:

- **Hasty generalizations** If your dorm room is robbed, a friend's car stolen from the student union parking lot, and a classmate's purse snatched on her way to class, you might assume that the campus is experiencing a crime wave. The evidence is compelling because it is immediate and personal. But it does not prove there is an increase in campus crime. In fact, crime could be dropping, and you and your friends may simply have the misfortune to fall into the declining pool of victims. Only a comparative review of police and security reports would prove if crime is increasing. Resist jumping to conclusions.

- **Absolute statements** Although it is important to convince readers by making strong assertions, avoid absolute claims that can be dismissed with a single exception. If you write, "All professional athletes are irresponsible," readers only need to think of a single exception to dismiss your argument. A qualified remark, however, is harder to disprove. The claim that "Many professional athletes are irresponsible" acknowledges that exceptions exist.

- **Non *sequitur* (it does not follow)** Avoid making assertions based on irrelevant evidence: "Jill Klein won an Oscar for best actress last year—she'll be great on Broadway." Although an actress might succeed on film, she may lack the ability to perform on stage before a live audience. The skills and style suited for film acting do not always translate well to the theater.

- **Begging the question** Do not assume what has to be proved: "These needless math classes should be dropped because no one uses algebra and geometry after they graduate." This statement makes an assertion, but it fails to prove that the courses are needless or that "no one" uses mathematics outside of academic settings.

- **False dilemma** Do not offer or accept only two alternatives to a problem: "Either employees must take a 20 percent wage cut, or the company will go bankrupt." This statement ignores other possible solutions such as raising prices, lowering production costs, selling unused assets, or increasing sales. If a wage cut is needed, does it have to be 20 percent? Could it be 15 percent or 10 percent? Before choosing what appears to be the better of two bad choices, determine if there are other options.

- **False analogy** Comparisons make weak arguments: "Marijuana should be legalized since Prohibition did not work." Marijuana and alcohol are different substances. Alcohol has been consumed by humans for thousands of years. Marijuana, however, has never had wide social acceptance. The fact that Prohibition failed could be used to justify legalizing anything that is banned, including assault weapons, child pornography, or crack cocaine.

- **Red herring** Resist the temptation to dodge the real issue by making emotionally charged or controversial statements: "How can you justify spending money on a new football stadium when homeless people are sleeping in the streets and terrorists are threatening to destroy us?" Homelessness and terrorism are genuine concerns but have little to do with the merits of a proposed stadium. The same argument could be used to attack building a park, a zoo, or an art gallery.

- **Borrowed authority** Avoid assuming that an expert in one field can be accepted as an authority in another: "Senator Goode claims Italy will win the World Cup." A respected senator may have no more insight into soccer than a cab driver or a hairdresser. Celebrity endorsements are common examples of borrowed authority.

- **Ad *hominem* (attacking the person)** Attack ideas, not the people who advocate them: "How can you accept the budget proposed by an alderman accused of domestic violence?" The merits of the budget have to be examined, not the person who proposed it.

- **Assuming past events will predict the future** The 2008 recession was caused, in part, because mortgage brokers believed that real estate prices would continue to rise 6 percent annually. When home values fell as much as 50 percent, millions of homeowners faced foreclosure and investors lost billions of dollars. Past trends cannot be assumed to continue into the future.

- **Ignoring alternative interpretations** Even objective facts can be misleading. If research shows that reports of child abuse have jumped 250 percent in the last ten years, does that mean that child abuse is on the rise? Could those numbers instead reflect stricter reporting methods or an expanded definition of abuse, so that previously unrecorded incidents are now counted?

- **"Filtering" data** If you begin with a preconceived thesis, you may consciously or unconsciously select evidence that supports your view and omit evidence that contradicts it. Good analysis is objective; it does not consist of simply collecting facts to support a previously held conviction. A list of high school dropouts who became celebrities does not disprove the value of a diploma.

- **Assuming that parts represent the whole** Just because one or more patients respond favorably to a new drug does not mean that it will cure all people suffering from the same disease. In the extreme, because individual men and women die does not mean the human race will eventually become extinct.

- **Assuming the whole represents each part** If 50 percent of students on campus receive financial aid, it does not mean you can assume that half the English majors receive aid. The student population in any given department may be less or more than the college average.

- **Mistaking a time relationship for a cause** (*post hoc, ergo propter hoc*) If your brakes fail after taking your car into the dealer for a tune-up, does that mean the mechanics are to blame? Can the president take credit for a drop in unemployment six months after signing a labor bill? Because events occur in time, it can be easy to assume an action that precedes another is a cause. The mechanics may not have touched your brakes, which were bound to wear out with or without a tune-up. A drop in unemployment could be caused by a decline in interest rates or an upsurge in exports and may have nothing to do with a labor bill. Do not assume events were caused by preceding events.

- **Mistaking an effect for a cause** Early physicians saw fever as a cause of disease rather than as an effect or symptom. If you observe that children with poor reading skills watch a lot of television, you might easily assume that television interferes with their reading. In fact, excessive viewing could be a symptom. Because they have trouble reading, they watch television.

STRATEGIES FOR ENHANCING CRITICAL THINKING

There is no quick method of enhancing critical thinking, but you can challenge yourself to move beyond first impressions and hasty generalizations by considering these questions:

1. **How much do you really know about this subject?** Do you fully understand the history, depth, and character of the topic? Are you basing your assumptions on objective facts or only on what you have read on blogs or heard on talk shows? Should you learn more by conducting research or interviewing people before making judgments?

2. **Have you looked at your topic closely?** First impressions can be striking but misleading. Examine your subject closely, ask questions, and probe beneath the surface. Look for patterns; measure similarities and differences.

3. **Have you rushed to judgment?** Collect evidence but avoid drawing conclusions until you have analyzed your findings and observations.

4. **Do you separate facts from opinions?** Don't confuse facts, evidence, and data with opinions, claims, and assertions. Opinions are judgments or inferences, not facts. Facts are reliable pieces of information that can be verified by studying other sources:

   FACT: This semester a laptop, petty cash, and an iPod were taken from the tutoring lab while Sue Harper was on duty.

   OPINION: Sue Harper is a thief.

   The factual statement can be proven. Missing items can be documented. The assumption that Sue Harper is responsible remains to be proven.

5. **Are you aware of your assumptions?** Assumptions are ideas we accept or believe to be true. It is nearly impossible to divorce ourselves from what we have been taught, but you can sharpen your critical thinking skills if you acknowledge your assumptions. Avoid relying too heavily on a single assumption—that IQ tests measure intelligence, that poverty causes crime, that television has a bad influence on children.

6. **Have you collected enough evidence?** A few statistics and quotations taken out of context may seem convincing, but they cannot be viewed as adequate proof. Make sure you collect enough evidence from a variety of sources before making judgments.

7. **Do you evaluate evidence carefully?** Do you apply common standards to evaluate the data you collect? Do you question the source of statistics or the validity of an eyewitness? The fact that you can find dozens of books about alien abductions does not prove they occur.

WRITING ACTIVITY

1. Review this list of topics and select one that you have strong opinions and feelings about.

the president	the war on terrorism	gun control
reality TV shows	gay marriage	NFL players
high school	your boss	homelessness
health insurance	landlords	online dating
cable news	lotteries	hybrid cars
global warming	welfare reform	job interviews

2. After selecting a topic, write a statement summarizing your attitudes about it. Write a full paragraph or list ideas or even words you associate with this subject.

3. Examine your comments carefully and consider these questions:

What do I really know about this topic?

Why do I feel this way?

Would other people call my views unfair or biased?

Are my views based on facts or assumptions?

Can I provide sufficient evidence to support my opinion?

Do I detect any logical fallacies in my response—hasty generalizations, red herrings, or mistaking a time relationship for a cause?

Do I need to conduct additional research before I can make a valid judgment?

Are there alternative opinions? Do they have any merit?

Could I organize a logical and convincing argument to persuade others to accept my point of view?

Examining and challenging your values, ideas, and opinions improves your ability to express yourself to others and anticipate their questions and objections.

Prewriting

Writing is not only a means of preparing a document but a way of thinking and exploring ideas. You can use a number of planning techniques to discover topics, define your thesis, and list needed support.

Freewriting records thoughts and impressions without interruption and without any concern for spelling, grammar, or punctuation. Freewriting should not be confused with writing a rough draft. Freewriting is like talking to yourself. It may have no direction, it may skip from topic to topic, and it may contradict itself. Freewriting is a bit like making a series of fast sketches before determining the subject matter of a large painting. The goal of freewriting is not writing a "paper" but simply discovering possible topics.

Overhearing a claim that the government was behind the influx of drugs in the inner city, a student sat at her computer and rapidly recorded a stream of thoughts on the topic of conspiracy theories:

> The CIA is behind the drug epidemic. The US government pays South Koreans to set up grocery stores in the ghetto. Every president since Nixon has lied about MIA's held captive in Southeast Asia. The Air Force lies about UFO sitings. The number of conspiracy theories is limitless. The lumber industry is against legalizing marijuana because hemp makes better paper than wood pulp. Roosevelt knew the Japanese were going to bomb Pearl Harbor but let it happen. The government either planned or knew about 9/11 but let it happen so that Bush could attack Iraq and grab their oil. Obama was born in Kenya. Conspiracies are endless. They are popular. They light up the blogosphere, create a lot of TV shows, and employ an army of theorists who move from talk show to talk show touting their books and their latest proof that the CIA or ilegal immigrants or the Fortune 500 is responsible for some horrible deed or social threat. No doubt some mad scientist in a govenment laboratory created AIDS and loosed it on the world. No doubt someone has cured cancer and has been kidnapped or killed so that millions of doctors and thousands of drug companies won't go out of business. Why? Why do people love these theories?
>
> Some people do need to believe that no lone asassin could have killed JFK. They cling to this belief, no matter what the evidence. Why? Maybe we need to believe in conspiracy theories. It

```
makes the evil in the world less frightening. We are not victims
of random choas, but of evil people who can theoretically be lo-
cated and exposed. To abandon conspiracy theories means accepting
chaos. Also it allows us to escape blame. If we put the blame for
all our problems on mysterious forces beyond our control, then we
can dodge personal responsiblity.
```

Although this freewriting is loose, repetitive, and misspelled, it moves from listing conspiracy theories to speculating about why people need to believe in them. The student now has something to focus on and a possible title: "Why We Need Conspiracy Theories."

Brainstorming is another prewriting process that can help you generate ideas and identify possible topics for further writing. As in freewriting, list your ideas as quickly as possible. Do not worry if your ideas are repetitive or irrelevant. Again, your purpose is not to outline a paper but simply to develop ideas.

Brainstorming can be used to discover a topic for an essay or to help a professional identify details that need to be included in a business letter or report. A composition student assigned a comparison/contrast essay might list as many ideas as possible in the hope of discovering a topic:

```
high school teachers/college professors
male/female attitudes about first dates
American/Japanese ideas about privacy
Puerto Ricans vs. Mexican Americans
Mexican-born vs. 1st generation Mex-Americans
English only vs. bilingual
Mexican-born English/1st generation Mex-American English
```

Through brainstorming or listing, the student has run through a number of ideas before focusing on a topic suited for a short paper: comparing the attitudes of Mexican-born Americans and their children toward English.

Even when the topic is defined, brainstorming can help writers identify important facts and details. The supervisor of a warehouse writing a report following a forklift accident could use brainstorming to make sure he or she produces a complete account that managers can use to examine the firm's legal liability, safety policies, employee training, and equipment use:

```
time/date/location of accident
Injured personnel-Alex Bolton, Sara Lopez (Medical Status)
911 call-get time from dispatcher
Bolton's forklift-last inspection (service log)
```

```
forklift load-stability (check manual)
Use of helmets
surveillance cameras (tapes)
accident witnesses
```

From this list, the supervisor identifies the information required to meet the needs of the readers.

<hr>

WRITING ACTIVITY

1. *Freewriting:* Select one of the following topics, and write for at least ten minutes. Do not worry about making sense or maintaining logical connections between ideas. Remember, this is not the rough draft of a paper but an attempt to develop ideas and discover topics.

downloading music	blind dates	camera phones and privacy
prisons	binge drinking	capital punishment
recycling	road rage	student loans
family values	car repair	media images of women

2. *Brainstorming:* Select one of the columns of ideas and build on it, adding your own ideas. Jot down your thoughts as quickly as possible. Do not worry if some of your ideas are off the topic.

men/women	success/money	vacation plans
dating	careers	plane/car
expectations	salary/income	hotel/meals
conflicts	risk/reward	budget/costs

<hr>

Clustering is a visual method of developing ideas. Instead of writing complete sentences or listing ideas, topics are grouped in circles and boxes. Visual markers such as arrows, question marks, and ink color can be used to organize and link ideas. Thinking about his sister's decision to adopt a baby from China, a student clustered a series of observations and questions:

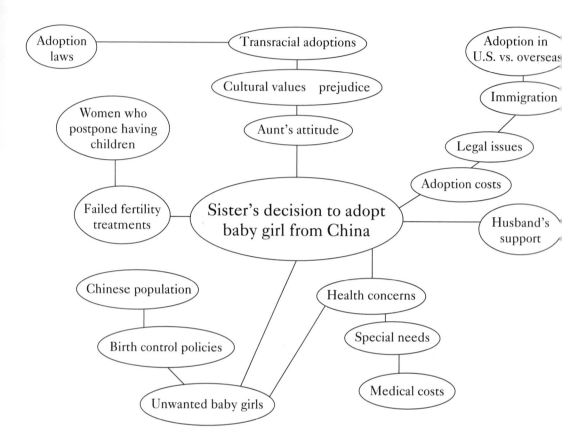

In this case, clustering helps chart the positive and negative elements of transracial adaption.

Asking questions is a method used by reporters and investigators to help identify critical information. For generations, newspaper reporters have been trained to ask the "five Ws": *Who? What? When? Where? Why?* Asking questions can help you identify topics and narrow your focus. A student considering writing a paper about Arthur Miller's play *Death of a Salesman* might list the following questions to help identify a topic for a short analytical paper:

```
              Death of a Salesman

What are Willy's values?
Is Willy a victim of society or of his own delusions?
What role does Uncle Ben play?
Is Willy's suicide caused by despair or a last attempt at success?
What impact does Willy's infidelity have?
Biff steals a suit and a fountain pen. What do these objects
  represent?
```

```
Linda knows Willy has lost his salary but does not confront him
  about it. Why?
Why does Miller compare Willy and Biff to Uncle Charlie and
  Bernard?
Is the play an attack on the American dream?
Why does Willy refuse to take a job from Charlie?
This play is world famous but the hero is abusive, selfish, and
  short-tempered. Why is the play so popular?
What is the purpose of the requiem at the end? How would the play
  be different without it?
```

By posing lists of questions, you can often identify key issues and provoke critical thinking that will lead to development of a thesis.

WRITING ACTIVITY

1. *Clustering:* Select one of the following topics. Use a large piece of paper to record and arrange your ideas. Group related ideas with circles or squares. Use arrows to connect ideas. You may use different colors, switch from pen to pencil, or mark major ideas with a highlighter. Whatever method you use, do not allow your artwork to overshadow your goal of developing ideas for a paper.

year-round school	identity theft	diets
child support	the American dream	women in combat
airport security	working out	teenage obesity
aging	Internet scams	outsourcing jobs

2. *Asking questions:* Select one of the following topics, and write a list of questions. Write as quickly as possible, and do not worry about being repetitive. Try to ask as many questions as you can to explore as many avenues as possible.

recent hit movie	gangs	credit cards
unions	suburbs	role models
teen pregnancy	rap music	bloggers' impact on politics
nightclubs	spring break	YouTube

Moving From Topic to Thesis

Good writing has a purpose. A paper is never "about" something; it must make a clear statement. Whether the topic is global warming, a first job, terrorism, or a high school football game, your writing should make a point or express an opinion. The *thesis* is the paper's main or controlling idea. A *thesis statement* presents the writer's position in a sentence or two and serves as the document's mission statement. *A thesis is more than a limited or narrowed topic—it expresses a point of view. It is a declaration stating your purpose.*

Topic	Narrowed Topic	Thesis Statement
gun control	handgun ban	*The city's proposed handgun ban will not prevent gang violence.*
online crime	consumer fraud	*Consumers will resist shopping on the Internet unless credit card security is assured.*
campus housing	rehabbing dorms	*Because of increased demand for on-campus housing, the fifty-year-old men's dorm should be rehabbed.*
terrorism	cyberterrorism	*Homeland Security must take greater steps to protect sensitive computer networks from cyber attacks.*

Elements of a Thesis Statement

Effective thesis statements share common characteristics:

They are generally stated in a single sentence. This statement forms the core of the paper and clearly and concisely states your point of view.

They express an opinion or point of view, not a topic or a fact. A thesis statement does more than announce what the paper is about; it makes a declaration. The statement *This paper is about teenage obesity* announces a topic. The sentence *One out of four teenagers is obese* presents a fact. A thesis expresses a point: *We must curb teenage obesity because it is responsible for the epidemic of juvenile diabetes, early heart disease, and misuse of diet pills.*

They limit the topic. A thesis statement can focus the paper by limiting the scope of the writer's concentration. *Television is bad for children* states an opinion but fails to target the paper, and can lead a writer to list only superficial observations. A defined thesis statement such as *Television action heroes teach children that violence is an acceptable method of resolving conflicts* guides the writer to develop a more engaging and original paper.

They indicate the kind of support that follows. Opinions require proof. The thesis *Because of declining enrollments, the costly film course should be cancelled* indicates an argument based on factual support, leading readers to expect enrollment and budget figures.

They organize supporting material. The thesis statement *Exercise is essential to control weight, prevent disease, and reduce stress* suggests the body of the paper will be presented in three parts.

Effective thesis statements are precisely worded. Because they express a writer's main idea in a single sentence, thesis statements must be accurately worded. General words like *good, bad, serious,* and *important* are vague and weak. The thesis statement *The college should improve dorm security to prevent crime* is not as effective as *The college should install deadbolt locks to deter break-ins,* which is both more accurate and easier to support.

Supporting the Thesis

Once you have determined your thesis, you can begin selecting supporting details. Writers support their theses using various kinds of evidence, ranging from personal observations to statistics. Because each kind of evidence has limitations, writers often present a blend of supporting details.

Personal observations are descriptive details and sensory impressions about a person, place, object, or condition. Writers can support a thesis by supplying readers with specific details. The thesis "Westwood High School must be renovated" can be supported with detailed observations about leaking roofs, faulty wiring, unsafe elevators, and peeling paint.

Personal experiences can provide convincing support. As a college student, you have direct insight into higher education. An Iraq War veteran has insights about combat and greater credibility than a commentator relying on media reports. Because personal observations and experiences are individual, writers often provide objective evidence such as facts or statistics to give their writing greater authority.

Examples are specific events, persons, or situations that represent a general trend, condition, or concept. A writer supporting the right to die might relate the story of a single terminal patient. The story of one small business could illustrate an economic trend. Because examples are isolated, they are often supplemented with facts and statistics.

Testimony consists of observations and statements by witnesses, participants, and experts. A paper about global warming might include quotations by environmentalists citing scientific studies and farmers reporting personal observations.

Facts are objective details that can be gathered or observed. The need for greater airport security can be demonstrated by counting security officers, noting defective surveillance cameras, and reviewing inspection reports.

Statistics are factual data expressed in numbers. A paper about identity theft might include statistics about the number of victims, the amount of money stolen, or the time it takes a person to restore his or her credit rating. Statistics can be easily manipulated or misinterpreted and should be used carefully.

Whatever evidence you select to support your thesis, make sure it is *relevant, accurate,* and *reliable.* Avoid taking facts, statistics, or quotations out of context. Make sure your evidence truly supports your thesis. Readers will only be persuaded by your support if you present it clearly and indicate where you obtained facts, quotations, and statistics.

Developing Outlines

Once you have assembled supporting details, you can create a plan or outline to guide your writing. Consider an outline as a rough sketch or road map to help organize ideas and guide your writing. A student familiar with life insurance might create an informal outline like this one to list reminders to guide a first draft:

```
            Whole Life and Term Insurance

     Whole Life
     - explain premiums
     - savings and loan options

     Term
     - no savings
     - lower rates
     Conclusion - last point
```

A formal outline, however, includes more detail, so prewriting can be refined into a clear framework for the first draft. Outlines should address the goals of the three main parts of any essay:

The introduction grabs attention, states the writer's goal, and indicates the kind of support to follow. Avoid introductions that simply announce a topic: *This paper is about life insurance. Life insurance is very important.* Writers use several techniques to create effective introductions:

Open with a thesis statement:

> Life insurance should form the core of any investment portfolio.

Begin with a fact or statistic:

> Two-thirds of 2,500 business owners surveyed only had enough life insurance to support their families for six months.

Use a quotation:

> Addressing consumers last month, Andrea Hernandez announced, "With the collapse of real estate values, couples can no longer consider the equity in their homes as a source of income in the event of a spouse's death."

Open with a brief narrative:

> Frank Monroe planned to leave his children a thriving software company. But without life insurance proceeds to cover the expenses of Frank's final illness and make up for lost income, his son was forced to sell the family business at a loss.

The body presents supporting details in a logical manner. Depending on the kind of paper you are writing, you can use a variety of methods to organize details:

Chronological order organizes details by time. Personal narratives, biographies, and historical events are usually presented as a chain of events.

Spatial order breaks details into major parts or types. An essay about alternative energy might be organized into three sections: wind, solar, and biofuels. A paper about life insurance could discuss insurance options for single adults, couples with small children, and people nearing retirement.

Degree of importance opens with the most important details and concludes with the least important, or begins with a minor detail and concludes with the most important. Your most significant ideas should open or close an essay, because that is where readers' attention is highest. Do not place these ideas in the middle of a document where readers may overlook them.

The conclusion brings the paper to a logical end and makes a final impression on the reader. Avoid simply repeating the introduction: *In conclusion,* *insurance should form the core of any investment portfolio.* There are several methods of creating an effective conclusion:

Present a call to action:

When you do your taxes this year, take time to review your life insurance needs.

End with a question to provoke thought:

How long could your family pay its bills in the event of your death?

Conclude with a quotation:

Speaking at a convention last month, Janet Liebling told investment counselors "All the media coverage of real estate and the stock market has led too many of us to overlook what should be the bedrock of our clients' investments—life insurance."

End with a final fact, statistic, claim, or prediction:

With an unpredictable stock market and falling housing prices, more investors are buying life insurance to provide security for their families.

In the next example, a student develops a formal outline using spatial order to compare two forms of life insurance:

Whole Life and Term Insurance

```
  I. Introduction: Whole life and term insurance
 II. Whole life insurance
     A. General description
        1. History
        2. Purpose
           a. Protection against premature death
           b. Premium payments include savings
     B. Investment feature
        1. Cash value accrual
        2. Loans against cash value
III. Term insurance
     A. General description
        1. History
        2. Purpose
           a. Protection against premature death
           a. Premium payments lower than whole life insurance
```

        B. Investment feature
            1. No cash accrual
            2. No loans against cash value
        C. Cost advantage
            1. Lower premiums
            2. Affordability of greater coverage
IV. Conclusion
        A. Insurance needs of consumer
            1. Income
            2. Family situation
            3. Investment goals and savings
            4. Obligations
        B. Investment counselors' advice about insurance coverage

HOW TO WRITE AN ESSAY

Many writers use a five-stage process that helps improve their writing and save time. As a beginning writer, you can benefit from following these guidelines. With experience, you can personalize your method of writing.

1. **Plan—establish context.** Once you have established your goal and thesis, determine how you will develop your paper in light of your readers' needs and the conventions of your discipline. Develop an outline listing the items needed to achieve your goal. Make sure the introduction and conclusion are effective and that the body of the paper is clearly organized.

2. **Write—get your ideas on paper.** After reviewing your plans, write as much as possible without stopping. Writing the first draft can be considered controlled freewriting. As you write, new ideas may occur to you. Record *all* your thoughts. Do not pause to check spelling or look up a fact, because doing so may break your train of thought. Underline words you think are misspelled and sentences that contain grammatical errors. Leave gaps for missing details. Place question marks next to items you want to double-check. Make notes to yourself rather than breaking your train of thought by stopping to look up facts or check errors.

3. **Cool—put your writing aside.** It is difficult to evaluate your work immediately after writing because much of what you wish to say is still fresh in your mind. Set your work aside. Work on other assignments, read, watch television, or take a walk to clear your mind. Afterward, you can return to your writing with greater objectivity.

4. **Revise—review your writing in context.** Before searching your paper for misspelled words or grammatical errors, examine it holistically. Review your

goal and plan. Examine any instructions you have received. Then read your paper. Does it clearly express your goal and support your thesis? Is it properly directed to your audience? Does it violate any principles in the discipline? Revision can mean rewriting the entire paper or merely reworking details.

5. **Edit—correct mechanical errors and polish style.** When you have a completed paper, examine your writing for grammatical errors and missing and misspelled words. In addition, review your diction. Eliminate wordy phrases and reduce repetition. Make sure ideas flow evenly and smoothly. *Reading a paper aloud can help identify errors and awkward sentences.*

These five stages are not neatly isolated. Writing, according to current research, is *recursive*—the steps overlap and occur simultaneously. As you write, you will find yourself brainstorming, editing, correcting spelling, and freewriting.

Each writing assignment is unique. For example, a narrative requires attention to chronology, while a division paper demands clear organization, and persuasion depends on the skillful use of logic. Each discipline represents a distinct discourse community. In literature courses, students are expected to provide original interpretations of literary works such as plays and novels. Students in the sciences are required to follow strict standards for gathering data, analyzing results, and presenting conclusions. Undoubtedly, you may find some papers more challenging than others. Because it is often difficult to determine how hard a particular assignment may be, it is advisable to start writing as soon as possible. Just ten minutes of prewriting will quickly reveal how much time and effort you need to devote to an assignment.

STRATEGIES FOR CREATING A COMPOSING STYLE

1. **Review past writing.** Consider how you have written in the past. Which papers received the highest and lowest grades in high school? Why? What can you recall about writing them? What mistakes did you make? What comments have teachers made about your work? Did you have trouble organizing or wording letters or reports you wrote at work?

2. **Experiment with composing.** Write at different times and places, using pen and paper or a computer. See what conditions enhance your writing.

3. **Study returned papers for clues.** Read your instructors' comments carefully. If your papers lack a clear thesis, devote more attention to prewriting and planning. If instructors fill your papers with red ink—circling misspelled words and underlining fragments—spend more time editing.

WRITING THE WHOLE COMPOSITION

The stages of the writing process are illustrated by a student developing a paper for a freshman composition class. Having read and discussed several essays concerning criminal justice, the class was instructed to turn in a short commentary debating the merits of a current legal issue.

Prewriting

The student began by exploring topics through prewriting. Note that her work blends several techniques, including brainstorming, freewriting, and clustering:

```
Topics:      criminal justice (issues)
             capital punishment
             pro/con gun control
             courtroom TV
             What is the impact of televised trials?
             Do TV trials educate the public?
             How does media attention affect juries?
             Victims and crime—are they forgotten?
             Who speaks for victims?
             Do prosecutors properly speak for victims?
```

Victim impact statements are increasingly a feature of modern trials as people are allowed to state their feelings about the crime and the criminal after he/she is convicted. Judges can consider the impact of the crime on the victim in sentencing.

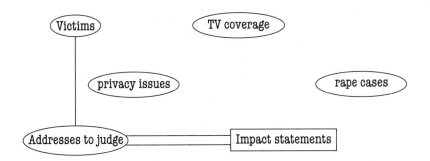

Sometimes victims ask for harsh punishment and sometimes they even ask for leniency and give the criminal, especially a young person a second chance...
Who is most impressive?
What about victims who can't speak well or don't know English?
What about families of homicide victims?
Victims without mourners? Less important?

Topic: Victim impact statements
Thesis: Although victim impact statements are supposed to
            empower the victims of crime, they may serve only to
            further marginalize the most helpless among us.

Planning

Victim Impact Statements

INTRO: Background of impact statements
            Definition
PRO: - empowers victims who feel forgotten
            - helps heal victims by addressing criminals
            - helps people regain control over their lives and
              move on
            - makes the human cost of a crime part of the sen-
              tencing decision.
CON: Question?
            Whose impact is more effective?
            Middle-class professional vs. welfare mom
END: Question, helpful or hurtful to victims?

First Draft with Revision Notes

In America today more and more victims of crime are being

allowed to address the court in terms of making what is called a

victim impact statment. These statements are very important in

sp
Wordy,
Awkward   making changes in the way people, the public, the media, and

judges look at crime and criminals. These statements can be writ-

ten or delivered orally.

Advocates of victim impact statements point to advantages.

First, these statements give people voices. For years people have

felt helpless. Prosecutors represent the state, not the individ-

sp   ual. They have been upset when prosacuters have arranged plee bargains without their OK. Some victims are still recovering from their injuries when they learn the guy who hurt them is walking off with probation.   *Wordy*

Therapists who work with victims also have been known to say that being able to <u>adress</u> the court helps with the healing   *sp* process. Victims of violent crime can feel powerless and vulnerable. So instead of suffering in silence, they are given the chance to talk to the criminal, to clear their chests, and get on with the rest of their lives. These statements allow judges to consider what sentences are appropriate. But giving victims a chance to speak raises some issues. What about the victims who cannot present themselves? **Add idea?**

[Victim impact statements may help victims who are smart to begin with but not help those who are not. **Expand ideas?**

Revision Notes
- Need stronger opening
- Check spelling
- Add examples

Revised Draft with Instructor's Annotations

Across America today more and more victims of crime are being allowed to address the court in terms of making what is called a   *vague, wordy* victim impact statement. These statements are very important and are changing the way the public, the media, and judges look at crim-

Define   inals. These statements can be written or delivered orally. *Be spe-cific. What is the purpose of these statements? Provide clear definition.*
This written or oral presentation to the court allows victims

to express their feelings to the judge after someone has been con-

victed of a crime. *Add examples*

use only with more than one point   Advocates of victim impact statements point to key advantages.

<u>First</u>, these statements give victims a voice. For years, victims

have felt helpless. Prosecutors represent the state, not the crime

sp   victim. Victims have been dismayed when <u>prosacuters</u> have arranged

plea bargains without their knowledge. Some victims are still re-

covering from their injuries when they learn the person who hurt

them pled to a lesser charge and received probation.

Therapists who work with victims also say that being able to

address the court helps with the healing process. Victims of

violent crime can feel powerless and vulnerable. Instead of

suffering in silence, they are given the chance to address the
Informal, delete
criminal, to <u>clear their chests</u>, and get on with the rest of

their lives.

Impact statements allow judges to consider what sentences are appropriate. In one case, a judge who planned to fine a teenager for shoplifting accepted the storeowner's suggestion of <u>waving</u> the _sp_ fine if the defendant completed his GED.

But giving victims a chance to speak raises some issues. What about the victim who is not articulate, who doesn't even speak English? Expand this final point.

Comments

A good topic, but the essay needs further development:

— Add a stronger attention getter at the opening to dramatize impact statements.

— Define what an impact statement is. You state they are important but do not fully explain what they are.

— You mention the advantages and disadvantages of impact statements but do not provide enough examples.

— The ending could raise more than one question. Reading your paper aloud can help you detect weak, awkward, and repetitive phrases.

Final Draft

The courtroom scene was riveting. One by one, the survivors of a deadly commuter-train shooting took the stand and addressed the man who had maimed them. Their voices quivering with emotion, they told the court how the gunman's actions changed their lives forever. Spouses and parents of the dead spoke of loss. There were tears, moments of intense anger, and quiet despair. Victim impact statements have become a common feature of criminal proceedings. Spoken in court or submitted in writing, these statements provide an opportunity for victims to be heard before sentencing.

Advocates of victim impact statements believe these declarations give victims a voice, an opportunity to be heard. Traditionally, victims have appeared in court only as witnesses subject to cross-examination. Prosecutors, victims soon learn, represent the state and not individuals. Still hospitalized after a brutal beating, a New Jersey restaurant owner learned from reading a newspaper that his assailants had plea-bargained to a lesser charge and received probation. Joining with other victims, he became an advocate for victims' rights, including impact statements.

Therapists who counsel victims of crime believe that addressing the court and taking an active role in the legal process instead of remaining passive witnesses helps people recover from a sense of helplessness and regain a measure of self-respect.

Impact statements allow judges to consider appropriate sentences. In a Florida case, a judge who intended to fine a teenager for shoplifting agreed with the storeowner's suggestion that the fine be waived if the defendant completed his GED.

But giving victims a chance to speak has led to ugly courtroom scenes that seem inappropriate in a democracy. In Milwaukee a sister of a young man murdered by Jeffrey Dahmer wailed and shrieked in contortions of pure rage. The relative of another murder victim shouted that he would execute the killer himself. Bailiffs had to restrain him as he begged the judge, "Just gimme five minutes with him!" Defense attorneys argue these harangues are unnecessary. What need is there to heap abuse upon a person about to lose his or her life or liberty? Can anger and harassment be considered healing?

But even restrained, well-reasoned impact statements raise troubling questions. What about the victim who is too impaired, too frightened, or too wounded to speak? Is his or her absence judged as indifference? What about those whose English is limited? What of those without friends or family? Should the drunk driver who kills a young professional missed by friends, family, and colleagues receive a tougher sentence than the drunk driver who kills a homeless man who dies unmourned, unmissed, and uncounted? Do we really want our courts and society to suggest that some lives are more significant than others?

Victim impact statements may help empower victims, especially the educated, the personally impressive, and the socially prominent. But these statements, unintentionally, may also further marginalize the most helpless among us, allowing forgotten victims to remain voiceless.

1. What have you found most challenging or difficult about writing? Discovering ideas? Getting started? Revising?

2. What comments have instructors made about your writing? Does a pattern exist? Have they suggested areas for improvement?

3. What are your writing habits? What could aid in improving your work and meeting deadlines? What ideas in this chapter might help you write more effectively?

WRITING ON A COMPUTER

If you have never written on a computer, take advantage of whatever opportunities your campus offers to learn word processing. Many colleges offer one-credit courses or free tutorials. If no course is available, ask a friend or classmate to show you how he or she uses a computer to write.

STRATEGIES FOR WRITING ON A COMPUTER

1. **Appreciate the advantages and limitations of using a computer.** Computers can speed up the writing process and allow you to add ideas, correct spelling, and delete sentences without having to retype an entire page. Computers, however, will not automatically make you a better writer. They cannot refine a thesis, improve your logic, or enhance critical thinking. *Don't confuse the neatness of the finished product with good writing.* An attractively designed document must still achieve all the goals of good writing.

2. **Learn the features of your program.** If you are unfamiliar with writing on a computer, make sure you learn how to move blocks of text, change formats, check spelling, and, most importantly, master the *print* and *save* functions. *Find out if your program has an* undo *function. This can save the day if you accidentally delete or "lose" some of your text.* This function simply undoes your last action, restoring deleted text or eliminating what you just added.

3. **Write in single space.** Most instructors require that papers be double-spaced, but you may find it easier to compose your various drafts in single space so that you can see more of your essay on the screen. You can easily change to double space when you are ready to print the final version.

4. **Date and color-code your drafts.** To make sure you do not accidentally turn in an earlier, unedited draft of a paper, always put today's date in the header to identify the most recent version. In writing and editing a longer paper, highlight passages and change colors. You might highlight passages needing grammatical editing in red and those needing fact checking or additional details in blue. Marking up drafts like this can make final editing easier. When you complete editing a section, change the color to black. When the entire document is free of red or blue paragraphs, you know you have fully edited the paper.

5. **Save your work.** If your program has an automatic save function, use it. Save your work to a CD or flash drive. If you are writing on a college or library computer and do not have a disc or flash drive, email your work to yourself, or print a hard copy. Don't let a power shortage or a keystroke error make you lose your work!

6. **Print drafts of your work as you write.** Computer screens usually allow you to view less than a page of text at a time. Although it is easy to scroll up and down through the text, it can be difficult to revise on the screen. You may find it easier to work with a hard copy of your paper. Consider double- or even triple-spacing before you print, so you will have room for handwritten notations.

7. **Keep backup copies of your work.** Flash drives can be damaged or lost. *Store important data on more than one device or save printed copies.*

8. **Make use of special features.** Most word processing applications allow you to count the number of words, check spelling, and use a built-in thesaurus. Some programs will aid you with grammar and usage rules.

9. **Use spell- and grammar checkers but recognize their limitations.** A spell-checker will go through your document and flag words it does not recognize, quickly locating many mistakes you might overlook on your own. *Spell-checkers do not locate missing words or recognize errors in usage, such as confusing* there *and* their *or* adopt *and* adapt. *Grammar checkers sometimes offer awkward suggestions and flag correct expressions as errors.* Reading your text aloud is still the best method of editing.

COLLABORATIVE WRITING

Writing often occurs in groups. Even when produced by a single person, writing may have to reflect the views of many people. Thomas Jefferson wrote the Declaration of Independence, but a committee including Jefferson, John Adams, Benjamin Franklin, and two others made forty-seven changes.

Franklin replaced Jefferson's original phrase (in italics) "we hold these rights to be *sound and undeniable*" with "*self-evident.*" More changes occurred when the declaration was presented to the entire Continental Congress. Jefferson's impassioned attack on slavery was eliminated to appease Southern representatives. In all, eighty-seven alterations were made to Jefferson's declaration before it was unanimously accepted. By the time John Hancock stepped forward to sign the Declaration of Independence, a quarter of Jefferson's original draft had been changed or deleted.

As a college student, you may be called on to work in a writing group. More and more professors assign collaborative writing projects, because writing in groups is common in business and industry. Most professionals work in groups or committees. The partners of a small software company seeking a new personnel director have to agree on the wording of a want ad. The sales team introducing a new product must determine what language to use on their website. Volunteers seeking government funding for a day care center must work together on a proposal.

Working in groups adds additional challenges to the writing process. The writing must express the ideas of different people. Viewpoints and personalities may clash. Even scheduling time for the group to meet may be challenging. Because people regard their writing as personal expression and are accustomed to working alone, it can be difficult for them to accept criticism.

But whether you are writing alone or in a group, the basic process remains the same. The writing must address the issue, meet the needs of the readers, and respect the conventions of the discipline or discourse community. To be effective, writing groups must achieve the "Three Cs" of group dynamics: *cohesion, cooperation,* and *compromise.* Members must have a clearly defined goal or task. They must be willing to meet and to work outside the group. Finally, and often most difficult, individuals must be willing to accept that their opinions may not prevail and be willing to drop or alter ideas they greatly value.

Strategies for Collaborative Writing

1. **Establish cohesion by stressing the goals, intended readers, and requirements of the writing project.** It is important for members of a writing group to feel trust so they can share ideas. In addition, they must be willing to offer and accept criticism.

2. **Keep the group focused on the task by creating a timeline.** People enjoy talking. Discussions can easily become generalized forums for spirited debate or the latest gossip. A target timeline can keep the group on track by outlining expected outcomes and reminding members of the deadline. The timeline should reflect stages in the writing process.

3. **Make meetings productive by setting goals and assigning tasks.** Meetings can easily degenerate into a series of discussion sessions, which, though interesting, may not produce the needed writing. Members should be assigned specific responsibilities: gathering research, conducting interviews, writing sample drafts. Each meeting should open with a goal statement of what is to be achieved. Meetings should end with a summary of what has been completed and an announcement of what must be accomplished at the next meeting.

4. **Designate one member to serve as a moderator or recorder.** One member of the group should serve as chair or recorder to document the progress of the group and serve as secretary to exchange messages between meetings.

5. **Avoid personalizing disagreements.** It is important to discuss opposing viewpoints in neutral terms. Avoid attaching ideas to individuals, which can lead to "us-against-them" conflicts.

6. **Take advantage of technology.** Students often have trouble finding common times to meet for social activities, let alone assignments. Consider how the group can maintain links through email and telephone conferences.

7. **Acknowledge contributions made by others by noting quotations and paraphrases or listing their names as coauthors.**

WRITER'S BLOCK

At some time almost everyone experiences writer's block—the inability to write. With a paper due in a few days, you may find yourself incapable of coming up with a single line or even unable to sit at your desk. You can feel frustrated, nervous, bored, tired, or anxious. The more time passes, and the more you think about the upcoming assignment, the more frustrated you can become.

Even professional authors sometimes find themselves unable to write. There is no magic cure for writer's block, but there are tactics that can help.

Strategies for Overcoming Writer's Block

1. **Recognize that writer's block exists.** When you have the time to write, write. If you have two weeks to complete an assignment, don't assume that you will be able to write well for fourteen days. Get as much writing as possible done when you can. If you delay work, you may find yourself unable to write as the deadline nears.

2. **Review your assignment.** Sometimes the reason you feel that you have nothing to say is that you have not fully understood the assignment. Read it carefully and turn the instructions into a series of questions to spark critical thinking.

3. **If you are having trouble selecting a topic, review the assignment for keywords and search the Internet.** See what web pages these keywords produce. If you don't have access to the Internet, look for these words in a dictionary or encyclopedia. Even wholly unrelated references can sometimes spark your imagination and help you develop ideas.

4. **Write anything.** The longer you delay writing, the harder it will be to start. If you have trouble focusing on your assignment, get into the mood for writing by sending an email to a friend. Use an online chat room to get into the rhythm of expressing yourself in writing.

5. **Discuss your assignment or goal with others.** Talking with a friend can often boost your confidence and reduce your anxiety about an assignment. A spirited discussion can generate free associations about your topic, helping you to view your subject from new angles.

6. **Force yourself to write for five minutes.** Sit down and write about your topic for five minutes nonstop. Let one idea run into another. If you have trouble writing about your topic, write about anything that comes to mind. Even writing nonsense will help you break the physical resistance you may have to sitting down and working with a pen or keyboard. Try to steer your experimental writing to the assigned task. If your draft is going nowhere, save your work and stop after five minutes. Take a walk or run some errands, then return to your writing. Sometimes seeing a word or phrase out of context will lead to significant associations.

7. **Lower your standards.** Don't be afraid to write poorly. Write as well as you can, making notes in the margin as you go along to remind yourself of areas that need revision. Remember that writing is recursive, so even badly written statements can form the foundation of a good paper.

8. **Don't feel obligated to start at the beginning.** If you find yourself unable to develop a convincing opening line or a satisfactory introduction, begin writing the body or conclusion of the paper. Get your ideas flowing.

9. **Switch subjects.** If you are bogged down on your English paper, start work on the history paper due next month. Writing well on a different subject may help you gain the confidence you need to return to a difficult assignment.

10. **Record your thoughts on tape or note cards.** If you find writing frustrating, consider talking into a tape recorder or listing ideas on index cards. You may find working with different materials an effective method of getting started.

11. **Try writing in a different location.** If you can't work at home because of distractions, go to the library or a quiet room. If the library feels stifling and intimidating, move to a less formal environment. You may discover yourself doing your best work while drinking coffee in a noisy student union.

12. **If you still have problems with your assignment, talk to your instructor.** Try to identify what is giving you the most trouble. Is it the act of writing itself, finding a topic, organizing your thoughts, or developing a thesis?

WRITING ACTIVITIES

1. Choose one of the following topics and use the five-step method described in this chapter to draft a short essay. *As you write, note which stages of the process pose the greatest challenges. Alter your composing style in any way that improves your writing.*

divorce	mandatory courses	televised trials
stepparents	charter schools	alternative energy
hate speech	volunteering	racial profiling
the insanity defense	college sports	minimum wage

2. Select an upcoming assignment and write a rough draft. Use this experience to identify topic areas that require the most attention. *Save your notes and draft for future use.*

3. Write an email to a friend about a recent experience. Before sending it, set it aside, letting it "cool." After two or three days, examine your draft for missing details, awkward or confusing phrases, misspelled words, and repetitious statements. *Notice how revision and editing can improve your writing.*

Avoid Plagiarism

In writing college papers, you may often include ideas, facts, and information from outside sources. Whenever you copy material or restate the ideas of others in your own words, you must indicate the source. Presenting the words or ideas of others as your own is called *plagiarism*, which is a serious academic offense. Students who submit plagiarized papers are frequently failed or expelled.

Strategies for Avoiding Plagiarism

1. **When you copy a source word for word, indicate it as a direct quote with quotation marks:**

   Original source

   The airbag is not the most important automotive safety device. It is a sober driver.

   William Harris, address before National Safety Council

   Quotation used in student paper:

   > Speaking before the National Safety Council, William Harris said, "The airbag is not the most important safety device. It is a sober driver."

2. **When you state the ideas of others in your own words, you still must acknowledge their source:**

   Paraphrase used in student paper:

   > William Harris has noted that a sober driver is a better safety device than an airbag.

3. **When working on drafts, color-code quotations and paraphrases to distinguish them from your own words.** In writing a paper over several days, you may forget where you used outside sources. Whenever you cut and paste material into a paper, color code it or place in bold as reminder that it needs to be treated as a quotation or a paraphrase in final editing.

4. **Always record the source of outside material.** When you cut and paste or paraphrase material, always copy the information needed to cite the source: the author, title, website or publication, dates, and page numbers.

   Refer to *A Writer's Guide to Documenting Sources* in the appendix for information on using and citing outside sources.

 Info Write provides additional information on the writing process.
cengage.learning.infowrite.com

2

CHAPTER THREE

CRITICAL READING

READING CRITICALLY

As a student, you are accustomed to reading to gain information. Cramming for a history exam, you read a textbook, hoping to extract the dates, facts, and concepts that will appear on the test. Reading a novel, you may allow yourself to be swept away by an exciting plot or an intriguing character. As a writer, however, you need to read critically; you need to read with a "writer's eye."

While most diners simply savor a new gourmet item, a chef wants to know the recipe. Visitors to a new office tower may marvel at the atrium, but an architect analyzes the support structure. Moviegoers gasp at an exciting car chase as film students review the director's editing technique. As a writer, you need to look at writing in much the same way. In addition to determining *what* an essay says, it is important to note how it is organized, how the writer overcame problems, and how language and detail contribute to its effect.

STRATEGIES FOR CRITICAL READING

When you pick up a magazine, you rarely read every article. You flip through the pages, letting your eyes guide you. A headline, a photograph, a graph, or a familiar name makes you pause and begin reading. If you become bored, you skip to the next article. Reading textbooks, you might skim over familiar sections to devote more time to new material.

In this course, however, you should read *all* the assigned selections carefully. Reading with a writer's eye, you will examine familiar works differently than readers seeking information. Critical reading, like writing, occurs best in stages.

First Reading

1. **Look ahead and skim selections.** Do not wait until the night before a class discussion to read assigned essays. Check your syllabus and skim through upcoming readings to get a general impression. Often, if you think about the authors and their topics, you can approach the essay more critically.

2. **Study the headnote and introduction.** Consider the author, the issue, the writing context. What readers does the writer seem to be addressing? What can you observe about the discourse community? Measure your existing knowledge about the author and subject.

3. **Suspend judgment.** Try to put your personal views aside as you read. Even if you disagree with the author's choice of topic, tone, or opinion, read the essay objectively. Remember, your goal is to understand how the writer states his or her point. Even if you reject an author's thesis, you can still learn useful techniques.

4. **Consider the title.** Titles often provide clues about the author's attitude toward his or her subject. Does the title label the essay, state a thesis, pose a question, or use a creative phrase to attract attention?

5. **Read the entire work.** Just as in writing the first draft, it is important to read the entire essay in one sitting if possible. Do not pause to look up an unfamiliar word at this stage. Instead, try to get the "big picture."

6. **Focus on understanding the writer's main point.** If possible, summarize the writer's thesis in your own words.

7. **Jot down your first impressions.** What do you think of this work? Do you like it? If so, why? If you find it dull, disturbing, or silly, ask why: What is lacking? How did the author fail in your eyes?

Put the essay aside, allowing it to cool. If possible, let two or three days pass before returning to the assignment. If the assignment is due the next day, read the selection early in the day and then turn to other work or run an errand so that you can come back to it with a fresh outlook.

Second Reading

1. **Review your first impressions.** Determine if your attitudes are based on biases or personal preferences rather than the writer's ability. Realize that an essay that supports your views is not necessarily well written. If you disagree with the author's thesis, try to put your opinions aside to evaluate objectively how well the writer presented his or her point of view. Don't allow your personal views to cloud your critical thinking. Appreciating an author's writing ability does not require you to accept his or her opinion.

2. **Read with a pen in your hand.** Make notes and underline passages that strike you as interesting, meaningful, offensive, or disturbing. Reading with a pen will prompt you to write, to be an active reader rather than a passive consumer of words.

3. **Look up unfamiliar words.** Paying attention to words can increase your vocabulary and enhance your appreciation of word choices.

4. **Analyze passages you found difficult or confusing during the first reading.** In many instances, a second reading can help you understand complex passages. If you still have difficulty understanding the writer's point, ask why. Would other readers also have problems comprehending the meaning? Could ideas be stated more directly?

5. **Review the questions at the end of the selection.** Considering the questions can help you focus on a closer, more analytical reading of the work. The questions are arranged in three groups:

Understanding Meaning:
What is the writer's purpose?
What is the thesis?
What audience is the writer addressing?
What is the author trying to share with his or her readers?

Evaluating Strategy:
How effective is the title?
How does the writer introduce the essay?
What evidence supports the thesis?
How does the writer organize ideas?
Where does the author use paragraph breaks?
What role does the writer play? Is the writer's approach subjective
    or objective?
How does the writer address possible objections or differing opinions?
How does the writer conclude the essay?
Does the author use any special techniques?

Appreciating Language:
How does the writer use words?
What does the language reveal about the intended readers?
What emotional impact do the words have?
How do the words establish the writer's tone?

6. **Summarize your responses in a point or two for class discussion.** Consider how you will express your opinions of the essay to fellow students. Be prepared to back up your remarks by citing passages in the text.

7. **Most importantly, focus on what this essay can teach you about writing.** How can this writer's style, way of organizing ideas, or word choice enrich your own writing? Though you may not wish to imitate everything you see, you can learn techniques to broaden your composing style.

8. **Think of how writers resolve problems you have encountered.** If you have trouble making an outline and organizing ideas, study how the essays in this book are arranged. If your instructor returns papers with comments about vague thesis statements and lack of focus, examine how the writers in this book develop controlling ideas.

Before Class Discussion

1. Before class discussion of an assigned essay, review the reading and your notes. Identify your main reactions to the piece. What do you consider the essay's strongest or weakest points?

2. Ask fellow students about their reactions to the writing. Determine whether their responses to the writer's thesis, tone, approach, and technique match yours. If their reactions differ from yours, review your notes to get a fresh perspective.

3. Be prepared to ask questions. Ask your instructor about unfamiliar techniques or passages you find confusing.

Above All, Read to Learn

Read the following essay by Cornel West and study how it has been marked during a critical reading. West is a highly organized writer who blends the use of several modes in this comparison essay on the current state of African American political leadership.

CORNEL WEST

Cornel West was a religion professor and Director of Afro-American Studies at Princeton University before he was appointed to the faculty at Harvard University. The author of Keeping Faith, Prophetic Fragments *and other books, West has specialized in writing on race in America.*

Black Political Leadership

CONTEXT: "Black Political Leadership" *appeared in West's best-selling 1994 book,* Race Matters. *In this section, West compares the current generation of black political leaders with leaders of the Civil Rights era. Although West's purpose is to compare, he uses a number of modes to develop his ideas.*

Black political leadership reveals the tame and genteel face of the black middle class. The black dress suits with white shirts worn by Malcolm X and Martin Luther King Jr. signified the seriousness of their deep commitment to black freedom, whereas today the expensive tailored suits of black politicians symbolize their personal success and individual achievement. Malcolm and Martin called for the realization that black people are somebodies with which America has to reckon, whereas black politicians tend to turn our attention to *their* somebodiness owing to *their* "making it" in America.

This crude and slightly unfair comparison highlights two distinctive features of black political leaders in the post–Civil Rights era: the relative lack of authentic anger and the relative absence of genuine humility. What stood out most strikingly about Malcolm X, Martin Luther King Jr., Ella Baker, and Fannie Lou Hamer was that they were almost always visibly upset about the condition of black America. When one saw them speak or heard their voices, they projected on a gut level that the black situation was urgent, in need of immediate attention. One even gets the impression that their own stability and sanity rested on how soon the black predicament could be improved. Malcolm, Martin, Ella, and Fannie were angry about the state of black America, and this anger fueled their boldness and defiance.

In stark contrast, most present-day black political leaders appear too hungry for status to be angry, too eager for acceptance to be bold, too self-invested in advancement to be defiant. And when they do drop their masks and try to get mad (usually in the presence of black audiences), their bold rhetoric is more performance than personal, more play-acting than heartfelt. Malcolm, Martin, Ella, and Fannie made sense of the black plight in a poignant and powerful manner, whereas most contemporary black political leaders' oratory appeals to black people's sense of the sentimental and sensational.

1
thesis/ opening

clothes as symbolic comparison

note use of italics

2
division

examples

3
shift/ transition

repetitive wording for emphasis

contrast

4
supplies
personal
definition

Similarly, Malcolm, Martin, Ella, and Fannie were examples of humility. Yes, even Malcolm's aggressiveness was accompanied by a common touch and humble disposition toward ordinary black people. <u>Humility is the fruit of inner security and wise maturity.</u> To be humble is to be so sure of one's self and one's mission that one can forego calling excessive attention to one's self and status. And, even more pointedly, to be humble is to revel in the accomplishments or potential of others—especially those with whom one identifies and

cause and
effect

to whom one is linked organically. The relative absence of humility in most black political leaders today is a symptom of the status-anxiety and personal insecurity pervasive in black middle-class America. In this context, even a humble vesture is viewed as a cover for some sinister motive or surreptitious ambition.

5

division
definition

<u>Present-day black political leaders can be grouped under three types: race-effacing managerial leaders, race-identifying protest leaders, and race-transcending prophetic leaders.</u> The first type is growing rapidly. The Thomas Bradleys and Wilson Goodes of black America have become a model for many black leaders trying to reach a large white constituency and keep a loyal black one. This type survives on sheer political savvy and thrives on personal diplomacy. This kind of candidate is the lesser of two evils in a political situation where the only other electoral choice is a conservative (usually white) politician. Yet this type of leader tends to stunt progressive development and silence the prophetic voices in the black community by casting the practical mainstream as the only game in town.

6

analysis

The second type of black political leader—race-identifying protest leaders—often view themselves in the tradition of Malcolm X, Martin Luther King Jr., Ella Baker, and Fannie Lou Hamer. Yet they are usually self-deluded. They actually operate more in the tradition of Booker T. Washington, by confining themselves to the black turf, vowing to protect their leadership status over it, and serving as power brokers with powerful nonblack elites (usually white economic or political elites, though in Louis Farrakhan's case it may be Libyan) to "enhance" this black turf. It is crucial to remember that even in the fifties, Malcolm X's vision and practice were international in scope, and that after 1964 his project was transracial—though grounded in the black turf. King never confined himself to being solely the leader of black America—even though the white press attempted to do so. And Fannie Lou Hamer led the National Welfare Rights Organization, not the Black Welfare Rights Organization. In short, race-identifying protest leaders in the post–Civil Rights era function as figures who white Americans must appease so that the plight of the black poor is overlooked and forgotten. When such leaders move successfully into elected office—as with Marion Barry—they usually become managerial types with large black constituencies, flashy styles, flowery rhetoric, and Booker T. Washington–like patronage operations within the public sphere.

Race-transcending prophetic leaders are rare in contemporary black America. *7* Harold Washington was one. The Jesse Jackson of 1988 was attempting to be *examples* another—yet the opportunism of his past weighed heavily on him. To be an elected official and prophetic leader requires personal integrity and political savvy, moral vision and prudential judgment, courageous defiance and organizational patience. The present generation has yet to produce such a figure. We have neither an Adam Clayton Powell Jr., nor a Ronald Dellums. This void sits like a festering sore at the center of the crisis of black *final effects* leadership—and the predicament of the disadvantaged in the United States and abroad worsens.

Using *The Sundance Reader*

The Sundance Reader is organized into nine chapters focusing on writers' goals. The readings in each section illustrate how writers achieve their purpose in different contexts. Each chapter opens with an explanation of the goal or mode. The first few readings in each chapter are brief, clear-cut examples of the mode and can serve as models for many of your composition assignments. The middle readings are longer and more complex and demonstrate writing tasks in a range of disciplines and writing situations. Each chapter ends with samples of applied writings taken from business, industry, and government to illustrate how writing is used beyond the classroom.

When reading entries, keep these general questions in mind:

1. **What is the writer's purpose?** Even writers pursuing the same goal—to tell a story or explain a process—have different intentions. What is the purpose of the story—to raise questions, motivate readers to take action, or change their point of view?

2. **What is the writer's thesis?** Does a clear thesis statement exist that you can highlight, or is it implied? Can you restate the thesis in your own words?

3. **Who are the intended readers?** Note the source of the article. What does it tell you about the readers? Does the writer direct it to a specific group or a general audience? What assumptions does the writer seem to make about the reader? What terms or references are defined? What knowledge does the writer expect his or her audience to possess?

4. **What evidence does the writer use to support the thesis?** Does the writer provide personal observation, statistics, studies, or the testimony of others to support his or her views?

5. **What is the nature of the discipline, profession, or writing situation?** What discipline is the writer addressing? Is he or she working within a

discipline or addressing readers in another discipline? Is the writer addressing general readers? Do special circumstances guide the way the writer develops the thesis, presents ideas, and designs the physical appearance of the writing?

6. **How successful is this writing in its context?** Does the writer achieve his or her goals while respecting the needs of the reader and the conventions of the discipline or situation? Do special circumstances explain why the author appears to "break" the rules of what most English courses consider "good writing"?

ANALYZING VISUAL IMAGES

We increasingly communicate in images. We are bombarded daily with advertisements in newspapers and magazines, on television and billboards. College textbooks, which thirty years ago consisted of only text, now feature graphs and photographs on nearly every page. Websites, once blocks of words, now include streaming video. Satellites allow journalists to broadcast from remote parts of the world. Cable news networks provide images of breaking events twenty-four hours a day. The personal computer and desktop publishing enable students and small-business owners to develop sophisticated multimedia

© BETTMANN/CORBIS

THE IMAGE AS ICON, ELVIS AUTOGRAPHS PHOTOGRAPHS FOR FANS

presentations rivaling those created by major corporations. Digital cameras allow people to transmit photos and video instantly worldwide.

Images can be used to grab attention, evoke an emotional response, record events, document conditions, record evidence, illustrate an idea or condition, establish a mood, or develop a context for discussion. Visual images command attention. They can be presented without comment or woven into the text of a written message.

Photographs, Film, and Video

Photographs, film, and video are compelling. There is an impression that "the camera does not lie." A written description of a person or a place never seems as objective or as accurate as a photograph. The camera, we believe, hides nothing. It tells the whole truth. It leaves nothing out. People writing reports about a car accident can exaggerate or minimize the damage, but a photograph, we believe, provides us with irrefutable evidence. Nevertheless, visuals can be highly subjective and often misleading. They require careful analysis to determine their meaning and reliability.

The impression a photograph or video makes is shaped by a number of factors: *perspective and contrast, context, timing and duplication, manipulation,* and *captions.*

Perspective and Contrast

How large is a group of a hundred? How tall is a twenty-story building? The impression we get of events, objects, and people depends on perspective, the angle and distance of the camera and the subject. A hundred protesters photographed in close-up will look like an overwhelming force. Fists raised, faces twisted in emotion, lunging toward the camera, they can appear all-powerful and unstoppable. Photographed from a distance, the crowd can seem small against a landscape of multistory buildings or acres of empty pavement. In contrast to large fixed objects, the protest can appear futile and weak. If ordinary people going about routine business are

CHARLES LINDBERGH, 1927

© CORBIS

JAMES DEAN IN TIMES SQUARE, 1955

© DENNIS STOCK, 1955/MAGNUM

shown in the foreground, the protesters, in contrast, may appear abnormal, ephemeral, even pathetic. A twenty-story building in a suburban neighborhood of two-story structures will loom over the landscape. Located in midtown Manhattan, dwarfed by skyscrapers, the same structure will seem undersized, less formidable, even homey in contrast. A luxury car photographed in front of a stately country home can appear as a desirable symbol of style, elegance, and taste. Parked next to a migrant farmworker's shack, the same car can appear oppressive, a symbol of tasteless greed, exploitation, and injustice. A mime shown entertaining small children will look wholesome, joyful, and playful. Posed next to a homeless man taking shelter in a cardboard box, a mime will look irrelevant, inane, even offensive.

An individual can appear large or small, weak or powerful, depending on perspective. Charles Lindbergh is shown in close-up on page 57. His face fills the frame. No other people, structures, or objects detract from his larger-than-life presence. In addition, he is photographed wearing his flight helmet and goggles, emblems of his famous 1927 transatlantic flight. His clear eyes look upward as if gazing to the horizon and the future. This photograph depicts a human being as powerful, in command of his environment. It is the type of image seen on movie posters and postage stamps, in official portraits and celebrity stills. Shown in isolation, any subject can appear dominant because there is nothing else to compare it to.

In contrast to Lindbergh's picture, the photograph of James Dean in Times Square was shot at some distance. Unlike Lindbergh, Dean is shown not in isolation but within an environment. Though he is at the center of the photograph, his stature is diminished by the urban landscape. Tall buildings rise above him. The iron fence on the right restricts his freedom of movement. In addition, the environment is hostile—dark, cold, and wet. Dean is hunched forward, his collar turned up against the wind, his hands buried in his pockets against the cold. The picture creates an image of brooding loneliness and alienation, suited to Dean's Hollywood image as a loner and troubled rebel.

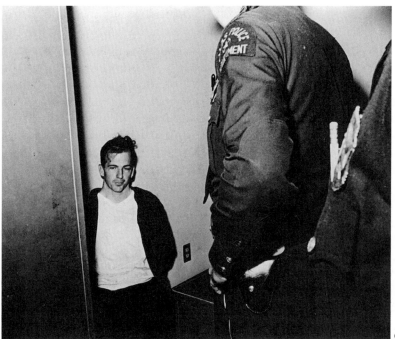

© AP PHOTO

LEE HARVEY OSWALD UNDER ARREST, DALLAS, 1963

The impression created of Lee Harvey Oswald is shaped by perspective. In the press photo taken shortly after his arrest, Oswald looks weak, subdued, cowardly. He is literally cornered, shown off-center at the edge of the frame. Though he is the subject of the photograph, he is markedly smaller in relation to the officers. The angle of the camera distorts the relative sizes of the figures so that the uniformed men in the foreground are oversized, their power and authority emphasized. The officer's badge appears larger than Oswald's head. The room is blank and featureless. Handcuffed and still disheveled from his arrest, Oswald is depicted as a disarmed menace, an assassin rendered harmless.

Context

Photographs and video images are isolated glimpses of larger events. A camera captures a split second of reality, but it does not reveal what happened before or after the image was taken. The photograph of a baseball player hitting a home run shows a moment of athletic triumph, but it does not reveal the player's batting average or who won the game. Photographs taken during a melee between police and demonstrators can capture a protester hurling a rock at a police officer or the officer striking back with a nightstick. A single striking image may distort our impressions of a larger event.

Motion picture and video cameras offer us a window onto the world, bringing world events into our homes—but it is a narrow window. During the hostage crisis in Iran in 1979, for example, television cameras continually showed violent demonstrations outside the American embassy, creating the impression that the entire nation was swept by a wave of anti-Americanism. American journalists, however, reported that only a block away they could walk through crowded streets and chat with passersby without incident. Aware of the power of image, protest groups around the world stage demonstrations for cameras to gain maximum media exposure.

Watching an evening of cable news creates the illusion that you are being well informed about world events. In thirty minutes, you see a conflict in the Middle East, a White House spokesperson, a senator commenting on the economy, a high-speed car chase in San Diego. But to a great extent cable news is limited to covering visual stories. Stories that are more complicated may not provide gripping visuals or may require too much explanation to make good television. Stories that break in developed countries within easy reach of media crews receive more coverage than events that occur in remote areas. Recent conflicts in the Middle East and Northern Ireland that claimed a few hundred lives a year received more coverage than a genocidal rebellion that killed hundreds of thousands in Rwanda or the ethnic cleansing that destroyed hundreds of villages in Sudan.

Juries have acquitted people caught on videotape buying drugs or engaged in violent assaults. Whereas the public only sees a dramatic segment, juries are often shown a videotape in its entirety. Defense attorneys place the tape in context by providing additional information about the people and events depicted. By raising doubts, they can persuade a jury to rethink what it has seen, questioning the tape's meaning and reliability.

Visual Connotations

Like words, images have connotations. They create emotional responses. Politicians are interviewed with flags and bookshelves in the background to demonstrate patriotism and indicate knowledge. Campaign commercials show candidates with their families, visiting the elderly, shaking hands with firefighters, or visiting veterans to link themselves with positive images. Ads and commercials will use provocative images of sex and violence to draw people's attention. Book covers and movie posters only vaguely associated with World War II often feature a large swastika because it is a symbol bound to attract attention.

Certain images become icons, symbols of an event, culture, attitude, or value. Reproduced in books and films, on murals and T-shirts, they serve to communicate a message with a single image. Marilyn Monroe's upswirled skirt symbolizes sex. The photograph of two African American athletes raising gloved fists at the 1968 Olympic Games became an icon of Black Power. The

World Trade Center attack has become an international symbol of terrorism. Often the icon takes on a meaning of its own, so that fiction can become reality. Although John Wayne never served in the military, his picture is often hung in Pentagon offices because his Hollywood image expresses values embraced by the military.

Timing and Duplication

Timing and duplication can enhance an image's impact and distort perceptions. If two celebrities meet briefly at a crowded special event and photographs of them shaking hands are widely reproduced over several months, it can create the impression they are close friends. The two figures become a single image repeatedly imprinted on the public, few recognizing that they are simply seeing the same moment from different angles. Stalin, Roosevelt, and Churchill only met on a few occasions during the Second World War, but the continual reproduction of photographs of them together helped create the image of the Big Three as a solid alliance against Hitler. Cable news reports of a suicide bombing, a shooting spree, or a car chase will recycle scenes over and over, often creating an exaggerated sense of their significance.

Manipulating Images

Just as painters in a king's court often depicted royalty in flattering poses without blemishes, photographers and filmmakers can use lighting, perspective, and contrast to alter perceptions of reality. Short actors can be made to seem taller on screen by lowering cameras or placing taller people in the background. Makeup and lighting can magnify or diminish facial features, improving someone's appearance. Even candid images can be carefully selected to show a subject in a positive light. Portraits and photographs of Kaiser Wilhelm and Joseph Stalin camouflaged the fact that both men had one arm that was noticeably shorter than the other. Wishing to project power and authority, both leaders wished to disguise their physical disability. Although most Americans knew that President Roosevelt had been stricken with polio, few were aware of how severely handicapped he actually was. The media did not release films of him in motion. Photographs and newsreels showed him standing or seated. The fact that he often had to be lifted out of cars or carried up steps was not made public. Although suffering from a painful back injury and Addison's disease, President Kennedy projected an image of youth and vigor by being shown in athletic contexts: playing touch football, swimming, or boating. Only a handful of photographs show Kennedy wearing the eyeglasses he needed for reading.

Photographs and film can be edited, revised, cut, and altered after the fact. A group photo can be reduced to focus on a single person. People and

© US ARMY SIGNAL CORPS/TIME & LIFE PICTURES/GETTY IMAGES

PRESIDENT WILSON AND GENERAL PERSHING. A RETOUCHER HAS PARTIALLY ERASED A FIGURE WALKING BE-
HIND THE TWO FAMOUS MEN, ALTERING VIEWERS' PERCEPTION OF A HISTORICAL EVENT. FREQUENTLY, NEGA-
TIVE OR DISTRACTING IMAGES ARE REMOVED FROM PHOTOGRAPHS TO ENHANCE THEIR EFFECT.

objects can be added or removed to alter the record of actual events. Leon
Trotsky was once a powerful Soviet leader, and was often photographed
standing next to Lenin. Wishing to obliterate his rival's role in the Russian
Revolution, Stalin had thousands of pictures retouched to remove Trotsky
from group photographs.

Today, with digital technology, images can be easily removed and inserted.
Photographs, motion pictures, and videos now have an increasing power to create their own reality, which may exaggerate, minimize, or distort actual events.

Gender and Cultural Issues

Images, like language, affect our perceptions. Historically, images have
reflected prevailing attitudes and biases. Words like *policeman, mankind,* and
mailman, and the universal use of *he* as a single pronoun, gave English a
distinct sexist stance. Historically, photographs focused on male activities,
actions, and behaviors, with women generally appearing as family members or
sex objects. Photographs taken of minorities often reflected and generated
stereotyped views, so that African Americans were often photographed in

subservient, patronized, or comic roles. Advertising has historically presented women as sexual objects or in a secondary role to men. Automobile ads still show men standing next to or driving a car, while women are draped across the hood as a kind of ornament. Soap ads depict men taking showers; women are posed lying in tubs. As gender roles change, popular culture and advertising alter our perceptions of men and women.

SOCIAL CHANGE REFLECTED BY A CLASH OF TRADITIONAL GENDER IMAGES. MAKEUP AND EARRINGS ARE DECIDEDLY FEMININE, IN STARK CONTRAST TO THE MASCULINE HARD HAT.

IN IRAN, A MALE PROFESSOR LECTURES FEMALE STUDENTS FROM BEHIND A SCREEN.

Perception and Analysis

Our analysis of images is shaped by our perceptions, both personal and cultural. A photograph taken in Iran depicts a male professor lecturing female seminary students from behind a screen. To Western eyes, this image can seem a shocking example of oppression and exclusion. To many Iranians, however, the image of women studying Islam represents inclusion and empowerment.

STRATEGIES FOR ANALYZING VISUAL IMAGES

1. **Examine the image holistically.** What does it represent? What is your initial reaction? Does it convey a message?

2. **Consider the nature of the image.** Is this a professional portrait or a candid press shot? Was this video taken at a prepared ceremony or a spontaneous event? Were people, images, or objects deliberately posed to make a statement?

3. **Examine perspective.** Is the subject depicted in close-up or at a distance? Does the subject appear in control of the environment, or does the background dominate the frame?

4. **Analyze contrasts and contexts.** Is the background supportive, neutral, or hostile to the subject? Does the image depict conflict or harmony?

5. **Examine poses and body language of human figures.** How are human figures depicted? What emotions do they seem to express?

6. **Look for bias.** Do you sense that the photographers were trying to manipulate the people or events depicted, casting them in either a favorable or negative light?

7. **Consider the larger context.** Does the image offer a fair representation of a larger event, or is it an isolated exception?

8. **Review the image for possible manipulation.** Could camera angles or retouching have altered what appears to be a record of actual events?

9. **Consider the story the image seems to tell.** What is the thesis of this image? What visual details or symbols help tell the story?

Info Write provides additional information on critical reading.
cengage.learning.infowrite.com

CHAPTER FOUR

NARRATION: RELATING EVENTS

WHAT IS NARRATION?

Narration seeks to answer the basic question "What happened?" The goal of narration is to tell a story. The Bible, Greek myths, Native American fables, novels, short stories, diaries, autobiographies, and history books are examples of narration. Narrative writing forms the heart of most newspaper articles. Narration is also one of the most common types of professional writing. Physicians write narration to record a patient's history or outline a course of treatment. Attorneys use narrative writing to relate the details of a crime or explain the rationale for a lawsuit. Government reports, grant proposals, sales brochures, and business plans generally include a section labeled "narrative" that provides the history of an organization or a summary of a current project.

The Writer's Purpose

Narration can be *subjective* or *objective*, depending on the writer's goal and context. Subjective narration focuses on personal impressions, thoughts, insights, and feelings. Often the writer is at the center of the narrative, either as a principal character or as a key witness. In "A Doctor's Dilemma" (page 74), James Dillard recounts the decisions he faced as a young physician when he rushed to aid an accident victim:

> I looked down again at the driver hanging from the windowsill. There were six empty beer bottles on the floor of the truck. I could smell the beer through the window. I knew I had to move him, to open his airway. I had no idea what neck injuries he had sustained. He could easily end up a quadriplegic. But I thought: he'll be dead by the time the ambulance gets here if I don't move him and try to do something to help him.

An image flashed before my mind. I could see the courtroom and the driver of the truck sitting in a wheelchair. I could see his attorney pointing at me and thundering at the jury: "This young doctor, with still a year left in his residency training, took it upon himself to play God. He took it upon himself to move this gravely injured man, condemning him forever to this wheelchair...." I imagined the millions of dollars in award money. And all the years of hard work lost. I'd be paying him off for the rest of my life. Amy touched my shoulder. "What are you going to do?"

Objective narration, on the other hand, is usually stated in the third person to give the writer's views a sense of neutrality. In objective narration, the author is not a participant but a collector and presenter of facts. In "Thirty-Eight Who Saw Murder and Didn't Call the Police" (page 91), Martin Gansberg chronicles a murder victim's last movements:

Twenty-eight-year-old Catherine Genovese, who was called Kitty by almost everyone in the neighborhood, was returning home from her job as manager of a bar in Hollis. She parked her red Fiat in a lot adjacent to the Kew Gardens Long Island Rail Road Station, facing Mowbray Place. Like many residents of the neighborhood, she had parked there day after day since her arrival from Connecticut a year ago, although the railroad frowns on the practice.

She turned off the lights of her car, locked the door, and started to walk the 100 feet to the entrance of her apartment at 82-70 Austin Street, which is in a Tudor building with stores on the first floor and apartments on the second.

The entrance to the apartment is in the rear of the building because the front is rented to retail stores. At night the quiet neighborhood is shrouded in the slumbering darkness that marks most residential areas.

Focus

Related to the writer's purpose is the narrative's focus. A biography of Abraham Lincoln could be a general account of his entire life or a psychological study of his problem with depression during the Civil War. A book about World War II could concentrate on military activities or on the role of women in the defense industry. An article on recycling may provide a survey of national trends or an in-depth study of a single city's program.

Focus determines the kinds of details the writer includes in the narrative and the types of evidence on which he or she relies. In writing a popular history about the sinking of the *Titanic*, Walter Lord based much of his narrative on memories of the survivors. This gave his book human interest and created a tense series of dramas as he recounted the ship's last hours. A nautical engineer writing a technical article explaining the sinking of the "unsinkable" luxury liner would pay attention to mechanical details, specific measurements, and statistics.

Chronology

Chronology, or time, is a central organizing element in narrative writing. Writers do not always relate events in a straight timeline. A biography, for instance, does not have to begin with birth and childhood. Writers often alter the time sequences of their stories to dramatize events or limit their topic. A biographer of Franklin D. Roosevelt might choose to highlight a key event or turning point in his life. The narrative might open with his polio attack, flash back to his childhood and early political career, then flash forward to his recovery and election to the presidency. Other writers find it more dramatic to begin a narrative at the end and then explain what led to this final event. The first chapter of a book about Czar Nicholas II could describe his execution and then flash back to the events leading to his downfall and death.

Each method of organizing a narrative has distinct advantages and disadvantages:

- **Beginning at the beginning** creates an open-ended narrative, providing readers with little hint of later events. Writers who relate complex stories with many possible causes can use a straight chronology to avoid highlighting a single event. Using a direct beginning-to-end approach is the most traditional method of telling a story. One of the difficulties with this method can be determining exactly when the narrative should start. Often the beginning of a story consists of incidental background information that readers may find uninteresting.

- **Beginning at the middle or at a turning point** can arouse reader interest by opening with a dramatic scene. This method of organization can focus on the chain of events, persuading readers to concentrate on a particular issue. This is a common pattern in nonfiction articles, biographies, and histories written for a general readership. Critics, however, can view this alteration of chronology as distorting. Not all historians, for instance, may agree that Roosevelt's illness was the "turning point" of his life. Some biographers might feel that focusing on his physical disability ignores his intellectual development or downplays his political role.

- **Beginning at the end** serves to dramatize the final event. When everything is presented in flashback, readers see events, actions, and thoughts in hindsight. The elements of suspense and randomness are removed, providing a stronger sense of cause and effect. Some readers will object to this method because it implies the final outcome was inevitable, when, in fact, events just as easily could have led to alternative endings.

STRATEGIES FOR READING NARRATION

When reading the narratives in this chapter, keep these questions in mind.

Understanding Meaning

1. What is the author's narrative purpose—to inform, enlighten, share a personal experience, or provide information required by the reader?

2. What is the writer's role? Is the author a participant or direct witness? Is he or she writing in a personal context, focusing on internal responses, or in a professional context, concentrating on external events?

3. What readership is the narration directed toward—general or specific? How much knowledge does the author assume readers have?

4. What is the nature of the discipline, discourse community, or writing situation? Is the narration objective or subjective? Does the original source of the narrative (newsmagazine, scientific journal, or government document) reveal anything about the context?

Evaluating Strategy

1. What details does the writer select to highlight? Are some items summarized or ignored?

2. What kind of support does the writer use—personal observation or factual documentation?

3. What is the sequence of events? How is the narration organized? Does the writer begin at the beginning, the end, or a midpoint?

4. Does the writer use flashbacks and flash-forwards?

5. What transitional devices does the writer use to advance the narrative? Does the author use time references such as "later that day" or "two months later"?

Appreciating Language

1. What does the level of language suggest about the writer's role, the intended readers, and the nature of the discipline or writing situation?

2. How does the writer use words to create tone and style? What do word choices suggest about the writer's attitude toward the subject?

SAMUEL SCUDDER

Samuel Scudder (1837–1911) was born in Boston and attended Williams College. In 1857, he entered Harvard, where he studied under the noted professor Louis Agassiz. Scudder held various positions and helped in founding the Cambridge Entomological Club. He published hundreds of papers and developed a comprehensive catalog of three centuries of scientific publications in mathematics and the natural and physical sciences. While working for the United States Geological Survey, he named more than a thousand species of fossil insects. Although later scientists would question some of his conclusions, much of Scudder's work is still admired for its attention to detail.

Take This Fish and Look at It

CONTEXT: *Today educators stress critical thinking, which begins with close observation. In this famous essay, Scudder relates the lesson in observation he learned under Professor Agassiz, whose teaching method was simple. Instead of lecturing, he directed his young student to "look again, look again." Note that Scudder omits details such as dates, addresses, and even Professor Agassiz's appearance.*

It was more than fifteen years ago that I entered the laboratory of Professor Agassiz, and told him I had enrolled my name in the Scientific School as a student of natural history. He asked me a few questions about my object in coming, my <u>antecedents</u> generally, the mode in which I afterwards proposed to use the knowledge I might acquire, and, finally, whether I wished to study any special branch. To the latter I replied that, while I wished to be well grounded in all departments of <u>zoology</u>, I purposed to devote myself specially to insects.

intro sets time

brief summary

"When do you wish to begin?" he asked.

uses dialogue

"Now," I replied.

This seemed to please him, and with an energetic "Very well!" he reached from a shelf a huge jar of specimens in yellow alcohol. <u>"Take this fish," he said, "and look at it; we call it a haemulon; by and by I will ask what you have seen."</u>

gives directions

With that he left me, but in a moment returned with explicit instructions as to the care of the object entrusted to me.

"No man is fit to be a naturalist," said he, "who does not know how to take care of specimens."

I was to keep the fish before me in a tin tray, and occasionally moisten the surface with alcohol from the jar, always taking care to replace the stopper tightly. Those were not the days of ground-glass stoppers and elegantly shaped exhibition jars; all the old students will recall the huge neckless glass bottles with their leaky, wax-besmeared corks, half-eaten by insects and begrimed with cellar dust. Entomology was a cleaner science than ichthyology, but the

example of the Professor, who had unhesitatingly plunged to the bottom of
the jar to produce the fish, was infectious; and though this alcohol had a "very
ancient and fishlike smell," I really dared not show any aversion within these
sacred precincts, and treated the alcohol as though it were pure water. Still
I was conscious of a passing feeling of disappointment, for gazing at a fish did
not commend itself to an ardent entomologist. My friends at home, too, were
annoyed when they discovered that no amount of eau-de-Cologne would
drown the perfume which haunted me like a shadow.

8   *first impression* In ten minutes I had seen all that could be seen in that fish, and started in
search of the Professor— who had, however, left the Museum; and when I re-
turned, after lingering over some of the odd animals stored in the upper apartment, my specimen was dry all over. I dashed the fluid over the fish as if to re-
suscitate the beast from a fainting fit, and looked with anxiety for a return of
the normal sloppy appearance. This little excitement over, nothing was to be
done but to return to a steadfast gaze at my mute companion. Half an hour
emphasizes boredom passed—an hour—another hour; the fish began to look loathsome. I turned it
over and around; looked it in the face—ghastly; from behind, beneath, above,
sideways, at three-quarters' view—just as ghastly. I was in despair; at an early
hour I concluded that lunch was necessary; so, with infinite relief, the fish was
carefully replaced in the jar, and for an hour I was free.

9   On my return, I learned that Professor Agassiz had been at the Museum,
but had gone, and would not return for several hours. My fellow students were
too busy to be disturbed by continued conversation. Slowly I drew forth that
hideous fish, and with a feeling of desperation again looked at it. I might not
use a magnifying glass; instruments of all kinds were interdicted. My two
hands, my two eyes, and the fish: it seemed a most limited field. I pushed my
finger down its throat to feel how sharp the teeth were. I began to count the
scales in the different rows, until I was convinced that was nonsense. At last a
discovers by drawing happy thought struck me—I would draw the fish; and now with surprise I
began to discover new features in the creature. Just then the Professor
returned.

10   "That is right," said he; "a pencil is one of the best of eyes. I am glad to notice, too, that you keep your specimen wet, and your bottle corked."

11   With these encouraging words, he added: "Well, what is it like?"

12   He listened attentively to my brief rehearsal of the structure of parts
whose names were still unknown to me: the fringed gill-arches and movable
operculum; the pores of the head, fleshy lips, and lidless eyes; the lateral
line, the spinous fins, and forked tail; the compressed and arched body.
When I finished, he waited as if expecting more, and then, with an air of disappointment:

13   "You have not looked very carefully; why," he continued more earnestly,
"you haven't even seen one of the most conspicuous features of the animal,

which is plainly before your eyes as the fish itself; <u>look again, look again!"</u> and he left me to my misery.

<u>I was piqued; I was mortified. Still more of that wretched fish!</u> But now I set myself to my task with a will and discovered one new thing after another, until I saw how just the Professor's criticism had been. The afternoon passed quickly; and when, towards its close, the Professor inquired: **14** *initial reaction*

"Do you see it yet?"   **15**

<u>"No," I replied, "I am certain I do not, but I see how little I saw before."</u>   **16**

"That is next best," said he, earnestly, "but I won't hear you now; put away your fish and go home; perhaps you will be ready with a better answer in the morning. I will examine you before you look at the fish."   **17**

This was disconcerting. Not only must I think of my fish all night, studying, without the object before me, what this unknown but most visible feature might be; but also, without reviewing my discoveries, I must give an exact account of them the next day. I had a bad memory; so I walked home by Charles River in a distracted state, with my two perplexities.   **18**

The cordial greeting from the Professor the next morning was reassuring; here was a man who seemed to be quite as anxious as I that I should see for myself what he saw.   **19**

"Do you perhaps mean," I asked, "that the fish has symmetrical sides with paired organs?"   **20**

His thoroughly pleased "Of course! Of course!" repaid the wakeful hours of the previous night. After he had discoursed most happily and enthusiastically—as he always did—upon the importance of this point, I ventured to ask what I should do next.   **21** *asks for help*

"Oh, look at your fish!" he said, and left me again to my own devices. In a little more than an hour he returned and heard my new catalogue.   **22**

"That is good, that is good!" he repeated; "but that is not all; go on"; and so for three long days he placed that fish before my eyes, forbidding me to look at anything else, or to use any artificial aid. <u>"Look, look, look," was his repeated injunction.</u>   **23** *repeated command*

<u>This was the best entomological lesson I ever had—a lesson whose influence has extended to the details of every subsequent study; a legacy the Professor had left to me, as he has left it to so many others, of inestimable value which we could not buy, with which we cannot part.</u>   **24** *thesis/value of lesson*

A year afterward, some of us were amusing ourselves with chalking outlandish beasts on the Museum blackboard. We drew prancing starfishes; frogs in mortal combat; hydra-headed worms; stately crawfishes, standing on their tails, bearing aloft umbrellas; and grotesque fishes with gaping mouths and staring eyes. The Professor came in shortly after, and was as amused as any at our experiments. He looked at the fishes.   **25** *flash-forward to humorous episode*

"Haemulons, every one of them," he said. "Mr. ———— drew them."   **26**

27   True; and to this day, if I attempt a fish, I can draw nothing but haemulons.

28   The fourth day, a second fish of the same group was placed beside the first, and I was bidden to point out the resemblances and differences between the two; another and another followed, until the entire family lay before me, and a whole legion of jars covered the table and surrounding shelves; the odor had become a pleasant perfume; and even now, the sight of an old, six-inch worm-eaten cork brings fragrant memories.

29   The whole group of haemulons was thus brought in review; and, whether engaged upon the dissection of the internal organs, the preparation and examination of the bony framework, or the description of the various parts, Agassiz's training in the method of observing facts and their orderly arrangement was ever accompanied by the urgent exhortation not to be content with them.

30   "Facts are stupid things," he would say, "until brought into connection with
conclusion some general law."

31   At the end of eight months, it was almost with reluctance that I left these friends and turned to insects; but what I had gained by this outside experience has been of greater value than years of later investigation in my favorite groups.

Understanding Meaning

1. What is the purpose of Scudder's narrative? What is he trying to impress on his reader? What makes this essay more than a simple "first day of school" story?

2. Why did the professor prevent Scudder from using a magnifying glass? What did Professor Agassiz mean when he said "a pencil is one of the best of eyes"?

3. What did Scudder find frustrating about Dr. Agassiz's teaching method?

4. *Critical Thinking*: How effective was Professor Agassiz's nineteenth-century teaching method? By directing a new student to "look again, look again," did he accomplish more than if he had required Scudder to attend a two-hour lecture on the importance of observation? Is close observation a discipline most of us lack? Can you consider detailed observation the first level of critical thinking?

Evaluating Strategy

1. How does Scudder focus his narrative? What details does he leave out?

2. Do his personal reactions to the smell and his frustrations dramatize an extremely passive event? How can a writer create action in a story where the events are mental or emotional?

3. How does Scudder recreate his sense of boredom and frustration?

4. *Blending the Modes*: How does Scudder use *description* of the fish, the specimen bottles, and the smells to provide readers with a clear impression of the laboratory?

Appreciating Language

1. Review Scudder's narrative. How much scientific language does he use in relating his story? What does this say about his readers?

2. This story has little action. Essentially, it is a story about a man interacting with a dead fish. What words add drama or humor to the narrative?

WRITING SUGGESTIONS

1. Apply Professor Agassiz's technique to a common object you might use every day. Spend five minutes carefully examining a clock radio, your watch, or a can of your favorite soft drink. Then write a brief description of what you have observed. List the features you have never noticed before.

2. Professor Agassiz gave his student little direction beyond a simple command. Write an essay relating an experience in which a parent, teacher, superior officer, or boss left you to act on your own. What problems did you encounter? Were you frustrated, afraid, or angry? Was it a learning experience?

3. *Collaborative Writing*: Working with three or four other students, select an object unfamiliar to the group. Allow each member to study the object and make notes. *Compare* your findings, and work to create a single *description* of it. Pay attention to the words you select to create an accurate, objective picture of the object. Notice the details you overlooked that others observed.

JAMES DILLARD

James Dillard is a physician who specializes in rehabilitative medicine. In this narrative, first published in the "My Turn" column in Newsweek, *he relates an incident that nearly ended his medical career.*

A Doctor's Dilemma

CONTEXT: *As you read this narrative, keep in mind how most people expect physicians to respond in a life-threatening emergency.*

1   It was a bright, clear February afternoon in Gettysburg. A strong sun and layers of down did little to ease the biting cold. Our climb to the crest of Little Round Top wound past somber monuments, barren trees, and polished cannon. From the top, we peered down on the wheat field where men had fallen so close together that one could not see the ground. Rifle balls had whined as thick as bee swarms through the trees, and cannon shots had torn limbs from the young men fighting there. A frozen wind whipped tears from our eyes. My friend Amy huddled close, using me as a windbreaker. Despite the cold, it was hard to leave this place.

2   Driving east out of Gettysburg on a country blacktop, the gray Bronco ahead of us passed through a rural crossroad just as a small pickup truck tried to take a left turn. The Bronco swerved, but slammed into the pickup on the passenger side. We immediately slowed to a crawl as we passed the scene. The Bronco's driver looked fine, but we couldn't see the driver of the pickup. I pulled over on the shoulder and got out to investigate.

3   The right side of the truck was smashed in, and the side window was shattered. The driver was partly out of the truck. His head hung forward over the edge of the passenger-side window, the front of his neck crushed on the shattered windowsill. He was unconscious and starting to turn a dusky blue. His chest slowly heaved against a blocked windpipe.

4   A young man ran out of a house at the crossroad. "Get an ambulance out here," I shouted against the wind. "Tell them a man is dying."

5   I looked down again at the driver hanging from the windowsill. There were six empty beer bottles on the floor of the truck. I could smell the beer through the window. I knew I had to move him, to open his airway. I had no idea what neck injuries he had sustained. He could easily end up a quadriplegic. But I thought: he'll be dead by the time the ambulance gets here if I don't move him and try to do something to help him.

6   An image flashed before my mind. I could see the courtroom and the driver of the truck sitting in a wheelchair. I could see his attorney pointing at me and

thundering at the jury: "This young doctor, with still a year left in his residency training, took it upon himself to play God. He took it upon himself to move this gravely injured man, condemning him forever to this wheelchair ... I imagined the millions of dollars in award money. And all the years of hard work lost. I'd be paying him off for the rest of my life. Amy touched my shoulder. "What are you going to do?"

The automatic response from long hours in the emergency room kicked in. 7 I pulled off my overcoat and rolled up my sleeves. The trick would be to keep enough traction straight up on his head while I moved his torso, so that his probable broken neck and spinal-cord injury wouldn't be made worse. Amy came around the driver's side, climbed half in, and grabbed his belt and shirt collar. Together we lifted him off the windowsill.

He was still out cold, limp as a rag doll. His throat was crushed and blood 8 from the jugular vein was running down my arms. He still couldn't breathe. He was deep blue-magenta now; his pulse was rapid and thready. The stench of alcohol turned my stomach, but I positioned his jaw and tried to blow air down into his lungs. It wouldn't go.

Amy had brought some supplies from my car. I opened an oversize intra- 9 venous needle and groped on the man's neck. My hands were numb, covered with freezing blood and bits of broken glass. Hyoid bone—God, I can't even feel the thyroid cartilage, it's gone ... OK, the thyroid gland is about there, cricoid rings are here ... we'll go in right here....

It was a lucky first shot. Pink air sprayed through the IV needle. I placed a 10 second needle next to the first. The air began whistling through it. Almost immediately, the driver's face turned bright red. After a minute, his pulse slowed down and his eyes moved slightly. I stood up, took a step back, and looked down. He was going to make it. He was going to live. A siren wailed in the distance. I turned and saw Amy holding my overcoat. I was shivering and my arms were turning white with cold.

The ambulance captain looked around and bellowed, "What the hell ... 11 who did this?", as his team scurried over to the man lying in the truck.

"I did," I replied. He took down my name and address for his reports. I had 12 just destroyed my career. I would never be able to finish my residency with a massive lawsuit pending. My life was over.

The truck driver was strapped onto a backboard, his neck in a stiff collar. 13 The ambulance crew had controlled the bleeding and started intravenous fluid. He was slowly waking up. As they loaded him into the ambulance, I saw him move his feet. Maybe my future wasn't lost.

A police sergeant called me from Pennsylvania three weeks later. Six days 14 after successful throat-reconstruction surgery, the driver had signed out, against medical advice, from the hospital because he couldn't get a drink on the ward. He was being arraigned on drunk-driving charges.

15   A few days later, I went into the office of one of my senior professors, to tell the story. He peered over his half glasses and his eyes narrowed. "Well, you did the right thing medically of course. But, James, do you know what you put at risk by doing that?" he said sternly. "What was I supposed to do?" I asked.

16   "Drive on," he replied. "There is an army of lawyers out there who would stand in line to get a case like that. If that driver had turned out to be a quadriplegic, you might never have practiced medicine again. You were a very lucky young man."

17   The day I graduated from medical school, I took an oath to serve the sick and the injured. I remember truly believing I would be able to do just that. But I have found out it isn't so simple. I understand now what a foolish thing I did that day. Despite my oath, I know what I would do on that cold roadside near Gettysburg today. I would drive on.

Understanding Meaning

1. What was Dillard's goal in publishing this narrative in a national newsmagazine?

2. Does this narrative serve to contrast ideals and reality? How does Dillard's oath conflict with his final decision?

3. Does the fact that the victim was drinking have an impact on your reactions to the doctor's actions? Does Dillard seem to show contempt for his patient?

4. *Critical Thinking*: Does this essay suggest that there is an undeclared war between doctors and lawyers? Do medical malpractice suits improve or diminish the quality of medicine? Are lawyers to blame for the author's decision to "drive on" next time?

Evaluating Strategy

1. *Blending the Modes*: Does this narrative also serve as a *persuasive* argument? Does Dillard's story make a stronger statement than a standard argumentative essay that states a thesis and presents factual support?

2. Does this first-person story help place the reader in the doctor's position? Is this a more effective strategy than writing an objective third-person essay about the impact of malpractice suits?

3. Why does Dillard mention that the patient later disobeyed his doctor's orders and left the hospital so that he could get a drink?

4. How do you think Dillard wanted his readers to respond to the essay's last line?

Appreciating Language

1. What words does Dillard select to dramatize his attempts to save the driver's life? How do they reflect the tension he was feeling? For example, Dillard uses the word "lucky." Do you think he wants readers to understand that emergency medicine depends on chance as well as skill?

2. What language does Dillard use to demonstrate what he was risking by trying to save a life?

3. What kind of people read *Newsweek*? Do you find this essay's language suitable?

WRITING SUGGESTIONS

1. Relate an emergency you experienced or encountered. Using Dillard's essay as a model, write an account capturing what you thought and felt as you acted.

2. Write a letter to the editor of *Newsweek* in response to Dillard's essay. Do you find his position tenable? Are you angry with a doctor who vows not to help accident victims? Or do you blame the legal community for putting a physician in this position?

3. *Collaborative Writing:* Discuss Dillard's essay with a number of students and list their reactions. Write a division paper outlining their views.

ANDREW BRAAKSMA

Andrew Braaksma was a junior at the University of Michigan when he wrote this essay, which won Newsweek's "Back to School" contest. His article appeared in September 2005.

Some Lessons from the Assembly Line

CONTEXT: *As you read this essay, consider your own working experiences while attending college. Do you think people's attitudes about jobs change during recessions? Is job satisfaction related to the general economy, the situation of peers, or the availability of other opportunities?*

1 Last June, as I stood behind the bright orange guard door of the machine, listening to the crackling hiss of the automatic welders, I thought about how different my life had been just a few weeks earlier. Then, I was writing an essay about French literature to complete my last exam of the spring semester at college. Now I stood in an automotive plant in southwest Michigan, making subassemblies for a car manufacturer.

2   I have worked as a temp in the factories surrounding my hometown every summer since I graduated from high school, but making the transition between school and full-time blue-collar work during the break never gets any easier. For a student like me who considers any class before noon to be uncivilized, getting to a factory by 6 o'clock each morning, where rows of hulking, spark-showering machines have replaced the lush campus and cavernous lecture halls of college life, is torture. There my time is spent stamping, cutting, welding, moving or assembling parts, the rigid work schedules and quotas of the plant making days spent studying and watching "SportsCenter" seem like a million years ago.

3   I chose to do this work, rather than bus tables or fold sweatshirts at the Gap, for the overtime pay and because living at home is infinitely cheaper than living on campus for the summer. My friends who take easier, part-time jobs never seem to understand why I'm so relieved to be back at school in the fall or that my summer vacation has been anything but a vacation.

4   There are few things as cocksure as a college student who has never been out in the real world, and people my age always seem to overestimate the value of their time and knowledge. After a particularly exhausting string of 12-hour days at a plastics factory, I remember being shocked at how small my check seemed. I couldn't believe how little I was taking home after all the hours I spent on the sweltering production floor. And all the classes in

the world could not have prepared me for my battles with the machine I ran in the plant, which would jam whenever I absent-mindedly put in a part backward or upside down.

As frustrating as the work can be, the most stressful thing about blue-collar life is knowing your job could disappear overnight. Issues like downsizing and overseas relocation had always seemed distant to me until my co-workers at one factory told me that the unit I was working in would be shut down within six months and moved to Mexico, where people would work for 60 cents an hour.

Factory life has shown me what my future might have been like had I never gone to college in the first place. For me, and probably many of my fellow students, higher education always seemed like a foregone conclusion: I never questioned if I was going to college, just where. No other options ever occurred to me.

After working 12-hour shifts in a factory, the other options have become brutally clear. When I'm back at the university, skipping classes and turning in lazy rewrites seems like a cop-out after seeing what I would be doing without school. All the advice and public-service announcements about the value of an education that used to sound trite now ring true.

These lessons I am learning, however valuable, are always tinged with a sense of guilt. Many people pass their lives in the places I briefly work, spending 30 years where I spend only 2 months at a time. When fall comes around, I get to go back to a sunny and beautiful campus, while work in the factories continues. At times I feel almost voyeuristic, like a tourist dropping in where other people make their livelihoods. My lessons about education are learned at the expense of those who weren't fortunate enough to receive one. "This job pays well, but it's hell on the body," said one co-worker. "Study hard and keep reading," she added, nodding at the copy of Jack Kerouac's "On the Road" I had wedged into the space next to my machine so I could read discreetly when the line went down.

My experiences will stay with me long after I head back to school and spend my wages on books and beer. The things that factory work has taught me—how lucky I am to get an education, how to work hard, how easy it is to lose that work once you have it—are by no means earth shattering. Everyone has to come to grips with them at some point. How and when I learned these lessons, however, has inspired me to make the most of my college years before I enter the real world for good. Until then, the summer months I spend in the factories will be long, tiring and every bit as educational as a French lit class.

Understanding Meaning

1. How did Braaksma's job in the factory differ from his life at college?

2. Why did Braaksma choose factory work over the less demanding part-time jobs his friends settled for?

3. What were the main lessons Braaksma learned from this job? Do you think many students only learn these lessons after they graduate and enter the workforce?

4. Why does Braaksma feel "a sense of guilt" about the lessons he learned?

5. What does Braaksma consider the "most stressful" aspect of working in a factory?

6. *Critical Thinking:* Braaksma states that factory work taught him what his life might have been like had he not attended college. Do you think many students drop out of high school or college because they do not appreciate how limited their options will be without an education?

Evaluating Strategy

1. *Blending the Modes:* How does Braaksma use *comparison* to develop his narrative? How can *comparison and contrast* demonstrate an idea or dramatize a writer's thesis?

2. What details does Braaksma include to highlight the difference between his life at college and his life in the assembly plant?

3. Braaksma quotes a coworker who tells him to "Study hard and keep reading." How does this comment support his thesis? Why did this advice from a factory worker have greater impact on Braaksma than "trite" public service announcements about the value of education?

4. *Critical Thinking:* Braaksma wrote this piece for a "Back to School" essay contest for a national magazine. How do you think this shaped his choice of topic? Were the lessons he learned relevant to a national audience? Why do you think the editors of *Newsweek* decided to publish this essay?

Appreciating Language

1. Do you think that Braaksma's word choice and tone are suited to a magazine like *Newsweek*? Why or why not?

2. What words and phrases does Braaksma use to characterize working in the factory and studying at college?

3. *Critical Thinking:* At one point Braaksma uses the phrase "skipping classes and turning in lazy rewrites" to describe his life at college. Do you think students are likely to identify with language like this or feel offended? Does the tone of this essay offer a condescending view of college life?

WRITING SUGGESTIONS

1. Using Braaksma's essay as a model, write a one- or two-page essay describing the lessons you learned from an experience working at a job, caring for a family member, moving into a new apartment, coping with a layoff, or traveling overseas.

2. Write a short narrative that tells the story of a typical day at your job. Focus on word choices to share with readers what your job is like. What stands out most about your average day? What is the most stressful thing you confront? What lessons does it teach you, if any?

3. *Collaborative Writing:* Discuss Braaksma's essay with a group of students. What lessons did they learn from their work experiences? Did jobs motivate them to take their educations more seriously? Collect a few short quotes, facts, or insights about jobs, then use them to create an email motivating high school students to stay in school. How can your work experiences demonstrate to teenagers that dropping out of school will limit their options in life?

MAYA ANGELOU

Born Marguerite Johnson in Saint Louis, Maya Angelou (1928–) has distinguished herself as a poet, autobiographer, and public performer. I Know Why the Caged Bird Sings (1970), the first in a series of memoirs, describes her harrowing youth in Arkansas. She has starred in an off-Broadway play, acted in the television miniseries Roots, and directed a feature film. When Bill Clinton was sworn in as president on January 20, 1993, she became only the second poet in American history (after Robert Frost) to read at a presidential inauguration.

Champion of the World

CONTEXT: *At a time in American history when sports teams were still racially segregated, Joe Louis inspired pride in African Americans when he defeated white men in the boxing ring. Notice how the people gathered together in a small store in a little town in Arkansas in the 1930s feel that the whole future of African Americans in America depends on the outcome of a boxing match.*

1 The last inch of space was filled, yet people continued to wedge themselves along the walls of the Store. Uncle Willie had turned the radio up to its last notch so that youngsters on the porch wouldn't miss a word. Women sat on kitchen chairs, dining-room chairs, stools, and upturned wooden boxes. Small children and babies perched on every lap available and men leaned on the shelves or on each other.

2 The apprehensive mood was shot through with shafts of gaiety, as a black sky is streaked with lightning.

3 "I ain't worried 'bout this fight. Joe's gonna whip that cracker like it's open season."

4 "He gone whip him till that white boy call him Momma."

5 At last the talking finished and the string-along songs about razor blades were over and the fight began.

6 "A quick jab to the head." In the Store the crowd grunted. "A left to the head and a right and another left." One of the listeners cackled like a hen and was quieted.

7 "They're in a clinch, Louis is trying to fight his way out."

8 Some bitter comedian on the porch said, "That white man don't mind hugging that niggah now, I betcha."

9 "The referee is moving in to break them up, but Louis finally pushed the contender away and it's an uppercut to the chin. The contender is hanging on, now he's backing away. Louis catches him with a short left to the jaw."

10 A tide of murmuring assent poured out the door and into the yard.

"Another left and another left. Louis is saving that mighty right...." 11
The mutter in the Store had grown into a baby roar and it was pierced by the
clang of a bell and the announcer's "That's the bell for round three, ladies and
gentlemen."

As I pushed my way into the Store I wondered whether the announcer gave 12
any thought to the fact that he was addressing as "ladies and gentlemen" all
the Negroes around the world who sat sweating and praying, glued to their
"master's voice."

There were only a few calls for RC Colas, Dr. Peppers, and Hires root 13
beer. The real festivities would begin after the fight. Then even the old
Christian ladies who taught their children and tried themselves to practice
turning the other cheek would buy soft drinks, and if the Brown Bomber's
victory was a particularly bloody one they would order peanut patties and
Baby Ruths also.

Bailey and I laid the coins on top of the cash register. Uncle Willie didn't 14
allow us to ring up sales during a fight. It was too noisy and might shake up the
atmosphere. When the gong rang for the next round we pushed through the
near-sacred quiet to the herd of children outside.

"He's got Louis against the ropes and now it's a left to the body and a right 15
to the ribs. Another right to the body, it looks like it was low.... Yes, ladies
and gentlemen, the referee is signaling but the contender keeps raining the
blows on Louis. It's another to the body, and it looks like Louis is going
down."

My race groaned. It was our people falling. It was another lynching, yet 16
another Black man hanging on a tree. One more woman ambushed and raped.
A Black boy whipped and maimed. It was hounds on the trail of a man running through slimy swamps. It was a white woman slapping her maid for being
forgetful.

The men in the Store stood away from the walls and at attention. Women 17
greedily clutched the babes on their laps while on the porch the shufflings
and smiles, flirtings and pinching of a few minutes before were gone. This
might be the end of the world. If Joe lost we were back in slavery and beyond
help. It would all be true, the accusations that we were lower types of human
beings. Only a little higher than apes. True that we were stupid and ugly and
lazy and dirty and unlucky and, worst of all, that God Himself hated us and
ordained us to be hewers of wood and drawers of water, forever and ever,
world without end.

We didn't breathe. We didn't hope. We waited.   18

"He's off the ropes, ladies and gentlemen. He's moving towards the cen- 19
ter of the ring." There was no time to be relieved. The worst might still
happen.

20   "And now it looks like Joe is mad. He's caught Carnera with a left hook to the head and a right to the head. It's a left jab to the body and another left to the head. There's a left cross and a right to the head. The contender's right eye is bleeding and he can't seem to keep his block up. Louis is penetrating every block. The referee is moving in, but Louis sends a left to the body and it's an uppercut to the chin and the contender is dropping. He's on the canvas, ladies and gentlemen."

21   Babies slid to the floor as women stood up and men leaned toward the radio.

22   "Here's the referee. He's counting. One, two, three, four, five, six, seven.... Is the contender trying to get up again?"

23   All the men in the store shouted, "NO."

24   "—eight, nine, ten." There were a few sounds from the audience, but they seemed to be holding themselves in against tremendous pressure.

25   "The fight is all over, ladies and gentlemen. Let's get the microphone over to the referee.... Here he is. He's got the Brown Bomber's hand, he's holding it up.... Here he is...."

26   Then the voice, husky and familiar, came to wash over us—"The winnah, and still heavyweight champeen of the world ... Joe Louis."

27   Champion of the world. A Black boy. Some Black mother's son. He was the strongest man in the world. People drank Coca-Colas like ambrosia and ate candy bars like Christmas. Some of the men went behind the Store and poured white lightning in their soft-drink bottles, and a few of the bigger boys followed them. Those who were not chased away came back blowing their breath in front of themselves like proud smokers.

28   It would take an hour or more before the people would leave the Store and head for home. Those who lived too far had made arrangements to stay in town. It wouldn't do for a Black man and his family to be caught on a lonely country road on a night when Joe Louis had proved that we were the strongest people in the world.

Understanding Meaning

1. How would you sum up in a single sentence Angelou's thesis? What is her purpose in telling this story?

2. What different moods do the people in the store experience as they listen to the fight?

3. In paragraph 16, when Joe Louis falls in the boxing ring, Angelou says, "It was our people falling." A few sentences later, in paragraph 17, she says, "This might be the end of the world." Why would a single boxing match have that much importance for African Americans in the 1930s?

4. In the last sentence, Angelou suggests that it would not be safe for an African American family to be traveling on a country road following the fight. Why?

5. *Critical Thinking:* Listening to the Joe Louis v. Primo Carnera fight drew African Americans together in a sense of community. What events in recent history drew members of a group together in a similar way? Did the events draw together only members of a single racial or ethnic group? Are there other events that are of such major importance that they draw together people in spite of racial and ethnic differences? For example, were you watching television with other people on September 11, 2001? What is a collective or shared experience?

Evaluating Strategy

1. This narrative tells the story of a boxing match, but it also tells how the people in the store reacted to the match. Notice the paragraphs that tell what is going on before the match begins and after it is over. How do those paragraphs help Angelou make her point in the essay?

2. Can you find words in the essay that appeal to all five of the senses: sight, hearing, taste, touch, and smell?

3. Angelou's essay is broken up into many short paragraphs. Why are there so many paragraph breaks? How does a narrative writer decide when to start a new paragraph?

Appreciating Language

1. In the second paragraph, Angelou uses a simile (a comparison using "like" or "as"), "The apprehensive mood was shot through with shafts of gaiety, as a black sky is streaked with lightning." How was Louis' victory like a streak of lightning for African Americans? Lightning can also be dangerous, of course. How does Angelou suggest the danger in the last paragraph?

2. In paragraph 12, why does Angelou find it ironic that the sports announcer uses the term "ladies and gentlemen"?

3. In paragraph 12, Angelou includes the phrase "their 'master's voice,'" which refers to RCA's famous logo of a dog listening to his owner's voice on an old-fashioned phonograph. How does the phrase suit a narrative about Southern blacks in the 1930s?

WRITING SUGGESTIONS

1. Choose an event from your past when you felt particularly proud or particularly ashamed. Use first person ("I") to tell the story in an essay modeled on Angelou's. Choose an event that took place in a short period of time, and provide only enough background for your readers to understand the context. Remember that your purpose is to tell not only *what* happened but also demonstrate how it made you *feel.*

2. Once you have written a draft of your narrative, go back and see where you might add more details that appeal to the senses of your reader.

3. *Collaborative Writing:* Exchange your draft with a partner and let him or her point out any places in the story where the facts are not clear. Ask your partner to tell you what he or she thinks your purpose was, and see if it matches what you intended.

RAMON "TIANGUIS" PÉREZ

Ramon "Tianguis" Pérez is an undocumented alien and does not release biographical information.

The Fender-Bender

CONTEXT: *This narrative, taken from Pérez's book* Diary of an Undocumented Immigrant, *illustrates how even a minor incident can affect the precarious existence of an undocumented alien. For Pérez, a few pieces of paper stand between a life in America and deportation.*

One night after work, I drive Rolando's old car to visit some friends, and then 1
head towards home. At a light, I come to a stop too late, leaving the front end
of the car poking into the crosswalk. I shift into reverse, but as I am backing
up, I strike the van behind me. Its driver immediately gets out to inspect the
damage to his vehicle. He's a tall Anglo-Saxon, dressed in a deep blue work
uniform. After looking at his car, he walks up to the window of the car I'm
driving.

"Your driver's license," he says, a little enraged. 2

"I didn't bring it," I tell him. 3

He scratches his head. He is breathing heavily with fury. 4

"Okay," he says. "You park up ahead while I call a patrolman." 5

The idea of calling the police doesn't sound good to me, but the accident 6
is my fault. So I drive around the corner and park at the curb. I turn off the
motor and hit the steering wheel with one fist. I don't have a driver's license.
I've never applied for one. Nor do I have with me the identification card
that I bought in San Antonio. Without immigration papers, without a driving
permit, and having hit another car, I feel as if I'm just one step away from
Mexico.

I get out of the car. The white man comes over and stands right in front of 7
me. He's almost two feet taller.

"If you're going to drive, why don't you carry your license?" he asks in an ac- 8
cusatory tone.

"I didn't bring it," I say, for lack of any other defense. 9

I look at the damage to his car. It's minor, only a scratch on the paint and a 10
pimple-sized dent.

"I'm sorry," I say. "Tell me how much it will cost to fix, and I'll pay for it; 11
that's no problem." I'm talking to him in English, and he seems to understand.

"This car isn't mine," he says. "It belongs to the company I work for. I'm 12
sorry, but I've got to report this to the police, so that I don't have to pay for the
damage."

13   "That's no problem," I tell him again. "I can pay for it."

14   After we've exchanged these words, he seems less irritated. But he says he'd prefer for the police to come, so that they can report that the dent wasn't his fault.

15   While we wait, he walks from one side to the other, looking down the avenue this way and that, hoping that the police will appear.

16   Then he goes over to the van to look at the dent.

17   "It's not much," he says. "If it was my car, there wouldn't be any problems, and you could go on."

18   After a few minutes, the long-awaited police car arrives. Only one officer is inside. He's a Chicano, short and of medium complexion, with short, curly hair. On getting out of the car, he walks straight towards the Anglo.

19   The two exchange a few words.

20   "Is that him?" he asks, pointing at me.

21   The Anglo nods his head.

22   Speaking in English, the policeman orders me to stand in front of the car and to put my hands on the hood. He searches me and finds only the car keys and my billfold with a few dollars in it. He asks for my driver's license.

23   "I don't have it," I answered in Spanish.

24   He wrinkles his face into a frown, and casting a glance at the Anglo, shakes his head in disapproval of me.

25   "That's the way these Mexicans are," he says.

26   He turns back towards me, asking for identification. I tell him I don't have that, either.

27   "You're an illegal, eh?" he says.

28   I won't answer.

29   "An illegal," he says to himself.

30   "Where do you live?" he continues. He's still speaking in English.

31   I tell him my address.

32   "Do you have anything with you to prove that you live at that address?" he asks.

33   I think for a minute, then realize that in the glove compartment is a letter that my parents sent to me several weeks earlier.

34   I show him the envelope and he immediately begins to write something in a little book that he carries in his back pocket. He walks to the back of my car and copies the license plate number. Then he goes over to his car and talks into his radio. After he talks, someone answers. Then he asks me for the name of the car's owner.

35   He goes over to where the Anglo is standing. I can't quite hear what they're saying. But when the two of them go over to look at the dent in the van, I hear the cop tell the Anglo that if he wants, he can file charges against me. The Anglo shakes his head and explains what he had earlier explained to me,

about only needing for the police to certify that he wasn't responsible for the accident. The Anglo says that he doesn't want to accuse me of anything because the damage is light.

"If you want, I can take him to jail," the cop insists. 36

The Anglo turns him down again. 37

"If you'd rather, we can report him to Immigration," the cop continues. 38

Just as at the first, I am now almost sure that I'll be making a forced trip 39 to Tijuana. I find myself searching my memory for my uncle's telephone number, and to my relief, I remember it. I am waiting for the Anglo to say yes, confirming my expectations of the trip. But instead, he says no, and though I remain silent, I feel appreciation for him. I ask myself why the Chicano is determined to harm me. I didn't really expect him to favor me, just because we're of the same ancestry, but on the other hand, once I had admitted my guilt, I expected him to treat me at least fairly. But even against the white man's wishes, he's trying to make matters worse for me. I've known several Chicanos with whom, joking around, I've reminded them that their roots are in Mexico. But very few of them see it that way. Several have told me how, when they were children, their parents would take them to vacation in different states of Mexico, but their own feeling, they've said, is, "I am an American citizen!" Finally, the Anglo, with the justifying paper in his hands, says goodbye to the cop, thanks him for his services, gets into his van, and drives away.

The cop stands in the street in a pensive mood. I imagine that he's trying to 40 think of a way to punish me.

"Put the key in the ignition," he orders me. 41

I do as he says. 42

Then he orders me to roll up the windows and lock the doors. 43

"Now, go on, walking," he says. 44

I go off taking slow steps. The cop gets in his patrol car and stays there, 45 waiting. I turn the corner after two blocks and look out for my car, but the cop is still parked beside it. I begin looking for a coat hanger, and after a good while, find one by a curb of the street. I keep walking, keeping about two blocks away from the car. While I walk, I bend the coat hanger into the form I'll need. As if I'd called for it, a speeding car goes past. When it comes to the avenue where my car is parked, it makes a turn. It is going so fast that its wheels screech as it rounds the corner. The cop turns on the blinking lights of his patrol car and leaving black marks on the pavement beneath it, shoots out to chase the speeder. I go up to my car and with my palms force a window open a crack. Then I insert the clothes hanger in the crack and raise the lock lever. It's a simple task, one that I'd already performed. This wasn't the first time that I'd been locked out of a car, though always before, it was because I'd forgotten to remove my keys.

Understanding Meaning

1. How serious is the accident? *Not that seriou*
2. Why does the van driver insist on calling the police?
3. What makes this incident a dangerous one for Pérez?
4. How does Pérez attempt to prevent the van driver from summoning the police?
5. Pérez answers the Chicano patrolman in Spanish. Was this a mistake? How did the officer treat Pérez?
6. *Critical Thinking:* Pérez implies that Chicanos have been offended when he has alluded to their Mexican roots; they insist on being seen as American citizens. What does this say about assimilation and identity? Does the Chicano officer's comments about Mexicans reveal contempt for immigrants? Have other ethnic groups—Jews, Italians, Irish—resented the presence of unassimilated new arrivals from their homelands?

Evaluating Strategy

1. Why is a minor incident like a fender-bender a better device to explain the plight of the undocumented immigrant than a dramatic one?
2. How does Pérez use dialogue to advance the narrative? Are direct quotations more effective than paraphrases? Why or why not?

Appreciating Language

1. What words does Pérez use to minimize the damage caused by the accident?
2. What word choices and images stress the importance of paper documents in the lives of aliens?

WRITING SUGGESTIONS

1. Write a short narrative essay detailing a minor event that provided insight into your life or social conditions. Perhaps you discovered your dependence on energy when your apartment lost power and you could not use your computer, watch television, or even open the garage door to get your car. A simple interaction with a homeless person may have caused you to question your assumptions about the poor.
2. *Collaborative Writing:* Working with a group of students, discuss your views on immigration and undocumented or "illegal" aliens. Take notes and write a brief statement outlining your views. If major differences of opinion exist, split the group into subgroups, and draft pro and con opinion statements.

MARTIN GANSBERG

Martin Gansberg (1920–1995) grew up in Brooklyn and worked as a reporter, editor, and book reviewer for the New York Times for over forty years. His 1964 article about a woman who was fatally stabbed while her neighbors watched but failed to call the police stunned readers and caused a national outrage. Psychologists blamed the impact of television for causing what they called "the bystander effect." Editorials cited the incident as sign of urban alienation and social apathy. Critics later claimed that Gansberg's article exaggerated events, and that his dramatic opening line created the false impression that the neighbors passively watched the entire incident from beginning to end. In fact, most witnesses only heard what they thought was a late-night argument, and the most vicious part of the attack occurred out of sight of many neighbors. The man convicted of the 1964 murder of Kitty Genovese, Winston Moseley, remains in prison. He was denied parole for the twelfth time in 2006.

Thirty-Eight Who Saw Murder and Didn't Call the Police

CONTEXT: *This article appeared four months after the assassination of President Kennedy, when many commentators and most of the public were troubled by social unrest, crime, violence, and a growing sense that America was, as some put it, a "sick society." Consider how today's cable news commentators and bloggers would react to a similar event.*

For more than half an hour 38 respectable, law-abiding citizens in Queens 1 watched a killer stalk and stab a woman in three separate attacks in Kew Gardens.

Twice their chatter and the sudden glow of their bedroom lights inter- 2 rupted him and frightened him off. Each time he returned, sought her out, and stabbed her again. Not one person telephoned the police during the assault; one witness called after the woman was dead.

That was two weeks ago today. 3

Still shocked is Assistant Chief Inspector Frederick M. Lussen, in charge of 4 the borough's detectives and a veteran of 25 years of homicide investigations. He can give a matter-of-fact recitation on many murders: But the Kew Gardens slaying baffles him—not because it is a murder, but because the "good people" failed to call the police.

"As we have reconstructed the crime," he said, "the assailant had three 5 chances to kill this woman during a 35-minute period. He returned twice to complete the job. If we had been called when he first attacked, the woman might not be dead now."

This is what the police say happened beginning at 3:20 a.m. in the staid, 6 middle-class, tree-lined Austin Street area:

7   Twenty-eight-year-old Catherine Genovese, who was called Kitty by almost everyone in the neighborhood, was returning home from her job as manager of a bar in Hollis. She parked her red Fiat in a lot adjacent to the Kew Gardens Long Island Rail Road Station, facing Mowbray Place. Like many residents of the neighborhood, she had parked there day after day since her arrival from Connecticut a year ago, although the railroad frowns on the practice.

8   She turned off the lights of her car, locked the door, and started to walk the 100 feet to the entrance of her apartment at 82-70 Austin Street, which is in a Tudor building with stores in the first floor and apartments on the second.

9   The entrance to the apartment is in the rear of the building because the front is rented to retail stores. At night the quiet neighborhood is shrouded in the slumbering darkness that marks most residential areas.

10   Miss Genovese noticed a man at the far end of the lot, near a seven-story apartment house at 82-40 Austin Street. She halted. Then, nervously, she headed up Austin Street toward Lefferts Boulevard, where there is a call box to the 102nd Police Precinct in nearby Richmond Hill.

11   She got as far as a streetlight in front of a bookstore before the man grabbed her. She screamed. Lights went on in the 10-story apartment house at 82-67 Austin Street, which faces the bookstore. Windows slid open and voices punctuated the early-morning stillness.

12   Miss Genovese screamed: "Oh, my God, he stabbed me! Please help me! Please help me!"

13   From one of the upper windows in the apartment house, a man called down: "Let that girl alone!"

14   The assailant looked up at him, shrugged, and walked down Austin Street toward a white sedan parked a short distance away. Miss Genovese struggled to her feet.

15   Lights went out. The killer returned to Miss Genovese, now trying to make her way around the side of the building by the parking lot to get to her apartment. The assailant stabbed her again.

16   "I'm dying!" she shrieked. "I'm dying!"

17   Windows were opened again, and lights went on in many apartments. The assailant got into his car and drove away. Miss Genovese staggered to her feet. A city bus, Q-10, the Lefferts Boulevard line to Kennedy International Airport, passed. It was 3:35 A.M.

18   The assailant returned. By then, Miss Genovese had crawled to the back of the building, where the freshly painted brown doors to the apartment house held out hope for safety. The killer tried the first door; she wasn't there. At the second door, 82-62 Austin Street, he saw her slumped on the floor at the foot of the stairs. He stabbed her a third time—fatally.

It was 3:50 by the time the police received their first call, from a man who 19
was a neighbor of Miss Genovese. In two minutes they were at the scene. The
neighbor, a 70-year-old woman, and another woman were the only persons on
the street. Nobody else came forward.

The man explained that he had called the police after much deliberation. 20
He had phoned a friend in Nassau County for advice, and then he had crossed
the roof of the building to the apartment of the elderly woman to get her to
make the call.

"I didn't want to get involved," he sheepishly told police. 21

Six days later, the police arrested Winston Moseley, a 29-year-old business 22
machine operator, and charged him with homicide. Moseley had no previous
record. He is married, has two children and owns a home at 133-19 Sutter
Avenue, South Ozone Park, Queens. On Wednesday, a court committed him
to Kings County Hospital for psychiatric observation.

When questioned by the police, Moseley also said that he had slain 23
Mrs. Annie May Johnson, 24, of 146-12 133d Avenue, Jamaica, on Feb. 29
and Barbara Kralik, 15, of 174-17 140th Avenue, Springfield Gardens, last
July. In the Kralik case, the police are holding Alvin L. Mitchell, who is said
to have confessed to that slaying.

The police stressed how simple it would have been to have gotten in touch 24
with them. "A phone call," said one of the detectives, "would have done it."
The police may be reached by dialing "0" for operator or SPring 7-3100.

Today witnesses from the neighborhood, which is made up of one-family 25
homes in the $35,000 to $60,000 range with the exception of the two apartment houses near the railroad station, find it difficult to explain why they
didn't call the police.

A housewife, knowingly if quite casually, said, "We thought it was a lovers' 26
quarrel." A husband and wife both said, "Frankly, we were afraid." They
seemed aware of the fact that events might have been different. A distraught
woman, wiping her hands in her apron, said, "I didn't want my husband to get
involved."

One couple, now willing to talk about that night, said they heard the first 27
screams. The husband looked thoughtfully at the bookstore where the killer
first grabbed Miss Genovese.

"We went to the window to see what was happening," he said, "but the 28
light from our bedroom made it difficult to see the street." The wife, still
apprehensive, added: "I put out the light and we were able to see better."

Asked why they hadn't called the police, she shrugged and replied: "I don't 29
know."

A man peeked out from a slight opening in the doorway to his apartment and 30
rattled off an account of the killer's second attack. Why hadn't he called the
police at the time? "I was tired," he said without emotion. "I went back to bed."

31   It was 4:25 A.M. when the ambulance arrived to take the body of Miss Genovese. It drove off. "Then," a solemn police detective said, "the people came out."

Understanding Meaning

1. What details of this murder transformed it from a local crime story into an event that captured national attention?

2. How did the duration of the attack add to the significance of the neighbors' failure to call the police?

3. What reasons did the residents of Kew Gardens give for not taking action?

4. Gansberg mentions that William Moseley is a married homeowner with two children. Would these details surprise readers? Do most people have stereotyped notions about violent criminals?

5. Gansberg describes the neighborhood as being middle class. Is this significant? Why or why not?

6. *Critical Thinking:* Do you think this article describes an isolated event or captures commonplace attitudes and behaviors? Would most people call 911 today? Have you or anyone you know reported a crime in progress? Do you believe that urban life and television violence have desensitized people to crime and led them to passively watch rather than help? Do you think the same situation could occur in a small town? Is it a fact of modern life or human nature that leads people to avoid getting involved?

Evaluating Strategy

1. What impact does the first line have? Although it states facts and not a point of view, can you consider it a thesis statement? Why or why not?

2. Gansberg includes details such as times and addresses. Why is this expected in a newspaper article? Does the author's inclusion of objective facts give the article greater authority?

3. Gansberg includes several direct quotations by neighbors explaining their actions that night. Are direct quotes more effective than paraphrases? Why?

4. *Critical Thinking:* Does the opening line imply to you that all the witnesses passively watched the attack from beginning to end? Do writers, especially reporters, have an ethical responsibility to be accurate? Do you believe some journalists distort or exaggerate events to make their stories more dramatic?

Appreciating Language

1. Gansberg uses passive voice to describe the actions of neighbors that night, stating "lights went out" and "windows opened." What impact does this have?

2. What verbs does Gansberg use to describe the victim's calls for help? What effect do they have?

3. What words does Gansberg use to describe the witnesses after the attack?

4. Gansberg uses the word "shrugged" to describe both the killer and a witness. Do you think this was deliberate? Why or why not?

WRITING SUGGESTIONS

1. Write a brief narrative about a recent incident and try objectively to reconstruct an accurate timeline of events. Include details about times, dates, locations, and participants suited for a newspaper report.

2. *Collaborative Writing:* Discuss Gansberg's article with a group of students. Are they aware of similar incidents? Have they observed people's reaction to the plight of a person in distress? Do they believe most people are apathetic to victims of violence? Why or why not? Use division to organize your group's responses. If the group comes up with opposing viewpoints, consider using comparison to prepare contrasting statements.

BLENDING THE MODES

GEORGE ORWELL

George Orwell was the pen name of Eric Blair (1903–1950), who was born in India, the son of a British official. Blair graduated from the prestigious Eton School but joined the Indian Imperial Police instead of attending a university. After four years of service in Burma, he left to pursue a writing career. His first book, Down and Out in Paris and London, *explored the plight of the poor and homeless during the Depression. His later books included* Animal Farm *and* Nineteen Eighty-Four.

Shooting an Elephant

CONTEXT: *As you read Orwell's narrative, consider what message about imperialism he was trying to communicate to his British readers. What is his implied thesis?*

1 In Moulmein, in Lower Burma, I was hated by large numbers of people—the only time in my life that I have been important enough for this to happen to me. I was sub-divisional police officer of the town, and in an aimless, petty kind of way, anti-European feeling was very bitter. No one had the guts to raise a riot, but if a European woman went through the bazaars alone somebody would probably spit betel juice over her dress. As a police officer, I was an obvious target and was baited whenever it seemed safe to do so. When a nimble Burman tripped me up on the football field and the referee (another Burman) looked the other way, the crowd yelled with hideous laughter. This happened more than once. In the end the sneering yellow faces of young men that met me everywhere, the insults hooted after me when I was at a safe distance, got badly on my nerves. The young Buddhist priests were the worst of all. There were several thousands of them in the town and none of them seemed to have anything to do except stand on street corners and jeer at Europeans.

2   All this was perplexing and upsetting. For at that time I had already made up my mind that imperialism was an evil thing and the sooner I chucked up my job and got out of it the better. Theoretically—and secretly, of course—I was all for the Burmese and all against their oppressors, the British. As for the job I was doing, I hated it more bitterly than I can perhaps make clear. In a job like that you see the dirty work of the Empire at close quarters. The wretched prisoners huddling in the stinking cages of the lock-ups, the grey, cowed faces of the long-term convicts, the scarred buttocks of the men who had been flogged with bamboos—all these oppressed me with an intolerable sense of guilt. But I could get nothing into perspective. I was young and ill educated and I had had to think out my problems in the utter silence that is imposed on every Englishman in the East. I did not even know that the British Empire is

dying, still less did I know that it is a great deal better than the younger empires that are going to supplant it. All I knew was that I was stuck between my hatred of the empire I served and my rage against the evil-spirited little beasts who tried to make my job impossible. With one part of my mind I thought of the British Raj as an unbreakable tyranny, as something clamped down, *in saecula saeculorum*, upon the will of prostrate peoples; with another part I thought that the greatest joy in the world would be to drive a bayonet into a Buddhist priest's guts. Feelings like these are the normal by-products of imperialism; ask any Anglo-Indian official, if you can catch him off duty.

One day something happened which in a roundabout way was enlighten- 3 ing. It was a tiny incident in itself, but it gave me a better glimpse than I had had before of the real nature of imperialism—the real motives for which despotic governments act. Early one morning the sub-inspector at a police station at the other end of the town rang me up on the phone and said that an elephant was ravaging the bazaar. Would I please come and do something about it? I did not know what I could do, but I wanted to see what was happening and I got on to a pony and started out. I took my rifle, an old .44 Winchester and much too small to kill an elephant, but I thought the noise might be useful *in terrorem*. Various Burmans stopped me on the way and told me about the elephant's doings. It was not, of course, a wild elephant, but a tame one which had gone "must." It had been chained up as tame elephants always are when their attack of "must" is due, but on the previous night it had broken its chain and escaped. Its mahout, the only person who could manage it when it was in that state, had set out in pursuit, but he had taken the wrong direction and was now twelve hours' journey away, and in the morning the elephant had suddenly reappeared in the town. The Burmese population had no weapons and were quite helpless against it. It had already destroyed somebody's bamboo hut, killed a cow, and raided some fruit-stalls and devoured the stock; also it had met the municipal rubbish van, and, when the driver jumped out and took to his heels, had turned the van over and inflicted violence upon it.

The Burmese sub-inspector and some Indian constables were waiting for 4 me in the quarter where the elephant had been seen. It was a very poor quarter, a labyrinth of squalid bamboo huts, thatched with palm-leaf, winding all over a steep hillside. I remember that it was a cloudy stuffy morning at the beginning of the rains. We began questioning the people as to where the elephant had gone, and, as usual, failed to get any definite information. That is invariably the case in the East; a story always sounds clear enough at a distance, but the nearer you get to the scene of events the vaguer it becomes. Some of the people said that the elephant had gone in one direction, some said that he had gone in another, some professed not even to have heard of any elephant. I had almost made up my mind that the whole story was a pack of lies, when we heard yells a little distance away. There was a loud, scandalised cry of "Go away, child! Go away this instant!" and an old woman with a switch in her hand came round the corner of a hut, violently shooing away a crowd of naked children. Some more women followed, clicking their tongues and exclaiming; evidently there was something there that the children ought not to have seen. I rounded the hut and saw a man's dead body sprawling in the mud. He was an Indian, a black Dravidian coolie, almost naked, and he could not have been dead many minutes. The people said that the elephant had come suddenly upon him round the corner of the hut, caught him with its trunk, put its foot on his back and ground him into the earth. This was the rainy season and the ground was soft, and his face had scored a trench a foot deep and a couple of yards long. He was lying on his belly with arms crucified and head sharply twisted to one side. His face was coated with mud, the eyes wide open, the teeth bared and grinning with an expression of unendurable agony. (Never tell me, by the way, that the dead look peaceful. Most of the corpses I have seen looked devilish.) The friction of the great beast's foot had stripped the skin from his back as neatly as one skins a rabbit. As soon as I saw the dead man I sent an orderly to a friend's house nearby to borrow an elephant rifle. I had already sent back the pony, not wanting it to go mad with fright and throw me if it smelled the elephant.

5   The orderly came back in a few minutes with a rifle and five cartridges, and meanwhile some Burmans had arrived and told us that the elephant was in the paddy fields below, only a few hundred yards away. As I started forward, practically the whole population of the quarter flocked out of their houses and followed me. They had seen the rifle and were all shouting excitedly that I was going to shoot the elephant. They had not shown much interest in the elephant when he was merely ravaging their homes, but it was different now that he was going to be shot. It was a bit of fun to them, as it would be to an English crowd; besides, they wanted the meat. It made me vaguely uneasy. I had no intention of shooting the elephant—I had merely sent for the rifle to defend myself if necessary—and it is always unnerving to have a crowd following you. I marched down the hill, looking and feeling a fool, with the rifle over my shoulder and an ever-growing army of people jostling at my heels. At the bottom, when you got away from the huts, there was a metalled road and beyond that a miry waste of paddy fields a thousand yards across, not yet ploughed but soggy from the first rains and dotted with coarse grass. The elephant was standing eighty yards from the road, his left side towards us. He took not the slightest notice of the crowd's approach. He was tearing up bunches of grass, beating them against his knees to clean them and stuffing them into his mouth.

6   I had halted on the road. As soon as I saw the elephant I knew with perfect certainty that I ought not to shoot him. It is a serious matter to shoot a working elephant—it is comparable to destroying a huge and costly piece of machinery—and obviously one ought not to do it if it can possibly be avoided.

And at that distance, peacefully eating, the elephant looked no more danger-ous than a cow. I thought then and I think now that his attack of "must" was already passing off; in which case he would merely wander harmlessly about until the mahout came back and caught him. Moreover, I did not in the least want to shoot him. I decided that I would watch him for a little while to make sure that he did not turn savage again, and then go home.

But at that moment I glanced round at the crowd that had followed me. It 7 was an immense crowd, two thousand at the least and growing every minute. It blocked the road for a long distance on either side. I looked at the sea of yellow faces above the garish clothes—faces all happy and excited over this bit of fun, all certain that the elephant was going to be shot. They were watching me as they would watch a conjuror about to perform a trick. They did not like me, but with the magical rifle in my hands I was momentarily worth watching. And suddenly I realized that I should have to shoot the elephant after all. The peo-ple expected it of me and I had got to do it; I could feel their two thousand wills pressing me forward, irresistibly. And it was at this moment, as I stood there with the rifle in my hands, that I first grasped the hollowness, the futility of the white man's dominion in the East. Here was I, the white man with his gun, standing in front of the unarmed native crowd—seemingly the leading actor of the piece; but in reality I was only an absurd puppet pushed to and fro by the will of those yellow faces behind. I perceived in this moment that when the white man turns tyrant it is his own freedom that he destroys. He becomes a sort of hollow, posing dummy, the conventionalized figure of a sahib. For it is the condition of his rule that he shall spend his life in trying to impress the "na-tives" and so in every crisis he has got to do what the "natives" expect of him. He wears a mask, and his face grows to fit it. I had got to shoot the elephant. I had committed myself to doing it when I sent for the rifle. A sahib has got to act like a sahib; he has got to appear resolute, to know his own mind and do definite things. To come all that way, rifle in hand, with two thousand people marching at my heels, and then to trail feebly away, having done nothing—no, that was impossible. The crowd would laugh at me. And my whole life, every white man's life in the East, was one long struggle not to be laughed at.

But I did not want to shoot the elephant. I watched him beating his bunch 8 of grass against his knees, with that preoccupied grandmotherly air that ele-phants have. It seemed to me that it would be murder to shoot him. At that age I was not squeamish about killing animals, but I had never shot an elephant and never wanted to. (Somehow it always seems worse to kill a *large* animal.) Besides, there was the beast's owner to be considered. Alive, the ele-phant was worth at least a hundred pounds; dead, he would only be worth the value of his tusks—five pounds, possibly. But I had got to act quickly. I turned to some experienced-looking Burmans who had been there when we arrived, and asked them how the elephant had been behaving. They all said the same thing: he took no notice of you if you left him alone, but he might charge if you went too close to him.

9   It was perfectly clear to me what I ought to do. I ought to walk up to within, say, twenty-five yards of the elephant and test his behavior. If he charged I could shoot; if he took no notice of me it would be safe to leave him until the mahout came back. But also I knew that I was going to do no such thing. I was a poor shot with a rifle and the ground was soft mud into which one would sink at every step. If the elephant charged and I missed him, I should have about as much chance as a toad under a steamroller. But even then I was not thinking particularly of my own skin, only the watchful yellow faces behind. For at that moment, with the crowd watching me, I was not afraid in the ordinary sense, as I would have been if I had been alone. A white man mustn't be frightened in front of "natives"; and so, in general, he isn't frightened. The sole thought in my mind was that if anything went wrong those two thousand Burmans would see me pursued, caught, trampled on, and reduced to a grinning corpse like that Indian up the hill. And if that happened it was quite probable that some of them would laugh. That would never do. There was only one alternative. I shoved the cartridges into the magazine and lay down on the road to get a better aim.

10   The crowd grew very still, and a deep, low, happy sigh, as of people who see the theatre curtain go up at last, breathed from innumerable throats. They were going to have their bit of fun after all. The rifle was a beautiful German thing with cross-hair sights. I did not then know that in shooting an elephant one should shoot to cut an imaginary bar running from ear-hole to ear-hole. I ought therefore, as the elephant was sideways on, to have aimed straight at his ear-hole; actually I aimed several inches in front of this, thinking the brain would be further forward.

11   When I pulled the trigger I did not hear the bang or feel the kick—one never does when a shot goes home—but heard the devilish roar of glee that went up from the crowd. In that instant, in too short a time, one would have thought, even for the bullet to get there, a mysterious, terrible change had come over the elephant. He neither stirred nor fell, but every line of his body had altered. He looked suddenly stricken, shrunken, immensely old, as though the frightful impact of the bullet had paralyzed him without knocking him down. At last, after what seemed a long time—it might have been five seconds, I dare say—he sagged flabbily to his knees. His mouth slobbered. An enormous senility seemed to have settled upon him. One could have imagined him thousands of years old. I fired again into the same spot. At the second shot he did not collapse but climbed with desperate slowness to his feet and stood weakly upright, with legs sagging and head drooping. I fired a third time. That was the shot that did for him. You could see the agony of it jolt his whole body and knock the last remnant of strength from his legs. But in falling he seemed for a

moment to rise, for as his hind legs collapsed beneath him he seemed to tower upwards like a huge rock toppling, his trunk reaching skyward like a tree. He trumpeted, for the first and only time. And then down he came, his belly towards me, with a crash that seemed to shake the ground even where I lay.

I got up. The Burmans were already racing past me across the mud. It was 12 obvious that the elephant would never rise again, but he was not dead. He was breathing very rhythmically with long rattling gasps, his great mound of a side painfully rising and falling. His mouth was wide open—I could see far down into caverns of pale pink throat. I waited a long time for him to die, but his breathing did not weaken. Finally I fired my two remaining shots into the spot where I thought his heart must be. The thick blood welled out of him like red velvet, but still he did not die. His body did not even jerk when the shots hit him, the tortured breathing continued without a pause. He was dying, very slowly and in great agony, but in some world remote from me where not even a bullet could damage him further. I felt that I had got to put an end to that dreadful noise. It seemed dreadful to see the great beast lying there, powerless to move and yet powerless to die, and not even to be able to finish him. I went back for my small rifle and poured shot after shot into his heart and down his throat. They seemed to make no impression. The tortured gasps continued as steadily as the ticking of a clock.

In the end I could not stand it any longer and went away. I heard later that 13 it took him half an hour to die. Burmans were arriving with dahs and baskets even before I left, and I was told they had stripped his body almost to the bones by the afternoon.

Afterwards, of course, there were endless discussions about the shooting 14 of the elephant. The owner was furious, but he was only an Indian and could do nothing. Besides, legally I had done the right thing, for a mad elephant has to be killed, like a mad dog, if its owner fails to control it. Among the Europeans opinion was divided. The older men said I was right; the younger men said it was a damn shame to shoot an elephant for killing a coolie, because an elephant was worth more than any damn Coringhee coolie. And afterwards I was very glad that the coolie had been killed; it put me legally in the right and it gave me a sufficient pretext for shooting the elephant. I often wondered whether any of the others grasped that I had done it solely to avoid looking a fool.

Understanding Meaning

1. What is Orwell's goal in relating this incident? What does this event symbolize?

2. What role does Orwell play in the narrative? How does his behavior as a police officer conflict with his personal views?

3. What are Orwell's attitudes toward the Burmese?

4. Orwell's readers were primarily British. What was he trying to impress upon them?

5. *Critical Thinking:* Consider Orwell's statement, "With one part of my mind I thought of the British Raj as an unbreakable tyranny ... with another part I thought that the greatest joy in the world would be to drive a bayonet into a Buddhist priest's guts." What does this admission reveal?

Evaluating Strategy

1. Orwell opens the essay with the statement, "I was hated by large numbers of people." What impact does this have on readers? Does it accomplish more than simply attracting attention?

2. How does Orwell balance his role between narrator and participant?

3. *Blending the Modes:* Where does Orwell use *description, comparison, analysis,* and *persuasion* within his narrative?

Appreciating Language

1. What metaphors does Orwell use in telling the story?

2. Underline the figurative language Orwell uses to describe the labored death of the elephant. What images does he use to create a sense of horror?

3. Orwell calls the Burmese "natives," "coolies," and "Burmans." He describes their huts as "squalid" and the rice paddies as a "miry waste." What does this suggest about his view of Asia?

WRITING SUGGESTIONS

1. *Critical Thinking:* Orwell relates an incident in which his role conflicted with his personal beliefs. Write a brief narrative about an event that placed you in a similar situation. Have your roles as parent, employee, manager, student, or friend caused you to act against your values? Have you ever been compelled to lie on behalf of others? In relating the story, clearly distinguish between the actions you took and your better judgment.

2. *Collaborative Writing:* Work with other students to create a short statement analyzing Orwell's message about political power and the nature of abusive governments. Have each member write a draft, then work together to combine ideas into a single statement. If there are major differences, develop a comparison or division paper to contrast or list opinions.

WRITING BEYOND THE CLASSROOM

WALTER LORD

Walter Lord (1917–2002) was born in Baltimore and studied history at Princeton University. He entered Yale Law School, but his studies were interrupted by World War II. After serving with the Office of Strategic Services, he returned to law school. He served as editor in chief of a business information service but soon turned to writing history. He tracked down and interviewed the sixty-three living survivors of the Titanic *and studied the ship's records to produce* A Night to Remember, *a minute-by-minute account of the doomed luxury liner. Lord's style of blending fact with tense human drama made his book a best seller. His later books include* Day of Infamy, *about the Japanese attack on Pearl Harbor, and* Incredible Victory, *which tells the story of the Battle of Midway.*

The Reconstructed Logbook of the *Titanic*

CONTEXT: A Night to Remember *tells the dramatic story of the famous liner that sank on its maiden voyage in 1912. Considered "unsinkable" by its builders, the* Titanic *had only twenty lifeboats for its 2,207 passengers. Rescuers located 705 survivors, many of them picked up in half-empty boats. To assist readers in following the chronology of events, Lord placed a reconstructed logbook of the ship in the appendix of his book.*

April 10, 1912   1
  12 noon Leaves Southampton dock; narrowly escapes collision with   2
  American liner *New York*.
  7:00 p.m. Stops at Cherbourg for passengers.   3
  9:00 p.m. Leaves Cherbourg for Queenstown.   4
April 11, 1912   5
  12:30 p.m. Stops at Queenstown for passengers and mail. One crewman 6
  deserts.
  2:00 p.m. Leaves Queenstown for New York, carrying 1316 passengers and 7
  891 crew.
April 14, 1912   8
  9:00 a.m. *Caronia* reports ice Latitude 42°N from Longitude 49° to 51°W. 9
  1:42 p.m. *Baltic* reports ice Latitude 41°51'N from Longitude 49°52'W.   10
  1:45 p.m. *Amerika* reports ice Latitude 41°27'N, Longitude 50°8'W.   11
  7:00 p.m. Temperature 43°.   12
  7:30 p.m. Temperature 39°.   13
  7:30 p.m. *Californian* reports ice Latitude 42°3'N, Longitude 49°9'W.   14
  9:00 p.m. Temperature 33°.   15
  9:30 p.m. Second Officer Lightoller warns carpenter and engine room to 16
  watch fresh water supply—may freeze up; warns crow's-nest to watch for ice.

17   9:40 p.m. *Mesaba* reports ice Latitude 42°N to 41°25'N, Longitude 49° to 50°30'W.
18   10:00 p.m. Temperature 32°.
19   10:30 p.m. Temperature of sea down to 31°.
20   11:00 p.m. *Californian* warns of ice, but cut off before she gives location.
21   11:40 p.m. Collides with iceberg Latitude 41°46'N, Longitude 50°14'W.
22 *April 15, 1912*
23   12:05 a.m. Orders given to uncover the boats, muster the crew and passengers.
24   12:15 a.m. First wireless call for help.
25   12:45 a.m. First rocket fired.
26   12:45 a.m. First boat, No. 7, lowered.
27   1:40 a.m. Last rocket fired.
28   2:05 a.m. Last boat, Collapsible D, lowered.
29   2:10 a.m. Last wireless signals sent.
30   2:18 a.m. Lights fail.
31   2:20 a.m. Ship founders.
32   3:30 a.m. *Carpathia's* rockets sighted by boats.
33   4:10 a.m. First boat, No. 2, picked up by *Carpathia*.
34   8:30 a.m. Last boat, No. 12, picked up.
35   8:50 a.m. *Carpathia* heads for New York with 705 survivors.

Understanding Meaning

1. What is the goal of presenting events in a timeline?

2. How does this log help readers to follow events in a complex story such as a disaster involving hundreds of people?

3. Why would this log be valuable to a board of inquiry investigating the disaster?

4. *Critical Thinking:* According to the log, it took forty minutes to launch the first lifeboat. Although the crew had more than two and one-half hours to evacuate the ship, fifteen hundred people were lost. Do these facts alone raise suspicion of incompetence?

Evaluating Strategy

1. Can such a log as this distort events by emphasizing time relationships instead of causal relationships?

2. How does a writer deal with events that do not have a clear time reference?

Appreciating Language

1. Why is word choice important in brief notations such as those in a log?

2. Can you locate any words that are not objective?

WRITING SUGGESTIONS

1. Reconstruct a log of the actions you took yesterday. Consider the problems that arise in attempting to explain events that did not occur in a specific time frame.

2. *Collaborative Writing:* Working with a group of students, read the log and discuss your impressions. Should a luxury liner be able to evacuate its passengers safely in two hours? Write a paragraph summarizing your group's discussion.

RESPONDING TO IMAGES

NEW ORLEANS FOLLOWING HURRICANE KATRINA, SEPTEMBER 2005

1. What are your first reactions to this photograph? Do you recall seeing images like this one on television following Hurricane Katrina? How did you and those around you respond to them?

2. How do you interpret the people's expressions and gestures?

3. Would this image be better suited to accompany an objective or a subjective narrative about the aftermath of the hurricane? Why?

4. *Visual Analysis:* How does the distress in the faces in the foreground contrast with the Superdome looming behind them? What image did the Superdome have? What did it represent? Did it become an ironic image following the hurricane?

5. Write a short narrative about two people in this picture. Add dialogue, inventing a conversation between the pair.

6. *Collaborative Writing:* Work with a group of students to create a caption for this photograph. Have each member write a caption, and then discuss

each one. Note how word choices imply different meanings or interpretations of the event. What words do students use to describe the people and the situation?

STRATEGIES FOR WRITING NARRATION

1. **Determine your purpose.** Does your narrative have a goal beyond simply telling a story? What details or evidence do readers need to accept your point of view? Before writing down a list of events, ask yourself why this experience was important? What do you want your readers to learn? What do you want them to remember?

2. **Define your role.** As a narrator, you can write in first person, either as the major participant in or a witness to events. You can use third person for greater objectivity, inserting personal opinions if desired.

3. **Consider your audience.** What are your readers' needs and expectations? How much background material will you have to supply? Which events will the audience find most impressive?

4. **Review the discipline or writing situation.** If you are writing a narrative report as an employee or agent of an organization, study samples to determine how you should present your story.

5. **Identify the beginning and end of your narrative.** You may find it helpful to place background information in a separate foreword or introduction, and limit comments on the ending to an afterword. This can allow the body of the paper to focus on a specific chain of events.

6. **Narrow the focus of your narrative if needed.** Your goal is not to tell readers *everything* that happened during a particular experience. If you are writing about the day your grandmother died, for instance, do not feel obligated to summarize the entire day, which might simply produce a list of events. You might develop a more interesting paper by selecting one episode, such as breaking the news to a relative or driving to the hospital. Think of your narrative as a clip from a movie, not the entire film.

7. **Select a chronological pattern.** After reviewing the context of the narrative, determine which pattern would be most effective for your purpose—using a straight chronology, opening with a mid- or turning point, or presenting the final events first.

8. **Include dialogue to dramatize interactions between people.** Rather than summarizing conversations between people, consider using direct quotations. Dialogue reveals word choices and tone to bring people to life.

9. **Make use of transitional statements.** To prevent readers from becoming confused, make clear transitional statements to move the narrative. Statements such as "later that day" or "two weeks later" can help readers follow the passage of time. Clear transitions are important if you alter chronological order with flashbacks and flash-forwards.

10. **Use consistent tense in narrating events.** Stories can be related in past or present tense. Avoid illogical shifts between past and present tense, as in "I *woke* up late and *see* it is snowing."

SUGGESTED TOPICS FOR WRITING NARRATION

GENERAL ASSIGNMENTS

Write a narrative on any of the following topics. Your narrative may contain passages making use of other modes, such as definition or comparison. Choose your narrative structure carefully, and avoid including minor details that add little to the story line. Use flashbacks and flash-forwards carefully. Transitional statements, paragraphing, and line breaks can help clarify changes in the chronology. Remember, a narrative can include dialogue, which can dramatize a conversation.

1. A job interview

2. Moving into your first dorm room or apartment

3. The events that led you to take a major action—quit a job, end a relationship, or join an organization

4. A sporting event you played in or observed (you may wish to limit the narrative to a single play)

5. A first date

6. An event that placed you in danger

7. An experience that led you to change your opinion about a friend or family member

8. A typical day at school or your job

9. The worst day of your high school or college career

10. An accident or medical emergency—focus on creating a clear, minute-by-minute chronology

WRITING IN CONTEXT

1. Imagine you are participating in an experiment in which psychologists ask you to write a journal recording your experiences in college. Specifically, the researchers are interested in measuring stressors students face—deadlines, lack of sleep, conflicts with jobs, financial pressures. Write a diary for a week, detailing instances when you experience stress. Be as objective as possible.

2. Write an email to a friend relating the events of a typical day in college. Select details your friend will find humorous or interesting.

3. Preserve on paper a favorite story told by your grandparents or other relatives. Include background details and identify characters.

4. You are accused of committing a crime last Tuesday. To establish an alibi, create a detailed log to the best of your recollection of the day's events and your movements.

Student Paper: Narration

This paper was written in response to the following assignment:

> Write a 350- to 500-word narrative essay based on personal experience or observation. Limit your topic, select details, and use figurative language to recreate the sights, sounds, smells, and moods you experienced.

First Draft with Instructor's Comments

weak intro

This paper is about a trip I made last spring to San Diego to visit my aunt and uncle. I saw a lot during that week but the most meaningful part I remember was a one day trip to Mexico. I think it really changed the whole way I think about things. Sometimes

//it's = 'it is'

its the minor things you remember as important.

delete, open with strong image

I got off the San Diego Trolley and I knew that I was going to

Run-on   this would make a better opening

wordy, vague, delete

start an adventure. Tijuana. As I neared the entrance to cross the

Avoid shift from past to present

border

boarder there is a priest with a plastic bowl. With a picture of

Fragment

some kids saying "feed Tijuana's homeless children." Yeah, right,

delete "to myself"

I think to myself, just another scam, this guy probably isn't even

a priest.

Awkward, revise or delete

Tijuana. Just the name of the city brings back a special smell.

A smell that you will only know if you have been there. It only

wordy, delete or shorten

vague, add details

takes one time and you can relate to what I am trying to say to you.

<u>A smell that will permeate your olfactory senses forever.</u>

Fragment

The smell was terrible.

sp

As <u>I</u> cross the <u>boarder</u> the first thing that hits <u>you</u> is the

avoid shift from "I" to "you"

smell I just mentioned. Then you witness the terrible suffering

add specific details—what is "terrible"?

and horrible poverty. It makes you realize how terrible many

people have it in this world.

Once I <u>get</u> past the few blocks of poverty and <u>handed</u> out all

I can, <u>I</u> wandered upon a busy little plaza where <u>you</u> could see all

kinds of people having fun and partying.

add details   Avoid shift, delete from "I" to "you"

As I continued my journey, I reached a bridge. The bridge was

why "horrible"?

horrible. Toward the midspan of the bridge, I experienced one of

the most touching moments in my whole life, one of those happy ones

where it's not clear <u>weather</u> you should laugh or cry. There was this   *whether*

little child playing the accordion and another one playing a guitar.

It was getting to be late, and I started to get ready to leave.

But this time as I passed the priest <u>I filled his plastic bowl with</u>

<u>the rest of my money.</u>   *Good image for ending*

Like I stated, this one afternoon is what I remember from my

whole trip. I still think about those people and the way they lived their lives. We as Americans take way too much for granted

and never realize how bad other people have it in this world

today. *wordy*

REVISION NOTES

This is a good topic for a narrative. There are changes you can make to create a stronger essay.

1. Delete the first and last paragraphs—they are vague and general. Let the experience speak for itself. Focus on the event rather than telling readers how significant it was.

2. Add details to explain general terms such as "horrible" and "terrible."

3. Avoid illogical shifts in time. Describe your actions in the past tense—"I got off the trolley," "I walked," or "I saw." You can use present tense to explain general ideas or impressions not restricted to this specific event—"Tijuana *is poor*."

4. Avoid awkward shifts from "I" to "you." Write "I walked into the plaza where *I* could see" instead of "I walked into the plaza where *you* could see."

Revised Draft

Spare Change

As I stepped off the San Diego Trolley, I knew I was going to embark on a great adventure. Tijuana. As I neared the entrance to the border, I saw a priest with a plastic bowl next to a picture of sad-looking kids. The caption of the picture said, "Feed Tijuana's homeless children." Yeah, right, I thought, just another scam. This man, I was convinced, probably was not even a priest.

Tijuana. Just the name of the city brings back a distinct smell, one that will permeate my olfactory senses forever. A thousand different scents compounded into one. It was the overwhelming smell of fast food, sweat, sewage, and tears.

As I crossed the border the first thing that hit me was the smell. Then I witnessed countless victims of unforgettable poverty and suffering. A man without legs sat on a worn cushion begging for money. A ragged woman with her children huddled around her stood on the corner and waved an old grease-stained wax cup at passersby. When I paused to put a dollar bill in her cup, I was immediately surrounded by dirty-faced children dressed in Salvation Army hand-me-downs, ripped pants, and mismatched shoes begging for money. Their hands searched my pockets for change, anything to buy food for the night.

Once I got past the few blocks of human suffering and handed out all I could, I wandered upon a busy little plaza. This place was reasonably clean and clear of trash. Deafening music poured from a row of flashy clubs, and I saw dozens of drunken young Americans stumbling around. Tourists, who had spent the day in the numerous outlet stores, trudged past, distressed and exhausted from a day of hard shopping. They lugged huge plastic bags jammed with discount jeans, shoes, purses, and blouses. A score of children held out little packs of colored Chiclets, a local gum they sold to Americans at whatever price the tourists could haggle them down to. It is pathetic to think tourists feel the need to haggle over the price of gum with a child, but this is Tijuana.

Tourists come from all over the world to drink, to shop, to haggle with children. This is just the way it is, the way it will always be. As I continued my journey, I reached a bridge. The bridge was horrible. Along the sides there was trash and rubbish. Towards the midspan of the bridge, I experienced one of the most touching moments of my life, one of those happy ones where I didn't know if I should shed a tear from happiness or out of despair. A small boy played an accordion and another played a guitar. He was singing a Spanish song, well actually, it sounded like he was screaming as his compadre strummed a guitar. He had a little cup in front of him, and I threw a coin into it. He just smiled and kept singing. I turned around and left, but as I passed the priest at the border, I filled his plastic bowl with the rest of my change.

QUESTIONS FOR REVIEW AND REVISION

1. This student was assigned a 350- to 500-word narrative in a composition class. How successfully does this paper meet this goal?

2. How does the student open and close the narrative? Does the opening grab attention? Does the conclusion make a powerful statement?

3. What devices does the student use to advance the chronology?

4. Most writers focus on visual details. This student includes the senses of sound and smell as well. How effective is this approach?

5. Did the student follow the instructor's suggestions? Do you see habitual errors the student should identify to improve future assignments?

6. Read the paper aloud. What changes would you make? Can you detect passages that would benefit from revision or rewording?

WRITING SUGGESTIONS

1. Using this essay as a model, write a short narrative about a trip that exposed you to another culture. Try to recapture the sights, sounds, and smells that characterized the experience.

2. *Collaborative Writing:* Ask a group of students to assign a grade to this essay and then explain their evaluations. What strengths and weaknesses does the group identify?

NARRATION CHECKLIST

Before submitting your paper, review these points:

1. Does the narrative have a clear focus?

2. Can readers follow the chronology of events?

3. Do you write in a consistent tense or time? Does your paper contain illogical shifts from past to present?

4. Does the narrative flow evenly, or is it bogged down with unnecessary detail?

5. Does your narrative maintain a consistent point of view? Do you switch from first to third person without reason?

6. Does your narrative suit your purpose, reader, discipline, or situation?

Info Write provides additional information on writing narration.
cengage.learning.infowrite.com

CHAPTER FIVE

DESCRIPTION: PRESENTING IMPRESSIONS

WHAT IS DESCRIPTION?

Description captures the essence of a person, place, object, or condition through sensory details. Nearly all writing requires description. Before you can narrate events, compare, classify, or analyze, you must provide readers with a clear picture of your subject. Dramatists open plays with set and character descriptions. Homicide detectives begin reports with descriptions of crime scenes. Before proposing expanding an airport, the writers of a government study must first describe congestion in the existing facility.

The way writers select and present details depends on context. Carl T. Rowan's article "Unforgettable Miss Bessie" (page 137), published in *Reader's Digest*, describes an influential teacher to a general audience reading for human interest:

> She was only about five feet tall and probably never weighed more than 110 pounds, but Miss Bessie was a towering presence in the classroom. She was the only woman tough enough to make me read *Beowulf* and think for a few foolish days that I liked it. From 1938 to 1942, when I attended Bernard High School in McMinnville, Tenn., she taught me English, history, civics—and a lot more than I realized.

Rowan's description includes facts about the teacher's height and weight, the courses she taught, and the name of the school. But Rowan's focus is her "towering presence" and the impact she had in shaping his life. Writing in the first person, Rowan places himself in the essay to build rapport with his readers.

This intimate portrait contrasts sharply with the description of Lee Harvey Oswald included in an FBI report:

> OSWALD was advised questions were intended to obtain his complete physical description and background. Upon repetition of the question as to his present employment, he furnished the same without further discussion.

RACE	White
SEX	Male
DATE OF BIRTH	October 18, 1939
PLACE OF BIRTH	New Orleans, Louisiana
HEIGHT	5' 9"
WEIGHT	140
HAIR	Medium brown, worn medium length, needs haircut
EYES	Blue-gray

Aside from noting that Oswald needed a haircut, the FBI agent never offers personal impressions and presents his observations in cold, factual statements. Unlike Rowan, who is writing to a general audience reading for entertainment, the FBI agent is preparing a report for a specialized reader who will use this information in a criminal investigation. The writer's statements will be scrutinized by investigators and attorneys. The inclusion of any personal impressions or colorful phrases would be unprofessional and subject to challenge.

The differences between the descriptions of Miss Bessie and Lee Harvey Oswald illustrate the differences between *objective* and *subjective* description.

Objective and Subjective Description

The purpose of *objective* description is to inform readers by accurately reporting factual details. Its language attempts to provide photographic realism of what people, places, things, and conditions are like. Research papers, business and government reports, and newspaper accounts of current events are objective. Objective description is effective when the writer's purpose is to present readers with information required to make an evaluation or decision. In many instances, it does not attempt to arouse a reader's interest since it is often written in response to reader demand.

Objective description focuses on facts and observable detail. *The Columbia Encyclopedia*, for example, offers readers this description of Chicago:

> Chicago (shĭkä'gō, shĭkô'gō), city (1990 pop. 2,783,726), seat of Cook Co., NE Ill., on Lake Michigan; inc. 1837. The third largest city in the United States and the heart of a metropolitan area of over 8 million people, it is the commercial, financial, industrial, and cultural center for a vast region and a midcontinental shipping point. A major Great Lakes port, it is also an historic rail and highway hub. O'Hare International Airport is the second busiest in the nation. An enormous variety of goods are manufactured in the area. Despite an overall decline in industry, Chicago has retained large grain mills and elevators, iron- and steelworks, steel fabricators, and meatpacking, food-processing, chemical, machinery, and electronics plants. The city has long been a publishing center; the Chicago *Tribune* is among the most widely read newspapers in the country.

In contrast to objective description, *subjective* description creates impressions through sensory details and imagery. Short stories, novels, essays, and opinion pieces use highly personal sensory details to create an individual sense of the subject. Instead of photographic realism, subjective description paints scenes, creates moods, or generates emotional responses. Providing accurate information is less important than giving readers a "feel" for the subject. In a subjective description of a car, the color, shape, ride, and the memories it evokes for the writer are more important than facts about horsepower, base price, and fuel efficiency.

Attempting to capture his view of Chicago, John Rechy compares the city to an expectant mother:

> You get the impression that once Chicago was like a constantly pregnant woman, uneasy in her pregnancy because she has miscarried so often. After its rise as a frontier town, plush bigtime madams, adventurers, and soon the titanic rise of the millionaires, the city's subsequent soaring population—all gave more than a hint that Chicago might easily become America's First City. But that title went unquestionably to New York. Brazenly, its skyscrapers, twice as tall as any in the Midwest city, symbolically invaded the sky. Chicago, in squat self-consciousness, bowed out. It became the Second City....

Rechy uses imagery and unconventional syntax to create a highly personalized view of the city. In the context of this essay written for a literary magazine, impression is more important than accuracy. Exact numbers, dates, and statistics are irrelevant to his purpose. The writer's purpose in subjective description is to share a vision or feeling, not to provide information.

Many writers blend the realism of objective description with the impressionistic details of subjective description to create striking portraits, such as Russell Miller's depiction of Chicago's State Street:

> Summer 1983. State Street, "that great street," is a dirty, desolate, and depressing street for most of its length. It runs straight and pot-holed from the Chicago city line, up through the black ghettos of the South Side, an aching wasteland of derelict factories pitted with broken windows, instant slum apartment blocks, vandalized playgrounds encased in chain-linked fencing, and vacant lots where weeds sprout gamely from the rubble and from the rusting hulks of abandoned automobiles. Those shops that remain open are protected by barricades of steel mesh. One or two men occupy every doorway, staring sullenly onto the street, heedless of the taunting cluster of skyscrapers to the north.

In this passage, details such as "vandalized playgrounds" are interwoven with expressions granting human emotions to inanimate objects, so wastelands are "aching" and skyscrapers "taunting." Blended descriptions such as this one are useful in strengthening subjective views with factual details. This style of writing is used by journalists and freelance authors writing to audiences who may be reading for both enjoyment and information.

Whether objective or subjective, all descriptive writing communicates through detail—through a careful selection and clear presentation of facts or impressions that serve the writer's purpose and impress readers.

The Language of Description

Words have power. The impact descriptive writing makes depends on *diction*, the writer's choice of words. Whether your description is objective, subjective, or a blend, the words you select should be *accurate*, *effective*, and *appropriate*. In choosing words, consider your purpose, readers, and discipline.

Use Words Accurately

Many words are easily confused. Should a patient's heart rate be monitored "continually," meaning at regular intervals such as once an hour, or "continuously," meaning without interruption? Is the city council planning to "adapt" or "adopt" a handgun ban? Some of the numerous pairs of frequently misused words follow:

allusion An indirect reference

illusion A false or imaginary impression

infer To interpret
imply To suggest

conscience A sense of moral or ethical conduct
conscious To be awake or aware of something

principle Basic law, rule, or concept
principal Something or someone important, as in school principal

affect To change or influence
effect A result; to achieve

When writing, consult a dictionary or review the usage section of a handbook to ensure you are using the correct word.

Use Words Effectively

You can improve the impact of your writing by using specific words, eliminating unnecessary words and diluted verbs, and avoiding clichés and inflated phrases. Often reading a paper aloud can help you "hear" wordy and ineffective sentences.

Use Specific Words

Specific words are direct and understandable. They communicate more information and make clearer impressions than do vague, abstract words:

ABSTRACT	SPECIFIC
motor vehicle	pickup truck
modest suburban home	three-bedroom colonial
human resources	employees
protective headgear	helmet
residential rental unit	studio apartment

Eliminate Unnecessary Words

Avoid cluttering your description with words that add little or no meaning:

WORDY	IMPROVED
at this point in time	now
few in number	few
consensus of opinion	consensus

thunderstorm activity	thunderstorms
winter months	winter
went to go to the store	went to the store
there are good jobs out there	there are good jobs
my favorite game to play	my favorite game

Avoid Diluted Verbs

Verbs convey action. Do not dilute their meaning by turning them into wordy phrases that weaken their impact and obscure the action they describe:

DILUTED VERB	IMPROVED
achieve purification	purify
render an examination of	examine
are found to be in agreement	agree
conduct an analysis	analyze

Avoid Clichés and Inflated Phrases

Description uses figurative language such as *similes* (comparisons using *like* or *as*) and *metaphors* (direct comparisons). To be effective, figurative language should create fresh and appropriate impressions. Avoid *clichés* (overly used expressions) and inflated phrases that distort through exaggeration:

CLICHÉ/INFLATED	IMPROVED
back in the day	in the past
pretty as a picture	attractive
straight from the shoulder	direct
as plain as day	obvious
terrible disaster	disaster
in the whole world today	today

Use Words Appropriately

Understand the Roles of Denotation and Connotation

All words *denote*, or indicate, a particular meaning. The words *home, residence,* and *domicile* all refer to where a person lives. Each has the same basic meaning or denotation, but the word *home* evokes personal associations of family, friends, and favorite belongings. *Domicile,* on the other hand, has a legalistic and official sound devoid of personal associations.

Connotations are implied or suggested meanings. Connotations often reflect the writer's purpose and opinion. A resort cabin can be described as a "rustic cottage" or a "seedy shack" depending on a person's point of view. The person who spends little money and shops for bargains can be praised for being "frugal" or ridiculed for being "cheap." A developer can be applauded for "draining a swamp to build homes" or condemned for "destroying a wetland to construct a subdivision." The Supreme Court's *Roe v. Wade* decision on abortion can be called a "protection that assures women's rights" or a "restriction that prevents states from passing laws." The following pairs of words and phrases have the same basic meaning or denotation, but their connotations create different impressions:

young	inexperienced
traditional	old-fashioned
brave	reckless
casual	sloppy
illegal aliens	undocumented workers
residential care facility	nursing home
unintended landing	plane crash
lied	misspoke
drilling for oil	exploring for energy
tax break	tax relief

Connotations shape meaning and, in many contexts, can be used to express opinion and influence readers. Depending on your point of view, graffiti can be seen as a "prank" or an "act of vandalism."

Be Conscious of Ethical Issues with Connotation

Words can be selected to dramatize or minimize an event or situation. This raises ethical issues. Because words such as *accident* and *explosion* might alarm the public, nuclear regulations substitute the terms *event* and *rapid disassembly.* When the space shuttle *Challenger* exploded in midair, the National Aeronautics and Space Administration (NASA) referred to a *major malfunction.* Writers in all disciplines have to weigh the moral implications of the words they choose.

STRATEGIES FOR READING DESCRIPTIONS

While reading the descriptions in this chapter, keep these questions in mind.

Understanding Meaning

1. What is the author's goal—to inform, enlighten, share personal observations, or provide information demanded by others? What is the writer's role? Is he or she writing from a personal or professional perspective?

2. Who is the intended audience—general or specific readers? How much knowledge does the author assume his or her readers have? Are technical terms defined? Does the description appear to have a special focus?

3. What is the nature of the discipline, discourse community, or writing situation? Is the description objective or subjective? Does the original source of the description (newsmagazine, scientific journal, or government document) reveal something about context?

Evaluating Strategy

1. What details does the writer select? Does he or she seem to ignore or minimize some details?

2. Does the description seek to establish a dominant impression? Which details support this impression?

3. How are details organized? Does the author use a particular method of grouping observations?

Appreciating Language

1. What level of language does the writer employ? Are technical terms used without explanation?

2. Does the language include connotations that shade reader reaction to the subject?

LANSING LAMONT

Lansing Lamont was born in New York City and was educated at Harvard College and the Columbia School of Journalism. He was a national political correspondent for Time *magazine from 1961 to 1968. He became deputy chief of* Time's *London bureau and later served as the magazine's Ottawa bureau chief. His best-selling book* Day of Trinity *(1965) told the story behind the development of the atom bomb during World War II. His second book* Campus Shock *(1979) examined American college life in the 1970s.*

The Bomb

CONTEXT: *In this section from* Day of Trinity *Lamont describes the first atomic bomb before its detonation in the New Mexico desert in July 1945. Note how Lamont includes both objective facts and subjective impressions of the bomb.*

The bomb rested in its cradle. 1

It <u>slept</u> upon a steel-supported oakwood platform, inside a sheet-metal 2 shack 103 feet above the ground: a <u>bloated black squid girdled with cables and</u> *subjective* <u>leechlike detonators</u>, each tamped with enough explosive to spark simultane- *animal* ously, within a millionth of a second, the final conflagration. <u>Tentacles</u> *imagery* emerged from the <u>squid</u> in a harness of wires connecting the detonators to a shiny aluminum tank, the firing unit.

Stripped of its coils, the bomb weighed 10,000 pounds. Its teardrop dimen- 3 sions were 4½ feet wide by 10½ feet long. Its guts contained two layers of *objective facts* wedge-shaped high-explosive blocks surrounding an inner core of precisely machined nuclear ingots that lay, as one scientist described them, like dia- monds in an immense wad of cotton. These ingots were made from a metal called plutonium.

At the <u>heart</u> of the bomb, buried inside the layers of explosive and pluto- 4 nium, lay the ultimate key to its success or failure, a metallic sphere no bigger than a ping-pong ball that even twenty years later would still be regarded a state secret: the initiator.

Within five seconds the initiator would trigger the sequence that hundreds 5 of shadows had gathered to watch that dawn. The bomb would either fizzle to a premature death or shatteringly christen a new era on earth.

Weeks, months, years of toil had gone into it. 6

The nation's finest brains and leadership, the cream of its scientific and en- 7 gineering force, plus two billion dollars from the taxpayers had built the squat monster on the tower for this very moment. Yet it had been no labor of love. There was not the mildest affection for it.

8   Other instruments of war bore dashing or maidenly names: Britain's "Spitfires"; the "Flying Tigers"; the "Gravel Gerties" and "Gypsy Rose Lees" that clanked across North Africa or blitzed bridgeheads on the Rhine; even the Germans' "Big Bertha" of World War I; and, soon, the Superfortress "Enola Gay" of Hiroshima, deliverer of an atomic bundle called "Little Boy."

9   The test bomb had no colorful nickname. One day its spawn would be known as "Fat Man" (after Churchill). But now its identity was cloaked in a welter of impersonal terms: "the thing," "the beast," "the device" and its Washington pseudonym, "S-1." The scientists, most of whom called it simply "the gadget," had handled it gently and daintily, like the baby it was—but out of respect, not fondness. One wrong jolt of the volatile melon inside its Dura-lumin frame could precipitate the collision of radioactive masses and a slow, agonizing death from radiation. Or instant vaporization.

10   The <u>monster</u> engendered the sort of fear that had caused one young sci-
use of witness   entist to break down the evening before and be escorted promptly from the
quotation   site to a psychiatric ward; and another, far older and wiser, a Nobel Prize winner, to murmur, as he waited in his trench, "I'm scared witless, absolutely witless."

Understanding Meaning

1. What dominant impression does Lamont make?

2. How did the scientists feel about the bomb they created?

3. What impact does the final quotation have?

4. *Critical Thinking:* Lamont notes that, unlike other weapons of WWII, the bomb was not given a colorful nickname. What does this imply? How does it set this weapon apart from the others that bore heroic or even whimsical names?

Evaluating Strategy

1. How does Lamont blend objective details and subjective impressions?

2. How does Lamont demonstrate how the scientists felt about the weapon?

Appreciating Language

1. What words create Lamont's dominant impression?

2. What role does animal imagery play in the description? How does it make the bomb appear as a "monster"?

WRITING SUGGESTIONS

1. Write a short description of an object like a car, house, or computer and use subjective impressions to bring it to life by comparing it to a person or animal. You might describe an old car as a "beast" or a guitar as a "best friend."

2. *Collaborative Writing:* Work with a group of students and write a short essay describing the threat of nuclear terrorism. What would happen if terrorists were able to place a nuclear weapon in a large American city? How would the nation and the public respond to a sudden, unexpected explosion that claimed a hundred thousand lives?

TRUMAN CAPOTE

Truman Capote (1924–1985) was born in New Orleans and first gained prominence as a writer of short stories. At age twenty-four he produced his first novel, Other Voices, Other Rooms, *which achieved international attention. His other works include* Breakfast at Tiffany's *and* A Tree of Night. *In 1965 he published* In Cold Blood, *which became an immediate best-seller. Based on extensive research and interviews,* In Cold Blood *told the story of the 1959 mass murder of a Kansas farm family and the fate of the killers. Although nonfiction, Capote's book read much like a novel.* In Cold Blood *helped shape a new school of journalism that uses the stylistic touches of fiction to relate wholly factual events.*

Out There

CONTEXT: *The opening pages of* In Cold Blood *describe the small town of Holcomb, Kansas, where the murders occurred. Capote spent a great deal of time in Holcomb and describes it almost as if it had been his own hometown.*

1 The village of Holcomb stands on the high wheat plains of western Kansas, a lonesome area that other Kansans call "out there." Some seventy miles east of the Colorado border, the countryside, with its hard blue skies and desert-clear air, has an atmosphere that is rather more Far Western than Middle West. The local accent is barbed with a prairie twang, a ranch-hand nasalness, and the men, many of them, wear narrow frontier trousers, Stetsons, and high-heeled boots with pointed toes. The land is flat, and the views are awesomely extensive; horses, herds of cattle, a white cluster of grain elevators rising as gracefully as Greek temples are visible long before a traveler reaches them.

2 Holcomb, too, can be seen from great distances. Not that there is much to see—simply an aimless congregation of buildings divided in the center by the main-line tracks of the Santa Fe Railroad, a haphazard hamlet bounded on the south by a brown stretch of the Arkansas (pronounced "Ar-kan-sas") River, on the north by a highway, Route 50, and on the east and west by prairie lands and wheat fields. After rain, or when snowfalls thaw, the streets, unnamed, unshaded, unpaved, turn from the thickest dust into the direst mud. At one end of the town stands a stark old stucco structure, the roof of which supports an electric sign—Dance—but the dancing has ceased and the advertisement has been dark for several years. Nearby is another building with an irrelevant sign, this one in flaking gold on a dirty window—Holcomb Bank. The bank closed in 1933, and its former counting rooms have been converted into apartments. It is one of the town's two "apartment houses," the second being a ramshackle mansion known, because a good part of the local school's faculty

lives there, as the Teacherage. But the majority of Holcomb's homes are one-story frame affairs, with front porches.

Down by the depot, the postmistress, a gaunt woman who wears a rawhide 3 jacket and denims and cowboy boots, presides over a falling-apart post office. The depot itself, with its peeling sulfur-colored paint, is equally melancholy; the Chief, the Super Chief, the El Capitan go by every day, but these celebrated expresses never pause there. No passenger trains do—only an occasional freight. Up on the highway, there are two filling stations, one of which doubles as a meagerly supplied grocery store, while the other does extra duty as a café—Hartman's Café, where Mrs. Hartman, the proprietress, dispenses sandwiches, coffee, soft drinks, and 3.2 beer. (Holcomb, like all the rest of Kansas, is "dry.")

And that, really, is all. Unless you include, as one must, the Holcomb 4 School, a good-looking establishment, which reveals a circumstance that the appearance of the community otherwise camouflages: that the parents who send their children to this modern and ably staffed "consolidated" school—the grades go from kindergarten through senior high, and a fleet of buses transport the students, of which there are usually around three hundred and sixty, from as far as sixteen miles away—are, in general, a prosperous people. Farm ranchers, most of them, are outdoor folk of very varied stock—German, Irish, Norwegian, Mexican, Japanese. They raise cattle and sheep, grow wheat, milo, grass seed, and sugar beets. Farming is always a chancy business, but in western Kansas its practitioners consider themselves "born gamblers," for they must contend with an extremely shallow precipitation (the annual average is eighteen inches) and anguishing irrigation problems. However, the last seven years have been years of droughtless beneficence. The farm ranchers in Finney County, of which Holcomb is a part, have done well; money has been made not from farming alone but also from the exploitation of plentiful natural-gas resources, and its acquisition is reflected in the new school, the comfortable interiors of the farmhouses, the steep and swollen grain elevators.

Until one morning in mid-November of 1959, few Americans—in fact, few 5 Kansans—had ever heard of Holcomb. Like the waters of the river, like the motorists on the highway, and like the yellow trains streaking down the Santa Fe tracks, drama, in the shape of exceptional happenings, had never stopped there. The inhabitants of the village, numbering two hundred and seventy, were satisfied that this should be so, quite content to exist inside ordinary life—to work, to hunt, to watch television, to attend school socials, choir practice, meetings of the 4-H Club. But then, in the earliest hours of that morning in November, a Sunday morning, certain foreign sounds impinged on the normal nightly Holcomb noises—on the keening hysteria of coyotes, the dry scrape of scuttling tumbleweed, the racing, receding wail of locomotive whistles. At the time not a soul in sleeping Holcomb heard them—four shotgun blasts that, all told, ended six human lives. But afterward the towns-people, theretofore sufficiently unfearful of each other to seldom trouble to lock their doors, found fantasy re-creating them over and again—those somber explosions that stimulated fires of mistrust in the glare of which many old neighbors viewed each other strangely, and as strangers.

Understanding Meaning

1. How much of Capote's description can be considered objective, and how much appears subjective?

2. Capote includes a great deal of factual detail—names of highways, the number of students in the high school, and Holcomb's population. What do these facts add to the description?

3. What does Capote attempt to capture in his description of Holcomb?

Evaluating Strategy

1. *Critical Thinking:* A key goal in the opening of any book is to get people's attention and motivate them to continue reading. How does Capote generate interest in describing a nondescript town?

2. What responses do the closing lines in this section of the story create?

Appreciating Language

1. How does the language of Capote's description differ from that of an encyclopedia or newspaper article?

2. *In Cold Blood* has sold millions of copies. What elements in Capote's style make his story about a crime in a small Kansas town so popular? What phrases strike you as being colorful or interesting?

WRITING SUGGESTIONS

1. Using Capote's description of Holcomb as a resource, write a purely objective, one-paragraph description of the town. Include as much factual detail as possible.

2. *Collaborative Writing:* Working with a group of students, rewrite a recent article from the local newspaper for a national audience, adding subjective details to arouse human interest. Include details about your community to give readers a feel for the location.

LUIS ALBERTO URREA

Luis Alberto Urrea was born in Tijuana to a Mexican father and American mother. He grew up in San Diego and attended the University of California. After graduation and a brief career as a movie extra, Urrea worked with a volunteer organization that provides food, clothing, and medical supplies to the poor of northern Mexico. In 1982 he taught writing at Harvard. His most recent novel, Into the Beautiful North, *was published in 2009, and he published a collection of short stories,* Six Kinds of Sky, *in 2002.*

Border Story

CONTEXT: *In this description of the Mexican-American border from* Across the Wire: Life and Hard Times on the Mexican Border *(1993), Urrea uses the device of second person to place his reader in the scene. By making "you" the "illegal," he seeks to dramatize and humanize the plight of the poor seeking a new life in the United States.*

At night, the Border Patrol helicopters swoop and churn in the air all along the line. You can sit in the Mexican hills and watch them herd humans on the dusty slopes across the valley. They look like science fiction crafts, their hard-focused lights raking the ground as they fly. 1

Borderlands locals are so jaded by the sight of nightly people-hunting that it doesn't even register in their minds. But take a stranger to the border, and she will *see* the spectacle: monstrous Dodge trucks speeding into and out of the landscape; uniformed men patrolling with flashlights, guns, and dogs; spotlights; running figures; lines of people hurried onto buses by armed guards; and the endless clatter of the helicopters with their harsh white beams. A Dutch woman once told me it seemed altogether "un-American." 2

But the Mexicans keep on coming—and the Guatemalans, the Salvadorans, the Panamanians, the Colombians. The seven-mile stretch of Interstate 5 nearest the Mexican border is, at times, so congested with Latin American pedestrians that it resembles a town square. 3

They stick to the center island. Running down the length of the island is a cement wall. If the "illegals" (currently, "undocumented workers"; formerly, "wetbacks") are walking north and a Border Patrol vehicle happens along, they simply hop over the wall and trot south. The officer will have to drive up to the 805 interchange, or Dairy Mart Road, swing over the overpasses, then drive south. Depending on where this pursuit begins, his detour could entail five to ten miles of driving. When the officer finally reaches the group, they hop over the wall and trot north. Furthermore, because freeway arrests would endanger traffic, the Border Patrol has effectively thrown up its hands in surrender. 4

5   It seems jolly on the page. But imagine poverty, violence, natural disasters, or political fear driving you away from everything you know. Imagine how bad things get to make you leave behind your family, your friends, your lovers; your home, as humble as it might be; your church, say. Let's take it further—you've said good-bye to the graveyard, the dog, the goat, the mountains where you first hunted, your grade school, your state, your favorite spot on the river where you fished and took time to think.

6   Then you come hundreds—or thousands—of miles across territory utterly unknown to you. (Chances are, you have never traveled farther than a hundred miles in your life.) You have walked, run, hidden in the backs of trucks, spent part of your precious money on bus fare. There is no AAA or Travelers Aid Society available to you. Various features of your journey north might include police corruption; violence in the forms of beatings, rape, murder, torture, road accidents; theft; incarceration. Additionally, you might experience loneliness, fear, exhaustion, sorrow, cold, heat, diarrhea, thirst, hunger. There is no medical attention available to you. There isn't even Kotex.

7   Weeks or months later, you arrive in Tijuana. Along with other immigrants, you gravitate to the bad parts of town because there is nowhere for you to go in the glittery sections where the *gringos* flock. You stay in a rundown little hotel in the red-light district, or behind the bus terminal. Or you find your way to the garbage dumps, where you throw together a small cardboard nest and claim a few feet of dirt for yourself. The garbage-pickers working this dump might allow you to squat, or they might come and rob you or burn you out for breaking some local rule you cannot possibly know beforehand. Sometimes the dump is controlled by a syndicate, and goon squads might come to you within a day. They want money, and if you can't pay, you must leave or suffer the consequences.

8   In town, you face endless victimization if you aren't streetwise. The police come after you, street thugs come after you, petty criminals come after you; strangers try your door at night as you sleep. Many shady men offer to guide you across the border, and each one wants all your money now, and promises to meet you at a prearranged spot. Some of your fellow travelers end their journeys right here—relieved of their savings and left to wait on a dark corner until they realize they are going nowhere.

9   If you are not Mexican, and can't pass as *tijuanense*, a local, the tough guys find you out. Salvadorans and Guatemalans are routinely beaten up and robbed. Sometimes they are disfigured. Indians—Chinantecas, Mixtecas, Guasaves, Zapotecas, Mayas—are insulted and pushed around; often they are lucky—they are merely ignored. They use this to their advantage. Often they don't dream of crossing into the United States: a Mexican tribal person would never be able to blend in, and they know it. To them, the garbage dumps and street vending and begging in Tijuana are a vast improvement over their

former lives. As Doña Paula, a Chinanteca friend of mine who lives at the Tijuana garbage dump, told me, "This is the garbage dump. Take all you need. There's plenty here for *everyone*!"

If you are a woman, the men come after you. You lock yourself in your 10 room, and when you must leave it to use the pestilential public bathroom at the end of your floor, you hurry, and you check every corner. Sometimes the lights are out in the toilet room. Sometimes men listen at the door. They call you "good-looking" and "bitch" and "*mamacita*," and they make kissing sounds at you when you pass.

You're in the worst part of town, but you can comfort yourself—at least 11 there are no death squads here. There are no torturers here, or bandit land barons riding into your house. This is the last barrier, you think, between you and the United States—*los Yunaites Estaites*.

You still face police corruption, violence, jail. You now also have a wide variety 12 of new options available to you: drugs, prostitution, white slavery, crime. Tijuana is not easy on newcomers. It is a city that has always thrived on taking advantage of a sucker. And the innocent are the ultimate suckers in the Borderlands.

Understanding Meaning

1. Urrea has called the border a "battlefield." How does his description illustrate this view?

2. What problems do the undocumented aliens face in their attempt to cross the border?

3. How are non-Mexican refugees treated in Tijuana?

4. What is the plight of refugee women on the border?

5. *Critical Thinking:* Urrea quotes a Dutch woman who used the term "un-American" to describe the border patrols. What is un-American about fences and helicopter patrols? Does this response to immigration clash with the Statue of Liberty's promise to welcome the tired and poor?

Evaluating Strategy

1. How effective is the use of the second person? Does it really put "you" in the scene? Does it help dramatize the plight of people many readers might choose to ignore?

2. What details does Urrea use to dramatize conditions along the border?

Appreciating Language

1. Throughout the description, Urrea uses lists—"beatings, rape, murder, torture, road accidents...." How effective are they? Can listing words become tedious?

2. Select the words that create the most powerful images of the border. Why do they make strong impressions?

1. Write an essay describing a place that highlights a social problem. Select a location of which you have personal knowledge, and try to convey through lists of details the conditions residents face.

2. *Collaborative Writing:* Ask a group of fellow students to respond to Urrea's account. Consider the issues his description of the border raises. Ask members to suggest how conditions could be improved, and then draft a short *persuasion* essay outlining your ideas.

JOSÉ ANTONIO BURCIAGA

José Antonio Burciaga (1940–1996) grew up in a synagogue in El Paso, where his father worked as a custodian. Burciaga served in the U.S. Air Force and then attended the University of Texas, where he earned a fine arts degree. Pursuing both art and literature, Burciaga was also active in Chicano affairs. His artwork was first exhibited in 1974. Two years later he published a collection of poetry called Restless Serpents, *followed by a variety of other publications.*

My Ecumenical Father

CONTEXT: *This essay, which first appeared in* Drink Cultura, *describes Burciaga's father, a man who maintained his ties to Mexican culture while taking pride in his American citizenship and developing a fierce devotion to the Jewish faith.*

¡Feliz Navidad! Merry Christmas! Happy Hanukkah! As a child, my season's 1 greetings were tricultural—Mexicano, Anglo, and Jewish.

Our devoutly Catholic parents raised three sons and three daughters in the 2 basement of a Jewish synagogue, Congregation B'nai Zion in El Paso, Texas. José Cruz Burciaga was the custodian and *shabbat goy*. A shabbat goy is Yiddish for a Gentile who, on the Sabbath, performs certain tasks forbidden to Jews under orthodox law.

Every year around Christmas time, my father would take the menorah out 3 and polish it. The eight-branched candleholder symbolizes Hanukkah, the commemoration of the first recorded war of liberation in that part of the world.

In 164 B.C., the Jewish nation rebelled against Antiochus IV Epiphanes, 4 who had attempted to introduce pagan idols into the temples. When the temple was reconquered by the Jews, there was only one day's supply of oil for the Eternal Light in the temple. By a miracle, the oil lasted eight days.

My father was not only in charge of the menorah, but for ten years he also 5 made sure the Eternal Light remained lit.

As children we were made aware of the differences and joys of Hanukkah, 6 Christmas and Navidad. We were taught to respect each celebration, even if they conflicted. For example, the Christmas carols taught in school. We learned the song about the twelve days of Christmas, though I never understood what the hell a partridge was doing in a pear tree in the middle of December.

We also learned a German song about a boy named Tom and a bomb— 7 O *Tannenbaum*. We even learned a song in the obscure language of Latin, called "Adeste Fideles," which reminded me of, *Ahh! d'este fideo*, a Mexican pasta soup. Though 75 percent of our class was Mexican American, we never sang a Christmas song in *Español*. Spanish was forbidden.

8   So our mother—a former teacher—taught us "Silent Night" in Spanish: *Noche de paz, noche de amor.* It was so much more poetic and inspirational.

9   While the rest of El Paso celebrated Christmas, Congregation B'nai Zion celebrated Hanukkah. We picked up Yiddish and learned a Hebrew prayer of thanksgiving. My brothers and I would help my father hang the Hanukkah decorations.

10   At night, after the services, the whole family would rush across the border to Juarez and celebrate the *posadas*, which take place for nine days before Christmas. They are a communal re-enactment of Joseph and Mary's search for shelter, just before Jesus was born.

11   To the *posadas* we took candles and candy left over from the Hanukkah celebrations. The next day we'd be back at St. Patrick's School singing, "I'm dreaming of a white Christmas."

12   One day I stopped dreaming of the white Christmases depicted on greeting cards. An old immigrant from Israel taught me Jesus was born in desert country just like that of the West Texas town of El Paso.

13   On Christmas Eve, my father would dress like Santa Claus and deliver gifts to his children, nephews, godchildren and the little kids in orphanages. The next day, minus his disguise, he would take us to Juarez, where we delivered gifts to the poor in the streets.

14   My father never forgot his childhood poverty and forever sought to help the less fortunate. He taught us to measure wealth not in money but in terms of love, spirit, charity and culture.

15   We were taught to respect the Jewish faith and culture. On the Day of Atonement, when the whole congregation fasted, my mother did not cook, lest the food odors distract. The respect was mutual. No one ever complained about the large picture of Jesus in our living room.

16   Through my father, leftover food from B'nai B'rith luncheons, Bar Mitzvahs, and Bat Mitzvahs found its way to Catholic or Baptist churches or orphanages. Floral arrangements in the temple that surrounded a Jewish wedding *huppah* canopy many times found a second home at the altar of St. Patrick's Cathedral or San Juan Convent School. Surplus furniture, including old temple pews, found their way to a missionary Baptist Church in *El Segundo Barrio.*

17   It was not uncommon to come home from school at lunchtime and find an uncle priest, an aunt nun, and a Baptist minister visiting our home at the same time that the Rabbi would knock on our door. It was just as natural to find the president of B'nai Zion eating beans and tortillas in our kitchen.

18   My father literally risked his life for the Jewish faith. Twice he was assaulted by burglars who broke in at night. Once he was stabbed in the hand.

19   Another time he stayed up all night guarding the sacred Torahs after anti-Semites threatened the congregation. He never philosophized about his ecumenism; he just lived it.

Cruz, as most called him, was a man of great humor, a hot temper, and a 20
passion for dance. He lived the Mexican Revolution and rode the rails during
the Depression. One of his proudest moments came when he became a U.S.
citizen.

On September 23, 1985, sixteen months after my mother passed away, my 21
father followed. Like his life, his death was also ecumenical. The funeral was
held at Our Lady of Peace, where a priest said the mass in English. My cousins
played mandolin and sang in Spanish. The president of B'nai Zion Congregation said a prayer in Hebrew. Members of the congregation sat with Catholics
and Baptists.

Observing Jewish custom, the cortege passed by the synagogue one last 22
time. Fittingly, father was laid to rest on the Sabbath. At the cemetery, in a
very Mexican tradition, my brothers, sisters, and I each kissed a handful of dirt
and threw it on the casket.

I once had the opportunity to describe father's life to the late, great Jewish 23
American writer Bernard Malamud. His only comment was, "Only in America!"

Understanding Meaning

1. What is a *shabbat goy?*

2. How did the author's family show respect to the congregation?

3. How did the author's family manage to blend respect for several
   cultures?

4. Burciaga points out that though he learned German and Latin
   songs in school, he was not allowed to sing in Spanish. What does
   this reveal about the educational system?

5. Why is the description of his father's funeral central to Burciaga's
   story?

6. *Critical Thinking:* What values does the ecumenical father represent?
   Are these values rare in our society? What lesson could this essay
   teach?

Evaluating Strategy

1. Would Bernard Malamud's comment, "Only in America," make a
   good title for this essay? Why or why not?

2. Burciaga offers an explanation of Hanukkah. What does this suggest
   about his intended audience?

3. *Blending the Modes:* Can this *description* be seen as an extended *definition* of "ecumenical"?

Appreciating Language

1. How did Burciaga's father define "wealth"?

2. Read through Burciaga's description and highlight his use of non-English words and phrases. How does he define them? What impact do all these unfamiliar words have?

WRITING SUGGESTIONS

1. Burciaga builds his description largely through details about his father's actions and behavior. Write a few paragraphs describing a person you know well. Try to capture what you consider the person's principal attributes by describing actions that reveal his or her values.

2. *Collaborative Writing:* Discuss this essay with a group of students. What do readers find most striking about this Mexican immigrant? Are his attitudes valuable to society? Is multiculturalism a trend today? Have each member write a few paragraphs explaining the significance of this essay. Read the responses aloud, and work to blend as many as possible in a short *analysis* of this essay.

CARL T. ROWAN

Carl T. Rowan (1925–2000) was born in Tennessee and received degrees from Oberlin College and the University of Minnesota. He worked for years as a columnist for the Minneapolis Tribune *and the* Chicago Sun Times, *expressing his views on a variety of issues, especially race relations. Rowan also served as the director of the United States Information Agency and was the ambassador to Finland.*

Unforgettable Miss Bessie

CONTEXT: *This article describing a schoolteacher originally appeared in* Reader's Digest, *where Rowan served as an editor. Rowan's account is personal, and much of his description focuses on the impact this teacher had on him and other disadvantaged students.*

She was only about five feet tall and probably never weighed more than 1 110 pounds, but Miss Bessie was a towering presence in the classroom. She was the only woman tough enough to make me read *Beowulf* and think for a few foolish days that I liked it. From 1938 to 1942, when I attended Bernard High School in McMinnville, Tenn., she taught me English, history, civics— and a lot more than I realized.

I shall never forget the day she scolded me into reading *Beowulf*. 2

"But Miss Bessie," I complained, "I ain't much interested in it." 3

Her large brown eyes became daggerish slits. "Boy," she said, "how dare you 4 say 'ain't' to me! I've taught you better than that."

"Miss Bessie," I pleaded, "I'm trying to make first-string end on the football 5 team, and if I go around saying 'it isn't' and 'they aren't,' the guys are gonna laugh me off the squad."

"Boy," she responded, "you'll play football because you have guts. But do 6 you know what *really* takes guts? Refusing to lower your standards to those of the crowd. It takes guts to say you've got to live and be somebody 50 years after all the football games are over."

I started saying "it isn't" and "they aren't," and I still made first-string end— 7 and class valedictorian—without losing my buddies' respect.

During her remarkable forty-four-year career, Mrs. Bessie Taylor Gwynn 8 taught hundreds of economically deprived black youngsters—including my mother, my brother, my sisters, and me. I remember her now with gratitude and affection—especially in this era when Americans are so wrought-up about a "rising tide of mediocrity" in public education and the problems of finding competent, caring teachers. Miss Bessie was an example of an in-formed, dedicated teacher, a blessing to children and an asset to the nation.

Born in 1895, in poverty, she grew up in Athens, Ala., where there was no 9 public school for blacks. She attended Trinity School, a private institution for blacks run by the American Missionary Association, and in 1911 graduated from the Normal School (a "super" high school) at Fisk University in Nashville. Mrs. Gwynn, the essence of pride and privacy, never talked about her years in Athens; only in the months before her death did she reveal that she had never attended Fisk University itself because she could not afford the four-year course.

10   At Normal School she learned a lot about Shakespeare, but most of all about the profound importance of education—especially for people trying to move up from slavery. "What you put in your head, boy," she once said, "can never be pulled out by the Ku Klux Klan, the Congress or anybody."

11   Miss Bessie's bearing of dignity told anyone who met her that she was "educated" in the best sense of the word. There was never a discipline problem in her classes. We didn't dare mess with a woman who knew about the Battle of Hastings, the Magna Carta and the Bill of Rights—and who could also play the piano.

12   This frail-looking woman could make sense of Shakespeare, Milton, Voltaire, and bring to life Booker T. Washington and W. E. B. DuBois. Believing that it was important to know who the officials were that spent taxpayers' money and made public policy, she made us memorize the names of everyone on the Supreme Court and in the President's Cabinet. It could be embarrassing to be unprepared when Miss Bessie said, "Get up and tell the class who Frances Perkins is and what you think about her."

13   Miss Bessie knew that my family, like so many others during the Depression, couldn't afford to subscribe to a newspaper. She knew we didn't even own a radio. Still, she prodded me to "look out for your future and find some way to keep up with what's going on in the world." So I became a delivery boy for the Chattanooga *Times*. I rarely made a dollar a week, but I got to read a newspaper every day.

14   Miss Bessie noticed things that had nothing to do with schoolwork, but were vital to a youngster's development. Once a few classmates made fun of my frayed, hand-me-down overcoat, calling me "Strings." As I was leaving school, Miss Bessie patted me on the back of that old overcoat and said, "Carl, never fret about what you *don't* have. Just make the most of what you *do* have—a brain."

15   Among the things that I did not have was electricity in the little frame house that my father had built for $400 with his World War I bonus. But because of her inspiration, I spent many hours squinting beside a kerosene lamp reading Shakespeare and Thoreau, Samuel Pepys and William Cullen Bryant.

16   No one in my family had ever graduated from high school, so there was no tradition of commitment to learning for me to lean on. Like millions of youngsters in today's ghettos and barrios, I needed the push and stimulation of a teacher who truly cared. Miss Bessie gave plenty of both, as she immersed me in a wonderful world of similes, metaphors, and even onomatopoeia.

She led me to believe that I could write sonnets as well as Shakespeare, or 17 iambic-pentameter verse to put Alexander Pope to shame.

In those days the McMinnville school system was rigidly "Jim Crow," and poor 18 black children had to struggle to put anything in their heads. Our high school was only slightly larger than the once-typical little red schoolhouse, and its library was outrageously inadequate—so small, I like to say, that if two students were in it and one wanted to turn a page, the other one had to step outside.

Negroes, as we were called then, were not allowed in the town library, ex- 19 cept to mop floors or dust tables. But through one of those secret Old South arrangements between whites of conscience and blacks of stature, Miss Bessie kept getting books smuggled out of the white library. That is how she introduced me to the Brontës, Byron, Coleridge, Keats, and Tennyson. "If you don't read, you can't write, and if you can't write, you might as well stop dreaming," Miss Bessie once told me.

So I read whatever Miss Bessie told me to, and tried to remember the things 20 she insisted that I store away. Forty-five years later, I can still recite her "truths to live by," such as Henry Wadsworth Longfellow's lines from "The Ladder of St. Augustine":

> The heights by great men reached and kept
> Were not attained by sudden flight.
> But they, while their companions slept,
> Were toiling upward in the night.

Years later, her inspiration, prodding, anger, cajoling, and almost osmotic 21 infusion of learning finally led to that lovely day when Miss Bessie dropped me a note saying, "I'm so proud to read your column in the Nashville *Tennessean*."

Miss Bessie was a spry 80 when I went back to McMinnville and visited her 22 in a senior citizens' apartment building. Pointing out proudly that her building was racially integrated, she reached for two glasses and a pint of bourbon. I was momentarily shocked, because it would have been scandalous in the 1930s and '40s for word to get out that a teacher drank, and nobody had ever raised a rumor that Miss Bessie did.

I felt a new sense of equality as she lifted her glass to mine. Then she re- 23 vealed a softness and compassion that I had never known as a student.

"I've never forgotten that examination day," she said, "when Buster Martin 24 held up seven fingers, obviously asking you for help with question number seven, 'Name a common carrier.' I can still picture you looking at your exam paper and humming a few bars of 'Chattanooga Choo Choo.' I was so tickled, I couldn't punish either of you."

Miss Bessie was telling me, with bourbon-laced grace, that I never fooled 25 her for a moment.

26   When Miss Bessie died in 1980, at age 85, hundreds of her former students mourned. They knew the measure of a great teacher: love and motivation. Her wisdom and influence had rippled out across generations.

27   Some of her students who might normally have been doomed to poverty went on to become doctors, dentists and college professors. Many, guided by Miss Bessie's example, became public-school teachers.

28   "The memory of Miss Bessie and how she conducted her classroom did more for me than anything I learned in college," recalls Gladys Wood of Knoxville, Tenn., a highly respected English teacher who spent 43 years in the state's school system. "So many times, when I faced a difficult classroom problem, I asked myself, *How would Miss Bessie deal with this?* And I'd remember that she would handle it with laughter and love."

29   No child can get all the necessary support at home, and millions of poor children get *no* support at all. This is what makes a wise, educated, warmhearted teacher like Miss Bessie so vital to the minds, hearts and souls of this country's children.

Understanding Meaning

1. What is Rowan's purpose in describing Miss Bessie? What makes this teacher significant to a middle-aged man?

2. What qualities of Miss Bessie does Rowan admire?

3. Does Rowan offer Miss Bessie as a role model? How does he demonstrate that she is an "asset to the nation"?

Evaluating Strategy

1. Rowan opens his essay with a physical description of Miss Bessie. Why are these details important to his purpose?

2. Why would this article appeal to readers of *Reader's Digest?* What values does it reinforce?

3. *Critical Thinking:* Would some people object to Rowan's article as being sentimental? Why or why not? Does this article suggest simple solutions to complex problems? Would a Miss Bessie be able to succeed in a modern urban high school?

Appreciating Language

1. Study the words Rowan uses in describing Miss Bessie. Which words have the most impact?

2. Rowan includes dialogue in his article. What do you notice about Miss Bessie's language? What does this add to the description?

WRITING SUGGESTIONS

1. Write a brief description of a teacher, employer, or coworker who greatly influenced your development. Provide specific examples of the lessons you learned.

2. *Collaborative Writing:* Working with three or four other students, discuss Miss Bessie's statement, "What you put in your head, boy, can never be pulled out by the Ku Klux Klan, the Congress or anybody." Use this quote as the headline of a poster urging people to read. Keep your message short. Read it aloud to hear how it sounds.

PAUL M. BARRETT

Paul M. Barrett has been a reporter and editor at the Wall Street Journal *for over eighteen years and now directs the investigating reporting team at* Business Week. *His books include* The Good Black: A True Story of Race in America *(1999) and* American Islam: The Struggle for the Soul of a Religion *(2007).*

American Islam

CONTEXT: *In this section from* American Islam, *Barrett provides readers with a general description of American Muslims. Note how he presents objective details to counter commonly held misconceptions about Islam in the United States.*

1 Most American Muslims are not Arab, and most Americans of Arab descent are Christian, not Muslim. People of South Asian descent—those with roots in Pakistan, India, Bangladesh, and Afghanistan—make up 34 percent of American Muslims, according to the polling organization Zogby International. Arab-Americans constitute only 26 percent, while another 20 percent are native-born American blacks, most of whom are converts. The remaining 20 percent come from Africa, Iran, Turkey, and elsewhere.

2 Muslims have no equivalent to the Catholic pope and his cardinals. The faith is decentralized in the extreme, and some beliefs and practices vary depending on region and sect. In America, Muslims do not think and act alike any more than Christians do. That said, all observant Muslims acknowledge Islam's "five pillars": faith in one God, prayer, charity, fasting during Ramadan, and pilgrimage to Mecca. Muslims are also united in the way they pray. The basic choreography of crossing arms, bowing, kneeling, and prostrating oneself is more or less the same in mosques everywhere.

3 The two major subgroups of Muslims, Sunni and Shiite, are found in the United States in roughly their global proportions: 85 percent Sunni, 15 percent Shiite. Ancient history still animates the rivalry, which began in the struggle for Muslim leadership after the Prophet Muhammad's death in 632. Shiites believe that Muhammad intended for only his blood descendants to succeed him. Muhammad's beloved cousin and son-in-law Ali was the only male relative who qualified. Ali's followers became known as Shiites, a derivation of the Arabic phrase for "partisans of Ali." Things did not go smoothly for them.

4 The larger body of early Muslims, known as Sunnis, a word related to Sunnah, or way of the Prophet, had a more flexible notion of who should succeed Muhammad. In 661, an extremist assassinated Ali near Najaf in what is now Iraq. Nineteen years later Sunnis killed his son, Hussein, not

far away in Karbala. These deaths permanently divided the aggrieved Shiite minority from the Sunni majority.

Sunnis historically have afflicted the weaker Shiites, accusing them of 5 shaping a blasphemous cult around Ali and Hussein. At the Karbala Islamic Education Center in Dearborn, Michigan, a large mural depicts mourning women who have encountered the riderless horse of Hussein after his final battle. "You see our history and our situation in this," says Imam Husham al-Husainy, a Shiite Iraqi émigré who leads the center. In Dearborn, Shiite Iraqis initially backed the American invasion to depose Saddam Hussein, who persecuted Iraq's Shiite majority. Most Sunnis in Dearborn condemned the war as an exercise in American imperialism.

Sufism, another important strain of Islam, is also present in the United 6 States. Sufis follow a spiritual, inward-looking path. Only a tiny percentage of American Muslims would identify themselves primarily as Sufis, in part because some more rigid Muslims condemn Sufism as heretical. But Sufi ideas crop up among the beliefs of many Muslims without being labeled as such. Sufism's emphasis on self-purification appeals to New Age seekers and has made it the most common avenue into Islam for white American converts such as Abdul Kabir Krambo of Yuba City, California. Krambo, an electrician who grew up in a conservative German Catholic family, helped build a mosque amidst the fruit arbors of the Sacramento Valley, only to see it burn down in a mysterious arson. Once rebuilt, the Islamic Center of Yuba City was engulfed again, this time by controversy over whether Krambo and his Sufi friends were trying to impose a "cult" on other worshipers.

Although there is a broad consensus that Islam is the fastest-growing reli- 7 gion in the country and the world, no one has provable numbers on just how many American Muslims there are. The Census Bureau doesn't count by religion, and private surveys of the Muslim population offer widely disparate conclusions. A study of four hundred mosques nationwide estimated that there are two million people in the United States "associated with" Islamic houses of worship. The authors of the survey, published in 2001 under the auspices of the Council on American-Islamic Relations (CAIR), a Muslim advocacy group, employed a common assumption that only one in three American Muslims associates with a mosque. In CAIR's view, that suggests there are at least six million Muslims in the country. (Perhaps not coincidentally the American Jewish population is estimated to be slightly below six million.) Other Muslim groups put the number higher, seeking to maximize the size and influence of their constituency.

Surveys conducted by non-Muslims have produced much lower estimates, 8 some in the neighborhood of only two million or three million. These findings elicit anger from Muslim leaders, who claim that many immigrant and poor black Muslims are overlooked. On the basis of all the evidence, a very crude range of three million to six million seems reasonable. Rapid growth of the Muslim population is expected to continue, fueled mainly by immigration and high birthrates and, to a lesser extent, by conversion, overwhelmingly by African Americans. In the next decade or two there probably will be more Muslims in the United States than Jews. Worldwide, the Muslim head count is estimated at 1.3 billion, second among religions only to the combined membership of Christian denominations.

9   American Muslims, like Americans generally, live mostly in cities and suburbs. Large concentrations are found in New York, Detroit, Chicago, and Los Angeles. But they also turn up in the Appalachian foothills and rural Idaho, among other surprising places. Often the presence of several hundred Muslims in an out-of-the-way town can be explained by proximity to a large state university. Many of these schools have recruited foreign graduate students, including Muslims, since the 1960s. In the 1980s Washington doled out scholarships to Arab students as part of a campaign to counter the influence of the 1979 Iranian Revolution. Some of the Muslim beneficiaries have stayed and raised families.

10   In New York, Muslims are typecast as cab drivers; in Detroit, as owners of grocery stores and gas stations. The overall economic reality is very different. Surveys show that the majority of American Muslims are employed in technical, white-collar, and professional fields. These include information technology, corporate management, medicine, and education. An astounding 59 percent of Muslim adults in the United States have college degrees. That compares with only 27 percent of all American adults. Four out of five Muslim workers earn at least twenty-five thousand dollars a year; more than half earn fifty thousand or more. A 2004 survey by a University of Kentucky researcher found that median family income among Muslims is sixty thousand dollars a year; the national median is fifty thousand. Most Muslims own stock or mutual funds, either directly or through retirement plans. Four out of five are registered to vote.

11   Relative prosperity, high levels of education, and political participation are indications of a minority population successfully integrating into the larger society. By comparison, immigrant Muslims in countries such as Britain, France, Holland, and Spain have remained poorer, less well educated, and socially marginalized. Western European Muslim populations are much larger in percentage terms. Nearly 10 percent of French residents are Muslim; in the United Kingdom the figure is 3 percent. In the more populous United States the Muslim share is 1 to 2 percent, depending on which Muslim population estimate one assumes. It's unlikely that American cities will see the sort of densely packed, volatile Muslim slums that have cropped up on the outskirts of Paris, for example.

12   America's social safety net is stingy compared with those of Western Europe, but there is greater opportunity for new arrivals to get ahead in

material terms. This may attract to the United States more ambitious immigrants willing to adjust to the customs of their new home and eager to acquire education that leads to better jobs. More generous welfare benefits in Europe allow Muslims and other immigrants to live indefinitely on the periphery of society, without steady jobs or social interaction with the majority. Europeans, who for decades encouraged Muslim immigration as a source of menial labor, have shown overt hostility toward the outsiders and little inclination to embrace them as full-fledged citizens. Partly as a result, violent Islamic extremism has found fertile ground in Western Europe.

Understanding Meaning

1. What are some of the more striking facts Barrett presents about American Muslims? Would most Americans be surprised to learn that most Muslims in this country are not Arabs and have higher-than-average incomes?

2. How does Barrett explain the difference between Sunni and Shia Muslims? What percentage of American Muslims are Sunni?

3. Barrett states that Muslims have a faith that is "decentralized in the extreme." What basic beliefs do most Muslims share?

4. Why is it difficult to ascertain exactly how many Americans are Muslim?

5. *Critical Thinking:* How is the Muslim American community different from those found in Western Europe? Does America's history of absorbing diverse immigrant groups create a different environment for Muslims? Why or why not?

Evaluating Strategy

1. How difficult is it to describe a religion objectively? Do you think Barrett is successful? Why or why not?

2. Which facts about American Muslims do you consider the most significant? How can a writer determine which facts are important and which are trivial?

3. *Blending the Modes:* How does Barrett use *comparison* to develop and organize his description?

Appreciating Language

1. Do you think Barrett uses objective and neutral language in describing American Muslims? Can you detect any terms some readers might find insensitive or biased?

2. Barrett states that some Muslims condemn Sufi Muslims as "heretics" trying to impose a "cult" on other Muslims. Look up the words "heretic" and "cult" in a dictionary. What do these words mean? Are these terms objective or subjective?

WRITING SUGGESTIONS

1. Write a *description* essay that objectively describes a group of people. You might provide details about the residents of your apartment building, coworkers, or members of a sports team. Use neutral language and include factual details.

2. *Collaborative Writing:* Working with a group of students, review Barrett's description and select three facts about American Muslims you think most significant. Which ones would surprise most Americans? Write a brief set of factual statements that might be used on billboards or blogs to educate the public.

BLENDING THE MODES

E.B.White

Elwyn Brooks White (1899–1985) was born in Mount Vernon, New York, and attended Cornell University. He was a regular contributor to the New Yorker *and* Harper's *magazine for fifty years. His articles achieved a reputation for their wit and style. White assisted Edmund Strunk in revising his popular book on writing,* Elements of Style. *He also gained popularity as a writer of children's literature. His books* Stuart Little *and* Charlotte's Web *have become classics.*

Once More to the Lake

CONTEXT: *First published in* Harper's *in 1941, "Once More to the Lake" describes White's nostalgic return to a boyhood vacation spot. As you read the essay, notice how White uses* comparison *and* narration *in developing his description.*

August 1941

One summer, along about 1904, my father rented a camp on a lake in Maine   1
and took us all there for the month of August. We all got ringworm from some kittens and had to rub Pond's Extract on our arms and legs night and morning, and my father rolled over in a canoe with all his clothes on; but outside of that the vacation was a success and from then on none of us ever thought there was any place in the world like that lake in Maine. We returned summer after summer—always on August 1 for one month. I have since become a salt-water man, but sometimes in summer there are days when the restlessness of the tides and the fearful cold of the sea water and the incessant wind that blows across the afternoon and into the evening make me wish for the placidity of a lake in the woods. A few weeks ago this feeling got so strong I bought myself a couple of bass hooks and a spinner and returned to the lake where we used to go, for a week's fishing and to revisit old haunts.

I took along my son, who had never had any fresh water up his nose and   2
who had seen lily pads only from train windows. On the journey over to the lake I began to wonder what it would be like. I wondered how time would have marred this unique, this holy spot—the coves and streams, the hills that the sun set behind, the camps and the paths behind the camps. I was sure that the tarred road would have found it out, and I wondered in what other ways it would be desolated. It is strange how much you can remember about places like that once you allow your mind to return into the grooves that lead back. You remember one thing, and that suddenly reminds you of another thing.

I guess I remembered clearest of all the early mornings, when the lake was cool and motionless, remembered how the bedroom smelled of the lumber it was made of and of the wet woods whose scent entered through the screen. The partitions in the camp were thin and did not extend clear to the top of the rooms, and as I was always the first up I would dress softly so as not to wake the others, and sneak out into the sweet outdoors and start out in the canoe, keeping close along the shore in the long shadows of the pines. I remembered being very careful never to rub my paddle against the gunwale for fear of disturbing the stillness of the cathedral.

3   The lake had never been what you would call a wild lake. There were cottages sprinkled around the shores, and it was in farming country although the shores of the lake were quite heavily wooded. Some of the cottages were owned by nearby farmers, and you would live at the shore and eat your meals at the farmhouse. That's what our family did. But although it wasn't wild, it was a fairly large and undisturbed lake and there were places in it that, to a child at least, seemed infinitely remote and primeval.

4   I was right about the tar: it led to within half a mile of the shore. But when I got back there, with my boy, and we settled into a camp near a farmhouse and into the kind of summertime I had known, I could tell that it was going to be pretty much the same as it had been before—I knew it, lying in bed the first morning, smelling the bedroom and hearing the boy sneak quietly out and go off along the shore in a boat. I began to sustain the illusion that he was I, and therefore, by simple transposition, that I was my father. This sensation persisted, kept cropping up all the time we were there. It was not an entirely new feeling, but in this setting it grew much stronger. I seemed to be living a dual existence. I would be in the middle of some simple act, I would be picking up a bait box or laying down a table fork, or I would be saying something, and suddenly it would be not I but my father who was saying the words or making the gesture. It gave me a creepy sensation.

5   We went fishing the first morning. I felt the same damp moss covering the worms in the bait can, and saw the dragonfly alight on the tip of my rod as it hovered a few inches from the surface of the water. It was the arrival of this fly that convinced me beyond any doubt that everything was as it always had been, that the years were a mirage, and that there had been no years. The small waves were the same, chucking the rowboat under the chin as we fished at anchor, and the boat was the same boat, the same color green and the ribs broken in the same places, and under the floorboards the same fresh-water leavings and debris—the dead hellgrammite, the wisps of moss, the rusty discarded fish-hook, the dried blood from yesterday's catch. We stared silently at the tips of our rods, at the dragonflies that came and went. I lowered the tip of mine into the water, tentatively, pensively dislodging the fly, which darted two feet away, poised, darted two feet back, and came to rest again a little

farther up the rod. There had been no years between the ducking of this dragonfly and the other one—the one that was part of memory. I looked at the boy,
who was silently watching his fly, and it was my hands that held his rod, my
eyes watching. I felt dizzy and didn't know which rod I was at the end of.

We caught two bass, hauling them in briskly as though they were mackerel, 6
pulling them over the side of the boat in a businesslike manner without any
landing net, and stunning them with a blow on the back of the head. When
we got back for a swim before lunch, the lake was exactly where we had left it,
the same number of inches from the dock, and there was only the merest suggestion of a breeze. This seemed an utterly enchanted sea, this lake you could
leave to its own devices for a few hours and come back to, and find it had not
stirred, this constant and trustworthy body of water. In the shallows, the dark,
water-soaked sticks and twigs, smooth and old, were undulating in clusters on
the bottom against the clean ribbed sand, and the track of the mussel was
plain. A school of minnows swam by, each minnow with its small individual
shadow, doubling the attendance, so clear and sharp in the sunlight. Some of
the other campers were in swimming, along the shore, one of them with a
cake of soap, and the water felt thin and clear and unsubstantial. Over the
years there had been this person with the cake of soap, this cultist, and here
he was. There had been no years.

Up to the farmhouse to dinner through the teeming, dusty field, the road 7
under our sneakers was only a two-track road. The middle track was missing,
the one with the marks of the hooves and the splotches of dried, flaky manure.
There had always been three tracks to choose from in choosing which track to
walk in; now the choice was narrowed down to two. For a moment I missed
terribly the middle alternative. But the way led past the tennis court, and
something about the way it lay there in the sun reassured me; the tape had
loosened along the backline, the alleys were green with plantains and other
weeds, and the net (installed in June and removed in September) sagged in
the dry noon, and the whole place steamed with midday heat and hunger and
emptiness. There was a choice of pie for dessert, and one was blueberry and
one was apple, and the waitresses were the same country girls, there having
been no passage of time, only the illusion of it as in a dropped curtain—the
waitresses were still fifteen; their hair had been washed, that was the only
difference—they had been to the movies and seen the pretty girls with the
clean hair.

Summertime, oh summertime, pattern of life indelible, the fade-proof lake, 8
the woods unshatterable, the pasture with the sweetfern and the juniper forever and ever, summer without end; this was the background, and the life
along the shore was the design, their tiny docks with the flagpole and the
American flag floating against the white clouds in the blue sky, the little paths
over the roots of the trees leading from camp to camp and the paths leading

back to the outhouses and the can of lime for sprinkling, and at the souvenir counters at the store the miniature birch-bark canoes and the postcards that showed things looking a little better than they looked. This was the American family at play, escaping the city heat, wondering whether the newcomers in the camp at the head of the cove were "common" or "nice," wondering whether it was true that the people who drove up for Sunday dinner at the farmhouse were turned away because there wasn't enough chicken.

9

It seemed to me, as I kept remembering all this, that those times and those summers had been infinitely precious and worth saving. There had been jollity and peace and goodness. The arriving (at the beginning of August) had been so big a business in itself, at the railway station the farm wagon drawn up, the first smell of the pine-laden air, the first glimpse of the smiling farmer, and the great importance of the trunks and your father's enormous authority in such matters, and the feel of the wagon under you for the long ten-mile haul, and at the top of the last long hill catching the first view of the lake after eleven months of not seeing this cherished body of water. The shouts and cries of the other campers when they saw you, and the trunks to be unpacked, to give up their rich burden. (Arriving was less exciting nowadays, when you sneaked up in your car and parked it under a tree near the camp and took out the bags and in five minutes it was all over, no fuss, no loud wonderful fuss about trunks.)

10

Peace and goodness and jollity. The only thing that was wrong now, really, was the sound of the place, an unfamiliar nervous sound of the outboard motors. This was the note that jarred, the one thing that would sometimes break the illusion and set the years moving. In those other summertimes all the motors were inboard; and when they were at a little distance, the noise they made was a sedative, an ingredient of summer sleep. They were one-cylinder and two-cylinder engines, and some were make-and-break and some were jump-spark, but they all made a sleepy sound across the lake. The one-lungers throbbed and fluttered, and the twin-cylinder ones purred and purred, and that was a quiet sound, too. But now the campers all had outboards. In the daytime, in the hot mornings, these motors made a petulant, irritable sound; at night, in the still evening when the afterglow lit the water, they whined about one's ears like mosquitoes. My boy loved our rented outboard, and his great desire was to achieve single-handed mastery over it, and authority, and he soon learned the trick of choking it a little (but not too much), and the adjustment of the needle valve. Watching him I would remember the things you could do with the old one-cylinder engine with the heavy flywheel, how you could have it eating out of your hand if you got really close to it spiritually. Motorboats in those days didn't have clutches, and you would make a landing by shutting off the motor at the proper time and coasting in with a dead rudder. But there was a way of reversing them, if you learned the trick, by cutting the switch and putting it on again exactly on the final dying revolution of the flywheel, so that it would kick back against the compression and begin reversing. Approaching a dock in a strong following breeze, it was difficult to slow up sufficiently by the ordinary coasting method, and if a boy felt he had complete mastery over his motor, he was tempted to keep it running beyond its time and then reverse it a few feet from the dock. It took a cool nerve, because if you threw the switch a twentieth of a second too soon you would catch the flywheel when it still had speed enough to go up past center, and the boat would leap ahead, charging bull-fashion at the dock.

We had a good week at camp. The bass were biting well and the sun shone   11
endlessly, day after day. We would be tired at night and lie down in the accumulated heat of the little bedrooms after the long hot day and the breeze would stir almost imperceptibly outside and the smell of the swamp drift in through the rusty screens. Sleep would come easily and in the morning the red squirrel would be on the roof, tapping out his gay routine. I kept remembering everything, lying in bed in the mornings—the small steamboat that had a long rounded stem like the lip of a Ubangi, and how quietly she ran on the moonlight sails, when the older boys played their mandolins and the girls sang and we ate doughnuts dipped in sugar, and how sweet the music was on the water in the shining night, and what it had felt like to think about girls then. After breakfast we would go up to the store and the things were in the same place—the minnows in a bottle, the plugs and spinners disarranged and pawed over by the youngsters from the boys' camp, the Fig Newtons and the Beeman's gum. Outside, the road was tarred and cars stood in front of the store. Inside, all was just as it had always been, except there was more Coca-Cola and not so much Moxie and root beer and birch beer and sarsaparilla. We would walk out with a bottle of pop apiece and sometimes the pop would backfire up our noses and hurt. We explored the streams, quietly, where the turtles slid off the sunny logs and dug their way into the soft bottom; and we lay on the town wharf and fed worms to the tame bass. Everywhere we went I had trouble making out which I was, the one walking at my side, the one walking in my pants.

One afternoon while we were there at that lake a thunderstorm came up.   12
It was like the revival of an old melodrama that I had seen long ago with childish awe. The second-act climax of the drama of the electrical disturbance over a lake in America had not changed in any important respect. This was the big scene, still the big scene. The whole thing was so familiar, the first feeling of oppression and heat and a general air around camp of not wanting to go very far away. In mid-afternoon (it was all the same) a curious darkening of the sky, and a lull in everything that had made life tick; and then the way the boats suddenly swung the other way at their moorings with the coming of a breeze out of the new quarter, and the premonitory

rumble. Then the kettle drum, then the snare, then the bass drum and cymbals, then the crackling light against the dark, and the gods grinning and licking their chops in the hills. Afterward the calm, the rain steadily rustling in the calm lake, the return of light and hope and spirits, and the campers running out in joy and relief to go swimming in the rain, their bright cries perpetuating the deathless joke about how they were getting simply drenched, and the children screaming with delight at the new sensation of bathing in the rain, and the joke about getting drenched linking the generations in a strong indestructible chain. And the comedian who waded in carrying an umbrella.

13   When the others went swimming my son said he was going in, too. He pulled his dripping trunks from the line where they had hung all through the shower and wrung them out. Languidly, and with no thought of going in, I watched him, his hard little body, skinny and bare, saw him wince slightly as he pulled up around his vitals the small, soggy, icy garment. As he buckled the swollen belt, suddenly my groin felt the chill of death.

Understanding Meaning

1. What is White's purpose in describing the resort? What lessons or observations does this journey reveal to him?

2. What are the key features of the lake? How much of it had changed in forty years?

3. White comments in the last line that he "felt the chill of death." How does viewing his son give White a sense of his mortality?

4. *Critical Thinking:* What role does time play in this description? What is White saying about the passage of time, the passage of life? How does watching a child grow affect a parent?

Evaluating Strategy

1. How does White use his son as a device for recalling his own youth?

2. Descriptions of places can become tedious lists of geographical details. How does White create action and bring the lake to life?

3. Writers usually rely on visual details to develop a description of a place. Locate places where White uses other sensory impressions. How effective are they?

4. *Blending the Modes:* Locate passages where White uses *comparison* and *narration*. How do they develop the essay? Could you classify this essay as *narration?*

Appreciating Language

1. White uses figurative language associated with nonnatural objects to describe the lake. For instance, he describes the lake as having the "stillness of a cathedral" and uses references to musical instruments—"the kettle drum, then the snare, then the bass drum and cymbals"—to capture the sound of a storm. What do these word choices suggest about his audience?

2. White uses brand names throughout his essay. What effect do references to Moxie, Fig Newtons, and Coca-Cola have?

WRITING SUGGESTIONS

1. Write an essay describing a place you revisited after a considerable lapse of time. Comment on what has and has not changed. Use as many sensory details as you can.

2. *Collaborative Writing:* Work with a group of students who share a common memory of a historical event or recent campus incident. Have each member write a brief narrative. Read each paper aloud to see how people recall and interpret events differently.

WRITING BEYOND THE CLASSROOM

BAYOU PRINTING

1500 Magazine Street
New Orleans, LA 70130
(504) 555-7100
www.bayouprinting.com

JOB ANNOUNCEMENT

Join a winning team!

Bayou Printing, New Orleans's largest independent chain of print shops, needs a creative, dynamic store manager to join our team.

Bayou offers successful managers unique opportunities unavailable in national firms:

- Performance bonuses
- Profit sharing
- Full medical and dental coverage
- Education benefits

Requirements:

- Experience in hiring, training, and supervising employees in a high-volume retail operation.
- Full knowledge of state-of-the-art printing technology.
- Strong leadership and communications skills.
- Proven ability to lower employee turnover and overhead costs.

To apply for this job and join our winning team, email us at www.bayouprinting.com.

Understanding Meaning

1. How does the ad describe Bayou Printing?

2. What are the most important requirements for the position?

3. What kind of person does Bayou Printing want to attract?

4. *Critical Thinking:* What are the limits of any want ad? Can a job be fully described in a few paragraphs? Why can't employers address all their interests and concerns?

Evaluating Strategy

1. Why does the ad first describe the job and then list the requirements?

2. How effective are the bulleted points?

Appreciating Language

1. What words does the ad use to describe the ideal candidate?

2. The ad uses the term "winning team." What impact does this term have? What is the company seeking to impress on applicants?

WRITING SUGGESTIONS

1. Write a want ad for a job you once had. Try to model yours after ones you have seen in the newspaper or online. Keep your ad as short as possible.

2. *Collaborative Writing:* Work with a group of students and write a want ad together. Imagine you are hiring a part-time employee to act as secretary for your writing group. Determine the skills needed, the major duties, and how the ad should be worded. If members have differences of opinion, craft more than one ad, and ask other students to choose the most effective ad.

MONICA RAMOS

Monica Ramos was born in New Orleans and managed a record store that was destroyed during Hurricane Katrina and never reopened. Realizing that record stores were losing business to downloading, she went to school to study printing and publishing. Having graduated with an associate's degree, she responded to the Bayou Printing ad reproduced in this chapter. Notice how she presents her unrelated work experience to describe her skills. Also notice that her resume uses bulleted lists of specific accomplishments to provide details that are easily read or skimmed.

The Resume of Monica Ramos

MONICA RAMOS
1455 Josephine Street #12
New Orleans, Louisiana 70118
(504) 555-6580
ramosm@nola.net

OBJECTIVE   Print Shop Manager

OVERVIEW   Associate's Degree in Printing and Publishing. Five years experience in all areas of retail management, including hiring, training, and motivating staff. Proven ability to lower overhead and increase sales through online marketing. Created new revenue streams for traditional business in declining markets.

EXPERIENCE   CORCORAN & BLACKWELL
2005-Present   *Executive Assistant* in 28-attorney law firm preparing documents and media to be presented in court. Worked 25 hours a week while attending college.
* Personally responsible for printing and assembling documents used in $75 million class-action lawsuit involving 6 attorneys and 9 paralegals.
* Assisted partners in developing new corporate website.

2000-2005   BOURBON STREET MUSIC
Manager of New Orleans' second-largest record store, supervising 35 employees. Reported directly to owners and investors.
* Increased profits 12% in first year through improved training and cost control.
* Worked with local bands to sell CDs and memorabilia at concerts to offset declining in-store sales.

* Created "CD-of-the-Month" club that coupled CD sales with concert tickets and free promotional items to develop new revenue stream.
* Assisted owners in transforming business from traditional retail box store to virtual multimedia enterprise.

EDUCATION   DELGADO COMMUNITY COLLEGE, New Orleans, LA
Associate's Degree in Printing and Publishing, 2010. Completed courses in editing, photo editing, desktop publishing, marketing, cost accounting, print purchasing, and personnel management.

* Experienced in operating and servicing all major brands of copiers.
* Maintained 3.5 GPA while working 25 hours a week.
* Personally raised $72,000 during alumni fund telemarketing campaign.

VOLUNTEER   GREATER NEW ORLEANS COUNCIL
WORK   Assisted with fund-raising drive to solicit
2006-2008   support from corporations and foundations to assist small business owners rebuilding after Katrina.

References available on request

Understanding Meaning

1. Compare this resume to the Bayou Printing want ad. Does it address the employer's needs?

2. What skills and experiences does Monica Ramos highlight? What are her important attributes? Why do you think she emphasizes her experience helping a business with "declining sales" when applying to a print shop?

Evaluating Strategy

1. One study revealed that the average executive devotes nine seconds to each resume on initial screening. Does this resume communicate its main points in a few seconds? Would it make a reader stop skimming and start reading?

2. How is the information arranged? Is it clear and easy to follow? Do you think the resume demonstrates the value of Ramos's unrelated experience managing a record store? Why or why not?

Appreciating Language

1. What is the tone of the resume? How do the words portray the applicant?

2. What device does Monica Ramos use to convey a sense of action?

WRITING SUGGESTIONS

1. Write your own resume, either a current one designed for student jobs or a professional one if you are graduating this semester.

2. *Collaborative Writing:* Meet with a group of students and have each member supply a resume. Discuss the merits of each resume you review. Talk about problems you have encountered. Take notes to improve your own resume. Your library or placement office may offer guides and computer programs to help you develop your resume.

RESPONDING TO IMAGES

SEATTLE STREET KIDS WITH GUN, 1983.

© MARY ELLEN MARK

1. Describe your first reactions to this picture. Do you feel anger, disgust, fear, concern? What kind of young people are drawn to guns?

2. This photograph was taken in 1983. What do you assume happened to the boys in the picture? Where might they be today?

3. How would you describe the attitudes shown by the boys in the photograph?

4. Write a brief story describing these boys' lives or situations. Use dialogue to construct a conversation.

5. *Visual Analysis:* What do the hats, hair, clothing, and demeanor suggest about the two boys?

6. *Collaborative Writing:* Discuss this photograph in a small group. How does each of you react to this picture? What do you see in the eyes of the boy on the left? Work together to create a brief paragraph describing your observations.

STRATEGIES FOR WRITING DESCRIPTION

1. **Determine your purpose.** What is your goal—to entertain a general audience or to provide information to colleagues, employees, superiors, or customers? What are the most important details needed to support your purpose?

2. **Define your role.** If you are expressing personal opinion, you are free to add subjective elements to your writing. You may wish to include yourself in the piece of writing by making personal references and writing in the first person. If you are writing as a representative of a larger body, objective language is usually more appropriate.

3. **Consider your audience.** Which type of description would best suit your readers—subjective impressions or objective facts? What needs and expectations does your audience have? What details, facts, statistics, or descriptions will influence readers the most?

4. **Review the discipline or writing situation.** Determine if you should use technical or specialized terminology. If you are writing for a profession, academic discipline, government agency, or corporation, use standard methods of developing ideas.

5. **Select details.** Having determined the context, select details that emphasize your purpose, impress your audience, and follow any guidelines in your discipline. Descriptions should have focus. Eliminate details that may be interesting in themselves but do not serve your purpose. What do you want readers to really know and remember about your subject?

6. **Organize details in an effective manner.** Good description is more than a collection of details. To be effective, your writing should be logically organized. You may organize details spatially by describing a house room by room or a city neighborhood by neighborhood. You may organize details in order of importance. If you use objective and subjective description, these details can alternate or be placed in separate sections.

7. **Avoid unnecessary detail or mechanical organization.** Descriptions have focus. A description of your apartment does not have to list every piece of furniture, explain how each room is decorated, or provide dimensions. In general, avoid writing descriptions that draw unnecessary attention to mechanical arrangements:

> *On the left-hand wall* is a bookcase. *To the right of the bookcase* is a stereo. *Around the corner of the stereo* stands an antique aquarium filled with tropical fish. *Above the aquarium* is a large seascape painting. Model ships line the windowsill. A cabinet *to the right of the window* is filled with seashells.

8. **Select key details to create a dominant impression.** A subjective description of a room can focus on a single theme:

> Although I live hundreds of miles from the ocean, my apartment has a seagoing motif. Beneath a sweeping seascape, a large antique aquarium dominates the living room, its colorful tropical fish flashing among rocks and shells I collected in Florida. Miniature schooners, windjammers, and ketches line the windowsill. The ornate glass cabinet intended for china houses my prize collection of Hawaiian seashells.

9. **Describe people and objects in action.** Descriptions can become stilted lists of facts or adjectives that describe a topic. You can bring your subject to life by including short narratives and showing people in action. *Show* rather than *tell* readers about your subject:

Original

Al Bryant was the best boss I ever worked for. He supervised the payroll office. He was smart, funny, generous, and patient. He knew all the payroll operations by heart. He had a fantastic eye for detail and problem solving. He was always patient with employees, no matter how upset they became. Confronted by a challenging problem, Al Bryant responded with grace, humor, and high-speed efficiency.

Improved

The payroll office came alive whenever Al Bryant stormed in, usually bearing a carton of fresh donuts and a bag of carrot sticks for his employees. He rarely sat in his office but instead spent his day roving past our cubicles, answering our questions, showing us shortcuts, and solving our problems. He never lost his patience when an employee banged on the door waving an incorrect check. Instead, he offered the employee a donut, grabbed the nearest terminal, and punched in data like a speed typist until he had cut the person a new check.

10. **Include quotations or dialogue.** A description can be made more interesting and effective by including direct quotes that state people's experiences and opinions in their own words.

SUGGESTED TOPICS FOR DESCRIPTIVE WRITING

GENERAL ASSIGNMENTS

Write a description on any of the following topics. Your description may contain passages demonstrating other modes, such as comparison or cause and effect. Select details carefully. Determine whether your description should rely on factual, objective support or subjective impressions. In choosing diction, be aware of the impact of connotation.

1. Your first apartment

2. The people who gather in a place you frequent—a coffee shop, store, tavern, library, or student union

3. How the recent recession affected a friend, your family, your neighborhood, or a business

4. The most desirable/least desirable place to live in your community

5. The most dangerous situation you have faced

6. The type of man/woman you find attractive

7. A consumer or social trend like online shopping, texting, or speed dating

8. A social problem you are confronting or believe is widely misunderstood or ignored

9. The most interesting or most unconventional person you have met in the past year

10. The best/worst party you have attended

WRITING IN CONTEXT

1. Imagine that your college has asked you to write a description of the campus for a brochure designed to recruit students. Your depiction should be easy to read and create a favorable impression.

2. Assume you write a column for an alternative campus newspaper. Develop a sarcastic description of the campus, the college administration, the faculty, or the student body.

3. Write an open letter to the student body of your high school describing what college life is like.

4. Imagine you are trying to sell your car. Write two brief ads, one designed for a campus flyer and the other for Craigslist.

Student Paper: Description

This descriptive paper was written in response to an assignment calling for "a brief description of a person, place, or thing."

First Draft with Instructor's Comments

Small or common items often mean more than we can usually appreciate or understand. <u>My car, for example.</u> I drive a 1969 Volks-
wagen bug. It is rusty, battered, and has a number of old bumper
stickers put on by members of my family.

wordy, delete

fragment

faulty parallelism

The outside of the car used to be cream but is now mostly rust.
Both front fenders are dented and have pits on them. The windshield has a crack on the passenger side. The original side view
mirror was lost and replaced with one originally from a Volvo. The
driver side door is a replacement from a junk yard and is gray
while the rest of the car is cream-colored. The running board on
the passenger side is bent and twisted. The back passenger side
fender is dented. The hood on the back of the car over the engine
is also a replacement part and is blue-gray in color.

The inside of the car <u>is also old</u>. The seats are split and have
been <u>tapped</u> up to cover tears and <u>wholes</u>. The glove compartment is
stuffed with papers, maps, and other items. The visors have old
parking permits from years ago when different people in my family
owned it. *general, be specific*

obvious

taped

holes

The VW bug is a junk pile on wheels, but it is in a way very
significant to me. It is like a history of my family on wheels.
You could say that it is like an heirloom that has passed from one
to another over three generations. It is old and junky. It is an
<u>embrassment</u> to drive to school <u>everyday</u> —but part of me loves the
old car. I like old styles and would love to drive the retro-
looking Mustang, but something about this old bug is special.
It is home. I may get another car, but I will never replace it.

vague

*embarrass-
ment*

every day

REVISION NOTES

*This could be the basis of an interesting description. Clearly, the car has special meaning to
you. You mention that it tells the history of your family and has had several owners.
Instead of focusing on describing the details of the car from front to back, think about using
chronology to show how the car changed over the years. Who owned it? Share details about
the car's past to <u>show</u> rather <u>tell</u> us why this vehicle is significant.*

This is a personal description of an object. Emphasize subjective as well as objective details. Create strong impressions about what you feel as well as what you see.

Revised Draft

My Bug

My father was in first grade when my Bug rolled off an assembly line in West Germany thirty-eight years ago. I have no idea what its original color was, but it has gone from gray to rust to black to cream during my lifetime. My '69 VW is not just a car but a family artifact.

My grandfather bought it in May 1969 as a second car for his wife. She drove it along the Jersey shore selling real estate for six years. The car followed the family west to San Francisco in 1975. My uncle then got the car and drove it to college in New Mexico. After graduating and getting a new car, he gave it to my dad, who was just learning how to drive. By now the car bore the tattoos of college bumper stickers, bent fenders, and rusted chrome. My dad had the car painted a light cream and invested in a new transmission. During a ski trip his freshman year, the Bug skidded off an icy mountain road in Colorado and rolled over. He had the dents pounded out and the car painted gray. It took my parents on their honeymoon. Two years later the battered Bug carried me home from the hospital. After my parents bought a van, the Bug was relegated to being a backup vehicle. When my mom got a new car, the Bug was retired to the garage.

Now it is mine. The fenders, though repainted, still bear the shallow depressions from the Colorado rollover. The windshield is pitted from stones that flew off a speeding gravel truck that nearly ran me off the road in Elko, Nevada, last year. The door handles are replacements I found on eBay. The car seats are patched with tape. Rust holes in the floor have been covered with cookie sheets. The dashboard sports the compass my mother glued on ten years ago so she would not get lost taking me to soccer games. The glove compartment is jammed with rumpled maps and snapshots from decades of family vacations and road trips.

My Bug is not the most glamorous vehicle in the college parking lot, but it has to be the most loved. It looks like a rolling homeless shelter to many. But to me it is a mobile family album. I love every ding and dent.

QUESTIONS FOR REVIEW AND REVISION

1. How interesting do you find this essay? How can a writer make the description of an object meaningful?

2. How does the student blend objective details and subjective impressions? Which are more important, in your view?

3. What is the student's goal in describing this car? What does he want readers to know?

4. How effective is the ending? Does it sum up the point of the essay?

5. Descriptions do not always have an identifiable thesis statement. How would you state the student's thesis?

6. Did the student follow the instructor's comments? Could you suggest other improvements?

7. Read the paper aloud. Are there any sentences that could be revised for clarity?

WRITING SUGGESTIONS

1. Write a description of your own car or one you are familiar with. What details would you want to share with readers? What makes this vehicle significant or memorable to you?

2. *Collaborative Writing:* Discuss this essay with a group of students. Have each member volunteer opinions on its strengths and weaknesses. Do members suggest revisions or a need for added detail?

DESCRIPTION CHECKLIST

Before submitting your paper, review these points:

1. **Have you limited your topic?**

2. **Do your supporting details suit your context? Should they be objective, subjective, or a blend?**

3. **Is your description focused and clearly organized, or is it only a random list of facts and observations?**

4. **Have you avoided including unnecessary details and awkward constructions?**

5. Does sensory detail include more than sight? Can you add impressions of taste, touch, sound, or smell?

6. Do you avoid overly general terms and focus on specific impressions? Have you created dominant impressions?

7. Do you *show* rather than *tell*? Can you add action to your description to keep it from being static?

8. Do you keep a consistent point of view?

9. Read your paper aloud. How does it sound? Do any sections need expansion? Are there irrelevant details to be deleted or awkward expressions to be revised?

Info Write provides additional information on writing description.
cengage.learning.infowrite.com

CHAPTER SIX

DEFINITION: ESTABLISHING MEANING

WHAT IS DEFINITION?

Effective communication requires that writers and readers have a shared language. Words and ideas must be *defined* clearly to eliminate confusion and misinterpretation. Definitions limit or explain the meaning of a term or concept. As a college student you have probably devoted much of your time to learning new words and their definitions. Fields such as chemistry, psychology, sociology, economics, law, and anatomy have technical terms that you must master in order to communicate within the discipline.

Clearly stated definitions play a critical role in professional and business writing. In order to prevent confusion, conflict, and litigation, many union contracts, insurance policies, sales agreements, and leases include definitions so all parties will share a common understanding of important terms. Government documents and business proposals contain glossaries to familiarize readers with new or abstract terms. Failing to understand a definition can be costly. A tenant who does not understand a landlord's definition of "excessive noise" may face eviction. The car buyer who misinterprets the manufacturer's definition of "normal use" can void his or her warranty.

The term *definition* leads most people to think of a dictionary. But defining entails more than looking something up. Definitions are not always precise or universally accepted. Distinctly different types of definitions exist. To be an effective writer in college and in your future profession, it is important to appreciate the range of definitions:

- **Standard definitions** are universally accepted and rarely subject to change. Words such as *tibia, dolphin, uranium, felony, turbine,* and *rifle* have exact meanings that are understood and shared by scholars, professionals, and the general public. Doctors, nurses, paramedics, and football coaches, for example, all recognize *tibia* as a specific bone in the body. Though different state legislatures might disagree on which specific crime constitutes a *felony*, they all accept its general concept.

- **Regulatory definitions** are officially designated terms and are subject to change. The National Football League, Internal Revenue Service (IRS), Federal Aviation Administration, Federal Communications Commission, school boards, labor organizations, the Catholic Church, and insurance companies issue definitions to guide policy, control operations, and make decisions. The IRS definition of *deductible meal allowance* can change yearly. Many states changed their definition of *drunk driving* by lowering the legal blood alcohol content from .10 percent to .08 percent. One health insurance company may pay for a liver transplant while another carrier refuses, defining the procedure *experimental*. Regulatory definitions may be universally accepted, but they can change or be limited to a specific region or discipline. The building codes of New York and San Francisco may have varying definitions of what makes buildings *structurally* sound. The medical definition of *insanity* varies greatly from the court-accepted, legal definition.

- **Evolving definitions** reflect changes in community attitudes, social values, governmental policy, and scientific research. In the nineteenth century corporal punishment was a routine feature of public school discipline. Today the same actions would be defined as *child abuse*. The term *date rape* defines incidents that generations ago would not be viewed as criminal assaults. Decades ago medical and psychology texts defined *homosexuality* as a mental disorder. Evolving definitions track social change but rarely shift as abruptly as regulatory definitions.

- **Qualifying definitions** limit meanings of words or concepts that are abstract or subject to dispute. How does one define an *alcoholic*? At what point do doctors label a patient *obese* or *senile*? Which young people are labeled *juvenile delinquents*? How does one define *genius*? In some fields organizations provide definitions. The American Medical Association may offer a definition of *alcoholism*. But unlike a regulatory term, physicians and researchers are free to dispute it and apply a different meaning altogether. Some definitions are hotly debated. Researchers, politicians, and social commentators continually argue about whether drug addiction and alcoholism should be defined as *disabilities*, which would entitle people with these conditions to receive benefits.

- **Cultural definitions** are shaped by the history, values, and attitudes of a national, ethnic, or religious group. Just as evolving definitions alter over time, cultural definitions differ from group to group. In some countries it is customary to offer cash gifts to officials as a *tribute*. In the United States the same action would be defined as an illegal *bribe*. People around the world embrace *freedom* but define it very differently. For most Americans *freedom* is defined in personal terms, meaning freedom of individual movement and expression. In other countries, people may define *freedom* in national terms, as protecting the independence and security of their homeland even if it means censorship and restricted personal liberties.

- **Personal definitions** are used by writers to express individual interpretations of words or ideas. Your concept of a good parent would be a personal definition. A writer can frame an entire essay in terms of a personal definition or establish a series of personal definitions at the outset of a narrative or persuasive paper. Writers often use personal definition as a method of stating their opinions.

- **Invented definitions** are created to identify a new or newly discovered idea, behavior, object, situation, or problem. The term *road rage* was invented to identify a situation in which a motorist violently overreacts to a minor traffic incident. Soon after, the word *air rage* was used to define the violent and rude behavior of frustrated airline passengers. The Internet has led to a number of invented definitions, including *chat room*, *online dating*, and *cyberstalking*. Janice Castro, for example, uses the term *Spanglish* (page 178) to identify a blend of English and Spanish spoken by many Hispanics.

Methods of Definition

Definitions can be established using a number of techniques:

1. **Defining through synonyms** is the simplest method of providing meaning for a word. Glossaries and dictionaries customarily use synonyms to define technical terms or foreign words. *Costal* refers to *ribs*. A *siesta* can be translated as a *nap*. A *casement* can be explained as a *window*.

2. **Defining by description** provides details about a thing or concept and gives readers a sense of what it might look, feel, taste, smell, or sound like. Defining a *costrel* as *a small flask with a loop or loops that is suspended from a belt* provides readers with a clear picture. Descriptive definitions also can demonstrate how something operates. An *airbag* can be defined as *a rapidly inflated cushion designed to protect automobile passengers in a collision.*

3. **Defining by example** provides specific illustrations to establish meaning. A *felony* can be defined as *a serious crime such as murder, rape, or burglary.* Examples can establish meaning through identification. Telling a fourth-grade class that an *adjective is a word that modifies a noun* will not be as effective as providing examples children can easily recognize—*red, fast, tall, silly, old-fashioned, hot.* Complex or abstract concepts are easier to comprehend if defined by example. Income tax instructions, for instance, often include numerous examples to define what is and is not deductible.

4. **Defining by comparison** uses analogies readers can understand to give meaning to something unfamiliar. A television reporter covering a space mission defined NASA terminology using comparisons viewers would readily understand. To explain the term *power down*, she remarked that the astronauts were *conserving power by turning off nonessential electrical devices, much like switching off the radio and windshield wipers on a car*. Because they can oversimplify complex ideas, comparative definitions must be used carefully.

5. **Extended definitions** qualify or limit the meaning of abstract, disputed, or highly complex words or concepts. Words such as *sin*, *love*, and *racism* cannot be adequately explained through synonyms, brief descriptions, or examples. A full description may require several paragraphs.

The Purpose of Definition

Definitions generally serve to establish meaning and to provide a common or shared understanding. But they also can be persuasive. Evolving definitions frequently indicate a break with past beliefs and suggest alternative interpretations. The first psychiatrists who defined *homosexuality* in terms of *sexual orientation* rather than as *deviancy*, *mental disorder*, or *sexual perversion* were clearly trying to persuade their readers to change their attitudes.

To transform public attitudes, writers frequently urge readers to redefine something, to change their perceptions and see striking a child as *abuse* instead of *spanking* or to accept graffiti as *street art* and not *vandalism*. Definitions can play a critical role in shaping opinions and making arguments. Drug addicts, for instance, can be defined in legalistic terms and viewed as *criminals* who should be imprisoned, or defined in medical terms as *patients* needing treatment.

Definition in Context

The way writers define subjects depends greatly on context. In defining *depression* for a marketing brochure, a psychotherapist directs an explanation to prospective clients:

> Depression is an internal state—a feeling of sadness, loss, "the blues," deep disappointment. *When it is more severe, you may have feelings of irritability, touchiness, guilt, self-reproach, loss of self-esteem, worthlessness, hopelessness, helplessness, and even thoughts of death and suicide.*

The definition is addressed to the reader, using the word "you," and focuses on personal "feelings" stated in general terms. In contrast, Jessica Kuper's *Encyclopedia of Psychology* offers a definition for mental health professionals:

Depression is a term used to describe a mood, a symptom, and syndromes of affective disorders. As a mood, it refers to a transient state of feeling sad, blue, forlorn, cheerless, unhappy, and/or down. As a symptom, it refers to a complaint that often accompanies a group of biopsychosocial problems. In contrast, the depressive syndromes include a wide spectrum of psychobiological dysfunctions that vary in frequency, severity, and duration.

The inclusion of words such as "affective disorders" and "biopsychosocial" indicate that this definition is intended for a specialized audience familiar with technical terms.

STRATEGIES FOR READING DEFINITIONS

In reading the definition entries in this chapter, keep these questions in mind.

Understanding Meaning

1. Which type of definition is the author developing—standard, regulatory, evolving, qualifying, cultural, or personal?

2. What is the author's purpose—to provide a definition to establish common ground, to explain a complex issue, or to persuade readers to alter their opinions?

3. What audience is the writer addressing—general readers or specialists? Does the audience need to know the definitions in order to base decisions or guide future actions?

4. What is the nature of the discipline or writing situation? Is the writer working within a strictly regulated profession or the general marketplace of ideas?

Evaluating Strategy

1. How does the writer define the word, object, or concept—through synonyms, descriptions, examples, or comparisons?

2. Is the definition limited to a specific incident or context, or can it be applied generally? Is the writer defining a particular person or a personality trait that could be shared by millions?

3. Does the writer supply personal examples, or does he or she rely on official sources to establish the definition?

Appreciating Language

1. What role do word choice and connotation play in establishing the definition?

2. What do the tone and level of language reveal about the writer's purpose and intended audience?

EILEEN SIMPSON

Eileen Simpson was a psychotherapist who struggled for years to overcome dyslexia, a reading disorder that affects more than 20 million Americans. She is the author of several books, including Poets in Their Youth, *a memoir of her marriage to the poet John Berryman. Other books based on her personal experiences explored problems of children growing up without parents. This section comes from her 1979 book,* Reversals: A Personal Account of Victory over Dyslexia.

Dyslexia

CONTEXT: *Simpson provides a standard definition of an existing term by examining its Greek and Latin roots and then demonstrates the effects dyslexia has on its victims. Notice that she supplies examples to help readers fully appreciate the implications of a widely misunderstood disorder.*

<u>Dyslexia (from the Greek, *dys*, faulty, + *lexis*, speech, cognate with the Latin</u> *legere*, to read), developmental or specific dyslexia as it's technically called, the disorder I suffered from, is the inability of otherwise normal children to read. Children whose intelligence is below average, whose vision or hearing is defective, who have not had proper schooling, or who are too emotionally disturbed or brain damaged to profit from it belong in other diagnostic categories. They, too, may be unable to learn to read, but they cannot properly be called dyslexics. *[opens with definition]* *[describes what dyslexia is not]*

For more than seventy years the essential nature of the affliction has been hotly disputed by psychologists, neurologists, and educators. It is generally agreed, however, that it is the result of a neurophysiological flaw in the brain's ability to process language. It is probably inherited, although some experts are reluctant to say this because they fear people will equate "inherited" with "untreatable." <u>Treatable it certainly is: not a disease to be cured, but a malfunction that requires retraining.</u> *[background]*

Reading is the most complex skill a child entering school is asked to develop. What makes it complex, in part, is that letters are less constant than objects. A car seen from a distance, close to, from above, or below, or in a mirror still looks like a car even though the optical image changes. The letters of the alphabet are more whimsical. Take the letter *b*. Turned upside down it becomes a *p*. Looked at in a mirror, it becomes a *d*. Capitalized, it becomes something quite different, a B. The M upside down is a W. The *E* flipped over becomes Ǝ. This reversed *E* is familiar to mothers of normal children who have just begun to go to school. The earliest examples of art work they bring home often have I LOVƎ YOU written on them. *[explains why reading is difficult]*

Dyslexics differ from other children in that they read, spell, and write letters upside down and turned around far more frequently and for a much longer *explains how dyslexics see letters* time. In what seems like a capricious manner, they also add letters, syllables, and words, or, just as capriciously, delete them. With palindromic words (was-saw, on-no), it is the order of the letters rather than the orientation they change. The new word makes sense, but not the sense intended. Then there are other words where the changed order—"sorty" for story—does not make sense at all.

5   The inability to recognize that g, g, and G are the same letter, the inability to maintain the orientation of the letters, to retain the order in which they appear, and to follow a line of text without jumping above or below it—all the results of the flaw—can make of an orderly page of words a dish of alphabet soup.

6   Also essential for reading is the ability to store words in memory and to retrieve them. This very particular kind of memory dyslexics lack. So, too, do they lack the ability to hear what the eye sees, and to see what they hear. If the eye sees "off," the ear must hear "off" and not "of," or "for." If the ear hears "saw," the eye must see that it looks like "saw" on the page and not "was." Lacking these skills, a sentence or paragraph becomes a coded message to which the dyslexic can't find the key.

7   It is only a slight exaggeration to say that those who learned to read without difficulty can best understand the labor reading is for a dyslexic by turning a page of text upside down and trying to decipher it.

8   While the literature is replete with illustrations of the way these children write and spell, there are surprisingly few examples of how they read. One, used for propaganda purposes to alert the public to the vulnerability of dyslexics in a literate society, is a sign warning that behind it are guard dogs trained to kill. The dyslexic reads:

a Wurring
Guard God
Patoly

example #1 demonstrates dyslexia

for

Warning
Guard Dog
Patrol

and, of course, remains ignorant of the danger.

9   Looking for a more commonplace example, and hoping to recapture the way I must have read in fourth grade, I recently observed dyslexic children at the Educational Therapy Clinic in Princeton, through the courtesy of Elizabeth Travers, the director. The first child I saw, eight-year-old Anna

(whose red hair and brown eyes reminded me of myself at that age), had just come to the Clinic and was learning the alphabet. Given the story of "Little Red Riding Hood," which is at the second-grade level, she began confidently enough, repeating the title from memory, then came to a dead stop. With much coaxing throughout, she read as follows:

> Grandma you a top. Grandma [looks over at picture of Red Riding Hood]. Red Riding Hood [long pause, presses index finger into the paper. Looks at me for help. I urge: Go ahead] the a [puts head close to the page, nose almost touching] on Grandma

example #2 of dyslexia

for

> Once upon a time there was a little girl who had a red coat with a red hood. Etc.

"Grandma" was obviously a memory from having heard the story read aloud. 10 Had I needed a reminder of how maddening my silences must have been to Miss Henderson, and how much patience is required to teach these children, Anna, who took almost ten minutes to read these few lines, furnished it. The main difference between Anna and me at that age is that Anna clearly felt no need to invent. She was perplexed, but not anxious, and seemed to have infinite tolerance for her long silences.

Toby, a nine-year-old boy with superior intelligence, had a year of tutoring 11 behind him and could have managed "Little Red Riding Hood" with ease. His text was taken from the *Reader's Digest's Reading Skill Builder*, Grade IV. He read:

> A kangaroo likes as if he had but truck together warm. His saw neck and head do not … [Here Toby sighed with fatigue] seem to feel happy back. They and tried and so every a tiger Moses and shoots from lonesome day and shouts and long shore animals. And each farm play with five friends…

example #3 of dyslexia

He broke off with the complaint, "This is too hard. Do I have to read any 12 more?"

His text was: 13

> A kangaroo looks as if he had been put together wrong. His small neck and head do not seem to fit with his heavy back legs and thick tail. Soft eyes, a twinkly little nose, and short front legs seem strange on such a large strong animal. And each front paw has five fingers, like a man's hand.

14   An English expert gives the following bizarre example of an adult dyslexic's performance:

example #4 of dyslexia

> An the bee-what in the tel mother of the biothodoodoo to the majoram or that emidrate eni eni Krastrei, mestriet to Ketra lotombreidi to ra from treido as that.

15   His text, taken from a college catalogue the examiner happened to have close at hand, was:

> It shall be in the power of the college to examine or not every licentiate, previous to his admission to the fellowship, as they shall think fit.

16   That evening when I read aloud to Auntie for the first time, I probably began as Toby did, my memory of the classroom lesson keeping me close to the text. When memory ran out, and Auntie did not correct my errors, I began to invent. When she still didn't stop me, I may well have begun to improvise in the manner of this patient—anything to keep going and keep up the myth that I was reading—until Auntie brought the "gibberish" to a halt.

Understanding Meaning

1. What basic definition does Simpson provide? What misinterpretation does she note can occur if a condition is considered "inherited"?

2. How does Simpson summarize controversies in the field of research? What do scientists from different disciplines agree on?

3. What is the implication to dyslexics and their parents that dyslexia is "not a disease to be cured," but "a malfunction that requires retraining"?

4. *Critical Thinking:* How can this disorder affect a child's development if it is not detected?

Evaluating Strategy

1. Why is it effective to provide an etymology of the word *dyslexia* at the opening? Does this help satisfy reader curiosity about a term many people have heard but do not fully understand?

2. How does Simpson's introduction of personal experience affect the definition? Does this add a human dimension to her definition, or does it detract from its objectivity? Would the inclusion of personal experience be appropriate in a textbook?

3. Do the examples of dyslexic reading dramatize the effects of this disorder? Would an explanation alone suffice to impress readers with the crippling effects of a reading disorder?

4. *Blending the Modes:* How does Simpson use *narration, description,* and *comparison* to develop her definition? What role can stories or case studies provide readers seeking to understand a complex subject?

Appreciating Language

1. Simpson is defining a complex disorder. How does her language indicate that she is seeking to address a general audience? Would the vocabulary differ in a definition written for psychology students?

2. Simpson cites an example of a dyslexic reading a warning sign as "propaganda." Does the use of this word weaken her argument that dyslexia is a serious condition? Why or why not?

3. How does Simpson define the term "palindromic"?

WRITING SUGGESTIONS

1. Write a concisely worded definition of dyslexia in your own words.

2. *Critical Writing:* Write an essay expressing your view on how dyslexics should be graded in college. Should students with dyslexia be allowed more time on essay tests, be offered special tutorial services, or be given alternative assignments and examinations? Can colleges accommodate students with disabilities while maintaining academic standards?

3. *Collaborative Writing:* Working with several other students, craft a brief explanation of dyslexia to be incorporated into a brochure for parents of children with learning disabilities. Keep your audience in mind, and avoid making negative comments that might upset parents.

JANICE CASTRO, DAN COOK, AND CRISTINA GARCIA

Janice Castro (1949–) is a journalist who became Time *magazine's first health policy reporter. In 1994 she published* The American Way of Health: How Medicine Is Changing and What It Means to You. *In addition to writing about medicine, she has published articles on topics ranging from pension plans to home-shopping. Castro is now the director of graduate journalism programs at Northwestern University's Medill School of Journalism. Dan Cook is a Los Angeles journalist and correspondent. Christina Garcia now works as a novelist. This essay appeared as part of a* Time *cover story about Hispanics.*

Spanglish

CONTEXT: *In this essay, the writers use an invented term to define a blend of English and Spanish spoken by a growing number of Americans. As you read their article, notice how they use* description, *ex-ample, and* comparison *to develop their definition.*

1   In Manhattan a first-grader greets her visiting grandparents, happily exclaiming, "Come here, *siéntate!*" Her bemused grandfather, who does not speak Spanish, nevertheless knows she is asking him to sit down. A Miami personnel officer understands what a job applicant means when he says, "*Quiero un part time.*" Nor do drivers miss a beat reading a billboard alongside a Los Angeles street advertising CERVEZA—SIX PACK!

2   This free-form blend of Spanish and English, known as Spanglish, is common linguistic currency wherever concentrations of Hispanic Americans are found in the U.S. In Los Angeles, where 55 percent of the city's 3 million inhabitants speak Spanish, Spanglish is as much a part of daily life as sunglasses. Unlike the broken-English efforts of earlier immigrants from Europe, Asia, and other regions, Spanglish has become a widely accepted conversational mode used casually—even playfully—by Spanish-speaking immigrants and native-born Americans alike.

3   Consisting of one part Hispanicized English, one part Americanized Spanish, and more than a little fractured syntax, Spanglish is a bit like a Robin Williams comedy routine: a crackling line of cross-cultural patter straight from the melting pot. Often it enters Anglo homes and families through the children, who pick it up at school or at play with their young Hispanic contemporaries. In other cases, it comes from watching TV; many an Anglo child watching *Sesame Street* has learned *uno dos tres* almost as quickly as one two three.

4   Spanglish takes a variety of forms, from the Southern California Anglos who bid farewell with the utterly silly "*hasta la* bye-bye" to the Cuban-American drivers in Miami who *parquean* their *carros*. Some Spanglish sentences are

mostly Spanish, with a quick detour for an English word or two. A Latino friend may cut short a conversation by glancing at his watch and excusing himself with the explanation that he must "*ir al* supermarket."

Many of the English words transplanted in this way are simply handier than their Spanish counterparts. No matter how distasteful the subject, for example, it is still easier to say "income tax" than *impuesto sobre la renta*. At the same time, many Spanish-speaking immigrants have adopted such terms as VCR, microwave, and dishwasher for what they view as largely American phenomena. Still other English words convey a cultural context that is not implicit in the Spanish. A friend who invites you to a *lonche* most likely has in mind the brisk American custom of "doing lunch" rather than the languorous afternoon break traditionally implied by *almuerzo*.

Mainstream Americans exposed to similar hybrids of German, Chinese, or Hindi might be mystified. But even Anglos who speak little or no Spanish are somewhat familiar with Spanglish. Living among them, for one thing, are 19 million Hispanics. In addition, more American high school and university students sign up for Spanish than for any other foreign language.

Only in the past ten years, though, has Spanglish begun to turn into a national slang. Its popularity has grown with the explosive increases in U.S. immigration from Latin American countries. English has increasingly collided with Spanish in retail stores, offices, and classrooms, in pop music and on street corners. Anglos whose ancestors picked up such Spanish words as *rancho, bronco, tornado*, and *incomunicado*, for instance, now freely use such Spanish words as *gracias, bueno, amigo*, and *por favor*.

Among Latinos, Spanglish conversations often flow more easily from Spanish into several sentences of English and back.

Spanglish is a sort of code for Latinos: the speakers know Spanish, but their hybrid language reflects the American culture in which they live. Many lean to shorter, clipped phrases in place of the longer, more graceful expressions their parents used. Says Leonel de la Cuesta, an assistant professor of modern languages at Florida International University in Miami: "In the U.S., time is money, and that is showing up in Spanglish as an economy of language." Conversational examples: *taipiar* (type) and *winshi-wiper* (windshield wiper) replace *escribir a máquina* and *limpiaparabrisas*.

Major advertisers, eager to tap the estimated $134 billion in spending power wielded by Spanish-speaking Americans, have ventured into Spanglish to promote their products. In some cases, attempts to sprinkle Spanish through commercials have produced embarrassing gaffes. A Braniff Airlines ad that sought to tell Spanish-speaking audiences they could settle back *en* (in) luxuriant *cuero* (leather) seats, for example, inadvertently said they could fly without clothes (*encuero*). A fractured translation of the Miller Lite slogan told readers the beer was "Filling, and less delicious." Similar blunders are often made by Anglos trying to impress Spanish-speaking pals. But if Latinos are amused by mangled Spanglish, they also recognize these goofs as a sort of friendly acceptance. As they might put it, *no problema.*

Understanding Meaning

1. What is Spanglish? Can you define it in a single sentence?

2. How does the concept of "Spanglish" differ from "broken English"?

3. Who uses Spanglish? What does it indicate about the growing Hispanic influence in the United States?

4. *Critical Thinking:* Many Americans advocate "English only" and oppose bilingual education. What does the emergence of Spanglish reveal about the status of English in America? Is there any danger that immigrants will fail to master English?

Evaluating Strategy

1. How do the authors use examples to create their definition?

2. How do the authors organize details to build a coherent essay?

3. How effective are the opening and closing paragraphs?

Appreciating Language

1. What do the tone and style of the essay suggest about the authors' attitude toward their subject?

2. The authors use the term "hybrid" to describe Spanglish. Is this an effective term? Why or why not?

3. *Critical Thinking:* The writers call Spanglish "slang." What is slang to you? Would you consider it an appropriate label for Spanglish?

WRITING SUGGESTIONS

1. Invent a word to represent something you have observed and support your definition with details. You might define "blind datism," "recycling phobia," or "texting withdrawal."

2. *Collaborative Writing:* Ask three or four students to identify a special kind of language they have encountered. Discuss samples and list examples, then write a short definition of "campus-ese," "first-date euphemisms," "parent-ese," or "online slang," for example.

ELLEN GOODMAN

Ellen Goodman (1941–) was born in Massachusetts and graduated from Radcliffe College. She worked for Newsweek *and the* Detroit Free Press *before joining the* Boston Globe *in 1967. Until her retirement in 2010, Goodman's column "At Large" was widely syndicated throughout the United States. As an essayist and television commentator, Goodman discussed feminism, changes in family life, sexual harassment, and male and female relationships. Her essays have been collected in several books, including* Close to Home, At Large, *and* Turning Points.

The Company Man

CONTEXT: *Instead of using a number of illustrations to develop a definition, Goodman presents a single, extended example of a person who fits her personal view of a workaholic.*

He worked himself to death, finally and precisely, at 3:00 A.M. Sunday 1 morning.

The obituary didn't say that, of course. It said that he died of a coronary 2 thrombosis—I think that was it—but everyone among his friends and acquaintances knew it instantly. He was a perfect Type A, a workaholic, a classic, they said to each other and shook their heads—and thought for five or ten minutes about the way they lived.

This man who worked himself to death finally and precisely at 3:00 A.M. 3 Sunday morning—on his day off—was fifty-one years old and a vice-president. He was, however, one of six vice-presidents, and one of three who might conceivably—if the president died or retired soon enough—have moved to the top spot. Phil knew that.

He worked six days a week, five of them until eight or nine at night, during 4 a time when his own company had begun the four-day week for everyone but the executives. He worked like the Important People. He had no outside "extracurricular interests," unless, of course, you think about a monthly golf game that way. To Phil, it was work. He always ate egg salad sandwiches at his desk. He was, of course, overweight, by 20 or 25 pounds. He thought it was okay, though, because he didn't smoke.

On Saturdays, Phil wore a sports jacket to the office instead of a suit, be- 5 cause it was the weekend.

He had a lot of people working for him, maybe sixty, and most of them liked 6 him most of the time. Three of them will be seriously considered for his job. The obituary didn't mention that.

But it did list his "survivors" quite accurately. He is survived by his wife, 7 Helen, forty-eight years old, a good woman of no particular marketable skills, who worked in an office before marrying and mothering. She had, according to her daughter, given up trying to compete with his work years ago, when the children were small. A company friend said, "I know how much you will miss him." And she answered, "I already have."

8   "Missing him all these years," she must have given up part of herself which had cared too much for the man. She would be "well taken care of."

9   His "dearly beloved" eldest of the "dearly beloved" children is a hard-working executive in a manufacturing firm down South. In the day and a half before the funeral, he went around the neighborhood researching his father, asking the neighbors what he was like. They were embarrassed.

10   His second child is a girl, who is twenty-four and newly married. She lives near her mother and they are close, but whenever she was alone with her father, in a car driving somewhere, they had nothing to say to each other.

11   The youngest is twenty, a boy, a high-school graduate who has spent the last couple of years, like a lot of his friends, doing enough odd jobs to stay in grass and food. He was the one who tried to grab at his father, and tried to mean enough to him to keep the man at home. He was his father's favorite. Over the last two years, Phil stayed up nights worrying about the boy.

12   The boy once said, "My father and I only board here."

13   At the funeral, the sixty-year-old company president told the forty-eight-year-old widow that the fifty-one-year-old deceased had meant much to the company and would be missed and would be hard to replace. The widow didn't look him in the eye. She was afraid he would read her bitterness and, after all, she would need him to straighten out the finances—the stock options and all that.

14   Phil was overweight and nervous and worked too hard. If he wasn't at the office, he was worried about it. Phil was a Type A, a heart-attack natural. You could have picked him out in a minute from a lineup.

15   So when he finally worked himself to death, at precisely 3:00 A.M. Sunday morning, no one was really surprised.

16   By 5:00 P.M. the afternoon of the funeral, the company president had begun, discreetly of course, with care and taste, to make inquiries about his replacement. One of the three men. He asked around: "Who's been working the hardest?"

Understanding Meaning

1. How does Goodman define a workaholic? Why does she assert that Phil's heart attack was directly related to his career?

2. What does Goodman's definition imply about the quality of Phil's life? What does she suggest that it was lacking?

3. What, if anything, seemed to have driven Phil?

4. Goodman mentions that Phil provided well for his widow. Is Phil, a hard-working vice-president who cares about his family, an ideal man in the eyes of many women? If Phil were African American or Hispanic, would he be viewed as a "role model"? Would a "company woman" be seen as a feminist?

5. *Critical Thinking:* Americans have long admired hard workers. Benjamin Franklin, Thomas Edison, Henry Ford, and Martin Luther King, Jr. became legendary for their accomplishments. On the other hand, Americans long for more leisure time. Is there a double standard? Do we want to spend more time with our friends and family but expect our doctors, lawyers, contractors, and stockbrokers to work overtime for us, meet our deadlines, and always be a phone call away?

Evaluating Strategy

1. Would Goodman's definition be stronger if she included more than one example?

2. What impact does the final paragraph have? How does this reinforce her point?

Appreciating Language

1. Goodman places certain phrases in quotation marks—"well taken care of" and "dearly beloved." What is the effect of highlighting these terms?

2. What does the term "company man" suggest? Would "church man" or "advocacy man" provoke different responses?

WRITING SUGGESTIONS

1. Develop your own definition of *workaholic*. Can it be defined in hours worked or by the degree of stress a job creates? Does an actor or writer working eighty hours a week to rehearse a play or write a novel fit the category of *workaholic*? Is a mother with young children by definition a workaholic?

2. *Collaborative Writing:* Speak with fellow students, then write a short statement in response to the question, "What do we owe our employers?"

ALISSA QUART

Alissa Quart is a contributing editor for Columbia Journalism Review, *where she writes a column. She has also written articles for* Newsweek, Mother Jones, *and the* New York Times Magazine. *Her books include* Branded: The Buying and Selling of Teenagers *(2003) and* Hothouse Kids *(2006). Quart was a Nieman Fellow at Harvard University in 2009–2010.*

Listening to Madness

CONTEXT: *This article, first published in* Newsweek *in 2009, explains why some mental patients reject the traditional definition of mental illness as a "disease," often embracing their condition as "unusual ways of processing information and emotion" and calling for an acceptance of what they call "mental diversity."*

1 "We don't want to be normal," Will Hall tells me. The 43-year-old has been diagnosed as schizophrenic, and doctors have prescribed antipsychotic medication for him. But Hall would rather value his mentally extreme states than try to suppress them, so he doesn't take his meds. Instead, he practices yoga and avoids coffee and sugar. He is delicate and thin, with dark plum polish on his fingernails and black fashion sneakers on his feet, his half Native American ancestry evident in his dark hair and dark eyes. Cultivated and charismatic, he is also unusually energetic, so much so that he seems to be vibrating even when sitting still.

2   I met Hall one night at the offices of the Icarus Project in Manhattan. He became a leader of the group—a "mad pride" collective—in 2005 as a way to promote the idea that mental-health diagnoses like bipolar disorder are "dangerous gifts" rather than illnesses. While we talked, members of the group—Icaristas, as they call themselves—scurried around in the purple-painted office, collating mad-pride fliers. Hall explained how the medical establishment has for too long relied heavily on medication and repression of behavior of those deemed "not normal." Icarus and groups like it are challenging the science that psychiatry says is on its side. Hall believes that psychiatrists are prone to making arbitrary distinctions between "crazy" and "healthy," and to using medication as tranquilizers.

3   "For most people, it used to be, 'Mental illness is a disease—here is a pill you take for it'," says Hall. "Now that's breaking down." Indeed, Hall came of age in the era of the book "Listening to Prozac." He initially took Prozac after it was prescribed to him for depression in 1990. But he was not simply depressed, and he soon had a manic reaction to Prozac, a not uncommon side effect. In his frenetic state, Hall went on to lose a job at an environmental

organization. He soon descended into poverty and started to hear furious voices in his head; he walked the streets of San Francisco night after night, but the voices never quieted. Eventually, he went to a mental-health clinic and was swiftly locked up. Soon after, he was diagnosed with schizophrenia. He was put in restraints and hospitalized against his will, he says. For the next year, he bounced in and out of a public psychiatric hospital that he likens to a prison. The humiliation and what he experienced as the failure of the medication were what turned him against traditional treatment. Since then, Hall has been asking whether his treatment was really necessary. He felt sloshily medicated, as if he couldn't really live his life.

Hall and Icarus are not alone in asking these questions. They are part of a new generation of activists trying to change the treatment and stigma attached to mental illness. Welcome to Mad Pride, a budding grassroots movement, where people who have been defined as mentally ill reframe their conditions and celebrate unusual (some call them "spectacular") ways of processing information and emotion.

Just as some deaf activists prefer to embrace their inability to hear rather than "cure" it with cochlear implants, members of Icarus reject the notion that the things that are called mental illness are simply something to be rid of. Icarus members cast themselves as a dam in the cascade of new diagnoses like bipolar and ADHD. The group, which now has a membership of 8,000 people across the U.S., argues that mental-health conditions can be made into "something beautiful." They mean that one can transform what are often considered simply horrible diseases into an ecstatic, creative, productive or broadly "spiritual" condition. As Hall puts it, he hopes Icarus will "push the emergence of mental diversity."

Embracing "mental diversity" is one thing, but questioning the need for medication in today's pillpopping world is controversial—and there have been instances in which those who experience mental extremes harm themselves or others. Icaristas argue that some of the severely mentally ill may avoid taking medication, because for some the drugs don't seem to help, yet produce difficult side effects. And while some side effects like cognitive impairment are surely debilitating, others are more subtle, such as the vague feeling that people are not themselves. Icaristas call themselves "pro-choice" about meds—some do take their drugs, but others refuse.

Mad pride has its roots in the mad-liberation movement of the 1960s and '70s, when maverick psychiatrists started questioning the boundaries between sane and insane, and patients began to resist psychiatric care that they considered coercive. But today the emphasis is on support groups, alternative health and reconsidering diagnostic labeling that can still doom patients to a lifetime of battling stigma. Icarus also frames its mission as a somewhat literary one—helping "to navigate the space between brilliance and madness." Even the name Icarus, with its origin in the Greek myth of a boy who flew to great heights (brilliance) but then came too close to the sun (madness) and hurtled to his death, has a literary cast.

8   Although Icarus and Hall focus on those diagnosed as mentally ill, their work has much broader implications. Talking to Hall, I was acutely aware just how much their stance reflects on the rest of us—the "normal" minds that can't read through a book undistracted, the lightly depressed people, the everyday drunks who tend toward volatility, the people who "just" have trouble making eye contact, those ordinary Americans who memorize every possible detail about Angelina Jolie.

9   After all, aren't we all more odd than we are normal? And aren't so many of us one bad experience away from a mental-health diagnosis that could potentially limit us? Aren't "normal" minds now struggling with questions of competence, consistency or sincerity? Icarus is likewise asking why we are so keen to correct every little deficit—it argues that we instead need to embrace the range of human existence.

10   While some critics might view Icaristas as irresponsible, their skepticism about drugs isn't entirely unfounded. Lately, a number of antipsychotic drugs have been found to cause some troubling side effects.

11   There are, of course, questions as to whether mad pride and Icarus have gone too far. While to his knowledge no members have gravely harmed themselves (or others), Hall acknowledges that not everyone can handle the Icarus approach. "People can go too fast and get too excited about not using medication, and we warn people against throwing their meds away, being too ambitious and doing it alone," he says.

12   But is this stance the answer? Jonathan Stanley, a director of the Treatment Advocacy Center, a nonprofit working to provide treatment for the mentally ill, is somewhat critical. Stanley, who suffers from bipolar illness with psychotic features, argues that medication is indispensable for people with bipolar disease or with schizophrenia. Stanley's group also supports mandatory hospitalization for some people suffering severe mental illness—a practice that Icarus calls "forced treatment."

13   Scholars like Peter Kramer, author of "Listening to Prozac" and "Against Depression," also take a darker view of mental extremes. "Psychotic depression is a disease," Kramer says. As the intellectual who helped to popularize the widespread use of antidepressants, Kramer is nonetheless enthusiastic about Icarus as a community for mad pride. Yet he still argues that mental-health diagnoses are very significant. "In an ideal world, you'd want good peer support like Icarus—for people to speak up for what's right for them and have access to resources—and also medication and deep-brain stimulation," he says.

14   For his part, Hall remains articulate, impassioned and unmedicated. He lives independently, in an apartment with a roommate in Oregon, where he

is getting a master's in psychology at a psychoanalytic institute. He maintains a large number of friendships, although his relationships, he says, are rather tumultuous.

Nevertheless, it's not so easy. Hall periodically descends into dreadful men- 15 tal states. He considers harming himself or develops paranoid fantasies about his colleagues and neighbors. Occasionally, he thinks that plants are communicating with him. (Though in his mother's Native American culture, he points out, this would be valued as an ability to communicate with the spirit world.)

On another night, I had dinner with eight Icarus members at a Thai restau- 16 rant in midtown Manhattan. Over Singha beer, they joked about an imaginary psychoactive medication called Sustain, meant to cure "activist burnout." It was hard to imagine at the dinner what Hall had suffered. While he and his "mad" allies were still clearly outsiders, they had taken their suffering and created from it an all-too-rare thing: a community.

Understanding Meaning

1. How would you define the "Mad Pride" movement?

2. Why do some mental patients reject the definition of their condition as a "disease" and refuse to take prescribed medications?

3. Does the fact that drugs often have serious side effects indicate that the condition they are designed to treat is not serious? Why or why not?

4. *Critical Thinking*: How difficult is it for parents, educators, employers, and medical professionals to determine who is mentally ill and needs intervention and treatment? When is someone "sick" and when is someone simply "different"?

Evaluating Strategy

1. Does the opening quotation make an effective introduction? Why or why not? Is a claim of not wanting to be "normal" bound to grab attention?

2. *Blending the Modes*: How does Quart use *comparison* to develop her article?

3. Quart uses numerous quotations in her essay. Is this an effective device? Why or why not?

Appreciating Language

1. What words do people in the Mad Pride movement use to describe their mental condition? What connotations do these words have? How does the choice of words reframe the definition of mental illness?

2. Look up the word *Icarus* in a dictionary or encyclopedia. Why might people in the Mad Pride movement decide to use this name? What does Icarus represent? Would others associate Icarus with self-destructive recklessness?

3. *Critical Thinking:* People with physical disabilities have rejected words like "invalid" or "cripple," which they believe belittle or degrade them. Is it natural that people with mental issues are sensitive about terms used by society to describe them or their condition?

WRITING SUGGESTIONS

1. Write a short essay examining how groups of people have changed widely held attitudes by changing the words used to define them. Why, for instance, did African Americans reject the word "Negro" during the Civil Rights movement of the 1960s? Why did feminists reject language that defined jobs using male and female terms, arguing that "mailmen," "policemen," and "stewardesses" should be called "letter carriers," "police officers," and "flight attendants"?

2. *Collaborative Writing:* Work with a group of students and develop your own definition of mental illness. When would your group define someone as being sick enough to require professional help? When, for instance, would you contact college administrators, family members, or mental health professionals about a classmate or roommate's behavior?

THOMAS SOWELL

Thomas Sowell (1930–) was born in North Carolina and received a BA in economics from Harvard College in 1958. He received an MA from Columbia University in 1959 and completed his PhD in economics at the University of Chicago in 1968. He has taught at Harvard University, Cornell University, and Amherst College. A syndicated newspaper columnist, Sowell has published over twenty books on education, economics, and public policy. His recent books include Controversial Essays *(2002),* Applied Economics: Thinking Beyond Stage One *(2003),* Affirmative Action Around the World: An Empirical Study *(2004), and* Intellectuals and Society *(2010).*

Needs

CONTEXT: *Sowell examines what politicians and the public mean when they use the word "need." Just what is a "need"?*

A group of UCLA economists were having lunch together one day at the faculty club. One of them, named Mike, got up to get himself some more coffee. Being a decent sort, he asked: 1

"Does anybody else here need coffee?" 2

"Need?!" another economist cried out in astonishment and outrage. 3

The other economists around the table also pounced on this unfortunate word, while poor Mike retreated to the coffee maker, like someone who felt lucky to escape with his life. 4

Partly this was good clean fun—or what passes for good clean fun among economists. But partly it was a very serious issue. 5

Someone is always talking about what we "need"—more child care centers, more medical research, more housing, more environmental protection. The list goes on and on. All the things we "need" would add up to far more than the gross national product. Obviously we cannot and will not get all the things we "need." 6

Why call them "needs" then? We obviously get along without them, simply because we have no choice. These "needs" are simply things we want—or that some of us want. Given that we cannot possibly have all the things we want, we have to make trade-offs. That is what economics is all about. 7

Words like *needs, rights,* or *entitlements* try to put some things on a pedestal, so that they don't have to face the reality of trade-offs. This is part of the higher humbug of politics. 8

Surely some things are really needs, you might say. If that is true, food must be one of those needs, since we would die without it. Huge agricultural surpluses are one result of this kind of mushy thinking. 9

10   There is obviously some amount of food that is urgently required to keep body and soul together. But the average American already takes in far more food than is necessary to sustain life—and in fact so much food as to make his lifespan shorter than it would be at a lower weight.

11   Like virtually everything else, food beyond some point ceases to be as urgently demanded and even ceases to be a benefit. When it reaches the point of being positively harmful, it can hardly be called a "need." That is why rigid words like *need* spread so much confusion in our thinking and havoc in our policies.

12   Prices force us into trade-offs, which is one of many reasons why the marketplace operates so much more efficiently than political allocation according to "need," "entitlement," "priorities" or other such rigid notions.

13   The real issue is almost never whether we should have nothing at all or some unlimited amount, or even some fixed amount of a particular good. The real issue is what kind of trade-off makes sense. That usually means having some of many things but not all we want of anything.

14   Prices tell us what the terms of the trade-offs are. Do we "need" more clothing? At some prices we do and at other prices we can get along with what we have. I happen to own these suits. But if clothing prices were one-tenth of what they are, I might have a wardrobe that would knock you dead.

15   My daughter used to make snide remarks about an old car that I drove for eight years. She stopped only when I told her that I could easily afford to get a new car, just by not paying her tuition. That's what trade-offs are all about.

16   If the government were giving out cars to those who "needed" them, I could have written an application that would have brought tears to your eyes. I could have gone on talk shows and worked up public sympathy over the ways my old jalopy was messing up my life—even threatening my life because the brakes failed completely twice.

17   If the taxpayers were paying for it, I would have "needed" a new car. But, since it was my money that was being spent, I had a brake job instead.

18   Politicians take advantage of our mushy thinking by promising to meet our "need" or by giving us a "right" or "entitlement" to this or that. But let's go back to square one. Politicians don't manufacture anything except hot air. Every "need" they meet takes away from some other "need" somewhere else.

19   Every job the government creates is supported by resources taken out of the private sector, where those same resources could have created another job— or maybe two other jobs, given the wastefulness of government.

20   "Needs" are a dangerous concept. Mike the economist suffered only a momentary embarrassment from using the word. Our whole economy and

society suffer much more from the mindless policies based on such misconceptions.

Understanding Meaning

1. How does Sowell define a *need*? How does a need differ from something we want? According to Sowell, why can't we get all the things we *need*?

2. Why does Sowell view *needs* as a *dangerous concept*?

3. How, in Sowell's view, does the word *need* cause *confusion in our thinking and havoc in our policies* (paragraph 11)?

4. Why does Sowell believe it is important to understand *prices* and *trade-offs* when considering needs?

5. *Critical Thinking:* How does the observation that Americans regard as necessities what other people view as luxuries fit into Sowell's thesis? Do many Americans define cars, TVs, computers, and cell phones as necessities?

Evaluating Strategy

1. What is the purpose of Sowell's opening narrative? How does it illustrate or introduce his point?

2. How does Sowell use his old car as an example to explain his point about needs and trade-offs?

3. What methods does Sowell use to establish his definition of need?

Appreciating Language

1. How does Sowell distinguish between a *need* and a *want*? Why is it important to understand the difference?

2. What does Sowell mean when he states that "Words like *needs*, *rights*, or *entitlements* try to put some things on a pedestal"? How do politicians use these words to make policy? If something is defined as a *right*, does that imply that it must be made available to every citizen even if he or she cannot pay for it?

WRITING SUGGESTIONS

1. Using Sowell's essay as a model, examine the definition of another concept such as *right*, *privilege*, *friend*, *patriotism*, or *duty*. What things do you define as basic rights that should be guaranteed to all citizens? What

is a privilege? Why do parents and driving instructors, for example, remind young people that driving is a *privilege* and not a *right*?

2. *Collaborative Writing:* Work with a group of students to explore personal definitions of a need. Ask each student to write down what they consider *needs* and compare lists. Are people's political beliefs directly related to what they define as a *need*?

JOSEPH C. PHILLIPS

Joseph C. Phillips (1962–) is an actor, writer, and social commentator. He appeared on The Cosby Show *from 1989 to 1991 and in several films, including* Strictly Business, Midnight Blue, *and* Let's Talk About Sex. *A syndicated newspaper columnist, Phillips has also written pieces for* Newsweek, Essence, Upscale, *and* USA Today. *He is also a regular contributor to the* Tavis Smiley Radio Show *broadcast on National Public Radio. He published his autobiography* He Talk Like A White Boy *in 2006.*

Who is Black?

CONTEXT: *In this opening passage from* He Talk Like a White Boy, *Phillips analyzes the definition of what it means to be black in America.*

Let me take you back—September 1974. A little Seals & Crofts playing on 1 the AM transistor radio, maybe some Three Dog Night. Denver, Colorado. This is where my story begins. Like so many autumn afternoons in Denver, the brightness of the sun belies the crisp chill in the air. Place Junior High school, eighth grade English class—not just regular English mind you, but *accelerated* English class. My teacher was Miss Smith. Her class stands in my mind as a monument, a shrine to all that is cold and cruel about this world.

I don't remember what the class discussion was about, but after an undoubt- 2 edly brilliant and insightful observation on my part, a black girl from across the room raised her hand and announced to the class, "He talk like a white boy!"

I don't know what this had to do with the discussion or why she felt the 3 need to share that little observation with the rest of the class. But one thing I do know is that in an accelerated English class, the teacher should have corrected her immediately.

"No, LaQueesha. Joseph speaks like a white boy! Class, repeat after me. 4 'Joseph speaks like a white boy.' Now, LaQueesha, you try."

"Miss Smith, Joseph speaks like a white boy!" 5

"Very good." 6

Bam! I was thrust into the spotlight. (And me not even knowin' how to 7 tap dance!)

What did LaQueesha mean? That I spoke clearly? Intelligently? That some 8 timbre was missing from my voice? At twelve, should one have timbre? I didn't know then and still don't know now. But that moment was not only the beginning of junior high school, it was the beginning of my life.

9   The man I am today has its genesis in that moment. In that instant I became acutely aware that I was different. Until that moment, I never realized there was something wrong with the way I spoke, that answering questions in class was acting "white."

10   I never knew how ugly, or hurtful, the words "Uncle Tom" were. In that moment, the tyranny of opinion—the notion that there are some people empowered to stand at the doors of a culture and determine who and who is not welcome—was made painfully clear to me. My definition of blackness—more accurately, my black self—was unimportant. That decision was left to the anointed, and no matter how idiotic, arcane, or nihilistic their definition, any deviation would be dealt with swiftly and decisively.

11   So there you have it. At the tender age of twelve, with no warning whatsoever, my membership credentials to the brotherhood were confiscated and ripped to shreds. The mere difference in how I spoke—the sound of my voice, my diction—clearly meant that I was trying to be something I wasn't, that I was an infiltrator, and that difference, real or perceived, made me an outsider.

12   I have been writing a weekly column for more than three years. During that time, I have occasionally received mail from people who disagree with me. The letters are mostly polite, even if they sometimes strain for that politeness. Like other folks who decide to offer their opinions for public scrutiny, I have also received my share of correspondence that is not so polite. The comments range in anger from "you have no idea who you are" and "your thoughts are dangerous to black people" to being called "Stepin Fetchit," a reference to the black film actor, Lincoln Perry, who was known for playing subservient shuffling servants to white masters in the 1920s, '30s, and '40s. I recently received an email from a group called Conscious Black Citizens for Negro Reform informing me that I had been nominated for the Sambo/Uncle Tom of the Year Award. According to the group's email, their objective is to "out" politicians, entertainers, and other public figures who are betraying the race.

13   It would appear that things have not changed all that much since eighth grade. These charges are quite frequently leveled anonymously and rarely, if ever, do they address the substance of whatever I allegedly said that makes me a traitor. Like the little girl in my eighth grade English class, they are content to simply comment on my lack of adherence to their definition of blackness. In their minds, I no longer *speak* like a white boy, I now *think* like a white boy.

14   The hazard with this type of collectivism is that the bar is always moving. An editor for one of the papers that publishes my column took offense at an essay I wrote in defense of a local proposition that would have outlawed California's collection of racial data. In the article, I made an appeal to begin taking steps to move beyond the artificial construct of race. For this gatekeeper, my stance was anti-black and unworthy of publication (though she was

outvoted by her editorial board and my piece was allowed to run as scheduled in spite of her objections). What does it say when appeals for brotherhood, once a mantra of the Yippie generation, are now deemed traitorous? It is a fool's game, one that honest men cannot win.

The criticism has also come from sources much closer to home. My older 15 sister, Lisa, whom I love dearly, tells me, "I'm ashamed to tell people that my little brother is a Republican!" She doesn't understand how my wife can bear to sleep with me. I have a younger sister who has alternately been a lesbian, a drug addict, in and out of mental hospitals, and on the run from debt collectors most of her adult life. But I have never heard Lisa say to her, "I am ashamed of you," or "I don't know how your husband sleeps with you." (Somewhere between the lesbianism and the drug addiction, baby sister decided she had to get married. It's all very complicated.) But *me* she is ashamed of.

Of course, I am a rather minor player in the cultural scheme of things and 16 I suspect very few people have ever heard of the Conscious Black Citizens for Negro Reform, nor are they likely to. I am also fairly certain that if push came to shove, my older sister would prefer me to be a Republican than a drug addict. At any rate, this is a microcosm of what happens in larger society.

Witness the treatment of Ward Connerly, the University of California re- 17 gent who authored and pushed through Proposition 209, the initiative that outlawed affirmative action in California. For daring to question the morality of affirmative action quotas and insisting that black children are capable of competing with white children, Connerly was called everything but a child of God. During a debate with then–California State Senator Dianne Watson (now congresswoman), the senator accused Connerly of being ashamed of his heritage, proof of which could be found in his marriage to a white woman. I had a discussion with another editor about a piece in which I only mentioned Connerly's name. The editor said that Connerly wakes up in the morning looking for ways to deny opportunities to black people. This editor added, "I hope he burns in hell." Pretty strong stuff.

John McWhorter, a former linguistics professor at Berkeley and a black 18 man, wrote a book entitled *Losing the Race: Self-Sabotage in Black America*. The *New York Times* review of his book concluded he really hadn't been exposed to African-American culture and was therefore not black enough to write about black people with authority. A fellow professor denounced him as a "rent-a-Negro." Shelby Steele, who had the temerity to suggest that current black leadership had grown rich on the currency of race, is sneered at. Walter Williams and Thomas Sowell, the economists who, among other things, have argued that the black middle class did not spring from affirmative action or the welfare state, are routinely ignored by the mainstream press and were miraculously not included in a list of public intellectuals compiled by "race expert" Michael Eric Dyson in his book *Race Rules*.

During a debate sponsored by the Maryland chapter of the NAACP, Republican candidate for lieutenant governor Mike Steele was pelted with Oreo cookies, referencing the Cabinet choices made by George W. Bush. Liberal attorney and talk-show host Gloria Allred referred to Colin Powell and Condoleezza Rice as "Uncle Tom types." And need we even begin to address the black community's complete ostracizing of Clarence Thomas, an associate justice on the United States Supreme Court?

19   The black monthly magazine *Ebony* refuses to include Justice Thomas on their list of "100 Most Influential Black Americans." One could easily make the argument that he is perhaps the *most* influential black person in America. The decisions he makes every day affect black Americans far more than the rather mundane edicts handed down by the heads of the black fraternities and sororities that are regularly included on the list. In an episode that displayed the utter absurdity of this thinking, an elementary school in Washington D.C. asked that Justice Thomas not appear at the school to speak to the children. Apparently a number of parents complained that he was not a proper role model. The schools had no such complaints, however, when they invited the crack-addicted, philandering former mayor of D.C., Marion Barry. Yep. Much better that the children should hear from a real black hero like Marion Barry than from a tyrant like Clarence Thomas—*Uncle* Thomas, as he is routinely referred to by black "leaders" like Al Sharpton.

20   The substance of the ideas put forth by these men is rarely argued. Their characters however, are routinely attacked and maligned. They are threatened with death! They aren't black. They are Toms, one and all! They are traitors to the race because they have chosen to think outside of the accepted black liberal dogma. They are—hide the women and children—CONSERVATIVES!

21   What remains unclear is who anointed these folks the right to stand at the door checking ideological credentials and confiscating the cultural membership cards of those who refuse to hoe rows on the liberal plantation? From whom do they get their authority? Quite simply, they have no authority except that which we grant to them.

Understanding Meaning

1. What did the statement "he talk like a white boy" reveal to Joseph Phillips?

2. What does Phillips mean by the "tyranny of opinion"?

3. How did Phillips begin to feel like an "outsider" or "infiltrator" in his own community?

4. Which African Americans, in Phillips' view, are labeled "Uncle Toms" and why? What does the term imply?

5. Why does Phillips' believe that *Ebony* magazine does not include Supreme Court Justice Clarence Thomas in its list of "100 Most Influential Black Americans"?

6. *Critical Thinking:* Do other groups have definitions of who should and should not be considered members? Do people have fixed definitions, for example, of what it means to be Jewish, Christian, Muslim, American, or patriotic? Do religious extremists, for instance, dismiss moderates as not being "real Christians" or not believing in the "true Islam"? How do people use definition as a way of repudiating opponents?

Evaluating Strategy

1. How does Phillips illustrate the way many African Americans define being black?

2. What objective facts does Phillips include to support his thesis?

3. Phillips lists a number of prominent African Americans who are labeled Uncle Toms. How does this support his point of view?

4. *Blending the Modes:* How does Phillips use *example* and *comparison* to develop his essay?

Appreciating Language

1. What does the term "Uncle Tom" mean? How does Phillips believe the term is used to enforce a common definition of blackness in America?

2. Phillips uses the term "membership credentials" and "membership cards" in relation to black identity. What is he saying about the definition of being black? Is he implying that people are not identified as being black by having black parents but by sharing a common set of beliefs or attitudes?

WRITING SUGGESTIONS

1. Write an essay about the importance of definition in cultural identity. Is being Jewish a religious or ethnic identity? Can someone be both an atheist and a Jew? Does someone have to attend a mosque and follow strict patterns of prayer and diet to be a Muslim? Who is more Hispanic, the first-generation Mexican American who does not speak Spanish or the Spanish speaker with only a single Hispanic grandparent? How does definition shape a community's identity, culture, and politics?

2. *Collaborative Writing:* Work with a group of students and conduct a simple exercise in definition. Ask the group to define who they consider a student. Would they limit their definition to include only full-time students? Would they consider someone taking a single noncredit computer class one night a week a student? If your college offered discount health insurance for students, who, in your group's view, should be eligible? If members of the group disagree, consider using comparison to craft opposing definitions or using classification to rank the most limited definition to the most liberal.

BLENDING THE MODES

MARIE WINN

Marie Winn was born in Czechoslovakia and grew up in New York. After completing her education at Radcliffe College, Winn began a career in publishing, writing and editing a number of children's books. While working with children's literature, she explored the effects television has on childhood development. She has written extensively on children and television, publishing articles in the New York Times *and* Village Voice. *In 1977 she published an influential study,* The Plug-In Drug: Television, Children and Family, *which was revised in 1985. Her other books include* Children without Childhood *(1983),* Unplugging the Plug-In Drug *(1987),* The Secret Life of Central Park *(1997), and* Red-Tails in Love: A Wildlife Drama in Central Park *(1998). In 2002 Winn published a 25th anniversary edition of* The Plug-In Drug *subtitled* Television, Computers, and Family Life.

TV Addiction

CONTEXT: *In building her case that television has negative effects, Winn first defines the term "addiction," then argues that television, like drugs and alcohol, damages those who allow it to consume their lives. Notice how Winn uses* narration, description, analysis, *and* cause and effect *to develop her definition.*

Cookies or Heroin?

The word "addiction" is often used loosely and wryly in conversation. People 1
will refer to themselves as "mystery-book addicts" or "cookie addicts."
E. B. White wrote of his annual surge of interest in gardening: "We are hooked
and are making an attempt to kick the habit." Yet nobody really believes that
reading mysteries or ordering seeds by catalogue is serious enough to be compared with addictions to heroin or alcohol. In these cases the word "addiction" is used jokingly to denote a tendency to overindulge in some pleasurable
activity.

People often refer to being "hooked on TV." Does this, too, fall into the 2
lighthearted category of cookie eating and other pleasures that people pursue
with unusual intensity? Or is there a kind of television viewing that falls into
the more serious category of destructive addiction?

Not unlike drugs or alcohol, the television experience allows the partic- 3
ipant to blot out the real world and enter into a pleasurable and passive
mental state. To be sure, other experiences, notably reading, also provide a
temporary respite from reality. But it's much easier to stop reading and
return to reality than to stop watching television. The entry into another
world offered by reading includes an easily accessible return ticket. The

entry via television does not. In this way television viewing, for those vulnerable to addiction, is more like drinking or taking drugs—once you start
it's hard to stop.

4   Just as alcoholics are only vaguely aware of their addiction, feeling that
they control their drinking more than they really do ("I can cut it out any
time I want—I just like to have three or four drinks before dinner"), many
people overestimate their control over television watching. Even as they put
off other activities to spend hour after hour watching television, they feel they
could easily resume living in a different, less passive style. But somehow or
other while the television set is present in their homes, it just stays on. With
television's easy gratifications available, those other activities seem to take too
much effort.

5   A heavy viewer (a college English instructor) observes:

> I find television almost irresistible. When the set is on, I cannot ig-
> nore it. I can't turn it off. I feel sapped, will-less, enervated. As I
> reach out to turn off the set, the strength goes out of my arms. So I
> sit there for hours and hours.

6   Self-confessed television addicts often feel they "ought" to do other
things—but the fact that they don't read and don't plant their garden or sew
or crochet or play games or have conversations means that those activities
are no longer as desirable as television viewing. In a way, the lives of heavy
viewers are as unbalanced by their television "habit" as drug addicts' or alcoholics' lives. They are living in a holding pattern, as it were, passing up
the activities that lead to growth or development or a sense of accomplishment. This is one reason people talk about their television viewing so rue-
fully, so apologetically. They are aware that it is an unproductive experience, that by any human measure almost any other endeavor is more
worthwhile.

7   It is the adverse effect of television viewing on the lives of so many people that makes it feel like a serious addiction. The television habit distorts
the sense of time. It renders other experiences vague and curiously unreal
while taking on a greater reality for itself. It weakens relationships by reducing and sometimes eliminating normal opportunities for talking, for communicating.

8   And yet television does not satisfy, else why would the viewer continue to
watch hour after hour, day after day? "The measure of health," wrote
the psychiatrist Lawrence Kubie, "is flexibility ... and especially the freedom
to cease when sated." But heavy television viewers can never be sated with
their television experiences. These do not provide the true nourishment that
satiation requires, and thus they find that they cannot stop watching.

A former heavy watcher, a filmmaker, describes a debilitating television 9 habit:

> I remember when we first got the set I'd watch for hours and hours, whenever I could, and I remember that feeling of tiredness and anxiety that always followed those orgies, a sense of time terribly wasted. It was like eating cotton candy; television promised so much richness, I couldn't wait for it, and then it just evaporated into air. I remember feeling terribly drained after watching for a long time.

Similarly a nursery-school teacher remembers her own childhood television 10 experience:

> I remember bingeing on television when I was a child and having that vapid feeling after watching hours of TV. I'd look forward to watching whenever I could, but it just didn't give back a real feeling of pleasure. It was like no orgasm, no catharsis, very frustrating. Television just wasn't giving me the promised satisfaction, and yet I kept on watching. It filled some sort of need, or had to do with an inability to get something started.

The testimonies of ex–television addicts often have the evangelistic over- 11 tones of stories heard at Alcoholics Anonymous meetings.

A handbag repair-shop owner says: 12

> I'd get on the subway home from work with the newspaper and immediately turn to the TV page to plan out my evening's watching. I'd come home and then we'd watch TV for the rest of the evening. We'd eat our dinner in the living room while watching, and we'd only talk every once in a while, during the ads, if at all. I'd watch anything, good, bad, or indifferent.
>
> All the while we were watching I'd feel terribly angry at myself for wasting all that time watching junk. I could never go to sleep until at least the eleven o'clock news, and then sometimes I'd still stay up for the late-night talk show. I had a feeling that I *had* to watch the news programs, even though most of the time nothing much was happening and I could easily find out what by reading the paper the next morning. Usually my wife would fall asleep on the couch while I was watching. I'd get angry at her for doing that. Actually, I was angry at myself.
>
> I had a collection of three years of back issues of different magazines, but I never got around to reading them. I never got around to

sorting or labeling my collection of slides I had made when traveling. I only had time for television. We'd take the telephone off the
hook while watching so we wouldn't be interrupted! We like classical music, but we never listened to any, never!

Then one day the set broke. I said to my wife, "Let's not fix it.
Let's just see what happens." Well, that was the smartest thing we
ever did. We haven't had a TV in the house since then.

Now I look back and I can hardly believe we could have lived
like that. I feel that my mind was completely mummified for all
those years. I was glued to that machine and couldn't get
loose, somehow. It really frightens me to think of it. Yes, I'm
frightened of TV now. I don't think I could control it if we had
a set in the house again. I think it would take over no matter
what I did.

13   Heavy television viewers often make comparisons between their viewing
habits and substance addictions. Several decades ago, a lawyer reported:

> I watch TV the way an alcoholic drinks. If I come home and sit
> in front of the TV, I'll watch any program at all, even if there's
> nothing on that especially appeals to me. Then the next thing I
> know it's eleven o'clock and I'm watching the Johnny Carson
> show, and I'll realize I've spent the whole evening watching TV.
> What's more, I can't stand Johnny Carson! But I'll still sit there
> watching him. I'm addicted to TV, when it's there, and I'm not
> happy about the addiction. I'll sit there getting madder and mad-
> der at myself for watching, but still I'll sit there. I can't turn it off.

14   Nor is the television addict always blind to the dysfunctional aspects of his
addiction. A homemaker says:

> Sometimes a friend will come over while I'm watching TV. I'll say,
> "Wait a second. Just let me finish watching this," and then I'll feel
> bad about that, letting the machine take precedence over people.
> And I'll do that for the stupidest programs, just because I *have* to
> watch, somehow.

15   In spite of the potentially destructive nature of television addiction, it is
rarely taken seriously in American society. Critics mockingly refer to television as a "cultural barbiturate" and joke about "mainlining the tube."
A spectacle called *Media Burn* perfectly illustrates the feeling of good fun

that often surrounds the issue of television addiction. The event, which took place in San Francisco when television was still a young medium, involved the piling up of forty-four old television sets in the parking lot of the Cow Palace, soaking them with kerosene, and applying a torch. According to the programs distributed before the event, everybody was supposed to experience "a cathartic explosion" and "be free at last from the addiction to television."

The issue of television addiction takes on a more serious air when the 16 addicts are our own children. A mother reports:

> My ten-year-old is as hooked on TV as an alcoholic is hooked on drink. He tries to strike desperate bargains: "If you let me watch just ten more minutes, I won't watch at all tomorrow," he says. It's pathetic. It scares me.

A number of years ago a mother described her six-year-old son's need to 17 watch:

> We were in Israel last summer where the TV stations sign off for the night at about ten. Well, my son would turn on the set and watch the Arabic stations that were still on, even though he couldn't understand a word, just because he had to watch *something*.

Other signs of serious addiction come out in parents' descriptions of their 18 children's viewing behavior:

> We used to have very bad reception before we got on Cable TV. I'd come into the room and see my eight-year-old watching this terrible, blurry picture and I'd say, "Heavens, how can you see? Let me try to fix it," and he'd get frantic and scream, "Don't touch it!" It really worried me, that he wanted to watch so badly that he was even willing to watch a completely blurred image.

Another mother tells of her eight-year-old son's behavior when deprived 19 of television:

> There was a time when both TV sets were out for about two weeks, and Jerry reached a point where I felt that if he didn't watch something, he was really going to start climbing the walls. He was fidgety and nervous. He'd crawl all over the furniture. He just didn't know what to do with himself, and it seemed to get

worse every day. I said to my husband, "He's having withdrawal symptoms," and I really think that's what it was. Finally I asked one of my friends if he could go and watch the Saturday cartoons at their house.

20   In the early 1980s Robin Smith, a graduate student at the University of Massachusetts in Amherst, conducted a research study on television addiction as part of a doctoral dissertation. Setting out to discover whether television viewing can truly be classified as an addiction according to a particular, narrow definition she had constructed from the work of various social scientists, Smith sent out a questionnaire to 984 adults in Springfield, Massachusetts, in which they were asked to rate their own behavior in regard to television viewing. Using a number of statistical tests to analyze the responses, the author concluded that the results failed to confirm that television addiction exists. "Television addiction does not appear to be a robust phenomenon," Smith wrote in that poetic yet obscure way academics sometimes have of expressing things.

21   Striving to understand why television is so widely considered an addiction, in the conclusion of her research paper Smith noted:

> ... the popularity of television as "plug-in drug" is enduring. One possible source of this image lies in the nature of viewing experience. The only study to date that examines the nature of the viewing experience in adults found that television watching, of all life activities measured in the course of one week, was the least challenging, involved the least amount of skill, and was most relaxing.

22   If television viewing is so bereft of value by most measures of well-being, and yet takes up the greatest part of people's leisure hours, it becomes moot whether it is defined as an addiction or simply a powerful habit. As psychologists Robert Kubey and Mihaly Csikszentmihalyi concluded in their book about the television experience: "A long-held habit becomes so ingrained that it borders on addiction. A person may no longer be watching television because of simple want, but because he or she virtually has to. Other alternatives may seem to become progressively more remote. What might have been a choice years earlier is now a necessity."

23   Robert Kubey explains further: "While television can provide relaxation and entertainment . . . it still rarely delivers any lasting fulfillment. Only through active engagement with the worlds we inhabit and the people in them can we attain for ourselves the rewards and meaning that lead to psychological well-being."

Understanding Meaning

1. How does Winn define "addiction"? How does addiction, in her view, differ from overindulgence in something pleasurable?

2. Describe the negative effects Winn sees in habitual television viewing.

3. How does the simple ease and accessibility of watching television versus going out to a movie contribute to making television so addictive?

4. One viewer Winn quotes states, "I had the feeling that I *had* to watch the news programs, that I *had* to know what was happening." Today are more people likely to feel almost obligated to watch television to be informed, to be a good citizen? Can the news be as dangerously addicting as entertainment shows?

5. *Critical Thinking:* Do you think that many of Winn's observations about television addiction describe people who feel compelled to spend hours on the Internet? Can cyberspace be just as addictive and just as harmful?

Evaluating Strategy

1. Why is it important for Winn to first define "addiction" before moving to her argument about television?

2. How effective is her use of interviews or case studies of television viewers? Is it important to hear from the "addicts" in their own words?

3. *Blending the Modes:* How much of this definition essay can be considered a *persuasive argument*? What role do *description*, *narration*, and *cause and effect* play in developing the definition?

Appreciating Language

1. Winn quotes one viewer who reports that television leaves him "sapped, will-less, enervated." How important are words like these to argue that television is addictive?

2. Winn repeatedly uses the word "sated." Look this up in a dictionary. Why is it a key word in defining an addiction?

3. *Critical Thinking:* Would some people object to applying the word "addiction" to an activity that is not life threatening? Drugs and alcohol, after all, lead to disease and early death. Does using the term in other contexts weaken its impact?

WRITING SUGGESTIONS

1. Write a short analysis of your own childhood experiences with television. How many hours did you watch a day? What were your favorite programs?

Did television add or detract from your development? Did you forgo studying, playing with other children, reading, or spending time with your family to watch television?

2. *Collaborative Writing:* Working with a group of other students, write a paper instructing parents step by step about how to monitor their children's viewing habits. How can parents prevent their children from becoming television addicts?

WRITING BEYOND THE CLASSROOM: TWO DEFINITIONS OF DEPRESSION

Definition is a critical feature of all professional writing. Professionals need common standards in order to communicate and operate efficiently. The way definitions are expressed depends on the writer's goal, the audience, and the discipline.

THE ENCYCLOPEDIA OF PSYCHOLOGY

CONTEXT: *This definition is taken from a specialized encyclopedia designed for mental health professionals. As a standard reference, it seeks to establish a common understanding of terms for people who must diagnose and treat patients with psychological problems.*

Depression

Description

In the United States, the word "depression" refers to everything from a transient mood state (feeling down) to the clinical disorder known as Major Depressive Disorder (MDD). In order to receive a diagnosis of MDD, a person must experience marked distress and a decrease in level of functioning. In addition, the two weeks preceding the examination must be characterized by the almost daily occurrence of a dysphoric mood (e.g., sadness) or a loss of interest or pleasure (anhedonia) in almost all activities. The individual must also experience at least four (only three if both dysphoric mood and anhedonia are both present) of the following seven symptoms nearly every day for the two week period: (a) significant weight change or change in appetite; (b) insomnia or hypersomnia; (c) psychomotor agitation or retardation; (d) fatigue or loss of energy; (e) feelings of worthlessness or of excessive or inappropriate guilt; (f) decreased concentration or indecisiveness; and (g) suicidal ideation, plan, or attempt (see American Psychiatric Association, 1994). Related disorders (i.e., other mood disorders) include Bipolar I and II (Manic-Depressive Disorder), dysthymia, and cyclothymia.

Prevalence and Costs

Major Depressive Disorder (MDD) is the most commonly diagnosed psychiatric disorder among adults, with lifetime prevalence rates of 20 to 25 percent for women and 9 to 12 percent for men. At any given point in time, the prevalence rates are about 6 percent for women and 3 percent for men. MDD is fairly rare among children, but it begins to manifest itself at puberty. Depression has been diagnosed with increased frequency among young people, so that in the current 16-to-25 age group, about 20 percent have already suffered from MDD. After late adolescence, the prevalence rates and gender differences are fairly constant over the human life span.

Depression tends to be a cyclical disorder. Among those who have had one episode, the probability of a second episode is 50 percent, and among those who have had two episodes, the probability of a third episode is 75 to 80 percent. After the third episode, the disorder is likely to plague the person on a chronic basis, though episodes of the disorder may come and go even without treatment. The episodes are painful both for the individuals with the disorder and for those around them. As noted, the disorder interferes with functioning in social and work situations. The costs are enormous to both the individual and society; for example, MDD is nearly always rated among the top five most expensive health problems.

DON D. ROSENBERG

CONTEXT: *This definition, written by a practicing psychologist, appeared in a brochure distributed in the waiting room of a Milwaukee mental health clinic. It is directed to the general public and seeks to explain the nature of depression to people seeking help for psychological problems they may have difficulty understanding.*

What is Depression?

Depression is <u>an internal state—a feeling of sadness, loss, "the blues," deep disappointment</u>. When it is more severe, you may have feelings of irritability, touchiness, guilt, self-reproach, loss of self-esteem, worthlessness, hopelessness, helplessness, and even thoughts of death and suicide. It may include such other feelings as <u>tearfulness, being sensitive and easily hurt, loss of interests, loss of sexual drive, loss of control in life, feeling drained and depleted, anger at yourself, and loss of the ability to feel pleasure.</u>

It may be accompanied by *physical symptoms* similar to the sense of profound loss, including:

* *loss of appetite*, often with weight loss, but sometimes we find increased eating

* *insomnia or early morning waking*, often 2–4 times per night, nearly every day, but sometimes we see a need to sleep excessively

* moving and speaking slows down, but sometimes we see *agitation*

* *fatigue or loss of energy* nearly every day

* *loss of concentration*, foggy and indecisive

* Sometimes it includes anxious and headachy feelings and also *frequent crying*.

Besides the <u>physical sensations</u> and <u>emotions of depression</u>, depressed people may *withdraw, may brood or ruminate about problems*, have trouble remembering things, wonder if they would be better off dead, and become very concerned about bodily symptoms and pains. They may be grouchy, sulking, restless, and unwilling to interact with family and friends.

Understanding Meaning

1. *The Encyclopedia of Psychology* is a reference text for mental health students and professionals. What is the purpose of its definition? How does

its definition differ from the clinic's definition, which is aimed at the general public?

2. What role does definition play in the treatment of any disorder? How is addressing professionals different from addressing potential patients?

3. Which are the objective statements in both definitions? Do both definitions agree on the basic elements of depression?

4. How does the brochure address its readers differently from the encyclopedia?

5. *Blending the Modes:* What *persuasive* elements are used in the brochure?

Evaluating Strategy

1. The brochure by Don Rosenberg uses italics, underlining, and asterisks for highlighting. What functions do these have? Discuss their suitability.

2. How does the brochure direct its message to the public and potential patients?

Appreciating Language

1. Does the purpose of the definition dictate the tone of the language in these two examples? Does the encyclopedia's *description* focus on objective, observable symptoms? Does the brochure seem to focus on feelings and emotions?

2. Would the language of the encyclopedia appear cold and unfeeling to a patient seeking help with depression?

WRITING SUGGESTIONS

1. Take a definition from the glossary section of a textbook, and write a version for a general audience of clients, consumers, or students.

2. Using information from the encyclopedia and brochure, write a definition of depression targeted to college students. Describe symptoms in terms students will readily identify.

3. *Collaborative Writing:* Discuss a common problem or issue with fellow students: job insecurity, lack of sleep, stressful family relationships, child care, or the fear of crime. Select a term you often overhear, and provide a clear definition for it. Have each member of the group list features of this term. Try to incorporate objective elements. Write the definition in two versions: one designed for an "official" publication such as the college catalog or textbook, the other for an informal handout.

RESPONDING TO IMAGES

ANTI-GAY MARRIAGE PROTEST IN BOSTON, 2004

1. What is your first impression of this photograph? Do you find this an effective form of protest? Does use of a 1 + 1 = _____ argument make a strong point or does it seem simplistic?

2. How important are definitions in law and public policy? How should our society define concepts such as marriage, stalking, child neglect, obscenity, or discrimination?

3. *Visual Analysis:* Note the wording of the sign. What connotations does the word "preserve" have? Does it imply that traditional marriage is imperiled? Would signs with negative messages be less effective?

4. *Critical Thinking:* Clearly the man in the photograph is holding his sign to the camera. In a visual society, do people feel they must condense their

points to something that can be captured on a billboard, website, or bumper sticker? Does it reduce complex ideas to simple phrases and sound bites?

5. *Collaborative Writing:* Working with a group of students, select a current political or social issue and discuss the role definition plays. Identify opposing points of view and write a definition statement that expresses each position. How, for instance, do people who argue over free speech define obscenity? How do people who debate gun control define the "right to bear arms"?

STRATEGIES FOR WRITING DEFINITIONS

1. **Determine your purpose.** Does your definition seek to provide a common language to prevent confusion, or does it seek to persuade readers by altering their perceptions?

2. **Define your role.** Your definition can be based on personal observation and opinion or standard principles and methods followed in a specific discipline or profession.

3. **Consider your audience.** What knowledge base do your readers have? Your definition should offer recognizable examples in language they will understand. Determine what uses your audience has for this definition. Will readers have to base decisions on your definition?

4. **Make extended definitions relevant.** Extended definitions depend on examples, illustrations, and narratives. The items you include to explain your topic should be relevant and understandable to your audience.

5. **Review special needs of the discipline or writing situation.** Each discipline can have a distinct history, research methodology, and set of concerns. Make sure your definition respects any special interests and addresses special needs.

6. **Use or refer to existing definitions.** Instead of attempting to create your own definition, you can adopt an existing one. If you accept the American Psychological Association's definition of *obsession*, you can simply restate the definition for readers. In using existing definitions, acknowledge their sources. If you disagree with an existing or official definition, restate it and then demonstrate how your interpretation differs.

7. **Make sure you *define* and not merely *describe* your topic.** Descriptions present information about a particular person, place, object, idea, or situation. Definitions must provide information about a "type" of person, place, object, idea, or situation.

8. **Include a clearly stated definition statement.** Definitions usually have a one-sentence statement that concisely summarizes the author's point: "Dyslexia ... is the inability of otherwise normal children to read." The statement can be placed at the opening or the closing of the essay.

SUGGESTED TOPICS FOR WRITING DEFINITIONS

GENERAL ASSIGNMENTS

Write a definition on any of the following topics. Your definition will probably contain other modes, such as *description*, *comparison*, and *narration*. Choose your terminology carefully, and avoid using words with misleading connotations. When defining complex and abstract concepts, consider defining extremes and then working toward the middle.

1. A successful professional in your career; define a good defense attorney, computer programmer, nurse, or teacher

2. A good relationship

3. Sexual harassment

4. Addiction

5. The perfect career

6. An educated person

7. A healthy lifestyle

8. The level of insanity at which a person should not be held criminally liable for his or her actions

9. A social problem or issue such as racial profiling, identity theft, elder abuse, or truancy

10. A hero or role model

WRITING IN CONTEXT

1. Imagine you have been asked to write a brief brochure about college life to be distributed to disadvantaged students at a high school. The principal stresses that she fears many of her students lack independent study skills and the discipline needed to succeed in college. Define the characteristics of a good college student, stressing hard work.

2. You have been asked to participate in a panel on sexual harassment. In preparation, provide two definitions of sexual harassment: one expressing attitudes, feelings, and statements you have observed and heard from males on campus, the other expressing attitudes, feelings, and emotions you have observed and heard from females. Try to be as objective as possible, and state any differences fairly.

Student Paper: Definition

This paper was written in response to the following assignment:

Invent a definition for a social issue or problem you have experienced. You may support your definition with factual research or personal observation. Make sure your paper clearly defines the subject and does not simply describe it.

First Draft with Instructor's Comments

Fathers are probably the most important people our lives   *delete; too general*

except may be for our mothers. They are supposed to teach us a

    maybe

lot. But my father was kind of a disappointment.   *vague*

Consider a stronger, tighter opening that gets to the point

    Like half the members of my generation, I am the product of

what used to be called a "broken home." My parents divorced when

I was eight. I lived with my mother all the time and would see

my father every other weekend. And every summer my dad took me

on a vacation lasting two weeks. *wordy, condense*

    My father, like many of his generation, was a Disneyland dad.

He always arrived on time, brought me stuff, and took me to places

I wanted. He bought me a lot of clothes and toys and gave me things

my mother would not get for me. He was always kind and generous.

But I found it disappointing that he gave me things and took me

places he never really acted like a real Dad. I think divorced   *redundant run-on* dads can be generous and responsible when it comes to paying

bills. I know my dad always came through when my mom told him she

needed money for us. When we needed school clothes or had to see

to the dentist he sent my mom extra money without any problems.

comma

But even so my Dad <u>never really acted like a real</u> Dad. He

have

redundant could <u>of</u> done so much more. Looking back, I really feel cheated.

My dad was there for me but he never acted like a real father just

a Disneyland Dad.

run on

REVISION NOTES

This paper is a <u>description</u>, not a <u>definition</u>. A description provides details about an individual person, place, or thing. Definition presents details about a type of person, place, or thing. You call your father a "Disneyland Dad." What exactly is a Disneyland Dad? You need to define that term. You can use your father as an illustrative example. Make sure your essay contains a clear definition of a "Disneyland Dad" that readers will be able to understand. For instance, Janice Castro defines "Spanglish" as "a free form of English and Spanish."

Revised Draft

Disneyland Dads

Like half the members of generation, I am the product of what used to be called a "broken home." My parents divorced when I was eight. I lived with my mother and saw my father on alternate week-ends and for two weeks during the summer.

My father, like many of his generation, was a classic Disney-land Dad. The Disneyland Dad is usually found at malls, little league fields, upscale pizza restaurants, and ice cream parlors. He is usually accompanied by a child busily eating food forbidden by Mom, wearing new clothes, or playing with expensive toys. The Disneyland Dad dispenses cash like an ATM and provides an endless supply of quarters for arcade games. Whether they are motivated by guilt, frustration, or an inability to parent, Disneyland Dads substitute material items for fatherly advice, guidance, and discipline.

While my mother furnished the hands-on, day-to-day parenting, my father remained silent. My mother monitored my eating habits, my friends, my grades, even the programs I watched on television. But without daily contact with my mother, my father found it difficult to make decisions about my upbringing. He was afraid of contradicting Mom. So he showered me with gifts and trips. He expanded my wardrobe, gave me my first pieces of real jewelry, introduced me to Broadway shows, and took me to Disneyland—but he did not help me with school, teach me about the job market, give me insight into boys, or allow me to be anything more than a spoiled consumer.

As I grew older, my relationship with my father became strained. Weekends with him were spent shopping, going to movies, playing tennis, and horseback riding—activities I loved, but activities that limited opportunities for anything but casual conversation.

Like most of my friends, I came to view my father as more of an uncle than a parent. He was a beloved family figure, someone who could be counted on for some extra cash, new clothes, a pizza. And like most of my friends, I was troubled by the gulf that widened between my father and myself. I talked, argued, and made up with my mother as I went through my teens. Both of us changed over the years. But my father remained the same—the generous but distant Disneyland Dad.

The Disneyland Dad is a neglected figure. While books and daytime talk shows focus on the plight of single moms, few people offer advice for the fathers. Men in our society are judged by success and conditioned to dispense tokens of their achievement to their children. We kids of divorce want all the things the Disneyland Dad can offer, but we really need his attention, his

guidance, his experience, his mentoring. Someone has to help
Disneyland Dads become fathers.

QUESTIONS FOR REVIEW AND REVISION

1. What tone does the term "Disneyland Dad" have? Is it suitable for a serious essay? What connotations does it suggest?

2. Does this student really "define" or merely "describe" Disneyland Dads?

3. Does the paper include enough details to outline the qualities of a Disneyland Dad?

4. The student uses quotation marks to highlight certain words. Do you find this an effective technique?

5. *Blending the Modes:* Where does the student use *narration* and *comparison* to develop the essay? Does the final paragraph state a *persuasive argument*?

6. Did the student follow the instructor's suggestions? Do you sense he or she appreciates the difference between description and definition?

7. Read the paper aloud. Can you detect awkward or vague passages that would benefit from revision?

WRITING SUGGESTIONS

1. Invent a term that defines a personality type, and illustrate it using a parent, friend, or coworker as an example.

2. *Collaborative Writing:* Discuss this paper with several students and collect ideas for a process paper that offers tips to teenage children on how to communicate with a Disneyland Dad.

DEFINITION CHECKLIST

Before submitting your paper, review these points:

1. Is your purpose clear—to inform or persuade?

2. Do you avoid defining a word with the same word, such as "a diffusion pump diffuses"?

3. Is your level of technical or professional language suited to your audience?

4. Does your definition provide enough information and examples so that readers can restate your thesis in their own words?

5. Are there existing definitions you can use for reference or contrast?

6. Do extended definitions contain illustrations, narratives, or comparisons that readers may either not recognize or misinterpret?

7. Do you state the essence of your definition in a short summary statement that readers can remember or highlight for future reference?

8. Are you really "defining" your subject or merely "describing" it?

Info Write provides additional information on the writing definition.
cengage.learning.infowrite.com

CHAPTER SEVEN

COMPARISON AND CONTRAST: INDICATING SIMILARITIES AND DIFFERENCES

WHAT IS COMPARISON AND CONTRAST?

Comparison and contrast answers the question: How are things alike or different? What distinguishes a gasoline engine from a diesel engine? Is it cheaper to buy or lease a car? What separates a misdemeanor from a felony? How does a bacterial infection differ from a viral one? What did Malcolm X and Martin Luther King Jr. have in common? Do men and women approach mathematics differently? How has a neighborhood changed in the last twenty years? All of these questions can be answered by comparing similarities and contrasting differences.

You have probably encountered essay questions that require comparison and contrast responses:

> Compare the industrial output of the North and South at the outbreak of the Civil War. Which side was better equipped to prosecute a protracted conflict?

> How do the rules of evidence differ in criminal and civil proceedings?

> Which arrangement offers business owners greater protection of personal assets—general or limited partnerships?

> Contrast Freud's dream theory with Jung's concept of the unconscious.

At the end of *The Great Gatsby*, Nick Carraway decides to return to the Midwest because he is too "squeamish" for the East. What differences did Fitzgerald see between the East and the Midwest?

Outline the principal differences between warm- and cold-blooded animals.

How did the role of the federal government change after WWII?

Comparison and contrast writing is commonly used to organize research papers. You might compare two short stories by Edgar Allan Poe in an English course, explain the differences between methods of depreciation in accounting, or contrast conflicting theories of childhood development for psychology. Comparison and contrast writing is also used by engineers to explain the fuel efficiency of different engines, by real estate developers to explore potential building sites, and by social workers to determine the best method of delivering medical services to the homeless.

The Purposes of Comparison and Contrast

Writers use comparison and contrast for four purposes:

1. **To draw distinctions between related subjects.** In many instances, comparison is used to eliminate confusion. Many people, for instance, mistake an *optician*, who makes and sells eyeglasses, for an *optometrist*, who performs eye examinations and prescribes lenses. Comparison can pair extended definitions to show readers the difference, for example, between air-cooled and water-cooled engines, African and Indian elephants, or cross-country and downhill skiing. When drawing distinctions, writers explain differences between similar subjects but do not choose one over the other.

2. **To recommend a choice between two things.** Television commercials compare competing products. Political campaign brochures urge voters to support a candidate over his or her rival. Articles in medical journals argue that one drug is more effective than another. Business proposals recommend one computer program or one security service over those of competitors. Government studies assert that one air-quality standard is preferable to another. The basic purpose of stating recommendations is to *persuade readers to make a choice*.

3. **To show how one subject has changed.** A television critic might argue that a TV series lacks the quality shown in its first season. A sportswriter might compare a team's performance this season with last season's. An employee might explain how a company has changed since it was

purchased by a multinational corporation. A student could use a "before and after" comparison to illustrate how a friend changed following the loss of a job or the death of a family member.

4. **To propose an idea, criticize a change, or make a prediction.** Writers can state an argument by comparing a problem with a proposed solution. A city engineer could describe current traffic jams and parking problems, then explain how widened streets and new parking garages could resolve congestion. A doctor could describe a patient's existing lifestyle as a cause of obesity, and then propose a diet and exercise program as solution. A congressman might criticize a policy intended to stimulate small businesses and create jobs by pointing out that in reality it has hurt entrepreneurs and caused layoffs. To show that a curriculum change has improved education, a principal could contrast students' previous test scores with their current performance. An environmentalist might predict how climate change will affect the planet by comparing current conditions with those expected in the future.

Organizing Comparison and Contrast Papers

When developing a paper using comparison and contrast, you must be sure your subjects share enough common points for meaningful discussion. You can compare two sports cars, two action adventure films, or two diets. But comparing a sports car to an SUV, an action film to a comedy, or a diet to plastic surgery is not likely to generate more than superficial observations. The entries in this chapter focus on related subjects, such as two immigrant sisters or two Civil War generals.

In addition, comparisons have to be carefully limited, especially when you are comparing broad or complex subjects. For contrasting the differences between American and Chinese cultures, Yi-Fu Tuan (page 228) limits the essay to demonstrating the different ways Americans and Chinese view space and place. By exploring this limited topic in depth, Yi-Fu Tuan reveals more about Chinese culture in a page or two than a twenty-page essay would that attempts to cover religion, politics, economics, history, and marriage customs. If you are comparing two presidents, you might focus your comparison on their relations with the press, the way they handled crises, or their trade policies.

Perhaps the most frustrating problem students face while writing comparison and contrast papers is organizing ideas. Without careful planning, you may find yourself awkwardly switching back and forth between subjects. Your reader may have difficulty following your train of thought and may confuse one subject with another. Whether they are drawing distinctions or making recommendations, writers use two methods of organizing comparison and contrast.

Subject-by-Subject

The *subject-by-subject* method divides the paper into two sections. Writers state all the information about topic A and then discuss topic B. Usually, the actual comparisons are drawn in the second part of the paper, where B is discussed in relation to A. In this short paper about two types of life insurance, the writer first explains whole life insurance, then discusses term insurance and draws distinctions between the two types. Since the purpose is to make distinctions, the conclusion does not offer a recommendation:

Whole Life and Term Insurance

Most life insurance companies offer a variety of life insurance products, investments, and financial services. Two of the most common policy types provided are whole life and term insurance.

Whole life insurance is the oldest and most traditional form of life insurance. Life insurance became popular in the nineteenth century as a way of protecting the buyer's dependents in the event of premature death. A purchaser would select a policy amount to be paid to his or her beneficiaries after his or her death. Payments called premiums were made on a yearly, quarterly, or monthly basis. As the policyholder paid premiums, the policy gained cash value. Part of the payment earned interest like money in a bank account. Insurance served as an investment tool, allowing people to save for retirement and giving them access to guaranteed loans. For a low interest fee, insurance holders could borrow against the cash value of their policies.

Term insurance, introduced in the twentieth century, serves the same basic purpose as whole life insurance, protecting the insured's dependents. Unlike whole life, however, no cash value accrues. In a sense the policyholder is "renting" insurance, buying only a death benefit. The advantage of term insurance is its low cost. Because there is no money set aside for investment, the premiums are lower. This allows a person to afford a larger policy. A term policy for $100,000 could be cheaper than a whole life policy for $50,000.

The type of insurance a person needs depends on his or her income, family situation, investment goals, savings, and obligations. Most investment counselors agree, however, that anyone with a spouse or children should have some form of life insurance protection.

Advantages and Disadvantages The subject-by-subject method is best suited to short papers. A twenty-page report organized this way would read much like two ten-page papers fastened together. It would be difficult for readers to remember enough of the first subject to appreciate how it differs from the second. This method, however, allows writers to compare abstract subjects with ease, especially when a subject has individual features the other does not share.

Point-by-Point

The *point-by-point* method organizes the comparison of A and B on a number of specific points. Following an introduction, A and B are discussed in a series of comparisons. Hotels, for example, have a number of common points: location, appearance, atmosphere, and room rates. In the following paper, the writer groups comments about the two hotels in each paragraph. For the recommendation, the writer states a clear preference in the opening and concluding paragraphs:

St. Gregory and Fitzpatrick Hotels

Campus organizations and academic conventions visiting the city hold special events in either the St. Gregory or Fitzpatrick. Both are large convention hotels, but for many reasons the St. Gregory is more desirable.

Opened in 1892, the St. Gregory is the oldest surviving hotel in the city. The Fitzpatrick is the newest, having opened just last spring. The St. Gregory has a commanding view of State Street. The Fitzpatrick is part of the $200 million Riverfront Centre.

The chief attraction of the St. Gregory is its famed domed lobby, ornamented with carved mahogany and elaborate brass and marble fittings. Admiral Dewey was presented with the key to the city here following his victory in Manila Bay in 1898. In contrast, the sleek Fitzpatrick is noted for its sweeping thirty-story atrium. The open lobby is banked with massive video screens.

The main lounge of the St. Gregory is the Pump Room, a plush, turn-of-the-century Irish bar decorated with gilt-framed paintings of the Emerald Isle. The Fitzpatrick features two bars. Homerun, a sports bar, is popular with local students and young professionals. The Exchange is a smaller, quieter bar that is a favorite of visiting executives. Copiers, fax machines, and computers are available in the nearby executive center.

Both hotels offer a range of room rates. The cheapest rooms at the St. Gregory are $95 a night. Though small, they are comfortable. The Fitzpatrick has only a dozen single traveler rooms for $125. Double rooms at the St. Gregory range from $175 to $250, depending on size and decor. All Fitzpatrick double rooms are identical and cost $195. In addition to convention rates,

the St. Gregory offers 20 percent student discounts. The Fitzpatrick does not offer student discounts.
    Both hotels provide excellent convention services. Since
most professors and academic delegates have access to university
computers and fax machines, they prefer the historic elegance of
the St. Gregory. Students especially appreciate discount rates
and the availability of public transport to the university.

Advantages and Disadvantages The point-by-point method is useful in organizing longer and more technical papers. The specific facts, statistics, and
quotes about A and B appear side by side. Readers of a long report about two
hotels, organized in a subject-by-subject manner, would be easily frustrated
because instead of seeing room rates compared in the same paragraph, they
might have to flip back a dozen pages. Point-by-point organization is helpful
when addressing multiple readers who may be interested in only a portion of
the paper. However, point-by-point papers about abstract subjects such as
two films or two novels might be difficult to organize because many important details about one subject may not appear in the second. For example,
one spy film might feature action scenes, while another focuses on psychological drama.
    As you read the essays in this chapter, you may note that many writers
blend both methods to develop their comparisons.

STRATEGIES FOR READING COMPARISON AND CONTRAST

*When reading the comparison and contrast entries in this chapter, keep
these questions in mind.*

Understanding Meaning

1. What is the writer's goal—to draw distinctions, recommend a choice,
   show how something has changed, or make a prediction?

2. What details does the writer present about each subject?

3. Who is the intended audience? Is the essay directed to a general or a specific reader?

4. Is the comparison valid? Is the writer comparing two subjects in a fair
   manner? Have any points been overlooked?

5. Does the author have an apparent bias?

6. If the comparison makes a recommendation, does the selection seem valid? What makes the chosen subject superior to the others? What evidence is offered?

Evaluating Strategy

1. What is the basic pattern of the comparison—subject by subject or point by point? Do variations occur?

2. Does the author use a device to narrow the topic or to advance the comparison?

3. Does the writer make use of visual aids? Are they effective?

Appreciating Language

1. Does the writer use connotations that ascribe positive or negative qualities to one or both of the items? How does the author describe the two subjects?

2. What do the diction, level of language, and use of technical terms reveal about the intended audience?

3. If suggesting a choice, how does the writer use language to highlight its desirability?

YI-FU TUAN

Yi-Fu Tuan (1930–) was born in China and later moved to the United States. He taught geography at the University of Wisconsin, specializing in the cultural differences between America and his native country. Since his retirement in 1998, Tuan has continued to write and give lectures. He published an autobiography in 1999 and Human Goodness *in 2008. He states that he writes "from a single perspective—namely that of experience." In this article published in* Harper's, *he compares the way people in two cultures view their environments.*

Chinese Space, American Space

CONTEXT: *Cultures as diverse as America's and China's have many points of difference. In attempting to provide insight into their differences in a brief essay, Yi-Fu Tuan focuses on the concept of space and location. Americans, he asserts, are less rooted to place and are future oriented. The Chinese, savoring tradition, are deeply tied to specific locations. Note that Yi-Fu Tuan devotes most of his essay to describing the less familiar Chinese houses and values.*

*American
space* 1   <u>Americans have a sense of space, not of place.</u> Go to an American home in ex-
Thesis urbia, and almost the first thing you do is drift toward the picture window. How
curious that the first compliment you pay your host inside his house is to say how
American lovely it is outside his house! He is pleased that you should admire his vistas.
home <u>The distant horizon is not merely a line separating earth from sky, it is a symbol
of the future. The American is not rooted in his place, however lovely: his eyes
are drawn by the expanding space to a point on the horizon, which is his future.</u>

2   <u>By contrast, consider the traditional Chinese home.</u> Blank walls enclose it.
Transition Step behind the spirit wall and you are in a courtyard with perhaps a miniature garden around a corner. <u>Once inside his private compound you are
wrapped in an ambiance of calm beauty, an ordered world of buildings, pavement, rock, and decorative vegetation. But you have no distant view:</u>
Chinese home <u>nowhere does space open out before you.</u> Raw nature in such a home is experienced only as weather, and the only open space is the sky above. The Chinese
is rooted in his place. When he has to leave, it is not for the promised land on
the terrestrial horizon, but for another world altogether along the vertical, religious axis of his imagination.

3   The Chinese tie to place is deeply felt. Wanderlust is an alien sentiment.
The Taoist classic *Tao Te Ching* captures the ideal of rootedness in place with
these words: "Though there may be another country in the neighborhood so
close that they are within sight of each other and the crowing of cocks and
barking of dogs in one place can be heard in the other, yet there is no traffic
between them; and throughout their lives the two peoples have nothing to do
Chinese place with each other." In theory if not in practice, farmers have ranked high in

Chinese society. The reason is not only that they are engaged in a "root" industry of producing food but that, unlike pecuniary merchants, they are tied to the land and do not abandon their country when it is in danger.

Nostalgia is a recurrent theme in Chinese poetry. An American reader of 4 translated Chinese poems may well be taken aback—even put off—by the frequency, as well as the sentimentality, of the lament for home. To understand the strength of this sentiment, we need to know that the Chinese desire for stability and rootedness in place is prompted by the constant threat of war, exile, and the natural disasters of flood and drought. Forcible removal makes the Chinese keenly aware of their loss. By contrast, Americans move, for the most part, voluntarily. Their nostalgia for hometown is really longing for a childhood to which they cannot return: in the meantime the future beckons and the future is "out there," in open space. <u>When we criticize American rootlessness, we tend to forget that it is a result of ideals we admire, namely, social mobility and optimism about the future. When we admire Chinese rootedness, we forget that the word "place" means both a location in space and position in society: to be tied to place is also to be bound to one's station in life, with little hope of betterment. Space symbolizes hope; place, achievement and stability.</u>

Final comments on American and Chinese values

Understanding Meaning

1. How does the author see a difference between "space" and "place"?

2. What do the traditional designs of American and Chinese homes reveal about cultural differences?

3. Why do the Chinese honor farmers?

4. What historical forces have shaped the Chinese desire for "rootedness"? How is American history different?

5. What negative aspects does Yi-Fu Tuan see in the Chinese sense of place?

Evaluating Strategy

1. The writer really devotes only a single paragraph to describing American concepts of space. Why? Is the essay out of balance? Discuss whether or not a comparison paper should devote half its space to each topic.

2. Is the author objective? Is it possible for a writer to discuss cultures without inserting a measure of bias?

Appreciating Language

1. What words does Yi-Fu Tuan use in describing the two cultures? Do they seem to differ in connotation?

2. Does the word "rootlessness" suggest something negative to most people? How does Yi-Fu Tuan define it?

3. Look up the word "wanderlust." How does a German term suit an essay comparing American and Chinese cultures?

WRITING SUGGESTIONS

1. If you have lived in or visited another country or region within the United States, write a brief essay outlining how it differs from your home. Just as Yi-Fu Tuan used the concept of space to focus a short article, you may wish to limit your comparison to discussing eating habits, dress, attitudes to work, music, or dating practices.

2. *Collaborative Writing:* Ask a group of students about their attitudes toward rootlessness and place. Determine how often students have moved in their lives. How many have spent their entire lives in a single house or apartment? Write a few paragraphs outlining the attitudes expressed by the group.

RACHEL CARSON

Rachel Carson (1907–1964) was a marine biologist known for the literary quality of her writing. She won critical acclaim with her first two books, The Sea Around Us *(1951) and* The Edge of the Sea *(1955). Then, in 1962, she hit the best-seller list with* Silent Spring, *a frightening exposé of the hazards that insecticides and weed killers were posing to both wildlife and human beings. As much as anything else, this one book can be said to have launched the modern environmental movement.*

A Fable for Tomorrow

CONTEXT: *Rapid industrialization both in manufacturing and in agriculture brought unprecedented material advantages to the developed world throughout the first half of the twentieth century. At the same time, insufficient notice was being taken of the damages such industrialization was inflicting on the natural environment. Although* Silent Spring *is a well-researched book by a reputable scientist, it is intended for a general audience. The following preface to that book is an imaginative rendering of the eventual consequences of continued indifference to the environment. Notice how Carson uses a before-and-after comparison to dramatize her warning.*

There was once a town in the heart of America where all life seemed to live 1 in harmony with its surroundings. The town lay in the midst of a checkerboard of prosperous farms, with fields of grain and hillsides of orchards where, in spring, white clouds of bloom drifted above the green fields. In autumn, oak and maple and birch set up a blaze of color that flamed and flickered across a backdrop of pines. Then foxes barked in the hills and deer silently crossed the fields, half hidden in the mists of the fall mornings.

Along the roads, laurel, viburnum and alder, great ferns and wildflowers de- 2 lighted the traveler's eye through much of the year. Even in winter the roadsides were places of beauty, where countless birds came to feed on the berries and on the seed heads of the dried weeds rising above the snow. The countryside was, in fact, famous for the abundance and variety of its bird life, and when the flood of migrants was pouring through in spring and fall people traveled from great distances to observe them. Others came to fish the streams, which flowed clear and cold out of the hills and contained shady pools where trout lay. So it had been from the days many years ago when the first settlers raised their houses, sank their wells, and built their barns.

Then a strange blight crept over the area and everything began to change. 3 Some evil spell had settled on the community: mysterious maladies swept the flocks of chickens; the cattle and sheep sickened and died. Everywhere was a shadow of death. The farmers spoke of much illness among their families. In the town the doctors had become more and more puzzled by new kinds of sickness appearing among their patients. There had been several sudden and unexplained deaths, not only among adults but even among children, who would be stricken suddenly while at play and die within a few hours.

4   There was a strange stillness. The birds, for example—where had they gone? Many people spoke of them, puzzled and disturbed. The feeding stations in the backyards were deserted. The few birds seen anywhere were moribund; they trembled violently and could not fly. It was a spring without voices. On the mornings that had once throbbed with the dawn chorus of robins, catbirds, doves, jays, wrens, and scores of other bird voices there was now no sound; only silence lay over the fields and woods and marsh.

5   On the farms the hens brooded, but no chicks hatched. The farmers complained that they were unable to raise any pigs—the litters were small and the young survived only a few days. The apple trees were coming into bloom but no bees droned among the blossoms, so there was no pollination and there would be no fruit.

6   The roadsides, once so attractive, were now lined with browned and withered vegetation as though swept by fire. These, too, were silent, deserted by all living things. Even the streams were now lifeless. Anglers no longer visited them, for all the fish had died.

7   In the gutters under the eaves and between the shingles of the roofs, a white granular powder still showed a few patches; some weeks before it had fallen like snow upon the roofs and the lawns, the fields and streams.

8   No witchcraft, no enemy action had silenced the rebirth of new life in this stricken world. The people had done it themselves.

9   This town does not actually exist, but it might easily have a thousand counterparts in America or elsewhere in the world. I know of no community that has experienced all the misfortunes I describe. Yet every one of these disasters has actually happened somewhere, and many real communities have already suffered a substantial number of them. A grim specter has crept upon us almost unnoticed, and this imagined tragedy may easily become a stark reality we all shall know.

10   What has already silenced the voices of spring in countless towns in America? This book is an attempt to explain.

Understanding Meaning

1. What sort of a world does Carson describe in the first two paragraphs of the essay?

2. Can you tell what causes the change between the world of the first two paragraphs and the world described next? What do you know about what caused the devastation?

3. What does Carson mean when she says the people had "done it themselves"?

4. What is Carson's purpose in providing this fictional account of destruction?

Evaluating Strategy

1. Note each reference to silence. How do all of those references relate to the title of the book Carson is introducing, *Silent Spring*?

2. How does Carson use a "before-and-after" comparison to make her point?

Appreciating Language

1. The first two paragraphs describe the town in almost fairy-tale language. In the remainder of the essay, which specific words help capture the negative atmosphere that Carson is trying to create?

2. Although Carson is a scientist, in this introduction she chose to use language that would be easily understood by the layperson. Why do you think she made that choice?

WRITING SUGGESTIONS

1. You may have seen specific places go through a transformation of the sort Carson describes on a smaller scale. Write two paragraphs in which you describe a place first as you once knew it and then as it exists now.

2. *Collaborative Writing*: Work with a group of students and develop an essay using a before-and-after strategy to describe how people change when they go through a transformation, such as getting married, losing a job, having a child, or buying a house.

SUZANNE BRITT

A native of Winston-Salem, North Carolina, Suzanne Britt holds an MA in English from Washington University in St. Louis. Her work has appeared in Sky Magazine, *the* New York Times, *the* Boston Globe, *and elsewhere. Her books include a history of Meredith College, where she teaches English, and two essay collections—*Skinny People Are Dull and Crunchy Like Carrots *(1982) and* Show and Tell *(1983). More recently, Britt has completed a novel and is currently writing poetry.*

Neat People vs. Sloppy People

CONTEXT: *In the following selection, Britt uses humorous exaggeration and fanciful speculation to defend sloppy living habits. Although her statements are not likely to be literally accepted by many readers, they constitute a kind of satirical rebuttal to the notion that cleanliness is next to godliness.*

1 I've finally figured out the difference between neat people and sloppy people. The distinction is, as always, moral. Neat people are lazier and meaner than sloppy people.

2 Sloppy people, you see, are not really sloppy. Their sloppiness is merely the unfortunate consequence of their extreme moral rectitude. Sloppy people carry in their mind's eye a heavenly vision, a precise plan, that is so stupendous, so perfect, it can't be achieved in this world or the next.

3 Sloppy people live in Never-Never Land. Someday is their métier. Someday they are planning to alphabetize all their books and set up home catalogs. Someday they will go through their wardrobes and mark certain items for tentative mending and certain items for passing on to relatives of similar shape and size. Someday sloppy people will make family scrapbooks into which they will put newspaper clippings, postcards, locks of hair, and the dried corsage from their senior prom. Someday they will file everything on the surface of their desks, including the cash receipts from coffee purchases at the snack shop. Someday they will sit down and read all the back issues of *The New Yorker*.

4 For all these noble reasons and more, sloppy people never get neat. They aim too high and wide. They save everything, planning someday to file, order, and straighten out the world. But while these ambitious plans take clearer and clearer shape in their heads, the books spill from the shelves onto the floor, the clothes pile up in the hamper and closet, the family mementos accumulate in every drawer, the surface of the desk is buried under mounds of paper, and the unread magazines threaten to reach the ceiling.

5 Sloppy people can't bear to part with anything. They give loving attention to every detail. When sloppy people say they're going to tackle the surface of

a desk, they really mean it. Not a paper will go unturned; not a rubber band will go unboxed. Four hours or two weeks into the excavation, the desk looks exactly the same, primarily because the sloppy person is meticulously creating new piles of papers with new headings and scrupulously stopping to read all the old book catalogs before he throws them away. A neat person would just bulldoze the desk.

Neat people are bums and clods at heart. They have cavalier attitudes to- 6 ward possessions, including family heirlooms. Everything is just another dust-catcher to them. If anything collects dust, it's got to go and that's that. Neat people will toy with the idea of throwing the children out of the house just to cut down on the clutter.

Neat people don't care about process. They like results. What they want to 7 do is get the whole thing over with so they can sit down and watch the rasslin' on TV. Neat people operate on two unvarying principles: Never handle any item twice, and throw everything away.

The only thing messy in a neat person's house is the trash can. The minute 8 something comes to a neat person's hand, he will look at it, try to decide whether it has immediate use and, finding none, throw it in the trash.

Neat people are especially vicious with mail. They never go through their 9 mail unless they are standing directly over a trash can. If the trash can is beside the mailbox, even better. All ads, catalogs, pleas for charitable contributions, church bulletins, and money-saving coupons go straight into the trash can without being opened. All letters from home, postcards from Europe, bills, and paychecks are opened, immediately responded to, then dropped in the trash can. Neat people keep their receipts only for tax purposes. That's it. No sentimental salvaging of birthday cards or the last letter a dying relative ever wrote. Into the trash it goes.

Neat people place neatness above everything, even economics. They are 10 incredibly wasteful. Neat people throw away several toys every time they walk through the den. I knew a neat person once who threw away a perfectly good dish drainer because it had mold on it. The drainer was too much trouble to wash. And neat people sell their furniture when they move. They will sell a La-Z-Boy recliner while you are reclining in it.

Neat people are no good to borrow from. Neat people buy everything in ex- 11 pensive little single portions. They get their flour and sugar in two-pound bags. They wouldn't consider clipping a coupon, saving a leftover, reusing plastic nondairy whipped cream containers, or rinsing off tin foil and draping it over the unmoldy dish drainer. You can never borrow a neat person's newspaper to see what's playing at the movies. Neat people have the paper all wadded up and in the trash by 7:05 a.m.

Neat people cut a clean swath through the organic as well as the inorganic 12 world. People, animals, and things are all one to them. They are so insensitive.

After they've finished with the pantry, the medicine cabinet, and the attic, they will throw out the red geranium (too many leaves), sell the dog (too many fleas), and send the children off to boarding school (too many scuff-marks on the hardwood floors).

Understanding Meaning

1. What thesis is Britt supporting in her essay?

2. What is it that makes sloppy people more moral, according to Britt?

3. Why do neat people come off as the "bad guys" in Britt's essay?

4. *Critical Thinking*: Is there some validity in what Britt says? What are neat people losing out on that sloppy people are not? Is there something worth-while in the goal of sloppy people, even if they never reach it?

Evaluating Strategy

1. Which organizational method does Britt use in this piece?

2. Britt states her thesis bluntly in paragraph 1. What effect does that have?

3. How does Britt achieve the humor that she does in the essay?

4. Why might Britt have decided to end the essay the way she did? What is she suggesting in her conclusion about neat versus sloppy people?

Appreciating Language

1. Which words that Britt chose show her bias in favor of the sloppy? Which show her bias against the neat?

2. What terms does she suggest that neat people associate with children in order to show how insignificant children are to them?

WRITING SUGGESTIONS

1. Write an essay in which you characterize yourself or someone you know as fitting into either Britt's description of a neat person or her description of a sloppy person.

2. *Collaborative Writing*: Working with a group of students, develop an essay that compares the characteristics of another pair of opposites: savers and spenders, punctual and unpunctual people, renters and homeowners, or happily and unhappily married people.

BRUCE CATTON

Bruce Catton (1899–1978) grew up listening to stories of Civil War veterans. His own college career was interrupted by service in World War I. Catton went to work as a reporter for the Cleveland Plain Dealer *and later served as information director for several government agencies. His interest in history, especially the Civil War, never flagged. In 1953, his book* A Stillness at Appomattox *became a best seller, and Catton received a Pulitzer Prize. He wrote several other books about the Civil War and edited* American Heritage *magazine for two decades.*

Grant and Lee

CONTEXT: *Perhaps no other essay is as widely anthologized as a sample of comparison writing as Catton's "Grant and Lee," which first appeared in a collection,* The American Story. *Directed to a general audience, the essay seeks to contrast the two most famous generals of the Civil War.*

When Ulysses S. Grant and Robert E. Lee met in the parlor of a modest house 1 at Appomattox Court House, Virginia, on April 9, 1865, to work out the terms for the surrender of Lee's Army of Northern Virginia, a great chapter in American life came to a close, and a great new chapter began.

These men were bringing the Civil War to its virtual finish. To be sure, 2 other armies had yet to surrender, and for a few days the fugitive Confederate government would struggle desperately and vainly, trying to find some way to go on living now that its chief support was gone. But in effect it was all over when Grant and Lee signed the papers. And the little room where they wrote out the terms was the scene of one of the poignant, dramatic contrasts in American history.

They were two strong men, these oddly different generals, and they repre- 3 sented the strengths of two conflicting currents that, through them, had come into final collision.

Back of Robert E. Lee was the notion that the old aristocratic concept 4 might somehow survive and be dominant in American life.

Lee was tidewater Virginia, and in his background were family, culture, and 5 tradition … the age of chivalry transplanted to a New World which was making its own legends and its own myths. He embodied a way of life that had come down through the age of knighthood and the English country squire. America was a land that was beginning all over again, dedicated to nothing much more complicated than the rather hazy belief that all men had equal rights and should have an equal chance in the world. In such a land Lee stood for the feeling that it was somehow of advantage to human society to have a pronounced inequality in the social structure. There should be a leisure class, backed by ownership of land; in turn, society itself should be keyed to the land as the chief source of wealth and influence. It would bring forth (according to this ideal) a class of men with a strong sense of obligation to the community; men who lived not to gain advantage for themselves, but to meet the solemn obligations which had been laid on them by the very fact that they were privileged. From them the country would get its leadership; to them it could look for the higher values—of thought, of conduct, of personal deportment—to give it strength and virtue.

6   Lee embodied the noblest elements of this aristocratic ideal. Through him, the landed nobility justified itself. For four years, the Southern states had fought a desperate war to uphold the ideals for which Lee stood. In the end, it almost seemed as if the Confederacy fought for Lee; as if he himself was the Confederacy ... the best thing that the way of life for which the Confederacy stood could ever have to offer. He had passed into legend before Appomattox. Thousands of tired, underfed, poorly clothed Confederate soldiers, long since past the simple enthusiasm of the early days of the struggle, somehow considered Lee the symbol of everything for which they had been willing to die. But they could not quite put this feeling into words. If the Lost Cause, sanctified by so much heroism and so many deaths, had a living justification, its justification was General Lee.

7   Grant, the son of a tanner on the Western frontier, was everything Lee was not. He had come up the hard way and embodied nothing in particular except the eternal toughness and sinewy fiber of the men who grew up beyond the mountains. He was one of a body of men who owed reverence and obeisance to no one, who were self-reliant to a fault, who cared hardly anything for the past but who had a sharp eye for the future.

8   These frontier men were the precise opposite of the tidewater aristocrats. Back of them, in the great surge that had taken people over the Alleghenies and into the opening Western country, there was a deep, implicit dissatisfaction with a past that had settled into grooves. They stood for democracy, not from any reasoned conclusion about the proper ordering of human society, but simply because they had grown up in the middle of democracy and knew how it worked. Their society might have privileges, but they would be privileges each man had won for himself. Forms and patterns meant nothing. No man was born to anything, except perhaps to a chance to show how far he could rise. Life was competition.

9   Yet along with this feeling had come a deep sense of belonging to a national community. The Westerner who developed a farm, opened a shop, or set up in business as a trader, could hope to prosper only as his own community prospered—and his community ran from the Atlantic to the Pacific and from Canada down to Mexico. If the land was settled, with towns and highways and accessible markets, he could better himself. He saw his fate in terms of

the nation's own destiny. As its horizons expanded, so did his. He had, in other words, an acute dollars-and-cents stake in the continued growth and development of his country.

And that, perhaps, is where the contrast between Grant and Lee becomes 10 most striking. The Virginia aristocrat, inevitably, saw himself in relation to his own region. He lived in a static society which could endure almost anything except change. Instinctively, his first loyalty would go to the locality in which that society existed. He would fight to the limit of endurance to defend it, because in defending it he was defending everything that gave his own life its deepest meaning.

The Westerner, on the other hand, would fight with an equal tenacity for 11 the broader concept of society. He fought so because everything he lived by was tied to growth, expansion, and a constantly widening horizon. What he lived by would survive or fall with the nation itself. He could not possibly stand by unmoved in the face of an attempt to destroy the Union. He would combat it with everything he had, because he could only see it as an effort to cut the ground out from under his feet.

So Grant and Lee were in complete contrast, representing two diametrically 12 opposed elements in American life. Grant was the modern man emerging; beyond him, ready to come on the stage, was the great age of steel and machinery, of crowded cities and a restless burgeoning vitality. Lee might have ridden down from the old age of chivalry, lance in hand, silken banner fluttering over his head. Each man was the perfect champion of his cause, drawing both his strengths and his weaknesses from the people he led.

Yet it was not all contrast, after all. Different as they were—in background, 13 in personality, in underlying aspiration—these two great soldiers had much in common. Under everything else, they were marvelous fighters. Furthermore, their fighting qualities were really very much alike.

Each man had, to begin with, the great virtue of utter tenacity and fidelity. 14 Grant fought his way down the Mississippi Valley in spite of acute personal discouragement and profound military handicaps. Lee hung on in the trenches at Petersburg after hope itself had died. In each man there was an indomitable quality ... the born fighter's refusal to give up as long as he can still remain on his feet and lift his two fists.

Daring and resourcefulness they had, too; the ability to think faster and 15 move faster than the enemy. These were the qualities which gave Lee the dazzling campaigns of Second Manassas and Chancellorsville and won Vicksburg for Grant.

Lastly, and perhaps greatest of all, there was the ability, at the end, to turn 16 quickly from war to peace once the fighting was over. Out of the way these two men behaved at Appomattox came the possibility of a peace of reconciliation. It was a possibility not wholly realized, in the years to come, but which did, in the end, help the two sections to become one nation again ... after a war whose bitterness might have seemed to make such a reunion wholly impossible. No part of either man's life became him more than the part he played in their brief meeting in the McLean house at Appomattox. Their behavior there put all succeeding generations of Americans in their debt. Two great Americans, Grant and Lee—very different, yet under everything very much alike. Their encounter at Appomattox was one of the great moments of American history.

Understanding Meaning

1. What does Catton see as the most striking differences between the two generals?

2. How did Grant and Lee differ in background and sense of allegiance?

3. What were the historical forces that shaped the two men?

4. What areas of similarity between the two does Catton detect?

5. *Critical Thinking:* Essentially Catton is telling the story of a confrontation between victor and vanquished, yet his account does not seem to depict the men as winner and loser. Catton does not dwell on what made Grant victorious or on the causes for Lee's defeat. What does this reveal about Catton's purpose?

Evaluating Strategy

1. How does Catton organize his comparison? Is this an effective method?

2. The Civil War was, in part, a battle over slavery. Catton does not mention this issue. Does his account appear to be ethically neutral, suggesting that neither the Union nor the Confederacy were morally superior in its war aims?

Appreciating Language

1. Does Catton appear to be neutral in his descriptions of the two men? What similes or metaphors does he use? Is the language balanced or biased?

2. What do the tone, level of language, and word choice suggest about Catton's intended audience?

WRITING SUGGESTIONS

1. Write an essay comparing two people you have known who are in the same profession. Compare two teachers, two coaches, two bosses, two landlords, or two coworkers. Try to focus on their personalities rather

than their appearance. You may limit your discussion to a specific attitude, situation, or activity. For example, compare how two teachers dealt with troublesome students, how two bosses motivated employees, or how two landlords maintained their properties.

2. *Collaborative Writing:* Work with a group of students to write a short dramatic scene based on Catton's essay. Use set descriptions to establish the locale, and invent dialogue. Discuss with members of the group how Lee and Grant might have sounded. What words would they have chosen? How would their vocabulary indicate their different backgrounds and personalities?

SHARON BEGLEY

Sharon Begley graduated from Yale University and joined Newsweek magazine in 1977 as an editorial assistant. After serving as an assistant editor in the late 1970s, she became a general editor in 1983. During her career at Newsweek, Begley wrote numerous articles on science and health issues. She left the magazine to write the "Science Journal" column for the Wall Street Journal. Five years later, Begley returned to Newsweek as a senior editor.

East Versus West: One Sees the Big Picture, Other Is Focused

CONTEXT: *In this* Wall Street Journal *article, Begley explains how a growing number of psychologists now believe that people from different cultures perceive things differently, remember different details, and make different associations.*

1   You ask two new acquaintances to tell you about themselves. The Japanese gent describes himself as "outgoing with his family," "competitive on the soccer field" and "serious at work." The Briton doesn't parse it so finely, saying he is "friendly, intellectual and goal-driven."

2   Then you ask each to decide which two—of a panda, a monkey and a banana—go together. The Japanese man selects the monkey and the banana; the Brit, the panda and the monkey.

3   Like many scholars of human thought since at least Hume and Locke, today's cognitive psychologists tend to be "universalists," assuming that everyone perceives, thinks and reasons the same way.

4   "There has long been a widespread belief among philosophers and, later, cognitive scientists that thinking the world over is basically the same," says psychologist Howard Gardner of Harvard University in Cambridge, Mass. Although there have always been dissenters, the prevailing wisdom held that a Masai hunter, a corporate raider and a milkmaid all see, remember, infer and think the same way.

5   But an ever-growing number of studies challenge this assumption. "Human cognition is not everywhere the same," concludes psychologist Richard E. Nisbett of the University of Michigan, Ann Arbor, in his new book, "The Geography of Thought: How Asians and Westerners Think Differently . . . and Why." Instead, he says, "the characteristic thought processes of Asians and Westerners differ greatly."

6   The book compares people from East Asia (Korea, China and Japan) with Westerners (from Europe, the British commonwealth and North America).

As the Monkey-Panda example shows, Westerners typically see 7 categories (animals) where Asians typically see relationships (monkeys eat bananas). Such differences in thinking can trip up business and political relationships.

The cognitive differences start with basic sensory perception. In one study, 8 Michigan's Taka Masuda showed Japanese and American students pictures of aquariums containing one big fast-moving fish, several other finned swimmers, plants, rock and bubbles. What did the students recall? The Japanese spontaneously remembered 60 percent more background elements than did the Americans. They also referred twice as often to relationships involving background objects ("the little frog was above the pink rock").

The difference was even more striking when the participants were asked 9 which, of 96 objects, had been in the scene. When the test object was shown in the context of its original surroundings, the Japanese did much better at remembering correctly whether they had seen it before. For the Americans, including the background was no help; they had never even seen it.

"Westerners and Asians literally see different worlds," says Prof. Nisbett. 10 "Westerners pay attention to the focal object, while Asians attend more broadly—to the overall surroundings and to the relations between the object and the field." These generalizations seem to hold even though Eastern and Western countries each represent many different cultures and traditions.

Because of their heightened perception of surroundings, East Asians attribute causality less to actors than to context. Little wonder, then, that West 11 and East see North Korea's nuclear threats very differently. "Understanding how other people think and see the world is crucial in international disputes," says psychologist Robert Sternberg of Yale University in New Haven, Conn.

Divergent East-West thinking also has produced some tense business conflicts. In the 1970s, Japanese refiners, having signed a contract to buy sugar 12 from Australia for $160 a ton, asked to renegotiate after world prices dropped. The Aussies refused. To the Asians, changing circumstances dictated changes in agreements; to the Westerners, a deal was a deal.

One striking east-west difference centers on drawing inferences. Imagine a 13 line graph plotting economic growth in which the rate of growth accelerates (that is, the line gets steeper to the right). Researchers asked college students in Ann Arbor and Beijing whether they thought the growth rate would go up, go down, or stay the same. The Americans were more likely to predict a continued rise, extrapolating trends, than were the Chinese, who saw trends as likely to reverse.

Westerners prefer abstract universal principles; East Asians seek rules appropriate to a situation. For example, when researchers in the Netherlands 14 asked people what to do about an employee whose work has been subpar for a year after 15 years of exemplary service, more than 75 percent of Americans and Canadians said to let her go; only 20 percent of Singaporeans and Koreans agreed.

15   Cognitive differences likely originate in child-rearing and social practices, but are far from hardwired: Asians living in the West and Westerners in Asia often find that their cognitive style goes native. Similarly, bicultural people, like those in Hong Kong with its British and Chinese history, show thinking patterns intermediate between East and West. That's a model that workplaces might do well to emulate, says Prof. Nisbett: The more cultural diversity and, hence, thinking styles in a workforce, the likelier it is to see problems clearly and solve them.

Understanding Meaning

1. What do traditional cognitive psychologists believe about the way humans think? Does it seem to fit prevailing attitudes about everyone being equal?

2. How do Asians and Westerners, according to some psychologists, think differently? How do their memories, associations, and judgments of a common experience differ?

3. What, in Begley's view, causes these differences? Are they "hard-wired" or formed by family and social forces?

4. *Critical Thinking:* How might different ways of perception change the way people respond to motion pictures, commercials, and political messages? Do you think that these findings may influence filmmakers and corporations? Might films be edited into Eastern and Western versions? Might advertising agencies develop different commercials to market the same products in Japan and the United States?

Evaluating Strategy

1. How does Begley organize her comparison? Are her transitions clear?

2. How effective is the "monkey–panda" example? Do you think it effectively demonstrates the ways Westerners and Asians think? How important are specific examples or illustrations?

3. Begley describes a 1970s trade dispute between Japan and Australia on page 243. Does this example illustrate the serious consequences differences in perception may have? Do you think different perceptions can explain, in part, international conflicts and failed diplomacy?

Appreciating Language

1. Begley uses the term "universalist." Can you define this term in your own words?

2. How would describe the general tone of Begley's article? Is it suited for a business-oriented publication like the *Wall Street Journal*? Why or why not?

WRITING SUGGESTIONS

1. Using the example of the Kenna and Lacy article on page 257, arrange Begley's observations about Eastern and Western ways of thinking in two columns.

2. *Collaborative Writing:* Discuss Begley's article with a group of students and answer this question: Can messages and images be developed to appeal to a universal audience, or are cultural and regional differences bound to lead people to respond differently to the same words and images? If members have different opinions, consider writing a comparison or classification essay to record their views.

BHARATI MUKHERJEE

Bharati Mukherjee was born in Calcutta and is now a distinguished professor at the University of California at Berkeley. In 1989 she became the first naturalized American citizen to win the National Book Critics Circle Award for Fiction for The Middleman and Other Stories. *Her other books include* Leave It to Me, The Holder of the World, Darkness, The Tiger's Daughter, Wife, Jasmine, *and* Desirable Daughters. *Much of her fiction and nonfiction commentary explores the diversity of immigrant experiences in the United States.*

Two Ways to Belong to America

CONTEXT: *This essay appeared in the* New York Times *in 1996 when Congress was debating bills that would greatly limit the benefits granted to legal immigrants. The debate gave Bharati Mukherjee an opportunity to compare her experience as a naturalized citizen with that of her sister who, though living and working in America for decades, preferred to remain an Indian national.*

1 This is a tale of two sisters from Calcutta, Mira and Bharati, who have lived in the United States for some 35 years, but who find themselves on different sides in the current debate over the status of immigrants. I am an American citizen and she is not. I am moved that thousands of long-term residents are finally taking the oath of citizenship. She is not.

2 Mira arrived in Detroit in 1960 to study child psychology and preschool education. I followed her a year later to study creative writing at the University of Iowa. When we left India, we were almost identical in appearance and attitude. We dressed alike, in saris; we expressed identical views on politics, social issues, love and marriage in the same Calcutta convent school accent. We would endure our two years in America, secure our degrees, then return to India to marry the grooms of our father's choosing.

3 Instead, Mira married an Indian student in 1962 who was getting his business administration degree at Wayne State University. They soon acquired the labor certifications necessary for the green card of hassle-free residence and employment.

4 Mira still lives in Detroit, works in the Southfield, Michigan, school system, and has become nationally recognized for her contributions in the fields of pre-school education and parent-teacher relationships. After 36 years as a legal immigrant in this country, she clings passionately to her Indian citizenship and hopes to go home to India when she retires.

5 In Iowa City in 1963, I married a fellow student, an American of Canadian parentage. Because of the accident of his North Dakota birth, I bypassed labor-certification requirements and the race-related "quota" system that

favored the applicant's country of origin over his or her merit. I was prepared for (and even welcomed) the emotional strain that came with marrying outside my ethnic community. In 33 years of marriage, we have lived in every part of North America. By choosing a husband who was not my father's selection, I was opting for fluidity, self-invention, blue jeans and T-shirts, and renouncing 3,000 years (at least) of caste-observant, "pure culture" marriage in the Mukherjee family. My books have often been read as unapologetic (and in some quarters overenthusiastic) texts for cultural and psychological "mongrelization." It's a word I celebrate.

Mira and I have stayed sisterly close by phone. In our regular Sunday 6 morning conversations, we are unguardedly affectionate. I am her only blood relative on this continent. We expect to see each other through the looming crises of aging and ill health without being asked. Long before Vice President Gore's "Citizenship U.S.A." drive, we'd had our polite arguments over the ethics of retaining an overseas citizenship while expecting the permanent protection and economic benefits that come with living and working in America.

Like well-raised sisters, we never said what was really on our minds, but we 7 probably pitied one another. She, for the lack of structure in my life, the erasure of Indianness, the absence of an unvarying daily core. I, for the narrowness of her perspective, her uninvolvement with the mythic depths or the superficial pop culture of this society. But, now, with the scapegoating of "aliens" (documented or illegal) on the increase, and the targeting of long-term legal immigrants like Mira for new scrutiny and new self-consciousness, she and I find ourselves unable to maintain the same polite discretion. We were always unacknowledged adversaries, and we are now, more than ever, sisters.

"I feel used," Mira raged on the phone the other night. "I feel manipulated 8 and discarded. This is such an unfair way to treat a person who was invited to stay and work here because of her talent. My employer went to the I.N.S. and petitioned for the labor certification. For over 30 years, I've invested my creativity and professional skills into the improvement of *this* country's preschool system. I've obeyed all the rules, I've paid my taxes, I love my work, I love my students, I love the friends I've made. How dare America now change its rules in midstream? If America wants to make new rules curtailing benefits of legal immigrants, they should apply only to immigrants who arrive after those rules are already in place."

To my ears, it sounded like the description of a long-enduring, comfort- 9 able, yet loveless marriage, without risk or recklessness. Have we the right to demand, and to expect, that we be loved? (That, to me, is the subtext of the arguments by immigration advocates.) My sister is an expatriate, professionally generous and creative, socially courteous and gracious, and that's as far as her Americanization can go. She is here to maintain an identity, not to transform it.

10   I asked her whether she would follow the example of others who have decided to become citizens because of the anti-immigration bills in Congress. And here, she surprised me. "If America wants to play the manipulative game, I'll play it too," she snapped. "I'll become a U.S. citizen for now, then change back to Indian when I'm ready to go home. I feel some kind of irrational attachment to India that I don't to America. Until all this hysteria against legal immigrants, I was totally happy. Having my green card meant I could visit any place in the world I wanted to and then come back to a job that's satisfying and that I do very well."

11   In one family, from two sisters alike as peas in a pod, there could not be a wider divergence of immigrant experience. America spoke to me—I embraced the demotion from expatriate aristocrat to immigrant nobody, surrendering those thousands of years of "pure culture," the saris, the delightfully accented English. She retained them all. Which of us is the freak?

12   Mira's voice, I realize, is the voice not just of the immigrant South Asian community but of an immigrant community of the millions who have stayed rooted in one job, one city, one house, one ancestral culture, one cuisine, for the entirety of their productive years. She speaks for greater numbers than I possibly can. Only the fluency of her English and the anger, rather than fear, born of confidence from her education, differentiate her from the seamstresses, the domestics, the technicians, the shop owners, the millions of hardworking but effectively silenced documented immigrants as well as their less fortunate "illegal" brothers and sisters.

13   Nearly 20 years ago, when I was living in my husband's ancestral homeland of Canada, I was always well employed but never allowed to feel part of the local Quebec or larger Canadian society. Then, through a Green Paper that invited a national referendum on the unwanted side effects of "nontraditional" immigration, the Government officially turned against its immigrant communities, particularly those from South Asia.

14   I felt then the same sense of betrayal that Mira feels now. I will never forget the pain of that sudden turning, and the casual racist outbursts the Green Paper elicited. That sense of betrayal had its desired effect and drove me, and thousands like me, from the country.

15   Mira and I differ, however, in the ways in which we hope to interact with the country that we have chosen to live in. She is happier to live in America as an expatriate Indian than as an immigrant American. I need to feel like a part of the community I have adopted (as I tried to feel in Canada as well). I need to put roots down, to vote and make the difference that I can. The price that the immigrant willingly pays, and that the exile avoids, is the trauma of self-transformation.

Understanding Meaning

1. What is the principal difference between the writer and her sister?

2. Why does the writer's sister prefer to remain an Indian national and not become an American citizen?

3. Can a person contribute to the American economy, society, and culture without becoming a citizen?

4. Why did Mukherjee become a citizen? How did that decision reflect her view of herself and of her position in American society?

5. Can you understand why the writer's sister feels "manipulated and discarded" by the suggestion that she should become a citizen? In your view, is her anger justified?

6. *Critical Thinking:* If your future career took you to France, would you consider becoming a French citizen or would you prefer to remain an American, even if you planned to live there for decades? Why? Would keeping your American citizenship show loyalty to your native country? If you renounced your American citizenship, would you feel you were rejecting your homeland?

Evaluating Strategy

1. Do you feel the device of comparing two sisters is an effective way of exploring different immigrant experiences? By using a person she loves and respects to represent a different viewpoint, does the writer avoid seeming overly biased?

2. Mukherjee wrote this as an op-ed piece for a major newspaper. Do you think she was effective in sharing her observations with the general public? What challenges do writers face when trying to address a complex topic in a brief newspaper editorial?

3. *Blending the Modes:* Where does Mukherjee use *description, narration,* and *cause and effect* to develop her comparison?

Appreciating Language

1. Mukherjee uses the word "mongrelization," stating, "It's a word I celebrate." Look up "mongrelization" in a dictionary. What connotations does it have? If Mukherjee celebrates this word, what does it reveal about her values and attitudes?

2. Mukherjee refers to her sister as an "expatriate." What connotation does this word have? Is the word neutral or does it have positive or negative connotations?

WRITING SUGGESTIONS

1. Use a comparison of two people to illustrate contrasting values. Compare two friends and their different attitudes about work or school. Contrast your spending habits with those of your mother. Compare the way you drive with your cousin's driving. Your essay may suggest that one person's values or methods are more desirable, or you may simply highlight their differences.

2. If you moved to another country to live and work, would you consider renouncing your American citizenship? Write an essay explaining your views.

3. *Collaborative Writing:* Discuss Mukherjee's essay with a group of students. Work together to develop a brief essay that outlines the pros and cons of becoming an American citizen. Only citizens can vote. Does the writer's sister deny herself the ability of choosing the leaders of the country she is living in? Ask members of the group whether they have any friends or relatives who decided either to become citizens or retain their original nationality.

CHRISTOPHER JENCKS

Christopher Jencks is the Malcolm Wiener Professor of Social Policy at Harvard University's Kennedy School of Government. He has taught at the University of Chicago, Northwestern University, and the University of California at Santa Barbara. His books include The Academic Revolution (*with David Reisman*), The Homeless, Inequality, Who Gets Ahead? *and* Rethinking Social Policy.

Reinventing the American Dream

CONTEXT: *In this article, which appeared in* The Chronicle of Higher Education *in 2008, Jencks compares the Republican and Democratic views of the American Dream and explains why both will have to be reinvented.*

The American Dream sounds like apple pie and motherhood. Everyone is for it. 1

But when everyone endorses an ideal, whether it's the American Dream, 2 equal opportunity, or justice, you can be pretty sure that they disagree about what the ideal means, and that the appearance of agreement is being achieved by talking past one another.

There are at least two competing versions of the American Dream, and 3 they are not only different but mutually incompatible. Perhaps even more alarming is the fact that they will both need to be reinvented if our children and grandchildren are to inhabit a livable planet.

In one version, this country is the place where anyone who builds a better 4 mousetrap can get rich. To do that, the mousetrap builder will need a lot of help: workers to make the mousetraps, salespeople to put them in the hands of consumers, and security guards to prevent the world from beating a path to the inventor's door and helping themselves. In order to get rich, mousetrap developers will also have to pay their workers far less than they make themselves. Otherwise there won't be enough money left over from mousetrap sales to make the inventor rich.

This version of the American Dream emphasizes individual talent and 5 effort. It favors freedom and opposes government regulation. And it belongs to the Republican Party.

Democrats have another version of the American Dream: Everyone who 6 works hard and behaves responsibly can achieve a decent standard of living. But the definition of a decent standard of living is a moving target. For those who came of age before 1950, it usually meant a steady job, owning a house in a safe neighborhood with decent schools, and believing that your children would have a chance to go to college even if you did not.

7   True, lots of people who worked hard and behaved responsibly didn't realize this dream. Blue-collar workers were laid off during recessions through no fault of their own, and their jobs often disappeared when technological progress allowed employers to produce more stuff with fewer workers. Still, more and more people achieved this dream between 1945 and 1970, so the Democratic version of the American Dream had broader appeal than the Republican version, in which a smaller number of people could get much richer.

8   Since the early 1970s, however, all that has changed.

9   The American economy has been under siege. Real per capita disposable income has continued to grow, but the average annual increase has fallen, from 2.7 percent between 1947 and 1973 to 1.8 percent between 1973 and 2005. Of course, even a 1.8 percent annual increase in purchasing power is far more than the human species achieved during most of its history, and it is also far more than we are likely to achieve in the future unless we do a lot of creative accounting.

10   What transformed the political landscape was not the slowdown in growth but the distributional change that accompanied it. From 1947 to 1973, the purchasing power of those in the bottom 95 percent of the income distribution rose at the same rate as per capita disposable income, about 2.7 percent a year. Among families in the top 5 percent, the growth rate was 2.2 percent. From 1973 to 2006, however, the average annual increase in the purchasing power of the bottom 95 percent was only .6 percent. The top 5 percent, in contrast, managed to maintain annual growth of 2.0 percent, which was almost the same as what they enjoyed before 1973.

11   That's a lot of numbers, but what my students at the Kennedy School call the "take-away" is pretty simple: After 1973, when economic growth slowed, America had a choice. We would have tried to share the pain equally by maintaining the social contract under which living standards had risen at roughly the same rate among families at all levels. Or we could have treated the slowdown in growth as evidence that the Democratic version of the American Dream didn't work, and that we should try the Republican version, in which we all look out for ourselves, some people get rich, and most get left behind.

12   We chose the Republican option.

13   That formulation is deceptive, of course, because voters did not have a clear choice. Many Democratic politicians accepted the Republican argument that the cure for slower growth was to make markets more competitive and government regulation less onerous. Very few Democrats argued that an adverse shift in the distribution of private-sector earnings was something the government should insure Americans against, like a Mississippi flood or a terrorist attack on the World Trade Center. In that respect the Democrats were very different from the parties of the left in Western Europe, but quite similar to the parties of the left in most other English-speaking countries.

One reason for Anglophone caution about protecting the citizenry from an 14
adverse shift in the distribution of income is that English-speaking economists
(which is to say almost all economists, even in non-English-speaking countries) were mostly blaming the rise in economic inequality on what they
called "skill-biased technological change." That argument was correct as far as
it went, but it didn't go very far and was therefore deeply misleading.

In their new book, *The Race Between Education and Technology* (Belknap 15
Press/Harvard University Press, 2008), Claudia Goldin and Lawrence F. Katz
argue—convincingly, in my view—that demand for skilled workers has indeed risen since 1973. But they also argue that demand for skilled workers rose
no faster after 1973 than it had between 1910 and 1973.

What changed was that before 1973, the supply of skilled workers grew at 16
about the same rate as demand, so relative wages were fairly stable. After 1973
the supply of skilled workers grew far more slowly, even though demand kept
rising. That imbalance played a significant role in raising inequality, at least
between 1975 and 2000.

Between 1940 and 1980, the number of years of school completed by the 17
average worker rose almost one year every decade (actually, .86 years).
Between 1980 and 2005, the increase was only half that (.43 years per
decade). If you exclude GEDs, administrative data indicate that high-school
graduation rates have hardly changed since the early 1970s. At the same time,
immigration has increased the supply of unskilled workers.

Those changes might not have led to a deterioration of wages and working 18
conditions among unskilled workers if we had tried to protect their livelihoods, but we didn't. Congress and presidents let the minimum wage lag farther and farther behind inflation from 1981 to 2006. Large employers and the
National Labor Relations Board made it harder to organize unions. Weaker
unions found it harder to protect their members, and that, in turn, reduced
the number of workers who wanted to join.

Again, this is a complicated story, but the take-away is pretty straightfor- 19
ward. Since 1973 both the federal government and the states have made less
effort to raise the educational attainment of the young. They have also made
less effort to protect the incomes of the less educated.

Why should that be? I'm not sure, but I have a hypothesis. Forty-some years 20
ago, I was attending a White House conference on higher education and ran
into Edmund G. (Pat) Brown, who was then governor of California, as we
waited for an elevator. I had been studying at the University of California, and
I asked him about the university's budget problems.

Brown, a Democrat, said the university always had budget problems when 21
the Democrats controlled the state. Having always thought of Democrats as
big spenders and friends of education, I was startled and asked why, just as we
reached his floor. His parting answer was (roughly): "Democrats want to spend

money on everything; Republicans only want to spend money on highways and the university, where they went and expect to send their children."

22   I don't know if that hypothesis holds up empirically, but I do think one big reason we have done so little to raise educational attainment since 1973 is that both federal and state budgets are much tighter. We cut the share of the gross domestic product going to national defense from 10 percent in 1959 to 5.5 percent in 1973 to 4.0 percent in 2006. But since 1973, that reduction has been more than offset by the government's increased spending on health care and Social Security. Even expenditures per student on K-through-12 education have risen faster than expenditures per student on higher education. According to the National Center for Education Statistics, expenditures per student in public elementary and secondary schools doubled between 1970–71 and 2000–1, even adjusted for inflation. Real expenditures per student in public colleges and universities rose only 35 percent during that period.

23   One alternative to keeping young people in school longer might have been to regulate the economy in ways analogous to what Germany, France, the Low Countries, and Scandinavia did to keep wages relatively equal. In truth, though, we would have had to both expand education and regulate the labor market to keep alive the Democratic version of the American Dream. Regulation arouses even more resistance from employers than does taxation. And unlike their European counterparts, American employers usually have something close to a veto over policy changes that don't involve national security.

24   Employers argue that regulating the market drives up costs and slows job growth. Growth statistics for the past 50 years offer some support for that claim. But since 1970, annual growth has been only about a tenth of a percentage point higher in inegalitarian countries than in egalitarian countries. To be sure, income is not all that matters, and dumb regulations can certainly slow job growth and generate high unemployment. But there is no reason why egalitarian regulations have to be dumb.

25   In any case, few Democratic politicians think voters would accept that approach to solving the economic problems of the bottom 95 percent, and I think they are right, at least in the short run. In the long run, a concerted effort to revive a Democratic version of the American Dream might change the rhetorical environment, but meanwhile, the Democrats would have to resign themselves to a long period in the wilderness, with no assurance that their strategy would ever appeal to most voters. Few politicians want to take such a risk.

26   In the long run, moreover, both the Democratic and Republican versions of the American Dream will have to be rethought. They both focus heavily on income and material consumption. The idea that we can keep raising our material standard of living without making most of the planet too hot for human habitation is, I think, mistaken. Even the idea that we have 20 or 30 years to make the necessary adjustments appears wrongheaded.

So I'm afraid reinventing the American Dream really means trying to wean 27 ourselves from the illusion that we all need and deserve more stuff. If we are to survive, we need a different definition of progress. That definition will need to focus on human needs like physical health, material security, individual freedom, and time to play with our children and smell the roses.

I'm not saying that material goods are unimportant. People need food to 28 sustain them, a home in which they can afford to live until they die, and medical advice when they are sick. But I'm not sure people my age (71) need a million-dollar machine to keep us alive another year or two. And I am quite sure that most of us could live without 85 percent of the stuff we buy in places other than grocery stores and gas stations.

An American Dream that doesn't destroy the planet will have to involve a 29 more-equal distribution of basic material goods. It will also have to involve more emphasis on the quality of the services we consume than on the quality of our possessions. Perhaps most important, it will have to involve more emphasis on what we can do for others and less emphasis on what we can get for ourselves.

There is just one small problem. I have no idea how to get from here to 30 there. That makes me a pessimist.

Understanding Meaning

1. How does Jencks describe the conflicting visions of the American Dream embraced by the Republican and Democratic parties? Do you detect any bias in his comparison? Which vision better represents your own definition of the American Dream?

2. How did the American economy change after 1973?

3. Why have workers' wages failed to rise?

4. *Critical Thinking:* Why does Jencks believe that both perceptions of the American Dream must be reinvented? Do both versions of American success require a level of consumption that is unsustainable?

Evaluating Strategy

1. How does Jencks use comparison to explain conflicting visions of the American Dream?

2. *Critical Thinking:* In two places Jencks states a number of statistics, then summarizes the main points in a simple explanation he calls the "takeaway." Do you think this is an effective way of connecting with readers who may not understand or remember complex data? Have professors used a similar technique giving lectures? Might some readers find this approach patronizing?

3. *Blending the Modes:* Where does Jencks use *narration, definition,* and *persuasion* to develop his essay?

4. Jencks ends his essay stating that he has no idea how to achieve the solutions he advocates. Does this weaken his argument? Might some readers be impressed by his honesty?

Appreciating Language

1. Does Jencks describe the opposing views of the American Dream in neutral terms? Do you detect any bias in his choice of words?

2. Jencks uses the term "egalitarian." How would you define this term?

3. How does Jencks want to redefine the term "progress"?

WRITING SUGGESTIONS

1. Write a short essay defining your vision of the American Dream. Do you follow Jencks' depiction of the Republican or the Democratic version or a blend?

2. *Collaborative Writing:* Discuss Jencks' essay with a group of students and ask them to respond to his argument that "reinventing the American Dream really means trying to wean ourselves from the illusion that we all need and deserve more stuff." Record students' responses and write an essay summarizing their views. If they have conflicting opinions, consider developing a comparison or classification essay.

PEGGY KENNA AND SONDRA LACY

Peggy Kenna and Sondra Lacy are communications specialists based in Arizona who work with foreign-born employees. In addition, they provide cross-cultural training to executives conducting international business. Kenna is a speech and language pathologist who specializes in accent modification. Kenna and Lacy have collaborated on a series of fifty-page booklets that compare American and foreign business organizations, habits, behaviors, and negotiating styles. Widely sold in airports, these booklets give Americans tips on doing business overseas.

Communication Styles: United States and Taiwan

CONTEXT: *This section from* Business Taiwan *contrasts American and Taiwanese styles of communicating. In designing their booklets for quick skimming, Kenna and Lacy use charts to highlight cultural differences.*

UNITED STATES	TAIWAN
• *Frank*	• *Subtle*
Americans tend to be very straightforward and unreserved. The people of Taiwan often find them abrupt and not interested enough in human relationships.	Frankness is not appreciated by the people of Taiwan. They particularly dislike unqualified negative statements.
• *Face saving less important*	• *Face saving important*
To Americans accuracy is important but errors are tolerated. Admitting mistakes is seen as a sign of maturity. They believe you learn from failure and therefore encourage some risk taking.	The Chinese do not like to be put in the position of having to admit a mistake or failure. They also do not like to tell you when they don't understand your point.
Americans believe criticism can be objective and not personal; however, all criticism should be done with tact.	You also should not admit too readily when you don't know something as it can cause you to lose face.

1 UNITED STATES

2 • *Frank*

3 Americans tend to be very straightforward and unreserved. The people of Taiwan often find them abrupt and not interested enough in human relationships.

4 • *Face saving less important*

5 To Americans accuracy is important but errors are tolerated. Admitting mistakes is seen as a sign of maturity. They believe you learn from failure and therefore encourage some risk taking.

6 Americans believe criticism can be objective and not personal; however, all criticism should be done with tact.

7 UNITED STATES

8 • **Direct eye contact**

9 Direct eye contact is very important to Americans since they need to see the nonverbal cues the speaker is giving. Nonverbal cues are a very important part of the American English language. Americans use intermittent eye contact when they are speaking but fairly steady eye contact when they are listening.

10 • **Direct and to the point**

11 Americans prefer people to say what they mean. Because of this, they sometimes tend to miss subtle nonverbal cues. Americans are uncomfortable with ambiguousness and don't like to have to "fill in the blanks." They also tend to discuss problems directly.

12

13

14 • **"Yes" means agreement**

15 Americans look for clues such as nodding of the head, a verbal "yes" or "uh huh" in order to determine if their arguments are succeeding.

TAIWAN

• **Avoid direct eye contact**

Holding the gaze of another person is considered rude.

• **Indirect and ambiguous**

People in Taiwan dislike saying "no." They may not tell you when they don't understand. They often hedge their answers if they know you won't like the answer. If they say something like, "We'll think about it," they may mean they aren't interested.

They dislike discussing problems directly and will often go around the issue, which can be frustrating for Americans.

The Chinese language (Mandarin) is so concise that the listener needs to use much imagination to "fill in the gaps."

• **"Yes" means "I hear"**

People in Taiwan do not judge information given to them so they do not indicate agreement or disagreement; they only nod or say "yes" to indicate they are listening to you. The people of Taiwan believe politeness is more important than frankness so they will not directly tell you "no." The closest they will come to "no" is "maybe."

Understanding Meaning

1. What appear to be the major differences between American and Taiwanese methods of communicating?

2. Why is it important for Americans to be sensitive about making direct eye contact with Taiwanese?

3. How do Americans and Taiwanese accept failure?

4. *Critical Thinking:* Why would this booklet be valuable to Americans visiting Taiwan on business? Does such a brief, to-the-point guide risk relying on stereotypes?

Evaluating Strategy

1. How easy is this document to read and review? How accessible would the information be if it were written in standard paragraphs?

2. What does the directness of the document reveal about the intended audience? Would it be suitable for a college classroom?

Appreciating Language

1. What language do the writers use in describing the Taiwanese? Do they attempt to be neutral, or does their word choice favor one nationality over another?

2. Kenna and Lacy suggest that many Taiwanese find Americans to be "abrupt." Is this a good word choice? Does the guide express common prejudices?

WRITING SUGGESTIONS

1. Using Kenna and Lacy's entry as a source, write a short, instructive process paper about how an American should present an idea or product in Taiwan. Assume you are writing to sales representatives traveling to Taiwan for the first time. Provide step-by-step suggestions for how they should conduct themselves from the moment they enter a seminar room to make a presentation.

2. *Collaborative Writing:* Working with a group of students, discuss the differences between high school teachers and college instructors, then develop a chart contrasting their attitudes toward absenteeism, late homework, tests, and research papers.

RESPONDING TO IMAGES

HENRY FORD II INTRODUCES THE 1949 FORD

CONTEXT: *The Ford Motor Company faced bankruptcy following World War II. In 1949 it introduced a streamlined car with many new features that became so popular it was called "the car that saved Ford." Over a million were produced.*

1. What is your first reaction to this photograph? What does this image represent to you? Is it a quaint image of an old-fashioned car or a reminder of a time when America dominated cutting-edge technology?

2. How could this image be used to illustrate a comparison between past and present?

3. Could Ford use this image today to remind car buyers, investors, and Congress that it has overcome adversity in the past? Would this image paired next to a modern Ford make an effective ad? Why or why not?

4. How have car ads changed in recent years? Once status symbols, cars are now associated with pollution, energy waste, government bailouts, and safety problems. How can a troubled auto company use images to overcome negative assumptions and win consumer confidence?

5. *Critical Thinking:* What kind of car do American automakers need to produce today to win back the market share they have lost to foreign companies?

6. *Collaborative Writing:* Discuss this image with other students. Work together and develop a new caption or a brief description to use this photo in an ad. What product or service would you promote with this picture— a TV show set in the Fifties, life insurance, a modern car, or a political organization lobbying for or against American corporations?

STRATEGIES FOR WRITING COMPARISON AND CONTRAST

1. **Determine your purpose.** Is your goal to explain differences between two topics, recommend one over the other, or show how a single subject has changed? Do you want readers to be informed, or do you wish them to make a choice?

2. **Consider your audience.** Before you can compare two items, you may have to explain background information. For example, before comparing two treatments for arthritis, it may be necessary to explain the nature of the disease and to define basic terminology.

3. **Determine which method would best suit your topic.** A short, nontechnical paper might be best organized using the subject-by-subject method. Longer works with facts and statistics that should be placed side by side are better developed using the point-by-point method.

4. **Make use of transitional statements.** To prevent confusion in writing comparison, use transitional statements carefully. You may wish to invent labels or titles to distinguish clearly the different subjects you are examining.

5. **Use visual aids to guide your readers.** Careful paragraphing, page breaks, bold or italic headings, and charts can help readers follow your comparison and prevent confusion.

SUGGESTED TOPICS FOR COMPARISON AND CONTRAST WRITING

GENERAL ASSIGNMENTS

Write a comparative paper on one of the following topics. You may use either subject-by-subject or point-by-point methods of organization. Clearly determine your purpose. Is your goal to inform or recommend?

1. High school versus college

2. Your best and worst jobs

3. Male and female student attitudes on dating/marriage/career/parenting

4. Working for a salary or an hourly wage

5. Two popular situation comedies

6. A sport team's performance this season compared to last season

7. Your favorite and least favorite college courses

8. Your parents' values and your own

9. Something you planned and the way it actually turned out

10. Before-and-after views of how a person, family, neighborhood, company, or social behavior changed over time or after a particular event

WRITING IN CONTEXT

1. Imagine you have been asked by a British newsmagazine to write an article explaining the pro-and-con attitudes Americans have about a controversial topic such as gun control, capital punishment, or health care. Your article should be balanced and objective and provide background information rather than express an opinion.

2. Write the text for a brief pamphlet directed to high school seniors comparing high school and college. You may wish to use a chart-like format.

3. Write a letter to a friend comparing the best and worst aspects of your college, dorm room, community, or job.

4. Examine a magazine or blog on cars, computers, or entertainment. Write a letter to the editor or blogger comparing the magazine or blog's best and worst features.

5. Compare two popular student clubs or restaurants for a review in the campus newspaper. Direct your comments to students interested in inexpensive entertainment.

Student Paper: Comparison and Contrast

This is a draft of a comparison paper a student wrote after reading several articles comparing different cultures. In addition to fulfilling a composition assignment, she considered using these ideas for a talk or display for an upcoming Saint Patrick's Day celebration.

First Draft with Instructor's Comments

Two Countries

At first glance Israel and Ireland would appear to have

nothing in common except their small size, but in fact they are

exaggeration — refine this statement, no two countries are ever "just alike"

just alike. Both countries are small but famous nations. They both

have the same kind of history. They share the same history of   *be more accurate*

oppression and a long struggle for independance. Both countries   *sp*

have dealt with terrorism and are important nations when it comes

to world politics, culture, and terrorism.

Maybe the most striking common thing about these countries is

refine this statement, are they "identical"??

that they have identical histories. Both countries only become

fully independent after WWII. Maybe the basic thing these countries   *word(s) missing?*

have is that the Irish and Jews have so much in common as a people.

run-on

In fact many Americans are Jewish and Irish and they see these

countries as special places that represent the roots of there   *sp/their*

ancestors. The Jews and Irish both have large communities all over the world and have played leading roles in countries from France

and England to Chile and Canada.

countries   Another thing that the <u>counties</u> have in common is the way

sp   <u>relgion</u>. has uniquely shaped their history and continues to play

a role in their modern social dynamics. The same conflict happens

Vague   in both countries over a range of important social and political
what
debates?   **be more specific**
issues. Some of these same debates happen in the United States

today.

Maybe the most striking issue of these two countries is the

role that the United States has played a part in trying to resolve

"have"   long-standing issues that <u>has</u> caused terrorism and other problems.
plural
needed   **Wordy, vague, explain in detail.**
Maybe what is most interesting about these countries is how

they went from being poor struggling counties just fifty years ago

to having the highest per capita incomes in their regions. They

are bound to be winners in the global economy.

REVISION NOTES

You have selected an interesting topic, but to create a meaningful comparison essay, you need to refine points and develop more support.

* No two countries are "just alike." For all the similarities you can draw between Ireland and Israel, readers can list dozens of differences. Admit that both are distinctly different nations with unique histories, then point out striking parallels. Parallel items are similar but not totally identical. Avoid absolute statements like "just alike" or "the same."

* *A comparison essay needs to be carefully structured. Create stronger paragraph introductions and transitions beyond saying "another thing." Write a stronger outline and clearly define what each paragraph will be about. Use paragraphs as building blocks that work together to build a coherent essay.*

* *Finally, in order for this essay to be more than just a list of casual observations, add specific details about each point you address. You might want to conduct some research to identify support.*

Revised Draft

Parallel States: Israel and Ireland

Despite obvious historical and cultural differences, Israel and Ireland share striking similarities. Both are small—each has a population of five to six million—yet significant nations. Israel is a narrow sliver of desert on the Mediterranean, a Middle Eastern country with negligible oil reserves. Ireland, an island on the fringe of Europe, is a neutral nation which played marginal roles in World War II and the Cold War.

Yet these nations have greater profiles than their larger and more powerful neighbors, largely because they represent homelands to vast diaspora populations. More Jews live in America than Israel; more Irish live in America than Ireland. American Jews and Irish were significant supporters of the Zionist and Republican movements that helped establish the modern independent states.

Their recent emergence as sovereign states indicates a shared legacy of oppression and occupation. Although both the Jews and the Irish have cultures thousands of years old, Israel and Ireland did not achieve full independence until after the Second World War. Israel was recognized by the United Nations in 1948. Though partitioned in 1922, Ireland was not officially declared a republic until 1949, ending eight hundred years of British influence.

Since their creation, Israel and Ireland have endured decades of violence and terrorism. Both nations have labored to maintain democratic rights while preserving security for their citizenry.

Both nations have dual identities. On one hand, both Israel and Ireland were founded as Western-style parliamentary democracies. Yet both are religious states. Israel is the Jewish

homeland. Ireland is a Catholic nation. The religious authorities—
the Catholic bishops and orthodox rabbis—believe citizens should
accept their views on marriage, divorce, abortion, censorship, and
civil customs. Secular forces, who view the religious orthodoxies
as tradition bound and male dominated, champion diversity and
tolerance. Issues such as the role of women and gay rights evoke
similar debates in Israel and Ireland as both nations struggle to
reconcile their political and religious traditions.

In recent years both nations have engaged in a peace process
to resolve long-standing conflicts in contested areas. In both
Northern Ireland and the West Bank, the populations are split by
religious, political, and cultural differences.

Recently the president of the United States, prompted by the
large number of Jews and Irish in America, played a pivotal role in
stimulating stalled peace talks. Negotiations in both regions were
difficult to conduct because Israeli and Northern Irish politicians
did not wish to recognize leaders of terrorist organizations.

By first inviting Yasser Arafat and Gerry Adams to the White
House, Bill Clinton helped transform their public images from terrorists to legitimate leaders so that other democratic leaders
could negotiate with them without appearing to endorse violence.

Despite ongoing tensions in both regions, Israel and Ireland
enjoy expanding tourism, particularly from millions of American
Jews and Irish who enjoy visiting homelands that represent their
heritage.

Economically, Israel and Ireland, both poor struggling countries just forty years ago, have become affluent high-tech power-
houses with rising per capita incomes and commanding places in the
global economy.

QUESTIONS FOR REVIEW AND REVISION

1. Is the thesis of this essay too general? Does the paper provide genuine insights or merely list obvious observations? Would it be better to develop a single issue fully, such as the role of religion in the two countries?

2. Would a revised introduction and conclusion provide greater focus?

3. What audience does the student seem to address?

4. *Critical Thinking:* To be effective, does a comparison paper have to accomplish more than merely list similarities? Should there be a greater purpose?

5. How effectively does the student organize the comparison? What role does paragraph structure play?

6. Does the student follow the instructor's suggestions? Is this version greatly improved over the first draft?

7. Read the paper aloud. Do you detect any passages that could be revised to reduce wordiness and repetition?

WRITING SUGGESTIONS

1. Write a 500-word essay comparing two nations, cities, or neighborhoods. Stress similarities of which most readers would be unaware.

2. *Collaborative Writing:* Discuss this paper with a group of students. Ask each member to suggest possible changes. Do they agree on which areas need improvement?

COMPARISON AND CONTRAST CHECKLIST

Before submitting your paper, review these points:

1. **Are your subjects closely related enough to make a valid comparison?**

2. **Have you identified the key points of both subjects?**

3. **Have you selected the best method of organizing your paper?**

4. **Is the comparison easy to follow? Are transitions clear?**

5. **Does the comparison meet reader needs and expectations?**

6. **Have you defined terms or provided background information necessary for readers to appreciate the comparison fully?**

7. **Is your thesis clearly stated and located where it will have the greatest impact?**

Info Write provides additional information about writing comparison and contrast.
cengage.learning.infowrite.com

CRITICAL ISSUES

- ◆ Health Care

- ◆ Immigration

- ◆ Criminal Justice

- ◆ Privacy in the Electronic Age

CONFRONTING ISSUES

Throughout our lives, we face issues that affect our jobs, our futures, our nation, and the planet we live on. In order to fully understand these issues and respond to them effectively, we need to analyze information, evaluate points of view, and express ideas and opinions clearly and logically.

You may already have strong views about many of the issues presented in this book. It is likely that you have heard them debated on television or discussed by family and friends. Good writers, however, do more than simply express what they feel or repeat what they have heard from others. To address complex and often controversial subjects, it is important to move beyond first impressions and immediate reactions.

LEARNING MORE ABOUT ISSUES

We are bombarded with information about issues through 24-hour cable news networks, newspapers, and the Internet. These sources, however, generally provide superficial and repetitive accounts of current events. To write meaningfully about issues, it is important to understand background information and appreciate different points of view.

Strategies For Learning More About Issues

1. **Get an overall description or history of the issue.** Try to get the "big picture" first by leaning the basics. What has been the history of immigration? Why do most Americans obtain health insurance through their employers? How many Americans are incarcerated?

2. **Understand key terms.** What is "identity theft"? Are there conflicting interpretations of "the right to privacy"? Do you understand terms such as "single payer," "universal coverage," or "preexisting condition"? What is a "green card"?

3. **Establish key facts.** People often discuss issues using misleading or obsolete data. To evaluate sources and write effectively, try to obtain recent and accurate data. How many immigrants enter the United States each year? How do international organizations determine infant mortality? How many people have a Facebook page?

4. **Distinguish objective, widely accepted facts from ideas subject to debate, controversy, or conflicting interpretation.** Experts may accept that millions of Americans lack proper health care but disagree over the role of government in providing coverage. Historians may agree that immigration benefited American society in the past but argue over

whether twenty-first century immigration policies will help or harm in the future. Try to find out what information most experts accept as valid. Determine what events, ideas, situations, or interpretations are debated or contested.

5. **Identify leading authorities, organizations, experts, commentators, activists, or participants.** Who are the major advocates of universal health care? Who opposes it? Who supports immigration reform? Who rejects it? What columnists, academics, or government officials have written about criminal justice or online privacy? If there is an active debate about this issue, who is on the pro side? Who are the major figures on the con side?

6. **Establish main schools of thought or points of disagreement.** What are the major differences between those who write about immigration? Why do people support or oppose mandatory sentences for drug dealers? What different approaches do experts advocate to counter cyberbullying? Is there a liberal or conservative point of view on this issue? Is this an argument between science and faith or between different visions of social justice?

STRATEGIES FOR FINDING INFORMATION ABOUT ISSUES

Although you may not have time to conduct extensive research about each issue you will study in this course, there are sources that will help you become a more informed reader and an effective writer.

1. **Review textbooks.** Textbooks offer brief overviews of subjects and often include endnotes, bibliographies, and footnotes directing you to additional sources.

2. **Survey encyclopedia articles.** A good encyclopedia will present background information and objective facts to give you an overview of an issue. Online encyclopedias have search features that allow you to enter keywords to generate a list of related articles.

3. **Review specialized encyclopedias, dictionaries, and directories.** A general encyclopedia such as *The Encyclopedia Britannica* may offer only brief commentaries on subjects and will not include minor people, events, or topics. The reference room of your library will likely have specialized encyclopedias that may contain multipage articles about a person or organization not even mentioned in general encyclopedias.

4. **Review indexes, databases, and abstracts.** Available in print, online, or on CD-ROM, these are valuable tools in obtaining information. Databases list articles. Many provide abstracts which briefly summarize

articles, usually in a single paragraph. Skimming abstracts allows you to review a dozen articles in the time it would take to locate a magazine and find a single article. Abstracts not only list the source of an article but also indicate its length and special features such as photographs or tables. Sources like *Chemical Abstracts*, *Psychological Abstracts*, and *Criminal Justice Abstracts* provide summaries in specific disciplines. Other databases are especially useful because they allow you to read and print entire articles. Many libraries subscribe to online services, such as InfoTrac, which list articles from thousands of general, business, and scholarly newspapers, journals, and magazines.

5. **Conduct an Internet search.** In addition to specific databases such as InfoTrac, you can use popular search engines such as Google, Alta Vista, Yahoo!, Excite, HotBot, and Bing to search for sources on the Internet. Each of these accesses millions of sites on the World Wide Web. These tools offer Web guides that organize sites by categories such as "arts and humanities," "education," or "news and media." You can also enter key words to generate focused lists.

Students unfamiliar with conducting Internet searches are often frustrated by the overwhelming list of unrelated "hits" they receive. Entering **Martin Luther King Jr.** may generate thousands of sites about **Billy Martin**, **Martin Luther**, and **King George III**.

Search engines usually provide tools to refine your search.

- Check the spelling of your search terms, especially names.

- Make the search words as specific as possible.

- Follow the directions to narrow your search:

  terrorism AND immigration *or* **terrorism + immigration** will list sites that include one or both words.

  terrorism NOT immigration *or* **terrorism − immigration** will list sites about terrorism that do not mention immigration.

  "Leopold and Loeb" will list only sites that include both names, eliminating documents about **King Leopold** or **Loeb Realty**.

- If you find it difficult to locate useful sources, ask a reference librarian for assistance.

HEALTH CARE

All health systems have pluses and minuses; all ration health care in some way. We ration it, harshly, by income and price. People with money and access command top-notch care. Those without scramble for what they can get. Big businesses negotiate good group health insurance. Small businesses are pushed against the wall. The healthy find private policies, the sick get kicked out. That's the American way.

Jane Bryant Quinn

A century ago, most physicians in the United States had only a fragmentary knowledge of medicine. Only 10 percent had a college degree. Some medical schools did not require applicants to have a high school diploma and granted a license with just six months training. Apprenticed to older doctors, medical students learned by observation. Little connection was made between research and practice. Equipped with dubious medicines and crude surgical techniques, doctors were frequently able to provide their patients with little more than emotional support.

The twentieth century saw a revolution in medical science, education, and technology. Extensive operations that required weeks of hospital care were replaced with minimally invasive procedures performed in outpatient clinics. New generations of drugs improved the quality of life for millions. Doctors became heroic figures, portrayed as selfless role models of skill, wisdom, and compassion. Americans came to expect immediate access to high-tech medical care.

Yet each year patients die or suffer injuries from medical malpractice. Surgeons make mistakes. Hospitals fail to follow postoperative procedures. Patients develop infections and drug interactions. According to an Institute of Medicine report, 98,000 hospital patients died from preventable medical errors in 1998. To protect themselves from lawsuits, doctors and hospitals carry malpractice insurance. In recent years, many doctors who have never been sued have seen their premiums rise from $30,000 to over $100,000 a year. In response, doctors have refused to treat high-risk patients, moved from states with high jury awards, or switched specialties to lower their rates. Leo Boyle argues that "the problem of medical malpractice is that it occurs far too often… killing more people than AIDS, breast cancer, or automobile crashes." Philip K. Howard insists the legal system has failed to address the problem, noting, "Most victims of error get nothing, while others win lottery-like jury awards even when the doctor did nothing wrong."

As medical technology has increased, so has its cost. The Centers for Medicare and Medicaid Services estimated that $2.34 trillion was spent on health care in the United States in 2008—$7,681 per person. Health care costs now represent 16 percent of the nation's economy. Combined, Medicare and Medicaid spent over $800 billion in 2008. The rising costs of health care are affecting American corporations. In 2005, General Motors reported that health care costs added $1,600 to the price of every vehicle sold. Providing health insurance for employees and retirees has made it harder for American corporations to compete with cheaper imports, further encouraging companies to send jobs overseas where both labor and benefits are cheaper.

Advances in medical technology have also continued to raise ethical questions about providing health care for the poor, using technology to extend the lives of the terminally ill, the pricing of new drugs, and fetal stem cell research.

Before reading these articles, consider these questions:

Examine the ads for doctors, hospitals, and malpractice attorneys in your local yellow pages. How do doctors and lawyers represent themselves to the public?

Is litigation the best way to redress medical malpractice? Does suing a few doctors on behalf of individual patients lead to reform or simply encourage doctors to practice "defensive medicine" and order unnecessary tests?

Do hospital dramas and drug commercials give the public unrealistic expectations of medical technology?

What kind of health care coverage, if any, do you or members of your family have?

Who should pay for the care of those who cannot afford health insurance?

Should patients or their families have the right to decide when to withdraw life support from the terminally ill or severely brain-damaged?

Should everyone in your family have a living will? If someone becomes incapacitated, who should make decisions about treatment? Do you feel you know how members of your family wish to be cared for in the event they become unable to communicate with their doctors?

E-READINGS ONLINE

Find each article by visiting the Premium Website, accessed through **CengageBrain.com.**

Katherine Baicker and Amitabh Chandra. *Defensive Medicine and Disappearing Doctors?*

Increases in malpractice insurance premiums and jury awards have led doctors to practice defensive medicine and limit their services.

Leo Boyle. *The Truth about Medical Malpractice*

The Association of American Trial Lawyers argues the malpractice crisis is not caused by litigation but by preventable medical error. Malpractice, Boyle asserts, kills more Americans each year than AIDS or breast cancer.

Health & Medicine Week. *Auto Manufacturers Say U.S. Must Solve Healthcare Crisis.*

With corporate health care costs rising 10 percent a year, the president of the United Auto Workers argues, "Our healthcare crisis is a national problem which demands a national solution" to keep America from losing its industrial base.

Dan Frosch. *Your Money or Your Life: When Getting Sick Means Going Broke.*

The middle class now accounts for nearly 90 percent of those declaring bankruptcy because of medical expenses.

Linda Stern. *Money: Grown Up and Uninsured.*

One-third of young adults lack health insurance, leading them to avoid seeing doctors and exposing them to crippling debts in the event of a medical emergency.

Jane Bryant Quinn. *Our 'Kindness Deficit' of Care: We Ration Health Care, Harshly, By Income and Price*

Those with generous medical benefits or money can afford top-notch care; the poor scramble for what they can get.

Jerry Adler and Jeneen Interlandi. *The Hospital That Could Cure Health Care*

The Cleveland Clinic, which provides high-quality, cost-efficient medicine, demonstrates how technology can both improve care and save money.

Jane Orient. *Fractured Healthcare: Americans Are Told That We Need "Universal Healthcare," But That Would Be Disastrous*

A physician argues that universal health care would only bring "universal health care rationing," longer waits for treatment, lower standards of care, and higher mortality rates for curable diseases.

K. J. Lee. *A Solution for America's Healthcare Crisis*

Health care costs could be lowered by eliminating waste and inefficiency and providing physicians and hospitals with "accurate, real-time, transparent data."

Christian Kryder. *The "F" Word in Healthcare: Eliminating Fraud Can Cut $250 Billion of Current Healthcare System Costs*

One health care dollar in ten is lost to fraud, which could be greatly reduced through making data transparent and developing fraud detection systems.

Bill Kettler. *Health Without Borders: Medical Tourism*

Seeking high quality, affordable health care, more Americans are going overseas for medical treatment.

US Newswire. *New Data Shows Obesity Costs Will Grow to $344 Billion by 2018.*

Because it is linked to the early onset of serious and expensive-to-treat diseases, obesity is a serious risk to the nation's health and economic well-being.

Michael Marschke. *To Die Well*

The elderly and dying should be given palliative care to provide comfort in their last days rather than aggressive procedures designed to cure them.

Jill Lepore. *The Politics of Death*

Medical technology has increased life expectancy and extended terminal illnesses so that "the longer we live, the longer we die." Over a quarter of Medicare money now pays for medical services in the final year of life.

Critical Reading and Thinking

1. Do you detect a "war" between doctors and lawyers?

2. Is there a better way of identifying and punishing incompetent or irresponsible physicians than costly litigation?

3. Does litigation force medical professionals to raise standards or does it only raise costs?

4. How has the cost of health care affected individuals, corporations, and the national economy?

5. Will upper-income professionals resist changes in health care policy in order to create a system that provides care for the uninsured because they fear losing some of their benefits?

6. Should health care coverage be linked to employment?

7. How important are statistics in these articles? Do they provide compelling evidence of a crisis? What role do case histories—stories about specific people—play in these articles? Is one kind of support more effective than another? Should writers rely on more than one type of evidence to develop persuasive arguments?

1. If you or someone you know has been involved in a medical malpractice case, write a short essay describing what you or they learned from the experience.

2. Draft a brief letter responding to one or more of the writers. Agree or disagree with the views expressed.

3. *Collaborative writing:* Review these articles with a group of students and discuss a single issue, such as medical malpractice, insurance benefits, medical costs, or the right to die. Develop an essay dividing the group's observations into categories or contrasting opposing viewpoints.

4. *Other modes*

   - Write a short *process* paper suggesting a fair method of handling malpractice cases.

   - Write a brief *definition* of "medical malpractice." What distinguishes malpractice from an honest error in judgment?

   - Develop a *cause-and-effect* essay detailing the causes and effects of rising health care costs. What are the causes—incompetent medical professionals, aggressive trial lawyers, patient expectations, or new technology? What are the effects on patients, the medical profession, public health, employers, the federal budget, and the American economy? You may limit your paper by discussing a single cause or effect.

   - Write a *persuasive* essay suggesting or more solutions to one aspect of the crisis in health care.

Research Paper

You can develop a research paper about the health care crisis by conducting further research:

- How much of the health care crisis is related to lifestyle issues such as smoking, obesity, diet, and alcohol and drug use? Can personal choices decrease the incidence of disease and lower family medical expenses?

- Would Americans accept a national health care system that would provide basic coverage for all citizens but limit treatment options?

- Will corporations trying to compete in the global economy pressure employees to accept lower health care benefits?

• Can advances in medical technology lower health care costs by diagnosing diseases at an earlier stage or identifying conditions that can be prevented with drugs or changes in lifestyle?

For Further Reading

To locate additional sources on health care, enter these search terms as Info-Trac subjects:

Health Insurance

Subdivisions: analysis

                          comparative analysis

                          demographic aspects

                          economic aspects

                          finance

                          forecasts and trends

Medical Malpractice Insurance

Subdivisions: analysis

                          cases

                          economic aspects

                          forecasts and trends

                          laws, regulations and rules

                          other

                          prices and rates

                          statistics

Additional Sources

Using a search engine such as Yahoo! or Google, enter one or more of the following terms to locate additional sources:

health care costs	medical malpractice
Medicare	medical malpractice insurance
health care crisis	national health insurance
right to die	euthanasia
living wills	HMOs

See Evaluating Internet Sources Checklist on page A-553.

IMMIGRATION

Immigration reform is perhaps the most important challenge facing America. How America resolves this challenge will not only determine what kind of country America will be, but whether or not America will remain a country at all.

Tom Tancredo

I reject the idea that America has used herself up in the effort to help outsiders in, and that now she must sit back exhausted, watching people play the cards fate has dealt them… We have no right to be content, to close the door to others now that we are safely inside.

Mario M. Cuomo

America is a nation of immigrants. Since its founding, the United States has absorbed waves of new arrivals from around the world. Settled primarily by the English, French, and Dutch in the seventeenth century, America attracted large numbers of Germans in the early nineteenth century. During the potato famine of the 1840s and 1850s, 1,700,000 Irish emigrated to the United States. Near the end of the century, millions more arrived from Italy and Eastern Europe. By 1910, 15 percent of American residents were foreign born.

These immigrants filled American cities, adding to their commerce and diversity. European immigrants provided the labor for the country's rapid industrial expansion. Chinese workers laid the railroad tracks that unified the nation and opened the West to economic expansion.

But immigrants also met with resistance. Groups like the Know-Nothings opposed the influx of Irish Catholics. As late as the 1920s, help-wanted ads in many newspapers contained the statement "No Irish Need Apply." California passed laws denying rights to the Chinese. Ivy League universities instituted quotas to limit the enrollment of Jewish students. Despite discrimination and hardships, these immigrants and their descendents entered mainstream American society and prospered. Today, some 40 percent of Americans can trace their roots to ancestors who passed through Ellis Island during the peak years of immigration a century ago.

The United States is now experiencing the largest increase in immigration in its history. Between 1990 and 2000 the number of foreign-born residents increased 57 percent, reaching 31 million in 2000. Today's immigrants come primarily from Mexico, Asia, and the Middle East. This new wave of immigration is changing the nation's demographics, so that Hispanics, not African Americans, are the largest minority group. Within decades, Muslims may outnumber Jews, making Islam America's second-largest religion.

This flow of immigrants, both legal and illegal, has fueled a debate about whether immigration benefits or hurts the United States. Supporters of immigration argue that immigrants offset a declining birthrate, adding the new workers and consumers needed to expand the nation's economy. Critics argue that the United States has a limited capacity to absorb immigrants, especially unskilled ones. Although immigrants provide employers with cheap labor, they burden the local governments that must provide them and their children with educational and health care services. Because of their numbers and historic ties to the land, Mexicans are changing the cultural fabric of the Southwest. In response, Americans concerned about national identity call for tighter border controls, restricted immigration, and the establishment of English as an official language.

Additionally, the terrorist attacks of September 11, 2001 led to new concerns about immigration, border controls, and national security.

Before reading these articles, consider these questions:

Where did your ancestors come from? Were they immigrants? Did they encounter discrimination when they arrived? Did they struggle to maintain their own language and culture or seek to assimilate into American society?

Should people who entered the country illegally be given legal status? Should amnesty be given to illegal immigrants who have lived and worked in the United States for several years?

Do wealthy countries like the United States have a moral obligation to accept immigrants? The United States has historically accepted immigrants fleeing war and oppression. After Castro assumed power, 250,000 Cubans fled to the United States. Tens of thousands of Vietnamese refugees entered the United States after the fall of South Vietnam. Does a prosperous nation have an obligation to absorb some of the world's poor?

How should the United States determine the number and type of immigrants allowed to enter the country each year? Should talented immigrants be given priority over the unskilled? Should the number of immigrants be limited during times of recession and high unemployment?

Does admitting immigrants improve the country by adding consumers and workers or weaken it by draining resources and burdening public services?

E-READINGS ONLINE

Find each article by visiting the Premium Website, accessed through **CengageBrain.com.**

Jon Meacham. *Who We Are Now*

The 1965 Immigration and Nationality Act signed by Lyndon Johnson will have profound consequences well into the twenty-first century, when whites will constitute only 47 percent of the population, making them the nation's largest minority group.

Robert J. Bresler. *Immigration: The Sleeping Time Bomb.*

Although past waves of immigrants have enriched this country, Bresler argues that unless immigration is limited our population could swell to 500 million in less than fifty years, reducing the quality of life for all citizens.

Christopher Gray. *Alien Nation: Common Sense about America's Immigration Disaster.*

Gray reviews three books analyzing the current immigration policy. America has 5 percent of the world's population but accepts 50 percent of the world's legal immigrants. The influx of a million immigrants a year may profoundly affect America's society, culture, economy, and values.

Robert Samuelson. *The Hard Truth of Immigration: No Society Has a Boundless Capacity to Accept Newcomers, Especially When Many of Them Are Poor and Unskilled Workers.*

Samuelson argues that immigration reform is needed to stem illegal immigration while granting legal status to illegal immigrants already living in the United States. "The stakes are simple," he argues, "will immigration continue to foster national pride and strength or will it cause more and more weakness and anger?"

Peter Duignan. *Do Immigrants Benefit America?*

Duigan believes that most of today's immigrants "will be an integral part of a revised American community" but warns that "past success does not guarantee that history will repeat itself."

August Gribbin. *Flow of Illegals "Inevitable": A Mexican Agency Predicts That the Mexican-born U.S. Population Will at Least Double, Up to 18 Million, by the Year 2030.*

The movement of Mexicans back and forth across the United States border follows a 200-year-old pattern that is deeply ingrained in Mexican culture.

Charlie Leduff. *Los Angeles County Weighs Cost of Illegal Immigration.*

Noting the growing costs of providing services for illegal immigrants, a Los Angeles County supervisor has proposed that illegal aliens obtain work permits and that their employers post bonds to pay for their health care.

Steven Camarota. *Our New Immigration Predicament.*

"Rather than changing our society to adapt to existing immigration," Camarota insists, "it would seem to make more sense to change the immigrant stream to fit our society."

Lawrence Brunner and Stephen M. Colarelli. *Immigration in the Twenty-First Century*

Viewing the United States as an organization, much like a corporation, Brunner and Colarelli argue it should admit talented immigrants, much like a company recruits employees.

Chi-an Chang. *Can Business Solve the Immigration Mess?*

Business owners claim they hire illegal immigrants not because they need "cheap labor" but because they seek "skilled craft workers."

Vivek Wadhwa. *Why Skilled Immigrants Are Leaving the U.S.*

Having started 52 percent of Silicon Valley's technology companies and contributed 25 percent of America's global patents, highly skilled immigrants are vital to the nation's economy and their loss threatens our country's future.

Warren Mass. *Immigration as a Win-Win Affair*

Immigration has benefited the nation's culture and economy—when it has been properly regulated and controlled.

Critical Reading and Thinking

1. What do authors see as the major costs and benefits of immigration?
2. What reasons do the authors give for the country's unwillingness to address illegal immigration?
3. What drives immigrants, both legal and illegal, to enter the United States?
4. How will the current wave of immigration change American society?
5. What motivates people to demand restrictions on immigration?

1. Write an essay about your own family history. Were you or your ancestors immigrants? When did they arrive? Did they encounter any discrimination or hardships? Did they assimilate into mainstream American society or seek to maintain ties to their native language, culture, and traditions?

2. *Collaborative writing:* Discuss immigration with other students and develop an essay presenting your group's views on one aspect of immigration—tightening border security, giving amnesty to illegal aliens, developing a guest worker program, or prosecuting employers who hire illegal aliens. If members have differing opinions, consider developing opposing statements.

3. *Other modes*

   • Write an essay that examines the language used to discuss illegal immigrants, such as "undocumented workers," "illegals," and "illegal aliens." Note the role that connotation plays in shaping attitudes toward illegal immigrants.

   • *Compare* current immigrants with those who entered Ellis Island a century ago.

   • Use *process* to explain how immigrants can obtain citizenship.

   • Write a *division* essay to outline the major problems that recent immigrants face in finding employment, housing, and health services in the United States.

   • Use *classification* to rank suggestions for immigration reform from the most to the least restrictive or from the most to the least acceptable to the public and politicians.

Research Paper

You can develop a research paper about immigration by conducting further research to explore a range of issues:

How effectively does law enforcement prosecute companies that hire illegal aliens?

How has concern about terrorism affected immigration policies? Do immigrants from Muslim countries face greater scrutiny? Has Homeland Security viewed the borders as potential weak spots?

What does current research reveal about the status of Mexican Americans? Are immigrants from Mexico entering the middle class at a similar rate to immigrants from other countries?

How will the new wave of immigrants influence American society, culture, economy, and foreign policy?

Examine the impact immigration has had on other developed countries, such as Canada, Britain, France, Germany, and Italy. What problems, if any, have immigrant populations posed in these nations?

For Further Reading

To locate additional sources on immigration, enter these search terms as Info-Trac subjects:

Immigrants

Subdivisions

analysis

behavior

cases

civil rights

economic aspects

education

laws, regulations and rules

personal narratives

political activity

psychological aspects

social aspects

statistics

Additional Sources

Using a search engine such as Yahoo! or Google, enter one or more of the following terms to locate additional sources:

immigration	green cards
visa lotteries	Ellis Island
citizenship	bilingual education
Mexican Americans	English only

See Evaluating Internet Sources Checklist on page A-553.

CRIMINAL JUSTICE

What Winston Churchill once said about democracy can probably also be said about the adversary system of criminal justice: It may well be the worst system of justice, "except [for] all the other [systems] that have been tried from time to time."

Alan M. Dershowitz

The system is seriously flawed. It disproportionately affects the poor and the African American community. It makes too many mistakes. Too many prisoners are unjustly placed on death row because of poor representation at trial. Too many others spend irretrievable chunks of their lives behind bars because of false identifications or shoddy police work or inadequate legal representation.

National Catholic Reporter

During the last decade violent crime has steadily dropped, particularly in major cities. Safer streets are one factor that has helped revitalize urban America, which has experienced a rapid growth in upscale housing and commercial redevelopment. At the same time, the nation's prison population has risen dramatically. Over six million citizens—1 in every 32 Americans—are in jail, on probation or parole, or in prison. While many Americans cite falling crime statistics as signs of progress, others, like Paul Butler, a former prosecutor, examine the social cost to those communities in which one in three males are under the supervision of the criminal justice system and more young men are in prison than in college:

These costs are both social and economic, and they include the large percentage of black children who live in female-headed, single-parent households; a perceived dearth of men "eligible" for marriage; the lack of male role models for black children, especially boys; the absence of wealth in the black community; and the large unemployment rate among black men.

Elizabeth Palmberg argues that the war on drugs has increased racial disparities in the criminal justice system, so that "four out of five state drug prisoners are African American or Latino, although these groups comprise only 22 percent of drug users ... and these disparities permeate every level of the criminal justice system, from policing to parole."

Popular television programs have highlighted the use of DNA to identify the guilty and exonerate the innocent. By proving the innocence of convicts,

DNA has demonstrated the unreliability of other forms of evidence such as eyewitness testimony. But even when DNA evidence conclusively proves that someone has been wrongly convicted, it does not always lead to immediate release. Bob Herbert noted in the *New York Times* that "once an innocent person is trapped in the system, it's extremely difficult to get him—or her—extricated." Complicating the use of DNA evidence is the fact that many of the current experts who testify in court have as little as two weeks' training.

The introduction of cameras in courtrooms in the 1990s allowed Americans who had only seen fictionalized courtroom dramas to witness real trials. Anna Quindlen argues that cameras should be allowed in courtrooms to let people see how the legal process "takes this messy stew of evidence and egos and transmutes it finally through order, instruction and deliberation into a system that gets it right a good bit of the time." In contrast, Jack Litman, a defense attorney, believes that cameras can intimidate witnesses and harm victims because "there is an enormous difference between . . . testifying before 12 people and 12 million people."

Before reading these articles, consider these questions:

Do you think the criminal justice system is basically fair to victims, witnesses, and defendants?

Do you think trials should be televised? Have you ever watched Court TV or other televised trials? What did you learn by watching actual courtroom proceedings? How do they differ from courtroom dramas?

Do you think juries should ever refuse to convict someone they know is guilty? In rare cases, juries have acquitted people they knew were guilty because they believed the law was unjust or that the defendant was unfairly charged. Can you think of any situations in which you would vote to acquit someone you knew was guilty?

Do celebrity and high-profile trials give the public a distorted view of the criminal justice system?

Have you ever served on a jury or appeared in court? How did your experiences shape your view of the criminal justice system?

E-READINGS ONLINE

Find each article by visiting the Premium Website, accessed through **CengageBrain.com.**

David Von Drehle. *Why Crime Went Away*

Despite the recession, crime has dropped to its lowest levels in over forty years, caused by an aging population, changes in the illegal drug trade, and the nation's soaring prison population.

Stuart Taylor Jr. *America's Prison Spree has Brutal Impact*

Over two million Americans are incarcerated at a cost of $60 billion a year. The impact on the black community, whose members have an incarceration rate eight times that of whites, has been devastating.

Anna Quindlen. *Lights, Camera, Justice for All*

Because the point of public trials was to let people in, Quindlen argues "in the 21st century, letting the people in means letting the cameras in."

Felicity Barringer. *Lawyers Are Divided on Cameras in the Courtroom*

Jack Litman, a defense attorney, questions the impact televised trials can have on witnesses and victims.

Leonard Post. *Citing Low Pay, Lawyers Refuse Indigent Cases.*

Because of low pay, many lawyers refuse to represent poor defendants, denying them adequate counsel and leading judges to dismiss charges against criminals when lawyers cannot be found to defend them.

Martin L. Haines. *Psst, Jurors: You Have the Power to Nullify*

Even when presented with conclusive evidence of a defendant's guilt, juries can refuse to convict, because "once a jury acquits, its verdict cannot be appealed, its deliberations are private and cannot be investigated, and no juror may be arrested for voting to acquit."

Paul Butler. *Black Jurors: Right to Acquit?*

A former federal prosecutor believes "that for pragmatic and political reasons, the black community is better off when some non-violent lawbreakers remain in the community rather than go to prison" and that black jurors have a "moral responsibility" to "emancipate some guilty black outlaws."

National Catholic Reporter. *Flawed Prison System Hurts Us All*

Noting that over six million Americans are currently in jail, on parole, or probation, the *National Catholic Reporter* argues that "we can't keep locking people away and trying to forget they exist. Humans, even those who have broken the law, deserve better, and even tough sentences eventually end."

Bob Herbert. *Trapped in the System*

Despite conclusive DNA evidence that he did not commit the crime he is accused of, Ryan Matthews remains on death row because "freeing someone who has been wrongfully convicted is a torturously slow and difficult process, with no guarantee at any time that it will end positively."

Adam Liptak. *You Think DNA Evidence Is Foolproof? Try Again*

DNA evidence has proven the unreliability of other forms of evidence, but it cannot create a "foolproof" system of justice because DNA tests are conducted by fallible technicians and presented in court by poorly trained "experts."

Thomas N. Faust. *Shift the Responsibility of Untreated Mental Illness Out of the Criminal Justice System*

Noting that 16 percent of inmates are severely mentally ill, the executive director of the National Sheriffs' Association argues that prisons "have started to become psychiatric hospitals."

David Rose. *Locked Up to Make Us Feel Better*

Petty criminals are increasingly given life sentences, not for crimes they committed, but to protect the public from their future behavior. As a result, prisons may soon house more inmates for "preventive detention" than murder.

Critical Reading and Thinking

1. What do the various authors see as strengths and weaknesses in the criminal justice system?

2. How has DNA evidence changed perceptions of the fairness of the criminal justice system?

3. What do some authors view as causes for racial disparities in the justice system?

4. What are the benefits and risks of televising trials?

5. Why do few Americans appear to be concerned about the large numbers of people in prison? Do people feel safer? Do they see imprisoning large numbers of mostly young and poor males as an acceptable trade-off for lowered crime rates?

WRITING SUGGESTIONS

1. Write an essay about one aspect of the criminal justice system that you have observed. Have you ever been a victim of crime, appeared in court,

or served on a jury? Describe your most surprising finding or observation. Was the system better or worse than you expected?

2. *Collaborative writing:* Working with other students, develop an essay outlining what your group believes would be the best ways to improve the criminal justice system to make sure victims are fairly treated and defendants adequately represented.

3. *Other modes*

- Write a *comparison* paper that contrasts the ways that different people view the police, courts, or prison system.
- Use a single trial, crime, defendant, or victim as an *example* of a problem in the criminal justice system.
- Write an essay that explores the *causes* or *effects* of racial disparities in sentencing offenders.
- Develop a *division* paper that discusses three or four of the most pressing challenges to the criminal justice system.
- Write a *classification* essay that outlines the most to least effective ways of dealing with people who break the law.

Research Paper

You can develop a research paper about the criminal justice system by conducting further research to explore a range of issues:

- Why has crime dropped?
- Why has the prison population expanded?
- What flaws in the justice system have been revealed by the use of DNA evidence? Has it, for example, led more people to oppose capital punishment?
- What representation do poor defendants receive in your area? Are state or local public defenders adequately funded and supported? Do the poor get fair trials?
- Examine media coverage of a sensational criminal trial. Are the stories balanced? Do you detect bias for or against the defendant, witnesses, the attorneys, or the victim?

For Further Reading

To locate additional sources on the criminal justice system, enter these search terms as InfoTrac subjects:

Criminal Justice, Administration of

Subdivisions: beliefs, opinions and attitudes

comparative analysis

economic aspects

evaluation

forecasts and trends

moral and ethical aspects

political aspects

public opinion

DNA Testing

Subdivisions: analysis

cases

laws, regulations and rules

methods

usage

Prisons

Subdivisions   analysis

demographic aspects

history

personal narratives

psychological aspects

social aspects

Additional Sources

Using a search engine such as Yahoo! or Google, enter one or more of the following terms to locate additional sources:

DNA testing	prisons	insanity defense
public defenders	televised trials	criminal justice system
capital punishment	parole	community service
Innocence Project	juvenile justice	mandatory sentencing

See Evaluating Internet Sources Checklist on page A-553.

PRIVACY IN THE ELECTRONIC AGE

> The Internet's greatest impact has been its ability to provide a voice
> for the many people who have no formal opportunity to speak in
> the real world.
>
> *Thomas A. Workman*

> Two years ago I warned that we were in danger of sleepwalking
> into a surveillance society. Today I fear that we are in fact waking up
> to a surveillance society that is already all around us.
>
> *Richard Thomas*

The Internet, cell phones, YouTube, MySpace, Facebook, and Twitter have
changed the fabric of modern life. Individuals can now operate corporations
from a laptop, conducting business worldwide without the need for an expensive office or support staff. Parents can keep track of children without having
to play phone tag. Corporations can keep in touch with employees and customers in real time. Accident victims can summon immediate help by cell
phone and be instantly located by GPS. Stolen automobiles and lost pets can
be tracked by satellite.

But these conveniences have eroded personal privacy. Cell phone
records can be used to track a person's location. The average New Yorker is
photographed twenty-three times a day by surveillance cameras in apartment lobbies, stores, elevators, and street corners. An embarrassing photograph taken at a party that once might have circulated in a single office or
high school can be posted online. Erin Andrews, a sportscaster, was secretly
videotaped undressing in her hotel room by a predator. Posted online
where it could be viewed, shared, and downloaded by anyone, the video
turned a single violation of privacy into a never-ending global personal
assault.

Today 70 percent of teenagers have online profiles, which often contain
personal information or potentially compromising postings. Few realize that
an innocent family snapshot posted on a personal page may reveal a house
number or a license plate that could be used by predators to stalk victims.

A survey of 500 adolescents revealed that over half had received emails
containing inappropriate sexual content. Ilene Berson, a professor of child and
family studies, finds that teenagers are especially vulnerable online because
for them "the Net is a kind of make-believe world where the regular expectations and rules don't seem to apply. They don't consider that once you turn off
the computer, it might spill over into their life."

Employers frequently examine job applicants' online profiles, as do attorneys who screen potential clients and witnesses for damaging or compromising postings. Alarmed that a simple Google search produces unflattering images or comments, many professionals hire companies specializing in cleaning up online reputations by deleting or burying negative information.

The Internet has raised First Amendment issues. Should high school teachers who post racist comments online or whose Facebook page depicts them drinking or behaving inappropriately be terminated or suspended? Should schools discipline students who slander principals with online parodies they produce at home?

The near-universal use of cell phone cameras and sites like YouTube have created a new global medium that can make anyone a journalist capable of recording a historical event for a worldwide audience. In 2009, cell phones could broadcast images of street demonstrations in Iran that the government tried to block and did not cover on its official media. Sites like YouTube and blogs allowed dissidents to disseminate information and inform the outside world. Later, Iranian security police tracked cell phone accounts and examined online postings to locate and detain dissidents. Ironically, the demonstrator who uses a cell phone camera to publicize a protest against a repressive regime also provides that regime with the evidence it needs to identify dissidents.

Before reading these articles, consider these questions:

Have you posted photographs or personal information on a MySpace or Facebook page? Have you considered if you have revealed too much of your identity?

Have you observed people taking pictures or videos of others at parties or public events without their knowledge? Would you feel violated if you discovered that someone had posted your picture online without your permission?

Should an employer evaluate applicants based on pictures they may have posted in high school or college?

Would you conduct an online search to locate information about a person before responding to a request for a date or hiring a babysitter?

Do cell phones and the Internet create citizen journalists who can bypass censorship or do they provide tools to distort events and manipulate perceptions of events?

Does the presence of surveillance cameras make you feel spied upon or protected?

E-READINGS ONLINE

Find each article by visiting the Premium Website, accessed through **CengageBrain.com.**

Sami Lais. *No More Secrets?*

With computers recording credit card purchases, GPS devices tracking their movements, and video surveillance cameras taping their behavior, people are daily losing any sense of privacy. More recently, "sexting" has led to blackmail, school suspensions, and prosecutions.

Jamie Malanowski. *Big Brother: How a Million Surveillance Cameras in London Are Proving George Orwell Wrong*

Not far from the flat where Orwell wrote his prophetic novel, thirty-two CCTV cameras run 24 hours a day, creating a "surveillance society" that has eroded privacy but given the public a greater sense of personal security.

John Caher. *No Warrant Needed for GPS Car-Tracking*

Because drivers have no expectation of privacy on the open road, a federal judge has ruled that the police do not need a warrant to use GPS devices to track a suspect.

Chloe Albanesius & Erik Rhey. *Are You on the Map?*

Online map services like Google Maps, which include street-view images of public buildings and private homes, concern citizens and security experts who fear these images can be used by predators and terrorists to target victims.

Mondaq Business Briefing. *"One of Our Laptops is Missing"—The Risks of Data Loss and How to Prevent It*

Lost or misused data can become a toxic liability for corporations and lead to fines and loss of reputations.

Thomas A. Workman. *The Real Impact of Virtual Worlds*

Students who post videos of themselves participating in risky or outrageous activities should be viewed as engaging in "misdirected recreation rather than purposeful misconduct."

Maria Giffen. *Online Privacy: When Your Life Goes Public*

Seventy percent of high school students have online profiles, and over half have posted their own photos, with little realization how their actions in cyberspace may affect their futures.

Nina Culver. *Pitfalls of Online Profile Content*

With only a first name, race, and town name provided on a MySpace page, a security consultant demonstrated to parents how he could quickly identify a student's full name, photograph, and home address. Even when teens limit the personal information they post online, they leave clues to their identity.

Sara Lipka. *The Digital Limits of "In Loco Parentis"*

Online postings of rowdy student behavior vex college administrators. "They know what to do with a drunken student," Lipka notes. "But what about a Facebook photo of a seemingly drunken student?"

Shannon P. Duffy. *The MySpace Suspensions*

Schools that have suspended students for posting lewd parodies of their principals on home computers have raised First Amendment Issues.

Healthcare Risk Management. *Cell Phone Cameras are Creating Liability Risk for Health Care Facilities*

Because employees have used cell phone cameras to violate the privacy of vulnerable patients, supervisors must monitor their presence in health care facilities that would never allow employees to carry traditional cameras.

Heidi Abegg. *Can Employers Check Social Networking Websites Prior to Hiring?*

Making hiring decisions based on applicants' online profiles raises privacy issues.

Betsy Boyd. *Candid Do's and Don'ts*

The volatile mix of cell phone cameras and YouTube have destroyed entertainers' careers and granted newcomers instant fame.

Douglas MacMillan. *A Twitter Code of Conduct*

To prevent leaks of sensitive data, blemished careers, and personal embarrassment, corporations must educate employees about what they should and should not Twitter.

Critical Reading and Thinking

1. What do the various authors see as the advantages and disadvantages of electronic devices?

2. How has the cell phone camera changed our notions of privacy?

3. What dangers do young people expose themselves to online?

4. Should teachers be suspended or terminated because their Facebook or MySpace pages show them partying and drinking away from school?

5. Should attorneys be allowed to introduce online profiles as evidence to discredit witnesses in court?

WRITING SUGGESTIONS

1. Write an essay about one aspect of the electronic age you have observed. Have you noticed anyone posting personal information or photographs on MySpace or Facebook that you think could have negative consequences? Do young people think before they post?

2. *Collaborative writing:* Work with a group of students and write a set of guidelines people should follow before posting on social networking sites.

3. *Other modes*

   • Write a *narrative* essay about a personal experience involving a cell phone or the Internet that illustrates the advantages or disadvantages of the electronic age.

   • Write a paper that outlines the *effects* of social networking.

   • Use *comparison* to identify the advantages and disadvantages of cell phone cameras, social networking sites, or GPS systems.

   • Write a *persuasive* paper supporting or criticizing schools that suspend students for posting online parodies accusing principals or teachers of criminal conduct.

   • Use *analysis* to study how the concept of privacy has changed in the electronic age.

Research Paper

You can develop a research paper about privacy in the electronic age by conducting further research to explore a range of issues:

- What cases about online postings have tested First Amendment rights?
- Do employers have the right to monitor employee use of company computers, cell phones, and other electronic devices?
- Have surveillance cameras lowered crime?
- Have terrorists used the Internet to recruit followers, disseminate propaganda, and plan attacks?
- Can police and courts effectively deter online stalking?

For Further Reading

To locate additional sources on privacy in the electronic age, enter these search terms as InfoTrac subjects:

Privacy

Subdivisions:
- analysis
- beliefs, opinions and attitudes
- cases
- political aspects
- public opinion
- social aspects

Cellular Telephones

Subdivisions:
- analysis
- laws, regulations and rules
- public opinion

Electronic Mail Systems

Subdivision:
- analysis
- ethical aspects
- laws, regulations and rules
- political aspects
- public opinion

Internet

Subdivisions:
- analysis
- beliefs, opinions and attitudes
- political aspects

Additional Sources

Using a search engine such as Yahoo! or Google, enter one or more of the following terms to locate additional sources:

surveillance cameras	GPS systems	Facebook
online predators	privacy	Twitter etiquette
email privacy	identity theft	data mining
YouTube	bloggers	Google

See Evaluating Internet Sources Checklist on page A-553.

CHAPTER EIGHT

ANALYSIS: MAKING EVALUATIONS

WHAT IS ANALYSIS?

Analysis moves beyond description and narration to make judgments or evaluations about persons, places, objects, ideas, or situations. A movie reviewer *describes* a new film and then *analyzes* it—critiquing the plot, acting, special effects, and social message. A historian *narrates* an event and then *evaluates* its lasting significance. Marketing executives *summarize* sales reports to *judge* the results of their advertising campaign. A psychiatrist *examines* a patient and then *diagnoses* the individual's mental condition.

Analysis often seeks to answer questions. Does aspirin prevent heart attacks? What are Vicki Shimi's chances of being elected governor? Is General Motors' new hybrid car fuel efficient? Does America have too many lawyers? Is addiction a disease? How effective were the poverty programs launched in the 1960s? What is the best way to remove asbestos from a public school? Is a defendant mentally competent to stand trial? Is the central figure of *Death of a Salesman*, Willy Loman, a victim of society or of his own delusions? The answers to all these questions require a careful gathering of information, critical thinking, and a clear presentation of the writer's thesis.

Analysis entails more than expressing an opinion or creating an impression. In an analytical paper, you cannot simply write, "I hated *A Streetcar Named Desire* because it was stupid," or "Welfare programs waste taxpayers' money." You must base your positions on observations and evidence. Why is the play stupid? What facts demonstrate that welfare programs are wasteful? When asked to write analytical papers, students often supply description and narration, summarizing a short story or describing a social problem. To keep your paper analytical, you can use the journalist's "Five Ws"—*Who? What? When? Where? Why?*—to develop your thesis. By answering questions, you are forced to find evidence and provide answers instead of simply retelling a story or describing a situation.

Subjective and Objective Analysis

The way writers develop analytical writing depends greatly on context. In many situations, writers rely wholly on personal observation and experience. Film critics, political columnists, book reviewers, fashion consultants, and social commentators tend to write subjective analysis. *Subjective analysis* is based on close observation and careful interpretation. The writer's points are supported by examples and illustrations he or she has chosen. Thomas Friedman, for example, analyzes America's foreign policy, arguing for a change in focus:

> Dick Cheney says President Obama is "trying to pretend that we are not at war" with terrorists. There is only one thing I have to say about that: I sure hope so.
>
> Frankly, if I had my wish, we would be on our way out of Afghanistan not in, we would be letting Pakistan figure out which Taliban they want to conspire with and which ones they want to fight, we would be letting the Israelis and Palestinians figure out on their own how to make peace, we would be taking $100 billion out of the Pentagon budget to make us independent of imported oil— nothing would make us more secure—and we would be reducing the reward for killing or capturing Osama bin Laden to exactly what he's worth: 10 cents and an autographed picture of Dick Cheney.

Objective analysis begins with close observations but seeks to answer questions through factual research. In objective analysis, the writer needs more than personal experience and anecdotal examples to support a position. In "How Television Distorts Reality" (page 317), Benjamin Radford analyzes newscasts to demonstrate that television disproportionately focuses on crime and disasters while paying minimal attention to other issues:

> Another study, this one headed by Syracuse University professor Robert Lissit, found that of 100 newscasts around the country, "nearly 30 percent of the news time was spent on crime and the courts. Ten percent was devoted to reporting calamities and natural disasters. Only 15 percent of the newscasts were devoted to government and politics. Health and medicine: about 7 percent. Race relations: 1.2 percent. Education: less than one percent." According to Lissit, crime gets a disproportionate amount of coverage not because it is important but because it is easy to cover: "A few

shots of the crime scene, a quick interview with a police officer, or someone in the neighborhood, and a quick reporter-on-camera standup. Summary, and that's the end of the story." Noncrime issues such as politics or education require more background and effort and usually can't be wrapped up in such a tidy, quick package.

Objective analysis is not limited to facts and statistics. Writers can balance numbers with interviews, personal examples, and anecdotal accounts. To dramatize the impact of overheard cell phone calls, Louis R. Mizell Jr. provides two cases of intercepted phone calls:

> Doctors and lawyers frequently discuss everyday business on cellular phones. In one case, a doctor was notified that a VIP patient had tested positive for AIDS. The information was intercepted, and before long, the VIP's medical status was common knowledge. In another case, a lawyer from Ohio reviewed a client's prenuptial agreement with a second lawyer who was using a cellular telephone. A teenage neighbor of the second lawyer intercepted the conversation. "Before long, the whole damn neighborhood knew about our secret wedding and my financial situation," said the angry groom-to-be.

The blending of statistics and personal interviews strengthens the analysis because the conclusions are drawn from more than one source of information.

The way writers develop their analytical writing is often influenced by their readers and their discipline. A widely respected restaurant critic will review a new cafe in wholly personal and subjective terms. But an engineer analyzing the structure of a hurricane-damaged bridge will use standard tests and procedures and will only provide conclusions clearly supported by scientific findings and observable detail. An attorney analyzing the admissibility of surreptitious recordings of suspects would base his or her opinion on Supreme Court rulings.

Detailed Observation

Analysis requires close observation, critical thinking, and in some instances outside research. If you have not read Samuel Scudder's "Take This Fish and Look at It" (page 69), you might wish to review it. This essay demonstrates the value of close observation. Good analysis cannot rely on first impressions. Before you can analyze a short story or a poem, you will have to read the work several times. If you are thinking of evaluating how women are depicted in television commercials, you may wish to videotape two or three evenings' worth of commercials and watch them several times rather than relying on memory. The more you observe about your subject, the more likely you will move from superficial observation to detecting details you may have previously overlooked.

Critical Thinking for Writing Analysis

Analytical writing can be challenging. Even the best writers often fall into common traps called *logical fallacies* and make errors in judgment. Following these guidelines can help you improve your analytical writing skills:

1. **Ask questions to avoid summarizing.** The most common error students make is mistaking summary or description for analysis. Asking questions such as *why?* or *who?* can help you avoid simply retelling the plot of a story rather than analyzing it. For example, before starting to write an analysis of Hemingway's short story "Hills Like White Elephants," you might develop questions. Answering a question such as "Who is the stronger character, the man or the woman?" will guide you toward evaluating the story rather than simply supplying a two-page summary.

2. **Limit the scope of your analysis.** Unless you are willing to devote months to research, it would be difficult to gather sufficient material to analyze a subject such as day care centers fully. You might restrict your topic to day care centers in one neighborhood or focus on a single issue such as licensing requirements.

3. **Evaluate sources for bias.** If you were analyzing the use of animals in medical research, you would not want to base your judgments solely on information from an animal rights group. When evaluating controversial subjects, you may be unable to obtain objective information, but you can achieve a measure of balance by examining data provided by individuals and organizations with opposing viewpoints.

4. **Apply common standards.** Analyzing data from different sources will be accurate only if all the sources have the same standards and definitions. If you were analyzing juvenile delinquency, you might face a problem if each study examined has a different definition of just who is a delinquent. Does one study include juveniles who skip school, while another only considers adolescents who commit felonies?

5. **Distinguish between opinion and fact.** Opinions are judgments or inferences, not facts. Facts are reliable pieces of information that can be verified by studying other sources:

OPINION:	John Smith is an alcoholic.
FACT:	John Smith drinks two martinis at lunch and frequents nightclubs on weekends.

The factual statement relies on observation. The writer's opinion of alcoholism is based on limited evidence and probably requires more support.

6. **Avoid hasty generalizations.** Generalizations should be based on adequate information, not a few instances that you may find dramatic or interesting. The fact that two friends had purses stolen in the student union last week and that your car was broken into this morning does not mean the college is in the grip of a crime wave. You would have to examine several months of police reports to determine whether an actual increase in campus crime has occurred.

7. **Consider alternative interpretations.** Facts do not always indicate what they imply at first glance. A rise in reported cases of child abuse may not indicate increasing violence against children, but instead better reporting. If a school has a low retention rate, does that indicate it is failing to address the needs of students or, instead, that it maintains such rigorous standards that only the best students graduate?

8. **Avoid "filtering" data.** If you begin with a preconceived thesis, you may consciously or unconsciously select evidence that supports your view and omit evidence that contradicts it. Good analysis is objective; it does not consist of simply collecting facts to support a previously held conviction.

9. **Do not assume that parts represent the whole.** Just because one or more patients respond favorably to a new drug does not mean that it will cure all people suffering from the same disease. In the extreme, because individual men and women die does not mean the human race will eventually become extinct.

10. **Do not assume that the whole represents each part.** If 50 percent of students on campus receive financial aid, it does not mean you can assume that half the English majors receive aid. The student population in any given department may be less or more than the college average.

11. **Avoid reasoning on false analogies.** Analogy or comparison essays often provide weak evidence because they overlook that no two situations are exactly alike. Avoid assuming, for example, that results from a study conducted in Japan provide valid evidence for researchers in the United States. Because airbags have been proven to save lives in car accidents does not mean they should be installed in airplanes.

STRATEGIES FOR READING ANALYSIS

As you read the analysis entries in this chapter, keep the following questions in mind.

Understanding Meaning

1. What is the author's purpose—to provide a personal opinion or an evaluation based on standard research methods?

2. What discipline is the writer operating in? What kinds of evidence and what analytical methods are presented?

3. Does the writer present sources for his or her evidence?

4. What does the original source of the entry indicate about the intended audience and discipline?

5. What is the most significant conclusion the author draws?

Evaluating Strategy

1. Does the writer rely on close observation, surveys, statistics, or expert testimony?

2. How were the data collected? Does the writer cite sources and supply footnotes?

3. Did the writer consider alternative interpretations?

4. Does the entry appear to be biased? Does the writer present facts to support a preconceived theory?

5. Does the writer avoid logical fallacies?

Appreciating Language

1. Do the author's choice of words and use of connotations indicate bias?

2. What language does the writer use in discussing people or organizations expressing different beliefs?

3. Are standard terms defined?

SHARON BEGLEY

Sharon Begley graduated from Yale University and joined Newsweek *magazine in 1977 as an editorial assistant. After serving as an assistant editor in the late 1970s, she became a general editor in 1983. During her career at* Newsweek, *Begley wrote numerous articles on science and health issues. She left the magazine to write the "Science Journal" column for the* Wall Street Journal. *Five years later, Begley returned to* Newsweek *as a senior editor.*

What's in a Word?

CONTEXT: *In this* Newsweek *article, Begley analyzes the way words may shape our thoughts and perceptions. Differences in cultural perceptions and attitudes can be explained, in part, by differences in language.*

<u>Language may shape our thoughts.</u>   *thesis*

    When the Viaduct de Millau opened in the south of France in 2004, this   1
tallest bridge in the world won worldwide accolades. German newspapers de-   2
scribed how it "floated above the clouds" with "elegance and lightness" and
"breathtaking" beauty. In France, papers praised the "immense" "concrete
giant." <u>Was it mere coincidence that the Germans saw beauty where the</u>   *example*
<u>French saw heft and power? Lera Boroditsky thinks not.</u>   *analytical*
                                                                                question

    A psychologist at Stanford University, she has long been intrigued by an   3
age-old question whose modern form dates to 1956, when linguist Benjamin
Lee Whorf asked whether the language we speak shapes the way we think and
see the world. If so, then language is not merely a means of expressing
thought, but a constraint on it, too. <u>Although philosophers, anthropologists,</u>   *expert*
<u>and others have weighed in, with most concluding that language does not</u>   *testimony*
<u>shape thought in any significant way, the field has been notable for a distress-</u>   *lack of data*
<u>ing lack of empiricism—as in testable hypotheses and actual data.</u>

    That's where Boroditsky comes in. In a series of clever experiments guided   4
by pointed questions, she is amassing evidence that, yes, language shapes
thought. The effect is powerful enough, <u>she says, that "the private mental</u>   *direct*
<u>lives of speakers of different languages may differ dramatically," not only when</u>   *quotation*
<u>they are thinking in order to speak, "but in all manner of cognitive tasks,"</u>
<u>including basic sensory perception. "Even a small fluke of grammar"—the</u>
<u>gender of nouns—"can have an effect on how people think about things in</u>
<u>the world," she says.</u>

    As in that bridge. <u>In German, the noun for bridge, *Brucke*, is feminine. In</u>   5
<u>French, *pont* is masculine. German speakers saw prototypically female features;</u>   *analysis of*
                                                                                words

<u>French speakers, masculine ones.</u> Similarly, <u>Germans describe keys (*Schlussel*)</u> <u>with words such as hard, heavy, jagged, and metal, while to Spaniards keys</u> <u>(*llaves*) are golden, intricate, little, and lovely. Guess which language construes</u> <u>key as masculine and which as feminine?</u> Grammatical gender also shapes how we construe abstractions. In 85 percent of artistic depictions of death and victory, for instance, the idea is represented by a man if the noun is masculine and a woman if it is feminine, says Boroditsky. Germans tend to paint death as male, and Russians tend to paint it as female.

rhetorical question

6   Language even shapes what we see. People have a better memory for colors if different shades have distinct names—not English's light blue and dark blue, for instance, but Russian's *goluboy* and *sinly*. Skeptics of the language-shapes-thought claim have argued that that's a trivial finding, showing only that people remember what they saw in both a visual form and a verbal one, but not proving that they actually see the hues differently. In an ingenious experiment, however, Boroditsky and colleagues showed volunteers three color swatches and asked them which of the bottom two was the same as the top one. Native Russian speakers were faster than English speakers when the colors had distinct names, suggesting that having a name for something allows you to perceive it more sharply. Similarly, Korean uses one word for "in" when one object is in another snugly (a letter in an envelope), and a different one when an object is in something loosely (an apple in a bowl). Sure enough, Korean adults are better than English speakers at distinguishing tight fit from loose fit.

analysis examples

7   In Australia, the Aboriginal Kuuk Thaayorre use compass directions for every spatial cue rather than right or left, leading to locutions such as "there is an ant on your southeast leg." The Kuuk Thaayorre are also much more skillful than English speakers at dead reckoning, even in unfamiliar surroundings or strange buildings. Their language "equips them to perform navigational feats once thought beyond human capabilities," Boroditsky wrote on Edge.org.

analysis example

8   <u>Science has only scratched the surface of how language affects thought.</u> In Russian, verb forms indicate whether the action was completed or not—as in "she ate [and finished] the pizza." In Turkish, verbs indicate whether the action was observed or merely rumored. Boroditsky would love to run an experiment testing whether native Russian speakers are better than others at noticing if an action is completed, and if Turks have a heightened sensitivity to fact versus hearsay. Similarly, while English says "she broke the bowl" even if it smashed accidentally (she dropped something on it, say), Spanish and Japanese describe the same event more like "the bowl broke itself." "When we show people video of the same event," says Boroditsky, "English speakers remember who was to blame even in an accident, but Spanish and Japanese speakers remember it less well than they do intentional actions. It raises questions about whether language affects even something as basic as how we construct our ideas of causality."

quotation

Understanding Meaning

1. Can you state Begley's thesis in your own words?

2. How, in Begley's view, do differences in language explain why the French and Germans described the same bridge in such different terms?

3. How does the gender of a word affect the way people see an idea, object, or concept?

4. Why does Lera Boroditsky believe the Kuuk Thaayorre of Australia have such a good sense of direction?

5. *Critical Thinking:* Does Begley's article indicate why precise and sensitive translations are necessary in order to conduct diplomatic negotiation? Might one language view a word in a positive light, while another sees it negatively?

Evaluating Strategy

1. What evidence does Begley use to support her thesis?

2. Are the examples Begley presents, such as words for keys or an action like a broken bowl, easy to understand?

3. Begley asks rhetorical questions. Is this an effective device? Why or why not? Could a writer pose too many questions?

4. *Critical Thinking:* Begley notes that "the field has been notable for a distressing lack of empiricism –as in testable hypotheses and actual data." Is this a significant admission? It is important for someone analyzing an issue to comment on the status of research or the quality of available evidence? Why or why not?

Appreciating Language

1. English does not have gender—everything is simply "the." Some languages, such as French, German, and Spanish, have masculine and feminine designations such as *der Mann* and *die Frau*. Should Begley have explained this more fully for English speakers who have never studied a foreign language? Why or why not?

2. *Critical Thinking:* Do you think there may be significant differences within the same language? Do men and women, blacks and whites, New Yorkers and Texans have different responses to the same words? Might, for example, the word "gun" lead people in Manhattan to think of crime and violence and remind people in Montana of hunting trips and family outings?

WRITING SUGGESTIONS

1. Analyze the language used to describe a recent event, issue, or controversy. What words were used in the press, on television, or by your friends to describe the firing of a football coach, a student protest, a new law, a change in policy, or the closing of a local company? Do you detect any bias? What words or phrases were the most significant, in your view, and what did they reveal about people's attitudes?

2. *Collaborative Writing:* Work with a group of students and analyze some common slang expressions. What do they suggest about the way members of your generation view themselves and the world around them? Write a short essay that uses specific examples. Do you perceive a common theme in the slang you hear on campus?

THOMAS FRIEDMAN

Thomas Friedman (1953-) was born in St. Louis Park, Minnesota, and graduated from Brandeis University with a degree in Mediterranean studies. Friedman joined the London bureau of United Press International after earning his master's degree. He later joined the New York Times *and covered the Middle East for several years. Friedman received a Pulitzer Prize for international reporting for his coverage of the 1982 Israeli invasion of Lebanon. In the late 1980s he covered the Palestinian Intifada and received another Pulitzer Prize. His books include* From Beirut to Jerusalem *(1989),* The Lexus and the Olive Tree *(1999),* The World is Flat *(2005) and* Hot, Flat, and Crowded *(2008).*

What's Our Sputnik?

CONTEXT: *In this* New York Times *article Friedman makes a reference to Sputnik. In 1957 the Soviet Union launched the world's first satellite, stunning the United States and shaking American self-confidence. The realization that the Soviets were technologically superior spurred the development of NASA, greater scientific research, and more technical scholarships.*

Dick Cheney says President Obama is "trying to pretend that we are not at war" 1
with terrorists. There is only one thing I have to say about that: I sure hope so.

Frankly, if I had my wish, we would be on our way out of Afghanistan not 2
in, we would be letting Pakistan figure out which Taliban they want to con-
spire with and which ones they want to fight, we would be letting Israelis and
Palestinians figure out on their own how to make peace, we would be taking
$100 billion out of the Pentagon budget to make us independent of imported
oil—nothing would make us more secure—and we would be reducing the reward for killing or capturing Osama bin Laden to exactly what he's worth: 10
cents and an autographed picture of Dick Cheney.

Am I going isolationist? No, but visiting the greater China region always 3
leaves me envious of the leaders of Hong Kong, Taiwan and China, who surely
get to spend more of their time focusing on how to build their nations than my
president, whose agenda can be derailed at any moment by a jihadist death
cult using exploding underpants.

Could we just walk away? No, but we must change our emphasis. The "war 4
on terrorists" has to begin by our challenging the people and leaders over there.
If they're not ready to take the lead, to speak out and fight the madness in their
midst, for the future of their own societies, there is no way we can succeed.
We'll exhaust ourselves trying. We'd be better off just building a higher wall.

As the terrorism expert Bruce Hoffman noted in an essay in The Washing- 5
ton Post: "In the wake of the global financial crisis, Al Qaeda has stepped up
a strategy of economic warfare. 'We will bury you,' Soviet Premier Nikita

Khrushchev promised Americans 50 years ago. Today, Al Qaeda threatens: 'We will bankrupt you.' " And they will.

6   Our presence, our oil dependence, our endless foreign aid in the Middle East have become huge enablers of bad governance there and massive escapes from responsibility and accountability by people who want to blame all their troubles on us. Let's get out of the way and let the moderate majorities there, if they really exist, face their own enemies on their own. It is the only way they will move. We can be the wind at their backs, but we can't be their sails. There is some hope for Iraq and Iran today because their moderates are fighting for themselves.

7   Has anyone noticed the most important peace breakthrough on the planet in the last two years? It's right here: the new calm in the Strait of Taiwan. For decades, this was considered the most dangerous place on earth, with Taiwan and China pointing missiles at each other on hair triggers. Well, over the past two years, China and Taiwan have reached a quiet rapprochement—on their own. No special envoys or shuttling secretaries of state. Yes, our Navy was a critical stabilizer. But they worked it out. They realized their own interdependence. The result: a new web of economic ties, direct flights and student exchanges.

8   A key reason is that Taiwan has no oil, no natural resources. It's a barren rock with 23 million people who, through hard work, have amassed the fourth-largest foreign currency reserves in the world. They got rich digging inside themselves, unlocking their entrepreneurs, not digging for oil. They took responsibility. They got rich by asking: "How do I improve myself?" Not by declaring: "It's all somebody else's fault. Give me a handout."

9   When I look at America from here, I worry. China is now our main economic partner and competitor. Sure, China has big problems. Nevertheless, I hope Americans see China's rise as the 21st-century equivalent of Russia launching the Sputnik satellite—a challenge to which we responded with a huge national effort that revived our education, infrastructure and science and propelled us for 50 years. Unfortunately, the Cheneyites want to make fighting Al Qaeda our Sputnik. Others want us to worry about some loopy remark Senator Harry Reid made about the shade of Obama's skin.

10   Well, what is our national project going to be? Racing China, chasing Al Qaeda or parsing Harry? Of course, to a degree, we need to both race China and confront Al Qaeda—but which will define us?

11   "Our response to Sputnik made us better educated, more productive, more technologically advanced and more ingenious," said the Johns Hopkins foreign policy expert Michael Mandelbaum. "Our investments in science and education spread throughout American society, producing the Internet, more students studying math and people genuinely wanting to build the nation."

12   And what does the war on terror give us? Better drones, body scanners and a lot of desultory T.S.A. security jobs at airports. "Sputnik spurred us to build

a highway to the future," added Mandelbaum. "The war on terror is prompting us to build bridges to nowhere."

We just keep thinking we can do it all—be focused, frightened and frivo- 13
lous. We can't. We don't have the money. We don't have the time.

Understanding Meaning

1. Why does Friedman hope that President Obama is pretending that America is not at war? What is his point?

2. What does Friedman see as the economic threat of terrorism?

3. What role does American dependence on foreign oil play in creating the
   problems in the Middle East?

4. How did Taiwan develop a strong economy despite its lack of resources?

5. *Critical Thinking:* Why does Friedman hope that Americans focus more on
   China than on Al Qaeda? In his view, why should China and not terrorism be our "Sputnik"?

Evaluating Strategy

1. How effective is Friedman's opening? Do you think he used the Dick
   Cheney quote to grab attention?

2. Friedman makes references to Sputnik. Do you think his essay would be
   stronger if he gave readers more background on an event that happened
   over fifty years ago?

3. How does Friedman use quotations to support his thesis?

4. How effective is the ending?

Appreciating Language

1. If you are unfamiliar with the word "Sputnik," look it up in an encyclopedia. What impact did this Russian word have during the Cold War? What
   did this word come to symbolize?

2. Consider the phrase Friedman uses in his last paragraph. Are Americans
   "focused, frightened and frivolous"? Why or why not?

WRITING SUGGESTIONS

1. Friedman uses the words "focused, frightened and frivolous" to describe
   American society. Choose one of these concepts and analyze evidence
   you see or do not see that illustrate this idea. Do hard-working entrepreneurs and students cramming for exams demonstrate focus? Does the

fascination with YouTube, reality TV shows, fashion trends, and pop music illustrate frivolous behavior?

2. *Collaborative Writing:* Work with a group of students and discuss whether the United States needs a new "Sputnik" to spark innovation and a new commitment to progress. What should this new Sputnik be in your view—health care, the deficit, the rise of China, global warming, poverty, or something else? Develop an essay outlining your views. If members of the group have differing views, consider writing a comparison essay to contrast opposing viewpoints or a division essay demonstrating a range of opinions.

FAREED ZAKARIA

Fareed Zakaria (1964-) was born in India and received his bachelor's degree from Yale and his doctorate from Harvard. He was managing editor of Foreign Affairs *magazine before becoming an editor at* Newsweek International. *He has appeared on ABC and CNN, where he hosts* Fareed Zakaria GPS. *His books include* From Wealth to Power *(1998),* The Future of Freedom *(2003), and* The Post-American World *(2008).*

Get Out the Wallets

CONTEXT: *Zakaria wrote this* Newsweek *article in August 2009 when economists were analyzing consumer spending to measure the extent of the 2008 recession. As Zakaria notes, the global economy has been driven largely by American consumption of imported goods.*

The world needs Americans to spend. 1

If I were told by the economic gods that I could have the answer to one question about the fate of the global economy, I know what I would ask. "When will the American consumer start spending again?" I know that doesn't sound as sophisticated as a question about industrial production, interest-rate fluctuations, or the Chinese stimulus plan, but it's the key to understanding when we will get out of this recession—and what the recovery is likely to look like. The rise of emerging powers like China, India, and Brazil is real. But for now, there is still just one 800-pound gorilla. The American consumer is the single largest factor at play in the global economy. Our spending is currently equal to the entire economies of China and India added together and then doubled. 2

The gorilla is showing some signs of life. It's rare for a statistical report to make news, but in late July, the release of the Case-Shiller Price Index was reported as the lead news story by both *The New York Times* and *The Wall Street Journal*. The report showed that the American housing market seems to have stopped declining. That's big news because the housing collapse has been the driving force behind both the economic recession and the financial crisis. Usually, recessions end with a return to spending on housing, automobiles, and appliances, followed by other consumer durables. 3

But this is not a usual recession. The United States entered this downturn with the average American deeply in debt. In 2007, total household debt was $13.8 trillion. Household debt per person nearly doubled between 1997 and 2007, from about $25,000 to $46,000. That means people might spend the next few years rebuilding their personal balance sheets, spending less, saving more. In fact, they're already doing that. The savings rate has shot up to almost 7 percent, the highest rate in 15 years. But many experts think that it 4 will have to get up to 8 or 9 percent—the historical average in the pre–credit bubble years—before Americans start spending again. That would mean either a longer recession or a much weaker recovery than most expect. The Chinese government is spending pots of money building bridges right now, German industries are retooling, but eventually they will all need to be able to export to Americans again.

5   We have come to believe that Americans are genetically coded to consume. In fact, it's not about DNA. Historically, Americans were seen as puritans, thrifty and hardworking. In the early 1970s, the American savings rate was more than 10 percent. But a change in economic conditions began to get Americans spending. Credit expanded dramatically in the last three decades, especially in the last eight years. The inflation of the 1970s left people worried that their savings could be wiped out. And a series of government policies and programs subsidized debt and expenditure and did nothing to reward savings.

6   The biggest of these, of course, is the tax deductibility of mortgage interest, which costs the country almost $100 billion every year. Please don't tell me it creates an ownership society. Margaret Thatcher eliminated a similar program in Britain, and Canada doesn't have one either—and both have the same home-owner-ship rates as America. The policy does not encourage home-owner-ship; it encourages the accumulation of debt.

7   The point is that people respond to incentives. Japan had a relatively low savings rate until the 1950s and '60s, when the government put in place policies that raised the savings rate. Conversely, as Tokyo has tried to get consumers to spend over the last two decades, Japan's savings rate has plummeted. The Chinese may or may not have a propensity to save, but their current high savings rate reflects a government policy to create high savings. In addition, objective factors matter. Chinese know that they do not have a government safety net, that they will have to pay for their own health care and retirement, and so they save. The Japanese, by contrast, are aging rapidly and retirees are spending down their savings at a rapid rate.

8   What does this mean for America? I doubt that the country will return to historically high savings rates. The baby boomers are aging, which means that they will save less and spend more. Credit is not nearly as available as it was two years ago, but compared with the rest of the world, America remains awash in easy access to cash—and at historically low interest rates. And perhaps most important, we have decided as a society to massively favor spending over saving. All the programs and incentives to pull out the wallet remain in place. For example, the United States is the only advanced industrial country that does not have a national sales tax. The American consumer will likely start spending sooner than many imagine. That's good for the world, but is it good for America?

Understanding Meaning

1. What impact do American consumers have on the world economy?

2. Americans are saving more than in recent years. Why is this seen as a negative?

3. How has the growth of consumer debt affected spending habits?

4. *Critical Thinking:* Zakaria states that the Chinese and Germans are waiting for American consumers to start spending again so they can export to the United States. Should American consumer spending also benefit American businesses, creating jobs and sparking demands for more advanced products? Is there a way to direct consumers to favor American-made products?

Evaluating Strategy

1. What figures does Zakaria use to demonstrate the magnitude of American spending in the global economy?

2. Economic analysis depends on numbers and statistics. Does Zakaria use figures in a way that the average reader can understand? What challenges do writers face in addressing complex issues that involve data and statistics?

3. How effective is Zakaria's final question?

Appreciating Language

1. Zakaria states that the tax deductibility of mortgage interest does not encourage "home-owner-ship" but "accumulation of debt." Consider the connotations these words have. Should the word "home owner" only refer to someone who actually owns his or her home outright? Is a person with a mortgage a "home owner" or a "debtor"?

2. Zakaria notes that historically Americans were viewed as "puritans, thrifty and hardworking." What three words might describe Americans today?

WRITING SUGGESTIONS

1. Write an essay that analyzes an aspect of consumer behavior. Have you observed people spending less, using credit more wisely, and saving more money? Have young people grown up with such easy access to cash through credit cards and ATMs that they have difficulty budgeting their money?

2. *Collaborative Writing:* Discuss consumer spending with a group of students and write a short essay that analyzes spending behavior they see on campus. Do they observe students routinely using credit cards to make discretionary purchases like DVDs, restaurant meals, and fashion items? Do lower-income students feel pressured by more-affluent peers to spend money they don't have to avoid feeling left out?

BENJAMIN RADFORD

Benjamin Radford (1970–) received a BA in psychology from the University of New Mexico in 1993. He is the managing editor of the science magazine Skeptical Inquirer *and editor in chief of the Spanish-language magazine* Pensar, *published in Argentina. Radford has published hundreds of articles on urban legends, the media, paranormal events, and critical thinking. His books include* Hoaxes, Myths, and Manias: Why We Need Critical Thinking, *with Robert E. Bartholomew (2003), and* Media Mythmakers: How Journalists, Activists, and Advertisers Mislead Us *(2003).*

How Television Distorts Reality

CONTEXT: *In this essay, Radford argues that television newscasts distort reality by emphasizing sensational events. Notice how he uses objective analysis to support his point of view.*

Television, by its very nature, distorts the reality it claims to reflect and report on. Events are compressed, highlighted, sped up. Thus a person who occasionally watches sports highlights on TV will likely see more home runs and touchdowns than a person who attends local games regularly; television viewers are likely to see more murders than a police detective, more serious car crashes than a tow truck driver, and more plane crashes than a crash investigator.

The amount of time devoted to crime coverage is widely disproportionate to the amount of crime that actually occurs. Professor Joe Angotti of the University of Miami found that nearly 30 percent of airtime is spent covering crime, courts, and cops. But airtime is finite, of course, and less "sexy" (but more important) topics lose out: Education, for example, got just 2 percent of airtime nationally in the newscasts surveyed. Race relations got just 1.2 percent. Angotti, formerly a senior vice president of NBC News, says of his findings, "It's unfortunate that body-bag journalism is what local news chooses to focus on at the expense of more important stories." Part of the problem is journalistic laziness. "Crime reporting is easy to do and doesn't require hardly any follow-up. Television journalists have to stand up and say we're here to tell people what they need to know," says Angotti. "Television news has abandoned its responsibility to do serious journalism in favor of sensational video."[1]

Another study, this one headed by Syracuse University professor Robert Lissit, found that of one hundred newscasts around the country, "nearly 30 percent of the news time was spent on crime and the courts. Ten percent was devoted to reporting calamities and natural disasters. Only 15 percent of the newscasts

[1]Terry Jackson, " 'Body-bag Journalism' Rules in Broadcast News, Study Says," *Miami Herald*, May 7, 1997.

were devoted to government and politics. Health and medicine: about 7 percent. Race relations: 1.2 percent. Education: less than 1 percent." According to Lissit, crime gets a disproportionate amount of coverage not because it is important but because it is easy to cover: "A few shots of the crime scene, a quick interview with a police officer or someone in the neighborhood, and a quick reporter-on-camera standup. Summary, and that's the end of story." Noncrime issues such as politics or education require more background and effort and usually can't be wrapped up in such a tidy, quick package.

4   Like Angotti, Lissit also dismisses the justification that news directors commonly give for such sanguineous fare: It's what the public wants. "Market-driven news is giving the viewers what the stations think they want. Some might ask if that isn't simply representative democracy at work: 'What could be more democratic than giving viewers what they want?' My answer: What could be more irresponsible, more cynical, and profoundly wrong?"[2]

5   Notice that the news media have, in a way, tied their own hands in trying to present "important" stories. Clearly, not everything that is reported on the news is newsworthy. But because viewers have been led to believe that what they see on the news *must* be important, news organizations can't be honest about their vacuous coverage without making liars of themselves. You'll never hear a journalist say, "We're still covering this story, but to be honest it's not very important." Instead, the rules of the profession require that each story be treated as important and relevant—otherwise why are they (and we) wasting time on it?

6   By and large, the news media (and entertainment media, for that matter) seek the broadest possible appeal. This makes sense; the more diverse the appeal, the larger the audience, and thus the more profitable a program is. But one side effect of this process is a dumbing-down and homogenizing of content. Programs that are too cerebral are doomed, while programs based on the basest instincts and interests—sex (*Baywatch*), violence (*World's Scariest Police Chases*), or sex *and* violence (*Jerry Springer*)—will thrive. Programmers frequently take this too far and insult the viewers' intelligence.

7   As *Newsweek's* Jonathan Alter wrote, "When news oozes 24 hours a day it's not really news anymore. The TV becomes ambient noise. The newspaper becomes wallpaper. Finding patterns of importance becomes hard. It's easier—and more profitable—just to make the consumer gape."[3]

The Media Paradox

8   Another consequence of the news perspective that contributes to the public's fears is what John Ruscio, a social psychologist at Elizabethtown College in Pennsylvania, calls "the media paradox": The more we rely on the popular

[2]"Ditching 'Body Bag Journalism,'" *Christian News Archives* [online], www.villagelife.org/church/archives/ucc_bodybagjournalism.html [October 22, 1997].

[3]Jonathan Alter, "In the Times of the Tabs," *Newsweek*, June 2, 1997.

media to inform us, the more apt we are to misplace our fears. The paradox is the combined result of two biases, one inherent in the news-gathering process, the other inherent in the way our minds organize and recall information.

As Ruscio explains: 9

> For a variety of reasons—including fierce competition for our patronage within and across the various popular media outlets—potential news items are rigorously screened for their ability to captivate an audience…. The stories that do make it through this painstaking selection process are then often crafted into accounts emphasizing their concrete, personal, and emotional content.[4]

In turn, the more emotional and vivid the account is, the more likely we are to remember the information. This is the first element, the *vividness bias:* Our minds easily remember vivid events.

The second bias lies in what psychologists term the *availability heuristic:* Our   10 judgments of frequency and probability are heavily influenced by the ease with which we can imagine or recall instances of an event. So the more often we hear reports of plane crashes, school shootings, or train wrecks, the more often we think they occur. But the bias that selects those very events makes them appear more frequent than they really are.

Imagine, for example, that a consumer group dedicated to travel safety es-   11 tablished a network of correspondents in every country that reported every train and bus wreck, no matter how minor, and broadcast daily pictures. Anyone watching that broadcast would see dozens of wrecks and crashes every day, complete with mangled metal and dead bodies, and would likely grow to fear such transportation. No matter that in general trains and buses are very safe; if you screen the news to emphasize certain vivid events, accidents will seem more dangerous and common than they actually are. That explains, in part, why many people fear flying even though they know that statistically it's one of the safest modes of transport: Though crashes are very rare, the vividness and emotion of seeing dramatic footage of crashed planes drowns out the rational knowledge of statistical safety.

The homicide rate is another example. Many people are surprised to learn   12 that the suicide rate is higher than the homicide rate: Nearly twice as many people die by their own hand than are killed by other people (the murder rate in the United States is 5.9 per 100,000; the suicide rate is 10.3 per 100,000). While murders make news, suicides are frequently ignored unless the victim is famous. This imbalance in news coverage leads many to believe that homicides are far more common than suicides, when in fact the opposite is true.[5]

---

[4]John Ruscio, "Risky Business," *Skeptical Inquirer* (March/April 2000): 24.
[5]"Mortality," in *Time Almanac 2003* (Boston: Information Please, 2002), p. 132.

13   The imbalance in media coverage is also due in part to the sensational nature of a murder. If a person is found killed by another, the story has only just begun: The police must look for the killer, determine a motive, find the weapon, arrest the killer, put him or her on trial, and so on. But when the killer *is* the victim, the story is over as soon as it starts. There will be no dramatic arrests or jailhouse confessions, just grief and perhaps memorials or a short quest for motive.

14   As a society we throw money at things we fear in order to fix them. But when we misplace our fears, we run the very real risk of wasting time and resources on insignificant problems. As author John Ross states," Are we then turning our backs on a raging inferno while we douse the flame of a match?"[6]

15   The news media do their best to raise alarm, even when no alarm is needed. The death of film director Alan Pakula is a good example. Pakula, director of many notable films, including *All the President's Men* and *Klute*, died in a freak freeway accident in November 1998. A vehicle in front of him ran over a piece of metal, which shot through his windshield, killing him. It was a sudden, horrific, one-in-a-million accident—yet the media reported it differently. While some reporters grudgingly admitted that the accident was very unusual, many others hyped the story. They tried to downplay the rarity of the accident, and rushed to air news segments revealing "hidden dangers on the highway." While trash on the roads is a threat, the number of drivers *ever* killed by road trash compared to, say, the number killed by falling asleep at the wheel or drunk driving in *a single month* is minuscule.

16   "A single death is a tragedy, a million deaths is a statistic," Joseph Stalin observed. The public and reporters latched onto Pakula's death because it was a single death of someone famous. And it's no accident that single deaths spark more outrage than many deaths. In 1994, more than 800,000 people were killed in genocidal ethnic clashes in Africa. Yet Americans took little notice of the carnage in Rwanda; they (and the news media) were much more interested in the murders of just two people: Nicole Brown Simpson and Ron Goldman.

17   John Ruscio explains why the news media prefer testimonials:

> Producers are aware that a scientific analysis is not as emotionally compelling as one (carefully chosen) individual's personal experience. Why does a television news reporter stand in front of a courthouse when sharing a landmark verdict reached earlier that day? Why does a weather correspondent endure frigid temperatures, sleet, and harsh wind on camera to inform us that a severe storm is in progress? Even superficial background elements appear to add a sense of realism and concreteness to a story.[7]

---

[6]John F. Ross, "Risk: Where Do Real Dangers Lie?" *Smithsonian* 26 (1995): 42–53.
[7]Ruscio, "Risky Business," p. 23.

Note that all this is done to promote the illusion of importance, and in the process the news media insult their audience's intelligence. Viewers are smart enough to know that a forecaster doesn't have to be actually standing outdoors to give them an accurate weather forecast.

Another example of the way in which the media emphasize the wrong risks 18 is in health care and disease prevention. Though the news media like to run stories on both real and alleged carcinogenic dangers lurking in our environments—such as toxic chemicals, cell phones, power lines, and radiation—health experts say that poor diet may be more likely to cause cancers. At a conference sponsored in part by the National Institute of Environmental Health Studies, it was reported that a lack of vitamins found in fruits and vegetables could be damaging people's DNA, increasing their susceptibility to cancer.

A California study found that only one-third of California residents reported 19 eating the minimum recommended amount of fruits and vegetables every day. This can lead to vitamin deficiencies, which has been shown to alter DNA. Bruce Ames, a professor of biochemistry at the University of California at Berkeley, said, "What is becoming clear is that there is a tremendous amount of DNA damage in people from not having their vitamins and minerals. People, when they think of cancer, they think of chemicals in the water or pesticide residue. I just think it's all a distraction."

Researchers have found that a lack of folic acid, a B vitamin, may influence 20 a person's susceptibility to leukemia; vitamin B_{12} deficiency has been shown to damage chromosomes, and still other research suggests that zinc and iron deficiencies may also result in genetic damage.[8]

These problems can be solved by simply eating well or taking a daily multi- 21 vitamin. Yet for the news media, this story isn't interesting. Telling people to eat right and take a vitamin just isn't eye-catching, not compared to showing footage of a leaking sewer pipe or pesticide spraying. Certainly there are real dangers from toxic chemicals and radiation. But the average news viewer has probably seen hundreds or thousands of reports on those dangers, and probably only a handful reminding them of the importance of eating a balanced meal.

The news bias causes us to misplace our fears in other ways as well. In his 22 book *Creating Reality*, journalist David Altheide notes,

> [D]ifferent news sources produce different stories. Police radio monitors, for example, provide crime news involving street crimes which frequently involve lower-class and minority group youth. But the story of crime is incomplete if it is only learned about through these sources. The image is presented, albeit unintentionally, that certain kinds of crime are not only committed by certain

---

[8]Maggie Fox, "U.S. Poor Said Damaging Health with Lack of Vitamins," Reuters [online], www.thevitamindigest.com/news/2000/oct1900uspoorsaid.htm [October 19, 2000].

groups of people, but that this is what the crime problem is about. White-collar crime and corporate rip-offs are not presented via police monitors, even though more money is involved than in dozens of $25–$100 robberies. Thus, the Phoenix media were reluctant to disclose that one of the area's largest banks was being investigated for passing illegal securities. If bank officials *are* eventually indicted, they will be interviewed in their plush offices. In all likelihood we will never see them "drug off" by police officers, handcuffed, disheveled, and looking ashamed.[9]

The white, middle-aged man or woman in a suit you happily sit across a business desk from is perhaps just as likely to rob you as the black youth you might cross the street to avoid—and they're likely to get much more money out of you than a mugger would.

Understanding Meaning

1. How do television newscasts, in Radford's view, distort reality? What stories are disproportionately covered and which issues are largely ignored?

2. How does the visual nature of television lead broadcasters to select which stories they will cover?

3. What does Radford mean by the term "availability heuristic"? Can you think of examples?

4. Why, in Radford's view, does television news devote so much coverage to homicides even though twice as many Americans take their own lives?

5. How does television news give the public distorted perceptions about crime?

6. *Critical Thinking:* Do you think twenty-four hour cable news channels such as CNN, MSNBC, and FOX NEWS have increased or decreased media distortion? Have competition and expanded broadcast time allowed television to explore more issues and study them in greater depth, or has it increased sensationalism as rival networks seek higher ratings?

Evaluating Strategy

1. What measurements or analytical tools does Radford use in examining television coverage?

2. Radford includes outside sources, including statistics and expert testimony. Does this give his article greater authenticity? Why is it important to include documentation?

---

[9]Altheide, *Creating Reality*, p. 191.

3. *Blending the Modes:* How does Radford use *comparison, example,* and *cause and effect* in developing his essay?

4. How effective is the conclusion? What impact does it have?

Appreciating Language

1. What tone and style does Radford use in describing the media? Do you detect any bias? Why or why not? Is it important for objective analysis to use neutral language?

2. Radford introduces terms such as "media paradox" and "vividness bias." Does he define these adequately? Can you explain them in your own words? Can you think of examples?

3. Look up the word "sensationalism." What does it mean? Can you think of recent stories that dominated the news that were sensational but had little significance?

WRITING SUGGESTIONS

1. Conduct your own analysis of one or more newscasts. Count the number of stories and use a stopwatch to measure the amount of time devoted to each one. Write an objective analysis of your findings. Which stories received the most coverage? Which stories received the least?

2. *Collaborative Writing:* Discuss the media with a group of students and examine how issues and events are covered by television news. What distortions or biases do students see? Are some stories given greater emphasis than they deserve? Are other issues ignored or given simplistic coverage? Record your comments and use division or classification to organize your group's observations.

SCOTT ROSENBERG

Scott Rosenberg grew up in Queens, New York, and worked as a theater and movie critic for the Boston Phoenix *and the* San Francisco Examiner. *In 1995 he helped found* Salon.com *and edited the online magazine's technology coverage. His books include* Dreaming in Code *(2008) and* Say Everything: How Blogging Began, What It's Becoming, and Why It Matters *(2010).*

Closing the Credibility Gap

CONTEXT: *In this* Nieman Reports *article, published in 2009, Rosenberg analyzes the issue of credibility of online sources. Often dismissed by print journalists, online sources, Rosenberg argues, can be verified for accuracy and bias.*

1 In November 1996, Pierre Salinger, former ABC News correspondent and White House press secretary to President John F. Kennedy, inspired a brief flurry of headlines when he stepped forward with what he claimed was dramatic news: He'd found documents proving that U.S. Navy missiles had shot down TWA Flight 800, which had crashed in the Atlantic Ocean earlier that year.

2 The FBI looked at Salinger's papers and identified them as identical to discredited documents that had been floating around the Internet's Usenet newsgroups for months.

3 Whoops! Salinger's snookering illustrated a common failing among journalists at that early point in the Internet's rise—a sort of online credulity syndrome. Somehow, he'd concluded that if information was published online and seemed real, it must be trustworthy. Once Salinger placed his imprimatur on the story, his credentials as a media insider ushered it past the usual checkpoints. It wound up all over cable news and front pages.

4 This sequence of events was plainly a failure of the journalistic process. But its coverage as news reframed it as a failure of the Internet. The problem, observers like Matthew Wald of the *New York Times* declared, was that the Web just can't be trusted: "It used to be called gossip. Now it takes the form of e-mail or Internet postings, and it has a new credibility."

5 As I read this coverage, I fumed. I'd already been online for half a decade, and I'd left my newspaper job a year before to help start Salon.com, a professional news magazine on the Web. I knew that the Internet sped up the diffusion of rumors—and that it also accelerated their debunking. Surely it behooved newsroom pros to grasp the dynamics of this unfamiliar but fascinating process. The flow of information was changing fast in front of us, and reporters, of all people, needed to become experts in navigating that flow.

Journalists should have been leaders in teaching others how to gauge the 6
trustworthiness of information in this exciting but anarchic new environment. Instead, they were making awful public mistakes themselves, such as
this one, and then scapegoating the Internet.

Breakdown of Trust

This Salinger flap set me on a trajectory, for the next several years, of chroni- 7
cling the triangular breakdown of trust I saw unfolding among the media, the
Web, and the general public. Journalists thought they could defend the reputation of their newspapers and broadcast outlets by trying to discredit the
upstart online world. Internet natives and recent immigrants to it lost respect
for many mainstream journalists, concluding that they were clueless about the
emerging online medium. Members of the public, instead of enjoying a
smooth transition guided by the journalists they knew and trusted, found
themselves asked to take sides in an intramedia feud.

In this melee, everyone lost. Today's newsrooms are full of journalists 8
with considerably more Web experience and online savvy than their prede-
cessors, but the "blame the Web" reflex is now deeply embedded in the
media-professional psyche, emerging on cue each time some hapless journalist makes a Salingeresque mistake.

Fortunately, we now have a wide range of reasonably sophisticated tools 9
and approaches for rating the quality of information on the Web. Here are a
few examples:

* Reliable online coverage documents its assertions with links to primary 10
  sources; the absence of such links is a red flag.
* Good bloggers lay out their backgrounds and biases in a stream of posts over 11
  the years, allowing readers to decide where they can be trusted and where
  they lose their bearings.
* Every page on Wikipedia—the collectively assembled and edited online ency- 12
  clopedia—has a "discussion" tab where users can see who has challenged what
  and a "history" tab that shows every change to the page's information.

The comments area found below most Web articles and posts provides a 13
natural space for give-and-take about possible errors, omissions and problems
with the coverage—and how a site handles such issues is another way to decide whom to trust.

Anonymous sources remain as suspect online as they are in any other medium, 14
but new opportunities to examine who links to any site and what they say about
it often yield insights, even about sites that don't tell us their authors' names.

15   These customs and practices for assessing the trustworthiness of information online have evolved in the years since Salinger's gaffe. Throughout that time, journalists have also often found themselves in a defensive crouch, unwilling or unable to embrace the Web's new techniques. Large media companies spent years discouraging outbound links from their Web sites, citing business reasons, and they still lag behind. Newsroom traditions of impersonality and aspirations to objectivity mean that most newspaper bylines remain opaque in comparison with the full profiles we have for our favorite bloggers. Newsroom culture remains committed to delivering a finished product to readers, so the Wikipedia-style "discussion" and "history" pages aren't an option. And the comments feature on most newspaper sites serves as an outlet for readers to vent frustration, rather than an arena for collaboration between readers and journalists.

16   All this has left editors and reporters employed by traditional news organizations scratching their heads, wondering how it is that their time-honored approaches have continued to lose trust and readers, while new-media upstarts multiply and thrive.

17   Earlier this year, a 22-year-old Dublin student inserted a bogus quote into the Wikipedia entry for composer Maurice Jarre, who had just passed away. Wikipedia's moderators did a pretty good job of removing the unsourced quotation, but not before it had been picked up by a depressingly high number of news outlets for use in their Jarre obituaries.

18   Surely, in 2009, working journalists must understand how to use Wikipedia. It was easy to discover that this quotation had been added to the Jarre page after the composer's passing; one click on the page's "history" tab brought up all the information you'd need. Apparently, not a single obit writer of the many who used the quotation bothered to make that simple inquiry.

19   The quotes would most likely have stood, uncorrected, had the student prankster not notified the publications of their error himself. That's depressing enough in itself. It's even sadder when we realize that, 13 years since Salinger's mistake, there are still so many journalists who know less than their readers do about how to read critically online.

Understanding Meaning

1. How did Pierre Salinger's 1996 gaffe illustrate a common journalistic failure in the Internet age?

2. Why does Rosenberg believe it is wrong for journalists to blame the Internet?

3. What strategies does Rosenberg suggest people use to verify online sources? Are these methods widely taught?

4. How can you determine if the information on Wikipedia is accurate?

5. *Critical Thinking:* As people become more adept at checking sources, do you think those spreading falsehoods will become more sophisticated by inventing sources, so that a slanderous posting appears to be supported by reputable evidence?

Evaluating Strategy

1. How effective is the opening example?

2. Rosenberg uses bullet points to highlight tools for examining online sources. Is this an effective device? How can a writer use visual markers to flag important material? Can a writer use too many?

3. Rosenberg makes the statement, "Surely, in 2009, working journalists must understand how to use Wikipedia." Why does he mention the year? What is Rosenberg trying to emphasize?

Appreciating Language

1. Does Rosenberg use any terms that readers unfamiliar with the Web would have problems understanding? What audience do you think he is seeking to address?

2. How would you define Rosenberg's term "'blame the Web' reflex"?

3. *Critical Thinking:* Rosenberg uses the terms "gossip" and "rumor." How would you define these terms? Do gossip and rumor ever become legitimate news items? If an untrue story becomes viral on the Internet, does it create its own reality and therefore become worthy of reporting?

WRITING SUGGESTIONS

1. Analyze the online sources for a rumor, controversy, or conspiracy theory. Consider sites that claim the Bush administration orchestrated the 9/11 attacks or those asserting that President Obama was born in Kenya. What evidence do they present? What sources do they list? Write a short essay based on your observations. Are these sites convincing to a sophisticated reader? Why or why not?

2. *Collaborative Writing:* Work with a group of students and develop a short process essay that lists in numbered steps strategies students should practice to evaluate online sources.

LOUIS R. MIZELL JR.

Louis R. Mizell Jr. was a special agent and intelligence officer for the U.S. State Department. He is now president of Mizell and Company, an international firm specializing in crime prevention. Mizell frequently appears on television commenting on home and personal security issues. He has published a series of books on personal safety. In 1998 he published Invasion of Privacy, *analyzing how modern technology has compromised personal privacy and security.*

Who's Listening to Your Cell Phone Calls?

CONTEXT: *Before reading this passage from* Invasion of Privacy, *consider how often you have used or have seen friends use cell phones. Do people assume their conversations are private?*

1   More than forty million cellular phones are currently in use in the United States, and the numbers are dramatically increasing each year.

2   On any given day, thousands of eavesdroppers intercept, record, and listen to conversations made from cellular and so-called cordless phones. These eavesdroppers include curious neighbors, business competitors, stalkers, journalists, private investigators, and even espionage agents.

3   In California, spies for hire cruise the highways of Hollywood and the Silicon Valley, hoping to steal valuable trade secrets from executives talking on their car phones. Armed with radio scanners, tabloid reporters in New York monitor conversations of the rich, famous, and infamous, hoping to get a front-page scoop. In Florida, a ham operator monitoring the poolside conversations of a prominent lawyer got incredible inside information on three divorce cases.

4   Cellular telephone conversations can be easily monitored by anyone with a radio scanner, but it is a violation of state and federal law to do so intentionally. A 1993 law made it illegal to make or sell radio scanners that pick up cellular calls, but the law didn't make it illegal to own the old scanners. Furthermore, it is rather easy, although illegal, to modify a legal police scanner so that it will pick up cellular conversations.

5   The problem is that there are hundreds of thousands of the old radio scanners in circulation and an equal number of people who don't care about the law. "How are they going to catch me and how are they going to prove it?" said one ham operator who listens to his neighbors' cellular conversations "just for the fun of it."

6   In truth, only a very small percentage of the people who have been monitored ever learn that their calls were intercepted. An even smaller percentage

of the perpetrators are ever caught. Curious kooks, corporate snoops, and spies for hire who use intercepted information are usually smart enough not to publicize where they got it.

"I really couldn't care less if someone listens to my conversations," said a 7 schoolteacher from Indiana. "I'm not discussing my love life or national security." One of the biggest problems concerning privacy and portable phones is that most people do not realize how even innocent information can be used by criminals and other opportunists. Another problem is that just because you don't care if someone is listening to your conversation, the person you are talking to might care very much.

Burglars are known to monitor the calls of people discussing evening or 8 weekend plans. Knowing that the occupants are going to be away, the burglars enter their homes.

Doctors and lawyers frequently discuss everyday business on cellular 9 phones. In one case, a doctor was notified that a VIP patient had tested positive for AIDS. The information was intercepted, and before long, the VIP's medical status was common knowledge. In another case, a lawyer from Ohio reviewed a client's prenuptial agreement with a second lawyer who was using a cellular telephone. A teenage neighbor of the second lawyer intercepted the conversation. "Before long, the whole damn neighborhood knew about our secret wedding and my financial situation," said the angry groom-to-be.

Stalking, or inappropriate pursuit, has become a dangerous epidemic in the 10 United States and is evolving into one of the most insidious threats to personal privacy. Many researchers estimate that more than 200,000 women, men, and children are currently being harassed, threatened, and endangered by stalkers.

Stalking may begin with an innocuous contact and then, through misinter- 11 pretation or delusion, the pursuer escalates to harassment, surveillance, threats, and sometimes murder.

I have been involved in seven cases and am aware of many more in which 12 stalkers intercepted cellular phone conversations and used the intelligence to harass their targets.

A jobless and toothless forty-one-year-old man, hooked on ampheta- 13 mines, became infatuated with a fifteen-year-old girl whom he first noticed at a state swimming competition. "He's really scary and keeps showing up wherever I go," explained the frightened swimmer. "It's like he always knows where I'm going to be."

The young lady had good reason to be scared; the man had a long history of 14 bizarre and criminal behavior. On one occasion, he burglarized a home and fell asleep in a teenage girl's bed. The horrified family called the police who arrested the man and confiscated handcuffs and a number of stolen house keys.

Released on good behavior, the "nonviolent" criminal was once again 15 free to victimize others. We can't prove what his ultimate plans were concerning our fifteen-year-old client, but we did prove that he had a scanner in his car and had recorded the swimmer's mother as she talked on various cell phones, including a car phone. Two of the taped conversations informed the stalker where his target would be. "I've got to pick my daughter up at McDonald's at 4:30," she mentioned to one friend. "The swim team is celebrating at the Hyatt tonight," she told her neighbor. Needless to say, the stalker showed up at both locations.

16   Eavesdropping on cellular phones is only one of the issues that worry privacy advocates. There is also concern that cellular phones will be used by police and sophisticated criminals to locate the caller.

17   Unbeknownst to most consumers, cellular phones are portable homing devices that allow police and others to pinpoint the caller's position. Police have used this tool to locate a wide range of criminals and kidnap victims. Privacy advocates worry that police will abuse this tool to spy on innocent citizens.

18   When a cellular phone is switched to the On position, it emits a low-power signal to the network to announce which cell site it is in. A cell site is a zone served by a single relay station and is generally several square miles in size. When a caller moves out of one cell site, the call is automatically switched to a different cell site.

19   By using a technique called triangulation, police are able to get a directional fix on the cellular signal and pinpoint the phone's cell site or location. This is the technique police used to locate the car owned by the slain father of basketball great Michael Jordan. Triangulation techniques have also been used by intelligence agencies to locate enemy radio sites and by ocean search-and-rescue teams to pinpoint the location of vessels.

20   There are dozens of cases in which triangulation techniques have assisted law enforcement worldwide.

21   When the Los Angeles police needed to locate O. J. Simpson during the now-famous highway chase, they received court-ordered help from a mobile phone company and were able to locate the Ford Bronco by tracing its cellular phone radio signal. In Colombia, ruthless drug boss Pablo Escobar was finally located and shot dead by police after they traced his mobile telephone's radio signal. Police in the United States located fugitive lawyer Nicholas Bissell, Jr., in Nevada on November 26, 1996, after tracing calls he made on his cellular telephone. Bissell was running from the law after being convicted of fraud, embezzlement, and abuse of power.

22   Another advantage of cellular tracing from a law enforcement perspective is that cellular phones can tell police not only where a suspect is going but also where he has been.

23   A federal drug informant is accused of booby-trapping a briefcase in an unsuccessful attempt to kill a U.S. prosecutor. Using the informant's cellular

phone records, prosecutors showed that he was in the same town on the same day where the would-be assassination kit was purchased.

Unlike hard-line telephones that most people have in their homes, cus- 24 tomers pay for each local cellular call. The billing record for each cellular call shows the cell site from which it was made.

Privacy advocates recognize that cellular call tracing can be a great tool for 25 law enforcement, but they argue that the bad will outweigh the good if police abuse their powers.

"Police have no right to know my location just because they reason that I 26 might be relevant to some investigation," explained a law-abiding political science professor. "I want to make sure police cannot track and follow a person using a mobile phone unless they obtain a full wiretap warrant." At present, police only need a simple subpoena, which is easier to obtain than a wiretap warrant, to legally intercept cell phone signals.

"I bet the good professor would change his mind real quickly if his daugh- 27 ter were kidnapped," countered a police captain. "We don't have the time, the resources, or the inclination to snoop on law-abiding citizens. . . . We only use cellular tools to catch criminals," he protested. "Shouldn't we be more worried about the way rapists and burglars invade our privacy and less worried about taking crime-fighting weapons from the police?"

Understanding Meaning

1. Why are cell phones easy to monitor? What makes them different from traditional telephones?

2. Why have laws banning police scanners that can pick up cell calls failed to curb illegal monitoring?

3. How can even innocent calls expose people to risk?

4. How do cell phones work as homing devices? How can police use them to track people's movements?

5. *Critical Thinking:* Can anyone be sure that his or her legal, medical, or financial records are secure? Even if you never use a cell phone, can you be sure that conversations by your lawyer, doctor, or broker are not being monitored?

Evaluating Strategy

1. How effective is the evidence Mizell presents? Do you find it convincing? Do you think it will change people's use of cell phones?

2. *Blending the Modes:* How does Mizell use *narration* and *cause and effect* in developing his analysis?

Appreciating Language

1. Mizell uses words such as "kook" in his essay. Does the use of slang make the essay easy to read, or does it detract from the seriousness of the subject?

2. Mizell's book is targeted to a wide audience. Do you find his style readable? Can you easily remember facts and details? Would the use of technical or legal terminology lend the article greater authority?

WRITING SUGGESTIONS

1. Write an essay analyzing how technology—cell phones, email, computers, the Internet, security video cameras—have robbed citizens of their privacy. Is there any way to protect people from stalkers and hackers who might monitor phone calls or illegally access computer files and post the information on a web page?

2. *Collaborative Writing:* Working with a group of students, review Mizell's article, and write a short process paper instructing consumers about cell phone use. Remind people to avoid discussing sensitive issues or providing information that could be used by burglars or stalkers.

JIM GEMMELL AND GORDON BELL

Jim Gemmell is a senior researcher at Microsoft Research whose work led to features of Windows XP, Windows Server 2008, and Bing.com. Gordon Bell is a principal researcher at Microsoft Research and a professor at Carnegie Mellon University. Their book Total Recall: How the E-Memory Revolution Will Change Everything *was published in 2009.*

The E-Memory Revolution

CONTEXT: *Gemmell and Bell wrote this article for* Library Journal, *a publication read by librarians coping with digital media that are changing the way records are created, collected, stored, and accessed.*

When Stanford University obtained the Buckminster Fuller archive, it heralded it as "one of the most extensive known personal archives in existence." Taking up 2000 linear feet of shelf space, including hundreds of thousands of pages and over 4000 hours of audio/video, Fuller's collection does indeed sound impressive. But Fuller, considered an eccentric for leaving behind such an enormous corpus, will be put to shame by the vast repository of electronic memories (e-memories) created by the average Joe of the next generation. And these e-memory archives will take up a lot less shelf space.

We are on the cusp of an era in which, if you choose, you can create e-memories of everything, forget nothing, and keep them in your own personal archive. You can have what we refer to as Total Recall. Souvenirs and mementos will belong to another era. More and more is being recorded about each one of us than ever before, and it is bound increasingly to include reading habits, health, location, and computer usage. Archivists, who are already beginning to deal with digital curation, will have to grapple less with physical objects and more with the potential analysis and distribution of the information those objects represent. And library patrons will be a new breed, "a digital person," with their own personal digital libraries of everything they've ever read, seen, and heard.

Three streams of technology are merging to bring about an imminent Total Recall revolution. The first is recording technology, beginning with the already ubiquitous digital cameras and cell phones that include cameras. They are the first few drops in a coming deluge of sensing devices that will include location tracking, environment-sensing (for example, temperature and humidity), and biometric sensing (via on-body devices today and someday via in-body devices). Furthermore, the trail of one's digital transactions can tell a detailed story—and not merely itemized credit card bills but phone call logs, email in-boxes, web browsing histories, movie rentals, and much more. We already have more digital records than we realize.

4   The second technology stream is the rapid increase in capacity and corresponding decrease in price for digital storage. Imagine an archive of everything you ever read or wrote—books, articles, web pages, emails, letters, and so on—along with 10 or 20 pictures a day and several hours of audio each day. Already, this would easily fit on a $100 hard drive. In a few years, it will fit in your cell phone. A few years after that, rolling video nonstop throughout life will be possible. We already have more digital storage than we realize.

5   The third stream is powerful software to take advantage of a lifetime of e-memories. Searching for words in your e-memories, like Google does on the web, is only the beginning. It will be possible to find things by cross-correlation, such as the document you read while in Phoenix, the picture taken by a relative, or the email you sent on that particularly cold day. And data-mining software will crunch through your life-log, finding patterns, trends, and connections. This third stream is where the most dramatic developments are occurring now.

Creating E-Memory Legacies

6 We don't expect very many people will record audio and video continuously throughout their lives. But virtually everyone will record much more audio and video, and the overall digital trail they leave behind will be even more expansive and detailed than it is now. Imagine if your great-great-grandfather had left behind as much video and audio as Buckminster Fuller, allowing you to hear the sound of his voice, identify his favorite sayings, and watch his mannerisms. Think also of looking through all his correspondence and seeing all his travels in detail down to each walk down the street. Suppose you could find ancestors similar to you and examine a detailed record of their health, including what they ate, how much exercise they took, and even a full history of their weight, blood pressure, blood glucose, and heart rate—recorded daily or even moment by moment.

7   With enough information about a person, it even becomes possible to simulate their responses in a dialog. Researchers at Carnegie Mellon University, Pittsburgh, have a program that lets you ask questions of Albert Einstein. You can chat with a virtual George Bush or Bart Simpson at MyCyberTwin.com. The scope of what you can discuss with Einstein, Bush, or Simpson is limited only by the source material. With a more comprehensive transcript of one's life, a very realistic simulation could be done. Imagine asking your great-great-grandfather about his first date with your great-great-grandmother.

Fundamental Human Values

Total Recall will impact more than just personal legacies; the legacy of re- 8
search projects will also be revolutionized. In the past, a paper or two might be
all that survived of a large research effort. In the future, all of the data, notes,
and correspondence will be preserved. Others will study it and add their own
observations. Someone may apply a fresh approach to the old data. This new
paradigm is already being tried in the world of science, yielding deeper insights and sometimes revealing flaws in earlier published work. And it should
be just as relevant in other fields, for example, history, where access to original source material will proliferate.

For the historian, e-memories will require mastering new computing skills. 9
There will be far too much material to view—you don't have enough time to
watch even one other person's life in its entirety. So, historians will become adept
at using data mining to ferret out the novel from the mundane and the significant
amid the trivia. Their scholarly community will draw increasingly on the tech-
nologies of database search, wikis, and Facebook. The human values that guide
their interpretations will always be fundamental, of course, but they are bound to
change as e-memories in a Total Recall world give an increasingly finer grain to
our understanding not only of ourselves but of other people in other ages.

Following Story Trails

The way that history and science—indeed any information—are consumed will 10
change. Whatever the topic, the entire corpus in gory detail will be available.
The first organizational step, though, will need to be in summaries and "story
trails." Summaries may be authored, but more often they will be automatically
created. We will want them even for our own life corpora, because being inti-
mately familiar with a vast collection will not prevent it from being intimidating.
Consider the automatic summarization made possible by a system from Dublin
City University, Ireland, that discerns between the novel and the mundane from
among tens of thousands of photos, GPS data, and other sensor values. Its output
is a summarized diary that highlights the interesting part of your day.

Story trails will take you from artifact to artifact with a narrative to guide 11
you. Think of it as a History Channel show but an interactive one that lets
you browse around like you surf the web and where you can look at more than
just the few seconds of video or a handful of selected photos. Imagine following a narrative of basketball star Michael Jordan's life and being able to follow
up on one brief mention to watch a game he played as a teenager. Every stat is
available, every second of every game, every interview. You end up in his baseball career and discover stories by others that provide fascinating perspectives.

And you find they take you off on other trails through history. By following up their trails you end up deep in baseball lore and eventually looking at historic pictures of Yankee Stadium.

12   A foretaste of this new way of consuming information comes from the World Wide Telescope, which includes authored guided tours through the universe. You might be taking a tour of spiral galaxies, stopping for a view of each galaxy to hear details, and then virtually flying through space to the next galaxy on your tour. You arrive at Andromeda and notice that it is also part of a tour of galaxies visible via amateur telescopes; clicking on that tour icon branches you off on a new trail through the universe. And at any point you can just roam around the stars as you please.

Innovations in Learning

13   A further change in information consumption will be the widespread adoption of electronic textbooks. While promised for years, e-texts are finally on the rise, with some colleges already offering textbooks on Kindle book readers and the governor of California advocating their adoption. E-texts will have many advantages, but an overlooked point is that they will put computing power into the hands of students, enabling them to create their own learning e-memories. The e-text should know what has been read and what hasn't. It can enable electronic highlighting and note-taking. It will record lab experiments and conversations with the teacher. Increasing use of electronic book readers and the ubiquity of notebook computers will propel the ascendency of e-texts, which will open the door to a new world of learning with Total Recall.

14   This will also impact all lifelong learners. The mother of an ADD son will have her own personal e-library of articles, books, advice, and notes that she will continually extend and reflect on as she gains greater insight into his particular needs. The youth baseball coach will ruminate over a corpus of practice plans, game footage, coaching seminars, and suggestions from his colleagues. The entrepreneur will have her own blend of college courses, seminars, articles, and life experience that she will grow and evolve over time.

Library Patrons in the Total Recall Era

15   All these changes mean a drastic alteration in the library patron of tomorrow. Imagine a patron today arriving with a truckload of books, magazines, and clippings, several helpers, and even a few librarians from other libraries. Virtually, electronically, this will be the Total Recall patron. In a way, patrons

will be the librarian of their own not insubstantial library. Still, most will lack expertise; they will likely be asking for help with advanced search, data mining, and making connections in the virtual world to the right experts. Patrons will ask for help building new connections with their truckload of e-memories, as it were, and may well give a librarian some access to their own memories to get this help.

And patrons won't just want to borrow works; they will want to absorb 16 them into their e-memories. Precious little will be able to protect copyright from personal copying: recording from pages, screens, and speakers will go from possible to trivial as miniaturized cameras and microphones meet powerful software to manage the recorded content. Bootleggers may be caught, small-scale sharing of copyrighted works may occasionally be detected, but personal copies will never be discovered.

Digital Curation Challenges

Digital archives come with their own unique challenges, particularly data loss, 17 data decay, and data entanglement. Backup and replication, thanks to market demand and competition, are rapidly approaching the affordability and ease of use that should make data loss a thing of the past. Data decay and data entanglement are more problematic.

Data decay occurs when the format you stored something in becomes obso- 18 lete and unreadable. It is hard to imagine a library owning every program needed to open every file type ever known. Rather than lose everything from an old spreadsheet, it is desirable to at least have a "print" version of the spreadsheet. The ability to calculate is lost, but at least the version as it would be printed can be easily retained in e-memory. Other interactive documents might be captured as video. In any event, care must be taken to preserve digital artifacts in formats likely to be long lived and to be constantly converting them into the latest generation of formats to avoid obsolescence. We expect software services to react to market demand to perform such conversion.

Data entanglement refers to the intermingling of work and private life and 19 the competing claims on e-memories that ensue. When we eventually part company with Microsoft, where we are currently both researchers, it will no doubt request that we perform an e-lobotomy of those memories associated with the company. However, the demarcation is not always clear. Are memories en route to a business meeting personal or corporate? And chat transcripts from our private accounts may mention company business, while corporate records could contain such personal tidbits as happy birthday greetings.

We question to what extent people will actually comply with requests for 20 e-memory purging, but whatever they do it is clear that data entanglement will be a thorny issue for the digital archivist. Just rounding up all of the bits of a person's life will be problematic as these lives are captured and archived on their own systems, on social web pages such as Facebook, and are part of other people's lives or organization archives. Yet, all of these bits, such as an occasional email missive, are needed to complete the stories.

21   Another issue is simply finding enough storage space. For an individual during his/her life, storage is not an issue, but any attempt to keep all the data stored by all individuals forever seems hopeless even though we have just come through a decade when storage has doubled annually. We cannot project continued exponential increases in storage capacity into the indefinite future. Nor can we count on increasing population to deal with storing past generations—especially when population grows most quickly in poor countries. No, storage will be finite, and we will have to answer who will get in the digital lifeboat. Do we want one full life or two half-lives? Will we trim video quality for one to make room for another? Or delete the repetitious bits: "same commute to work as usual-video/GPS/auto information deleted"?

22   However we answer such questions, many more lives will still be digitally preserved, each in ever-greater fidelity.

Your Life as a Library, Not a Museum

23 Most physical artifacts will collect dust prior to being ultimately discarded or sold as antiques. Digital artifacts will be found and enjoyed and collect no dust at all. One woman we know sells tiaras on eBay. In the 20th century, she could never have found enough customers to make a business of it. In the Internet era, she has global reach. The Beatles have made a lot of additional money by selling outtakes of obscure videos of themselves. The interested student of history will soon be finding digitally stored artifacts of, say, World War II in far greater quantities than is now possible. People looking for an ancestor whom few others care about will be especially advantaged. E-memories are just so much more accessible.

24   We horrify archivists when we talk about digitizing things and then throwing them away. Of course, one need not destroy the physical object after making a digital copy, but one of the most enjoyable aspects of Total Recall is the reduction of clutter; it is especially satisfying to shred one's papers and eliminate rows of filing cabinets and shelves. When curators come to deal with our archives, they will surely find hundreds fewer physical objects because of Total Recall. But they will have hundreds of thousands of additional digital artifacts. Whether you agree that is a highly positive trade-off, it is surely coming.

25   The benefits of e-memories will extend across the life of the individual and throughout society. These benefits, along with the technological trends

that make e-memories affordable and convenient, make the Total Recall era inevitable. Your life, in so far as it is information, is about to become totally accessible to you. The skills and passions of librarians will be invaluable in this new age.

Understanding Meaning

1. What do Gemmell and Bell mean by "Total Recall"? How will it affect libraries and average citizens? Do you see advantages and disadvantages to having an ability to totally recall events, documents, and personal records?

2. What three streams of technology are causing the "Total Recall revolution"?

3. How will the digital revolution change the jobs of librarians and archivists? Why will they be "invaluable" in the future?

4. What ethical issues does the digital revolution create?

5. *Critical Thinking:* Will the digital revolution create more transparency, or will dishonest people simply avoid recording their activities or craft messages so artfully that they can camouflage their intent?

Evaluating Strategy

1. How do Gemmell and Bell dramatize how little space digital records require in contrast to traditional documents and videotapes?

2. How do Gemmell and Bell use examples to illustrate how the digital revolution will change people's lives in the future?

3. *Blending the Modes:* Where do the authors use *comparison*, *division*, and *narration* to develop their analysis?

Appreciating Language

1. Gemmell and Bell are Microsoft researchers writing to librarians, some of whom may not be familiar with digital technology. Do you think their word choices are suited to a nontechnical audience? Did you find any terms that need definition or further explanation?

2. Can you define Gemmell and Bell's terms "Total Recall," "story trails," and "data entanglement" in your own words?

WRITING SUGGESTIONS

1. Write an essay that examines one issue raised by the Total Recall revolution. How will access to detailed patient records revolutionize medical

research? Will the availability of so much personal data lead to abuses? Does the focus on collecting and storing data overlook the importance of interpretation and analysis? Can data be misread or filtered to support preexisting positions? Will critical thinking skills be more important in the future? Why or why not?

2. *Collaborative Writing:* Discuss Gemmell and Bell's article with a group of students and develop a comparison paper listing the positive and negative effects of the Total Recall revolution, or write a process paper outlining a set of ethical standards for recording, collecting, storing, and accessing personal data.

WRITING BEYOND THE CLASSROOM

Alton Enterprises

Analysis is frequently used in professional writing, as in this report, to examine problems and propose solutions.

ALTON ENTERPRISES
www.altonenterprises.com

CONFIDENTIAL

Preliminary Security Analysis

Date May 15, 2010
Submitted to Carmen Gonzalez
Submitted by Samuel Goldman

Background

The president of Alton Enterprises requested a preliminary security analysis to determine whether a full security review is required.

Recommendation

Based on personal observations made May 1–3, I strongly recommend a full review of all Alton Enterprises' security procedures to prevent accidents, cancellation of government contracts, and increased insurance premiums.

Examples of Security Lapses Observed May 1–3, 2010

Physical Safety

- On three occasions visitors and family members of employees were allowed to enter work areas, which specifically violates company policy and federal work rules.
- On May 2, only two security guards were present in the main plant. Alton's contracts with the federal government require at least four guards on duty at all times.
- Employee cars were parked in a fire lane on the night of May 2.

Data Security

- Confidential reports were left untended in the copy room.
- Employee laptops containing classified Defense Department specifications were left untended and running in the break room.
- Twenty-two employees are missing security clearance files.

Conclusion

These lapses indicate a clear need for an immediate and thorough review of Alton Enterprises' security policy and procedures.

Understanding Meaning

1. What is the purpose of Goldman's analysis?

2. What evidence does Goldman present to support his conclusion?

3. How could security lapses affect Alton Enterprises?

4. *Critical Thinking:* How could a document like this affect an individual or organization that did not respond to it in a timely fashion?

Evaluating Strategy

1. Why do you think Goldman labeled this report "Confidential"? How could a leak of this document adversely affect the management of Alton Enterprises?

2. How effective is the use of bullet points? Would this analysis have the same impact if written as a standard business letter in traditional paragraphs? Why or why not?

3. Goldman puts the date in large letters. Does this serve to dramatize the fact that all the lapses he observed occurred over three days?

Appreciating Language

1. How would you characterize the tone and style of Goldman's report?

2. Does Goldman's use of terms like "strongly recommend" and "immediate and thorough" suit his purpose? Can a writer use language that is overly dramatic? Can a writer be dismissed as being an alarmist?

WRITING SUGGESTIONS

1. Using Goldman's report as a model, write a short analysis based on personal observations. You might document environmental problems in your neighborhood, list safety and health issues at your job or campus, note the way a company or product is advertised on television, study the way popular blogs or websites address a specific issue, or analyze the strengths and weaknesses of a sports team.

2. *Collaborative Writing:* Discuss this report with a group of students and write a process paper that lists in order of importance the actions Alton Enterprises should take. Why would it be important to generate documents showing that the company is taking immediate steps to address the problems Goldman observed?

RESPONDING TO IMAGES

CELL PHONE CAMERA IMAGE OF STREET DEMONSTRATION, TEHRAN, JUNE 2009

1. What is your first reaction to this image?

2. How have camera cell phones and Internet sites like YouTube changed media? Can governments that censored television and newspapers in the past control citizens using online media?

3. *Critical Thinking:* How can television networks verify the validity of video posted online? Should they only broadcast what they can independently verify or should they simply air videos with disclaimers and allow viewers to judge for themselves? Do you see possible abuses or hoaxes?

4. Neda, the young woman depicted in the video, became an international symbol of Iranian repression. Do camera cell phones and the Internet mean that more stories will be covered in the future? Can a single gripping image or brief video distort as well as dramatize an event?

5. As camera cell phones become more universal, do you think eyewitnesses in court will have a greater impact on a jury when they can supplement their testimony about an accident or crime with a video they made of the event?

6. *Visual Analysis:* Some networks initially blurred the face of the dying Neda. Does video shot by non-journalists raise ethical concerns about privacy?

7. Write an essay analyzing how camera cell phones have changed our notions of privacy. How would you feel if you attended a public event like a football game or a demonstration and later discovered that someone had taped you without your knowledge and placed the video online? Would your reaction be different if the video had been taken at a private party in someone's home? Why or why not?

8. *Collaborative Writing:* Discuss this photograph with a group of students. Do they see advantages and disadvantages to personal videos of news events that are posted online? Write a comparison essay outlining what they see as the pros and cons.

STRATEGIES FOR WRITING ANALYSIS

1. **Determine your purpose.** Does your analysis seek to explain the parts of a complex object, issue, condition, or situation, or does it seek to identify a reason, a cause, or a solution to a problem? Persuasive analysis requires greater attention to context.

2. **Define your role.** Are you expressing personal opinion supported by facts and examples of your own choosing, or are you following the dictates of a specific discipline? When writing in a professional role, use standard methods and tools of analysis. If you use unconventional methods, explain your rationale, and be prepared for criticism.

3. **Consider your audience.** In addition to evaluating your readers' knowledge base, you should consider their perceptual world. Are your readers likely to be receptive or hostile to your conclusions? What kind of evidence will most impress them?

4. **Limit your subject.** Analysis requires close study, and an ill-defined topic likely will lead to confusion.

5. **Gather appropriate sources, data, and information.** The strength of your analysis will depend on the quantity and quality of the information you examine. Avoid making judgments on limited data. Evaluate the sources of your data for possible flaws, oversights, or bias.

6. **Be open to alternative interpretations.** Do not make general statements based on data without entertaining alternative interpretations. Consider possible data you may have overlooked.

7. **Apply the rules of critical thinking, and avoid the logical fallacies.**

SUGGESTED TOPICS FOR
WRITING ANALYSIS

GENERAL ASSIGNMENTS

Write an analysis on any of the following topics. Your analysis will require careful thinking, observation, and possibly outside research. Remember to avoid the logical fallacies and to qualify your remarks.

1. Affordable student housing (Define "affordable" in your area.)

2. Current movies (Use newspaper or online listings as a source.)

3. Status of women in your college's faculty and administration

4. The principal problem facing fellow students

5. The political climate on your campus

6. Airport security

7. Your generation's attitude toward the war in Afghanistan, the Civil Rights movement, or any other historical event

8. Racial profiling

9. The effect of divorce on children

10. America's role in international affairs

WRITING IN CONTEXT

1. Assume you have been asked by the campus newspaper to analyze how students feel about abortion, gun control, or another controversial issue. Design a method to gather and analyze data. Indicate what methods you would use, such as focus groups, surveys, or personal interviews.

2. Analyze the image of women, the elderly, black males, businesspeople, or any other group presented in popular television shows. Include as many examples as possible in your analysis.

3. Analyze editions of the largest newspaper in your area to determine the amount of attention given to international events versus domestic news. Explain your research methods—the number of editions reviewed and the methods of measurement (number of articles or amount of space).

Student Paper: Analysis

This paper was written in response to the following assignment: Analyze the meaning or significance of a social, educational, or political issue. Your essay should analyze a subject by exploring causes, effects, or deeper meanings, not merely superficial description.

First Draft with Instructor's Comments

Endless War

*awkward,
a lot*

wordy

unclear

run-on

it?

*Explain
this point.*

When George Bush used the word "war" to describe the fight against terrorism, <u>he created in the mindsets of aloot of people that there would eventually be an a final end.</u> <u>So many people are wondering</u> when it will end, what will a victory be? But this war is not like other wars. <u>Because we won WWII and the occupations of Germany, Italy, and Japan created stable democracies people like to see it as a kind of role model.</u>

Because the war in Iraq did not turn out like Italy there are a lot of questions. Most people don't think Iraq had much to do with 9/11. Osama bin Laden and Saddam had little or nothing in common except maybe a hatred of the United States.

*fragment
satellites*

A war on terrorism is not like other wars. <u>Although it might use armed forces to bomb targets and high tech surveillance equipment like spy satitllites.</u> Most of the conflicts and important battles are fought in secret. Cutting off funding to radical groups and eliminating key personnel, even if that means kidnapping and assassination, is the way terrorism will be fought. It will be a secret war mostly.

*explain,
add details*

The country is not prepared to fight this kind of war. But it is like other things we call wars, like the war on drugs or the war on organized crime. These conflicts go on and <u>on and</u> no one pretends there will be any victory any time soon. So this war against terror will go on and on.

run-on

REVISION NOTES

The war on terrorism is a good topic to analyze. An analysis essay, however, must have a clearly defined topic. This paper raises a number of ideas but does not explore them in any depth. An analysis—even a subjective analysis—is more than a collection of random thoughts on a particular subject.

Narrow your topic. A short essay cannot address everything you know about a subject. A good way to focus an analysis essay is to ask yourself a question:

 —Is "war" the appropriate term for this conflict?

 —Is military force the best way to counter terrorism?

 —When will anyone declare victory?

 —How will a long war on terrorism change society, civil liberties, immigration?

Because many people do not consider the Iraq war part of the war on terror, you might need to explain your position more clearly.

Revised Draft

Endless War

Since President Bush declared a war on terror, it is unlikely that any future president will be able to declare victory or even an armistice. The war on terror can never end because billions of people in the world see America as a target. In a global economy, the poor and disaffected, Muslims and non-Muslims alike, see the United States as an imperial power that exploits their people, defames their values, and supports corrupt regimes. All this resentment only has to inspire a handful of fanatics to create a serious terrorist threat. Today's terrorists come from the Arab world. Tomorrow's terrorists could come from the poor of South America, Asia, or even Europe. Today's terrorists wage war to protect their vision of Islam. Tomorrow's terrorists could wage war in the name of the environment, hunger, poverty, or the world's failure to accept their conspiracy theories about UFOs.

Northern Ireland is a small region with the population of Milwaukee County, yet it produced enough IRA terrorists at one point to require 30,000 British troops, metal detectors on the streets, barricades, helicopter patrols, and constant counterterrorism intelligence. A handful of terrorists can paralyze a society and cripple an economy.

As the only superpower and an emblem of what many people in the world fear and resent, America and its interests will always be targets unless there is a major shift in our relationship with people we do not understand, often demonize, and frequently insult through our ignorance.

So the war against terrorism will go on and on. Future presidents may trim funding here and there, but Homeland Security will likely become as American as Social Security because no one can predict when an attack can occur. Lyndon Johnson declared a war on poverty forty-five years ago, and no has proclaimed victory yet. You might as well ask when the Urban League and NAACP plan to disband. At what point will African American leaders announce that racism is over? When will NOW declare victory over sexism and go out of business?

Because terrorism does not depend on nation states, mass organizations, or institutional support, it is unpredictable. Timothy McVeigh was able to kill over one hundred people and destroy millions of dollars worth of property in Oklahoma City with a rented truck and bomb made of fertilizer and diesel fuel. Tomorrow's terrorists will likely have access to nuclear and biological weapons so that the next rental truck that explodes in a city street could kill tens of thousands and contaminate whole neighborhoods for decades. That prospect will keep this war going even if the Arab-Israeli conflict is resolved, democracy and prosperity sweep the Arab world, and America elects a Muslim president. Terrorists in Algeria and Afghanistan have killed thousands of fellow Muslims because they failed to embrace their extremist form of Islam. And it will only take a handful of extremists to stage an attack that will dwarf the events of September 11. No one will dare proclaim victory over terrorism any more than anyone will claim to have won the war against racism, organized crime, or poverty.

QUESTIONS FOR REVIEW AND REVISION

1. Is the student's thesis clear? Can you restate it in your own words?

2. Does the student provide sufficient proof to support the thesis?

3. How effective are the introduction and conclusion? Would you suggest any changes? Why or why not?

4. The student includes an example about Northern Ireland. Does this provide effective support? Why or why not?

5. The student compares the war on terrorism to wars on organized crime, poverty, and racism. Do you find this comparison effective? Why or why not?

6. Read the paper aloud. Do you detect any sentences or paragraphs that could be revised for greater clarity?

WRITING SUGGESTIONS

1. Write an essay analyzing a current fad, trend, or common behavior. Include key details, and suggest the cause or significance of your subject.

2. *Collaborative Writing:* Discuss this essay with a group of students, and work together to develop a statement on terrorism. Do they believe any future president will announce the war on terrorism has ended? Why or why not? Record the group's comments using comparison or division and classification to organize their observations.

ANALYSIS CHECKLIST

Before submitting your paper, review these points:

1. **Is the topic clearly limited?**

2. **Is your approach appropriate for the writing context?**

3. **Do you present enough evidence?**

4. **Have you evaluated sources for inaccuracy or bias?**

5. **Have you avoided errors in logic?**

6. **Are your research methods clearly explained?**

7. **Do you clearly present the results of your analysis?**

8. **Have you considered alternative interpretations?**

Info Write provides additional information on writing analysis.
cengage.learning.infowrite.com

CHAPTER NINE

DIVISION AND CLASSIFICATION: SEPARATING INTO PARTS AND RATING CATEGORIES

WHAT ARE DIVISION AND CLASSIFICATION?

Division separates a subject into parts; **classification** rates subjects on a scale. Both are used to make complex subjects easier to understand and help in decision making. Poorly written division and classification, however, can misinform and mislead readers. Division and classification can be based on official and objective designations established by researchers, government agencies, corporations, organizations, or experts. They can also be created by individuals to express personal observations and opinions.

Division

If you enter a hospital, you will probably see signs directing you to different departments, for example, cardiology, radiology, psychiatry, and pediatrics. Universities consist of separate colleges, such as business and liberal arts. American literature can be divided into courses by historical era (nineteenth- and twentieth-century writers), by genre (poetry, fiction, and drama), or by special interest (women's literature, black literature, and science fiction). Discount stores organize products into housewares, clothing, linens, and other departments. Corporations place personnel into different divisions, such as design, production, maintenance, marketing, sales, and accounting. If you call your cable company's 800 number, a recorded voice may direct you to press one number for billing and another for technical support.

Division makes complicated subjects easier to comprehend and work with. The human body is overwhelmingly intricate. In order to understand how it functions, medical disciplines divide it into systems: digestive, respiratory, nervous, musculoskeletal, reproductive, and others. By studying individual systems, medical students come to a fuller understanding of how the whole body operates. Crime is such a vast social problem that writers discuss it in terms of traditional divisions—robbery, car theft, homicide, fraud, and so on—or invent their own categories, dividing crime by causes: power, greed, identity, and revenge.

The website Depression-help-resource.com, for instance, uses division to explain widely accepted types of depression:

> **Post Partum Depression** – Major depressive episode that occurs after having a baby. Depressive symptoms usually begin within four weeks of giving birth and can vary in intensity and duration.
>
> **Seasonal Affective Disorder (SAD)** – A type of depressive disorder which is characterized by episodes of major depression which reoccur at a specific time of year (e.g. fall, winter). In the past two years, depressive periods occur at least two times without any episodes that occur at a different time.
>
> **Anxiety Depression** – Not an official depression type (as defined by the DSM). However, anxiety often also occurs with depression. In this case, a depressed individual may also experience anxiety symptoms (e.g. panic attacks) or an anxiety disorder (e.g., PTSD, panic disorder, social phobia, generalized anxiety disorder).

In contrast, Judith Viorst (page 358) uses division to distinguish seven types of friends she has observed, inventing categories such as "convenience friends" and "part-of-a-couple friends" to explain her personal views of friendship.

Division writing can present a series of descriptions or definitions and organize a set of narratives, processes, or persuasive arguments.

Critical Thinking for Writing Division

Dividing any subject can be challenging. Would it make more sense to explain American politics to a foreign visitor in terms of political parties or specific issues? Would you group used cars by year, by price, or by model? The goal of division is to make a complicated subject easier to understand.

When writing division, follow these guidelines:

1. **Identify whether your division is official or personal.** Explain the rationale of your division, stating whether you are using a method established by others or creating one of your own.

2. **Avoid oversimplifying your subject.** You have no doubt seen magazine articles announcing three kinds of bosses, four types of marriages, or five

methods of child rearing. Writers often invent descriptive or humorous labels, warning you to avoid "the toxic controller" or advising you how to negotiate with the "whiny wimp." Although these divisions can be amusing and insightful, they can trivialize or oversimplify a subject. Not all people or situations can neatly fit into three or four types. *When discussing complex topics, inform readers of possible exceptions to your categories.* You can indicate exceptions by simply adding the word "most" to your introduction: "*Most* students belong to one of the following categories..."

3. **Indicate the size of each type or group.** If you write that students pay for college in three ways—by scholarships, loans, and personal savings—many readers may assume that a third of students pay their own way, when, in fact, they may constitute less than 1 percent of the whole. To prevent misleading readers, explain the size of each group. If you cannot give precise percentages, indicate the groups' general size: "The vast majority of students rely on loans, while only a very small minority are able to finance their education with personal savings."

4. **Select a method of division that includes all parts of the whole.** If you divide college students into three types, for example, make sure everyone on campus is included in one of the groups. Eliminate potential gaps. You cannot simply divide students into Protestants, Catholics, and Jews if some are agnostics or Muslims. Every member or part of the whole must be accounted for.

5. **Make sure individual parts fit only one category.** If you were to divide businesses by geographical region—north, south, east, and west—how would you handle a company with operations on both coasts? If items can fit in more than one category, your method of division is not suited to your subject. It might be better to discuss businesses in terms of their gross sales, products, or size rather than location.

6. **Avoid categories that include too many differences.** If you were examining people of different ages, it could make sense to write about people in groups from thirty to forty or fifty to sixty. But an age category of sixty to seventy would include both working and retired people—both those still paying into Social Security and those receiving benefits. It might be more accurate to break this group into people who are sixty to sixty-five and those who are sixty-five to seventy.

7. **Indicate possible exceptions or changes.** Divisions may not be hard or fast. After explaining the three ways students pay for college, you might point out that some students could use all three methods in the same semester. In some instances students start college with enough scholarship money to pay for their freshman year, use their own savings to pay for a later semester, and then rely on loans until graduation.

Classification

Like division, classification breaks a complex subject into parts. But for classification, the categories are ranked or rated according to a single standard. Teachers grade tests A, B, C, D, or F according to the number of correct answers. Car insurance companies set prices based on drivers' ages, past accidents, and the value of their vehicles. Fire departments rank fires as one, two, three, four, or five alarms to determine how much equipment to send. Prisons are classified minimum, medium, and maximum security. During the football season, teams are ranked by their wins and losses.

Classification helps people to make decisions and to direct actions. Classifications can set prices, establish salaries, and in some cases save lives. The importance of classification is demonstrated by the use of triage in emergency medicine. When a hospital is flooded with accident victims, doctors place patients into three categories: those who will die with or without immediate medical attention, those who will survive without emergency care, and those who will survive only if treated without delay. The last group is given priority to ensure that doctors do not waste time on the dying or those with minor injuries.

Like division, classification can be objective and official or personal. The movie listings in a newspaper may display a number of stars next to an R rated film. The R rating, officially established by the MPAA (see page 394), is an official classification that will appear in every newspaper listing, television commercial, theater trailer, poster, and website. The number of stars, however, will vary with each newspaper, reflecting the personal opinion of a local critic.

The National Weather Service, for example, uses the Saffir-Simpson Hurricane Wind Scale measuring sustained wind speeds of one minute to officially rank hurricanes in five clearly defined categories:

Category 1 (74–95 mph) *Very dangerous winds will produce some damage.* Large branches of trees will snap and shallow-rooted trees can be toppled.

Category 2 (96–110 mph) *Extremely dangerous winds will cause extensive damage.* Many shallowly rooted trees will be snapped or uprooted and block numerous roads.

Category 3 (111–130 mph) *Devastating damage will occur.* Many trees will be snapped or uprooted, blocking numerous roads.

Category 4 (131–155 mph) *Catastrophic damage will occur.* Most trees will be snapped or uprooted and power poles downed. Fallen trees and power poles will isolate residential areas.

Category 5 (over 155 mph) *Catastrophic damage will occur.* Nearly all trees will be snapped or uprooted and power poles downed. Fallen trees and power poles will isolate residential areas.

In contrast, James Austin (page 368) uses classification to explain his personal view that there are four levels of chance or luck, ranging from "pure blind luck" that benefits anyone to "luck that is peculiar to one person."

Critical Thinking for Writing Classification

As with division writing, classification requires careful planning. To avoid common problems, follow these guidelines:

1. **Avoid confusing division with classification.** Perhaps the most frequent mistake students make in writing classification papers is simply dividing a subject into parts. *Classification not only divides a subject into parts but also rates the parts on a scale.*

2. **Establish a clearly defined standard of measurement.** To successfully teach writing, for example, an English professor must provide students with a clear understanding of what distinguishes an A paper from a B paper. Even if you are making up your own categories, each one should be clearly defined so that readers understand what distinguishes one from the other.

3. **Explain whether the classification is objective and official or personal.** Inform readers if your classification method is universally accepted or is subject to controversy. Some classifications may be clearly defined because they are based on precise measurements, such as credit scores. The classification of depression into mild, moderate, and severe levels may be more subjective and less universally accepted. If you are creating your own classification, make sure you clearly explain your method of ranking subjects.

4. **Do not mix standards.** You can classify automobiles, for instance, from the cheapest to the most expensive, from the safest to the most dangerous, or from the most fuel efficient to the least fuel efficient. But you cannot write a classification essay that rates cars as being either safe, fuel efficient or expensive since many cars could be both expensive and fuel efficient.

5. **Arrange categories in order.** Organize the categories so that they follow a ladder-like pattern, such as judging items from the best to the worst, the cheapest to the most expensive, or the newest to the oldest.

6. **Provide enough categories to include all parts of the whole.** If you were to classify cars as being either American or foreign, how would you account for Toyotas produced in the United States or Chryslers assembled in Mexico?

7. **Explain if subjects can change categories.** Not all subjects can be permanently labeled. A student's grade point average can change from one semester to another. A consumer's credit rating will rise and fall. The five categories of hurricanes are clearly fixed, but an individual storm will move up and down the scale as a tropical storm gathers enough speed to be officially called a hurricane, then move from category 1 to 2 or 3 as it increases force, then fall back to category 1 as it loses strength, and eventually fall off the scale as it ceases to be called a hurricane and becomes nothing more than an ordinary rainstorm. *Make sure readers do not mistakenly assume that items subject to change have fixed designations.*

USING DIVISION AND CLASSIFICATION

In many cases, people use both division and classification to make decisions and explain ideas or actions. A travel guide might divide local restaurants by type—seafood, steak, Italian, or Mexican—and then classify them by quality or price range. A financial planner could present clients with different types of investments—stocks, bonds, and mutual funds–and then classify each by risk or rate of return. A nutritionist designing a diet for a weight loss program would first divide foods into groups, such as grains and vegetables, then classify how many calories a dieter should consume of each. A first aid manual might use division to explain the different causes of burns—contact with heat, radiation, chemicals, or electricity—and then use classification to rank them first, second, or third degree based on their severity. In answering a 911 call, a dispatcher uses division to determine whether the emergency requires a police, fire department, or ambulance response. With further information, he or she might use classification to measure the size or severity of the emergency to determine how many police officers or paramedics to send.

STRATEGIES FOR READING DIVISION AND CLASSIFICATION

As you read the division and classification entries in this chapter, keep the following questions in mind.

Understanding Meaning

1. What is the writer trying to explain by dividing or classifying the topic? Does the division or classification help you understand the subject better than a simple description would?

2. Do the divisions risk oversimplifying the subject?

3. Do the classification essays have a clearly defined standard?

4. Do the standards seem fair? Do they adequately measure what they claim to evaluate?

Evaluating Strategy

1. How does the writer introduce or set up the division or classification?

2. How does the author use definitions and examples to create distinct categories?

3. Does the writer use standard divisions and classifications accepted by a particular discipline or profession, or invent new ones?

4. Does the writer use division or classification to explain a topic, or is it used as a device to recommend one item over another?

Appreciating Language

1. What does the level of language reveal about the writer's discipline and intended audience?

2. What words does the author use to describe or define standards of classification? Do you detect a bias?

JUDITH VIORST

Judith Viorst (1936–) is best known for the columns she writes for Redbook. *She has published several children's books, including* Alexander and the Terrible, Horrible, No Good, Very Bad Day *(1982) and* Sad Underwear and Other Complications *(1995). She has also written a number of collections of light verse, including* It's Hard to Be Hip Over Thirty and Other Tragedies of Modern Life *(1970),* How Did I Get to Be Forty and Other Atrocities *(1984), and* Suddenly Sixty and Other Shocks of Later Life *(2000). She has also published a novel,* Murdering Mr. Monti: A Merry Little Tale of Sex and Violence *(1994).*

Friends, Good Friends—and Such Good Friends

CONTEXT: *Before reading this essay, consider the friends you have had in your life. Did they belong to different types? Were school friends different from neighborhood friends or friends met through relatives?*

introduction definition of "friend"

1   Women are friends, I once would have said, when they totally love and support and trust each other, and bare to each other the secrets of their souls, and run—no questions asked—to help each other, and tell harsh truths to each other (no, you can't wear that dress unless you lose ten pounds first) when harsh truths must be told.

2   Women are friends, I once would have said, when they share the same affection for Ingmar Bergman, plus train rides, cats, warm rain, charades, Camus, and hate with equal ardor Newark and Brussels sprouts and Lawrence Welk and camping.

division into types

3   In other words, I once would have said that a friend is a friend all the way, but now I believe that's a narrow point of view. <u>For the friendships I have and the friendships I see are conducted at many levels of intensity, serve many different functions, meet different needs and range from those as all-the-way as the friendship of the soul sisters mentioned above to that of the most nonchalant and casual playmates.</u>

4   <u>Consider these varieties of friendship:</u>

type #1 examples.

5   1. Convenience friends. These are women with whom, if our paths weren't crossing all the time, we'd have no particular reason to be friends: a next-door neighbor, a woman in our car pool, the mother of one of our children's closest friends or maybe some mommy with whom we serve juice and cookies each week at the Glenwood Co-op Nursery.

6   Convenience friends are convenient indeed. They'll lend us their cups and silverware for a party. They'll drive our kids to soccer when we're sick. They'll

take us to pick up our car when we need a lift to the garage. They'll even take our cats when we go on vacation. As we will for them.

But we don't, with convenience friends, ever come too close or tell too much; we maintain our public face and emotional distance. "Which means," says Elaine, "that I'll talk about being overweight but not about being depressed. Which means I'll admit being mad but not blind with rage. Which means that I might say that we're pinched this month but never that I'm worried sick over money." [7]

But which doesn't mean that there isn't sufficient value to be found in these friendships of mutual aid, in convenience friends. [8]

2. Special-interest friends. These friendships aren't intimate, and they needn't involve kids or silverware or cats. Their value lies in some interest jointly shared. And so we may have an office friend or a yoga friend or a tennis friend or a friend from the Women's Democratic Club. [9] *type #2 examples*

"I've got one woman friend," says Joyce, "who likes, as I do, to take psychology courses. Which makes it nice for me—and nice for her. It's fun to go with someone you know and it's fun to discuss what you've learned, driving back from the classes." And for the most part, she says, that's all they discuss. [10]

"I'd say that what we're doing is *doing* together, not being together," Suzanne says of her Tuesday-doubles friends. "It's mainly a tennis relationship, but we play together well. And I guess we all need to have a couple of playmates." [11]

I agree. [12]

My playmate is a shopping friend, a woman of marvelous taste, a woman who knows exactly *where* to buy *what*, and furthermore is a woman who always knows beyond a doubt what one ought to be buying. I don't have the time to keep up with what's new in eyeshadow, hemlines and shoes and whether the smock look is in or finished already. But since (oh, shame!) I care a lot about eyeshadow, hemlines and shoes, and since I don't *want* to wear smocks if the smock look is finished, I'm very glad to have a shopping friend. [13]

3. Historical friends. We all have a friend who knew us when ... maybe way back in Miss Meltzer's second grade, when our family lived in that three-room flat in Brooklyn, when our dad was out of work for seven months, when our brother Allie got in that fight where they had to call the police, when our sister married the endodontist from Yonkers and when, the morning after we lost our virginity, she was the first, the only, friend we told. [14] *type #3 examples*

The years have gone by and we've gone separate ways and we've little in common now, but we're still an intimate part of each other's past. And so whenever we go to Detroit we always go to visit this friend of our girlhood. Who knows how we looked before our teeth were straightened. Who knows how we talked before our voice got un-Brooklyned. Who knows what we ate before we learned about artichokes. And who, by her presence, puts us in touch with an earlier part of ourself, a part of ourself it's important never to lose. [15]

16   "What this friend means to me and what I mean to her," says Grace, "is having a sister without sibling rivalry. We know the texture of each other's lives. She remembers my grandmother's cabbage soup. I remember the way her uncle played the piano. There's simply no other friend who remembers those things."

17   4. Crossroads friends. Like historical friends, our crossroads friends are important for *what was*—for the friendship we shared at a crucial, now past, time of life. A time, perhaps, when we roomed in college together; or worked as eager young singles in the Big City together; or went together, as my friend Elizabeth and I did, through pregnancy, birth and that scary first year of new motherhood.

type #4 examples

18   Crossroads friends forge powerful links, links strong enough to endure with not much more contact than once-a-year letters at Christmas. And out of respect for those crossroads years, for those dramas and dreams we once shared, we will always be friends.

19   5. Cross-generational friends. Historical friends and crossroads friends seem to maintain a special kind of intimacy—dormant but always ready to be revived—and though we may rarely meet, whenever we do connect, it's personal and intense. Another kind of intimacy exists in the friendships that form across generations in what one woman calls her daughter-mother and her mother-daughter relationships.

type #5 examples

20   Evelyn's friend is her mother's age—"but I share so much more than I ever could with my mother"—a woman she talks to of music, of books and of life. "What I get from her is the benefit of her experience. What she gets—and enjoys—from me is a youthful perspective. It's a pleasure for both of us."

21   I have in my own life a precious friend, a woman of 65 who has lived very hard, who is wise, who listens well; who has been where I am and can help me understand it; and who represents not only an ultimate ideal mother to me but also the person I'd like to be when I grow up.

22   In our daughter role we tend to do more than our share of self-revelation; in our mother role we tend to receive what's revealed. It's another kind of pleasure—playing wise mother to a questing younger person. It's another very lovely kind of friendship.

23   6. Part-of-a-couple friends. Some of the women we call our friends we never see alone—we see them as part of a couple at couples' parties. And though we share interests in many things and respect each other's views, we aren't moved to deepen the relationship. Whatever the reason, a lack of time or—and this is more likely—a lack of chemistry, our friendship remains in the context of a group. But the fact that our feeling on seeing each other is always, "I'm *so* glad she's here" and the fact that we spend half the evening talking together says that this too, in its own way, counts as a friendship.

type #6 examples

24   (Other part-of-a-couple friends are the friends that came with the marriage, and some of these are friends we could live without. But sometimes, alas,

she married our husband's best friend; and sometimes, alas, she *is* our husband's best friend. And so we find ourself dealing with her, somewhat against our will, in a spirit of what I'll call *reluctant* friendship.)

7. Men who are friends. I wanted to write just of women friends, but the women I've talked to won't let me—they say I must mention man-woman friendships too. For these friendships can be just as close and as dear as those that we form with women. Listen to Lucy's description of one such friendship: "We've found we have things to talk about that are different from what he talks about with my husband and different from what I talk about with his wife. So sometimes we call on the phone or meet for lunch. There are similar intellectual interests—we always pass on to each other the books that we love—but there's also something tender and caring too." 25 type #7 examples

In a couple of crises, Lucy says, "he offered himself for talking and for helping. And when someone died in his family he wanted me there. The sexual, flirty part of our friendship is very small, but *some*—just enough to make it fun and different." She thinks—and I agree—that the sexual part, though small, is always *some*, is always there when a man and a woman are friends. *26*

It's only in the past few years that I've made friends with men, in the sense of a friendship that's *mine*, not just part of two couples. And achieving with them the ease and the trust I've found with women friends has value indeed. Under the dryer at home last week, putting on mascara and rouge, I comfortably sat and talked with a fellow named Peter. Peter, I finally decided, could handle the shock of me minus mascara under the dryer. Because we care for each other. Because we're friends. *27*

8. There are medium friends, and pretty good friends, and very good friends indeed, and these friendships are defined by their level of intimacy. And what we'll reveal at each of these levels of intimacy is calibrated with care. We might tell a medium friend, for example, that yesterday we had a fight with our husband. And we might tell a pretty good friend that this fight with our husband made us so mad that we slept on the couch. And we might tell a very good friend that the reason we got so mad in that fight that we slept on the couch had something to do with that girl who works in his office. But it's only to our very best friends that we're willing to tell all, to tell what's going on with that girl in his office. 28 levels of friendship classified by intimacy

The best of friends, I still believe, totally love and support and trust each other, and bare to each other the secrets of their souls, and run—no questions asked—to help each other, and tell harsh truths to each other when they must be told. *29*

But we needn't agree about everything (only 12-year-old girl friends agree about *everything*) to tolerate each other's point of view. To accept without judgment. To give and to take without ever keeping score. And to *be* there, as I am for them and as they are for me, to comfort our sorrows, to celebrate our joys. *30*

Understanding Meaning

1. What was Viorst's original view of women friends? How did she define them?

2. How do convenience friendships differ from special-interest friendships? Are they both superficial relationships in many ways? Why or why not?

3. Viorst states that she did not want to include men in her article, but her female friends insisted that man–woman friendships should be included. Does this reflect a social change? Do you think women today have more friendships with men, especially in the workplace, than their mothers or grandmothers did?

4. *Critical Thinking:* Viorst writes almost exclusively about female friendship. Do you think that men, too, have the same types of friends—convenience friends, special-interest friends, historical friends, and so on? Are male friendships different?

Evaluating Strategy

1. Viorst divides friends into types rather than classifying them from best friends to acquaintances. Does her approach make more sense? Can friendships change? Can a convenience friend over time become your best friend?

2. Viorst mentions other women in her essay. Does this make her observations more effective? If she limited her commentary to only her friends, would the essay be as influential?

3. *Blending the Modes:* Where does Viorst use *description* and *comparison* to develop her essay?

4. *Critical Thinking:* Viorst wrote this essay in 1977. Since then, has technology created new communities and new friendships? Should online friends be included?

Appreciating Language

1. This essay first appeared in *Redbook*. Is there anything in her word choices or tone that indicates she was writing to a female audience?

2. Consider the words we use to describe people we include in our lives: "friend," "acquaintance," "colleague," "partner," "pal." Do men and women define these words differently?

WRITING SUGGESTIONS

1. Write a short essay about the types of friendships you have developed. Have you maintained many friendships that began in childhood? Why or why not?

2. Write a classification essay categorizing people who only take from friends, those who share with friends, and those who only seem to give in relationships. Provide examples of each type.

3. *Collaborative Writing:* Discuss Viorst's essay with a group of students. Do her comments seem to apply exclusively to women's friendships? Why or why not? Write a brief comparison paper contrasting the different ways men and women develop friendships. Is one gender more competitive? Do men or women seem to have or need more friends?

MARTIN LUTHER KING JR.

Martin Luther King Jr. (1929–1968) was a leading figure in the civil rights movement in the 1950s and 1960s. A noted minister, King blended his deeply felt religious values and his sense of political and social justice. He created the Southern Christian Leadership Conference, organized many demonstrations, and lobbied for voting rights. In 1964 he received the Nobel Peace Prize. He was assassinated in 1968.

Three Ways of Meeting Oppression

CONTEXT: *In this section from his 1958 book* Stride toward Freedom, *King classifies three ways oppressed people have responded to oppression. King uses classification to rate which response is the most effective and concludes his comments by persuading readers to accept his choice.*

1 Oppressed people deal with their oppression in three characteristic ways. One way is acquiescence: The oppressed resign themselves to their doom.

2 They tacitly adjust themselves to oppression, and thereby become conditioned to it. In every movement toward freedom some of the oppressed prefer to remain oppressed. Almost 2,800 years ago Moses set out to lead the children of Israel from the slavery of Egypt to the freedom of the promised land. He soon discovered that slaves do not always welcome their deliverers. They become accustomed to being slaves. They would rather bear those ills they have, as Shakespeare pointed out, than flee to others that they know not of. They prefer the "fleshpots of Egypt" to the ordeals of emancipation.

3 There is such a thing as the freedom of exhaustion. Some people are so worn down by the yoke of oppression that they give up. A few years ago in the slum areas of Atlanta, a Negro guitarist used to sing almost daily: "Been down so long that down don't bother me." This is the type of negative freedom and resignation that often engulfs the life of the oppressed.

4 But this is not the way out. To accept passively an unjust system is to cooperate with that system; thereby the oppressed become as evil as the oppressor. Noncooperation with evil is as much a moral obligation as is cooperation with good. The oppressed must never allow the conscience of the oppressor to slumber. Religion reminds every man that he is his brother's keeper. To accept injustice or segregation passively is to say to the oppressor that his actions are morally right. It is a way of allowing his conscience to fall asleep. At this moment the oppressed fails to be his brother's keeper. So acquiescence—while often the easier way—is not the moral way. It is the way of the coward. The Negro cannot win the respect of his oppressor by acquiescing; he merely increases the oppressor's arrogance and contempt. Acquiescence is interpreted as proof of the Negro's inferiority. The Negro cannot win the respect of the white people of the South or the peoples of the world

if he is willing to sell the future of his children for his personal and immediate comfort and safety.

A second way that oppressed people sometimes deal with oppression is to resort to physical violence and corroding hatred. Violence often brings about momentary results. Nations have frequently won their independence in battle. But in spite of temporary victories, violence never brings permanent peace. It solves no social problem; it merely creates new and more complicated ones.

Violence as a way of achieving racial injustice is both impractical and immoral. It is impractical because it is a descending spiral ending in destruction for all. The old law of an eye for an eye leaves everybody blind. It is immoral because it seeks to humiliate the opponent rather than win his understanding; it seeks to annihilate rather than to convert. Violence is immoral because it thrives on hatred rather than love. It destroys community and makes brotherhood impossible. It leaves society in monologue rather than dialogue. Violence ends by defeating itself. It creates bitterness in the survivors and brutality in the destroyers. A voice echoes through time saying to every potential Peter, "Put up your sword."* History is cluttered with the wreckage of nations that failed to follow this command.

If the American Negro and other victims of oppression succumb to the temptation of using violence in the struggle for freedom, future generations will be the recipients of a desolate night of bitterness, and our chief legacy to them will be an endless reign of meaningless chaos. Violence is not the way.

The third way open to oppressed people in their quest for freedom is the way of nonviolent resistance. Like the synthesis in Hegelian philosophy, the principle of nonviolent resistance seeks to reconcile the truths of two opposites—acquiescence and violence—while avoiding the extremes and immoralities of both. The nonviolent resister agrees with the person who acquiesces that one should not be physically aggressive toward his opponent; but he balances the equation by agreeing with the person of violence that evil must be resisted. He avoids the nonresistance of the former and the violent resistance of the latter. With nonviolent resistance, no individual or group need submit to any wrong, nor need anyone resort to violence in order to right a wrong.

It seems to me that this is the method that must guide the actions of the Negro in the present crisis in race relations. Through nonviolent resistance the Negro will be able to rise to the noble height of opposing the unjust system while loving the perpetrators of the system. The Negro must work passionately and unrelentingly for full stature as a citizen, but he must not use

---

*The apostle Peter had drawn his sword to defend Christ from arrest. The voice was Christ's, who surrendered himself for trial and crucifixion (John 18:11).

inferior methods to gain it. He must never come to terms with falsehood, malice, hate, or destruction.

10   Nonviolent resistance makes it possible for the Negro to remain in the South and struggle for his rights. The Negro's problem will not be solved by running away. He cannot listen to the glib suggestion of those who would urge him to migrate en masse to other sections of the country. By grasping his great opportunity in the South he can make a lasting contribution to the moral strength of the nation and set a sublime example of courage for generations yet unborn.

11   By nonviolent resistance, the Negro can also enlist all men of good will in his struggle for equality. The problem is not a purely racial one, with Negroes set against whites. In the end, it is not a struggle between people at all, but a tension between justice and injustice. Nonviolent resistance is not aimed against oppressors but against oppression. Under its banner consciences, not racial groups, are enlisted.

Understanding Meaning

1. Briefly describe the three ways people respond to oppression, according to King. Do you know of a fourth or fifth way? Do people, for instance, respond to oppression by blaming each other?

2. Humility is a Christian value. How does King, a minister, argue that humble acceptance of injustice is immoral?

3. King admits that nations have won freedom through violence, but why does he reject it for African Americans?

4. *Critical Thinking:* King defines the third way as a blend or synthesis of the first two. Why does he argue that this last manner is the most successful? What are its advantages?

Evaluating Strategy

1. Why does King use classification to suggest a solution instead of writing a direct persuasive argument?

2. How does King use his religious values as a way of arguing the desirability of his choice?

3. What transition statements does King use to direct his readers?

Appreciating Language

1. How does King define the difference between "acquiescence" and "nonviolent resistance"?

2. What does King's use of Biblical analogies and reference to Hegelian philosophy reveal about his intended audience?

WRITING SUGGESTIONS

1. Use King's essay as a model to write your own classification paper revealing the way people generally respond to a common issue or problem—the death of a loved one, the loss of a job, the discovery that a partner has been unfaithful, or the experience of being victimized. Rank the responses from the least effective to the most effective.

2. *Collaborative Writing:* Discuss King's classification with a group of students. How many people suffering oppression appear to be following his "third way"? Have a member of the group take notes, then work together to draft a short paper dividing or classifying, if possible, your group's responses.

JAMES AUSTIN

Dr. James Austin (1925–) graduated from Harvard Medical School and is a specialist in neurology. He devoted more than twenty years to research on the brain. While serving as professor and chair of the Department of Neurology at the University of Colorado Medical School, he received the American Association of Neuropathologists Prize. Austin has also earned a reputation as a writer with an ability to make complicated scientific issues understandable to general readers.

Four Kinds of Chance

CONTEXT: *James Austin has written widely on the role of chance or luck in scientific discovery. In this article, written for the* Saturday Review *(1974), he classifies the four kinds of chance that occur in scientific research. Luck, he explains, is not as simple as drawing a winning hand in poker. As you read the article, consider how many of the varieties of chance you have experienced.*

1 What is chance? Dictionaries define it as something fortuitous that happens unpredictably without discernable human intention. Chance is unintentional and capricious, but we needn't conclude that chance is immune from human intervention. Indeed, chance plays several distinct roles when humans react creatively with one another and with their environment.

2 We can readily distinguish four varieties of chance if we consider that they each involve a different kind of motor activity and a special kind of sensory receptivity. The varieties of chance also involve distinctive personality traits and differ in the way one particular individual influences them.

3 Chance I is the pure blind luck that comes with no effort on our part. If, for example, you are sitting at a bridge table of four, it's "in the cards" for you to receive a hand of all 13 spades, but it will come up only once in every 6.3 trillion deals. You will ultimately draw this lucky hand—with no intervention on your part—but it does involve a longer wait than most of us have time for.

4 Chance II evokes the kind of luck Charles Kettering had in mind when he said: "Keep on going and the chances are you will stumble on something, perhaps when you are least expecting it. I have never heard of anyone stumbling on something sitting down."

5 In the sense referred to here, Chance II is not passive, but springs from an energetic, generalized motor activity. A certain basal level of action "stirs up the pot," brings in random ideas that will collide and stick together in fresh combinations, lets chance operate. When someone, *anyone*, does swing into motion and keeps on going, he will increase the number of collisions between events. When a few events are linked together, they can then be exploited to have a

fortuitous outcome, but many others, of course, cannot. Kettering was right. Press on. Something will turn up. We may term this the Kettering Principle.

In the two previous examples, a unique role of the individual person was either lacking or minimal. Accordingly, as we move on to Chance III, we see blind luck, but in camouflage. Chance presents the clue, the opportunity exists, but it would be missed except by that one person uniquely equipped to observe it, visualize it conceptually, and fully grasp its significance. Chance III involves a special receptivity and discernment unique to the recipient. Louis Pasteur characterized it for all time when he said: "Chance favors only the prepared mind." 6

Pasteur himself had it in full measure. But the classic example of his principle occurred in 1928, when Alexander Fleming's mind instantly fused at least five elements into a conceptually unified nexus. His mental sequences went something like this: (1) I see that a mold has fallen by accident into my culture dish; (2) the staphylococcal colonies residing near it failed to grow; (3) the mold must have secreted something that killed the bacteria; (4) I recall a similar experience once before; (5) if I could separate this new "something" from the mold, it could be used to kill staphylococci that cause human infections. 7

Actually, Fleming's mind was exceptionally well prepared for the penicillin mold. Six years earlier, while he was suffering from a cold, his own nasal drippings had found their way into a culture dish, for reasons not made entirely clear. He noted that nearby bacteria were killed, and astutely followed up the lead. His observations led him to discover a bactericidal enzyme present in nasal mucus and tears, called lysozyme. Lysozyme proved too weak to be of medical use, but imagine how receptive Fleming's mind was to the penicillin mold when it later happened on the scene! 8

One word evokes the quality of the operations involved in the first three kinds of chance. It is *serendipity*. The term describes the facility for encountering unexpected good luck, as the result of: accident (Chance I), general exploratory behavior (Chance II), or sagacity (Chance III). The word itself was coined by the Englishman-of-letters Horace Walpole in 1754. He used it with reference to the legendary tales of the Three Princes of Serendip (Ceylon), who quite unexpectedly encountered many instances of good fortune on their travels. In today's parlance, we have usually watered down *serendipity* to mean the good luck that comes solely by accident. We think of it as a result, not an ability. We have tended to lose sight of the element of sagacity, by which term Walpole wished to emphasize that some distinctive personal receptivity is involved. 9

There remains a fourth element in good luck, an unintentional but subtle personal prompting of it. The English prime minister Benjamin Disraeli summed up the principle underlying Chance IV when he noted that "we make our fortunes and we call them fate." Disraeli, a politician of considerable 10 practical experience, appreciated that we each shape our own destiny, at least to some degree. One might restate the principle as follows: *Chance favors the individualized action.*

11   In Chance IV the kind of luck is peculiar to one person, and like a personal hobby, it takes on a distinctive individual flavor. This form of chance is one-man-made, and it is as personal as a signature…. Chance IV has an elusive, almost miragelike, quality. Like a mirage, it is difficult to get a firm grip on, for it tends to recede as we pursue it and advance as we step back. But we still accept a mirage when we see it, because we vaguely understand the basis for the phenomenon. A strongly heated layer of air, less dense than usual, lies next to the earth, and it bends the light rays as they pass through. The resulting image may be magnified as if by a telescopic lens in the atmosphere, and real objects, ordinarily hidden far out of sight over the horizon, are brought forward and revealed to the eye. What happens in a mirage then, and in this form of chance, not only appears farfetched but indeed is farfetched.

12   About a century ago, a striking example of Chance IV took place in the Spanish cave of Altamira.[1] There, one day in 1879, Don Marcelino de Sautuola was engaged in his hobby of archaeology, searching Altamira for bones and stones. With him was his daughter, Maria, who had asked him whether she could come along to the cave that day. The indulgent father had said she could. Naturally enough, he first looked where he had always found heavy objects before, on the *floor* of the cave. But Maria, unhampered by any such preconceptions, looked not only at the floor but also all around the cave with the open-eyed wonder of a child! She looked up, exclaimed, and then he looked up, to see incredible works of art on the cave ceiling! The magnificent colored bison and other animals they saw at Altamira, painted more than 15,000 years ago, might lead one to call it "the Sistine Chapel of Prehistory." Passionately pursuing his interest in archaeology, de Sautuola, to his surprise, discovered man's first paintings. In quest of science, he happened upon Art.

13   Yes, a dog did "discover" the cave, and the initial receptivity was his daughter's, but the pivotal reason for the cave paintings' discovery hinged on a long sequence of prior events originating in de Sautuola himself. For when we dig into the background of this amateur excavator, we find he was an exceptional person. Few Spaniards were out probing into caves 100 years ago. The fact that he—not someone else—decided to dig that day in the cave of Altamira was the culmination of his passionate interest in his hobby. Here was a rare man whose avocation had been to educate himself from scratch, as it were, in the science of archaeology and cave exploration. This was no simple passive recognizer of blind luck when it came his way, but a man whose

---

[1]The cave had first been discovered some years before by an enterprising hunting dog in search of game. Curiously, in 1932 the French cave of Lascaux was discovered by still another dog.

unique interests served as an active creative thrust—someone whose own actions and personality would focus the events that led circuitously but inexorably to the discovery of man's first paintings.

Then, too, there is a more subtle manner. How do you give full weight to 14 the personal interests that imbue your child with your own curiosity, that inspire her to ask to join you in your own musty hobby, and that then lead you to agree to her request at the critical moment? For many reasons, at Altamira, more than the special receptivity of Chance III was required—this was a different domain, that of the personality and its actions.

A century ago no one had the remotest idea that our caveman ancestors were 15 highly creative artists. Weren't their talents rather minor and limited to crude flint chippings? But the paintings at Altamira, like a mirage, would quickly magnify this diminutive view, bring up into full focus a distant, hidden era of man's prehistory, reveal sentient minds and well-developed aesthetic sensibilities to which men of any age might aspire. And like a mirage, the events at Altamira grew out of de Sautuola's heated personal quest and out of the invisible forces of chance we know exist yet cannot touch. Accordingly, one may introduce the term *altamirage* to identify the quality underlying Chance IV. Let us define it as the facility for encountering unexpected good luck as the result of highly individualized action. Altamirage goes well beyond the boundaries of serendipity in its emphasis on the role of personal action in chance.

Chance IV is favored by distinctive, if not eccentric, hobbies, personal life- 16 styles, and modes of behavior peculiar to one individual, usually invested with some passion. The farther apart these personal activities are from the area under investigation, the more novel and unexpected will be the creative product of the encounter.

Understanding Meaning

1. What are the four categories of chance?

2. What is meant by "blind" or "dumb" luck? Give some examples from your own life.

3. What is the Kettering Principle? Would Edison's famous trial-and-error experiments to discover a filament for the incandescent light bulb fit this kind of chance?

4. How does the Pasteur principle differ from the Kettering Principle?

5. How did the dog's discovery of a cave differ from "blind luck" or Chance I?

6. *Critical Thinking:* How often have you discovered things by chance? What role has chance played in your career and education? Does understanding Austin's four kinds of chance enhance your ability to be "lucky" in the future? Can you "make your own kind of luck"?

Evaluating Strategy

1. What principle does Austin use to divide chance into four categories?

2. What examples does Austin use to illustrate each type? Are they accessible by a general audience?

3. Would a chart aid in explaining the four types of chance?

4. *Blending the Modes:* How does Austin make use of *definition* and *narration* in developing his classification essay?

Appreciating Language

1. How much technical language does Austin include?

2. *Critical Thinking:* Is part of Austin's task in this article to invent new terms to create categories of chance? Do most of our words for chance—"luck," "fortune," "lot"—all suggest the same meaning?

WRITING SUGGESTIONS

1. List a number of instances in your life you considered lucky. Using Austin's four categories, write a paper categorizing your experiences. Have you ever gotten past Chance I?

2. *Collaborative Writing:* Discuss the role of chance with a group of students. Do many people use the idea of chance to dismiss the accomplishments of others? Do people use luck as an excuse for not trying? Talk about these issues, and then collaborate on a short paper suggesting how Austin's concept of chance should be taught to children.

BILL WASIK

Bill Wasik is a senior editor of Harper's Magazine. *His book* And Then There's This: How Stories Live and Die in Viral Culture *was published in 2009. In 2006, Wasik revealed that he had anonymously organized the first flash mobs in New York in 2003.*

Our Friend the Smear

CONTEXT: *Wasik published this article in* Harper's Magazine *just before the 2004 presidential election when John Kerry and John Edward were running against George Bush and Dick Cheney, who were seeking a second term. Kerry was dogged by commercials sponsored by an organization called Swift Boat Veterans for Truth that called into question his Vietnam service. Using this case as an example, Wasik breaks smears into four phases.*

However much we might prefer our elections to be decided on the issues, 1 victory on November 2 will almost certainly belong to the side that propagates the most effective smear. For this reason, it is worthwhile to develop our understanding of the smear and of its peculiar niche in our political ecosystem. What is it that allows the smear to thrive? What are its haunts and its habits? To answer these questions, let us examine the life cycle of a particularly robust smear—the ad campaign of the Swift Boat Veterans for Truth—within the confines of a single TV network (ABC). As we will see, the life cycle of a smear has four distinct phases.

1. Gestation. In order to survive in the twenty-four-hour news cycle, the 2 smear must develop two defenses or else perish. The first is that it seem new, and in this it enjoys a natural advantage over the truths with which it must compete. Most truths about a presidential candidate have been reported to the point that they seem, to reporters and editors, like commonplaces; a story that "everybody knows" is in danger of being left behind as reporters "move on."

The second defense is that the smear seem solid, and this is merely a question 3 of time. With luck (or careful planning) the smear will soon develop a defensive layer of fact—for example, when a candidate makes a pre-eruptive denial, which the media can immediately report, along with the smear itself. In the case of the Swift Boat smear, its benefactors supplied its factual shell by taking out ads, a legitimate news event. And thus, on or around August 5, was a smear born. From the next day's *Good Morning America*:

> DIANE SAWYER: Well, this morning, we're turning now to a new hot 4 potato being passed around on the campaign trail. A group of Vietnam veterans is casting a shadow on John Kerry's war record, and ABC's Jake Tapper has a report on all this from Washington. Jake?

5   JAKE TAPPER: Good morning, Diane. Well, these anti-Kerry Vietnam veterans have launched a very controversial new ad in a few key battleground states, slamming John Kerry's record as a soldier.

6   **2. Controversy as story.** Once a smear has been accepted into the ecosystem, journalists can simply report on the dispute; e.g., the ad was a "hot potato," "very controversial." This approach allows the smear to grow quickly: if the story is the controversy, then reporters must adopt a mechanical evenhandedness, by which lies and truth are granted equal time. Thus ABC's next major treatment of the Swift Boat story, August 9 on *Nightline*, began with a series of clips juxtaposing the Swift Boat ads with the words of Kerry supporters. The voiceover from ABC anchor Michel Martin: "John Kerry, the decorated war hero . . . Or John Kerry, war fraud?" In his introductory remarks, Martin elaborated:

7   [A]lmost thirty years after the war ended, many people cannot even agree on the facts. Especially when those facts become part of the political battlefield. John Kerry has been campaigning with his comrades from Vietnam, to make the case that he is ready to be commander in chief. And now an opposing group of veterans has challenged him and his record. Here's ABC's Jake Tapper.

8   Only after another sustained barrage of disagreeing vets (four anti-Kerry, two pro-) did Tapper upset the magnificent equipoise with this:

9   The Kerry campaign calls the charges wrong, offensive, and politically motivated, and points to naval records that seemingly contradict the charges. Adding to the murkiness about these many accusations is the fact that when Kerry faced similar questions about his Silver Star during his 1996 Senate race, two of the swift-boat veterans opposing him now defended him then.

10   Later, Tapper informed viewers that funding for the Swift Boat ads had been provided by a Republican donor with close ties to Karl Rove. In the sophisticated wordplay of the controversy-as-story, this fact, as with the naval records and the rest, was taken not to exonerate the accused but to further add to the "murkiness."

11   **3. Story as story.** Once a smear has survived a few weeks, it can begin to subsist as the basis for itself. The classic indication that a smear has reached this stage is when a candidate is "dogged by a story that will not go away." When *Nightline* rejoined the Swift Boat story on August 19, anchor Chris Bury in fact marked the transition with just those words. After rehashing the ad and the controversy, he then dove into a lengthy meta-analysis:

12   So how did one TV ad, which appeared in only three states, become a national story that would not go away? More on that when we come back.

13   During this later stage, repetition replaces controversy in nourishing the smear. In the three weeks leading up to the Republican Convention, portions

of the Swift Boat Veterans for Truth ad—with its short, repetitive statements such as "John Kerry is no war hero," "John Kerry has not been honest about what happened in Vietnam," "John Kerry lied to get his Bronze Star"—were replayed on twenty-six different network and cable news programs, not even counting those on Fox News.

4. Story as story line. With ubiquity, the smear has reached its final, ma- 14 ture state. The Swift Boat story indeed will dog Kerry for the remainder of the campaign, no matter how thoroughly and frequently it is discredited. It now resonates, in the sense that Ted Koppel used the word on September 1, in the following exchange on *Nightline* with comedian Jon Stewart:

KOPPEL: The problem, Jon, is—and here is where I think the Republicans 15 have got John Kerry dead to rights . . . when he came out there and said "John Kerry, reporting for duty," when he has made every public appearance in recent memory in the presence of his band of brothers, when there is not a public appearance that doesn't in some way reflect on the Vietnam experience, then the Vietnam experience becomes central.

STEWART: Absolutely relevant, but that doesn't make the lies true.   16

KOPPEL: No . . . But it makes them particularly resonant.   17

Why, in the end, do some smears "resonate" while others falter? The 18 answer, quite simply, is that successful smears travel in herds. The Swift Boat smear now makes its lair within a vast and welcoming habitat of Republican smears, which together provide the permanent media talking points for "why some people oppose Kerry": untrustworthy flip-flopper, weak on terrorism, may have lied about his medals. Political strategists praise the Republicans for their "message discipline," and this is especially earned with respect to their smears, to the unwavering story line by which they have maligned John Kerry. Whereas smears from the left have been equally vigorous, as a brood they are far less harmonious—Bush is portrayed one day as a nefarious genius, the next as a dimwitted puppet; one day as an upper-crust plutocrat, the next as a pious yokel. The right, by contrast, displays an integrity of character assassination. Kerry's greatest enemy on Election Day will not be President Bush but his pack of smears, which will be nothing if not exceptionally well bred.

Understanding Meaning

1. What are the four phases of a political smear in Wasik's view?

2. What two elements does a smear have to contain in order to get media coverage?

3. How do reporters help a smear grow by covering "the smear as story"? How does trying to be even-handed and fair actually propel smears?

4. How does a smear "subsist as the basis for itself"?

5. Why, in Wasik's view, do some smears resonate with the public and others do not?

6. *Critical Thinking*: Do you think that political smears will be more common now that they can be broadcast online and do not need media coverage or expensive ad campaigns to reach the public?

Evaluating Strategy

1. How does Wasik use division to organize his article? How important are the names or labels given to a step or stage?

2. Wasik focuses his essay on a single smear launched against a single candidate. Would his article be more effective if he included more examples, perhaps balancing smears made against both Democrats and Republicans? Why or why not?

3. Wasik includes direct quotes from television news broadcasts. Do they effectively illustrate his view of smears?

Appreciating Language

1. What do the tone and style of Wasik's article suggest about his audience?

2. Consider the word "smear." What connotation does it have? Can a political candidate attempt to dismiss legitimate criticism by calling it a "smear campaign"? Why or why not?

WRITING SUGGESTIONS

1. Using Wasik's essay as a model, describe different phases of a process you have observed. What are the phases of a job interview, a divorce settlement, the grief process, quitting smoking, or getting out of debt?

2. *Collaborative Writing*: Discuss Wasik's article with a group of students, then use division to detail ways voters can identify smears or to classify types of smears from most to least effective.

THOMAS H. BENTON

Thomas H. Benton is the pseudonym of an associate professor of English at a Midwestern liberal arts college.

The Seven Deadly Sins of Students

CONTEXT: *Before reading this essay, consider if you have observed student behavior that you find unacceptable or self-destructive. How seriously do the students on your campus take their education?*

I've been teaching for about 10 years now, and, of course, I was a student for 1
20 years before that. So I have some experience observing my students' sins, and perhaps even more experience committing them.

The sins that I see in the everyday life of the typical college student are not 2
great ones. Most of the time, they don't seem like "sins" at all, even if one accepts the religious significance of the term. But they spring from thoughts and behaviors that, over time, become habits.

Enabled by institutions, students repeatedly take the path of least resistance, 3
imagining they are making creative compromises with duty that express their unique talents. So they choose self-indulgence instead of self-denial, and self-esteem instead of self-questioning. They do not understand that those choices will eventually cause more unhappiness than the more difficult paths they chose not to walk.

The traditional model of the "Seven Deadly Sins" provides a helpful means 4
of categorizing—and perhaps simplifying—the complicated and cumulative experience I am trying to describe:

Sloth: Students often postpone required readings and assigned preparations, 5
making it hard for them to understand their classes the next day. Gradually, lectures and discussions that were once interesting start to seem boring and irrelevant, and the temptation to skip classes becomes greater and greater, especially when the classes are in the morning. Sometimes students arrive late with—in my opinion—insufficient shame, closing the door behind them with a bang. Slothful students regard themselves as full of potential, and so they make a bargain: "I will be lazy now, but I will work hard later." Like St. Augustine, students say to themselves, "Let me be chaste, but not yet." More on lust later.

Greed: Students often pursue degrees not for the sake of learning itself but 6
with the aim of getting a better-paying job, so they can buy a bigger house and fancier cars than those owned by their parents and their neighbors. That often leads to greed for grades that they have not earned. Some students cheat on exams or plagiarize their papers; others, sometimes the most diligent, harass

professors into giving them grades unjustified by their performance. The goal of such cheaters and grade-grubbers is not the reality of achievement but the appearance of it. They will then apply to graduate programs or entry-level jobs that they do not really desire and for which they are not really qualified. They want to be lawyers, but they are bored by law courses. They want to be doctors, but they do not care about healing people. They want to go into business, not to provide useful products and services, but to get rich by any means necessary. And so they come to believe that no one has integrity and that there is no basis—other than the marketplace—by which value can be judged.

7   Anger: Seemingly more often than in the past, professors encounter students who are angered by challenging assignments, which they label—with bureaucratic self-assurance—"unfair" or even "discriminatory." When students do not succeed, they sometimes conclude that their professors are "out to get them" because of some vague prejudice. Students feel entitled to deference by professors who "work for them and should act like it." They do not come to office hours for clarification about an A-; instead, they argue that they are paying a lot of money and, therefore, deserve a high grade, and, if you don't give it to them, they will "complain to management," as if they were sending back food in a restaurant. One hears rumors of cars and homes vandalized by angry students. But perhaps the easiest places to find uncensored student rage are the anonymous, libelous evaluations of faculty members found online at Web sites such as RateMyProfessors.com. Often those evaluations say less about the quality of a teacher than they do about the wounded pride of coddled students. More on that topic soon.

8   Lust: I have seen students come to classes barefoot, with bare midriffs and shoulders, in boxer shorts, bathing suits, and other kinds of clothes that, even by fairly casual standards, are more appropriate for streetwalking than higher learning. When did liberation from uniforms transform itself into the social demand that one prepare to be ogled in the classroom? It is hardly a surprise that on RateMyProfessors.com, students are asked to rate their professors' "hotness"—in other words, the teachers' worthiness to be sexually fantasized about by bored students. Even in high-school classes, as an observer of novice teachers, I have overheard lewd remarks about female teachers from denizens of the back row who fear no rebuke because none is forthcoming from the current culture.

9   Gluttony: It hardly needs saying that most colleges struggle to control alcohol consumption by students and the embarrassing incidents and tragedies that result from it. But there are other manifestations of gluttony these days. For example, when did it become acceptable for students to eat and drink in class as if they were sitting in a cafeteria? Nowadays, I occasionally encounter a student who thinks it's OK to consume a large, messy, and odorous meal in class. I once saw a student eat an entire rotisserie chicken, a tub of mashed potatoes with gravy, several biscuits, and an enormous soft drink during the

first 10 minutes of a lecture. I felt like a jester in the court of Henry VIII. It seems hard these days to find a student in class whose mouth is not stuffed with food. Such students will often say that they have no other time to eat, but previous generations—who were no less busy—managed to consume small snacks between classes. That is why colleges have vending machines.

Envy: I think competition is a good thing in education; up to a point, it 10 encourages students to work harder and excel. But the envious student, perhaps daunted by some temporary setback, comes to believe that education is "a rigged game." Envy is the voice of resignation that cringes at the success of one's peers: "Listen to her, trying to impress the teacher, like she's so brilliant. I hate her." Envy is the feeling that no one "earns" anything because there are no objective criteria of accomplishment; and, as a result, success and failure seem to be based on political and personal preferences. But envy is not limited to differences in effort and ability. Even more pervasive is a sense of unjustified economic inequality, but, it seems to me, the fashionable students in their convertibles who jeer the commuters at the bus stop commit a greater sin than those who envy their money.

Pride: I once asked a group of 20 students how many thought they were "bet- 11 ter than their parents"? All of them raised their hands. I didn't ask, but I assume they all believed they were better than their teachers too. They would rise higher, be more successful, and transcend the limitations of their elders. We read this belief in our students' expressions: "What you know is not worth learning. They're just your opinions anyway. I am young. I have infinite potential. You are old. And you're just a college professor. But I will be rich and famous someday." They have rarely been given a realistic assessment of their abilities and prospects. Out of this pride—nurtured by the purveyors of unearned self-esteem, personal grievance, dumbed-down courses, and inflated grades (often in the guise of liberality)—the opportunity to earn an education is squandered by prideful students who can make a potential heaven seem like hell.

The concept of the "Seven Deadly Sins" comes out of the Christian tradi- 12 tion, but it also has value as an ethical guide or at least as a means of avoiding unhappiness. Increasingly, as a professor who teaches undergraduates, I believe that one of the paramount purposes of a liberal-arts education is to help young people acquire the wisdom to escape those sins, especially the last one from which the others often spring.

A liberal-arts education, as I see it, is not about acquiring wealth and oppor- 13 tunities to further indulge one's desires. Nor is it about cultivating in students an insular, idolatrous view of their nation, ethnic group, gender, or religion. It is also not about celebrating the so-called "great tradition" of authors, philosophers, and artists.

It is about the recognition, ultimately, of how little one really knows, or can 14 know. A liberal-arts education, most of all, fights unmerited pride by asking students to recognize the smallness of their ambitions in the context of human history, and more. Whether it is grounded in faith or not, a liberal-arts education should help students to combat the Seven Deadly Sins with the "Seven Contrary Virtues" of diligence, generosity, patience, chastity, moderation, contentment, and, most important of all, humility.

15   Of course, moral perfection seldom arrives at graduation, even in the best of cases. I teach the courses, and yet I must present myself, at last, as the "Chief of Sinners." The behaviors I observe in students often reflect the deeper drives—the resentments and weaknesses—of their teachers. Perhaps the impulse to identify the sins of others reflects a corruption more serious than any I have described here. And that is why, next month, I will sermonize on the "Seven Deadly Sins of Professors."

Understanding Meaning

1. What is Benton's thesis? Can you state it in your own words?

2. In Benton's view, what are the students' principal "sins"?

3. What does Benton consider the goal of a liberal arts education? What, in his opinion, should not be considered goals?

4. How are students, in Benton's view, cheating themselves by avoiding "the more difficult paths"?

5. Do you think the behaviors Benton objects to are limited to college campuses? Why or why not?

6. *Critical Thinking:* Do some of these "sins," such as wearing revealing clothing or eating in class, concern social etiquette rather than academic achievement? Is a casually dressed student necessarily casual or unprofessional about his or her studies? In the days of rigid dress codes (some colleges required male students to wear jackets and ties to class), were students more dedicated and responsible?

Evaluating Strategy

1. How effective is Benton's title and method of division?

2. Benton states in the introduction that he has committed many of these "sins" himself. Is this important? Does this admission prevent his essay from simply being a sarcastic diatribe?

3. *Critical Thinking:* How can a writer criticize a group of people without appearing to be mean-spirited, biased, or hypocritical? How are students likely to react when a professor describes them as wanting to be lawyers but being "bored by law courses" or wanting to be doctors but not caring about "healing people"?

4. Benton does not use his real name. Do you think announcing that he is using a pseudonym raises questions about his motives or credibility?

Appreciating Language

1. Look up the word "sin" and the term "seven deadly sins" in dictionaries or encyclopedias. What do these terms mean? What are their connotations? Do you think these words are suited for an article in an academic magazine? Why or why not?

2. How would you characterize the general tone and style of the article? What words and phrases does Benton use to describe students?

WRITING SUGGESTIONS

1. Using Benton's article as a model, develop an essay that delineates the "seven deadly sins" of American consumers, homeowners, renters, employees, employers, parents, or drivers.

2. *Collaborative Writing:* Discuss Benton's essay with a group of students and formulate a response. Do members of your group agree or disagree with Benton's points? Use division to develop responses to each of Benton's seven deadly sins. If members disagree, consider using comparison to create opposing essays.

WILLIAM LUTZ

William Lutz (1940-) was born in Racine, Wisconsin, and received his bachelor's degree from the Dominican College of Racine and his master's degree from Marquette University. He received his doctorate in 1971 from the University of Nevada, Reno. He taught at Rutgers University's Camden, New Jersey, campus. From 1980 to 1994 Lutz edited the Quarterly Review of Doublespeak. *His books include* The Age of Communication *(1974),* Doublespeak: From "Revenue Enhancement" to "Terminal Living" *(1989), and* The Cambridge Thesaurus of American English *(1994).*

Four Kinds of Doublespeak

CONTEXT: *George Orwell coined the term "doublespeak" in his novel* Nineteen Eighty-Four *to refer to the way an oppressive society used language to disguise its actions. Lutz uses the term to describe the way governments, corporations, and individuals use language to obscure rather than express facts and ideas.*

1 There are no potholes in the streets of Tucson, Arizona, just "pavement deficiencies." The Reagan Administration didn't propose any new taxes, just "revenue enhancement" through new "user's fees." Those aren't bums on the street, just "nongoal oriented members of society." There are no more poor people, just "fiscal underachievers." There was no robbery of an automatic teller machine, just an "unauthorized withdrawal." The patient didn't die because of medical malpractice, it was just a "diagnostic misadventure of a high magnitude." The U.S. Army doesn't kill the enemy anymore, it just "services the target." And the doublespeak goes on.

2   Doublespeak is language that pretends to communicate but really doesn't. It is language that makes the bad seem good, the negative appear positive, the unpleasant appear attractive or at least tolerable. Doublespeak is language that avoids or shifts responsibility, language that is at variance with its real or purported meaning. It is language that conceals or prevents thought; rather than extending thought, doublespeak limits it.

3   Doublespeak is not a matter of subjects and verbs agreeing; it is a matter of words and facts agreeing. Basic to doublespeak is incongruity, the incongruity between what is said or left unsaid, and what really is. It is the incongruity between the word and the referent, between seem and be, between the essential function of language—communication—and what doublespeak does— mislead, distort, deceive, inflate, circumvent, obfuscate.

How to Spot Doublespeak

4 How can you spot doublespeak? Most of the time you will recognize doublespeak when you see or hear it. But, if you have any doubts, you can identify doublespeak just by answering these questions: Who is saying what to whom,

under what conditions and circumstances, with what intent, and with what results? Answering these questions will usually help you identify as doublespeak language that appears to be legitimate or that at first glance doesn't even appear to be doublespeak.

First Kind of Doublespeak

There are at least four kinds of doublespeak. The first is the euphemism, an 5
inoffensive or positive word or phrase used to avoid a harsh, unpleasant, or distasteful reality. But a euphemism can also be a tactful word or phrase which avoids directly mentioning a painful reality, or it can be an expression used out of concern for the feelings of someone else, or to avoid directly discussing a topic subject to a social or cultural taboo.

When you use a euphemism because of your sensitivity for someone's feel- 6
ings or out of concern for a recognized social or cultural taboo, it is not doublespeak. For example, you express your condolences that someone has "passed away" because you do not want to say to a grieving person, "I'm sorry your father is dead." When you use the euphemism "passed away," no one is misled. Moreover, the euphemism functions here not just to protect the feelings of another person, but to communicate also your concern for that person's feelings during a period of mourning. When you excuse yourself to go to the "rest room," or you mention that someone is "sleeping with" or "involved with" someone else, you do not mislead anyone about your meaning, but you do respect the social taboos about discussing bodily functions and sex in direct terms. You also indicate your sensitivity to the feelings of your audience, which is usually considered a mark of courtesy and good manners.

However, when a euphemism is used to mislead or deceive, it becomes 7
doublespeak. For example, in 1984 the U.S. State Department announced that it would no longer use the word "killing" in its annual report on the status of human rights in countries around the world. Instead, it would use the phrase "unlawful or arbitrary deprivation of life," which the department claimed was more accurate. Its real purpose for using this phrase was simply to avoid discussing the embarrassing situation of government-sanctioned killings in countries that are supported by the United States and have been certified by the United States as respecting the human rights of their citizens. This use of a euphemism constitutes doublespeak, since it is designed to mislead, to cover up the unpleasant. Its real intent is at variance with its apparent intent. It is language designed to alter our perception of reality.

The Pentagon, too, avoids discussing unpleasant realities when it refers to 8
bombs and artillery shells that fall on civilian targets as "incontinent ordnance." And in 1977 the Pentagon tried to slip funding for the neutron bomb unnoticed into an appropriations bill by calling it a "radiation enhancement device."

Second Kind of Doublespeak

9   A second kind of doublespeak is jargon, the specialized language of a trade, profession, or similar group, such as that used by doctors, lawyers, engineers, educators, or car mechanics. Jargon can serve an important and useful function. Within a group, jargon functions as a kind of verbal shorthand that allows members of the group to communicate with each other clearly, efficiently, and quickly. Indeed, it is a mark of membership in the group to be able to use and understand the group's jargon.

10   But jargon, like the euphemism, can also be doublespeak. It can be—and often is—pretentious, obscure, and esoteric terminology used to give an air of profundity, authority, and prestige to speakers and their subject matter. Jargon as doublespeak often makes the simple appear complex, the ordinary profound, the obvious insightful. In this sense it is used not to express but impress. With such doublespeak, the act of smelling something becomes "organoleptic analysis," glass becomes "fused silicate," a crack in a metal support beam becomes a "discontinuity," conservative economic policies become "distributionally conservative notions."

11   Lawyers, for example, speak of an "involuntary conversion" of property when discussing the loss or destruction of property through theft, accident, or condemnation. If your house burns down or if your car is stolen, you have suffered an involuntary conversion of your property. When used by lawyers in a legal situation, such jargon is a legitimate use of language, since lawyers can be expected to understand the term.

12   However, when a member of a specialized group uses its jargon to communicate with a person outside the group, and uses it knowing that the nonmember does not understand such language, then there is doublespeak. For example, on May 9, 1978, a National Airlines 727 airplane crashed while attempting to land at the Pensacola, Florida airport. Three of the fifty-two passengers aboard the airplane were killed. As a result of the crash, National made an after-tax insurance benefit of $1.7 million, or an extra 18¢ a share dividend for its stockholders. Now National Airlines had two problems: It did not want to talk about one of its airplanes crashing, and it had to account for the $1.7 million when it issued its annual report to its stockholders. National solved the problem by inserting a footnote in its annual report which explained that the $1.7 million income was due to "the involuntary conversion of a 727." National thus acknowledged the crash of its airplane and the subsequent profit it made from the crash, without once mentioning the accident or the deaths. However, because airline officials knew that most stockholders in the company, and indeed most of the general public, were not familiar with legal jargon, the use of such jargon constituted doublespeak.

Third Kind of Doublespeak

A third kind of doublespeak is gobbledygook or bureaucratese. Basically, such 13 doublespeak is simply a matter of piling on words, of overwhelming the audience with words, the bigger the words and the longer the sentences the better. Alan Greenspan, then chair of President Nixon's Council of Economic Advisors, was quoted in *The Philadelphia Inquirer* in 1974 as having testified before a Senate committee that "It is a tricky problem to find the particular calibration in timing that would be appropriate to stem the acceleration in risk premiums created by falling incomes without prematurely aborting the decline in the inflation-generated risk premiums."

Nor has Mr. Greenspan's language changed since then. Speaking to the 14 meeting of the Economic Club of New York in 1988, Mr. Greenspan, now Federal Reserve chair, said, "I guess I should warn you, if I turn out to be particularly clear, you've probably misunderstood what I've said." Mr. Greenspan's doublespeak doesn't seem to have held back his career.

Sometimes gobbledygook may sound impressive, but when the quote is 15 later examined in print it doesn't even make sense. During the 1988 presidential campaign, vice-presidential candidate Senator Dan Quayle explained the need for a strategic-defense initiative by saying, "Why wouldn't an enhanced deterrent, a more stable peace, a better prospect to denying the ones who enter conflict in the first place to have a reduction of offensive systems and an introduction to defensive capability? I believe this is the route the country will eventually go."

The investigation into the Challenger disaster in 1986 revealed the dou- 16 blespeak of gobbledygook and bureaucratese used by too many involved in the shuttle program. When Jesse Moore, NASA's associate administrator, was asked if the performance of the shuttle program had improved with each launch or if it had remained the same, he answered, "I think our performance in terms of the liftoff performance and in terms of the orbital performance, we knew more about the envelope we were operating under, and we have been pretty accurately staying in that. And so I would say the performance has not by design drastically improved. I think we have been able to characterize the performance more as a function of our launch experience as opposed to it improving as a function of time." While this language may appear to be jargon, a close look will reveal that it is really just gobbledygook laced with jargon. But you really have to wonder if Mr. Moore had any idea what he was saying.

Fourth Kind of Doublespeak

The fourth kind of doublespeak is inflated language that is designed to make 17 the ordinary seem extraordinary; to make everyday things seem impressive; to give an air of importance to people, situations, or things that would not normally be considered important; to make the simple seem complex. Often this kind of doublespeak isn't hard to spot, and it is usually pretty funny. While car mechanics may be called "automotive internists," elevator operators members of the "vertical transportation corps," used cars "pre-owned" or "experienced cars," and black-and-white television sets described as having "non-multicolor capability," you really aren't misled all that much by such language.

18   However, you may have trouble figuring out that, when Chrysler "initiates a career alternative enhancement program," it is really laying off five thousand workers; or that "negative patient care outcome" means the patient died; or that "rapid oxidation" means a fire in a nuclear power plant.

19   The doublespeak of inflated language can have serious consequences. In Pentagon doublespeak, "pre-emptive counterattack" means that American forces attacked first; "engaged the enemy on all sides" means American troops were ambushed; "backloading of augmentation personnel" means a retreat by American troops. In the doublespeak of the military, the 1983 invasion of Grenada was conducted not by the U.S. Army, Navy, Air Force, and Marines, but by the "Caribbean Peace Keeping Forces." But then, according to the Pentagon, it wasn't an invasion, it was a "predawn vertical insertion."

Understanding Meaning

1. How does Lutz define "doublespeak"? Can you think of recent examples you have heard?

2. What is "euphemism," and why does Lutz suggest that this form of doublespeak is acceptable and often a sign of "courtesy and good manners"?

3. What is jargon and how can it be misused to hide or obscure meaning? Do some people use jargon to confuse voters, customers, or clients?

4. What are the potential dangers of "gobbledygook" and "inflated language"? Can you think of recent examples?

5. *Critical Thinking:* What ethical issues do reporters and journalists face when presented with corporate or government press releases that use doublespeak? Should they explain to readers that "revenue enhancement" means "raising taxes," or that "soldiers withdrawing to a secure position" are actually "retreating," or that "personnel restructuring" means "layoffs"? Do controversial political issues produce competing forms of doublespeak?

Evaluating Strategy

1. Do you think Lutz provides a clear definition of "doublespeak"? Why or why not? Can you define it in your own words?

2. Does Lutz clearly distinguish among each kind of doublespeak?

3. Does Lutz provide sufficient examples to illustrate each type? Can you think of your own examples of doublespeak that would fit each of his four categories?

4. *Blending the Modes:* Where does Lutz use *narration, description, definition, process,* and *cause and effect* to develop his division essay?

Appreciating Language

1. Look up the words "circumvent" and "obfuscate." Are these effective words to use in a description or definition of doublespeak?

2. When, in Lutz's view, does euphemism become doublespeak? Can trying to spare someone's feelings or address a controversial issue diplomatically lead to harmful doublespeak?

WRITING SUGGESTIONS

1. Write an essay describing uses of doublespeak you have encountered. Did a high school use euphemisms to describe students who misbehaved or dropped out? Did an employer refer to fired employees as being "non-retained"? Did a local politician or community organization prefer to call a neighborhood "low income" rather than a "slum"? Have you heard convicted criminals or their attorneys admit to "making bad choices" rather than "committing crimes"?

2. Write a short analysis of the way a current political or social issue is discussed on television or on the Web. Can you detect evidence of doublespeak? Do controversial issues lead opponents to accuse each other of using doublespeak?

3. *Collaborative Writing:* Working with a group of students, practice doublespeak by translating these sentences into more neutral and less dramatic statements:

My client got drunk, drove into a school bus, and injured three children.

Our company will immediately fire fifty workers.

The mayor wants to raise taxes on homeowners.

BLENDING THE MODES

ANDRÉS MARTIN

Andrés Martin received his medical degree from Anahuac University in 1990 and is currently a professor of child psychiatry and psychiatry at Yale University and the Director of Medical Studies of the Yale Child Study Center. In 2006, he was appointed an editor of the Journal of the American Academy of Child and Adolescent Psychiatry *and became its editor in chief in 2008.*

On Teenagers and Tattoos

CONTEXT: *In this 2000 article, which first appeared in* Reclaiming Children and Youth, *Martin describes three psychological motivations that drive adolescents to seek the permanence of tattoos.*

> The skeleton dimensions I shall now proceed to set down are copied verbatim from my right arm, where I had them tattooed, as in my wild wanderings at that period, there was no other secure way of preserving such valuable statistics.
>
> —Melville/*Moby Dick*

1 Tattoos and piercing have become a part of our everyday landscape. They are ubiquitous, having entered the circles of glamour and the mainstream of fashion, and they have even become an increasingly common feature of our urban youth. Legislation in most states restricts professional tattooing to adults older than 18 years of age, so "high end" tattooing is rare in children and adolescents, but such tattoos are occasionally seen in older teenagers. Piercings, by comparison, as well as self-made or "jailhouse" type tattoos, are not at all rare among adolescents or even among school-age children. Like hairdo, makeup, or baggy jeans, tattoos and piercings can be subject to fad influence or peer pressure in an effort toward group affiliation. As with any other fashion statement, they can be construed as bodily aids in the inner struggle toward identity consolidation, serving as adjuncts to the defining and sculpting of the self by means of external manipulations. But unlike most other body decorations, tattoos and piercings are set apart by their irreversible and permanent nature, a quality at the core of their magnetic appeal to adolescents.

2 Adolescents and their parents are often at odds over the acquisition of bodily decorations. For the adolescent, piercing or tattoos may be seen as personal and beautifying statements, while parents may construe them as oppositional and enraging affronts to their authority. Distinguishing bodily adornment from self-mutilation may indeed prove challenging, particularly

when a family is in disagreement over a teenager's motivations and a clinician is summoned as the final arbiter. At such times it may be most important to realize jointly that the skin can all too readily become but another battleground for the tensions of the age, arguments having less to do with tattoos and piercings than with core issues such as separation from the family matrix. Exploring the motivations and significance belying tattoos (Grumet, 1983) and piercings can go a long way toward resolving such differences and can become a novel and additional way of getting to know teenagers. An interested and nonjudgmental appreciation of teenagers' surface presentations may become a way of making contact not only in their terms but on their turfs: quite literally on the territory of their skins.

The following three sections exemplify some of the complex psychological   3
underpinnings of youth tattooing.

Identity and the Adolescent's Body

Tattoos and piercing can offer a concrete and readily available solution for   4
many of the identity crises and conflicts normative to adolescent development. In using such decorations, and by marking out their bodily territories, adolescents can support their efforts at autonomy, privacy, and insulation. Seeking individuation, tattooed adolescents can become unambiguously demarcated from others and singled out as unique. The intense and often disturbing reactions that are mobilized in viewers can help to effectively keep them at bay, becoming tantamount to the proverbial "Keep Out" sign hanging from a teenager's door.

Alternatively, feeling prey to a rapidly evolving body over which they   5
have no say, self-made and openly visible decorations may restore adolescents' sense of normalcy and control, a way of turning a passive experience into an active identity. By indelibly marking their bodies, adolescents can strive to reclaim their bearings within an environment experienced as alien, estranged, or suffocating or to lay claim over their evolving and increasingly unrecognizable bodies. In either case, the net outcome can be a resolution to unwelcome impositions: external, familial, or societal in one case; internal and hormonal in the other. In the words of a 16-year-old girl with several facial piercings, and who could have been referring to her body just as well as to the position within her family: "If I don't fit in, it is because I say so."

Incorporation and Ownership

Imagery of a religious, deathly, or skeletal nature, the likenesses of fierce animals or imagined creatures, and the simple inscription of names are some of   6
the time-tested favorite contents for tattoos. In all instances, marks become

not only memorials or recipients for dearly held persons or concepts: they strive for incorporation, with images and abstract symbols gaining substance on becoming a permanent part of the individual's skin. Thickly embedded in personally meaningful representations and object relations, tattoos can become not only the ongoing memento of a relationship, but at times even the only evidence that there ever was such a bond. They can quite literally become the relationship itself. The turbulence and impulsivity of early attachments and infatuations may become grounded, effectively bridging oblivion through the visible reality to tattoos.

7   Case Vignette: "A," a 13-year-old boy, proudly showed me his tattooed deltoid. The coarsely depicted roll of the dice marked the day and month of his birth. Rather disappointed, he then uncovered an immaculate back, going on to draw for me the great "piece" he envisioned for it. A menacing figure held a hand of cards: two aces, two eights, and a card with two sets of dates. "A's" father had belonged to Dead Man's Hand, a motorcycle gang named after the set of cards (aces and eights) that the legendary Wild Bill Hickock had held in the 1890s when shot dead over a poker table in Deadwood, South Dakota. "A" had only the vaguest memory of and sketchiest information about his father, but he knew he had died in a motorcycle accident: The fifth card marked the dates of his birth and death.

8   The case vignette also serves to illustrate how tattoos are often the culmination of a long process of imagination, fantasy, and planning that can start at an early age. Limited markings, or relatively reversible ones such as piercings, can at a later time scaffold toward the more radical commitment of a permanent tattoo.

The Quest for Permanence

9 The popularity of the anchor as a tattoo motif may historically have had to do less with guild identification among sailors than with an intense longing for rootedness and stability. In a similar vein, the recent increase in the popularity and acceptance of tattoos may be understood as an antidote or counterpoint to our urban and nomadic lifestyles. Within an increasingly mobile society, in which relationships are so often transient—as attested by the frequencies of divorce, abandonment, foster placement, and repeated moves, for example—tattoos can be a readily available source of grounding. Tattoos, unlike many relationships, can promise permanence and stability. A sense of constancy can be derived from unchanging marks that can be carried along no matter what the physical, temporal, or geographical vicissitudes at hand. Tattoos stay, while all else may change.

10   Case Vignette: A proud father at 17, "B" had had the smiling face of his 4-month-old baby girl tattooed on his chest. As we talked at a tattoo

convention, he proudly introduced her to me, explaining how he would "always know how beautiful she is today" when years from then he saw her semblance etched on himself.

The quest for permanence may at other times prove misleading and offer 11 premature closure to unresolved conflicts. At a time of normative uncertainties, adolescents may maladaptively and all too readily commit to a tattoo and its indefinite presence. A wish to hold on to a current certainty may lead the adolescent to lay down in ink what is valued and cherished one day but may not necessarily be in the future. The frequency of self-made tattoos among hospitalized, incarcerated, or gang-affiliated youths suggests such motivations: A sense of stability may be a particularly dire need under temporary, turbulent, or volatile conditions. In addition, through their designs teenagers may assert a sense of bonding and allegiance to a group larger than themselves. Tattoos may attest to powerful experiences, such as adolescence itself, lived and even survived together. As with Moby Dick's protagonist, Ishmael, they may bear witness to the "valuable statistics" of one's "wild wandering(s)": those of adolescent exhilaration and excitement on the one hand; of growing pains, shared misfortune, or even incarceration on the other.

Adolescents' bodily decorations, at times radical and dramatic in their presen- 12 tation, can be seen in terms of figuration rather than disfigurement, of the natural body being through them transformed into a personalized body (Brain, 1979). They can often be understood as self-constructive and adorning efforts, rather than prematurely subsumed as mutilatory and destructive acts. If we bear all of this in mind, we may not only arrive at a position to pass more reasoned clinical judgment, but become sensitized through our patients' skins to another level of their internal reality.

References

Brain, R. (1979). *The decorated body*. New York: Harper & Row. Grumet, G. W. (1983). Psychodynamic implications of tattoos. American Journal of Orthopsychiatry, 53, 482–492.

Understanding Meaning

1. What three motivations does Martin see driving teenagers to get tattoos? Do these same motivations explain other adolescent behaviors, such as joining gangs, engaging in sexual activity, or taking drugs? Could they also explain drives for athletic, academic, or artistic achievement?

2. What problems do clinicians face when they are called to arbitrate a dispute between parents and children?

3. How does a tattoo help a teenager "reclaim" his or her changing body?

4. How do symbolic markings help a teenager incorporate abstractions into his or her life?

5. Why does the permanence of a tattoo appeal to adolescents?

6. *Critical Thinking:* Teenagers have always sought to express themselves and follow fads through music, hair, makeup, and fashion—all of which they can shed as they mature and seek new identities or develop new interests. How are tattoos different? Do you think tattoo artists have an ethical responsibility to counsel teenage clients, especially those seeking radical and highly visible tattoos? What does the popularity of tattoo removal reveal about choices adolescents make?

Evaluating Strategy

1. As a psychiatrist, how does Martin address the issue of teenagers and tattoos? Does he appear to strive for objectivity, or does he take a position? Do you think many adults would expect a medical professional to side with parents and oppose body modification?

2. How does Martin use division to organize his article? How effective are the labels he creates to describe each motivation?

3. Martin opens his essay with a reference to *Moby Dick.* Is this an effective technique to introduce his topic? Why or why not?

4. *Blending the Modes:* Where does Martin use *narration, analysis,* and *definition* to develop his division article?

Appreciating Language

1. Consider the tone of Martin's last paragraph, which states that tattoos can be seen as "figuration rather than disfigurement." Does he appear to legitimize adolescent drives for body modification? Might some parents insist on defining body medication as "mutilation" and a sign of "self-destructive" behavior?

2. Consider the word "tattoo." What connotations and associations does it have? Do you think people under twenty-five have a different reaction to the word itself than their parents do? Do the terms "body art" and "permanent decoration" evoke different responses?

3. *Critical Thinking:* What challenges do psychiatrists, psychologists, and therapists face when writing about controversial or sensitive issues like

body modification, drug use, or sexual behavior? Can the use of objective language make the writer appear to accept or condone actions that many see as immoral?

WRITING SUGGESTIONS

1. If you or someone you know has a tattoo, describe the motivations that led to this decision. Did any of the reasons Martin cites play a role?

2. Imagine that a friend emails you stating he or she is thinking of getting a radical and highly visible tattoo. Write an email stating your views. How would your friend's background and personality shape your response?

3. *Collaborative Writing*: Discuss tattoos with a group of students. Do they or their friends regret getting tattoos? Work together to write a short process paper for a student life website asking students to think carefully before getting tattooed. You may present your advice as a list of questions if you wish.

MOTION PICTURE ASSOCIATION OF AMERICA

The Motion Picture Association of America was founded in 1922 as the trade association of the American film industry. The organization's initial goal was to curb widespread criticism of motion pictures by improving the public image of the movie industry. It established production codes to counter state and local censorship boards that threatened to disrupt film distribution. In 1968 the MPAA, in partnership with theater owners, developed a rating system for motion pictures to alert the public, especially parents, of objectionable content.

CONTEXT: *The Red Carpet Ratings Service emails parents the ratings of newly released films. The announcement on page 395, designed to resemble a movie poster, appeared on the MPAA website.*

Understanding Meaning

1. Who is the target audience for this announcement?

2. What method of classification does the MPAA use to rate films?

3. *Critical Thinking*: Why does a trade organization representing motion pictures feel the need to rate its own products? Does this strike you as being self-defensive or, instead, socially responsible? Do you think many parents would like to see a rating system for music? Why or why not?

Evaluating Strategy

1. How effective is the design of this announcement?

2. What does the title "Parents: Stay Ahead of the Curve!" suggest to you? What parental concerns does it address?

3. *Critical Thinking*: How might a movie studio executive use this announcement to answer critics of the film industry?

Appreciating Language

1. What does the phrase *Red Carpet* suggest? Do you think it makes an effective name for this service? Why or why not?

2. Do you think the wording of the classifications is clear? What is the difference between "not suitable" and "inappropriate," or "suggesting guidance" and "strongly cautioning"? Do you think these labels provide accurate information for parents making decisions about what movies their children should and should not see?

3. The MPAA originally used X as its most restrictive designation. It changed the listing to NC-17 in the 1980s. What connotation does X-rated have? Why would the MPAA want to eliminate this term?

1. Write an essay about your experiences with movie ratings. Did your parents restrict the movies you were allowed to see as a child based on the ratings? If you have children, do you use ratings to select movies? Why or why not?

2. *Collaborative Writing*: Work with a group of students to establish a similar rating system for music. Which artists and groups would your group rate PG or R? If members disagree, develop opposing statements.

RESPONDING TO IMAGES

SYMBOLS OF THREE FAITHS, 2006

1. What is your first impression of this photograph?

2. Could you use this image as a book cover, billboard, or poster? Would it grab attention? What message would it communicate in your eyes? Are there places in the world where a poster like this would be largely accepted and others where it might provoke protest?

3. What does this photograph reveal about the power of symbols? What visual connotations do these images represent?

4. *Visual Analysis:* Does presenting three religions in a similar fashion suggest equality? Might some people be offended, believing that their faith is superior or correct? Why or why not?

5. Write an essay classifying the ways people might respond to this image.

6. *Collaborative Writing:* Share this image with a group of students and ask each to write a caption before you discuss the photograph. What do the captions suggest? Can reactions to an image like this reveal people's perceptual worlds? Can a photograph like this act like a Rorschach test measuring an individual's values? Why or why not?

STRATEGIES FOR DIVISION AND CLASSIFICATION WRITING

1. **Determine which mode you will use.** Which method will best suit your purpose: dividing your subject into subtopics or measuring subtopics against a common standard? Do you need to use both methods to explain your subject?

2. **Select an effective method of division.** If you were writing about improving the public schools, for example, it might be more effective to divide the paper by discipline, discussing how to improve math skills, writing ability, and knowledge of geography rather than improving elementary schools, junior high schools, and high schools.

3. **Avoid divisions that oversimplify or distort meaning.** Your paper should aid in helping readers grasp a complex subject without trivializing or misstating the issues. You may wish to qualify your division and explain to readers that exceptions and situations may exist where the division may not apply. Indicate the size or significance of each category and explain if it is possible for a specific item to fit more than one category or change categories over time.

4. **Avoid overlapping categories.** When writing both division and classification, make sure the categories are distinct. Do not separate cars into "domestic, foreign, and antique models," because antique cars would clearly have to belong to the first two groups.

5. **Use a single, clearly defined standard to classify subjects.** Classification relies on a clearly stated standard that is used to measure all the items you discuss. Avoid mixing standards. In some instances you may have to explain or justify why you are using a particular standard.

6. **In classification writing, make sure all topics fit into *one* category.** In a properly written classification paper, every unit should fit only one category. For example, a term paper is either an A− or a B+. In addition, make sure no items are left over that cannot be logically placed.

7. **Explain whether your division or classification is official or personal.** Tell readers who established or uses the division or classification method you are using, or explain the division or classification method you created to express your personal views.

SUGGESTED TOPICS FOR DIVISION AND CLASSIFICATION WRITING

Division

Write a *division* essay on any of the following topics. Your division may make use of standard categories or ones you invent. Remember to clearly state the way you are dividing your subject. Each subject or example should be supported with definitions, brief narratives, or descriptions.

1. Dates you have had

2. Student housing on and off campus

3. Baseball, basketball, or football teams

4. Popular music

5. The ways people cope with a problem, such as a divorce, a job loss, or the death of a family member

Classification

Write a *classification* essay on any of the following topics. Make sure to use a single method of rating the subtopics, from best to worst, easiest to hardest, or least desirable to most desirable, for example:

1. Jobs you have had

2. Student services, including health, police, food, etc.

3. Vacation destinations

4. Bosses or professors you have known

5. Talk shows or news programs

Division and Classification

Write an essay that uses both *division* and *classification* on any of the following topics. Make sure you clearly separate your topic into parts and use a clear method of classification; for example,

1. *Divide* SUVs, hybrid cars, or any other product into popular brands, then *classify* price ranges for each.

2. *Classify* students from A to F, and then *divide* each level into types. A students, for instance, could include those who study hard, those who had

taken related courses, and those who benefited from parents active in that discipline. F students could include those who never attend class and those who study as hard as they can but fail every test.

3. *Divide* a subject like terrorism or pollution into different types, and then *classify* the threats of each type from most to least serious.

4. *Divide* television shows into different types, and then *classify* specific shows in each group from your most to least favorite.

5. *Classify* football, baseball, or basketball teams into best, average, and worst by their wins and losses, then *use division* to draw distinctions between teams in each level. Do some winning teams owe their success to one or more star players, skilled coaching, or weak opponents?

WRITING IN CONTEXT

1. Assume you have been asked by a national magazine to write about students' political attitudes. You may develop your essay by division or classification. You can discuss politics in general terms of liberalism and conservatism or restrict your comments on students' attitudes toward a particular issue, such as abortion, capital punishment, or health care.

2. Write a humorous paper about campus fashion by dividing students into types. Invent titles or labels for each group, and supply enough details so that readers can readily fit the people they meet into one of your categories.

Student Paper: Division and Classification

This paper was written in response to the following assignment:

Write a 500-word paper classifying people, objects, or issues you have observed on campus. Make sure that you develop and adequately describe meaningful categories.

First Draft with Instructor's Comments

Hispanics on Campus

Delete the opening three lines—focus on the subject in your title, Hispanics on campus.

Like most groups, Hispanics are subject to stereotypes in the media. You see images of gangs, Mexican bandits, and wetbacks as if they tell the whole story of a complex and varied group. In college it is no different. Students, faculty, and administrators here tend to refer to "Hispanics" as if all Latino and Latina students belonged to a single homogenous group. But there are several different and very distinct groups. They are each different and unique. *avoid repetition*

Maybe the most politically active Hispanic students are the immigrants and children of immigrants. Many are low income. For a lot of them English is a second language and a barrier. These students feel alienated to mainstream American culture and want to assert their distinct identity.   *explain in fuller detail*   *"from"*   *need stronger transition*

Then there's another, very different group. The largest group of Hispanics are middle-class American born students, many of whom don't speak Spanish and have never been to Mexico in their whole lives. *Expand commentary*   *delete*

Then you have the group I belong to. These are people I call "invisible Hispanics" because of intermarriage they may not have Hispanic-sounding names or look "Spanish" even though they know alot about their heritage, culture, and language. I have blonde hair but speak Spanish and visit Mexico yearly.   *avoid "you have" phrases*   *run-on*   *"a lot"*   *add details*

Then you have those students who are exchange students from Central and South America. Many of them speak other languages like Italian or French. They hang out more with other foreign students. You are more likely to find them at the International House than at the Hispanic Cultural Center.   *avoid "you have"*   *slang*

Vague   It is important to understand these differences to prevent misunderstanding and discrimination. Not all Hispanics think alike. By understanding differences we can see how much we really have more in common.

REVISION NOTES

You have selected an interesting topic. Your essay, however, is not a classification essay. Remember, a classification essay must rank or grade items on a scale—not simply break a subject into parts or types. You can classify students from poorest to richest, youngest to oldest, most to least gifted, etc.

*   *Consider ranking Hispanic students on a common scale that will explain their differences. How are the immigrants different from the foreign students, the middle-class students, and the students you call "invisible"?*

*   *State your classification method in the first paragraph and provide clearer introductions and transitions for each group you describe. Avoid simply stating "another group is" or "then you have" to introduce the next type.*

Revised Draft

Hispanics on Campus

Students, faculty, and administrators tend to refer to "Hispanics" as if all Latino and Latina students belonged to a single homogeneous group. Actually, there are four distinct groups of Hispanic students. Outsiders may only see slight discrepancies in dress and behavior, but there are profound differences which occasionally border on suspicion and hostility. Their differences are best measured by their attitude toward and their degree of acceptance of mainstream American values and culture.

The least assimilated group of Hispanic students are politically active immigrants or children of immigrants. These are the students who sponsored the recent protest against Western Civilization courses. Most of them were born in Mexico or Puerto Rico. English is their second language and a perceived cultural barrier. Because of this, they tend to see European culture as oppressive, an arbitrary hurdle blocking their progress. They are keenly sensitive to the negative stereotypes of Hispanics and resent media portrayals of bandits, drug dealers, and gang members.

Equally alien to American culture but less politically active are the foreign students from Latin America. Whether they are from Mexico, Chile, or Argentina, they speak excellent English. Many have lived or studied in Europe. As citizens of their native countries, they have no insecurities about their ethnic identities and seem willing to mix socially with Americans but only if they share their upper-class values. Unlike immigrants, they feel connected to European culture. Many speak French and German in addition to Spanish and Italian. They are more likely to spend their free time at the International House than the Hispanic Center.

The most assimilated and largest group of Hispanic students are second and third generation Latinos and Latinas. Few speak more than a few Spanish phrases. Many pronounce their names with an Anglo accent, so that they say "Rammer-ez" for Ramirez. They interact with all students and consider themselves Americans. Their parents work for IBM, sell real estate, or own restaurants. These students are rarely politically active. They use the terms "Chicano," "Latino," and "Mexican American" interchangeably. Although many participate in Hispanic cultural activities on campus, they avoid political rallies. Only a few consider themselves radical, and some, especially the Cuban Americans, are extremely conservative.

There is a group of Hispanics who are so assimilated into mainstream American culture that I call them invisible. Because of intermarriage, many Hispanics have last names like O'Brien, Edelman, and Kowalski. My father is third-generation Irish. While working on an engineering project in Mexico, he met my mother, who ironically had an Irish grandmother. I was born in San Diego but spent almost every summer in Cancun with my aunt. I speak and write Spanish. I subscribe to Mexican magazines. I serve on numerous Hispanic organizations. But because of my blonde hair and my last name, Callaghan, I am frequently viewed as an outsider by Hispanics who don't speak Spanish.

QUESTIONS FOR REVIEW AND REVISION

1. What's the student's thesis?

2. How does the student define her standard of measurement?

3. What value does this classification have in understanding Hispanic students?

4. Is each class of students clearly defined? Can you think of any students you know who would not fit into one of the categories?

5. Does the student include enough examples or descriptions to explain each category of students fully?

6. Read the essay aloud. Can you detect weak or awkward passages that need revision? How effectively did the student follow the instructor's suggestions?

WRITING SUGGESTIONS

1. Using this paper as a model, write a similar classification paper about students on your campus. Classify students by academic performance, school spirit, support of athletic teams, or involvement in campus activities or politics. Remember to use a single standard or method of evaluation.

2. *Collaborative Writing*: Discuss this essay with other students. Do students in other ethnic groups fit a pattern similar to the Hispanics at the writer's college? Work together to select a group, and write a short paper that classifies them into different types.

DIVISION AND CLASSIFICATION CHECKLIST

Before submitting your paper, review these points:

1. Have you clearly defined your goal—to write a division, classification, or division and classification paper?

2. Do you make meaningful divisions or classifications, or does your paper oversimplify a complex subject?

3. Are your categories clearly defined?

4. Do you avoid overlapping categories?

5. Do you use parallel patterns to develop categories and items?

6. In division, do you explain the size and significance of each category?

7. In classification, do you use a single standard of evaluation?

8. Do all the parts of your subject clearly fit into a single category? Are there any items left over?

9. Do you explain possible exceptions or changes?

Info Write provides additional information on writing division and classification. cengage.learning.infowrite.com

CHAPTER TEN

PROCESS:EXPLAINING HOW THINGS WORK AND GIVING DIRECTIONS

WHAT IS PROCESS?

Process writing shows how things work or how specific tasks are accomplished. The first type of process writing demonstrates how a complex procedure takes place. Biology textbooks describe how the heart operates by separating its actions into a series of stages. This chain-of-events explanation also can illustrate how an engine works, how inflation affects the economy, how the IRS audits an account, how a bill becomes a law, how a volcano forms, or how police respond to a 911 call. This kind of process writing is a directed form of narration that explains step by step how a procedure or event occurs.

The second type of process writing instructs readers how to complete a specific task. Recipes, employee manuals, textbooks, and home repair articles provide readers with step-by-step directions to bake a cake, process an insurance claim, set up a stereo system, write a research paper, lose weight, or fix a leaking roof. These instructions are challenging to create because writers may be unable to determine how much background information to provide and may easily forget a critical piece of information.

Explaining How Things Work

Just as division writing seeks to explain an abstract or complex subject by separating it into smaller categories, process writing separates the workings of complicated operations into distinct parts. In explaining how humans developed different skin colors, Marvin Harris (page 421) describes the way the body absorbs sunlight:

> As it falls on the skin, sunshine converts a fatty substance in the
> epidermis into vitamin D. The blood carries vitamin D from the

skin to the intestines (technically making it a hormone rather than a vitamin), where it plays a vital role in the absorption of calcium. In turn, calcium is vital for strong bones. Without it, people fall victim to the crippling diseases rickets and osteomalacia. In women, calcium deficiencies can result in a deformed birth canal, which makes childbirth lethal for both mother and fetus.

In writing explanations, it is important to consider the knowledge base of your readers. You may have to define technical terms; make use of illustrative analogies, such as comparing the heart to a pump; and tell brief narratives so that readers understand the process. Some writers will use an extended analogy, comparing a nuclear power plant to a teakettle or a computer virus to a brush fire. One of the challenges of explanatory writing can be deciding which details to leave out and where to make separations.

Critical Thinking for Writing Explanations

1. **Study the process carefully.** Note principal features that need emphasis. Identify areas that are commonly confused or might be difficult for readers to understand.

2. **Determine how much background information is needed.** Your readers may require, for example, a basic knowledge of how normal cells divide before being able to comprehend the way cancer cells develop. In some instances, you may have to address common misconceptions. If you were to explain criminal investigation methods, you first might have to point out how actual police operations differ from those depicted on television.

3. **Determine the beginning and end of the process.** In some cases, the process may have an obvious beginning and end. Leaves emerge from buds, flower, grow, turn color, and fall off. But the process of a recession may have no clear-cut beginning and no defined end. If you were to write a paper about the process of getting a divorce, would you stop when the final papers are signed or continue to discuss alimony and child visitation rights? When does a divorce end?

4. **Separate the process into logical stages.** Readers will naturally assume all the stages are equally significant unless you indicate their value or importance. Minor points should not be overemphasized by being isolated in separate steps.

5. **Alert readers to possible variations.** If the process is subject to change or alternative forms, present readers with the most common type. Indicate,

either in the introduction or in each stage, that exceptions or variations to the pattern of events exist.

6. **Use transitional phrases to link the stages.** Statements such as "*at the same time,*" "*two hours later,*" and "*if additional bleeding occurs*" help readers follow explanations.

7. **Stress the importance of time relationships.** Process writing creates a slow-motion effect that can be misleading if the chain of events naturally occurs within a short period. You can avoid this confusion by opening with a "real-time" description of the process:

> The test car collided with the barrier at thirty-five miles an hour. In less than a tenth of a second the bumper crumpled, sending shock waves through the length of the vehicle as the fenders folded back like a crushed beer can. At the same instant sensors triggered the air bag to deploy with a rapid explosion so that it inflated before the test dummy struck the steering wheel.

The rest of the paper might repeat this process for four or five pages, slowly relating each stage in great detail.

8. **Use images, details, narratives, and examples to enrich the description of each stage.** Give readers a full appreciation of each stage by describing it in details they can grasp. Avoid long strings of nonessential, technical language. Use comparisons and narratives to provide readers with clear pictures of events and situations.

9. **Review the final draft for undefined technical terms.** Use a level of language your readers understand. Include technical terms only when necessary, and define ones your readers may not know or may find confusing.

Giving Directions

Directions are step-by-step instructions guiding readers to accomplish a specific goal or task. Process writing can include directions for buying a house or negotiating a loan. In "Fender Benders: Legal Do's and Don'ts" (page 417), Armond D. Budish gives drivers specific instructions on what to do if they are involved in a minor traffic accident:

> 1. **Stop! It's the Law.** No matter how serious or minor the accident, stop immediately. If possible, don't move your car—especially if someone has been injured. Leaving the cars as they were when the

accident occurred helps the police determine what happened. Of course, if your car is blocking traffic or will cause another accident where it is, then move it to the nearest safe location.

When giving instructions, you may find it helpful to add visual aids such as bold type, capital letters, and underlining, as well as pictures, graphs, and charts. Visual aids are commonly used in documents that must be read quickly or referred to while working. A recipe printed in standard paragraphs instead of lists and numbered steps would be extremely difficult for someone to follow while cooking. The instructions for cleaning car battery terminals on page 441 illustrate how directions can be arranged for quick, accurate reading.

Critical Thinking for Writing Directions

1. **Appreciate your responsibility.** When you give directions, you may assume a legal responsibility. If consumers or employees are injured or suffer losses following your directions, they may sue or claim damages. You cannot defend yourself after the fact by arguing that people should have known about a hazard you failed to warn them about.

2. **Write to your readers.** Determine your readers' current knowledge. They may require background information to understand the process. Readers may also have misconceptions that must be cleared up. Define and explain important terms.

3. **Make sure the directions are self-contained.** Your document should contain *all* the information needed for readers to carry out the task. *Readers should not be directed to another source for information to complete the process.*

4. **Alert readers to potential hazards.** Use all capital letters, underlining, or italics to highlight warnings and disclaimers. Warn readers about any dangers to themselves, their property, or the environment. In addition to cautioning people about physical dangers, alert them about potential legal liabilities. Remind readers to check local zoning laws or inspection requirements before remodeling their home and refer to a car's warranty before modifying their engine.

5. **Explain the cost of materials or time required to complete the process.** Homeowners thinking of installing a redwood deck might begin a project only to discover they cannot afford all the supplies needed to finish the job. Someone making a dessert for the first time may be unable to judge how much time it will take to prepare. List estimated costs or the time required in a subtitle or the first paragraph so readers can make an informed decision before proceeding. In estimating the time required, remember

that readers performing the process for the first time will take longer than an experienced professional will.

6. **Consider using numbered steps.** Readers find it easier to follow numbered steps and can mark their places if interrupted. Numbered steps also allow you to eliminate wordy transitional statements such as "The next thing you should do is . . . ."

7. **Emphasize verbs.** Begin instructions with action verbs to dramatize what readers should do: "Set the oven at 350 degrees. . . ." or "Call your supervisor. . . ."

8. **Provide complete instructions.** Readers will be performing this process for the first time and will only have your instructions to guide them. If you tell readers "place the cake in the oven for 30 minutes or until done," they will have no idea what the cake is supposed to look like at that point— should it be evenly browned, or can the center remain soft? When is it "done"? Directions should be precise:

   Bake at 350°F for 35 minutes or until edges are golden brown (Note: Center of cake may remain soft).

9. **Alert readers of possible events they may misinterpret as mistakes.** If, during the process, an engine may give off smoke or a computer slow down, readers may assume they have made a mistake or used the wrong or defective materials. Tell readers what to anticipate:

   Attach legs to desk top with screws. (NOTE: Legs will remain loose until final assembly.)

10. **Give negative instructions.** Tell readers what *not* to do, especially if you know people have a tendency to misinterpret instructions, ignore safety warnings, skip difficult steps, or substitute cheaper materials.

11. **Use maps, charts, diagrams, and photographs to help readers visualize directions.**

12. **Proofread carefully.** Make sure the names, dates, addresses, room numbers, and prices you list are accurate. *Before distributing instructions that are over a year old, verify that the information is current and correct.*

13. **Test directions before distributing them.** Because it is easy to overlook details or write misleading instructions, have other people review your document. Before emailing directions to 500 employees, you might want to send it to 20 employees and ask them if they have any questions. Send follow-up emails or call this test group to see whether there are any corrections or changes that should be made before you distribute the directions to everyone.

STRATEGIES FOR READING PROCESS

As you read the process entries in this chapter, keep these questions in mind.

Understanding Meaning

1. What is the writer's goal, to explain or to instruct?

2. Is the goal clearly stated?

3. What are the critical steps in the process?

4. What errors should readers avoid?

Evaluating Strategy

1. What is the nature of the intended audience?

2. How much existing knowledge does the writer assume readers have? Are terms explained?

3. What are the beginning and ending points of the process? Are these clearly defined?

4. How are steps or stages separated? Are the transitions clear?

5. Does the writer use paragraph breaks, numbers, bold type, or other visual prompts? Are these skillfully used?

6. Are instructions easy to follow?

7. Does the writer demonstrate the significance of the process or the value of his or her advice?

Appreciating Language

1. Are technical terms clearly defined and illustrated?

2. Does the writer use language that creates clear images of what is being explained?

MORTIMER ADLER

Mortimer Adler (1902–2001) was born in New York City. He taught psychology at Columbia University, and then moved to Chicago, where he taught the philosophy of law for more than twenty years. He resigned from the University of Chicago in 1952 to head the Institute for Philosophical Research in San Francisco. His books include How to Read a Book *and* Philosopher at Large: An Intellectual Autobiography. *Adler became famous as an editor of the* Encyclopedia Britannica *and leader of the Great Books Program of the University of Chicago. This program encouraged adults from all careers to read and discuss classic works. This essay first appeared in the* Saturday Review of Literature *in 1940.*

How to Mark a Book

CONTEXT: *Before reading Adler's essay, consider your own reading habits. Do you read with a pen in your hand? Do you scan a work first or simply begin with the first line? Do you take notes? Do you have problems remembering what you read?*

You know you have to read "between the lines" to get the most out of anything. I want to persuade you to do something equally important in the course of your reading. I want to persuade you to "write between the lines." Unless you do, you are not likely to do the most efficient kind of reading.   *1*
introduction

<u>I contend, quite bluntly, that marking up a book is not an act of mutilation but of love.</u>   *2*
thesis

You shouldn't mark up a book which isn't yours. Librarians (or your friends) who lend you books expect you to keep them clean, and you should. If you decide that I am right about the usefulness of marking books, you will have to buy them. Most of the world's great books are available today, in reprint editions, at less than a dollar.   *3*
disclaimer

<u>There are two ways in which one can own a book. The first is the property right you establish by paying for it, just as you pay for clothes and furniture. But this act of purchase is only the prelude to possession. Full ownership comes only when you have made it a part of yourself, and the best way to make yourself a part of it is by writing in it</u>. An illustration may make the point clear. You buy a beefsteak and transfer it from the butcher's icebox to your own. But you do not own the beefsteak in the most important sense until you consume it and get it into your bloodstream. I am arguing that books, too, must be absorbed in your bloodstream to do you any good.   *4*
defines "full ownership"

<u>Confusion about what it means to *own* a book leads people to a false reverence for paper, binding, and type—a respect for the physical thing—the craft of the printer rather than the genius of the author.</u> They forget that it is possible for a man to acquire the idea, to possess the beauty, which a great book   *5*

describes "false reverence for paper"

contains, without staking his claim by pasting his bookplate inside the cover. Having a fine library doesn't prove that its owner has a mind enriched by books; it proves nothing more than that he, his father, or his wife, was rich enough to buy them.

6   There are three kinds of book owners. The first has all the standard sets and best-sellers—unread, untouched. (This deluded individual owns wood pulp and ink, not books.) The second has a great many books—a few of them read through, most of them dipped into, but all of them as clean and shiny as the day they were bought. (This person would probably like to make books his own, but is restrained by a false respect for their physical appearance.) The third has a few books or many—every one of them dog-eared and dilapidated, shaken and loosened by continual use, marked and scribbled in from front to back. (This man owns books.)

classifies three types of book owners

7   Is it false respect, you may ask, to preserve intact and unblemished a beautifully printed book, an elegantly bound edition? Of course not. I'd no more scribble all over a first edition of *Paradise Lost* than I'd give my baby a set of crayons and an original Rembrandt! I wouldn't mark up a painting or a statue. Its soul, so to speak, is inseparable from its body. And the beauty of a rare edition or of a richly manufactured volume is like that of a painting or a statue.

8   But the soul of a book *can* be separated from its body. A book is more like the score of a piece of music than it is like a painting. No great musician confuses a symphony with the printed sheets of music. Arturo Toscanini reveres Brahms, but Toscanini's score of the C-minor Symphony is so thoroughly marked up that no one but the maestro himself can read it. The reason why a great conductor makes notations on his musical scores—marks them up again and again each time he returns to study them—is the reason why you should mark your books. If your respect for magnificent binding or typography gets in the way, buy yourself a cheap edition and pay your respects to the author.

9   Why is marking up a book indispensable to reading? First, it keeps you awake. (And I don't mean merely conscious; I mean wide awake.) In the second place, reading, if it is active, is thinking, and thinking tends to express itself in words, spoken or written. The marked book is usually the thought-through book. Finally, writing helps you remember the thoughts you had, or the thoughts the author expressed. Let me develop these three points.

explains need to write as you read

10   If reading is to accomplish anything more than passing time, it must be active. You can't let your eyes glide across the lines of a book and come up with an understanding of what you have read. Now an ordinary piece of light fiction, like say, *Gone with the Wind*, doesn't require the most active kind of reading. The books you read for pleasure can be read in a state of relaxation, and nothing is lost. But a great book, rich in ideas and beauty, a book that raises and tries to answer great fundamental questions, demands the most active reading of which you are capable. You don't absorb the ideas of John

defines "active reading"

Dewey the way you absorb the crooning of Mr. Vallee. You have to reach for them. That you cannot do while you're asleep.

If, when you've finished reading a book, the pages are filled with your notes, you know that you read actively. The most famous active reader of great books I know is President Hutchins, of the University of Chicago. He also has the hardest schedule of business activities of any man I know. He invariably reads with a pencil, and sometimes, when he picks up a book and pencil in the evening, he finds himself, instead of making intelligent notes, drawing what he calls "caviar factories" on the margins. When that happens, he puts the book down. He knows he's too tired to read, and he's just wasting time. 11

But, you may ask, why is writing necessary? Well, the physical act of writing, with your own hand, brings words and sentences more sharply before your mind and preserves them better in your memory. To set down your reaction to important words and sentences you have read, and the questions they have raised in your mind, is to preserve those reactions and sharpen those questions. 12 *why write?*

Even if you wrote on a scratch pad and threw the paper away when you had finished writing, your grasp of the book would be surer. But you don't have to throw the paper away. The margins (top and bottom, as well as side), the endpapers, the very space between the lines, are all available. They aren't sacred. And, best of all, your marks and notes become an integral part of the book and stay there forever. You can pick up the book the following week or year, and there are all your points of agreement, disagreement, doubt, and inquiry. It's like resuming an interrupted conversation with the advantage of being able to pick up where you left off. 13

And that is exactly what reading a book should be: a conversation between you and the author. Presumably he knows more about the subject than you do; naturally, you'll have the proper humility as you approach him. But don't let anybody tell you that a reader is supposed to be solely on the receiving end. Understanding is a two-way operation; learning doesn't consist in being an empty receptacle. The learner has to question himself and question the teacher. He even has to argue with the teacher, once he understands what the teacher is saying. And marking a book is literally an expression of your differences, or agreements of opinion, with the author. 14 *reading as conversation*

There are all kinds of devices for marking a book intelligently and fruitfully. Here's the way I do it: 15

1. *Underlining:* of major points, of important or forceful statements.

2. *Vertical lines at the margin:* to emphasize a statement already underlined.

3. *Star, asterisk, or other doo-dad at the margin:* to be used sparingly, to emphasize the ten or twenty most important statements in the book. (You

uses numbered steps and italics for easy reading

may want to fold the bottom corner of each page on which you use such marks. It won't hurt the sturdy paper on which most modern books are printed, and you will be able to take the book off the shelf at any time and, by opening it at the folded-corner page, refresh your recollection of the book.)

4. *Numbers in the margin:* to indicate the sequence of points the author makes in developing a single argument.

5. *Numbers of other pages in the margin:* to indicate where else in the book the author made points relevant to the point marked; to tie up the ideas in a book, which, though they may be separated by many pages, belong together.

6. *Circling of key words or phrases.*

7. *Writing in the margin, or at the top or bottom of the page, for the sake of:* recording questions (and perhaps answers) which a passage raised in your mind; reducing a complicated discussion to a simple statement; recording the sequence of major points right through the book. I use the end-papers at the back of the book to make a personal index of the author's points in the order of their appearance.

16 The front end-papers are, to me, the most important. Some people reserve them for a fancy bookplate. I reserve them for fancy thinking. After I have finished reading the book and making my personal index on the back end-papers, I turn to the front and try to outline the book, not page by page, or point by point (I've already done that at the back), but as an integrated structure, with a basic unity and an order of parts. This outline is, to me, the measure of my understanding of the work.

17   If you're a die-hard anti-book-marker, you may object that the margins, the space between the lines, and the end-papers don't give you room enough. All right. How about using a scratch pad slightly smaller than the page-size of the book—so that the edges of the sheets won't protrude? Make your index, outlines, and even your notes on the pad, and then insert these sheets permanently inside the front and back covers of the book.

18   Or, you may say that this business of marking books is going to slow up your reading. It probably will. That's one of the reasons for doing it. Most of us have been taken in by the notion that speed of reading is a measure of our intelligence. There is no such thing as the right speed for intelligent reading. Some things should be read quickly and effortlessly, and some should be read slowly and even laboriously. The sign of intelligence in reading is the ability to read *goal of* different things according to their worth. <u>In the case of good books, the point *reading good* is not to see how many of them you can get through, but rather how many can *books* get through you—how many you can make your own.</u> A few friends are better

than a thousand acquaintances. If this be your aim, as it should be, you will not be impatient if it takes more time and effort to read a great book than it does a newspaper.

You may have one final objection to marking books. You can't lend them to 19 your friends because nobody else can read them without being distracted by your notes. Furthermore, you won't want to lend them because a marked copy is a kind of intellectual diary, and lending it is almost like giving your mind away.

If your friend wishes to read your *Plutarch's Lives, Shakespeare,* or *The Feder-* 20 *alist Papers,* tell him gently but firmly to buy a copy. You will lend him your car *conclusion* or your coat—but your books are as much a part of you as your head or your heart.

Understanding Meaning

1. In Adler's view, when do you really *own* a book? What makes a book truly yours? What makes a book like a steak?

2. What does Adler mean by the "soul" of a book? How does respecting it differ from respecting its "body"?

3. Why is it important, in Adler's view, to write as you read?

4. *Critical Thinking:* This essay was first published more than seventy years ago. Are Adler's suggestions any different from the study skills you may have learned in high school or college?

Evaluating Strategy

1. What audience is Adler addressing?

2. *Blending the Modes:* Where does Adler use *comparison, description,* and *classification* in developing this essay?

3. Adler provides seven suggestions that are stated in italics and numbered. If this advice were written in a standard paragraph, would it be as effective? Why or why not?

Appreciating Language

1. The *Saturday Review of Literature* had a general but highly literary readership, much like that of today's *New Yorker* or *Vanity Fair.* Does the tone and style of the article seem suited to this audience?

2. Are there any words, phrases, references, or expressions in this seventy-year-old article that need updating?

1. Using Adler's seven suggestions, write a brief one-page guide to active reading directed to high school students.

2. *Collaborative Writing:* Adler presents tips for active reading. Work with a group of students and discuss their experiences in studying for examinations. Record your ideas and suggestions, and then write a well-organized list of tips to help new students develop successful study skills.

ARMOND D. BUDISH

Armond D. Budish is an attorney and consumer-law reporter. He practices law in Ohio, where he writes columns on consumer issues for the Cleveland Plain Dealer. *He has also published articles in* Family Circle *magazine. His book* How to Beat the Catastrophic Costs of Nursing Home Care *was published in 1989, and his latest book is* Avoiding the Medicaid Trap *(1996).*

Fender Benders: Legal Do's and Don'ts

CONTEXT: *As you read this article, notice how Budish makes use of numbered steps and bold type to make this* Family Circle *article easy to skim.*

The car ahead of you stops suddenly. You hit the brakes, but you just can't stop in time. Your front bumper meets the rear end of the other car. *Ouch!* 1

There doesn't seem to be any damage, and it must be your lucky day because the driver you hit agrees that it's not worth hassling with insurance claims and risking a premium increase. So after exchanging addresses, you go your separate ways. 2

Imagine your surprise when you open the mail a few weeks later only to discover a letter from your "victim's" lawyer demanding $10,000 to cover car repairs, pain and suffering. Apparently the agreeable gentleman decided to disagree, then went ahead and filed a police report blaming you for the incident and for his damages. 3

When automobiles meet by accident, do you know how to respond? Here are 10 practical tips that can help you avoid costly legal and insurance hassles. 4

1. **Stop! It's the Law.** No matter how serious or minor the accident, stop immediately. If possible, don't move your car—especially if someone has been injured. Leaving the cars as they were when the accident occurred helps the police determine what happened. Of course, if your car is blocking traffic or will cause another accident where it is, then move it to the nearest safe location. 5

   For every rule there are exceptions, though. If, for example, you are rear-ended at night in an unsafe area, it's wisest to keep on going and notify the police later. There have been cases in which people were robbed or assaulted when they got out of their cars. 6

2. **Zip Loose Lips.** Watch what you say after an accident. Although this may sound harsh, even an innocent "I'm sorry" could later be construed as an 7

admission of fault. Also be sure not to accuse the other driver of causing the accident. Since you don't know how a stranger will react to your remarks, you run the risk of making a bad situation worse.

8   Remember, you are not the judge or jury; it's not up to you to decide who is or is not at fault. Even if you think you caused the accident, you might be wrong. For example: Assume you were driving 15 miles over the speed limit. What you probably were not aware of is that the other driver's blood-alcohol level exceeded the legal limits, so he was at least equally at fault.

9   **3. Provide Required Information.** If you are involved in an accident, you are required in most states to give your name, address and car registration number to: any person injured in the accident; the owner, driver or passenger in any car that was damaged in the accident; a police officer on the scene. If you don't own the car (say it belongs to a friend or your parents), you should provide the name and address of the owner.

10   You must produce this information even if there are no apparent injuries or damages and even if you didn't cause the accident. Most states don't require you to provide the name of your insurance company, although it's usually a good idea to do so. However, *don't* discuss the amount of your coverage—that might inspire the other person to "realize" his injuries are more serious than he originally thought.

11   What should you do if you hit a parked car and the owner is not around? The law requires you to leave a note with your name, and the other identifying information previously mentioned, in a secure place on the car (such as under the windshield wiper).

12   **4. Get Required Information.** You should obtain from the others involved in the accident the same information that you provide them with. However, if the other driver refuses to cooperate, at least get the license number and the make and model of the car to help police track down the owner.

13   **5. Call the Police.** It's obvious that if it's a serious accident in which someone is injured, the police should be called immediately. That's both the law and common sense. But what if the accident seems minor? Say you're stopped, another car taps you in the rear. If it's absolutely clear to both drivers that there is no damage or injury, you each can go your merry way. But that's the exception.

14   Normally, you should call the police to substantiate what occurred. In most cities police officers will come to the scene, even for minor accidents, but if they won't, you and the other driver should go to the station (of the city where the accident occurred) to file a report. Ask to have an officer check out both cars.

15   If you are not at fault, be wary of accepting the other driver's suggestion that you leave the police out of it and arrange a private settlement. When

you submit your $500 car-repair estimate several weeks later, you could discover that the other driver has developed "amnesia" and denies being anywhere near the accident. If the police weren't present on the scene, you may not have a legal leg to stand on.

Even if you *are* at fault, it's a good idea to involve the police. Why? Because a police officer will note the extent of the other driver's damages in his or her report, limiting your liability. Without police presence the other driver can easily inflate the amount of the damages. 16

6. **Identify Witnesses.** Get the names and addresses of any witnesses, in case there's a legal battle some time in the future. Ask bystanders or other motorists who stop whether they saw the accident; if they answer "yes," get their identifying information. It is also helpful to note the names and badge numbers of all police officers on the scene. 17

7. **Go to the Hospital.** If there's a chance that you've been injured, go directly to a hospital emergency room or to your doctor. The longer you wait, the more you may jeopardize your health and the more difficult it may be to get reimbursed for your injuries if they turn out to be serious. 18

8. **File a Report.** Every driver who is involved in an automobile incident in which injuries occur must fill out an accident report. Even if the property damage is only in the range of $200 to $1,000, most states require that an accident report be filed. You must do this fairly quickly, usually in 1 to 30 days. Forms may be obtained and filed with the local motor vehicle department or police station in the city where the accident occurred. 19

9. **Consider Filing an Insurance Claim.** Talk with your insurance agent as soon as possible after an accident. He or she can help you decide whether you should file an insurance claim or pay out of your own pocket. 20

For example, let's say you caused an accident and the damages totaled $800. You carry a $250 deductible, leaving you with a possible $550 insurance claim. If you do submit a claim, your insurance rates are likely to go up, an increase that will probably continue for about three years. You should compare that figure to the $550 claim to determine whether to file a claim or to pay the cost yourself. (Also keep in mind that multiple claims sometimes make it harder to renew your coverage.) 21

10. **Don't Be Too Quick to Accept a Settlement.** If the other driver is at fault and there's any chance you've been injured, don't rush to accept a settlement from that person's insurance company. You may not know the extent of your injuries for some time, and once you accept a settlement, it's difficult to get an "upgrade." Before settling, consult with a lawyer who handles personal injury cases. 22

23   When you *haven't* been injured and you receive a fair offer to cover the damage to your car, you can go ahead and accept it.

Understanding Meaning

1. What problems can motorists run into if they are careless about handling even minor accidents?

2. What are some of the most important things you should do if involved in a fender bender?

3. Why should you go to the hospital even if you have what appears to be a minor injury?

4. *Critical Thinking:* Should this article be printed as a pamphlet and distributed to drivers' education classes? Have you known anyone who has encountered difficulties that could have been avoided if he or she had followed the writer's advice?

Evaluating Strategy

1. How does Budish arouse reader attention in the opening?

2. How effective are the numbered steps? Would the article lose impact if it were printed in standard paragraphs?

3. How easy is this article to remember? Can you put it down and recall the main points?

Appreciating Language

1. This article was written for *Family Circle*. Does the choice of language appear targeted to a female audience?

2. Why does Budish, who is an attorney, avoid legal terminology?

3. Does Budish's language create concrete images that make strong impressions and dramatize his subject?

WRITING SUGGESTIONS

1. Using this article as a model, provide the general public with a similar list of tips to prevent heart disease, deter muggers, prepare children for school, save money for retirement, or provide tips on a topic of your choice.

2. *Collaborative Writing:* Work with a group of students to provide tips for new students on campus. Use peer review to make sure you do not overlook details in writing your student guide.

MARVIN HARRIS

Marvin Harris (1927–2001) was born in Brooklyn and received degrees from Columbia University. After teaching at Columbia for many years, Harris moved to the University of Florida, where he served as a graduate research professor in anthropology. Harris conducted research in Harlem, Africa, South America, and Asia. He published several scholarly works but is best known for books written for general readers, such as Cows, Pigs, Wars, and Witches: The Riddles of Culture *and* Cannibals and Kings: The Origins of Cultures. *Much of Harris's work focused on how people's basic needs for food and shelter influence their culture.*

How Our Skins Got Their Color

CONTEXT: *In this essay from* Our Kind: Who We Are, Where We Came From, Where We Are Going *(1988), Harris explains how human beings developed different skin colors. In reading this account, determine how he addresses a topic laden with controversy.*

Most human beings are neither very fair nor very dark, but brown. The extremely fair skin of northern Europeans and their descendants, and the very black skins of central Africans and their descendants, are probably special adaptations. Brown-skinned ancestors may have been shared by modern-day blacks and whites as recently as ten thousand years ago. 1

Human skin owes its color to the presence of particles known as melanin. The primary function of melanin is to protect the upper levels of the skin from being damaged by the sun's ultraviolet rays. This radiation poses a critical problem for our kind because we lack the dense coat of hair that acts as a sunscreen for most mammals. Hairlessness exposes us to two kinds of radiation hazards: ordinary sunburn, with its blisters, rashes, and risk of infection; and skin cancers, including malignant melanoma, one of the deadliest diseases known. Melanin is the body's first line of defense against these afflictions. The more melanin particles, the darker the skin, and the lower the risk of sunburn and all forms of skin cancer. This explains why the highest rates for skin cancer are found in sun-drenched lands such as Australia, where light-skinned people of European descent spend a good part of their lives outdoors wearing scanty attire. Very dark-skinned people such as heavily pigmented Africans of Zaire seldom get skin cancer, but when they do, they get it on depigmented parts of their bodies—palms and lips. 2

If exposure to solar radiation had nothing but harmful effects, natural selection would have favored inky black as the color for all human populations. But the sun's rays do not present an unmitigated threat. As it falls on the skin, sunshine converts a fatty substance in the epidermis into vitamin D. The 3 blood carries vitamin D from the skin to the intestines (technically making it a hormone rather than a vitamin), where it plays a vital role in the absorption of calcium. In turn, calcium is vital for strong bones. Without it, people fall victim to the crippling diseases rickets and osteomalacia. In women, calcium deficiencies can result in a deformed birth canal, which makes childbirth lethal for both mother and fetus.

4   Vitamin D can be obtained from a few foods, primarily the oils and livers of marine fish. But inland populations must rely on the sun's rays and their own skins for the supply of this crucial substance. The particular color of a human population's skin, therefore, represents in large degree a trade-off between the hazards of too much versus too little solar radiation: acute sunburn and skin cancer on the one hand, and rickets and osteomalacia on the other. It is this trade-off that largely accounts for the preponderance of brown people in the world and for the general tendency for skin color to be darkest among equatorial populations and lightest among populations dwelling at higher latitudes.

5   At middle latitudes, the skin follows a strategy of changing colors with the seasons. Around the Mediterranean basin, for example, exposure to the summer sun brings high risk of cancer but low risk for rickets; the body produces more melanin and people grow darker (i.e., they get suntans). Winter reduces the risk of sunburn and cancer; the body produces less melanin, and the tan wears off.

6   The correlation between skin color and latitude is not perfect because other factors—such as the availability of foods containing vitamin D and calcium, regional cloud cover during the winter, amount of clothing worn, and cultural preferences—may work for or against the predicted relationship. Arctic-dwelling Eskimos, for example, are not as light-skinned as expected, but their habitat and economy afford them a diet that is exceptionally rich in both vitamin D and calcium.

7   Northern Europeans, obliged to wear heavy garments for protection against the long, cold, cloudy winters, were always at risk for rickets and osteomalacia from too little vitamin D and calcium. This risk increased sometime after 6000 B.C., when pioneer cattle herders who did not exploit marine resources began to appear in northern Europe. The risk would have been especially great for the brown-skinned Mediterranean peoples who migrated northward along with the crops and farm animals. Samples of Caucasian skin (infant penile foreskin obtained at the time of circumcision) exposed to sunlight on cloudless days in Boston (42°N) from November through February produced no vitamin D. In Edmonton (52°N) this period extended from October to March. But further south (34°N) sunlight was effective in producing vitamin D in the middle of the winter. Almost all of Europe lies north of 42°N. Fair-skinned, nontanning individuals who could utilize the weakest and briefest doses of sunlight to synthesize vitamin D were strongly favored by natural

selection. During the frigid winters, only a small circle of a child's face could be left to peek out at the sun through the heavy clothing, thereby favoring the survival of individuals with translucent patches of pink on their cheeks characteristic of many northern Europeans....

If light-skinned individuals on the average had only 2 percent more chil- 8 dren survive per generation, the changeover in their skin color could have begun five thousand years ago and reached present levels well before the beginning of the Christian era. But natural selection need not have acted alone. Cultural selection may also have played a role. It seems likely that whenever people consciously or unconsciously had to decide which infants to nourish and which to neglect, the advantage would go to those with lighter skin, experience having shown that such individuals tended to grow up to be taller, stronger, and healthier than their darker siblings. White was beautiful because white was healthy.

To account for the evolution of black skin in equatorial latitudes, one has 9 merely to reverse the combined effects of natural and cultural selection. With the sun directly overhead most of the year, and clothing a hindrance to work and survival, vitamin D was never in short supply (and calcium was easily obtained from vegetables). Rickets and osteomalacia were rare. Skin cancer was the main problem, and what nature started, culture amplified. Darker infants were favored by parents because experience showed that they grew up to be freer of disfiguring and lethal malignancies. Black was beautiful because black was healthy.

Understanding Meaning

1. What is Harris's thesis?

2. What is the "natural" color for human skin?

3. What caused people to develop different complexions?

4. What role did sunlight play in human evolution?

5. *Critical Thinking:* What impact could this scientific explanation of skin color have on debates about race and discrimination? Can biological aspects of humanity be separated from social, cultural, political, or psychological attitudes?

Evaluating Strategy

1. How does Harris organize his essay?

2. What research does Harris use to support his views?

3. *Blending the Modes:* Where does Harris use *narration, comparison,* and *definition* in his explanation?

Appreciating Language

1. How does Harris define "melanin"?

2. Does Harris's selection of words describing color contain connotations that suggest a bias? Is his essay wholly objective? How often does he use words such as "white" and "black"?

3. Would the average newspaper reader be able to understand this essay? What does the level of language suggest about the intended audience?

WRITING SUGGESTIONS

1. Using this essay for background information, draft a brief explanation about skin color for an elementary school brochure on race relations. Use easily understood language, and employ comparisons and short narratives to explain scientific principles. Avoid words that may have negative connotations.

2. *Critical Writing:* Write an essay analyzing the effect reading this essay had on you. Did it affect your attitudes toward people of different races? Does the knowledge that all humans probably once shared the same complexion change the way you view yourself?

3. *Collaborative Writing:* Discuss Harris's essay with a group of students. What role does a scientific explanation of skin color have in addressing racial problems? Would it be beneficial to share this information with children? Record members' reactions and create a short statement about the importance of understanding the origins of skin color. If members disagree, consider developing pro and con responses.

ANNE WEISBORD

Anne Weisbord has a master's degree in education and served as director of Career Services at Hahnemann University in Philadelphia before beginning a career as a private career counselor. Widely published, she has appeared on radio and television providing advice on careers, job search strategies, and interviewing. In this article, written for Nurse Extra, Weisbord tells nurses how to write effective resumes.

Resumes That Rate a Second Look

CONTEXT: *Although directed to nurses, Weisbord's advice applies to most professionals. As you read the article, notice how her terse, to-the-point phrases mirror the kind of writing found on most resumes.*

In today's business and professional environment—in which healthcare positions can be eliminated STAT—every nurse should have a resume ready to send to potential employers. 1

The purpose of the resume is to get you a job interview. Employers use resumes to screen out undesirable, or less desirable, candidates. Your resume should summarize your skills and experience, and convince employers of the value they will gain in hiring you. It's an advertisement for yourself, and as with all ads, it should generate interest and motivate the reader. 2

Before you prepare your resume, take a few moments to consider your marketable skills. Identify the strengths and accomplishments that are relevant to the position you are seeking, and present them as succinctly and as clearly as possible. You'll need to organize all of this information in no more than two pages, in an easy-to-read, attractive format. Beyond this, there are really no hard-and-fast rules about writing resumes. 3

Let's look at the standard components of the traditional resume that presents your relevant nursing background in reverse chronological order. 4

1. **Personal identification.** You need include only your name, degree, and your professional certification, address, and phone number. Omit date of birth, marital status, and health; these can be discriminatory factors in hiring. 5

2. **Career objective.** This is optional. If you know *exactly* what you want to do, you can use a phrase that describes the type and level of position you are seeking. An objective might be "Nurse Coordinator in Pediatrics," or "Nurse Manager, ICU." However, if you would consider a variety of positions, skip the objective and use only a summary. 6

3. **Summary.** Describe your background in a few punchy sentences. This is the "hook" that will pique the reader's interest in the rest of the resume. 7

8   **4. Professional experience.** List names, places, job titles, and dates of employment. Link your experience to your summary or objective. Stress accomplishments and emphasize responsibilities that will impress the potential employer. Use brief phrases with vivid verbs and nouns to describe the skills essential to each position. Omit obvious duties. Emphasize accomplishments with bullets.

9   As you go back into your work history, present fewer details. When you first became a nurse, you naturally had fewer responsibilities. Devote more space to higher-level, more professional duties.

10   **5. Education.** If you are a recent graduate with little nursing experience, put education before professional experience. Always list the most recent school, degree or certificate program and work backward. Do include honors or academic awards. Don't list high school. If you have a college degree, the employer will assume you earned a high-school diploma.

11   **6. Professional certification(s).** List certifications in reverse chronological order or organize them according to specialty areas.

12   **7. License(s).** List only the state and title of each professional license. Don't give your license number(s). You will be asked to provide them later in the interview process.

13   **8. Activities.** No one will hire you for a healthcare position based on your interest in golf or coin collecting, but volunteer community involvement shows positive personal characteristics. Be careful about listing political or religious activities. Your reader may have biases against your persuasions.

14   Remember that your resume serves as a first impression of you. To a potential employer, your coffee-stained copy or your misspellings say something about your attention (or lack of attention) to detail, your neatness, and even your attitude. Also, modesty is not an asset in a resume. Toot your own horn!

Understanding Meaning

1. Summarize Weisbord's key points on resumes.

2. What is the purpose of a resume? Why does this seemingly obvious fact need to be explained? Do many people have misconceptions about resumes?

3. What information does Weisbord suggest omitting? Why?

4. *Critical Thinking:* What is the context of a resume? How does this document reflect the roles of writer, audience, and discipline?

Evaluating Strategy

1. How effective is the format of Weisbord's article?

2. Weisbord tells readers "there are really no hard-and-fast rules about writing resumes." Why is this important?

3. How does her article mirror the document she is training readers to write?

Appreciating Language

1. How effective are Weisbord's style and choice of words? Is the article readable?

2. How does Weisbord's emphasis on verbs, "*Describe* your background...." and "*List* names, places...." (italics added), reflect the kind of language found on most resumes?

WRITING SUGGESTIONS

1. If you have not written a resume already, draft one, adopting Weisbord's advice.

2. *Collaborative Writing:* Meet with a group of students and review each other's resumes. Select the best features you discover, and then write a brief process essay explaining step-by-step how to create an effective resume.

EUGENE RAUDSEPP

Eugene Raudsepp was president of Princeton Creative Research Inc., based in New Jersey. An expert on job interviewing techniques, Raudsepp published over fifty articles in National Business Employment Weekly *between 1984 and 1995, and wrote over seven hundred articles for publications around the world. His books include* Creative Growth Games *(1977),* How to Create New Ideas for Corporate Profit and Personal Success *(1982),* The World's Best Thoughts on Success and Failure *(1981), and* What the Executive Should Know About Creating and Selling Ideas *(1966).*

Seeing Your Way Past
Interview Jitters

CONTEXT: *This article, directed toward engineers, instructs candidates to use a psychological technique called visualization to improve their performance during job interviews.*

1   It is not unusual to experience a mild attack of nerves before a job interview. But there are engineers whose interview jitters are intense enough to be harmful. They have such overwhelming apprehension and fear that they either become tongue-tied or proceed to talk themselves out of the job. Even many capable and articulate engineers act stiff and awkward in interviews, often fidgeting or sitting on the edge of the chair.

2   When we're anxious, we frequently become self-conscious spectators of our own behavior during interviews, observing and judging our every utterance and movement. This not only makes us more anxious and less convincing, but also divides our attention.

3   Excessive self-consciousness is particularly true among engineers who go to interviews with a do-or-die attitude. Trying too hard to succeed increases tension and reduces effectiveness. "The self-imposed pressure of trying to ace an interview can make some people focus too much on how they look and act," says Steven Berglas, a psychiatry instructor at Harvard Medical School. He feels that those who are overly conscious of their grooming, speech, body language, and other interviewing behavior frequently "suppress those elements of their personality that won them the interview in the first place."

4   Perfectionist engineers particularly experience high anxiety during job interviews. Because they have a strong need to do well and have such inflated expectations of their own performance, any real or imaginary deviation from their self-imposed high, and often unrealistic, standards triggers excessive nervousness and self-critical ruminations. From one slight, innocuous mistake they automatically assume the entire interview will turn out badly.

This anticipation often drives them to behaviors and statements that 5 would seem self-sabotage to an innocent bystander.

REDUCING TENSION

Although you may feel your blood pressure rise, palms moisten, and stomach 6 tighten before an important interview, you can control these reactions.

According to H. Anthony Medley, author of *Sweaty Palms: The Neglected* 7 *Art of Being Interviewed*, there are four sound reasons why you have nothing to fear but fear itself, and they can help you keep an interview in perspective:

1. The interview centers on the subject you know best: yourself.

2. If you've done your homework, you have a decided advantage: You know more about the interviewer's company than it knows about you.

3. Interviewers expect job candidates to be a bit nervous.

4. You have nothing to lose. You didn't have the job offer before the interview, so if you don't have it afterward, you're no worse off.

Some interview failures may be inevitable. Most engineers have experienced at 8 least one. The important point is to refrain from exaggerating the importance of an interview situation. Also, if possible, generate several interviews; don't pin your hopes on just one. A winning-at-all-costs attitude seldom wins a job offer. 9

It is detrimental to adopt a confrontational stance with the interviewer. If you feel overly tense or belligerent, it is helpful to pretend that the interviewer is a good friend. A little make-believe can go a long way toward calming hostile feelings.

One interesting method of lessening interview stress is suggested by 10 Lawrence Darius, president of Corporate Communication Skills Inc., New York. He is convinced that one of the more effective ways to overcome interview jitters is to separate yourself from your performance. "Just as an actor or actress creates the character in a script, you must try to create a character for the position you're seeking," he explains. "You probably have an image of the ideal engineer or, better yet, of the perfect candidates for the job. How do they differ from you? How do they walk, talk, and act?"

Daralee Schulman, a New York City–based career counselor, teaches her 11 clients to relax before an interview by doing this exercise: "Visualize a serene and beautiful scene, perhaps a moonlit beach, while becoming aware of the rhythm of your breathing. On each breath in, think 'I am' and on each breath out, think 'calm.' Ten repetitions of 'I am calm' breathing done in the reception area before an interview can ease your tension." A "reliving" of a past interview in which you did well boosts your self-confidence, too.

12   A more advanced and exceedingly effective breathing technique is offered by Dan Lang, who conducts stress-reducing workshops in New York. First, exhale totally, imagining that you are relaxing all your tension. Next, close your mouth and place your right thumb on your right nostril so that it is completely closed. Then slowly and deeply inhale and exhale through your left nostril a couple of minutes, or 25 to 30 times. This enables you to tap into the right hemisphere of your brain, particularly the limbic part that governs emotions. You will experience an immediate reduction of fear and anxiety, resulting in a more relaxed, in-charge feeling.

THE POWER OF VISUALIZATION

13   Many top athletes experience almost overwhelming stress before important events. However, most of them have learned—through the new sports psychology of visualization—how to manage performance anxiety, improve concentration, and enhance athletic performance.

14   Tennis champion Chris Evert, for example, used to carefully and repeatedly visualize every detail of an upcoming championship match in her mind's eye. She pictured her opponent's style and form, and then visualized how she would counter and respond to every possible maneuver or tactic.

15   Golf great Jack Nicklaus programs his "bio-computer" for success this way: "I never hit a shot, even in practice, without having a sharp, in-focus picture of it in my head. It's like a color movie. First, I 'see' the ball where I want it to finish. I 'see' the ball going there: its path, trajectory, and shape. The next scene shows me making the kind of swing that will turn the previous image into reality."

16   There are significant emotional parallels between sports and job interviews. Through visualizing your ideal interview performance, you can build confidence and reduce anxiety to manageable levels.

17   Visualization of a successful interview is impressed upon the memory. When the actual event happens, there is complete confidence of success, as if one had done it before with a positive outcome.

Understanding Meaning

1. Does Raudsepp suggest engineers suffer from more anxiety at interviews than other professionals?

2. Describe the process of visualization in your own words. Why does it work?

3. Why does "trying too hard" often defeat a candidate interviewing for a job?

4. What does Raudsepp tell engineers not to do?

5. *Critical Thinking:* Could these techniques aid students facing an oral exam or essay test? Could visualizing your completed paper help in the writing process?

Evaluating Strategy

1. How effective are the examples Raudsepp uses for support?

2. How does Raudsepp reinforce his views with quotes from other authorities? Why is this important when giving advice?

Appreciating Language

1. What kind of language does Raudsepp use in explaining psychological techniques to engineers? How might this article be stated if written for a psychology journal?

2. Would the tone and style of the article help ease a reader's anxiety about facing a job interview? Explain.

WRITING SUGGESTIONS

1. Write a narrative essay about a job interview you have had. At the end, provide a brief analysis of your performance. Could it have been better?

2. *Collaborative Writing:* Discuss job interview experiences with a group of students. Ask the members about the toughest questions they were asked. Have the members suggest possible answers. Collect the comments, and collaborate on a process paper: "How to Handle Tough Questions in a Job Interview."

LIZ GRINSLADE

Liz Grinslade is vice president of MSI Healthcare, a national executive search firm that specializes in locating professionals for health care providers. In this 1993 article published in Healthcare Financial Management, *she tells executives how to evaluate a job opportunity.*

Evaluating a Job Opportunity

CONTEXT: *Grinslade's advice is directed toward health care professionals but applies to almost anyone considering a job offer. Her article is important because for some people, taking the wrong job can do more damage to their careers than not being hired.*

1 For financial managers, as well as other job candidates, the decision to accept or reject a position offered during the job hunting process can be a difficult one. However, if eight basic areas are investigated and considered, the decision to accept or reject an offer can be made more easily. During the job interview, the job candidate should try and obtain information that will help answer the following questions:

1. Will the work be fulfilling and challenging?

2. What skills are necessary to be successful at the job? If the skills are not already possessed, can they readily be developed?

3. Is the facility stable? Is the position stable?

4. Is the management philosophy acceptable?

5. Is there good chemistry between the job candidate and the hiring manager and prospective coworkers?

6. Is the location satisfying?

7. Will there be opportunities for continuing growth and new challenges?

8. Is the compensation fair and equitable?

2 The answers to these questions can lead a job candidate to the right decision.

3 *What skills are necessary to be successful at the job? If the skills are not already possessed, can they readily be developed?* The candidate should consider the scope of responsibilities of the position, as well as the expectations of others, including the facility's administrator, board of directors, and hiring manager. The candidate should try and determine if these expectations are realistic. One way to gather relevant information is to ask what was liked and what was disliked about the performance of the employee previously in the position.

Lynn Boltuch, business office director at Mount Sinai Medical Center of   4
Greater Miami, Miami, Florida, suggests that job applicants try to ascertain
whether a company is genuinely anxious to hire someone who can make
changes to improve operations. Has the company identified specific problems
in a department that need to be solved? If the company is seeking a turn-
around specialist, will the person hired be given the autonomy, resources, and
support needed to make necessary changes? How many layers of management
will be involved in making decisions? What are the administrator's overall
goals for the position? Are schedules established for implementation of
change and does meeting the schedule seem feasible? Are staffing levels
adequate?

Is the facility stable? Is the position stable? Employers expect a job applicant to   5
inquire about a facility's current financial condition. (For independent
verification, a Medicare cost report on U.S. healthcare facilities is available for
$75 through the Center for Healthcare Industry Performance Studies—
CHIPS—in Columbus, Ohio.) If recent financial reports have not been positive, consider the trend. Is the facility's financial position cyclical and approaching an upswing or does an ongoing downslide seem probable? While
asking about the financial picture, the job candidate should note not only what
the hiring manager says but also the confidence level of his or her response.

There are other aspects of stability that should be explored. For instance,   6
the candidate should try to ascertain why the position is open. Has someone
been promoted within the system or has there been a "revolving door" of
CFOs who could not work with the administrator or the board? What are the
market conditions? Are there two other competing hospitals of similar or
larger size in the immediate service area? And how tough is the managed care
environment?

Is the management philosophy acceptable? Is there good chemistry between the job   7
candidate and the hiring manager and prospective coworkers? Overall job satisfaction may rest with the answers to these questions. To assess the management
philosophy, the candidate should inquire about the priorities for the position
and how they should be accomplished. Job candidates should be able to adapt
to new ways of doing things and, just as important, organizations should be
open to employees' suggestions for change.

The job candidate also should ask other staff members, such as the chief op-   8
erating officer or director of personnel, about the administrator's management
style. How does the administrator react in different situations? Is he or she
emotional and erratic? Does he or she avoid confrontations at all costs?
Boltuch says one factor that determines how well a job candidate will enjoy
working with a hiring manager is noting how the manager makes the candidate feel upon entering the office for the first interview. Did the manager
make the candidate feel at ease or "on display"?

9   When it comes to evaluating the chemistry between the candidate and the management team and other coworkers, the candidate should make a point of meeting as many people he or she would come in contact with in a position as soon as possible. Meeting off-site is preferable. A lot more can be learned over a casual lunch than in a potential coworker's office. "Gut" feelings should be given strong consideration when evaluating the position.

10   *Is the location satisfying?* If accepting the position means moving to another city, the job candidate should make a list of important considerations, including climate, affordability, quality of school systems, proximity to family and friends, potential cultural and recreational activities, and educational opportunities. The needs of the candidate's spouse should not be forgotten.

11   Cost of living also can be a significant factor to weigh in making a decision. Using the cost-of-living index, produced by the American Chamber of Commerce Researchers Association, the candidate can compare the relative cost of living in a city. The index is updated quarterly and is available at most libraries.

12   *Will there be opportunities for continuing growth and new challenges?* By asking about the organizational structure of a facility, a potential career path can be outlined. Are there higher positions within the company that can be pursued in the future? Have specific situations been mentioned where individuals have been promoted internally? Does the organization provide tuition reimbursement for advanced degrees? Does the organization support/pay for membership in professional associations? In addition to paying for membership, does the organization also allow for time off to attend meetings or serve as a volunteer on committees? All of these factors can indicate the potential for future advancement.

13   *Is the compensation fair and equitable?* The candidate should gather information about competitive salary structures from mentors, human resource departments, executive recruiters, and professional associations. HFMA periodically surveys and publishes salary data for CFOs and patient accounts managers. But money is only one of many factors to consider.

14   The old "rule of thumb" requiring a certain percentage of increase in compensation to change jobs is no longer valid. Many healthcare financial professionals accept lateral salary moves or even lower salaries to gain valuable experience from a particular position. Opting for a higher salary at the expense of quality of life or job satisfaction can be a poor trade-off.

Understanding Meaning

1. What key issues should people consider before accepting a job?

2. In their eagerness to accept jobs, what problems can people create for themselves?

3. What questions should an applicant ask about the employer?

4. Why does Grinslade suggest that a high salary is sometimes worth passing over?

5. *Critical Thinking:* Does Grinslade's article suggest that many people, including skilled professionals, are too passive in the job process? Do people fail to interview their potential employers? Are they too trusting? Do you think many people feel they will be perceived as being rude or ungrateful if they seem critical of an organization offering them a job?

Evaluating Strategy

1. How effectively is the article organized? Are points easy to follow?

2. How does Grinslade use transitions?

3. Grinslade offers sources for gaining further information. Do many other writers fail to do this?

Appreciating Language

1. This article is directed to financial managers in the health care industry. Would it require much rewriting to be reprinted in a sales, engineering, or computer magazine?

2. Grinslade uses clichés such as "rule of thumb" and "'gut' feelings." Are these appropriate phrases in this context?

WRITING SUGGESTIONS

1. Have you ever been burned by a job that did not work out? Were you hired, only to find that the company was facing bankruptcy or that you would not receive the equipment or resources needed to do the job? Write a narrative essay about your experience.

2. *Collaborative Writing:* Meet with a group of students, and discuss experiences, both good and bad, with job opportunities. Take notes, and write a process essay similar to Grinslade's offering advice on evaluating job offers. You may wish to target your essay to college students seeking part-time or summer jobs.

MALCOLM X

Malcolm X (1925–1964) was born Malcolm Little in Omaha, Nebraska, where his father was a preacher. While in prison for robbery, Malcolm Little converted to the Black Muslim faith. He changed his last name to X to reject his "slave name" and demonstrate African Americans' loss of heritage. He became a rising force in the Nation of Islam, and in 1963 was named its first "national minister." After a trip to Mecca, he converted to orthodox Islam and rejected the racial views advocated by Black Muslims. He founded the Muslim Mosque, Inc., in 1964. A year later, he was shot and killed at a Harlem rally.

My First Conk

CONTEXT: *In this section of his autobiography, Malcolm X explains the process of "conking," or straightening hair, popular with some African Americans in the 1940s and 1950s. As you read this essay, note how Malcolm X explains the process, and then uses it as an example to develop an analysis and persuasive argument about black identity.*

1   Shorty soon decided that my hair was finally long enough to be conked. He had promised to school me in how to beat the barbershops' three- and four dollar price by making up congolene, and then conking ourselves.

2   I took the little list of ingredients he had printed out for me, and went to a grocery store, where I got a can of Red Devil lye, two eggs, and two medium-sized white potatoes. Then at a drugstore near the poolroom, I asked for a large jar of Vaseline, a large bar of soap, a large-toothed comb and a fine-toothed comb, one of those rubber hoses with a metal spray-head, a rubber apron and a pair of gloves.

3   "Going to lay on that first conk?" the drugstore man asked me. I proudly told him, grinning, "Right!"

4   Shorty paid six dollars a week for a room in his cousin's shabby apartment. His cousin wasn't at home. "It's like the pad's mine, he spends so much time with his woman," Shorty said. "Now, you watch me—"

5   He peeled the potatoes and thin-sliced them into a quart-sized Mason fruit jar, then started stirring them with a wooden spoon as he gradually poured in a little over half the can of lye. "Never use a metal spoon; the lye will turn it black," he told me.

6   A jelly-like, starchy-looking glop resulted from the lye and potatoes, and Shorty broke in the two eggs, stirring real fast—his own conk and dark face bent down close. The congolene turned pale-yellowish. "Feel the jar," Shorty

said. I cupped my hand against the outside, and snatched it away. "Damn right, it's hot, that's the lye," he said. "So you know it's going to burn when I comb it in—it burns bad. But the longer you can stand it, the straighter the hair."

He made me sit down, and he tied the string of the new rubber apron 7 tightly around my neck, and combed up my bush of hair. Then, from the big Vaseline jar, he took a handful and massaged it hard all through my hair and into the scalp. He also thickly Vaselined my neck, ears and forehead. "When I get to washing out your head, be sure to tell me anywhere you feel any little stinging," Shorty warned me, washing his hands, then pulling on the rubber gloves, and tying on his own rubber apron. "You always got to remember that any congolene left in burns a sore into your head."

The congolene just felt warm when Shorty started combing it in. But then 8 my head caught fire.

I gritted my teeth and tried to pull the sides of the kitchen table together. 9 The comb felt as if it was raking my skin off.

My eyes watered, my nose was running. I couldn't stand it any longer; 10 I bolted to the washbasin. I was cursing Shorty with every name I could think of when he got the spray going and started soap-lathering my head.

He lathered and spray-rinsed, lathered and spray-rinsed, maybe ten or 11 twelve times, each time gradually closing the hot-water faucet, until the rinse was cold, and that helped some.

"You feel any stinging spots?"　　　　　　　　　　　　　　　　　　　12

"No," I managed to say. My knees were trembling.　　　　　　　　　13

"Sit back down, then. I think we got it all out okay."　　　　　　　　14

The flame came back as Shorty, with a thick towel, started drying my head, 15 rubbing hard. "*Easy, man, easy!*" I kept shouting.

"The first time's always worst. You get used to it better before long. You took 16 it real good, homeboy. You got a good conk."

When Shorty let me stand up and see in the mirror, my hair hung down in 17 limp, damp strings. My scalp still flamed, but not as badly; I could bear it. He draped the towel around my shoulders, over my rubber apron, and began again Vaselining my hair.

I could feel him combing, straight back, first the big comb, then the fine- 18 tooth one.

Then, he was using a razor, very delicately, on the back of my neck. Then 19 finally, shaping the sideburns.

My first view in the mirror blotted out the hurting. I'd seen some pretty 20 conks, but when it's the first time, on your own head, the transformation, after the lifetime of kinks, is staggering.

The mirror reflected Shorty behind me. We both were grinning and on top 21 of my head was this thick, smooth sheen of shining red hair—real red—as straight as any white man's.

22   How ridiculous I was! Stupid enough to stand there simply lost in admiration of my hair now looking "white," reflected in the mirror in Shorty's room. I vowed that I'd never again be without a conk, and I never was for many years.

23   This was my first really big step toward self-degradation: when I endured all of that pain, literally burning my flesh to have it look like a white man's hair. I had joined that multitude of Negro men and women in America who are brainwashed into believing that the black people are "inferior"—and white people "superior"—that they will even violate and mutilate their God-created bodies to try to look "pretty" by white standards.

24   Look around today, in every small town and big city, from two-bit catfish and soda-pop joints into the "integrated" lobby of the Waldorf-Astoria, and you'll see conks on black men. And you'll see black women wearing these green and pink and purple and red and platinum-blonde wigs. They're all more ridiculous than a slapstick comedy. It makes you wonder if the Negro has completely lost his sense of identity, lost touch with himself.

25   You'll see the conk worn by many, many so-called "upper class" Negroes, and, as much as I hate to say it about them, on all too many Negro entertainers. One of the reasons that I've especially admired some of them, like Lionel Hampton and Sidney Poitier, among others, is that they have kept their natural hair and fought to the top. I admire any Negro man who has never had himself conked, or who has had the sense to get rid of it—as I finally did.

26   I don't know which kind of self-defacing conk is the greater shame—the one you'll see on the heads of the black so-called "middle class" and "upper class," who ought to know better, or the one you'll see on the heads of the poorest, most downtrodden, ignorant black men. I mean the legal minimum-wage ghetto-dwelling kind of Negro, as I was when I got my first one. It's generally among these poor fools that you'll see a black kerchief over the man's head, like Aunt Jemima; he's trying to make his conk last longer, between trips to the barbershop. Only for special occasions is this kerchief-protected conk exposed—to show off how "sharp" and "hip" its owner is. The ironic thing is that I have never heard any woman, white or black, express any admiration for a conk. Of course, any white woman with a black man isn't thinking about his hair. But I don't see how on earth a black woman with any race pride could walk down the street with any black man wearing a conk—the emblem of his shame that he is black.

27   To my own shame, when I say all of this I'm talking first of all about myself—because you can't show me any Negro who ever conked more faithfully than I did. I'm speaking from personal experience when I say of any black man who conks today, or any white-wigged black woman, that if they gave the

brains in their heads just half as much attention as they do their hair, they would be a thousand times better off.

Understanding Meaning

1. What motivated black people to endure the painful conking process?

2. Why does Malcolm X see the conk as an "emblem of shame"?

3. Why is Malcolm X especially disturbed by the sight of conks worn by middle-class and professional African Americans?

4. *Critical Thinking:* A century ago, Jewish immigrants from Eastern Europe were urged, often by American Jews, to shave their beards and discard traditional clothing in order to assimilate in the New World. Are these changes harmless adaptations to a new culture, or do they represent a form of self-loathing and denial? Do you see current examples of men and women altering their identity?

Evaluating Strategy

1. Malcolm X opens the essay with a story told without commentary. Do you find it effective to first explain the process, and then discuss its social significance?

2. How does Malcolm X use dialogue to bring the narrative to life?

3. *Blending the Modes:* Where does Malcolm X use *narration, analysis,* and *argument* to develop his process essay?

4. *Critical Thinking:* Social critics generally comment on social behavior from a distance. How does the story of his own conking give Malcolm X greater insight into black self-degradation? If he had not introduced his own experiences, what effect would the last four paragraphs have?

Appreciating Language

1. What language does Malcolm X use to dramatize the pain of being conked?

2. At one point, Malcolm X states he was "brainwashed." Why is this a key term? How, in his view, did popular culture "brainwash" generations of African Americans to admire "whiteness" and despise black identity?

3. Malcolm X uses the word "shame" repeatedly. How do you define "shame"?

WRITING SUGGESTIONS

1. Write a short essay about a process you have experienced—such as getting your ears pierced, applying for a loan, trying out for a team, or auditioning for a part. First describe the process; then comment on what you learned about yourself and society.

2. *Collaborative Writing:* Discuss the last sentence of the essay with a number of students. Do many people—of all races—devote more attention to their hair than their brains? Write a list of examples showing how people seek to alter their appearance to achieve a new identity.

LUCILLE TREGANOWAN

Auto expert Lucille Treganowan (1930–) operates Transmissions by Lucille, a chain of repair shops in Pittsburgh, Pennsylvania. She also appears on the popular PBS television series Lucille's Car Care Clinic. *In 1996 she published a book on auto repair,* Lucille's Car Care, *written in collaboration with Gina Catanzarite, the producer of her television series.*

Cleaning Battery Terminals

CONTEXT: *As you read the following instructions from* Lucille's Car Care, *think about whether or not you would find it easy to follow them. Do they seem clear and detailed enough for someone who has never performed this procedure before?*

Corrosion around the battery terminals affects the way electrical currents are conducted, and if the corrosion is severe it can even prevent the car from starting. Sometimes you'll be able to see a kind of whitish powder develop on the terminals, but most problems are caused by corrosion you *can't* see at the contact surfaces between the terminal and the post.

You will need:

A 12-inch or 56-inch box wrench or an open-end wrench from your tool kit or a small ratchet wrench designed specifically for side terminals. Use a 10M (metric measurements) wrench for imports.

screwdriver or battery cable terminal puller

battery terminal cleaner brush

rag

water and baking soda solution

petroleum jelly

NOTE: *Never* smoke cigarettes or use anything that might spark around a battery.

To avoid electrical shock, perform the following procedure in the following sequence:

1. Use the wrench to loosen the nuts on the battery terminals at the end of the cable. Be sure to note which is the negative terminal and which is the positive terminal. They will be clearly marked, and the positive cable is almost always red.

2. Use the battery cable terminal puller to remove the negative terminal. If you do not own this tool, use your fingers to work the cable back and forth until it is loosened, or insert a screwdriver underneath the terminal and gently pry it up.

3. Use the battery terminal cleaner brush to scrub the inside of the hole in the terminal. Brush until the surface is shiny like new metal. Then fit the other side of the tool over the battery post and rotate it until the metal shines.

4. Dip a rag in the water/baking soda solution and clean the top of the battery, removing metal particles that were brushed off the terminal and posts.

5. Repeat Step 2 through 4 with the positive terminal.

6. Return the terminals to the proper posts, positive *first*, then negative. Tighten the bolts until you cannot turn the terminal any more.

7. Apply a light coating of petroleum jelly to the outside of the terminals to fight future corrosion buildup.

Understanding Meaning

1. Why is it important to make sure that a car's battery terminals are clean?

2. What is the point of the warning note that precedes the numbered list of instructions?

3. Why is it important to note "which is the negative terminal and which is the positive terminal"?

4. Why is the final step to apply petroleum jelly to the cleaned terminals?

Evaluating Strategy

1. Why do you think these instructions begin with a list of items one will need to perform the task? Would they be harder or easier to follow without this opening list?

2. How effectively organized are the instructions? Can they be quickly understood?

3. How do numbered points and typeface variations affect the way you read these instructions?

Appreciating Language

1. What does the level of diction and word choice suggest about the intended audience?

2. Does the author successfully avoid overly technical language that some readers might find difficult?

WRITING SUGGESTIONS

1. Write a set of instructions on first aid, car or home repair, or campus security to be read in an emergency. Use visual aids and short, direct sentences to communicate in as few words as possible.

2. *Collaborative Writing:* Analyze the effectiveness of Treganowan's instructions with a group of students. Have members read the instructions, and then close their books. One person should refer to the instructions and quiz the group on the steps. Note how much people remembered, and identify areas that more than one person forgot. Based on your group's experiences, work collaboratively to write a short analysis, suggesting changes for greater readability if needed.

RESPONDING TO IMAGES

© KATE KUNZ/CORBIS

1. What is your immediate response to this photograph? Does it symbolize opportunity or desperation? Does the photograph's connotation change with the economy and unemployment rate? Can a symbol inspire hope in one person and despair in another? Why or why not?

2. Would this image make a good poster? Why or why not? What might it announce or advertise?

3. *Visual Analysis:* The photographer carefully arranged a newspaper want ad, a resume, and a pen and laptop. Are these items arranged to suggest a process or action—moving from reading an ad to writing a resume and emailing it? Can still images be made to demonstrate action? Why or why not?

4. *Collaborative Writing:* Discuss this image with a group of students. Would they use it to promote a college placement office? Why or why not? What caption would they add?

STRATEGIES FOR PROCESS WRITING

1. **Define your goal—to explain or to instruct.** Is your purpose to explain how something takes place or to instruct readers about how to accomplish a specific task?

2. **Evaluate your audience's existing knowledge.** How much does your audience know about the subject? Do any common misconceptions need to be clarified? What terms should be defined?

3. **Define clear starting and ending points.** When does this process begin? What is the end? Readers must have a clear concept of the beginning and end, especially in instructions.

4. **Separate the process into understandable stages or steps.** To explain a process, it is important to break it down into a chain of separate events that makes the process understandable without distorting it. When giving instructions, do not include too many operations in a single step.

5. **Number steps for clarity in the instructions.** Instructions are easier to follow if organized in numbered steps. If interrupted, readers can easily mark their places and later resume the process without confusion.

6. **Consider using visual aids.** Large print, capital letters, bold or italic type, and underlining can highlight text. Graphs, drawings, diagrams, and photographs can be beneficial to reinforce both explanatory writing and instructions.

7. **Measure readability of instructions.** Instructions, especially directions people will have to refer to while working, should communicate at a glance. Short sentences and wide spacing between steps are used in cookbooks and repair manuals so a person working in a kitchen or garage can read the text at a distance.

8. **Test your writing.** Because it is easy to skip steps when explaining a process you are familiar with, it is important to have other people read your writing. Other readers can be objective and easily detect missing information.

SUGGESTED TOPICS FOR PROCESS WRITING

GENERAL ASSIGNMENTS

Write a process paper on any of the following topics. Assume you are writing for a general, college-educated audience. You may develop your explanation using narratives, comparisons, and definitions. Explain the process as a clearly stated chain of events. Draw from your own experiences.

1. How the university processes student applications

2. The operation of an appliance such as a microwave, refrigerator, or washing machine

3. The process of a disease or disability

4. The way small children learn to talk

5. The method your employer uses in training

6. The stages of childbirth

7. How a computer virus infects a computer

8. The way corporations market a new product

9. The way the body loses fat through diet or exercise

10. How networks select television programs

Write a process paper giving directions to complete a specific task. You may wish to write your instructions in numbered steps rather than standard paragraphs. Remember to highlight any safety hazards.

1. How to protect your computer against viruses

2. How to purchase a new or used car at the best price

3. How to improve your credit score

4. How to quit smoking

5. How to find a job or prepare for a job interview

6. How to handle sexual harassment on campus or in a job

7. How to prevent identity theft

8. How to operate a drill press, microscope, or other piece of industrial or scientific equipment

9. How to treat a second-degree burn or other injury

10. How to monitor a child's use of the Internet

WRITING IN CONTEXT

1. Imagine you have been selected to write a section for a student handbook instructing freshmen how to register for classes. Write a step-by-step paper giving complete instructions. Give exact room numbers, times, and locations. You may wish to refer to a campus map. When you complete a draft of your paper, review it carefully to see if you have left out any pieces of essential information.

2. Select a process you learned on a job, and write instructions suitable for training a new employee. Consider how your job may have changed. Give trainees the benefit of your experience, and add tips that might not be included in the standard job descriptions. Warn readers, for instance, of common problems that arise.

3. Select a process from one of your textbooks and rewrite it for a sixth-grade class. Simplify the language and use analogies sixth graders would understand.

STUDENT PAPER: PROCESS

This paper was written in response to the following assignment:
Write a 500-word process paper providing directions to accomplish a specific task. You may include graphs, charts, diagrams, or numbered steps.

First Draft with Instructor's Comments

Home Safety

Use more specific title, "Home Safety" could refer to avoiding accidents in the home.

Homeowners are generally only concerned about security when

wordy, shorten opening sentences

they plan to take a vacation. When they take off for a week or two

to the mountains or down the shore, they install additional locks,

what do timers do?

set timers, purchase sophisticated monitoring systems, talk to

neighbors, and hope their homes will not be robbed while they are

good points enjoying themselves. But the reality is different. Most homes are

not burglarized while their owners are thousands of miles away.

wordy, cut Most houses are robbed before 9 p.m., often while their owners are

near or inside the residence. Your house is more likely to be

robbed while you are grilling in the backyard or watching a foot-

ball game than when you are on a cruise or camping trip.

There are things you can do to make your home burglar proof.

Revise—you can't guarantee to make anyplace "burglar proof"—Qualify remark

The most important thing you can do is to take steps in case

a burglary does happen. You will have to prove any loss. So it makes sense to make a list of your valuables. Photograph or video- *Good advice*

tape each room in your house. Keep receipts of major purchases.

Store these in a safe deposit box. Review your insurance to see if

special items like furs, artwork, or coin collections are covered. *Good tip!*

It is also important to identify valuables. Engrave computers,

televisions, cameras, stereos, and DVD players with your name or

an identifying number. Police often discover stolen property but

have no way of contacting the owner.

A really important thing to remember is to always lock your

doors. Nothing is more tempting to a criminal than an open garage

door or unlatched screen door. <u>Lock up even when you plan to visit</u>   *wordy, break up and shorten*

<u>a neighbor for "just a minute" because that "minute" can easily turn</u>

<u>into a half an hour, giving a burglar plenty of time for a burglary.</u>

Many people buy very expensive and high-tech security systems

but leave them off most of the time because they are so hard to

use. A cheap alarm system used 24-7 is better than one used just   *slang*

¶ New paragraph, different topic

now and then. It can also be important to trim shrubbery around

doors and windows to keep burglars from having a hiding place.

It is very important to network with neighbors and let them

<u>know what is going on.</u> Let neighbors know if you expect   *vague*

deliveries or contractors. Thieves have posed as moving crews, casually looting a house and loading a truck while neighbors looked on.

Thieves are usually reluctant to leave the first floor, which usually has a number of exits. They don't like going into attics or basements where they might get trapped, so that is where to hide valuables.

And finally, call the police the moment you discover a break-in. If you return home and find evidence of a break in—do not go inside the home. The thieves, who could be armed <u>with weapons,</u> might still be inside. Use your cell phone or go to a neighbor's to call the police. Never attempt to confront a burglar yourself. No personal possession is worth risking death or a disabling injury.

Delete —not needed

REVISION NOTES

This is a good topic, but your instructions could be made clearer and easier to follow.

* Qualify your opening remark. No one can promise to make a home "burglar-proof" but you can suggest ways to reduce the risk of break-ins.
* Number steps and use titles to highlight each of your suggestions. Stress verbs to highlight actions readers should take. Numbered steps can reduce wordy and repetitive transitional statements like "another important thing is."

Revised Draft

Securing Your Home

Homeowners frequently think of security only when planning a vacation. Leaving home for a week or two, they install additional locks, set timers to trigger lights, purchase sophisticated monitoring systems, alert neighbors, and hope their homes will not be robbed in their absence. But most homes are robbed before 9 p.m., often while their owners are near or inside the residence. Your house is more likely to be robbed while you are grilling in the backyard or watching a football game in a basement rec room than when you are on a cruise or camping trip.

Although it is impossible to make any home "burglar-proof," there are some actions you can take to protect your home and property:

1. Document your assets.
    Make a list of your valuables. Photograph or videotape each room in your home. Keep receipts of major purchases. Store these and other important records in a safe deposit box so you can prove any losses. Review your insurance policies to see if special items like furs, artwork, or coin collections are covered.

2. Identify valuables.
    Engrave computers, televisions, cameras, stereos, and DVD players with your name or an identifying number. Police often discover stolen property but have no way of contacting the owners.

3. *Always* lock your doors.
    Nothing attracts a thief more than an open garage or unlatched screen door. Lock up even when you plan to visit a neighbor for "just a minute." That "minute" can easily become half an hour, plenty of time for a burglary to occur. Don't leave doors open if you are going to be upstairs or in the basement.

4. Install only security systems you will use.
    Many homeowners invest in expensive, high-tech security systems that are so cumbersome they leave them off most of the time. A cheap alarm system used twenty-four hours a day

provides more protection than a state-of-the-art system used randomly.

5. **Trim shrubbery around entrances and windows.**
   Don't provide camouflage for burglars. Thieves can easily conceal themselves behind foliage while jimmying doors and windows.

6. **Network with neighbors.**
   Let neighbors know if you expect deliveries, house guests, or contractors. Thieves have posed as moving crews, casually looting a house and loading a truck while neighbors looked on.

7. **Store valuables in attics and basements.**
   Thieves are reluctant to venture beyond the ground floor, which usually offers numerous exits in case of detection. Attics and basements, therefore, provide more security for valuable or hard to replace items.

   Finally, call the police the moment you discover a burglary has occurred. If you return home and find evidence of a break-in—*do not go inside!* The thieves, who could be armed, might still be on the premises. Use a cell phone or ask a neighbor to call the police. Never attempt to confront a burglar yourself. No personal possession is worth risking death or a disabling injury.

QUESTIONS FOR REVIEW AND REVISION

1. The student offers seven directions. Would these be easier to recall if emphasized by the subtitle "Seven Tips to Keep Your Home Secure"? Would it be better to introduce the steps stating "there are seven actions you can take" instead of "some actions"? Why or why not?

2. What misconceptions does the student address?

3. How important is the final warning?

4. The student writes in the second person, directly addressing the readers. Would the paper be less effective if written in third person? Why or why not?

5. Do the level of language, diction, and tone suit the intended audience?

6. Did the student follow the instructor's suggestions?

7. Read the paper aloud. Is this document easy to read and easy to remember? Could revisions increase its clarity?

WRITING SUGGESTIONS

1. Using this paper as a model, write a set of instructions directed to a general audience about improving the performance of your car, installing a new computer program, planning a trip or a wedding, losing weight, choosing a pet, preparing for a job interview, or another topic of your choice.

2. *Collaborative Writing:* Discuss this paper with other students. Using some of its ideas, work together to write a brief set of instructions on securing a dorm room or an apartment.

PROCESS CHECKLIST

Before submitting your paper, review these points:

1. Is the process clearly defined?

2. Do you supply background information that readers need?

3. Is the information easy to follow? Is the chain of events or the steps logically arranged?

4. Could the text be enhanced by large print, all capital letters, bold or italic type, diagrams, charts, or photographs?

5. Are your instructions complete? Do readers know when one step is over and another begins?

6. Do your instructions alert readers to normal changes they might mistake for errors?

7. Are hazards clearly stated?

8. Do you tell readers what not to do?

9. Did you verify that names, phone numbers, dates, prices, and email addresses are current and correct?

10. Did you use peer review to test your document?

 Info Write provides additional information on process writing.
cengage.learning.infowrite.com

CHAPTER ELEVEN

CAUSE AND EFFECT: DETERMINING REASONS AND MEASURING OR PREDICTING RESULTS

WHAT IS CAUSE AND EFFECT?

What causes terrorism? How will Katrina affect the future of New Orleans? What caused the collapse of subprime mortgages? How will health care reform affect the deficit? Would a handgun ban lower street crime? Can a Supreme Court ruling prevent frivolous lawsuits? What causes autism? Will a new school policy prevent bullying? The answers to these questions call for the use of *cause and effect*, writing that seeks either to establish reasons why something occurred or measure or predict results.

Historians devote much of their time to determining the causes of events. What caused the Civil War? Why did Hitler rise to power? What led to the women's movement of the 1970s? Historians also consider the ramifications of events and policies and speculate about the future. What impact did the growth of suburbs after World War II have on cities? Did a tax cut create jobs? Has a drug treatment program been successful? Will another oil crisis occur? How will a change in American foreign policy increase chances for peace in the Middle East? What will happen in Iraq?

Nearly all professions and disciplines engage in cause-and-effect reasoning. Marketers try to determine why a product succeeded. Engineers work to discover why a test engine failed. Medical researchers measure the results of a new treatment. City planners predict the effect a major earthquake would have on emergency services. Educators consider whether curriculum changes will improve Scholastic Aptitude Test scores. Federal Aviation Administration (FAA) investigators examine wreckage to establish why a plane crashed.

Many of the research papers you will be assigned in college and the letters and reports you will write in your future career will be developed using cause and effect. Identifying the reasons why something occurred can be formidable. Determining future outcomes, no matter how much data are examined or how many experiments are conducted can remain largely guesswork.

Deduction and Induction

Writers often formulate cause-and-effect papers using deduction and induction. *Deduction* is a form of logic in which a *major premise* or general rule is applied to a *minor premise* or specific instance in order to reach a *conclusion*. You may be familiar with this classic example of deduction:

MAJOR PREMISE:	All cows are mammals.
MINOR PREMISE:	Bessie is a cow.
CONCLUSION:	Bessie is a mammal.

This illustration, though famous, fails to show the practical value of deduction. Other examples should give you an idea of how often we use deduction:

MAJOR PREMISE:	All full-time students are eligible for financial aid.
MINOR PREMISE:	Sandra Lopez is a full-time student.
CONCLUSION:	Sandra Lopez is eligible for financial aid.
MAJOR PREMISE:	The student health plan is only available to California residents.
MINOR PREMISE:	Amy Kwan is a resident of New York.
CONCLUSION:	Amy Kwan cannot join the student health plan.

Deduction can be used to solve problems and answer questions: Are dental exams deductible on my income tax return? Can I sublet my apartment? Will the college give me a refund if I drop a class in the fourth week? Each of these questions forms a minor premise. The IRS rules, apartment leases, and college policies you consult for answers serve as major premises. Deduction can be used to help determine both causes and effects.

Was a plane crash caused by a defective part?

MAJOR PREMISE:	FAA regulations consider this part defective if three bolts are missing.

MINOR PREMISE:	One bolt was missing from this part.
CONCLUSION:	This part was not defective.

How will an increase in bus fares affect ridership?

MAJOR PREMISE:	Bus ridership declines with fare increases.
MINOR PREMISE:	The city authorized a fifty-cent fare increase.
CONCLUSION:	Bus ridership will likely decline.

Problems occur with deductive reasoning if the major and minor premises are not precisely stated. The statement "All full-time students are eligible for financial aid" might be clearer if it included a definition of who is considered a full-time student: "All students taking twelve credits or more are eligible for financial aid." Other problems arise if the major premise is subject to interpretation. A warranty for snow tires might refuse to cover "improper use." Is off-road driving considered "improper"? How much damage can be considered "normal wear and tear"? Some major premises may prove to be false or require qualification:

MAJOR PREMISE:	Democrats are anti-business.

Are *all* Democrats anti-business? What is meant by *anti-business?*

MAJOR PREMISE:	Gun control reduces crime.

Can this be proven? Could a drop in crime in a city that passed gun control be caused by other factors—a decrease in unemployment, a shift in population, or more effective policing? How is "crime" defined?

Induction, unlike deduction, does not open with a major premise. Instead, it presents and interprets data and then makes a conclusion:

```
        X  X  X  X  X
          X  X  X  X
     X  X  X  X   X
          X  X  X
          X    X    X
     _____
```

X = Data

Inductive Leap —— Conclusion

The Xs in the diagram could represent reports of stolen cars, the number of computers sold last month, blood tests of patients taking a new fertility drug, satellite photographs, interviews with consumers, or evidence collected at a crime scene. Based on a review of the evidence, a conclusion is drawn: car thefts are increasing in the suburbs, the new fertility drug damages red blood cells, coastline erosion is worse than it was last year, the consumers' major complaint is poor service, or the murder suspect is a Caucasian female with O-positive blood and dyed hair.

As these examples illustrate, effective induction requires a large body of valid evidence to achieve reasonable conclusions. Ford Motor Company would have to interview more than a handful of Focus owners to determine customer satisfaction. Medical researchers must rule out other reasons for damaged red blood cells. As the diagram notes, the movement from specific details to conclusion requires an *inductive leap*. No matter how much evidence is discovered and examined, no absolute assurance can be made that the conclusion is totally true.

The best demonstration of inductive reasoning takes place in a courtroom. In a criminal case, the prosecutor tells members of the jury that if they examine all the evidence they will conclude that the defendant is guilty *beyond a reasonable doubt*. The defense attorney will attempt to raise doubt by providing alternative interpretations and by introducing conflicting evidence. He or she will tell the jury that *reasonable doubt* exists and that not enough evidence has been found to reach a conclusion of guilt.

Establishing Causes

By the 1920s, surgeons and physicians began noticing that many of their patients with lung cancer were heavy smokers. An observable association was discovered but there was no clear proof of a cause-and-effect relationship. Not all lung cancer patients smoked, and millions of smokers were free of the disease. Though scientists were concerned, they had no evidence that smoking *caused* cancer. In fact, throughout the 1930s and 1940s cigarette ads featured endorsements by doctors who claimed that the calming effect of nicotine reduced stress and prevented stomach ulcers. It was not until 1964 that researchers assembled enough data to convince the Surgeon General of the United States to proclaim cigarette smoking a health hazard.

In some instances, causes can be established through investigation and research. Doctors can diagnose an infection as the cause of a fever. Accountants can study financial records to discover why a company lost money. But many controversial issues remain subject to debate for decades. Why are American schools failing to educate children? John Taylor Gatto (page 466) examined the issue, determining that television and schools cause detrimental effects on children's lives:

Two institutions at present control our children's lives—television and schooling, in that order. Both of these reduce the real world of wisdom, fortitude, temperance, and justice to a never-ending, non-stop abstraction. In centuries past, the time of a child and adolescent would be occupied in real work, real charity, real adventures, and the real search for mentors who might teach what one really wanted to learn.

When evaluating a writer attempting to establish a cause, consider the amount of evidence, the degree of objective analysis, and the willingness to qualify assertions. If General Motors saw an increase in car sales after a major promotional campaign, does it prove the commercials were successful? Could additional sales be attributed to a change in interest rates, easier credit, a price increase in imported cars, or a surge in consumer confidence? It would take careful research to determine if the advertising directly contributed to the sales results.

Measuring and Predicting Results

Measuring results tries to answer a question: what happened? Have the efforts of Mothers Against Drunk Driving changed public attitudes and behaviors about driving under the influence? How has downloading songs changed the music industry? Did an antismoking education program prove effective? Like establishing causes, measuring results requires careful research. Could you measure smoking rates of young people who participated in the program and those who did not? If young people who participated in the program smoked less or began smoking at a later age, would these be considered signs of success?

Predicting results requires careful critical thinking. In 1936 the *Literary Digest* predicted that Alf Landon would defeat Franklin Roosevelt in his bid for a second term as president. The editors based their prediction on a detailed telephone survey. By randomly selecting names from phone books and asking people whom they planned to vote for, the surveyors assumed they would get an accurate prediction. Their responses, from men and women, government employees and business executives, Italians and Jews, farmers and factory workers, and young and old, strongly indicated a preference for Landon. But their research failed to predict the outcome of the election accurately because the survey method did not measure a significant population. In 1936 many Americans could not afford telephones, and these economically deprived voters tended to favor Roosevelt.

Predicting future outcomes can be challenging because evidence may be difficult to collect or may be subject to various interpretations. In addition, numerous unforeseen factors can take place to alter expected events. A school board that determines to close schools because of a declining birthrate may fail to account for an influx of immigrants or the closure of private schools that would place more students into the public system.

Peter Moskos (page 482) argues that because addictive drugs are dangerous, they should be legalized to regulate and reduce their use. Legalization of drugs, he predicts, would reduce both crime and consumption:

> Illegal drug dealers sell to anyone. Legal ones are licensed and help keep drugs such as beer, cigarettes, and pharmaceuticals away from minors. Illegal dealers settle disputes with guns. Legal ones solve theirs in court. Illegal dealers fear police. Legal ones fear the IRS.
>
> Less use. Regulation can reduce drug use. In two generations, we've halved the number of cigarette smokers not through prohibition but through education, regulated selling, and taxes. And we don't jail nicotine addicts. Drug addiction won't go away, but tax revenue can help pay for treatment.... It's unlikely that repealing federal drug laws would result in a massive increase in drug use....

In contrast, Lee P. Brown (page 485) argues that legalization would not reduce demand:

> Some argue that drug enforcement should be replaced by a policy of "harm reduction," which emphasizes decriminalization and medical treatment over law enforcement and interdiction. But people do not use drugs simply because they are illegal. Equally significant, effective enforcement reduces drug supply, increases price, lowers the numbers of users, and decreases hard-core drug use. There is an inverse relationship between the price of cocaine and the number of people seeking emergency room treatment...
>
> Legalization does not get to the problem's core.... it fails to answer why more drug availability would not lead to more drug use and more devastating consequences.

When examining writing that predicts future effects, consider the amount of evidence presented, the recognition of other factors that may affect results, and the use of critical thinking.

CRITICAL THINKING FOR CAUSE-AND-EFFECT WRITING

When writing cause-and-effect essays, avoid these common traps, many of which are known as logical fallacies.

1. **Avoid mistaking a time relationship for a cause** (*post hoc, ergo propter hoc*). If your brakes fail after you take your car into the dealer for an oil change, does that mean the mechanics are to blame? Can the president

take credit for a drop in unemployment six months after signing a labor bill? Because events occur in time, it can be easy to assume an action that precedes another is a cause. The mechanics may not have touched your brakes, which were bound to wear out with or without an oil change. A drop in unemployment could be caused by a decline in interest rates or an upsurge in exports and may have nothing to do with a labor bill. *Do not assume events were caused by preceding events.*

2. **Do not mistake an effect for a cause.** Early physicians saw fever as a cause of disease rather than as an effect or symptom. If you observe that children with poor reading skills watch a lot of television, you might easily assume that television interferes with their reading. In fact, excessive viewing could be a symptom. Because they have trouble reading, they watch television.

3. **Do not confuse associations with causes.** For years researchers argued that marijuana use led to heroin addiction. The evidence was clear. Nearly every heroin addict interviewed admitted to starting with marijuana. But since most addicts also drank beer, smoked cigarettes, chewed gum, and attended high school, this association could not alone be considered proof. Associations can be compelling and command attention, but they are not proof of a cause-and-effect relationship.

4. **Anticipate unexpected changes.** Many researchers qualify their predictions with the statement "all things being equal, we can anticipate ..." But conditions never remain frozen. An increase in a school's test scores following a curriculum change could be caused by student computer use at home or the arrival of gifted transfer students rather than anything the school did.

5. **Avoid "slippery slope" interpretations.** Do not assume that changes will start a trend that will snowball without restraint. If the government allows euthanasia for the terminally ill, you cannot argue that eventually all the elderly and handicapped will be put to death.

6. **Realize that past performance, though an important factor, cannot predict future results.** In early 2008 the price of oil hit $100 a barrel. Production was lagging and the growing energy demand from China assured experts that prices would continue to increase. Throughout the spring oil prices rose, reaching $125 by May. In July oil climbed to $145, and a few analysts predicted oil would soon reach $200 a barrel. High gasoline prices led Americans to drive less, lowering demand. Months later a financial crisis shook world markets as banks collapsed and evidence of a global recession mounted. In February 2009 the price of oil dropped to $34 a barrel. *Past trends cannot be assumed to continue into the future.*

7. **Be aware of unintended consequences.** Policies or actions taken for one purpose may cause something unplanned or unanticipated to occur. The

demilitarized zone created to separate North and South Korea inadvertently created a valuable wildlife sanctuary because humans were prevented from entering the territory. The banning of smoking in hotels for health reasons may have decreased fires caused by the careless use of smoking materials. Programs to improve education may have led schools to improve their scores by making their tests easier or expelling lower-performing students.

STRATEGIES FOR READING CAUSE AND EFFECT

When reading the cause-and-effect entries in this chapter, keep these questions in mind.

Understanding Meaning

1. Is the writer seeking to establish a cause or to measure or predict results?

2. What is the source of the evidence? A writer opposed to atomic power who cites only studies commissioned by an anti-nuclear group is not as credible as one who presents data collected by neutral organizations.

3. Are alternative interpretations possible? Does a rise in the number of people receiving food stamps mean an increase in poverty, or does it reflect better government assistance?

Evaluating Strategy

1. Does the writer mistake a result for a cause? A survey revealing that 90 percent of batterers in domestic violence cases are abusing alcohol might lead to a call for more treatment centers. In fact, alcohol abuse and domestic violence may both result from unemployment.

2. Does the writer assume past trends will continue into the future?

3. Does the essay rest on unproven assumptions?

4. Does the writer demonstrate skills in critical thinking?

5. Does the author use narratives or comparisons to demonstrate his or her conclusions?

Appreciating Language

1. Does the author's choice of words indicate bias?

2. How does the writer introduce technical terms? Are definitions supplied?

3. What do the tone and style of the entry suggest about the intended audience?

JOHN BROOKS

John Brooks (1920–1993) published his first novel, The Big Wheel, in 1949. His second novel, The Man Who Broke Things, appeared in 1958. Brooks's nonfiction book about corporations in the 1980s, The Takeover Game, became a best seller. Brooks, who served as a trustee of the New York Public Library for fifteen years, contributed articles to the New Yorker for four decades.

The Effects of the Telephone

CONTEXT: In this brief essay, Brooks outlines how the telephone has shaped human lives and perceptions. Before reading this article, consider what your life would be like without a telephone. How much do you depend on the phone?

What has the telephone done to us, or for us, in the hundred years of its existence? _{1 opening question}

A few effects suggest themselves at once. It has saved lives by getting rapid word of illness, injury, or famine from remote places. By joining with the elevator to make possible the multistory residence or office building, it has made possible—for better or worse—the modern city. By bringing about a quantum leap in the speed and ease with which information moves from place to place, it has greatly accelerated the rate of scientific and technological change and growth in industry. _{2 obvious effects}

Beyond doubt it has crippled if not killed the ancient art of letter writing. It has made living alone possible for persons with normal social impulses; by so doing, it has played a role in one of the greatest social changes of this century, the breakup of the multigenerational household. It has made the waging of war chillingly more efficient than formerly. Perhaps (though not provably) it has prevented wars that might have arisen out of international misunderstanding caused by written communication. Or perhaps—again not provably—by magnifying and extending irrational personal conflicts based on voice contact, it has caused wars. ₃ _{possible effects}

Certainly it has extended the scope of human conflicts, since it impartially disseminates the useful knowledge of scientists and the babble of bores, the affection of the affectionate and the malice of the malicious. ₄

But the question remains unanswered. The obvious effects just cited seem inadequate, mechanistic; they only scratch the surface. Perhaps the crucial effects are evanescent and unmeasurable. Use of the telephone involves personal risk because it involves exposure; for some, to be "hung up on" is among the worst of fears; others dream of a ringing telephone and wake up with a pounding heart. The telephone's actual ring—more, perhaps, than any other ₅

psychological effects sound in our daily lives—evokes hope, relief, fear, anxiety, joy, according to our expectations. The telephone is our nerve-end to society.

6   In some ways it is in itself a thing of paradox. In one sense a metaphor for *paradoxical effects* the times it helped create, in another sense the telephone is their polar opposite. It is small and gentle—relying on low voltages and miniature parts—in times of hugeness and violence. It is basically simple in times of complexity.

7   It is so nearly human, re-creating voices so faithfully that friends or lovers need not identify themselves by name even when talking across oceans, that to ask its effects on human life may seem hardly more fruitful than to ask the effect of the hand or the foot. The Canadian philosopher Marshall McLuhan—one of the few who have addressed themselves to these ques- *closing* tions—was perhaps not far from the mark when he spoke of the telephone as *quotation* creating "a kind of extra-sensory perception."

Understanding Meaning

1. What does Brooks see as the dominant effects of the telephone? Have there been negative consequences?

2. Why does Brooks see the telephone as "a thing of paradox"?

3. *Critical Thinking:* What lessons about the telephone can be applied to the Internet? Does cyberspace connect people in more ways than the typical one-on-one connection a telephone provides?

Evaluating Strategy

1. Most people have grown up with telephones. Many carry cell phones in pockets and purses. How does Brooks prompt readers to question something they take for granted? Could you imagine writing a similar essay about cars, ballpoint pens, or supermarkets?

2. *Critical Thinking:* Brooks states that the telephone and elevator made the high-rise and the modern city possible. Does this suggest that it can be difficult to isolate a single cause? Do technological and social changes intertwine and interact to create unintended results?

Appreciating Language

1. Brooks calls the telephone "nearly human." How does he personalize a communication instrument, linking it to human emotions?

2. Brooks avoids technical language in his essay. Would the introduction of scientific terminology weaken his essay?

3. Consider Brooks's observation that the "telephone is our nerve-end to society." Does the telephone link you to others, or to the world? Can we

think of phone lines as nerves that make our society and economy function by transmitting information?

WRITING SUGGESTIONS

1. Using Brooks's article as a model, write your own essay explaining the effects of another common invention. How did the modern newspaper or the Sears catalog change life in the nineteenth century? How did shopping malls, freeways, and suburbs shape life in the twentieth century?

2. *Collaborative Writing*: Work with a group of students to discuss the effects computers have on children and society. Develop a list of positive and negative effects and write a brief essay comparing the benefits and dangers.

JOHN TAYLOR GATTO

John Taylor Gatto taught in New York City public schools for twenty-five years and was named the city's Teacher of the Year three times. He has published several books about public education, including Dumbing Us Down, The Exhausted School, and The Empty Child. Since leaving teaching, Gatto has become a public speaker, addressing audiences at the White House and NASA's Goddard Space Flight Center.

Why Schools Don't Educate

CONTEXT: *In this section of a speech Gatto presented after receiving an award, he outlines the effects television and schools have had on children. As you read his list, consider if there could be other causes for the symptoms he describes.*

1 Two institutions at present control our children's lives—television and schooling, in that order. Both of these reduce the real world of wisdom, fortitude, temperance, and justice to a never-ending, nonstop abstraction. In centuries past, the time of a child and adolescent would be occupied in real work, real charity, real adventures, and the real search for mentors who might teach what one really wanted to learn. A great deal of time was spent in community pursuits, practicing affection, meeting and studying every level of the community, learning how to make a home, and dozens of other tasks necessary to becoming a whole man or woman.

2 But here is the calculus of time the children I teach must deal with:

3 Out of the 168 hours in each week, my children must sleep 56. That leaves them 112 hours a week out of which to fashion a self.

4 My children watch 55 hours of television a week, according to recent reports. That leaves them 57 hours a week in which to grow up.

5 My children attend school 30 hours a week; use about 8 hours getting ready, going, and coming home; and spend an average of 7 hours a week in homework—a total of 45 hours. During that time they are under constant surveillance, have no private time or private space, and are disciplined if they try to assert individuality in the use of time or space. That leaves 12 hours a week out of which to create a unique consciousness. Of course my kids eat, too, and that takes some time—not much, because we've lost the tradition of family dining. If we allot 3 hours a week to evening meals we arrive at a net amount of private time for each child of 9 hours.

6 It's not enough. It's not enough, is it? The richer the kid, of course, the less television he watches, but the rich kid's time is just as narrowly proscribed by a broader catalogue of commercial entertainments and his inevitable assignment to a series of private lessons in areas seldom of his choice.

And these things are, oddly enough, just a more cosmetic way to create de- 7
pendent human beings, unable to fill their own hours, unable to initiate lines
of meaning to give substance and pleasure to their existence. It's a national
disease, this dependency and aimlessness, and I think schooling and television
and lessons—the entire Chautauqua idea—have a lot to do with it.

Think of the things that are killing us as a nation: drugs, brainless compe- 8
tition, recreational sex, the pornography of violence, gambling, alcohol, and
the worst pornography of all—lives devoted to buying things—accumulation
as a philosophy. All are addictions of dependent personalities and that is what
our brand of schooling must inevitably produce.

I want to tell you what the effect is on children of taking all their time—time 9
they need to grow up—and forcing them to spend it on abstractions. No reform
that doesn't attack these specific pathologies will be anything more than a facade.

1. The children I teach are indifferent to the adult world. This defies the experience of thousands of years. A close study of what big people were up
   to was always the most exciting occupation of youth, but nobody wants to
   grow up these days, and who can blame them? Toys are us.

2. The children I teach have almost no curiosity, and what little they do have
   is transitory; they cannot concentrate for very long, even on things they
   choose to do. Can you see a connection between the bells ringing again and
   again to change classes, and this phenomenon of evanescent attention?

3. The children I teach have a poor sense of the future, of how tomorrow is
   inextricably linked to today. They live in a continuous present; the exact
   moment they are in is the boundary of their consciousness.

4. The children I teach are ahistorical; they have no sense of how the past
   has predestined their own present, limiting their choices, shaping their
   values and lives.

5. The children I teach are cruel to each other; they lack compassion for
   misfortune, they laugh at weakness, they have contempt for people whose
   need for help shows too plainly.

6. The children I teach are uneasy with intimacy or candor. They cannot deal
   with genuine intimacy because of a lifelong habit of preserving a secret self
   inside an outer personality made up of artificial bits and pieces, of behavior
   borrowed from television or acquired to manipulate teachers. Because they
   are not who they represent themselves to be, the disguise wears thin in the
   presence of intimacy, so intimate relationships have to be avoided.

7. The children I teach are materialistic, following the lead of schoolteachers who materialistically "grade" everything—and television mentors who
   offer everything in the world for sale.

8. The children I teach are dependent, passive, and timid in the presence of new challenges. This timidity is frequently masked by surface bravado or by anger or aggressiveness, but underneath is a vacuum without fortitude.

10   I could name a few other conditions that school reform will have to tackle if our national decline is to be arrested, but by now you will have grasped my thesis, whether you agree with it or not. Either schools, television, or both have caused these pathologies. It's a simple matter of arithmetic. Between schooling and television, all the time children have is eaten up. That's what has destroyed the American family; it no longer is a factor in the education of its own children.

Understanding Meaning

1. How, in Gatto's view, are television and schools linked in children's lives?

2. How has television affected children's views of the world?

3. Gatto states that schoolchildren are "cruel" and "passive." Can one be both cruel and passive? Can pent-up energy and stunted creativity lead children to express themselves in bursts of selfish violence?

4. Gatto observes that children are materialistic. How much of this is caused by television and how much by the values of their parents?

5. Do Gatto's observations explain why many people advocate school choice and homeschooling?

6. *Critical Thinking:* Gatto remarks that "children live in a continuous present" without a sense of past and future. Is this a natural attribute of childhood or something induced by television? Doesn't television teach children something about history, even if what it teaches is simplified and distorted?

Evaluating Strategy

1. How effective is Gatto's use of numbered steps?

2. All of Gatto's eight points open with "The children I teach ..." Is this repetition suited to a speech? Does it help hammer home his ideas to a listening audience? Does it seem less effective in print?

3. What risk does a writer run in criticizing children? How might parents respond?

Appreciating Language

1. Gatto uses the word "ahistorical." How would you define this term?

2. Gatto calls "being devoted to buying things" the "worst pornography of all." Is "pornography" an effective word choice?

WRITING SUGGESTIONS

1. Write your own essay detailing the effects television has had on your generation or your children's. Do your observations match Gatto's?

2. Write a brief narrative about an elementary school experience that truly taught you something. Did it occur in the context of the traditional classroom?

3. *Collaborative Writing:* Discuss Gatto's article with a group of students. Record their observations about school reform. Select the major ideas you come up with and write a letter to the local school board suggesting ways to improve education.

TANNER STRANSKY

Tanner Sransky writes for Entertainment Weekly *and has published articles about television, books, and motion pictures. He previously worked at the* New York Post *and* Teen People. *His book* Find Your Inner Ugly Betty: 25 Career Lessons for Young Professionals Inspired by TV Shows *was published in 2008.*

Who Killed Miss America?

CONTEXT: *In this 2010 article Stransky examines the reasons for the loss of public interest in the Miss America Pageant, which was once a national television event akin to the Academy Awards. No longer broadcast on a major network, the beauty pageant draws little more than a tenth of the viewers it did twenty years ago. Once major celebrities, today's Miss Americas are largely unknown.*

1   IN 1991, WHEN KATIE STAM was just 5 years old, growing up in Seymour, Ind., you could spy the pint-size beauty cutting cereal boxes into princess crowns and fashioning sashes out of thick ribbons with her favorite cousin. You could also spy Stam, in mid-September of that year, watching her beloved Miss America pageant on NBC with 26.7 million other television viewers. "We would pretend we were Miss America," she remembers fondly, noting that her family gathered around the television annually for the show. "We had the most amazing connection with the pageant. It was such a big deal to us." And to the rest of the country. The Miss America pageant was a true television event, close to the Oscars and the Super Bowl.

2   No longer. When current Miss America Stam, now 23, traded in her homemade crown for the real deal last January on TLC, only 3.5 million viewers tuned in, a stunning drop of 87 percent from when she was a little girl. And now, on Jan. 30 (at 8 p.m. on TLC), Stam will relinquish her title as a new Miss America is crowned. The question is, will anyone notice? The pageant's days of dominating watercooler conversations are long gone.

3   So who, or what, killed Miss America? Blame the decline of Western civilization, says Mario Lopez, who will be hosting the show for a third time. Decades ago, the Miss America pageant was a rare chance to see a little skin and sexuality on TV—but now that's everywhere. "There are so many things these days, like Maxim, where you can check out beautiful women," says Lopez. The bathing-suit competition sure seems a lot less risqué when compared with the half-naked ladies now cavorting in hot tubs on scores of reality TV shows. Even feminists have a hard time getting worked up about Miss America these days. "As a feminist, I want to rejoice in the fact that the Miss America pageant has less viewers," says author Jessica Valenti, "but I find it

kind of difficult to, because I have a feeling those millions of viewers are just watching The Bachelor."

And indeed they are. While Miss America could easily be considered the 4 original reality competition show, it has been completely eclipsed by its 21st-century offspring. Viewers used to argue the merits of Miss Montana versus Miss Rhode Island; now they're on either Team Kris or Team Adam. Fans used to sit wondering whether Miss Arkansas would get the crown; now they can't wait to find out which woman receives the final rose of the evening. Ericka Dunlap has seen both sides. She won Miss America in 2003 and came in third on the most recent edition of CBS' The Amazing Race. "People have the option to not watch perfection personified," says Dunlap of the gravitation away from pageants to reality TV. "They just want to watch entertaining television, so we enter into some trash, like the dating reality shows filled with these girls who are willing to bicker and fight." She may have a point: The biggest notoriety Miss America has received in the past 30 years was in 1984, when nude photos surfaced of reigning queen (and now Ugly Betty star) Vanessa Williams, who was subsequently forced to abdicate her title.

How, then, can Miss America keep up with the times, and tastes, of TV au- 5 diences? Originally reluctant to change (which led to its break with ABC in 2004), the pageant has finally gotten a subtle but important makeover: In 2006, the show moved to Las Vegas from its longtime home of Atlantic City in a bid to dazzle younger viewers. And in 2008 and 2009, TLC (after grabbing the show from CMT) produced lead-up reality shows to gather interest in the contestants and build them as personalities viewers could grow attached to. "We recognized that the difficulty with our show was that people didn't get to know these contestants," says Art McMaster, president and CEO of the Miss America Organization. Additionally, TLC introduced American Idol-style "America's Choice" voting, which allows some of the pageant's top 15 finalists to be chosen by viewers. Stam and her runner-up both made the finals through this program.

The nipping and tucking continues in 2010. Producers are trying a one- 6 hour behind-the-curtain special (hosted by What Not to Wear's Clinton Kelly) to air the night before the pageant. Viewers will see the preliminary competitions, which have never been shown in the organization's 89-year history. And then there's the long-standing goal of keeping Miss America a pseudo-celebrity. This past year, Stam rode a float in the Macy's Thanksgiving Day Parade—the first Miss America to do so in nearly a decade. "I have said from the moment I started that Miss America needs to be on the cover of Elle magazine," she says, "and she needs to make appearances on the hottest TV shows, like The Office or CSI." (One well-known TV producer, however, told EW he "doesn't care about Miss America unless there's something juicy or scandalous about her.")

7   Ultimately, the organizers behind the show know their treasured pageant will never again draw 30 million viewers. And they seem okay with that future. "As long as we can provide good ratings to our television partner and keep them happy, we feel like we can really showcase this pageant a lot better in years to come," McMaster says. "This is one of the last great American icons. They may not have seen the pageant, but everybody knows that name, Miss America." But for how long?

Understanding Meaning

1. What, in Stransky's view, caused the decline in the pageant's popularity?

2. Feminists once viewed the Miss America Pageant, with its swimsuit competition and emphasis on beauty, as a sign of sexism. Why have they lost interest in this event?

3. How has the pageant tried to change with the times?

4. *Critical Thinking:* Does the decline of interest in the beauty pageant suggest society no longer sees women as sex objects, or does it indicate that the pageant has simply been supplanted by television shows that more blatantly exploit women's sexuality?

Evaluating Strategy

1. What facts does Stransky present to demonstrate the pageant's loss of popularity?

2. How effective is Stransky's final question? Does an essay that concludes with a question rather than a statement provoke more critical thinking? Why or why not?

Appreciating Language

1. Stransky wrote this article for *Entertainment Weekly*. What do his tone and choice of words suggest about the magazine's readership?

2. Consider the term "Miss America." What connotations does it have? Do people who have never watched the pageant and cannot name the current Miss America use the term as a symbol? What does it represent to you?

WRITING SUGGESTIONS

1. Using Stransky's article as a model, write a short essay explaining the popularity of reality programs like *Big Brother* or *The Bachelor*. Why do people,

who once tuned into television shows to see stars, watch everyday people compete to win a prize or a bachelor's approval?

2. *Collaborative Writing:* Discuss Stransky's article with a group of students. Do they see other reasons for the pageant's loss of popularity? Do young girls still see beauty queens as role models? Have more explicit depictions of women and sexuality made beauty contests seem old-fashioned? Have the contests failed to interest a more diverse American public? Record the group's observations and write a short essay summarizing their views.

DIANA BLETTER

Diana Bletter (1957–) was born in New York City and received a degree in comparative literature from Cornell University in 1978. A freelance writer, Bletter has published articles in the International Herald Tribune, Mademoiselle, Newsday, *and numerous other periodicals. Bletter and Samia Zina helped organize Dove of Peace, an organization of Arab and Jewish women.*

I Refuse to Live in Fear

CONTEXT: *In this 1996 article, Bletter describes the effect terrorism has had on Israelis. She notes that in some ways terrorism has united Jewish and Arab Israelis because "terrorists target everyone."*

1 For most of my life, I thought a shoe box was just a shoe box. Until the afternoon I discovered that it could also be considered a lethal weapon.

2 This is what happened: I had just gone shopping for shoes—one of my favorite pastimes—in the small Mediterranean town of Nahariyya in northern Israel, where I've lived for the last five years. I sat down on a bench to change into my new purchase. I was so busy admiring my feet that I left the shoe box (with my old shoes) on the bench. Fifteen minutes later, I suddenly remembered it and turned back. When I approached the street, I saw crowds of people, barricades and at least five policemen.

3 "What happened?" I asked.

4 "Everyone's been evacuated. Someone reported a suspicious object on a bench down the street."

5 "Oh, no!" I shouted. "My shoes!"

6 Had I arrived even a few seconds later, a special bomb squad—complete with robot—would have imploded my shoe box to deactivate what could have been a bomb hidden inside. The policeman shook his finger at me. "This is the Middle East!" he said angrily. "You can't be careless like that!"

Reality Bites, Hard

7 Moving to Israel from America's tranquil suburbia has taught me about living with the threat of terrorism, something we Americans—after the bomb at Atlanta's Olympic Games and the explosion of TWA Flight 800—are finally being forced to think about on our own turf. The brutal fact of a terrorist attack is that it shatters the innocent peace of our days, the happy logic of our lives. It inalterably changes the way we live.

8 I can no longer daydream as I walk down a street—now I know that, to stay alive, I have to remain aware of who and what surrounds me. As my fiancé always tells me, "Your eyes are your best friends!" and I use them to keep track of emergency exits, the closest windows, the nearest heavy object that could be used in self-defense.

I used to be a reflexive litter-grabber—in my hometown, I never hesitated   9
to pick up a coffee cup from the sidewalk and toss it in a nearby garbage can.
In Israel, I've learned not to touch litter and to stay away from garbage cans—
on several occasions, bombs have been placed in them. If I see a knapsack,
shopping bag or—yes—a shoe box left unattended, I now do three things:
One, ask passers-by if they forgot the package; two, get away from it as fast as
I can; and three, report it to the police.

Necessary Inconveniences

Living in a country where terrorism is always a possibility means that at   10
every entrance to a public place, guards search every bag. I forgot this the first
time I walked into Nahariyya's lone department store; a guard stopped me to
look through my pocketbook. "How could I have shoplifted?" I asked. "I
haven't set foot in the store." Then I remembered that in America, people
worry about what someone might sneak *out* of a store; in Israel, people worry
what weapons or bombs someone might sneak *in* to a store.

The first few days after a terrorist attack seem very quiet. Since all of Israel   11
is only the size of New Jersey, everybody usually knows someone who was hurt
or killed. The nation slips into mourning: People avoid going out, attending
parties, sitting in cafés.

Gradually, though, daily life returns to normal. Israelis (and now, Ameri-   12
cans) have to prove again and again to potential terrorists that we're not
giving in to our fears. If we voluntarily restrict our movements and our lives,
terrorists have vanquished us.

During the latest hostilities in Lebanon (whose border is about seven miles   13
from Nahariyya), Samia Zina, my dear friend—and a Muslim Arab—dreamed
about me, one of those vivid dreams that seems prophetic when you wake. She
dreamed that the fighting had forced her to flee her home, and that I'd hidden
her and her children in my house (and I certainly would have, had the night-
mare been a reality). The next day, Samia popped by to tell me her dream and
give me the two stuffed chickens she'd been moved to cook for me.

"Thank you," I said, astonished by the food and the dream. "But I know you   14
would have hidden me, too."

Terrorists attempt to divide people by fear, but in our community they've   15
brought so-called enemies together: Even Arabs and Jews watch out for each
other in public places, knowing that terrorists target everyone. By resisting the
temptation to become paranoid and isolated, by sticking up for one another,
we remain undefeated.

Understanding Meaning

1. What did the shoe box incident teach Bletter about terrorism?

2. How did living in Israel change the way Bletter walks down a street?

3. What three things does she do if she spots an unattended shopping bag or knapsack on the street?

4. What impact has terrorism had on relations between Israeli Arabs and Jews?

5. How, in Bletter's view, can people defeat terrorism?

6. *Critical Thinking:* This article was written before the 9/11 attacks. Do you think Americans have changed the way they live because of terrorism? Why or why not? Do Americans only think of terrorism when going through airports? Would an abandoned shopping bag or backpack on campus worry you? Why or why not?

Evaluating Strategy

1. How effective is Bletter's opening narrative?

2. How does Bletter use comparison to develop her essay? How is life in Israel different from life in the United States?

3. What examples does Bletter present to show the effect terrorism has had on her behavior?

Appreciating Language

1. Bletter never defines "terrorism" in her essay. How would you define the term? Could a bomb planted in a public place and intended to kill pedestrians be called anything other than a "terrorist" device?

2. This article first appeared the women's magazine *Mademoiselle*. Do you think Bletter's tone and style is suited to her audience? Why or why not?

WRITING SUGGESTIONS

1. Write an essay describing how a recent incident affected your life or the lives of people you know. Did a recent drunk driving accident change the way students drink at parties? Has a recent crime made people more cautious? Have news reports about the economy changed the way people spend money or use credit cards? Has a popular television show inspired students to change their majors?

2. *Collaborative Writing:* Discuss Bletter's essay with a group of students and consider the effect a major terrorist attack would have on the American people. After 9/11, do people expect that someday there will be another spectacular attack that kills thousands? Would the use of biological or nuclear weapons produce more panic and fear than hijacked planes or conventional bombs? Why or why not?

BRENT STAPLES

Brent Staples (1951–) was born in Chester, Pennsylvania, and graduated from Widener University in 1973. He received a doctorate in psychology from the University of Chicago in 1982. After writing for several Chicago publications, he joined the New York Times in 1985 and became a member of its editorial board in 1990. He has also contributed articles to Ms. and Harper's. In 1994 he published a memoir, Parallel Time: Growing Up in Black and White, recalling a childhood of poverty and violence.

Black Men and Public Space

CONTEXT: *In this Harper's article Staples recounts the effects he has had on white pedestrians. As a black male, he realized he had the power to cause fellow citizens to alter their behavior by simply walking in their direction.*

My first victim was a woman—white, well dressed, probably in her early twenties. I came upon her late one evening on a deserted street in Hyde Park, a relatively affluent neighborhood in an otherwise mean, impoverished section of Chicago. As I swung onto the avenue behind her, there seemed to be a discreet, uninflammatory distance between us. Not so. She cast back a worried glance. To her, the youngish black man—a broad 6 feet 2 inches with a beard and billowing hair, both hands shoved into the pockets of a bulky military jacket—seemed menacingly close. After a few more quick glimpses, she picked up her pace and was soon running in earnest. 1

Within seconds she disappeared into a cross street. 2

That was more than a decade ago. I was 22 years old, a graduate student 3 newly arrived at the University of Chicago. It was in the echo of that terrified woman's footfalls that I first began to know the unwieldy inheritance I'd come into—the ability to alter public space in ugly ways. It was clear that she thought herself the quarry of a mugger, a rapist, or worse. Suffering a bout of insomnia, however, I was stalking sleep, not defenseless wayfarers. As a softy who is scarcely able to take a knife to a raw chicken—let alone hold one to a person's throat—I was surprised, embarrassed, and dismayed all at once. Her flight made me feel like an accomplice in tyranny. It also made it clear that I was indistinguishable from the muggers who occasionally seeped into the area from the surrounding ghetto. That first encounter, and those that followed, signified that a vast, unnerving gulf lay between nighttime pedestrians—particularly women—and me. And I soon gathered that being perceived as dangerous is a hazard in itself. I only needed to turn a corner into a dicey situation, or crowd some frightened, armed person in a foyer somewhere, or make an errant move after being pulled over by a policeman. Where fear and weapons meet—and they often do in urban America—there is always the possibility of death.

4   In that first year, my first away from my hometown, I was to become thoroughly familiar with the language of fear. At dark, shadowy intersections, I could cross in front of a car stopped at a traffic light and elicit the *thunk, thunk, thunk, thunk* of the driver—black, white, male, or female—hammering down the door locks. On less traveled streets after dark, I grew accustomed to but never comfortable with people crossing to the other side of the street rather than pass me. Then there were the standard unpleasantries with policemen, doormen, bouncers, cabdrivers, and others whose business it is to screen out troublesome individuals *before* there is any nastiness.

5   I moved to New York nearly two years ago and I have remained an avid night walker. In central Manhattan, the near-constant crowd cover minimizes tense one-on-one street encounters. Elsewhere—in SoHo, for example, where sidewalks are narrow and tightly spaced buildings shut out the sky—things can get very taut indeed.

6   After dark, on the warrenlike streets of Brooklyn where I live, I often see women who fear the worst from me. They seem to have set their faces on neutral, and with their purse straps strung across their chests bandolier-style, they forge ahead as though bracing themselves against being tackled. I understand, of course, that the danger they perceive is not a hallucination. Women are particularly vulnerable to street violence, and young black males are drastically overrepresented among the perpetrators of that violence. Yet these truths are no solace against the kind of alienation that comes of being ever the suspect, a fearsome entity with whom pedestrians avoid making eye contact.

7   It is not altogether clear to me how I reached the ripe old age of 22 without being conscious of the lethality nighttime pedestrians attributed to me. Perhaps it was because in Chester, Pennsylvania, the small, angry industrial town where I came of age in the 1960s, I was scarcely noticeable against a backdrop of gang warfare, street knifings, and murders. I grew up one of the good boys, had perhaps a half-dozen fistfights. In retrospect, my shyness of combat has clear sources.

8   As a boy, I saw countless tough guys locked away; I have since buried several, too. They were babies, really—a teenage cousin, a brother of 22, a childhood friend in his mid-twenties—all gone down in episodes of bravado played out in the streets. I came to doubt the virtues of intimidation early on. I chose, perhaps unconsciously, to remain a shadow—timid, but a survivor.

9   The fearsomeness mistakenly attributed to me in public places often has a perilous flavor. The most frightening of these confusions occurred in the late 1970s and early 1980s, when I worked as a journalist in Chicago. One day, rushing into the office of a magazine I was writing for with a deadline story in

hand, I was mistaken for a burglar. The office manager called security and, with an ad hoc posse, pursued me through the labyrinthine halls, nearly to my editor's door. I had no way of proving who I was. I could only move briskly toward the company of someone who knew me.

Another time I was on assignment for a local paper and killing time before 10 an interview. I entered a jewelry store on the city's affluent Near North Side. The proprietor excused herself and returned with an enormous red Doberman pinscher straining at the end of a leash. She stood, the dog extended toward me, silent to my questions, her eyes bulging nearly out of her head. I took a cursory look around, nodded, and bade her good night.

Relatively speaking, however, I never fared as badly as another black male 11 journalist. He went to nearby Waukegan, Illinois, a couple of summers ago to work on a story about a murderer who was born there. Mistaking the reporter for the killer, police officers hauled him from his car at gunpoint and but for his press credentials would probably have tried to book him. Such episodes are not uncommon. Black men trade tales like this all the time.

Over the years, I learned to smother the rage I felt at so often being taken 12 for a criminal. Not to do so would surely have led to madness. I now take precautions to make myself less threatening. I move about with care, particularly late in the evening. I give a wide berth to nervous people on subway platforms during the wee hours, particularly when I have exchanged business clothes for jeans. If I happen to be entering a building behind some people who appear skittish, I may walk by, letting them clear the lobby before I return, so as not to seem to be following them. I have been calm and extremely congenial on those rare occasions when I've been pulled over by the police.

And on late-evening constitutionals I employ what has proved to be an excel- 13 lent tension-reducing measure: I whistle melodies from Beethoven and Vivaldi and the more popular classical composers. Even steely New Yorkers hunching toward nighttime destinations seem to relax, and occasionally they even join in the tune. Virtually everybody seems to sense that a mugger wouldn't be warbling bright, sunny selections from Vivaldi's *Four Seasons*. It is my equivalent of the cowbell that hikers wear when they know they are in bear country.

Understanding Meaning

1. What is Staples's thesis? What is he saying about race, class, crime, prejudice, and fear in our society?

2. What is Staples's attitude toward the way women responded to his presence? What caused their reactions?

3. Staples reports that both African American and white drivers locked their doors when they encountered him. What is he saying about racial perceptions and fear?

4. How do you interpret the conclusion? Would people be reassured by a black man whistling classical music? What does this say about prejudice, racial profiling, and stereotyping? What else would make a black man appear less threatening—singing spirituals, carrying the *Wall Street Journal*, walking a poodle? Why?

5. *Critical Thinking*: Would a white man walking through an African American neighborhood produce similar results? Would residents respond differently than if he were black? Would a Hispanic, an Asian, an orthodox Jew produce similar or different results?

Evaluating Strategy

1. What is the impact of the first sentence?

2. Staples shifts the chronology several times. How does he prevent readers from becoming confused? How important are transitional statements and paragraph breaks to maintaining a coherent essay?

3. *Blending the Modes*: How does Staples use *narration*, *comparison*, and *example* in developing his essay?

Appreciating Language

1. Staples avoids using words such as "racist," "prejudice," and "stereotype" in his essay. Do words like these tend to be inflammatory and politically charged? Would they detract from his message?

2. What does the tone and style of the essay suggest about the response Staples hoped to achieve from his readers? Do you sense he was trying to reach white or African American readers?

WRITING SUGGESTIONS

1. Write an essay narrating your own experiences in public space. You can explore how you cause others to react to your presence or how location affects your behavior. What happens when you cross the campus late at night, drive alone, or enter a high-crime neighborhood? Would the police and public see you as a likely victim or a probable perpetrator?

2. *Collaborative Writing*: Discuss this essay with a group of students. Consider if a white man in shabby clothing or a black man in a business suit would provoke the same or different responses in white pedestrians. Is class or race the defining factor in producing fear? Is age an issue? Has the public been influenced to see young black men as threatening? Would a

middle-aged black man provoke different reactions? Why or why not? Develop an outline for a sociological experiment that measures people's reaction to a variety of test figures engaged in the same actions. Write a process paper explaining how your group might conduct the experiment and evaluate the results.

OPPOSING VIEWPOINTS: LEGALIZING DRUGS

PETER MOSKOS

Peter Moskos is a former Baltimore police officer and Harvard graduate who is now an assistant professor at the John Jay College of Criminal Justice and the CUNY Graduate Center in the Department of Sociology. In his book Cop in the Hood *(2008), which describes his experiences as a police officer in East Baltimore, Moskos called for reforming the legal system and legalizing drugs.*

Too Dangerous Not to Regulate

CONTEXT: *In this* U.S. News & World Report *article, published in 2008, Moskos argues that the war on drugs has resulted in increased addiction, gang violence, and human suffering. Legalizing and regulating drugs, he predicts, would lessen drug use.*

1   Drugs are bad. So let's legalize them.

2   It's not as crazy as it sounds. Legalization does not mean giving up. It means regulation and control. By contrast, criminalization means prohibition. But we can't regulate what we prohibit, and drugs are too dangerous to remain unregulated.

3   Let's not debate which drugs are good and which are bad. While it's heartless to keep marijuana from terminally ill cancer patients, some drugs—crack, heroin, crystal meth—are undoubtedly bad. But prohibition is the issue, and, as with alcohol, it doesn't work. Between 1920 and 1933, we banned drinking. Despite, or more likely because of, the increased risk, drinking became cool. That's what happens when you delegate drug education to moralists. And crime increased, most notoriously with gangland killings. That's what happens when you delegate drug distribution to crooks. Prohibition of alcohol ended in failure, but for other drugs it continues.

4   Law enforcement can't reduce supply or demand. As a Baltimore police officer, I arrested drug dealers. Others took their place. I locked them up, too. Thanks to the drug war, we imprison more people than any other country. And America still leads the world in illegal drug use. We can't arrest and jail our way to a drug-free America. People want to get high. We could lock up everybody and still have a drug problem. Prisons have drug problems.

5   Illegal production remains high. Since 1981, the price of cocaine has dropped nearly 80 percent. Despite the ongoing presence of U.S. and other troops, Afghanistan has been exporting record levels of opium, from which heroin is made. Poor farmers may not want to sell to criminals, but they

need to feed their families, and there is no legal market for illegal drugs. Al Qaeda in Afghanistan, the FARC in Colombia, and drug gangs in Mexico all rely on drug prohibition. A legal drug trade would do more to undermine these terrorists than military action would. If we taxed drugs, profits would go to governments, which fight terrorists.

Illegal drug dealers sell to anyone. Legal ones are licensed and help keep   6 drugs such as beer, cigarettes, and pharmaceuticals away from minors. Illegal dealers settle disputes with guns. Legal ones solve theirs in court. Illegal dealers fear police. Legal ones fear the IRS.

Less use. Regulation can reduce drug use. In two generations, we've halved   7 the number of cigarette smokers not through prohibition but through education, regulated selling, and taxes. And we don't jail nicotine addicts. Drug addiction won't go away, but tax revenue can help pay for treatment.

The Netherlands provides a helpful example. Drug addiction there is con-   8 sidered a health problem. Dutch policy aims to save lives and reduce use. It succeeds: Three times as many heroin addicts overdose in Baltimore as in all of the Netherlands. Sixteen percent of Americans try cocaine in their life-time. In the Netherlands, the figure is less than 2 percent. The Dutch have lower rates of addiction, overdose deaths, homicides, and incarceration. Clearly, they're doing something right. Why not learn from success? The Netherlands decriminalized marijuana in 1976. Any adult can walk into a legally licensed, heavily regulated "coffee shop" and buy or consume top-quality weed without fear of arrest. Under this system, people in the Netherlands are half as likely as Americans to have ever smoked marijuana.

It's unlikely that repealing federal drug laws would result in a massive in-   9 crease in drug use. People take or don't take drugs for many reasons, but apparently legality isn't high on the list. In America, drug legalization could happen slowly and, unlike federal prohibition, not be forced on any state or city. City and state governments could decide policy based on their needs.

The war on drugs is not about saving lives or stopping crime. It's about yes-   10 teryear's ideologues and future profits from prison jobs, asset forfeiture, court overtime pay, and federal largess.

We have a choice: Legalize drugs, or embark on a second century of failed   11 prohibition. Government regulation may not sound as sexy or as macho as a "war on drugs," but it works better.

Understanding Meaning

1. What is Moskos's thesis? Can you state it in your own words?

2. Why does Moskos believe that legalizing drugs should not be seen as a surrender in the fight against drugs?

3. What effect would legalizing drugs have on terrorists?

4. Why does Moskos believe that legalizing drugs would not increase their use?

5. *Critical Thinking:* Why does Moskos see the war on drugs as a failure? Why cannot law enforcement stop illegal drug use?

Evaluating Strategy

1. How effective is Moskos' introduction?

2. How does Moskos use comparisons to support his thesis? Are they effective? Can a writer rely too much on analogies?

3. How does Moskos address opposing arguments?

4. *Critical Thinking:* How does Moskos use his experience as a police officer to establish his credibility as an authority on drugs?

Appreciating Language

1. Does the word "legalization" suggest acceptance or approval? How does Moskos try to define the word?

2. Moskos refers to beer and cigarettes as "drugs." Do you think many readers will equate beer with heroin? Why or why not?

WRITING SUGGESTIONS

1. Using Moskos' article as a model, write a cause-and-effect essay that analyzes the success or failure of a social or government policy. Has school choice improved education? Have drunk driving laws changed people's behavior?

2. *Collaborative Writing:* Working with a group of students, discuss Moskos's article and determine if you agree or disagree with his view. Write an essay stating your group's views. If members have conflicting opinions, consider developing a comparison paper stating opposing viewpoints.

LEE P. BROWN

Lee P. Brown (1937–) earned a degree in criminology from Fresno State University in 1960. He earned a master's degree in criminology from the University of California–Berkeley, from which he also received his doctorate in 1970. He headed police departments in Atlanta, Houston, and New York City before becoming the first African American mayor of Houston, Texas, in 1997. In 1993 he served as the Director of the Office of National Drug Control Policy (the nation's "drug czar") under President Clinton.

End the Demand, End the Supply

CONTEXT: *In this article, which appeared with Peter Moskos's article in* U.S. News & World Report *in 2008, Brown rejects Moskos's call for the legalization of drugs.*

Illegal drugs continue to be a major problem in America. They will never be 1
legalized, and they should not be.

Advocates of legalization argue that drug prohibition only makes things 2
worse. They argue that crime, the spread of HIV, and violence are major consequences of drug prohibition. But these represent only part of the damage
caused by drug use. Consider drug-exposed infants, drug-induced accidents,
and loss of productivity and employment, not to mention the breakdown of
families and the degeneration of drug-inflicted neighborhoods. These too are
consequences of drugs.

Others argue that drugs affect only the user. This is wrong. No one familiar 3
with alcohol abuse would suggest that alcoholism affects the user solely. And
no one who works with drug addicts will tell you that their use of drugs has not
affected others—usually family and friends.

Some argue that drug enforcement should be replaced by a policy of "harm 4
reduction," which emphasizes decriminalization and medical treatment over
law enforcement and interdiction. But people do not use drugs simply because
they are illegal. Equally significant, effective enforcement reduces drug supply,
increases price, lowers the number of users, and decreases hard-core drug use.
There is an inverse relationship between the price of cocaine and the number
of people seeking emergency room treatment.

Legalization advocates claim widespread support. But the fact is that there 5
is no broad public or political outcry for the decriminalization of drugs.

Contrary to what the advocates of legalization say about the European 6
models, decriminalization has not worked there. The Dutch policy of "responsible" drug use has resulted in thousands of foreigners going to the
Netherlands to buy drugs. These users then commit crimes to support their

habits and drain Dutch taxpayers to provide treatment for their addictions. The number of marijuana and heroin users has increased significantly.

7   The British experience of controlled distribution of heroin resulted in the doubling of the number of recorded new addicts every 16 months between 1960 and 1967. That experiment was ended.

8   A 1994 resolution opposing drug legalization in Europe that was signed by representatives of several European cities stated in part that "the answer does not lie in making harmful drugs more accessible, cheaper and socially accept-able. Attempts to do this have not proven successful."

9   Supply and demand. An effective drug policy must focus on reducing the demand for drugs through prevention, education, and treatment without overlooking enforcement and working with source countries. That was the policy that I developed while serving as the nation's "drug czar" under President Clinton. The formula is simple: no demand, no supply.

10   In 1988, the House Select Committee on Narcotics Abuse and Control, chaired by Rep. Charles Rangel, a New York Democrat, held hearings on the possible legalization of drugs. The questions asked by Rangel then are equally relevant today: Which drugs would we legalize—heroin, cocaine, metham-phetamines, and PCP, as well as marijuana? What would we do with addicts? Would we support their habit for life or pay for their treatment? What would we do about those who are only experimenting? Would legalization contribute to their addiction? What would prevent a black market from emerging?

11   Because these and other questions cannot be answered to the satisfaction of the U.S. public and our lawmakers, America will never legalize drugs.

12   Legalization does not get to the problem's core. In seeking to satisfy the few, it subverts the best interests of all. In purporting to provide a quick, simple, costless cure for crime and violence, it fails to answer why more drug availabil-ity would not lead to more drug use and more devastating consequences.

13   We must, however, change our drug policy and view drug use as a public health problem, not just a problem for the criminal justice system.

Understanding Meaning

1. What is Brown's thesis? Can you state it in your own words?

2. How does Brown counter Moskos's argument that decriminalization has lowered drug use in Europe?

3. How, in Brown's view, does effective law enforcement decrease drug use?

4. Why does Brown believe that legalization would have negative conse-quences?

5. *Critical Thinking:* Are there any points on which Moskos and Brown agree?

Evaluating Strategy

1. How does Brown introduce his personal experience to establish credibility?

2. *Blending the Modes:* How does Brown use *comparison* to develop his cause-and-effect essay?

3. Brown argues that law enforcement reduces supply. Would his argument be stronger if he included facts or statistics to support this assertion? Why or why not?

Appreciating Language

1. Brown places words like "harm reduction" and "responsible" in quotation marks. What impact does this have? What is he trying to suggest about these terms?

2. *Critical Thinking:* Brown uses the term "supply and demand" as being critical to combating drug use. Do you think many programs simply focus on one aspect of the issue, such as cutting demand through education or limiting supply by arrests and seizures? Would society have to stress both supply and demand for such programs to be effective? Why or why not?

WRITING SUGGESTIONS

1. Using Moskos's and Brown's articles as models, write a short essay stating your prediction about the legalization of drugs. If drugs were legalized but regulated like alcohol or cigarettes, would more people use drugs? Would it reduce crime by eliminating gangs? Would it make the drug problem better or worse?

2. *Collaborative Writing:* Discuss Moskos's and Brown's articles with a group of students and ask which author they find more convincing and why. Write a short essay reflecting the ideas of your group. If members disagree, consider writing a comparison essay presenting pro and con views.

WRITING BEYOND THE CLASSROOM

THOMAS JEFFERSON ET AL.

During the hot summer of 1776, the Second Continental Congress met in Philadelphia. Following a call for a resolution of independence from Britain, John Adams, Thomas Jefferson, Benjamin Franklin, Robert Livingston, and Roger Sherman were charged with drafting a declaration. Jefferson wrote the original draft, which was revised by Adams and Franklin before being presented to the entire Congress. After further changes, the Declaration of Independence was adopted and signed.

The Declaration of Independence

CONTEXT: *The Declaration of Independence presents a theory of government greatly influenced by the concept of natural rights espoused by Locke and Rousseau and then provides evidence that the British have failed to respect these rights. Notice that most of the declaration is a list of grievances or reasons for the colonies to seek independence.*

1   *In Congress, July 4, 1776. The unanimous Declaration of the thirteen united States of America,*

2   When in the Course of human events, it becomes necessary for one people to dissolve the political bands which have connected them with another, and to assume among the powers of the earth, the separate and equal station to which the Laws of Nature and of Nature's God entitle them, a decent respect to the opinions of mankind requires that they should declare the causes which impel them to the separation.

3   We hold these truths to be self-evident, that all men are created equal, that they are endowed by their Creator with certain unalienable Rights, that among these are Life, Liberty and the pursuit of Happiness.

4   That to secure these rights, Governments are instituted among Men, deriving their just powers from the consent of the governed,

5   That whenever any Form of Government becomes destructive of these ends, it is the Right of the People to alter or to abolish it, and to institute new Government, laying its foundation on such principles and organizing its powers in such form, as to them shall seem most likely to effect their Safety and Happiness. Prudence, indeed, will dictate that Governments long established should not be changed for light and transient causes; and accordingly all experience hath shown, that mankind are more disposed to suffer, while evils are sufferable, than to right themselves by abolishing the forms to which they are accustomed. But when a long train of abuses and usurpations, pursuing invariably the same Object evinces a design to

reduce them under absolute Despotism, it is their right, it is their duty, to throw off such Government, and to provide new Guards for their future security.

Such has been the patient sufferance of these Colonies; and such is now the 6 necessity which constrains them to alter their former Systems of Government. The history of the present King of Great Britain is a history of repeated injuries and usurpations, all having in direct object the establishment of an absolute Tyranny over these States. To prove this, let Facts be submitted to a candid world.

He has refused his Assent to Laws, the most wholesome and necessary for 7 the public good.

He has forbidden his Governors to pass Laws of immediate and pressing 8 importance, unless suspended in their operation till his Assent should be obtained; and when so suspended, he has utterly neglected to attend to them.

He has refused to pass other Laws for the accommodation of large districts 9 of people, unless those people would relinquish the right of Representation in the Legislature, a right inestimable to them and formidable to tyrants only.

He has called together legislative bodies at places unusual, uncomfortable, 10 and distant from the depository of their public Records, for the sole purpose of fatiguing them into compliance with his measures.

He has dissolved Representative Houses repeatedly, for opposing with 11 manly firmness his invasions on the rights of the people.

He has refused for a long time, after such dissolutions, to cause others to 12 be elected; whereby the Legislative powers, incapable of Annihilation, have returned to the People at large for their exercise; the State remaining in the mean time exposed to all the dangers of invasion from without, and convulsions within.

He has endeavored to prevent the population of these States; for that pur- 13 pose obstructing the Laws for Naturalization of Foreigners; refusing to pass others to encourage their migrations hither, and raising the conditions of new Appropriations of Lands.

He has obstructed the Administration of Justice, by refusing his Assent to 14 Laws for establishing Judiciary powers.

He has made Judges dependent on his Will alone, for the tenure of their 15 offices, and the amount and payment of their salaries.

He has erected a multitude of New Offices, and sent hither swarms of 16 Officers to harrass our people, and eat out their substance.

He has kept among us in times of peace, Standing Armies without the 17 Consent of our legislatures.

He has affected to render the Military independent of and superior to the 18 Civil power.

19   He has combined with others to subject us to a jurisdiction foreign to our constitution, and unacknowledged by our laws; giving his Assent to their Acts of pretended Legislation:

20   For quartering large bodies of armed troops among us:

21   For protecting them, by a mock Trial, from punishment for any Murders which they should commit on the Inhabitants of these States:

22   For cutting off our Trade with all parts of the world:

23   For imposing Taxes on us without our Consent:

24   For depriving us in many cases, of the benefits of Trial by Jury:

25   For transporting us beyond Seas to be tried for pretended offences:

26   For abolishing the free System of English Laws in a neighboring Province, establishing therein an Arbitrary government, and enlarging its Boundaries so as to render it at once an example and fit instrument for introducing the same absolute rule in these Colonies:

27   For taking away our Charters, abolishing our most valuable Laws, and altering fundamentally the Forms of our Governments:

28   For suspending our own Legislatures, and declaring themselves invested with power to legislate for us in all cases whatsoever.

29   He has abdicated Government here, by declaring us out of his Protection and waging War against us.

30   He has plundered our seas, ravaged our Coasts, burnt our towns, and destroyed the lives of our people.

31   He is at this time transporting large Armies of foreign Mercenaries to complete the works of death, desolation and tyranny, already begun with circumstances of Cruelty & perfidy scarcely paralleled in the most barbarous ages, and totally unworthy the Head of a civilized nation.

32   He has constrained our fellow Citizens taken Captive on high Seas to bear Arms against their Country, to become the executioners of their friends and Brethren, or to fall themselves by their Hands.

33   He has excited domestic insurrections among us, and has endeavored to bring on the inhabitants of our frontiers, the merciless Indian Savages, whose known rule of warfare is an undistinguished destruction of all ages, sexes, and conditions.

34   In every stage of these Oppressions We have Petitioned for Redress in the most humble terms: Our repeated Petitions have been answered only by repeated injury. A Prince, whose character is thus marked by every act which may define a Tyrant, is unfit to be the ruler of a free people.

35   Nor have We been wanting in attentions to our British brethren. We have warned them from time to time of attempts by their legislature to extend an unwarrantable jurisdiction over us. We have reminded them of the circumstances of our emigration and settlement here. We have appealed to their

native justice and magnanimity, and we have conjured them by the ties of our common kindred to disavow these usurpations, which would inevitably interrupt our connections and correspondence. They too have been deaf to the voice of justice and consanguinity. We must, therefore, acquiesce in the necessity, which denounces our Separation, and hold them, as we hold the rest of mankind, Enemies in War, in Peace Friends.

We, therefore, the Representatives of the united States of America, in General Congress, Assembled, appealing to the Supreme Judge of the world for the rectitude of our intentions, do, in the Name, and by Authority of the good People of these Colonies, solemnly publish and declare, That these United Colonies are, and of Right ought to be, Free and Independent States; that they are Absolved from all Allegiance to the British Crown, and that all political connection between them and the State of Great Britain, is and ought to be totally dissolved; and that as Free and Independent States, they have full Power to levy War, conclude Peace, contract Alliances, establish Commerce, and to do all other Acts and Things which Independent States may of right do. 36

And for the support of this Declaration, with a firm reliance on the protection of divine Providence, we mutually pledge to each other our Lives, our Fortunes and our sacred Honor. 37

Understanding Meaning

1. What were the principal causes for the Congress to declare independence?

2. Why do Jefferson and the other authors argue that these grievances could not be resolved in any other fashion?

3. *Critical Thinking:* When was the last time you read the Declaration of Independence? Do some items strike you as relevant to current conditions? Should Americans be more familiar with a document that helped create their country establish its values?

Evaluating Strategy

1. How does the Declaration of Independence use induction and deduction?

2. How much space is devoted to the list of causes? Is enough evidence provided to support severing ties with Britain?

3. The causes are placed in separate paragraphs rather than combined. What impact does this have?

Appreciating Language

1. How does the document refer to the king?

2. This document was drafted in 1776. How readable is it today? How has language changed in two hundred years?

WRITING SUGGESTIONS

1. Write a personal analysis of the Declaration of Independence. What do you think is the most significant feature of the document? What does the phrase "Life, Liberty and the pursuit of Happiness" mean to you?

2. *Collaborative Writing:* Discuss the declaration with a group of students. Does the current government reflect the ideals of Jefferson? How has America changed since 1776? For further discussion, look up the original draft, which contained a passage denouncing slavery, a passage Jefferson had to delete to pacify Southern delegates. Develop a statement with other students expressing your opinion of the Declaration of Independence's importance in the twenty-first century.

RESPONDING TO IMAGES

FORECLOSURE SIGN, TEXAS, 2008

© COURTNEY PERRY/DALLAS MORNING NEWS/CORBIS

1. What is your first reaction to this picture? What words come to mind?

2. Does this photograph illustrate a national crisis or a family crisis or both?

3. Could you imagine using this photograph as a political campaign poster? What caption could accompany it? How could a caption shape the picture's message?

4. *Critical Thinking:* Who do you think is most responsible for the mortgage crisis—officials who deregulated the financial industry, irresponsible lenders, or people who bought houses they knew they could not afford?

5. *Visual analysis:* How does the sign contrast with the house? Does it appear to attack or call into question homeownership? What does the house represent?

6. *Collaborative Writing:* Discuss this photograph with a group of students and have each one write a caption. What does each person's caption represent? Can a photograph like this serve as a kind of Rorschach test that reveals an individual's perceptual world?

STRATEGIES FOR CAUSE-AND-EFFECT WRITING

1. **Determine your goal.** Are you attempting to explain a cause or to measure or predict future outcomes?

2. **Evaluate your reader's needs.** What evidence does your reader's require in order to accept your conclusions? Are government statistics more impressive than the testimony of experts? Does any background information or do any definitions need to be presented?

3. **Offer logical, acceptable evidence.** Present support that comes from reliable sources readers will accept. Present evidence in a clearly organized manner. Use brief narratives or analogies to dramatize data.

4. **Review your use of deduction or induction.** Does your major premise contain unproven assumptions? Is it clearly stated, or is it subject to different interpretations? Does your inductive leap move beyond reasonable doubt? Do you provide enough evidence to support your inductive conclusion?

5. **Qualify assertions and conclusions.** A writer who admits that alternative interpretations or conflicting evidence exists can appear more credible to readers than one who narrowly insists he or she has the only possible conclusion.

6. **Evaluate sources.** Do not allow yourself to assume automatically that everything you read is valid. Experts have made errors of judgment. Read books, articles, websites, and studies carefully. Look for signs of bias, unproven assumptions, or mistakes in logic. Do writers support their claims with sufficient and reliable evidence? Do they document their sources? *Look for what is missing.*

7. **Use other modes to organize information.** It may be beneficial to use narrative, comparison, extended definition, or division and classification to present your cause-and-effect thesis.

SUGGESTED TOPICS FOR CAUSE-AND-EFFECT WRITING

GENERAL ASSIGNMENTS

Write a cause-and-effect paper on any of the following topics. Your paper may use other modes to organize and present evidence. Cause-and-effect papers usually require research. It is possible to use cause and effect in less formal papers, in which you offer personal experience and observations as examples. However, the more objective facts you can cite, the stronger your writing will be.

Write a paper explaining the cause(s) of the following topics:

1. Teenage pregnancy

2. Sexual harassment

3. Divorce

4. The success or failure of a local business

5. The victory or defeat of a political candidate

Write a paper measuring or predicting the effects of the following topics:

1. The information superhighway

2. Immigration

3. A parent's loss of a job

4. Tuition increases

5. The election of a particular candidate

WRITING IN CONTEXT

1. Analyze in a short essay a recent event on campus, in your community, or at your place of work. Examine what caused this event to take place. If several causes exist, you may use division to explain them or classification to rank them from the most important to the least important.

2. Write a letter to the editor of the campus newspaper predicting the effects of a current policy change, incident, or trend in student behavior.

3. Imagine a job application that asks you to write a 250-word essay presenting your reasons for choosing your career. Write a 1-page essay that lists your most important reasons. As you write, consider how an employer would evaluate your response.

Student Paper: Cause and Effect

This paper was written in response to the following assignment:

Write an essay explaining the causes or analyzing the effects of a social phenomenon, technological change, economic problem, or political issue. You might discuss causes for the popularity of a fad, the effect of the Internet on political campaigns, or reasons behind recent protests over immigration policies.

First Draft with Instructor's Comments

Clearer introduction needed

Why do so many people throughout the world who once used to

? dream of coming to America now hate it. It seems like all we hear

delete about these days is how much people all over the world now hate

Avoid repetition

the US. Anti-American feelings seem to have swept the whole globe

in the last decade. Sure, "Yankee, Go Home!" was a cliché protest

sign, but now it's all over.

vague, add specific examples Many people say that the reasons people in the world hate

unclear, what people?

us vary a lot. Take for example, US military presence throughout

DELETE Europe, Asia, Africa, and South America, for instance. People

hostile to the United States see US Navy ships dock in their

ports. Sixty years after WWII America still has bases in England

and Germany.

Another reason is American popular culture. Maybe all the sex

and violence Hollywood, Hip Hop, and TV puts out troubles minis-

Run-on ters, rabbis, and priests in this country, but it assaults the mindsets of Muslims throughout the world. We know that all the

<u>stuff</u> Hollywood <u>puts out</u> is fantasy. We see normal Americans work-

ing, going to school, raising kids, and paying bills.   *too informal*

But in other countries the only Americans they see are Tony

Soprano and the *Sex in the City* girls. All they know about us are

sex, greed, and violence. So when their kids begin to sing along

with Britney or wear their hair like Paris, <u>these people go nuts</u>

and see it like the end of their culture.

<u>All of this has been said before</u>. I think maybe one reason the   *Too general,*
                                                                        vague

hatred of the US has gone up in the last twenty years has to do

with the Cold War ending. This is something we did not expect or

understand. Expand this point

REVISION NOTES

Your essay lists common reasons why people in other countries resent the United States. It does not say much that is new. It restates the obvious. Your last paragraph, however, introduces an idea that might give you something original and interesting to write about. Focus on this reason. How did the end of the Cold War cause a rise in anti-American sentiment around the globe?

Revised Draft

Why They Hate Us

In the days following the attacks of September 11, 2001, many shocked Americans wondered why people hated the United States. The horror of watching planes flying into buildings was matched by the disbelief and anger many felt watching people in the Middle East dancing in the streets, honking car horns, and passing out candy to children like it was a holiday. Polls taken in the Middle East revealed that large numbers of people approved of Osama bin Laden and viewed the hijackers not as terrorists but heroes and martyrs. As President Bush prepared for the war in Iraq, many Europeans began criticizing the United States. Polls in Germany and France showed that many Europeans believed the CIA was responsible for the 9/11 attacks. Seeing former allies view the United States with suspicion and hostility troubled many Americans.

Why do they all hate us? Scholars, reporters, and diplomats have given us a lot of reasons. They suggest that anti-Americanism is caused by jealousy, fears of modernity, support for Israel, and the sense that Western culture is eroding traditional customs and values.

But none of these reasons is new. America has been making movies that offend foreign tastes for eighty years. The United States has supported Israel since 1948. The main cause for rising anti-Americanism, I think, is the end of the Cold War. For almost fifty years the world was dominated by two superpowers—the United States and Soviet Union. The conflict made America look less threatening and violent in contrast to a Communist dictatorship that killed and jailed millions.

People in West Germany may have grumbled about being under America's shadow, but they only had to look over the Berlin Wall to realize it was a lot better than being in East Germany under Soviet domination. There was no comparison between living in North or South Korea, either. Arabs and other Muslims may have resented America's support for Israel, but they knew the United States believed in the freedom of religion. The Soviets were officially atheists and denounced all religion. The spread of American influence may have weakened Islamic values, but the growth of Soviet-sponsored Communist movements in Pakistan, Iran, Indonesia, and Algeria threatened to abolish Islam.

The Cold War made America look like the lesser of two evils. We were the good cop in a good cop-bad cop scenario. People resented American power and influence, but had reasons to fear the Communists.

Now that the Cold War is over, the world has only one super-power. We no longer look like the good cop or the lesser evil. To many people in the world the United States is a global bully, an economic giant, and a cultural titan—all of which make other nations feel weak, intimidated, and second-rate. And no people like feeling second-rate.

QUESTIONS FOR REVIEW AND REVISION

1. What is the student's thesis? Can you state it in your own words?

2. Does the student present enough evidence to support the thesis? What, if anything, could strengthen this essay?

3. How effective is the opening? Does it grab attention and dramatize the student's subject? What changes, if any, would you make?

4. *Blending the Modes:* How does the student use *narrative, comparison,* and *persuasion* to develop the essay?

5. Did the student follow the instructor's suggestions? Did the student develop an original topic?

6. Read the essay aloud. Do you detect any informal or unclear sentences that could be more clearly stated?

WRITING SUGGESTIONS

1. Using the student's essay as a model, describe the causes for another phenomenon—the popularity of reality television shows, a campus fad, rising consumer debt, the prices of homes in your area, the local job market, or differences between male and female attitudes on a certain subject.

2. *Collaborative Writing:* Discuss the student essay with a group of students and suggest ways for the United States to counter anti-Americanism around the world. What can the government, foundations, corporations, nonprofit organizations, and individuals do to improve America's image?

CAUSE-AND-EFFECT CHECKLIST

Before submitting your paper, review these points:

1. **Is your thesis clearly stated?**

2. **Are causes clearly stated, logically organized, and supported by details?**

3. **Are conflicting interpretations disproven or acknowledged?**

4. **Are effects supported by observation and evidence? Do you avoid sweeping generalizations and unsupported conclusions?**

5. Do you anticipate future changes that might alter predictions?

6. Do you avoid making errors in critical thinking, especially errors such as making hasty generalizations and confusing time relationships with cause and effect?

7. Have you tested your ideas through peer review?

Info Write provides additional information on writing cause and effect
cengage.learning.infowrite.com

CHAPTER TWELVE

ARGUMENT AND PERSUASION

WHAT IS ARGUMENT AND PERSUASION?

We are bombarded by argument and persuasion every day. Newspaper editorials encourage us to change our opinions about immigration, gun control, taxes, or terrorism. Sales brochures try to convince us to invest in stocks or buy life insurance. Fund-raising letters ask us to contribute to homeless shelters or the local symphony. Billboards, magazine ads, and television commercials urge us to buy automobiles and soft drinks. Political candidates solicit our votes. Public service announcements warn us against smoking and drunk driving.

As a student, you have to develop persuasive arguments in essays and research papers to demonstrate your skills and knowledge. After graduation you will need a persuasive resume and cover letter to secure job interviews. In your career you will have to impress clients, motivate employees, justify decisions, and propose new ideas to superiors with well-stated arguments and persuasive appeals.

Arguments are assertions designed to convince readers to accept an idea, adopt a solution, take action, or change their way of thinking. Writers use reason and facts to support their arguments, often disproving or disputing conflicting theories or alternative proposals in the process. Attorneys prepare written arguments stating why a client has a valid claim or deserves a new trial. Scientists present the results of experiments to argue for new medical treatments or to disprove current assumptions. Economists assemble data to support arguments to raise or lower interest rates.

The way writers present evidence depends on their discipline or profession. Each field has specific methods and standards of presenting evidence and stating arguments.

The audience plays a critical role in the way writers shape an argument, especially when they suspect that readers hold viewpoints opposed to theirs or might be prejudiced against them or the groups they represent. In directing an argument to readers, writers often use persuasion, making emotional or dramatic statements that stir people's passions and beliefs. Advertisers use sex appeal to sell everything from toothpaste to cars. Commercials for charities flash 800 numbers over images of starving children to motivate people to make donations. In creating persuasive arguments, you should consider the perceptual world of your readers (see page 9).

Persuasive Appeals

Writers traditionally use three basic appeals to convince readers to accept their ideas or take action: **logic, emotion,** and **ethics**. Because each appeal has advantages and disadvantages, writers generally use more than one.

Logic supports a point of view or proposed action through reasoned arguments and a presentation of evidence:

facts *observable and verifiable details such as stock prices, rainfall measurements, or the number of cars sold last year*

historical documents *records such as trial transcripts, letters, email, government and corporate reports, blueprints, contracts, resolutions, minutes of meetings, laws, and regulations*

test results *findings established by experiments or standard research methods*

statistics *data represented by numbers and percentages*

expert testimony *opinions or statements made by respected authorities*

eyewitness testimony *statements by those who experienced or witnessed events and situations*

surveys *measurements of public opinion or sample audiences*

Logic is widely used in academic, business, and government reports.

ADVANTAGES: Provides evidence needed for major decisions, especially group decisions. Factual evidence is transferable. Those convinced by research or statistics can share that data to persuade others.

DISADVANTAGES: Demands a high degree of reader attention, concentration, time, and specialized knowledge. Logical arguments are often complex, and data can be difficult to present in brief messages.

Emotion uses images, sensations, or shock appeals to lead people to react in a desired manner. Emotional appeals call on people's deeply felt needs and desires:

Creativity *to achieve recognition through self-expression and originality*

Success *to attain money, fame, status, or fulfillment*

Independence *the drive to be unique, to stand out, and to be individual*

Conformity *the desire to be part of a group, to be included, and to be "in"*

Endurance *to achieve satisfaction by bearing burdens others could not or feeling successful by simply surviving*

Fear *to resist, avoid, or defeat threats to the self or society, such as cancer, crime, or terrorism*

Preservation *to save or maintain traditions, values, artifacts, or the environment from loss or damage*

Popularity *to be known, recognized, accepted, attractive, or desired by the opposite sex*

Emotional appeals are found most frequently in public relations, political campaigns, marketing, and advertising. Emotional appeals are not logical. Persuasive messages often use conflicting emotional appeals to motivate people. Recruiting commercials simultaneously urge men and women to conform by joining a regimented team and to achieve independence by being "one of the few, the proud, the brave."

ADVANTAGES: Produces immediate results.

DISADVANTAGES: Has limited impact, can backfire, and provides limited factual support for readers to share with others.

Ethics use shared values to influence people. Ethics may call on reasoning but do not rest wholly on logical analysis of data. Like emotional appeals, ethics reflect deeply held convictions rather than personal motivations:

Religion *the desire to follow the rules and behavior espoused by one's faith, such as to be a good Christian or an observant Jew.*

Patriotism *the urge to place one's country before personal needs: "Ask not what your country can do for you; ask what you can do for your country."*

Standards *the desire to be a good citizen, a good lawyer, or a good parent; to express the higher ideals of a community, profession, or family role.*

Humanitarianism *a secular appeal to help others, protect the weak, or be a "citizen of the world."*

Ethical appeals form the basis of many sermons, editorials, and political speeches.

ADVANTAGES:	Can be very powerful, especially if the writer is addressing an audience with the same value system
DISADVANTAGES:	Dependent on readers who accept the principles espoused by the writer. A Muslim cleric's appeal, for example, may have little impact on Catholics or atheists.

Blending Appeals

To create effective persuasive messages, writers frequently blend factual details with emotionally charged human-interest stories. A fund-raising email for a children's shelter might use the emotional story of a single child to arouse sympathy, provide facts and statistics to demonstrate the severity of the problem, and then conclude with an ethical appeal for financial support:

	MAKE A DIFFERENCE
Emotion *human interest story demonstrating a problem*	Thirteen-year-old Sandy Lopez will not have to sleep in a doorway tonight. Abandoned by abusive parents, she spent six weeks living in subway stations and alleys before she came to Safe Haven. Today she has a warm bed, clean clothes, and regular meals. She is back in school, making friends, and studying music.

| Logic
factual support
presenting a solution	Since 1986 Safe Haven has helped thousands of homeless children find shelter, counseling, and support. Eighty percent of our clients complete high school and almost a third graduate from college.
	But Safe Haven has only 90 beds and every day has to turn away dozens of the 2,000 homeless children who live in the streets, where they often succumb to drugs, prostitution, and alcohol abuse. To meet the growing need, Safe Haven needs your help to build a new dorm, hire more counselors, and expand its job training center.
Ethics
moral call to action	Living in one of the richest cities in the world, can we ignore the children who sleep in our streets? Make a difference. Contribute to Safe Haven today.

Appealing to Hostile Readers

Perhaps most challenging is attempting to persuade a hostile audience: readers you anticipate having negative attitudes toward you, the organization you represent, or the ideas you advocate. Although no technique will magically convert opponents into supporters, you can overcome a measure of hostility and influence those who may still be undecided with a few approaches:

1. **Openly admit differences.** Instead of attempting to pretend no conflict exists, openly state that your view may differ from that of your readers. This honest admission can win a measure of respect.

2. **Responsibly summarize opposing viewpoints.** By fairly restating your opponents' views, you force readers to agree with you and demonstrate impartiality.

3. **Avoid making judgmental statements.** Do not label your opponents' ideas with negative language. Use neutral terms to make distinctions. If you call your ideas intelligent and your readers' ideas naïve or stupid, you will have difficulty getting people to accept your points because in the process they will have to accept your insults as being valid.

4. **Point to shared values, experiences, and problems.** Build common bridges with your readers by demonstrating past cooperation and common goals.

5. **Ask your readers to keep an open mind.** Don't demand or expect to convert readers. However, almost everyone will agree to try to be open-minded and receptive to new ideas, so you can suggest that what is needed is a reasonable debate about issues, rather than arguments or accusations.

6. **Work to overcome negative stereotypes.** Play the devil's advocate, and determine what negative stereotypes your readers might have about you and your ideas. Then work to include examples, references, and evidence in your paper to counter negative assumptions.

CRITICAL THINKING FOR WRITING ARGUMENT AND PERSUASION

Perhaps no other form of writing demands more critical thinking than argument and persuasion. When using logical, emotional, and ethical appeals, avoid the logical fallacies (see pages 302-303).

STRATEGIES FOR READING ARGUMENT AND PERSUASION

When reading the argument and persuasion entries in this chapter, keep these questions in mind:

Understanding Meaning

1. What is the author's thesis? What does he or she want readers to accept?

2. How credible is the thesis? Does it make sense? Are alternatives discussed?

3. How does the writer characterize those who advocate differing views? Does the writer appear to have an unfair bias?

Evaluating Strategy

1. Which appeals are used—logic, emotion, or ethics?

2. Do the appeals seem to work with the intended audience?

3. Are the factual details interesting, believable, and effective?

4. Does the writer present relevant and sufficient evidence to support his or her thesis?

5. Are emotional appeals suitable, or do they risk backfiring or distorting the issue?

6. Are the logical fallacies avoided?

7. Does the writer appear to anticipate rejection or approval?

Appreciating Language

1. What role does connotation play in shaping arguments using logical, emotional, or ethical appeals?

2. What does the author's choice of words suggest about the intended audience?

3. Does word choice indicate a bias? Does the writer use inflammatory or derogatory language to dismiss opposing views instead of debating their merits or offering proof?

ANNA QUINDLEN

Anna Quindlen (1952–) graduated from Barnard College in 1974 and began working as a reporter in New York City. After writing articles for the New York Post, *she took over the "About New York" column for the* New York Times. *In 1986 she started her own column, "Life in the Thirties." Her collected articles were published in* Living Out Loud *in 1988. She has written numerous op-ed pieces for the* Times *on social and political issues and in 1992 received the Pulitzer Prize. The following year she published another collection of essays,* Thinking Out Loud: On the Personal, the Political, the Public, and the Private. *Quindlen has also written three novels,* Object Lessons, One True Thing, *and* Black and Blue.

Stuff is Not Salvation

CONTEXT: *Anna Quindlen published this* Newsweek *article in 2008, a time when a severe recession caused rising unemployment, foreclosures, and business failures. Addressing the economic collapse, she questioned Americans' habitual consumerism.*

1

opening question

As the boom times fade, an important holiday question surfaces: why in the world did we buy all this junk in the first place?

2

dramatic example

What passes for the holiday season began before dawn the day after Thanksgiving, when a worker at a Wal-Mart in Valley Stream, N.Y., was trampled to death by a mob of bargain hunters. Afterward, there were reports that some people, mesmerized by cheap consumer electronics and discounted toys, kept shopping even after announcements to clear the store.

3

consumption as sickness

These are dark days in the United States: the cataclysmic stock-market declines, the industries edging up on bankruptcy, the home foreclosures and the waves of layoffs. But the prospect of an end to plenty has uncovered what may ultimately be a more pernicious problem, an addiction to consumption so out of control that it qualifies as a sickness. The suffocation of a store employee by a stampede of shoppers was horrifying, but it wasn't entirely surprising.

4

comparison

Americans have been on an acquisition binge for decades. I suspect television advertising, which made me want a Chatty Cathy doll so much as a kid that when I saw her under the tree my head almost exploded. By contrast, my father will be happy to tell you about the excitement of getting an orange in his stocking during the Depression. The depression before this one.

5

A critical difference between then and now is credit. The orange had to be paid for. The rite of passage for a child when I was young was a solemn visit to the local bank, there to exchange birthday money for a savings passbook. Every once in a while, like magic, a bit of extra money would appear. Interest. Yippee.

6

debt

The passbook was replaced by plastic, so that today Americans are overwhelmed by debt and the national savings rate is calculated, like an algebra equation, in negatives. By 2010 Americans will be a trillion dollars in the hole on credit-card debt alone.

But let's look, not at the numbers, but the atmospherics. Appliances, toys, clothes, gadgets. Junk. There's the sad truth. Wall Street executives may have made investments that lost their value, but, in a much smaller way, so did the rest of us. "I looked into my closet the other day and thought, why did I buy all this stuff?" one friend said recently. A person in the United States replaces a cell phone every 16 months, not because the cell phone is old, but because it is old-ish. My mother used to complain that the Christmas toys were grubby and forgotten by Easter. (I didn't even really like dolls, especially dolls who introduced themselves to you over and over again when you pulled the ring in their necks.) Now much of the country is made up of people with the acquisition habits of a 7-year-old, desire untethered from need, or the ability to pay. The result is a booming business in those free-standing storage facilities, where junk goes to linger in a persistent vegetative state, somewhere between eBay and the dump.   *7*

question repeated

Oh, there is still plenty of need. But it is for real things, things that matter: college tuition, prescription drugs, rent. Food pantries and soup kitchens all over the country have seen demand for their services soar. Homelessness, which had fallen in recent years, may rebound as people lose their jobs and their houses. For the first time this month, the number of people on food stamps will exceed the 30 million mark.   *8*

need for "real things"

Hard times offer the opportunity to ask hard questions, and one of them is the one my friend asked, staring at sweaters and shoes: why did we buy all this stuff? Did anyone really need a flat-screen in the bedroom, or a designer handbag, or three cars? If the mall is our temple, then Marc Jacobs is God. There's a scary thought.   *9*

question repeated

The drumbeat that accompanied Black Friday this year was that the numbers had to redeem us, that if enough money was spent by shoppers it would indicate that things were not so bad after all. But what the economy required was at odds with a necessary epiphany. Because things are dire, many people have become hesitant to spend money on trifles. And in the process they began to realize that it's all trifles.   *10*

Here I go, stating the obvious: stuff does not bring salvation. But if it's so obvious, how come for so long people have not realized it? The happiest families I know aren't the ones with the most square footage, living in one of those cavernous houses with enough garage space to start a homeless shelter. (There's a holiday suggestion right there.) And of course they are not people who are in real want. Just because consumption is bankrupt doesn't mean that poverty is ennobling.   *11*

thesis example

But somewhere in between there is a family like one I know in rural Pennsylvania, raising bees for honey (and for the science, and the fun, of it), digging a pond out of the downhill flow of the stream, with three kids who   *12*

example

somehow, incredibly, don't spend six months of the year whining for the toy du jour. (The youngest once demurred when someone offered him another box on his birthday; "I already have a present," he said.) The mother of the household says having less means her family appreciates possessions more. "I can give you a story about every item, really," she says of what they own. In other words, what they have has meaning. And meaning, real meaning, is *final point* what we are always trying to possess. <u>Ask people what they'd grab if their house were on fire, the way our national house is on fire right now. No one ever says it's the tricked-up microwave they got at Wal-Mart.</u>

Understanding Meaning

1. What is Quindlen's thesis? Can you state it in your own words?

2. What does Quindlen blame, in part, for what she calls an "acquisitions binge"?

3. What does Quindlen mean by the need for "real things"? What things matter in her opinion?

4. How did credit, in her view, fuel consumption?

5. Whom does Quindlen see as the happiest families? Why?

6. *Critical Thinking:* Consumer spending accounts for 60–70 percent of the American economy. Walmart is the nation's largest employer. Can we cut back on spending without causing more unemployment and business failures? Are we trapped in a vicious circle of credit and spending? What would it take to change our economy?

Evaluating Strategy

1. Quindlen restates the question, "Why did we buy all this stuff," three times. Is this an effective device? Why or why not? Do you think she senses that many of her readers have asked themselves similar questions?

2. How effective is Quindlen's opening example? Does the trampling death of a shopper illustrate her point?

3. What facts does Quindlen include to support her thesis? Are they convincing? Why or why not?

4. *Blending the Modes:* Where does Quindlen use *narration* and *comparison* to develop her argument?

Appreciating Language

1. Quindlen uses words like "stuff" or "junk" to describe people's personal possessions. What impact do these words have? Do you know people who

spend money on something "they have to have," only to call it "my junk" or "my stuff" a few months later?

2. For some Americans, is the shopping mall a "temple"? Why or why not?

3. What words does Quindlen use to describe the happiest families she knows?

4. *Critical Thinking:* Consider the words in Quindlen's title. Do many people see "stuff" as "salvation"? Do we buy things because we "need" them or because we think they will make us happy, more popular, or enriched?

WRITING SUGGESTIONS

1. Write a short essay about shopping habits you have observed. Do you know people who purchase items they never use or buy clothes they never wear? Is shopping itself a kind of hobby or social activity? Is "going to the mall" something to do, like going to a movie? Is this behavior normal or do you see it as something harmful?

2. *Collaborative Writing:* Discuss Quindlen's remark that "meaning, real meaning, is what we are always trying to possess" with a group of students. What do they think this statement means? Do people buy "stuff" because it is easier to attain than something more abstract like love, respect, or happiness? Summarize the students' views in a short essay. If they have differing interpretations, use comparison or division to organize their comments.

MAGGIE JACKSON

Maggie Jackson earned a B.A. in English from Yale University in 1982 and a graduate degree in international politics with highest honors from the London School of Economics in 1990. She is a columnist for the Boston Globe *and has written for many national publications, including the* New York Times, BusinessWeek, Utne Reader, *and* Gastronomica. *Her books include* What's Happening to Home? Balancing Work, Life and Refuge in the Information Age *(2002) and* Distracted: The Erosion of Attention and the Coming Dark Age *(2008).*

Distracted: The New News World and the Fate of Attention

CONTEXT: *In George Gissing's 1891 novel* New Grub Street, *an editor proposed to create a newspaper for readers "incapable of sustained attention." People, he argued, want only "bits" of stories, scandals, jokes, and statistics. "Their attention," he claimed, "can't sustain itself beyond two inches.... Even chat is too solid for them; they want chit-chat." In the twenty-first century, according to Jackson, attention span has dwindled further in the multimedia "data floods" that split our concentration and erode our ability to think.*

1 Last summer, I was a passenger in a car barreling down a Detroit highway when I noticed a driver speeding past us, a magazine propped up beside his steering wheel. Perhaps most amazingly, I was the only person in my group who was surprised by this high-speed feat of multitasking.

2 Today, it's rare to give anything our full attention. Our focus is fragmented and diffused, whether we're conversing, eating, working, minding our kids—or imbibing the news. A new hypermobile, cybercentric and split-focused world has radically changed the context of news consumption—and shifted the environment for newsgathering as well. Attention is the bedrock of deep learning, critical thinking, and creativity—all skills that we need to foster, not undercut, more than ever on both sides of the newsmaking fence. And as we become more culturally attention-deficient, I worry about whether we as a nation can nurture both an informed citizenry—and an informative press.

3 It's easy to point first to rising data floods as a culprit for our distraction. More than 100 million blogs and a like number of Web sites, not to mention 1.8 million books in print, spawn so much information that, as Daniel Boorstin observes, data begin to outstrip the making of meaning. "We are captives of information," writes the cultural historian Walter Ong, "for uninterrupted information can create an information chaos and, indeed, has done so, and quite clearly will always do so."

Yet sense-making in today's information-rich world is not just a matter of 4
how much we have to contend with but, more importantly, how we
approach the 24/7 newsfeed that is life today. Consider the Detroit driver; where
was he consuming media, and how much focus was he allotting to the task?

Increasingly, Americans are on the go, whatever they're doing. Just 5
14 percent of us move each year, yet the average number of miles that we
drive annually has risen 80 percent during the past two decades. The car-as-
moving-den, the popularity of power bars and other portable cuisine, the
rise of injuries related to "textwalking," all of these—and more—attest to
our collective hyperactivity. And as "We relentlessly hurry through our days
toting hand-held foods and portable gadgets, at the same time we keep one
ear or eye on multiple streams of news-bytes.

Fragmented Attention

As a term, "multitasking" doesn't quite do justice to all the ways in which 6
we fragment our attention. Split-focus is sometimes simply the result of living
in a highly mediated world. More than half of children ages eight to 18 live in
homes where a television is on most of the time, an environment linked to
attention difficulties and lowered parent-child interaction. In public spaces
from elevators to taxis, screens packed with flickering words and images are
increasingly hard to avoid. Despite reconnaissance forays up and down
airports, I usually have to succumb to an inescapable TV blare while waiting
to fly. Former Microsoft executive Linda Stone deems ours a landscape of
"continuous partial attention." Tuning in and out is a way of life.

But split focus also occurs when we hopscotch from one task or person to 7
another, as most famously exemplified by the lethal crash of a California com-
muter train, apparently because the rail engineer at the helm was texting. Our
veneration of multitasking can be traced in part to the influential efficiency
guru Frederick W. Taylor, who counseled that factory work could be speeded
up if broken down into interchangeable parts. As well, we live in an era where
we seem to believe that we can shape time at will. We ignore age-old rhythms
of sun and season, strain to surpass our biological limitations, and now seek to
break the fetters of mechanized time by trying to do two or more things at
once. Multitasking is born of a post-clock era.

The result on the job is "work fragmentation," according to Gloria Mark, 8
an informatics professor at the University of California, Irvine and a leader
in the field of "interruption science." In studies across a range of industries,
she and other researchers have found that office workers change tasks on
average every three minutes throughout the day. An e-mail, instant message,
phone call, colleague's question, or a new thought prompts an interruption.
Once interrupted, it takes nearly 25 minutes to return to an original task.
Half of the time, people are interrupting themselves.

9   The risks are clear. "If you're continually interrupted and switching thoughts, it's hard to think deeply about anything," Mark once observed to me. "How can you engage with something?"

10   In our rapid-fire, split-focus era, are we able to process, filter and reflect well on the tsunamis of information barraging us daily? Are we hearing, but not listening? If this continues to be the way we work, learn and report, could we be collectively nurturing new forms of ignorance, born not from a dearth of information as in the past, but from an inability or an unwillingness to do the difficult work of forging knowledge from the data flooding our world?

11   I see worrisome signs that our climate of distraction undermines our ability to think deeply. Consider that nearly a third of workers are so busy or interrupted that they often feel they do not have time to reflect on the work that they do, according to the Families and Work Institute. David M. Levy, a professor at the University of Washington, has even held a high-level MacArthur Foundation-funded conference tellingly called, "No Time to Think." And for all their tech-fluency, younger generations often have trouble evaluating and assessing information drawn from the Web, studies show. For example, a new national exam of information literacy, the Educational Testing Service's "iSkills" assessment test, found that just half of college students could judge the objectivity of a Web site, and just over a third could correctly narrow an overly broad online search.

Multitasking and the News

12   News consumption fares no better, according to a small but in-depth recent study of 18- to 34-year-olds commissioned by The Associated Press. The 18 participants, who were tracked by ethnographers for days, consumed a "steady diet of bite-size pieces of news," almost always while multitasking. Their news consumption was often "shallow and erratic," even as they yearned to go beyond the brief and often repetitive headlines and updates that barraged them daily. Participants "appeared debilitated by information overload and unsatisfying news experiences," researchers observed. Moreover, "when the news wore them down, participants in the study showed a tendency to passively receive versus actively seek news."

13   This is a disturbing portrait: multitasking consumers uneasily "snacking" on headlines, stuck on the surface of the news, unable to turn information into knowledge.

14   Are consumers lazy? Are the media to blame? Or is Google making us stupid, as a recent Atlantic magazine cover story asked? It's far too simplistic to look for a single culprit, a clear-cut driver of such changes. Rather, helped by influential tools that are seedbeds of societal change, we've built a culture over generations that prizes frenetic movement, fragmented work, and instant answers. Just today, my morning paper carried a front-page story about efforts "in a new age of impatience" to create a quickboot computer. Explained one tech executive,

"It's ridiculous to ask people to wait a couple of minutes" to start up their computer. The first hand up in the classroom, the hyper-businessman who can't sit still, much less listen—these are markers of success in American society.

Of course, the news business has always been quick, fast and fueled by multitasking. Reporters work in one of the most distracting of milieus—and yet draw on reserves of just-in-time focus to meet deadlines. Still, perhaps today we need to consider how much we can shrink editorial attention spans, with our growing emphasis on "4D" newsgathering, Twitter-style reporting, and newsfeeds from citizen bloggers whose influence far outstrips any hard-won knowledge of the difficult craft of journalism. It's not just news consumers who are succumbing to a dangerous dependence on what's first up on Google for making sense of their world.

Ultimately, our new world does more than speed life up and pare the news down. Most importantly, our current climate undermines the trio of skills—focus, awareness and planning/judgment—that make up the crucial human faculty of attention. When we split our focus, curb our awareness, and undercut our ability to gain perspective, we diminish our ability to think critically, carry out deep learning, or be creative. Can we afford to create an attention-deficient economy or press, or build a healthy democracy from a culture of distraction? Absolutely not.

Understanding Meaning

1. Why is the lack of attention significant in the information age? Does Jackson believe that there is a paradox—the more data that are made available to us, the less we actually know?

2. Jackson states that "it's rare to give anything our full attention." Have you noticed that people feel driven to attempt to do more than one thing at a time? Do you see students studying while watching television or listening to music? Is focusing on one thing at a time too challenging or difficult for some people?

3. Jackson discusses what Gloria Mark calls "work fragmentation." Do jobs require people to split their focus? Have companies tried to make employees more productive by assigning them a variety of competing tasks and responsibilities? Have you observed people using a cell phone while driving or talking to a customer as they read their email?

4. What does Jackson see as the risks of multitasking? How many times have you forgotten or overlooked something important while trying to accomplish several assignments at once?

5. How does multitasking affect our consumption of news? Do you notice that cable news broadcasts fragment our attention by running one-sentence

updates at the bottom of the screen or showing sidebar graphics while conducting a live interview? Are we, as Jackson suggests, receiving a stream of "bite-size pieces of news" that creates a series of superficial glimpses of events rather than a full understanding of problems and issues?

6. Because people have such short and superficial attention spans, do you think politicians feel they have to reduce their messages to bumper-sticker phrases people can quickly remember and repeat? Does the lack of focus and "deep thinking" make it difficult for politicians to discuss complex issues such as health care, the economy, or foreign policy intelligently?

7. *Critical Thinking:* Does the habit of multitasking also affect our personal relationships? Do you know people who attempt to hold a conversation with one person while talking with someone else on a cell phone? Do we increasingly accept the idea that no one deserves our undivided attention?

Evaluating Strategy

1. How effective is Jackson's opening? How does this example introduce her subject and illustrate her thesis?

2. How does Jackson present her thesis? Can you restate it in your own words?

3. What evidence does Jackson provide to support her views?

4. *Blending the Modes:* Where does Jackson use *narration, comparison, analysis,* and *cause and effect* to develop her argument?

5. Jackson ends her article by posing a question and then answering it. Is this an effective device? Why or why not?

Appreciating Language

1. Jackson places key terms, such as "textwalking," "work fragmentation" and "continuous partial attention," in quotation marks. Is this an effective way to highlight words? Can a writer emphasize too many words or phrases?

2. Jackson uses phrases such as "data floods" and "tsunamis of information." How do these images support her thesis?

3. Jackson refers to the term "multitasking" several times. What connotation does this word have? Do you know people who see "multitasking" as an important skill? Do they pride themselves on their ability to juggle competing tasks?

WRITING SUGGESTIONS

1. In 1946 George Orwell observed that in "many English homes the radio is literally never turned off":

   > . . . I know people who will keep the radio playing all through a meal and at the same time continue talking just loudly enough for the voices and music to cancel out. This is done for a definite purpose. The music prevents the conversation from becoming serious or even coherent, while the chatter of voices stops one from listening attentively to the music and thus prevents the onset of that dreaded thing, thought.

   Do people fill their lives with a flow of distracting images and sounds so they do not have to think, confront problems, or ask themselves troubling questions? Write an essay explaining how people use distractions to avoid having to think.

2. *Collaborative Writing:* Discuss Jackson's article with a group of students and write a short process essay describing ways schools can teach students to overcome "continuous partial attention" with focus and concentration. Refer to Samuel Scudder's "Take This Fish and Look at It" (page 69). Your group might list a set of concentration or critical thinking exercises. How can schools teach students to concentrate and think critically?

BLENDING THE MODES

MARY SHERRY

Mary Sherry (1940–) writes from her experience as a parent, a writer, and a teacher. She writes articles and advertising copy, owns a small publishing firm in Minnesota, and for many years has taught remedial and creative writing to adults.

In Praise of the "F" Word

CONTEXT: *Social promotion is not a new concept. For years teachers have passed students who should not have passed because of the social stigma associated with being left behind by one's peers. President George W. Bush, in fact, even pushed a major educational incentive called No Child Left Behind. The goal of having every child succeed is a noble goal. The reality for some students, however, is that they have no motivation to try very hard to succeed unless they feel that failure is a real possibility. In this 1991 article from* Newsweek, *Sherry argues that simply failing students who do not try would provide the motivation they might need to take school seriously.*

1   Tens of thousands of 18-year-olds will graduate this year and be handed meaningless diplomas. These diplomas won't look any different from those awarded their luckier classmates. Their validity will be questioned only when their employers discover that these graduates are semiliterate.

2   Eventually a fortunate few will find their way into educational repair shops—adult-literacy programs, such as the one where I teach basic grammar and writing. There, high-school graduates and high-school dropouts pursuing graduate-equivalency certificates will learn the skills they should have learned in school. They will also discover they have been cheated by our educational system.

3   As I teach, I learn a lot about our schools. Early in each session I ask my students to write about an unpleasant experience they had in school. No writers' block here! "I wish someone would have made me stop doing drugs and made me study." "I liked to party and no one seemed to care." "I was a good kid and didn't cause any trouble, so they just passed me along even though I didn't read well and couldn't write." And so on.

4   I am your basic do-gooder, and prior to teaching this class I blamed the poor academic skills our kids have today on drugs, divorce and other impediments to concentration necessary for doing well in school. But, as I rediscover each time I walk into the classroom, before a teacher can expect students to concentrate, he has to get their attention, no matter what distractions may be at hand. There are many ways to do this, and they have much to do with teaching style. However, if style alone won't do it, there is another way to show who holds the winning hand in the classroom. That is to reveal the trump card of failure.

I will never forget a teacher who played that card to get the attention of   5
one of my children. Our youngest, a world-class charmer, did little to develop
his intellectual talents but always got by. Until Mrs. Stifter.

Our son was a high school senior when he had her for English. "He sits in   6
the back of the room talking to his friends," she told me. "Why don't you
move him to the front row?" I urged, believing the embarrassment would get
him to settle down. Mrs. Stifter looked at me steely-eyed over her glasses. "I
don't move seniors," she said. "I flunk them." I was flustered. Our son's academic
life flashed before my eyes. No teacher had ever threatened him with that
before. I regained my composure and managed to say that I thought she was
right. By the time I got home I was feeling pretty good about this. It was a radical
approach for these times, but, well, why not? "She's going to flunk you," I
told my son. I did not discuss it any further. Suddenly English became a priority
in his life. He finished out the semester with an A.

I know one example doesn't make a case, but at night I see a parade of stu-   7
dents who are angry and resentful for having been passed along until they
could no longer even pretend to keep up. Of average intelligence or better,
they eventually quit school, concluding they were too dumb to finish. "I
should have been held back" is a comment I hear frequently. Even sadder are
those students who are high-school graduates who say to me after a few weeks
of class, "I don't know how I ever got a high-school diploma."

Passing students who have not mastered the work cheats them and the em-   8
ployers who expect graduates to have basic skills. We excuse this dishonest behavior
by saying kids can't learn if they come from terrible environments. No
one seems to stop to think that—no matter what environments they come
from—most kids don't put school first on their list unless they perceive something
is at stake. They'd rather be sailing.

Many students I see at night could give expert testimony on unemploy-   9
ment, chemical dependency, abusive relationships. In spite of these difficulties,
they have decided to make education a priority. They are motivated by
the desire for a better job or the need to hang on to the one they've got. They
have a healthy fear of failure.

People of all ages can rise above their problems, but they need to have a   10
reason to do so. Young people generally don't have the maturity to value education
in the same way my adult students value it. But fear of failure, whether
economic or academic, can motivate both.

Flunking as a regular policy has just as much merit today as it did two gen-   11
erations ago. We must review the threat of flunking and see it as it really is—
a positive teaching tool. It is an expression of confidence by both teachers and
parents that the students have the ability to learn the material presented to
them. However, making it work again would take a dedicated, caring conspiracy
between teachers and parents. It would mean facing the tough reality that

passing kids who haven't learned the material—while it might save them grief for the short term—dooms them to long-term illiteracy. It would mean that teachers would have to follow through on their threats, and parents would have to stand behind them, knowing their children's best interests are indeed at stake. This means no more doing Scott's assignments for him because he might fail. No more passing Jodi because she's such a nice kid.

12   This is a policy that worked in the past and can work today. A wise teacher, with the support of his parents, gave our son the opportunity to succeed—or fail. It's time we return this choice to all students.

Understanding Meaning

1. What was Sherry's purpose in writing the essay? Does she have in mind certain types of students? Are there students who should be excluded from her plan?

2. When Sherry discusses the students she works with in night school, what reasons does she say they had for not doing well in school? How do they feel about their education?

3. Why are the students Sherry teaches motivated to learn what they failed to learn when they were younger?

4. Why does Sherry call the threat of failure a positive teaching tool?

5. Why would it take a concerted effort of parents and teachers for her suggestion to work?

6. *Critical Thinking:* Do you feel that the threat of failure would motivate students to do better in school than they would without that threat? Is Sherry right in thinking that students do not perceive failure to be a real threat? Have things changed since Sherry published this essay in 1991?

Evaluating Strategy

1. Is the title effective in grabbing attention? Why or why not?

2. *Blending the Modes:* Sherry makes use of her own son as an example. Is he representative of high school students who don't do as well as they could in school?

3. How does Sherry establish herself as someone who has a right to express an opinion on this subject? In other words, how does she present a trustworthy ethos?

4. Would students in grades K–12 be able to get past their emotional response to failing and understand its logic? If you failed a course and were told it would be good for you in the long run, would you agree?

Appreciating Language

1. What does Sherry mean when she refers to failure as the "trump card" of education?

2. What does Sherry suggest with her term "educational repair shops" in the second paragraph?

3. Is Sherry's tone and style suited to a news magazine like *Newsweek?* Why or why not?

WRITING SUGGESTIONS

1. Write a short essay that agrees or disagrees with Sherry's argument about failing students.

2. *Collaborative Writing:* Discuss Sherry's essay with a group of students and ask them about the grading policies in their high schools. Were failing grades given routinely or rarely? Were students passed based on attendance? Write a short essay organizing the group's observations using division or classification.

MARTIN JACQUES

Martin Jacques (1945–) was born in Britain and graduated with honors from Manchester University. From 1977 to 1991 he edited Marxism Today. *He has been a contributor to the* Times, *the* Sunday Times, *the* Guardian, *and the* New Statesman. *He was a visiting professor at Renmin University in Beijing and is currently a visiting fellow at the London School of Economics. In 2009 he published* When China Rules the World: The Rise of the Middle Kingdom and the End of the Western World.

When China Rules the World

CONTEXT: *In this excerpt from* When China Rules the World *Martin Jacques argues that by 2050 China will be the world's largest economy, with the United States and India vying for second place. The world, once dominated by Western nations like Britain, France, and Germany, will be influenced by the rising economies of Mexico, Brazil, and Indonesia.*

1 Since 1945 the United States has been the world's dominant power. Even during the Cold War its economy was far more advanced than, and more than twice as large as, that of the Soviet Union, while its military capability and technological sophistication were much superior.[1] Following the Second World War, the US was the prime mover in the creation of a range of multinational and global institutions, such as the United Nations, the International Monetary Fund and NATO, which were testament to its new-found global power and authority. The collapse of the Soviet Union in 1991 greatly enhanced America's pre-eminent position, eliminating its main adversary and resulting in the territories and countries of the former Soviet bloc opening their markets and turning in many cases to the US for aid and support. Never before, not even in the heyday of the British Empire, had a nation's power enjoyed such a wide reach. The dollar became the world's preferred currency, with most trade being conducted in it and most reserves held in it. The US dominated all the key global institutions bar the UN, and enjoyed a military presence in every part of the world. Its global position seemed unassailable, and at the turn of the millennium terms like 'hyperpower' and 'unipolarity' were coined to describe what appeared to be a new and unique form of power.

2   The baton of pre-eminence, before being passed to the United States, had been held by Europe, especially the major European nations like Britain, France and Germany, and previously, to a much lesser extent, Spain, Portugal and the Netherlands. From the beginning of Britain's Industrial Revolution

in the late eighteenth century until the mid twentieth century, Europe was to shape global history in a most profound manner. The engine of Europe's dynamism was industrialization and its mode of expansion colonial conquest. Even as Europe's position began to decline after the First World War, and precipitously after 1945, the fact that America, the new rising power, was a product of European civilization served as a source of empathy and affinity between the Old World and the NewWorld, giving rise to ties which found expression in the idea of the West[2] while serving to mitigate the effects of latent imperial rivalry between Britain and the United States. For over two centuries the West, first in the form of Europe and subsequently the United States, has dominated the world.

We are now witnessing an historic change which, though still relatively in its infancy, is destined to transform the world. The developed world–which for over a century has meant the West (namely, the United States, Canada, Western Europe, Australia and New Zealand) plus Japan – is rapidly being overhauled in terms of economic size by the developing world.[3] In 2001 the developed countries accounted for just over half the world's GDP, compared with around 60 percent in 1973. It will be a long time, of course, before even the most advanced of the developing countries acquires the economic and technological sophistication of the developed, but because they collectively account for the overwhelming majority of the world's population and their economic growth rate has been rather greater than that of the developed world, their rise has already resulted in a significant shift in the balance of global economic power. There have been several contemporary illustrations of this realignment. After declining for over two decades, commodity prices began to increase around the turn of the century, driven by buoyant economic growth in the developing world, above all from China, until the onset of a global recession reversed this trend, at least in the short run.[4] Meanwhile, the stellar economic performance of the East Asian economies,with their resulting huge trade surpluses, has enormously swollen their foreign exchange reserves. A proportion of these have been invested, notably in the case of China and Singapore, in state-controlled sovereign wealth funds whose purpose is to seek profitable investments in other countries, including the West. Commodity-producing countries, notably the oil-rich states in the Middle East, have similarly invested part of their newly expanded income in such funds. Sovereign wealth funds acquired powerful new leverage as a result of the credit crunch, commanding resources which the major Western financial institutions palpably lacked.[5] The meltdown of some of Wall Street's largest financial institutions in September 2008 underlined the shift in economic power from the West, with some of the fallen giants seeking support from sovereign wealth funds and the US government stepping in to save the mortgage titans Freddie Mac and Fannie Mae partly in order to reassure countries like China, which had invested huge sums of money in them: if they had

3

withdrawn these, it would almost certainly have precipitated a collapse in the value of the dollar. The financial crisis has graphically illustrated the disparity between an East Asia cash-rich from decades of surpluses and a United States cash-poor following many years of deficits.

4   According to projections by Goldman Sachs, the three largest economies in the world by 2050 will be China, followed by a closely matched America and India some way behind, and then Brazil, Mexico, Russia and Indonesia.[6] Only two European countries feature in the top ten, namely the UK and Germany in ninth and tenth place respectively. Of the present G7, only four appear in the top ten. In similar forecasts, PricewaterhouseCoopers suggest that the Brazilian economy could be larger than Japan's, and that the Russian, Mexican and Indonesian economies could each be bigger than the German, French and UK economies by 2050.[7] If these projections, or something similar, are borne out in practice, then during the next four decades the world will come to look like a very different place indeed.

Understanding Meaning

1. What is Jacques's thesis? Can you state it in your own words?

2. Why does Jacques believe the United States will lose its superpower status?

3. How, in his view, will the developed Western world change by 2050?

4. What role does Asian investment in the United States play in the coming economic change that Jacques predicts?

5. *Critical Thinking:* Jacques's title makes a declarative statement, asserting that it is only a matter of time until China rules the world, though he admits this change is "in its infancy." Would his argument be more convincing if his title posed the question, "Will China Rule the World?" Why or why not?

Evaluating Strategy

1. What impact does the title have? Do you think Jacques meant to grab attention, shock, challenge, or even anger some readers?

2. What evidence does Jacques present to support his thesis?

3. *Critical Thinking:* Jacques is making projections forty years into the future. Given that many unanticipated events could arise, does he risk making errors in logic such as "slippery slope" assertions? Does he assume that recent trends will continue into the future? Would his argument be stronger if he qualified his thesis by repeating statements like "if these trends continue" or "if nothing is done"? Why or why not? Does Jacques appear to suggest that there is nothing the United States can do to prevent the outcome he predicts?

Appreciating Language

1. Consider the word "rule." What does it suggest? Does the world's wealthiest nation necessarily become the world's largest military or political force? Does the idea of another country "ruling" the world appear threatening to many Americans?

2. Look up "unipolarity." What does the word mean? Is Jacques suggesting the world is moving from an American "unipolarity" to a Chinese one?

WRITING SUGGESTIONS

1. Using Jacques's article as a model, write an essay that argues how the future will be different from the present. How will colleges and universities change by 2050? What will the American family be like in forty years? How will the Internet reshape the way we live our lives? If current trends continue, how will your job, your community, your way of life change by 2050?

2. *Collaborative Writing:* Discuss Martin Jacques's article with a group of students. Do they find his argument interesting, factual, or threatening? Summarize the views of the group in a short essay. If students have differing views, consider using comparison to organize opposing viewpoints or classification to reflect a range of opinions.

MINXIN PEI

Minxin Pei (1957-) was born in Shanghai, China, and studied at Shanghai International Studies University, the University of Pittsburgh, and Harvard University. He taught at Princeton University from 1992–1998. Formerly a senior associate in the China Program at the Carnegie Endowment for International Peace, Pei is currently the director of the Keck Center for International and Strategic Studies at Claremont McKenna College. His books include From Reform to Revolution: The Demise of Communism in China and the Soviet Union *(1994) and* China's Trapped Transition: The Limits of Developmental Autocracy *(2006).*

Why China Won't Rule the World

CONTEXT: *In this* Newsweek *article, published in December 2009, Pei questions Martin Jacques's view that China will eventually rule the world. China, he argues, faces many challenges that may limit its future growth and global influence.*

1   Conventional wisdom can be devilishly hard to dispute. For example, most pundits agree that the Great Recession helped China more than any other state. At first glance, this claim seems obviously true. Unlike the United States and the other major Western powers, which saw their economies plummet and their financial institutions come close to ruin, the Chinese economy has kept on growing. Chinese financial institutions, considered technically insolvent only a few years ago, now boast balance sheets and market capitalizations that Western banks can only dream of. With its economy expected to grow at 9 percent in 2010, China will soon surpass Japan as the world's second-largest economy (measured in U.S. dollars). Pundits like Martin Jacques, a veteran British journalist, are predicting that China will soon rule the world—figuratively, if not literally.

2   Yet before declaring this the Chinese century, you might want to take another look at what's actually taken place in the country over the past year.

3   One of the strangest things about predictions of Chinese dominance is that they tend to impress everyone but the Chinese themselves. Take China's supposedly miraculous economic recovery. While the international business community has practically run out of words to praise Beijing's handling of the crisis, Chinese leaders haven't stopped worrying. They fret that their banks have gone on a reckless lending binge; Liu Mingkang, China's chief bank regulator, warned in September that "all sorts of risks have risen" as a result. He's right. In the first half of 2009, Chinese banks shelled out roughly $1.2 trillion, creating a potential tidal wave of future nonperforming loans. State-owned enterprises (SOEs) used much of the money to speculate in the real-estate and stock markets and to

make questionable expansions; as a result, Dragonomics, a Beijing-based consultancy, now estimates that as much as one sixth of all the bank loans made between 2008 and 2010 could end up not paying off. Yet Beijing is still wary of shutting off the spigot, lest China prove unable to keep growing without it.

Its leaders' frequently voiced trepidation may be overstated. Perhaps the officials are simply being modest or trying to soothe Western worries about the so-called China Threat. It's far more likely, however, that China's leaders are actually telling the truth. They know their country has indeed pulled off the world's most impressive recovery. But they also know that's a relative accomplishment—and China has paid a huge long-term price in the process. In addition to sowing the seeds for future dud loans, its investment-focused stimulus policies have exacerbated the country's economic imbalances by creating new productive-capacities—factories and the like—without really boosting China's anemic household consumption. In other words, Chinese plants may be cranking out even more TVs, cars, and toys than before, but no Chinese are buying them. Loosened bank credit has mainly benefited SOEs, allowing these inefficient behemoths to expand at the expense of the private sector, which has been given little access to the government's largess.

Meanwhile, China has yet to confront what has become an enormous overcapacity for producing cheap goods. During the boom, when Americans were hungry for these products, Chinese exports registered double-digit growth year after year, accounting for nearly a quarter of the country's net GDP growth. Now that nervous and debt-ridden U.S. consumers have virtually shut their pocketbooks, China can no longer expect them to snap up its wares. To account for this change, Beijing must embark on some painful restructuring, shuttering many export-oriented factories and strengthening the social safety net to boost household consumption (which remains stuck below 40 percent of GDP). China's leaders know all this. But they've yet to take the plunge.

Dig a bit deeper, and it becomes very difficult to pin down just how exactly China has gained so much from the crisis. Its failures are much more evident. Take Beijing's lack of success in snapping up prized assets overseas. For several years, Chinese leaders have aimed to secure foreign natural resources by acquiring effective control of or stakes in oilfields, mining companies, and commodity producers in other countries. Beijing is convinced that such moves are essential for its long-term security. Yet opposition by Western politicians, entrenched multinationals, and vigilant governments in developing countries has stymied many attempts by cash-flush Chinese SOEs to execute their government's master plan. During the first months of the crisis, these SOEs and China's sovereign-wealth fund did nab modest stakes in a few minor natural-resource companies. But they failed to score a big hit, and there were some embarrassing failures. In late 2008, for example, Chinalco (a state-owned Chinese aluminum company) reached a tentative agreement to pay

$19.5 billion to increase its stake in Rio Tinto, a global mining giant. But fierce shareholder opposition and the skepticism of Australian regulators doomed the deal, to Beijing's intense frustration. To borrow a colorful Chinese proverb, Chinalco saw its "cooked duck fly away." This ignominious setback served as an uncomfortable reminder of the humiliation of 2005 when CNOOC, one of China's state-owned oil companies, was prevented from taking over Unocal, an American energy producer, by congressional opposition.

7   Another puzzle: if China is so strong, why doesn't it show more leadership in addressing global problems? While Chinese officials show up at almost every important gathering of world leaders, and their opinions and support are eagerly solicited, they consistently maintain a low profile, preferring to focus on guarding their national interests and skipping opportunities to showcase their soft power. At the G20 summit in London in April 2009, for example, the only thing China cared about was keeping Hong Kong off the list of offshore tax havens being scrutinized. Beijing's coffers may be bulging with $2.1 trillion in foreign-currency reserves, but it is not exactly offering to spend that cash on common crises. Besides calling for a new international reserve currency, China has remained mostly silent on how to reform the global financial system. Nor did it take charge in advance of the make-or-break Copenhagen climate-change conference in December 2009. Beijing's foreign policy remains stuck in a reactive mode; if this is a superpower, no one's told the Politburo yet.

8   Still, most Chinese leaders seem unconcerned with their inability to translate strength into real gains on the international stage. That's because they're far more concerned with domestic stability. Yet here again the news is hardly reassuring. Antigovernment riots and collective protests throughout China are on the rise.

9   Corruption remains rampant. More than a dozen senior officials, ranging from a vice minister of public security to several CEOs of giant SOEs, were arrested in 2009. The political maneuvering for the next succession, due in 2012, has already begun, making Chinese leaders all the more cautious—even a tiny misstep between now and then could be politically catastrophic.

10   The worst news on this front has been the reemergence of ethnic separatism in China's restive, but resource-rich, border regions. The bloody riots of July 2009 in Urumqi, the capital of Xinjiang, killed nearly 200 and wounded more than 1,000, making it China's worst ethnic conflict in three decades. Coupled with the Tibet problem, the challenge by the Uighurs to Chinese rule will preoccupy the minds of Beijing's ruling elites for years to come—and keep their sights firmly fixed on matters domestic.

11   All this helps explain why, while China's leaders may be mightily relieved to have escaped the worst consequences of the world economic crisis, they see no cause to celebrate. True, the crunch enabled China to close the economic gap with its badly ravaged rivals, particularly the U.S. and Japan. And popular perceptions of new Chinese strength have allowed China's leaders to bask

in the global limelight and flaunt their elevated international status to the Chinese public. Deep down, however, Chinese leaders are no fools. They understand perfectly well how tough are the challenges they still face—and how quickly fortune can turn. If only foreigners knew this as well. Of course, the Chinese are thrilled that everyone *thinks* they're the biggest winner. The truth, however, is that they're more like the least-bad losers—and they know it.

Understanding Meaning

1. How do Pei's views of China's future differ from those of Martin Jacques?

2. Why, in Pei's opinion, is China's growth not likely to continue in the future?

3. Martin Jacques views China's lending and investment as a powerful leverage tool to use against the United States. Why does Pei see it as a potential liability?

4. How has American consumer behavior benefited China's growth, in Pei's opinion? Could changes in American buying habits affect China's future? Why or why not?

5. What domestic issues does Pei identify that could affect China's future?

6. *Critical Thinking*: When nations invest and lend money overseas, does that give them power over other countries or make them vulnerable to decisions made by people they can influence but not really control? Are China's trillions of dollars of investment in the West a source of power or a potential vulnerability?

Evaluating Strategy

1. What evidence does Pei present to support his thesis?

2. Does Pei, who was born in China, have greater credibility than a Western scholar who has only studied or visited China? Why or why not?

3. *Critical Thinking*: Does a writer have an easier task questioning why a prediction might not come true than making a bold assertion? Why or why not?

Appreciating Language

1. Pei uses the term "conventional wisdom" in the first sentence. Is that a negative term? When people refer to "conventional wisdom," do they usually suggest that it is wrong?

2. Look up the word "pundit." How does it differ from "expert" or "scholar"? Does Pei try to dismiss those he disagrees with by calling them "pundits"?

3. What does Pei mean when he calls the Chinese "the least-bad losers"?

1. Using Pei's article as a model, write an essay that questions recent predictions or "conventional wisdom" about young people, jobs, family life, the American work ethic, or a political issue.

2. *Collaborative Writing*: Discuss Jacques and Pei's articles about China with a group of students. Which author do they believe is more credible, and why? Write a short essay outlining the views of your group. If students have conflicting opinions, use comparison to present opposing viewpoints.

ARMSTRONG WILLIAMS

Armstrong Williams (1959–) is a talk show host and columnist who has written on a range of issues concerning African Americans. His recent books include Beyond Blame: How We Can Succeed by Breaking the Dependency Barrier *(1995) and* Letters to a Young Victim: Hope and Healing in America's Inner Cities *(1996). Williams is a frequent commentator on cable news programs.*

Hyphenated Americans

CONTEXT: *In this column, Williams argues against Americans retaining an ethnic identity that empha-sizes separateness and erodes allegiance to a common civil society.*

Over the past year, small, trite hyphens have been appearing on the campaign 1
trail: Bush courts the African-American vote; the Muslim-American vote will make the difference in Michigan; Gore simultaneously appeals to California's Asian-American population and New York's Jewish-American community; Nader attempts to tap into the Native-American segment of our voting pop-ulace. Like deadly spores, these hyphens are replicating everywhere, supplant-ing our identities as Americans with a tribal ID card.

Hopefully now, our elected president will make a renewed effort to regard 2
the citizens of this country not as rival clans, but as humans. To understand the importance of this issue, follow me for a moment, from the political to the personal. With little cultural debate, much of the country now chooses to de-fine themselves not as Americans, but as the proud embodiments of various tribes. We no longer share this vast country. Instead, there is a nation for blacks and a nation for Asians and a nation for gays and Hispanics, one for Jews and whites, with each tribe pledging allegiance not to a unified nation-state, but to their own subjective cultural identity.

So what exactly is a hyphenated-American? No one really asks. They 3
understand only that Americans must not be called "Americans" in this day and age. To do so would be to violate the tenets of political correct-ness, and to invite disaster—at least at suburban dinner parties. Those who dare find strength in their authentic experiences, rather than always trying to go about things as an -American might, are deemed traitors to their tribe and soon find themselves joined to no one. This is the new cultural narrative in America: what matters is not your unique experience as a human-American, but rather your ability to identify with some vague tribal concept.

4   Of course, there are those who swell with pride at being hyphenated-Americans. They would argue that those small hyphens keep intact their unique struggles and heritage. Such people might even point to the important symbolic function that such a hyphen serves: it pushes the hyphenated-American experience into the mainstream, therefore reducing any cultural hangover from America's less tolerant past.

5   In reality though, the argument for rooting oneself in a tribal identity seems terribly destabilizing to the concept of multicultural unity. To insist that we are all hyphenated Americans is pretty much the same thing as asserting that no one is an American. The major implication: your America is not my America. The idea of civic unity becomes clouded as hyphenated-Americans increasingly identify with their cultural "I," rather than the civic "we." The great hope that our civil rights leaders had about getting beyond the concept of warring tribes and integrating to form a more perfect union falls by the wayside of these small hyphens.

6   I fear that we are reverting from a highly centralized country to a set of clans separated by hyphens. Herein lies the danger: when you modify your identity to distinguish it from other clans, you tend to modify your personal attitudes as well. You make the "others" what you need them to be, in order to feel good about your own little tribe. The best in the other "tribes" therefore becomes obscured, as does any unity of understanding. Instead, we distill the cultural "others" into the most easily identifiable symbols: Blacks as criminals; Asians as isolationists; Italians as gangsters; Muslims as fanatics; Jews as stingy; Latin Americans as illegal immigrants; whites as racists. We perpetuate these stereotypes when we willingly segregate ourselves into cultural tribes, even when we know that in our individual lives, we are so much more than this.

7   Our cultural prophets once dreamt of achieving a nation not of warring tribes, but of humans. Presently, we fail this vision, and we fail ourselves.

Understanding Meaning

1. What observations did Armstrong make during the 2000 presidential campaign? What troubled him the most?

2. Why does Armstrong view ethnic identities as damaging to the nation and civic society?

3. Do you observe that many people on your campus or neighborhood prefer to see themselves as African Americans, Hispanics, Jews, or Irish Americans rather than "Americans"?

4. Does identification with an ethnic heritage always imply a political point of view? Why or why not?

5. *Critical Thinking:* Is an ethnic identity undercut by other associations and influences? Do the poor and unemployed of all ethnic groups have more in common with each other than with middle-class professionals with whom they share a common ancestry? Why or why not? Do New Yorkers have a geographical identity that distinguishes them from people of the same ethnicity who live in Texas or Oregon? Do entrepreneurs, doctors, teachers, police officers, and landlords have shared interests that overcome ethnic identities? Can a highly technological and complex society like the United States really break up along ethnic lines?

Evaluating Strategy

1. Williams opens his essay by observing political campaigns. Is this an effective device? Does it reveal how politicians view the voting public?

2. Can you easily summarize Williams's thesis in a single sentence? Why or why not? Is his point clearly stated?

Appreciating Language

1. How does Williams define "hyphenated Americans"? How does he define "multicultural society"?

2. Williams uses the terms "tribe" and "clan" to describe ethnic groups and ethnic loyalty. What connotations do these words have? Do some people find terms like "tribal" and "clan" demeaning or offensive?

3. Williams places the word "other" in quotation marks. Today many commentators use the term "other" to describe people who are seen as outsiders, enemies, or threats. Look up this word in a dictionary. What does the word "other" mean to you? What connotations does it have?

WRITING SUGGESTIONS

1. Write a short essay explaining the way you choose which political candidates to vote for. Does your ethnic identity influence the way you vote? Are you more likely to support candidates who share your background? Why or why not?

2. *Collaborative Writing:* Working with a group of students, discuss Williams's essay and ask each member if he or she agrees or disagrees with his position on ethnic identity. Write an essay that summarizes your group's views, using classification to organize their views from those who strongly agree to those who strongly disagree with Williams's argument.

JULIANNE MALVEAUX

Julianne Malveaux (1953–) was born in San Francisco. She studied economics at Boston College and later attended the Massachusetts Institute of Technology, where she received a PhD in economics in 1980. She has published articles on economics and social policy in Ms., Essence, Emerge, and The Progressive. Her recent books include Sex, Lies and Stereotypes: Perspectives of a Mad Economist (1994) and Wall Street, Main Street, and the Side Street: A Mad Economist Takes a Stroll (1999).

Still Hyphenated Americans

CONTEXT: *Malveaux wrote this column in response to the question, "Why celebrate Black History Month?" Malveaux argues that African Americans are only celebrating the hyphenated status history gave them.*

1 "Why are we still celebrating Black History Month," the young white woman asks me. Until then, our airplane conversation had been casual, companionable. We'd spoken of trivia for nearly an hour, of changed travel conditions, the flight delay, of the plastic knives we'd been handed. My seatmate, a California college student, was traveling to Washington, D.C. to visit friends, and brimmed over with questions about sightseeing in Washington. Then she lowered her voice just a bit, asked if I minded an "awkward" question, and asked about Black History Month.

2 I didn't know whether to chuckle or to scream. Seventy-five years after Dr. Carter G. Woodson established Negro History week in 1926, folks are still wondering why we should commemorate black history. We need look no further than the words of one of our nation's most-quoted African Americans, Dr. Martin Luther King, Jr., who wrote, "The mistreatment of the Negro is as old as the most ancient history book, and as recent as today's newspaper." As long as African American life and history are not fully represented on newspaper pages, in the broadcast media, or in the history books, it makes sense to commemorate African American History Month.

3 The Association for the Study of Afro-American Life and History annually selects a black history month theme. Their website, www.asalh.com, lists themes for the next several years. This year, the theme is The Color Line Revisited: Is Racism Dead? I shared the theme with my young seatmate who assured me that class, not race, is what separates Americans. Rubbing shoulders in the first class cabin of the plane, she wondered, "You can't honestly say you've been discriminated against in your life, have you?"

4 Discrimination is an institutional, not an individual phenomenon. How else but discrimination do we explain the differentials between African

American and white income, unemployment rates, and homeownership levels. Those simple statistics make it clear that African Americans and whites have very different realities. If the overall unemployment rate were 9.8 percent, as the black rate was in January, we'd be talking about a depression and designing programs to put people back to work. Instead, President Bush's new budget cuts employment and training programs from $225 million to $45 million, a cut of nearly 80 percent. These programs, targeted to some of our nation's largest cities, provide important training to high-risk young people, many of whom are African American. To cut such programs at this time is tantamount to cutting the defense budget in wartime, but we know that President Bush has done no such thing. Indeed, while job-training funds are being slashed by millions of dollars, the President proposes increasing defense spending by $48 billion more this year.

The nation's indifference to high black unemployment rates speaks to the 5 difference in our realities. Many whites see themselves as Americans, while African Americans are hyphenated only because our realities are hyphenated. We'll feel like "regular" Americans when we have "regular" experiences (meaning no racial profiling, among other things), when our "regular" history is reflected in our nation's statuary (how many cities literally have no public monuments to African American people) and libraries.

The unemployment rate difference isn't the only place the color line is drawn. 6 Seventy-one percent of all whites own their homes, compared to 48 percent of African Americans. The gap is a function of redlining and discrimination in lending, both of which have been convincingly demonstrated by contemporary research. But when a home is the largest asset in most people's portfolio, too many African Americans are denied the opportunity to accumulate wealth when they can't buy homes. Restrictive covenants no longer prevent people from owning, but implicitly restrictive lending policies are as effective today as racist covenants were two generations ago.

To be sure, the color line is fuzzier than it has ever been. Our airwaves fre- 7 quently broadcast the lifestyles of the black and beautiful—the Oprah Winfreys, Michael Jordans, Condoleeza Rices and Colin Powells of the world. As proud as we are of African American icons, it would be foolhardy to suggest that all black people share experiences with these icons. At the other end, one in four African Americans and 40 percent of African American children live in poverty. Is racism real? No question. We commemorate Black History Month because it is an important way to recognize the many contributions African American people have made to our nation, because our nation, despite the progress it has made, still fails to systematically acknowledge black history. Until our textbooks spill over with stories of the slaves who built our nation's capital, the African American patriots who fought and died for our country, and the African American scientists whose inventions have shaped our lives, I will gleefully commemorate African American History Month. I shouldn't be the only one celebrating, African American history is American history! We hyphenated Americans are merely celebrating the hyphen that history handed us.

Understanding Meaning

1. Why does Malveaux argue that Black History Month should be celebrated?

2. What does Malveaux mean by "institutional" discrimination? Why does she reject the idea that social problems are "about class, not race"?

3. When, in her view, will African Americans be able to feel like "regular Americans"?

4. *Critical Thinking:* Malveaux comments on the "black and beautiful" celebrities like Oprah Winfrey, Michael Jordan, and Colin Powell. Do you think the presence of successful African Americans leads people to believe that racism no longer exists?

Evaluating Strategy

1. How does Malveaux use comments of the white passenger to open her essay? Is this a valuable device with which to introduce a controversial issue?

2. What facts and statistics does Malveaux use to support her thesis? Why is factual support important in this essay?

Appreciating Language

1. How does Malveaux define "hyphenated Americans"?

2. Are Malveaux's diction, tone, and style suited for a newspaper column that many people will skim rather than read? What challenges do columnists face in writing about complex and difficult issues?

WRITING SUGGESTIONS

1. Write a letter agreeing or disagreeing with Malveaux's column. Could you argue that other groups, such as Hispanics and Asians, are far less represented in the nation's history books, media, and public institutions?

2. *Collaborative Writing:* Discuss Malveaux's column with a group of students and ask if public schools should teach American history by highlighting ethnic differences, or by weaving them into a single unified version of our past. Should black history be taught separately? Why or why not? Write an essay summarizing your group's view. If students have differing opinions, use comparison or division and classification to organize their opinions.

WRITING BEYOND THE CLASSROOM

COVENANT HOUSE

Covenant House is the nation's largest shelter program for homeless youth. Begun in 1969 by a priest who took in six runaways during a blizzard, the program has grown to serve thousands each year. The agency is supported almost entirely by donations from individuals.

Covenant House Needs Your Help

As you read this web page soliciting support, notice how examples are used to dramatize the plight of homeless youth and illustrate the program's services.

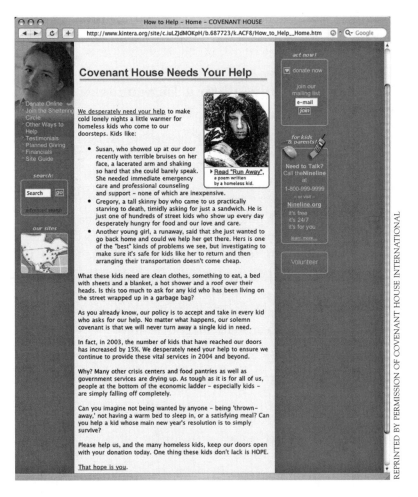

Understanding Meaning

1. What services does Covenant House provide?

2. Why does Covenant House need financial support?

3. Why do homeless youths face greater challenges today?

4. What is the mission of Covenant House?

Evaluating Strategy

1. What purpose do examples serve? Is it important to provide names of those served? Why or why not?

2. What role do statistics play? Is it important to balance examples with factual detail?

3. How effective is the visual impact of this web page? Do you find it easy to read? Does it communicate at a glance? Does the photograph grab attention and demonstrate the severity of the problem of homeless young people?

Appreciating Language

1. Does this level of diction seem appropriate for a mass audience?

2. Do you think using the word "kid" is effective? Why or why not? Might some readers object to this term?

WRITING SUGGESTIONS

1. Develop the text for a fund-raising brochure or web page using examples for support. Determine which examples would both dramatize a social problem and demonstrate how the organization works to solve it.

2. *Collaborative writing:* Discuss this web page with a group of students, and then develop a process essay that explains, step by step, how you would conduct a national fund-raising campaign to draw attention to the problem of homeless youth and encourage donations.

RESPONDING TO IMAGES

SIGN WARNING DRIVERS ABOUT ILLEGAL IMMIGRANTS

1. What is your initial reaction to this sign?

2. What does a sign like this illustrate?

3. What is your impression of the silhouette figures? Does using visual images avoid having to use words that express a political bias, such as "illegal aliens" or "undocumented worker"? Does the sign only warn drivers about people crossing the highway? Is the notion that these people are "illegal aliens" only implied? Could the same sign be posted outside a football stadium, beach, or amusement park? Why or why not?

4. Might some people find this sign offensive? Why or why not? Will some compare it to deer crossing signs? Will others think of "Children at Play" signs?

5. *Visual Analysis:* The sign depicts a man, a woman, and child in flight. What were the designers trying to suggest? Would a single figure or a group of male adults arouse different reactions? Why or why not? Does this image suggest most illegal immigrants are crossing the border as families?

6. Write a short essay stating how the United States should handle illegal border crossings.

7. *Collaborative Writing:* Before discussing this image with a group of students, have each person write down an immediate reaction and supply a caption for the photograph. Have each member of the group read his or her response; then, discuss the impact word choice has on meaning. Write an essay describing your group's impressions. If members have conflicting reactions, use comparison or division and classification to organize their views.

STRATEGIES FOR WRITING ARGUMENT AND PERSUASION

1. **Determine your purpose.** Clearly establish your thesis, and define what ideas you want readers to accept and what actions you want them to take. Do not try to recommend too many separate actions in one document.

2. **Evaluate your readers carefully.** Examine the perceptual world of your audience. Do barriers to your message exist that must be overcome? What information do your readers need in order to accept your ideas?

3. **Determine which appeals will be effective.** Recognize the advantages and disadvantages of each appeal, and consider blending more than one.

4. **Craft your introductions and conclusions carefully.** Your opening paragraphs must arouse interest and prepare readers for your argument or appeal. Your conclusion should end with a statement that will motivate readers to accept your ideas or take the action you recommend.

5. **Present factual detail in ways readers can understand.** In presenting facts and statistics, use methods such as analogies and narratives to dramatize their significance.

6. **Verify sources.** Before using as evidence a quote or statistic you heard on television or read on a blog, determine if it is stated accurately and comes from a reliable source.

7. **Do not mistake propaganda for persuasion.** Do not assume that hurling accusations, using questionable facts, or employing shock tactics will make your argument or appeal successful. People dislike feeling manipulated, and often potential supporters will find overstated appeals objectionable and offensive.

SUGGESTED TOPICS FOR WRITING ARGUMENT AND PERSUASION

GENERAL ASSIGNMENTS

Write a persuasive argument to a general audience on one of the following topics. You may use one or more appeals. You can frame your paper in the form of an essay, a letter, a flyer, or an advertisement.

1. Community and police relations
2. The drinking age
3. The way colleges prepare or fail to prepare graduates for the job market
4. Bullying
5. School choice
6. Labor unions
7. Social networking sites like Facebook and MySpace
8. Out-of-wedlock births
9. Sexual harassment
10. The deficit

Select one of the following issues, and craft a persuasive essay targeted to one of the audiences listed.

Issues: Medicare reform, distribution of condoms in public schools, school prayer, bilingual education, recycling, gun control, legalization of drugs

Audiences: Suburban residents, retired schoolteachers, small business owners, an organization of minority police officers, inner-city health care providers

WRITING IN CONTEXT

1. Imagine you have become close to a highly respected member of your community. This person is well regarded by your family and may have a

key role in your future. He or she invites you to join an organization that actively supports a view on abortion that is opposite to yours. Write a letter persuading this person to accept your reasons for declining the offer. Try to make your disagreement known without creating animosity.

2. Write a letter to the editor of the campus newspaper about an issue that you have heard discussed but that no one else seems willing to raise. Urge the community to pay attention.

Student Paper: Argument and Persuasion

This paper was written in response to the following assignment:

Write a 500–750-word persuasive essay about a current social or political issue. Avoid writing about subjects such as abortion or capital punishment unless you can provide a new or unique angle. Document your use of any outside sources.

First Draft with Instructor's Comments

This college, like many others, has and needs a Black Student

weak, vague, what does everyone "seem to think"??

Union. <u>It has nothing to do with what everyone seems to think it</u>

<u>has</u>. A lot of people who make <u>these claims</u> have never even both-

what claims?

explain what they saw "in the paper"

ered to visit the Black Student Union or bothered to check the

facts they saw in the paper.

Revise this paragraph for clarity

People say black students are getting paid to run their

organization, <u>which is so totally not the case</u>. In fact, the Black

wordy, informal

Student Union only receives money to operate a study center that,

in fact, serves lots of non-blacks because the <u>Acamdemic</u> Support

SP

Center. The union received money last year, but most of it went to

Words missing?

fix the building, which does belong to the university.

Many people criticize the Black Student Center for <u>foresting</u>

fostering?

racial discrimination. This is not the case. We live in integrated

Well stated

dorms, attend integrated classes, and play on integrated teams.

The few hours a week a student might spend at the BSU hardly

Provide specific examples.

threatens to create racial isolation. Other students have

specialized centers, and no one seems bothered about that.

explain more, expand In addition, people have accused the BSU of being a hotbed of

radical politics. I see no evidence of this.

Black students need the BSU. Black students are a minority on

this campus. It is easy for them to feel alienated and isolated.

And they are at high risk for failure. Dean Smith says "Since only

one of eight black males entering a university will graduate, it

is imperative that we seek remedies to support their academic

achievement and professional advancement." And the BSU does just

Source data? that. Weak Black students have problems finding friends and build-

Clarify;— too wordy ing positive reinforcement networks that provide needed personal

support. Because few of their friends in high school were college-

bound, they had to isolate themselves and study on their own. This

habit, however, is not always the best strategy in college. Many

students benefited from "social promotion" and when they get to

wordy college, they discover that their A's and B's were really more

equal to C's and D's in better suburban schools. The Black Student

Union offers African American students a place to relax, to inter-

act with older students, and work to make the university a more

hospitable place to minorities.

Works Cited

Smith, Dean. *Black Males in Crisis*. New York: Dial Press, 2009

REVISION NOTES

You have an interesting topic for a persuasive essay, but you need to make several improvements to produce a truly effective paper.

1. You mention that the Black Student Union has critics and refer to the recent newspaper article. Expand this point. Explain the claims and criticisms of those who oppose the Black Student Union, then disprove or discount them point by point.

2. You need to provide additional factual support to counter charges that the Union is getting too much money.

3. You need to document the sources fully. You list the Smith book in Works Cited but do not show the page reference for the quote you use. See MLA guidelines.

4. Finally, read your draft out loud. Missing words, awkward sentences, and wordy phrases are easier to hear than see.

Revised Draft

Why a Black Student Union?

Before any controversial issue can be discussed, there is usually a certain amount of misinformation to deal with. This is clearly the case with the Black Student Union. Many students have voiced concern and written letters to the editor since the college paper revealed that $540,000 was being allocated to the Union (Kane 1). The article stated that $52,000 was going to salaries, making the Black Student Union the only student organization with a paid staff.

First of all, the bulk of the money allocated to the Union is dedicated to renovating the building, which is university property. Constructed in 1962, the building has not had major repairs since 1974. Roof leaks, first reported to the administration three years ago, have led to substantial and costly damage. In addition, it is the only building that was not retrofitted with new heating and air conditioning systems in 1996 (*CSU* 22). Also, the building still does not comply with the Americans with Disabilities Act. Wheelchair ramps must be installed by court order (*CSU* 23).

Second, no one at the Union receives a salary for student activities. Five graduate students are paid to tutor remedial classes. Given the lack of space in the cramped Academic Support Center, use of the Black Student Union makes sense and creates more openings in the Center. Many non-black students attend classes and remedial seminars at the Union. Less than half the graduates of the Internet course last semester were African American (Kane 2).

But there are other objections to the Union. Why should blacks have their own facility? Many on campus see the presence of a black student union as a kind of self-imposed apartheid. The Union has also been criticized for being the center of racially hostile militancy.

The Black Student Union hardly threatens to impose a new kind of segregation. We live in integrated dorms, attend integrated classes, participate in integrated sports, and serve on mostly white and Asian academic committees. The few hours a week a student might spend at the BSU hardly threatens racial isolation—any more than the women's center risks ending coeducation or the Newman Center pits Catholics against Protestants. From my own observations, I see little evidence of the radical and extremist politics Union opponents mention. The most popular event the Black Student Union holds is Career Week when black students line up to meet representatives from AT&T, IBM, US Bank, and 3M. Most students are concerned about academic performance and career options rather than radical politics. True, the Union has sponsored some controversial speakers, but so has the university itself. Much of the "extremist literature" cited in a campus editorial is not distributed by the Union. The Union receives a lot of free literature in the mail, which has been traditionally displayed in the lobby. When it was brought to the attention of the board that some of the pamphlets were anti-Semitic, members took quick steps to screen incoming publications and discard "hate literature."

The real purpose of the Union is to assist African Americans to succeed on campus. Comprising less than 5 percent of the student body, blacks easily feel alienated, particularly those who graduated from predominantly black high schools. According to Dean Smith, "Since only one of eight black males entering a university

will graduate, it is imperative that we seek remedies to support
their academic achievement and professional advancement" (12).
Many black students have difficulty forming friendships and joining organizations. Often there were only a handful of college-
bound students in their schools. To survive, they had to isolate
themselves, studying alone to avoid associating with peers resentful of their dedication to academics. Outcasts in high school,
these students find college bewildering. They are not accustomed
to participating in class or working in groups. They often discover that they are woefully unprepared for college. Coming from
schools with 50-75 percent dropout rates, many suffered from "social promotion." They discover that their A's and B's are only
equal to C's and D's in better suburban schools. The Black Student
Union offers African American students a place to relax, interact
with older students, and work to make the university a more hospitable place to minorities.

Given the history of discrimination and disadvantage faced by
African Americans, the Union can be a positive asset. Is it a
crutch, an undeserved luxury? No one can deny that black students
feel handicapped on campus. No one complains about the cost of
wheelchair ramps and elevators which benefit a handful of physically disabled students. Why should we ignore the crippling legacy
of racism?

Works Cited

*CSU Facilities Report: 2009. California State University Budget
Office.* California State University, 2009. Web. 5 May 2011
Kane, Kelly. "BSU Funding Furor." *Campus Times* 1 May 2009: 1-2.
Print.
Smith, Dean. *Black Males in Crisis.* New York: Dial, 2009. Print.

QUESTIONS FOR REVIEW AND REVISION

1. What is the student's thesis?

2. What negative assumptions does the student seek to address? How does he counter them?

3. What audience does the writer appear to address? What appeals does the student use?

4. How much of the paper consists of responses to opponents' criticisms? Is this a useful device?

5. How effective is the conclusion? Does comparing disabled students to African Americans make a valid point? Would you suggest an alternative ending?

6. Read the paper aloud. Are there passages that should be deleted or expanded?

7. Did the student follow the instructor's suggestions?

WRITING SUGGESTIONS

1. Using this paper as a model, write a similar essay taking a position on a current campus controversy. Assume you are addressing a hostile audience. Respond to their objections without criticizing or demeaning those who disagree with your thesis.

2. *Collaborative Writing*: Discuss this paper with a group of students. Have a member record comments by the group. Work together to write a short statement approving or disapproving of the concept of establishing separate student unions. If members disagree, consider writing pro and con versions.

ARGUMENT AND PERSUASION CHECKLIST

Before submitting your paper, review these points:

1. Is your message clearly defined?

2. Does your paper meet readers' needs? Do you provide the support they need in order to accept your thesis?

3. Do you support your views with adequate evidence from reliable sources?

4. Do you anticipate reader objections and alternative points of view?

5. Do you balance the strengths and weaknesses of logical, ethical, and emotional appeals?

6. Do you avoid overstated, sentimental, or propagandistic appeals?

7. Do you avoid preaching to the converted? Will only those who already agree with you accept your arguments?

8. Do you make it easy for undecided readers to accept your position without feeling manipulated or patronized?

9. Have you tested your argument with peer review?

 Info Write provides additional information on argument and persuasion.
cengage.learning.inforwrite.com

APPENDIX A: A WRITER'S GUIDE TO DOCUMENTING SOURCES

WHAT IS DOCUMENTATION?

Many of the papers you will write in college require documentation—*a systematic method of acknowledging borrowed words and ideas.* Academic disciplines, publications, and professions have specific methods of documenting sources. When assigned a documented paper, make sure you understand the system your instructor expects.

WHY DOCUMENT SOURCES?

Whatever their discipline or topic, writers document outside sources for three main reasons:

1. **To avoid charges of plagiarism.** *Plagiarism* (derived from the Latin word for "kidnapping") refers to stealing or using the words, ideas, or artistic work of others without giving them credit. Some students find it difficult to believe that copying a few paragraphs from *The World Book* or using statistics found on a website can be considered a "crime." But using sources without credit is a theft of intellectual property. Most colleges have strict policies about plagiarism. Instructors routinely fail students who plagiarize papers. Many universities expel students who submit plagiarized assignments. Charges of plagiarism have ruined the careers of famous scholars and diminished the reputation of political figures. Hollywood studios, screenwriters, novelists, rock singers, and rap stars have been sued for stealing ideas, words, or lyrics of other artists. As a writer,

you can protect yourself from charges of plagiarism by noting outside sources. *Accurate documentation clearly distinguishes your work from that of others so no one can accuse you of cheating.*

2. **To support a thesis.**   Citing sources not only protects you from charges of cheating but also makes your writing more effective. To convince readers to accept your thesis, it is important to provide them with evidence. In court, lawyers prove cases by presenting eyewitnesses, expert testimony, and exhibits. As a writer, you can persuade readers to accept your point of view if you provide proof. *The more controversial your thesis, the more your readers will demand supporting evidence from credible sources.*

3. **To help readers learn more.**   Your citations not only protect you from plagiarism and strengthen your argument but also show readers where they can obtain additional information by listing periodicals, books, and websites.

WHEN TO DOCUMENT

Students are often confused about what they have to document.

What *Not* to Document

First, you do not have to document all the sources you use. Even if you look up something in an encyclopedia or on a website, you do not have to note its use if the information belongs to what researchers call *the realm of common knowledge*:

1. **Common expressions or famous quotations.**   You don't need to list the Bible or your edition of Shakespeare if you simply check the wording of a quotation by Jesus or Hamlet. If you refer to statements readers are familiar with, such as Martin Luther King Jr.'s "I have a dream" or John F. Kennedy's "Ask not what your country can do for you—ask what you can do for your country," you don't have to note their original source. *Less familiar statements, especially controversial ones readers might doubt or question, must be documented.*

2. **Common facts not subject to change and available in numerous sources.**   You don't have to list *The Encyclopedia Britannica* as a source if you use it to look up where George Washington was born, when *Death of a Salesman* opened on Broadway, when Malcolm X died, or the height of Mount Everest. General facts such as these are not subject to change and are readily available in thousands of books, almanacs, biographies, textbooks, and websites. No one will accuse you of stealing information

that is considered standard and widely known by millions of people. *Facts subject to change or dispute such as the population of Denver, the number of people on death row, or income tax regulations must be documented.*

What to Document

In almost every other case, you must acknowledge the use of outside sources:

1. **Direct quotations.**   Whenever you copy word for word the spoken or written words of others, you must use quotation marks or indented paragraphs to distinguish them from your own text; you must also indicate the source.

2. **Indirect quotations or paraphrases.**   Even if you don't copy information, but do restate the author's ideas in your own words, you must acknowledge the source. Changing a few words in a quotation or summarizing several pages in a paragraph does not alter the fact that you are using ideas and information taken from another source. Although you don't use quotation marks, you need to indicate that you have borrowed from an outside source.

3. **Specific facts, statistics, and numbers.**   Facts will only be acceptable to readers if they know where they came from. If you state, "Last year eighteen innocent men were sentenced to death for crimes they did not commit," readers will demand the source of this number.

4. **Graphs, charts, photographs, and other visual aids.**   Indicate the source of any visual aid you reproduce in your paper. If you create your own graphics based on statistics, you must indicate their source.

Evaluating Internet Sources Checklist

As you search for sources online, determine their value and reliability:

✔ **Source:** What is the domain name of the source? The URL—the site's Internet address—can help you evaluate an online source:

Domain	Source
.com	company or for profit organization
.edu	college or university
.gov	federal government
.mil	military
.net	Internet provider or individual
.ny.us	New York state government
.org	nonprofit organization or individual

Does a reputable organization sponsor the site? Is this organization likely to be impartial in its examination of the information? Does the organization benefit from persuading you to accept its position? Do you detect inflammatory language that reveals bias or prejudice? If a search leads you to a single posting, examine the organization's home page, which may contain information about its staff, mission, and orientation. Use the name of the organization or author as a search term and examine the responses it generates.

✔ **Authorship:** Does the site mention the author or webmaster? This information is often noted at the bottom of the site's home page, but does not always appear on internal pages. Does the author or webmaster include an email address? An email to the author or webmaster can yield valuable insights

✔ **Credibility:** If you are able to identify the site's author, can you also determine whether he or she has significant knowledge about the topic? Does the site present objective information or express personal opinion? Does the author include his or her résumé?

- To check if the author has also published books, check your library's online catalog or Amazon.com (www.amazon.com), which lists books and often includes reader reviews.

- Place the author's full name in quotation marks and use it as a search term using a search engine like Google or Yahoo! to locate biographical information.

✔ **Purpose:** Can you determine the site's intended purposes? Is the site designed to present all available evidence? Does it seem to take a side? Is the site intended to inform readers or to sell a product or service?

✔ **Audience:** Does the site expect its reader to have an opinion before visiting the site? Does the site encourage its reader to form an opinion based solely on the information presented? Or does the site invite further investigation by providing links to related sites?

✔ **Language:** Is the information presented in a manner that allows virtually any reader to understand it? Is specialized terminology included? Does its presence have a negative effect on the presentation on the general reader's comprehension?

✔ Is the tone and style objective and professional? Does the site refute or question opposing views using evidence, or does it attempt to dismiss opponents with inflammatory or derogatory language?

✔ **Presentation:** Has the site been planned and designed well? Is it easy to navigate? Are the links active, current, and relevant? Does the text reflect that careful planning has been devoted to it, including thorough proofreading? Don't allow impressive graphics, sound, and video to substitute for accuracy in the information.

✔ **Timeliness:** Many sites are not dated, making it difficult to determine the currency of the information. If dates do not appear, test links to see if they are still active. Place key terms and phrases in quotations and use them as search terms using search engines, such as Google or Yahoo!, to determine dates and perhaps locate sources that are more recent.

✔ **Critical Thinking:** Do you detect errors in critical thinking, such as hasty generalizations, dependence on anecdotal evidence, faulty comparisons, false authorities, or attacking personalities?

USING QUOTATIONS

Direct quotations should be used sparingly. Remember, the goal of your paper is to express your thoughts and opinions, not present a collection of other people's ideas. There are times, however, when direct quotations can be powerful additions to your essay. Use direct quotations

1. When presenting a significant statement by an authority or eyewitness

2. When the statement is unique or memorable

3. When the idea conflicts with the mainstream of thought or common knowledge

4. When the original statement is well written and more compelling than a paraphrase or summary

5. When readers may doubt a controversial point of view or question that a certain person made the statement

Direct quotations have to be integrated into the text of an essay in a clear, sensible manner and be documented.

1. Indicate short direct quotations (1–4 lines) by placing them in quotation marks followed by a parenthetical citation:

> According to Lester Armstrong, "The university failed to anticipate the impact of state budget cuts" (17).

Indicate long direct quotations (more than 4–5 lines) by placing them in indented paragraphs without quotation marks. Indent ten spaces on the left side and introduce with a colon:

According to Lester Armstrong, higher education suffered greatly during the recession:

> The university failed to anticipate the impact of state budget cuts. As a result, construction on the new stadium was halted. Twenty-five administrators were laid off. Plans to expand the computer labs, bilingual programs, and adult night school were scrapped. The library budget was slashed by 24 percent, and two day care centers were closed. The century-old Main Hall, which was scheduled for an extensive refurbishing, was given only cosmetic repairs and painting. (17)

2. Link direct quotations with your text. Avoid isolated quotations:

Incorrect

Children are greatly affected by violence on television. **"By the time a child graduates from high school, he or she has witnessed over 18,000 homicides on television" (Smith 10).** Young people come to view violence, even murder, as a reasonable method of resolving conflicts.

Blend direct quotations into your text by introducing them:

Revised

Children are greatly affected by violence on television. **"By the time a child graduates from high school,"** Jane Smith notes, **"he or she has witnessed over 18,000 homicides on television" (10).** Young people come to view violence, even murder, as a reasonable method of resolving conflicts.

3. You may edit quotations to eliminate redundant or irrelevant material. Indicate deleted words within a sentence by inserting an *ellipsis* (three spaced periods). If the ellipsis occurs at the end of the sentence, place three spaced periods after the final period.

Original Text

George Washington, who was heading to New York to confer with his leading advisors, agreed to meet with Franklin in Philadelphia on June 10.

Edited Quote

As Smith notes, "George Washington . . . agreed to meet with Franklin in Philadelphia . . ."

Deletions should only remove unneeded information; they should not alter the meaning of the text by removing qualifications or changing a negative statement into a positive one. It is unethical to alter the quotation **"We should, only if everything else fails, legalize drugs"** to read, **"We should . . . legalize drugs."**

4. Insert words or other information to prevent confusion or avoid grammatical errors. For instance, if a direct quote refers to a Frank Obama by his last name and you are concerned readers will confuse him with President Obama, you may insert his first name, even though it does not appear in the original text.

Original Text

Hoping to ease tensions in the Middle East, **Obama** called for UN peacekeepers to patrol the West Bank.

Quotation

"Hoping to ease tensions in the Middle East, **[Frank] Obama**," according to *Newsweek*, "called for UN peacekeepers to patrol the West Bank" (14).

If you delete words or phrases, you may have to insert words to prevent a grammar error:

Original Text

Poe and other writers of his generation were influential in shaping a new, truly American literature.

Quotation

According to Sydney Falco, "**Poe** . . . **[was]** influential in shaping a new, truly American literature" (64).

5. Explain, if necessary, the significance of the person or source you are quoting:

Maria Gomez, **who investigated over two hundred crashes for the FAA,** notes that "technology cannot replace human perception in reducing accidents."

Wall Street Dreamers, **a twenty-year study compiled by a panel of professors from the Harvard Business School and sixteen investment bankers,** claims "speculation can be curbed and channeled but never removed from the market."

USING PARAPHRASES

Paraphrases are indirect quotes. You must document your use of sources, even when you do not copy the text word for word. If you read two or three pages of a history book and summarize its points in a single paragraph, document your use of that source. Although you did not directly reproduce any words or sentences, the ideas you present are not your own and should be documented:

Original Text

More than 10,000 of New York's 29,000 manufacturing firms had closed their doors. Nearly one of every three employables in the city had lost his job. An estimated 1,600,000 New Yorkers were receiving some form of public relief. Many of those fortunates who had kept their jobs were "underemployed," a euphemism for the fact that they worked two or three days a week or two weeks a month—or, if they worked full time, were paid a fraction of their former salaries; stenographers, earning

$35 to $40 per week in 1928, were averaging $16 in 1933; Woolworth's was paying full-time salesladies $6 per week.

Robert Caro, The Power Broker 323–324

Paraphrase

The Depression devastated New York City. A third of the manufacturers shut down operations, and over a million and a half New Yorkers were on relief. Those with jobs saw their hours cut and their salaries slashed **(Caro 323–324)**. Conditions in Chicago, Los Angeles, and San Francisco were similar.

Parenthetical references should be placed immediately after the paraphrased material at an appropriate pause or at the end of the sentence.

USING MLA DOCUMENTATION

The MLA style, developed by the Modern Language Association, is the preferred documentation method used in language and literature courses. In the MLA system, outside sources are listed alphabetically at the end of the paper in a "Works Cited" list and parenthetical citations are placed after direct quotations and paraphrases.

NOTE: Print and online MLA guides created before 2009 use underlining instead of italics and require inclusion of full URLs. If you have any questions about MLA documentation, refer to the current guide, *The MLA Handbook for Writers of Research Papers,* 7th edition.

Building a Works Cited List

List all sources you refer to under the title "Works Cited" at the end of your paper. Items are listed alphabetically by author's last name or first significant word in the title:

General Guidelines

Print Sources:

Author, last name first: **Twain, Mark**

Title (in quotation marks for articles and other short works; in italics for books and other long works)

Name of magazines or newspapers in italics for articles: **Newsweek**

City and publisher for books: **New York: Random** (Words like *House, Books, Publishers,* and *Inc.* are omitted from the names of publishers. University presses are designated with UP: **Ohio State UP.**

Volume and issue number for magazine articles if available

Date of publication (day, month, and year for newspaper articles; year for books)

Inclusive page numbers for articles

Medium: **Print.**

Online Sources:

Author, last name first

Title (in quotation marks for short works from a larger work; in italics for independent works)

Name of website in italics: ***Modern Language Association***

Publisher of website (use **n.p.** if none is available)

Date (use **n.d.** if none is listed)

Medium: **Web**

Date of access (the date you downloaded or printed the website)

Sample formats

A book by a single author:

Smith, John. *The City*. New York: Putnam, 2002. Print.

A book by two or three authors:

Smith, John, and Naomi Wilson. *The New Suburb*. New York: Western, 2001. Print.

(Only the first author is listed last name, first name.)

A book with more than three authors:

Smith, John, et al. *Urban Housing*. Chicago: Chicago UP, 2000. Print.

A work in an anthology:

Miller, Arthur. *Death of a Salesman*. *American Literature 1945–2000*. Eds. Keisha Sahn and Wilson Goodwin. New York: Dial, 2001. 876–952. Print.

An encyclopedia article:

"China." *The World Book*. 2009 ed. Print.

(Volume and page numbers are not needed in encyclopedia references.)

A periodical article with a single author:

Smith, John. "Urban Planning Today." *American Architect* 25 Oct. 1999: 24–29. Print.

A *newspaper article without an author:*

"Mideast Crisis Boils Over." *The Washington Post* 22 May 2002: 54+. Print.

(If an article starts on one page, then skips to others, list the first page with a plus sign.)

A *television program:*

"Oil Boom." Narr. Morley Safer. *Sixty Minutes.* CBS. WCBS, New York. 27 Jan. 2002. Television.

(Include both network and local station with date of broadcast.)

An *online article:*

Wilkins, Robert. "Reflections on Milton." *Michigan Literary Review* Sep. 1998. n. pag. Web. 22 Feb. 2002.

(Use n. pag. for items without page numbers.)

An *article from an online database:*

Miller, John. "The New China." *Time* 5 May 2010 n. pag. *Online Sources.* Web. 10 May 2010.

An *email:*

Hennessey, Richard. "Re: Urban Planning Conference." Message to Sean Brugha. 22 June 2001. E-mail.

(Provide name of writer; title of message in quotation marks, recipient, and date.)

In-text Citations

As you include direct quotations and paraphrases in your paper, cite their use with parenthetical notations. These citations should be brief but accurate.

If you mention an author or source in your text, you only need to add a page number:

> **Winston Hachner** has noted, "The Internet has provided us with a dilemma of choice" **(874)**.

(Note: Place the period after the parenthetical citation.)

If you do not mention the source, include the author's last name or title with page numbers:

> The Internet has given us more choices than we can process **(Hachner 874)**. The sheer volume of information can overwhelm, confuse, and strangle businesses accustomed to defined channels of communication **("Internet" 34–35)**.

Sources without page references do not require parenthetical notes if cited in the text:

During a *Sixty Minutes* interview in 2002, Randall Pemberton argued, "A terrorist attack in cyberspace can cripple our economy."

You can avoid long, cumbersome parenthetical notes by citing titles or several authors in the text:

As stated in the *Modern Directory of Modern Drama*, "August Wilson has emerged as one of the nation's most powerful dramatic voices" (13). Jacobson and Marley view him as a dominant force in shaping the country's perceptions of the African American experience (145–146).

Sources and Sample Documented Essay

Read through the excerpts taken from a book, an article, and a website and note how the student uses and notes these sources.

Book Excerpt

From *How to Survive College* by Nancy Hughes, published by Academic Press, New York City, 2009.

HOW TO SURVIVE COLLEGE   176

Today credit card companies bombard incoming freshmen with credit card offers. Card companies operate on campuses, often in student unions and dorm lobbies. Giving out free hats, T-shirts, coffee mugs, and pizza coupons, they encourage students to sign up for cards. Companies generally issue cards to any student over eighteen whether he or she has a job or not. Faced with the need for books, clothes, computer supplies, and student fees, many students quickly apply for cards and ring up charges. At Northwestern University nearly 10 percent of incoming freshmen had maxed out at least one credit card by the end of their first semester.

Actual purchases, however, are often not the culprit. The ability to use a credit card to get cash from an ATM leads many students to live well beyond their means, getting into debt $40 or $60 at a time. Miranda Hayes, who graduated with $7,500 in credit card debts, had made only $2,000 in purchases. "I charged a computer my freshman year and all my books," she admits. "The rest was all cash from an ATM that went for movies, beer, pizzas, bus fare, my cell phone, health club dues, and interest."

Magazine Article

From "University of Wisconsin Takes Up the Issue of Student Credit Card Debt" in *Cardline*, June 11, 2009, page 1.

Cardline June 11, 2009   1

UNIVERSITY OF WISCONSIN TAKES UP THE ISSUE OF STUDENT CREDIT CARD DEBT

The Board of Regents for the University of Wisconsin System, which operates the state's 13 four-year schools and 14 two-year schools, was expected to discuss credit card solicitation today, a spokesperson for the UW-Madison tells Cardline. The discussion was promoted by the release in May of a 15-page, UW-commissioned report, "Student Credit Card Debt and Policies on Credit Card Solicitation on the University of Wisconsin," which said that 40 percent of its students owe credit card balances of $1,000 or more. It's not clear what action the regents, who are meeting at the UW's Milwaukee campus, will take, but three of its campuses have adopted formal policies regarding credit card solicitations and others have informal ones. The report recommends that the regents adopt rules that are consistent system-wide. Some UW administrators take a much harsher attitude. They wanted credit card solicitation banned altogether, but the report said such a ban might violate the law. The UW commissioned the report following several national studies, including one by the General Accounting Office. Newspapers also regularly reported on the issue. The report gathered its data through telephone interviews with staff members, student surveys and anecdotal information. It found that between 62 and 71 percent of students had at least one credit card. A UW Student Spending and Employment Survey found that of those who responded to it, 40 percent of students owed credit card debts of $1,000 to $5,000, and 10 percent owed over $5,000. The high card debt takes a toll on some students. Although the campuses don't . . . .

A Website

From "Top Ten Student Money Mistakes" by Blythe Terrell on Young Money, updated at http://www.youngm.oney.com/money_management/spending/020809_02, and accessed March 21 2009

✉ **MAIL**   🖨 **PRINT**

▶ careers

▶ consumer issues

▶ credit & debt

▶ entertainment

▶ entrepreneurship

▶ financial aid

▶ investing

▶ lifestyles

▶ money management

▶ technology

▶ travel

▶ wheels

Top Ten Student Money Mistakes

By Blythe Terrell, University of Missouri

For many students, college is the first major land-mark on the path to independence. Moving away from home means no more curfews, no asking for permission, and no parents looking over their shoulders. It also means that the liberty-seeking college kid is now free to make his or her own mistakes.

In such an environment, money management often becomes an issue. Knowing how to avoid these problems is the key to beating them. Here are ten common mistakes students make, and how you can avoid them.

1. **Making poor choices about which credit cards to get.** Credit card companies set up booths on college campuses, offering T-shirts and other items to anyone who will sign up for a card. Although the deals can seem fantastic, students must look into the card's repayment terms carefully. "When students get credit cards, two things can happen," said Stephen Ferris, professor of finance at the University of Missouri–Columbia. "One, they don't read the fine print and see what they're paying. And they're paying a lot. Or they use it until it's maxed out." It is absolutely necessary to pay your credit cards on time each month, added Ferris.

2. **Letting friends pressure them into spending money.** College life is full of opportunities to spend money, finals-week smorgasbords, an evening out with friends, road trips and vacations . . . Not knowing how to say "no" can cause students to spend money they just do not have. "If you can't afford it, just say no," says David Fingerhut, a financial adviser with Pines Financial in St. Louis.

> 3. **Not setting up a budget.** If they have a set
>   amount of money, they must plan ahead and
>   know how much they can spend each month. "It
>   has to work on paper before it works in real life,"
>   Fingerhut said.
>
> 4. **Not seeking out the best bank rates.** Banks
>   offer many different kinds of checking and sav-
>   ings accounts, but some charge fees that others
>   do not. It is essential for students to do research
>   and not simply go with the closest, most acces-
>   sible bank, Ferris said.

Student Essay

College Students and Debt

Students graduating in debt is
nothing new. Few students or their
parents have enough money to pay as
they go. Even students with scholarships take on debts to pay for college expenses. But in recent years
tens of thousands of students have
added to their financial burdens by
amassing credit card debts. Colleges,
which allow credit card companies to
student thesis operate on campus, must regulate the
way they advertise and educate
students on managing their money.

topic sentence Arriving on campus, freshmen encounter credit card promoters in stu-
Paraphrase dent unions and dorms. Offering stu-
facts stating dents free gifts, the various card
problem companies urge students to sign up
for credit cards. Card companies will
issue cards to any college student
citation showing who is at least eighteen (Hughes 176).
author and page Credit cards have become extremely
popular with students. Currently
62-71 percent of college students

have at least one credit card
("University" 1).

     Many students are unsophisti-
cated when it comes to using credit.
Whether making a purchase or obtaining a cash advance, they rarely calculate how interest charges or ATM
fees will inflate their balance. In
many cases, students get deep into
debt not by making major purchases,
but by withdrawing costly cash advances. Many students share the fate
of Miranda Hayes, who amassed a
$7,500 credit card debt, noting,
"I charged a computer my freshman
year and all my books. The rest was
all cash from an ATM that went for
movies, beer, pizzas, bus fare, my
cell phone, health club dues, and
interest" (qtd. Hughes 1).

     The University of Wisconsin,
among others, is considering establishing new policies to regulate
credit card promotions on campus
("University" 1). But the real service colleges can give students is to
prepare them for the responsibilities
of adult life by including financial
planning seminars that focus on
credit cards, budgets, and loans.
Stephen Ferris, a finance professor,
points out that when students sign up
for cards, "they don't read the fine
print and see what they are paying.
And they're paying a lot" (qtd. Terrell). Students don't consider interest rates, let peer pressure guide
their spending, and fail to set up
budgets (Terrell).

specific fact cited

topic sentence

example supporting thesis

quote within quote cited

paraphrase

topic sentence

quote within cited expert citation

paraphrase

conclusion

restatement of thesis

Ultimately, students are responsible. Away from home for the first
time, they have to learn to manage
their time, ignore distractions and
peer pressure, and use credit wisely.
Parents and colleges can provide information and give advice, but as
adults, college students must take
responsibility for the decisions
they make.

Works Cited

Hughes, Nancy. *How to Survive College.* New York:
    Academic, 2005. Print.

Terrell, Blythe. "Top Ten Student Money Mistakes."
    Young Money, 21 Mar. 2009. n. pag. Web. 10 May
    2010.

"University of Wisconsin Takes Up the Issue of
    Student Credit Card Debt." *Cardline* 11 June
    2009: 1. Print.

USING APA DOCUMENTATION

The APA style, developed by the American Psychological Association, is
the preferred documentation method used in social sciences, including
psychology, sociology, political science, and history. In the APA style, outside sources are listed alphabetically at the end of the paper in a reference
list and parenthetical citations are placed after direct quotations and paraphrases.

For complete details, refer to *The Publication Manual of the American
Psychological Association*, 6th edition.

Building a Reference List

List all sources you refer to under the title "References" at the end of your
paper. Items should be alphabetized by authors' last names, or by the first
significant word of their titles if no author is listed.

General Guidelines

Print Sources:

Author, last name first and initials for first and middle names: **Twain, M.**

Date of publication in parentheses (year, month, and day for newspaper articles; year for books): **Twain, M. (1888).**

Title (in regular font for articles and other short works; in italics for books and other long works, capitalizing only the first word, the first word after a colon, and proper names.

Images and stories of the new China.

Title of magazine and newspaper articles in italics, capitalizing the first word and all significant words: ***The American Journal of Psychology.*** City and publisher for books: **San Diego, CA: Academic Press**

Volume and issue number for magazines if available.

Inclusive page numbers for articles.

Online Sources

Author's last name, initials for first and middle names.

Date.

Title (in regular font for short works from a larger work; italics

for independent works capitalizing the first word and proper nouns).

Retrieval source (including full URL): **Retrieved from http://www.princeton.edu/publications/cent.asian.studies.html**

Sample formats

A book by a single author:

Smith, J. (2002). *The city.* New York, NY: Putnam Press.

A book by two authors:

Smith, J., & Wilson, N. (2001). *The new suburb.* New York, NY: Western Publishing.

(Both authors listed by last name, initial.)

A book with six or seven authors:

Smith, J., Wilson, S., Franco, W., Kolman, R., Westin, K., & Dempsey, F.. (2000). *Urban housing.* Chicago, IL: Chicago University Press.

(All authors listed by last name, initial.)

A book with eight or more authors:

> Smith, J., Wilson, S., Franco, W., Kolman, R., Westin, K., Dempsey, F....Smith, K. (2000). *Urban housing.* Chicago, IL: Chicago University Press.
>
> *(First six authors listed by last name, initial, followed by ellipsis [. . .], followed by last author.)*

A work in an anthology:

> Miller, A. (2001). Depression in the adolescent male. In J. P. Meyers, J. Reed, & R. Rank (Eds.), *The psychology of youth: Problems and solutions* (pp. 87–99). New York, NY: The Dial Press.

An encyclopedia article:

> Depression. (1998). In *The World Book* (Vol. 13, pp. 324–325). Chicago IL: World Book.

A periodical article with a single author:

> Smith, J. (1999, October 25). Urban planning today. *American Architect.* 24–29.

A newspaper article without an author:

> Mideast crisis boils over. (2002, May 22). *The Washington Post,* pp. 54, 58, 78, 89–92.
>
> *(If an article starts on one page, then skips to others, list all pages.)*

A television program:

> Paulus, G. (Executive Producer). (2002, January 27). The mind. [Television series]. New York: WNET.

An online article:

> Wilkins, R. (1998, March). Reflections on depression. *Michigan Science Review.* 9, 116–123. Retrieved from http://www.umichigan.edu/scireview.html

A corporate or organizational website without dates:

> New York City Health Department. (n.d.). Bioterrorism. Retrieved from http://www.nychd.org/bioterrorism. html

Article on CD-ROM:

> Albania. (2001) In *Oxford Encyclopedia of Education.* 3rd. ed. [CD-ROM]. Oxford, UK: Oxford University Press.

An email:

> Email and other correspondence are not included in references but are listed within the text by referring to the writer and date.

In-text Citations

When you include quotations and paraphrases in your paper, cite their use with parenthetical notations listing author and year. These citations should be brief but accurate:

> Hachner (2002) noted, "The Internet provides us with a dilemma of choice" (p. 12).
>
> *(Note: Place the period after the parenthetical citation.)*

Wellman (2000) compares two common therapies for treating depression. (Note: No page references cited for paraphrases.)

For sources without authors, include the titles in the text or a parenthetical citation:

> *Psychology Year in Review* (2002) presents new theories on addiction. A recent article reveals a genetic predisposition to narcotic dependence ("Genetic Maps," 2002). (Include only years even if day and month are available.)

If a work has three, four, or five authors, cite all authors by only last names in the first reference:

> Bodkin, Lewis, Germaine, and Neimoller (2001) dispute commonly held views of addiction.

In subsequent references, cite only the first author:

> Bodkin et al. (2001) found no single factor in determining predisposition to alcoholism.

For works with six or more authors, cite only the first author in first and subsequent references:

> Bryant et al. (2001) analyzed census figures to determine demographic changes.

STRATEGIES FOR AVOIDING COMMON DOCUMENTATION PROBLEMS

1. **Use outside sources sparingly.**   A good essay is not a collection of quotations and paraphrases. The focus of your paper should be your thesis, supporting ideas, and commentary. Avoid using long direct quotations that can be summarized in short paraphrases. *The fact that you find many interesting sources in the library or on the Internet does not mean that you should include everything you find in your paper. Be selective.*

2. **Take careful notes and collect documentation information when you locate valuable sources.**   Make sure you copy direct quotations carefully word for word and do not distort their meaning by taking ideas out

of context. Place direct quotations in quotation marks. If you photocopy a book or periodical, make sure you record the author's name and all publication information needed to document the sources. If you print an article from the Internet, make sure you record the full website address and the date. If you cut and paste online material directly into your paper, highlight it in a different color to distinguish it from the rest of your text while writing and editing. After accurately documenting the source, change the color to black.

3. **Select sources carefully.**   Avoid sources that appear biased, outdated, or poorly presented. Remember that all books, periodicals, and websites were created by human beings who may be misinformed or prejudiced. Avoid basing your entire paper on a single source. Do not assume that all sources are of equal value. Use critical thinking skills to measure the significance of the sources you locate.

4. **Comment on the quality and quantity of sources.**   Let readers know the results of your research. If sources are limited, outdated, or fragmentary, explain this situation to readers. If you find conflicting evidence or theories, objectively summarize the differences and justify your decisions in selecting sources. Don't assume direct quotations can speak for themselves. Don't insert sources into your essay without commenting on their value and demonstrating how they support your thesis.

5. **Clearly distinguish your ideas from those of others.**   Accurate documentation, transitional statements, and paragraph breaks can help readers understand which ideas are solely yours and which originate from outside sources.

6. **Blend quotations and paraphrases into your text to avoid awkward shifts.**   There should be smooth transitions between your ideas and those of others.

7. **Be sure to use the documentation system your instructor expects.**

INFORMAL DOCUMENTATION

Even if an assignment does not require formal documentation, you can add credibility to a personal essay by informally noting outside sources:

> According a recent report on CNN, the number of college students working full-time has almost doubled since 2008.

> The *New York Times* reports that more consumers paid for major purchases using cash in 2010 than 2009.

> Students have repeatedly complained about the online registration   system (*Campus Times*).

APPENDIX B: A WRITER'S GUIDE TO REVISING AND EDITING

WHAT ARE REVISING AND EDITING?

After completing a first draft, you may be tempted to check your essay for misspelled words and missing commas. But before *editing* your paper to correct mechanical errors, you should *revise* your work. *Revising* means "to see again." Before focusing on details, first look at the big picture. Review your assignment and goal, then revise paragraphs and edit sentences and words.

REVISING THE ESSAY

Review the Assignment and Your Goal

Before looking at your first draft, review the assignment and your goal. Read over any instructor requirements or guidelines. What does the assignment call for? What does your instructor expect? What should your paper accomplish? What does it have to contain? Review your own notes and outline. What is your goal? What do you want to say? What do you want your paper to achieve?

Review the Whole Essay

Read the paper aloud. How does it sound? What ideas or facts are missing, poorly stated, or repetitive? Highlight areas that need improvement and delete paragraphs that are off topic or merely restate ideas.

- Does your draft meet the needs of the assignment?
- What are the most serious defects?

- Have you selected an appropriate method of organizing your essay? Would a chronological approach be better than division? Should you open with your strongest point or reserve it for the conclusion?

Examine the Thesis

Does your paper have a clear thesis, a controlling idea—or is it simply a collection of facts and observations? Does the essay have a point?

- If your paper has a thesis statement, read it aloud. Is it clearly stated? Is it too general? Can it be adequately supported?

- Where have you placed the thesis? Would it be better situated elsewhere in the essay? Remember, the thesis does not have to appear in the first paragraph.

- If the thesis is implied rather than stated, does the essay have a controlling idea and a sense of direction? Do details and your choice of words provide readers with a clear impression of your subject?

Review Topic Sentences and Controlling Ideas

Each paragraph should have a clear focus and support the thesis.

- Review the controlling idea for each paragraph.

- Do all the paragraphs support the thesis?

- Are there paragraphs that are off the topic? You may have developed interesting ideas, recalled an important fact or quote, or told a compelling story—but if these details don't directly relate to the thesis, they do not belong in this essay.

Review the Sequence of Paragraphs

While writing, you may have discovered new ideas or diverted from your plan, altering the design of the essay. Study your paragraphs and determine whether their order serves your purpose.

- Should paragraphs be rearranged to maintain chronology or to create greater emphasis?

- Does the order of paragraphs follow your train of thought? Should some paragraphs be preceded by those offering definitions and background information?

Revise the Introduction

The opening sentences and paragraphs of any document are critical. They set the tone of the paper, announce the topic, arouse reader interest, and establish how the rest of the essay is organized. Because you cannot always predict how you will change the body of the essay, you should always return to the introduction and examine it before writing a new draft.

Introduction Checklist

- Does the introduction clearly announce the topic?

- Does the opening paragraph arouse interest?

- Does the introduction limit the topic and prepare readers for what follows?

- If the thesis appears in the opening, is it clearly and precisely stated?

- Does the language of the opening paragraph set the proper tone for the paper?

- Does the introduction address reader concerns, correct possible misconceptions, and provide background information so that readers can understand and appreciate the evidence that follows?

Revise Supporting Paragraphs

The paragraphs in the body of the essay should support the thesis, develop ideas, or advance the chronology.

Supporting Paragraphs Checklist

- Does each paragraph have a clear focus? Does it need a stronger topic sentence stating the controlling idea?

- Should the topic sentence be placed elsewhere in the paragraph? Would it be better at the end rather than the beginning?

- Is the controlling idea supported with enough evidence?

- Is the paragraph logically organized? Would a different structure be more effective for unifying ideas?

- Are there irrelevant or repeated details that should be deleted?

- Do paragraph breaks signal major transitions? Should some paragraphs be combined and others broken up?

Revise the Conclusion

Not all essays require a separate concluding paragraph. A narrative may end with a final event. A comparison may conclude with the last point.

Conclusion Checklist

- Does the conclusion end the paper on a strong note? Will it leave readers with a final image, question, quotation, or fact that will challenge them and lead them to continue thinking about your subject?

- Does the conclusion simply repeat the introduction or main ideas? Is it necessary? Should it be shortened or deleted?

- If your purpose is to motivate people to take action, does the conclusion give readers specific directions?

REVISING PARAGRAPHS

First drafts often produce weak paragraphs that need stronger topic sentences and clearer support:

First Draft

The automobile changed America. Development increased as distances were reduced. People moved outward from the city to live and work. Highways and bridges were built. Travel increased and greater mobility led to rapid population shifts, causing growth in some areas and declines in others. Cars created new industries and demands for new services.

Revision Notes

The automobile changed America. Development increased as distances were reduced. People moved outward from the city to live and work. Highways and bridges were built. Travel in-

explain which areas?

creased <u>and greater mobility led to</u> rapid population shifts, causing growth in some areas and declines in others. Cars cre-

give examples

ated new industries and demands for new services.

too vague, needs tighter topic sentence. Improve sentence variety.

Second Draft

The automobile reshaped the American landscape. As millions of cars jammed crowded streets and bogged down on unpaved roads, drivers demanded better highways. Soon great bridges spanned the Hudson, Delaware, and Mississippi to accommodate the flood of traffic. The cities pushed beyond rail and trolley lines, absorbing farms, meadows, and marshland. The middle class abandoned the polluted congestion of the city for the mushrooming suburbs that offered greater space and privacy. Gas stations, garages, parking structures, drive-in movies appeared across the country. Motels, chain stores, and fast food restaurants catered to the mobile public. Shopping malls, office towers, factories, and schools appeared in the new communities, all of them surrounded by what the cities could not offer—free parking.

EDITING SENTENCES

After revising the main elements of the draft, you can edit sentences to eliminate errors and improve clarity.

Common Grammar Errors

When editing drafts, look for common grammar errors:

Fragments

Fragments are incomplete sentences. Sentences require a subject and a verb and must state a complete thought:

Tom works until midnight.	**sentence**
Tom working until midnight	**fragment (incomplete verb)**
Works until midnight.	**fragment (subject missing)**
Because Tom works until midnight.	**fragment (incomplete thought)**

Notice that even though the last item has a subject, *Tom*, and a verb, *works*, it does not state a complete thought.

Run-ons and Comma Splices

Run-ons and comma splices are incorrectly punctuated compound sentences. Simple sentences (independent clauses) can be joined to create compound sentences in two ways:

1. Link with a **semicolon (;)**

2. Link with a **comma (,) + and, or, yet, but,** or **so**

```
I was born in Chicago, but           correct
   I grew up in Dallas.
I studied French; Jan took Italian.  correct
We have to take a cab my battery is dead.  run-on
Jim is sick, the game is canceled.   comma splice
```

Subject-Verb Agreement

Subjects and verbs must match in number. Singular subjects use singular verbs and plural subjects use plural verbs:

```
The boy walks to school.        singular
The boys walk to school.        plural
The cost of drugs is rising.    singular (the subject is cost)
Two weeks is not enough time    singular (amounts of time
                                   and money are singular)
The jury is deliberating.       singular (group subjects are
                                   singular)
The teacher or the students     plural (when two subjects
   are invited                     are joined with or, the subject
                                   nearer the verb determines
                                   whether it is singular or plural)
```

Pronoun Agreement

Pronouns must agree or match the nouns they represent:

```
Everyone should cast his or her vote.     singular
The children want their parents to call.  plural
```

The most misused pronoun is *they. They* is a pronoun and should clearly refer to a noun. Avoid unclear use of pronouns as in, "Crime is rising. Schools are failing. *They* just don't care." Who does *they* refer to?

Dangling and Misplaced Modifiers

To prevent confusion, modifiers—words and phrases that add information about other words—should be placed near the words they modify.

```
Rowing across the lake,          dangling (who was rowing?
   the moon rose over the water.    the moon?)
Rowing across the lake, we saw the  correct
   moon rise over the water.
```

She borrowed the car and drove to school, which was illegal, and was fired.	**misplaced** (what was *illegal*, borrowing the car or driving to school?)
She *illegally* borrowed the car and drove to school and was fired.	**correct**

Faulty Parallelism

Pairs and lists of words and phrases should match in form:

Jim is tall, handsome, and an athlete.	**not parallel** (list mixes adjectives and a noun)
Jim is tall, handsome, and athletic.	**parallel** (all adjectives)
We need to paint the bedroom, shovel the walk, and the basement must be cleaned.	**not parallel** (The last item does not match with *to paint* and to *shovel*.)
We need to *paint* the bedroom, *shovel* the walk, and *clean* the basement.	**parallel** (all verb phrases)

Awkward Shifts in Person
Avoid awkward shifts in person:

We climbed the tower and you could see for miles.	**awkward shift from *we* to *you***
We climbed the tower and *we* could see for miles.	**correct**
If *a student* works hard, *you* can get an A.	**awkward shift from *student* to *you***
If *you* work hard, *you* can get an A.	**correct**

Awkward Shifts in Tense
Avoid awkward shifts in tense (time):

Hamlet *hears* from a ghost, then he avenged his father.	**awkward shift from present to past**
Hamlet *heard* from a ghost, then he *avenged* his father.	**correct (both past)**
Hamlet *hears* from a ghost, then he *avenges* his father.	**correct (both present)**

IMPROVING SENTENCES

Along with editing the grammar of your draft, examine the sentences in each paragraph. Read each sentence separately to make sure it expresses the thoughts you intended.

Sentence Checklist

- Does the sentence support the paragraph's controlling idea? Could it be eliminated?

- Are key ideas emphasized through specific words and active verbs?

- Are secondary ideas subordinated?

- Are the relationships between ideas clearly expressed with transitional expressions?

- Do the tone and style of the sentence suit your reader and the nature of the document?

Be Brief

Sentences lose their power when cluttered with unnecessary words and phrases. When writing the rough draft, it is easy to slip in expressions that add nothing to the meaning of the sentence.

Original:	In today's modern world, computer literacy is essential to entering into the job market.
Improved:	Computer literacy is essential to entering the job market.

Phrases that begin with *who is* or *which were* can often be shortened:

Original:	Viveca Scott, *who was an ambitious business leader*, doubled profits, *which stunned her stockholders*.
Improved:	Viveca Scott, an ambitious business leader, stunned her stockholders by doubling profits.

Delete Wordy Phrases

Even skilled writers use wordy phrases in trying to express themselves in a first draft. When editing, locate phrases that can be replaced with shorter phrases or single words:

Wordy

Then you have a lot of students out there with a lot of debt.

Improved

Many students are deep in debt.

Wordy	Improved
at that period of time	then
in this day and age	now
in the near future	soon
winter months	winter
round in shape	round
blue in color	blue
for the purpose of informing	to inform
render an examination of	examine
make an analysis	analyze
started to pack	packed
went to go to work	went to work

Eliminate Redundancy

Repeating or restating words and ideas can have a dramatic effect, but it is a technique that should be used sparingly and only when you wish to emphasize a specific point.

Redundant: The computer has revolutionized education, revolutionizing delivery systems, course content, and teaching methods.

Improved: The computer has revolutionized educational delivery systems, course content, and teaching methods.

Avoid Placing Minor Details in Separate Sentences

Sentences should express ideas, not simply state a minor detail that can be incorporated into a related sentence:

Awkward

The mayor demanded a new budget. This was on Tuesday.
I bought a Corvette. It was red.

Improved

```
The mayor demanded a new budget on Tuesday.
I bought a red Corvette.
```

Vary Sentence Types

You can keep your writing interesting and fresh by altering types of sentences. Repeating a single kind of sentence can give your writing a monotonous predictability. A short sentence isolates an idea and gives it emphasis, but a string of choppy sentences explaining minor details robs your essay of power. Long sentences can subordinate minor details and show the subtle relationships among ideas, but they can become tedious for readers to follow.

Unvaried:
```
Mary Sanchez was elected to the assembly. She
worked hard on the budget committee. Her work
won her respect. She was highly regarded by the
mayor. People responded to her energy and drive.
She became popular with voters. The mayor de-
cided to run for governor. He asked Mary Sanchez
to manage his campaign.
```

Varied:
```
Mary Sanchez was elected to the assembly. Her hard
work on the budget committee won her respect, es-
pecially from the mayor. Voters were impressed by
her drive and energy. When the mayor decided to
run for governor, he asked Mary Sanchez to manage
his campaign.
```

EDITING WORDS

Your writing will improve when you make careful decisions about *diction*, the choice of appropriate words.

Diction Checklist

- Are the words accurate? Have you chosen words that precisely reflect your thinking?

- Is the level of diction appropriate? Do your words suit the tone and style of the document?

- Do connotations suit your purpose or do they detract from your message?

- Are technical terms clearly defined?
- Do you use specific rather than abstract words?

Use Words Precisely

Many words are easily confused. Should a patient's heart rate be monitored *continually* (meaning at regular intervals, such as once an hour) or *continuously* (meaning without interruption)? Is the city council planning to *adapt* or *adopt* a budget? Did the mayor make an *explicit* or *implicit* statement?

Your writing can influence readers only if you use words that accurately reflect your meaning. There are numerous pairs of frequently confused words:

allusion	an indirect reference
illusion	a false or imaginary impression
infer	to interpret
imply	to suggest
conscience (noun)	a sense of moral or ethical conduct
conscious (adjective)	awake or aware of something
principle	a basic law or concept
principal	something or someone important, such as school *principal*
affect (verb)	to change or modify
effect (noun)	a result

Use Specific Words

Specific words communicate more information and make clearer impressions than abstract words, which express only generalized concepts.

Abstract	Specific
motor vehicle	pickup truck
modest suburban home	three-bedroom colonial
individual	boy
protective headgear	helmet
residential rental unit	studio apartment
digestive ailment	heartburn
educational facility	high school

Avoid Sexist Language

Sexist language either ignores the existence of one gender or promotes negative attitudes about men or women.

Replace sexist words with neutral terms:

Sexist	Nonsexist
mankind	humanity
postman	letter carrier
policeman	police officer
chairman	chairperson

Avoid using male pronouns when nouns refer to both genders. The single noun *man* takes the single male pronoun *he*. If you are writing about a boys' school, it is appropriate to substitute "he" for the noun "student." But if the school includes both males and females, both should be represented:

> Every student should try *his or her* best.
> All students should try *their* best.

Plural nouns take the pronouns *they* and *their*, avoiding wordy *he or she* and *his or her* constructions.

Avoid Clichés

Clichés are worn-out phrases. Once creative or imaginative, these phrases, like jokes you have heard more than once, have lost their impact. In addition, clichés allow simplistic statements to substitute for genuine thought:

white as snow	back in the day	acid test
perfect storm	in the thick of it	on pins and needles
evil as sin	dead heat	crushing blow
viable option	bottom line	all that jazz
crack of dawn	calm before the storm	dog-tired

Use Appropriate Levels of Diction

The style and tone of your writing are shaped by the words you choose. Your goal, your reader, the discourse community, and the document itself usually indicate the kind of language that is appropriate. Informal language that might be acceptable in a note to a coworker may be unsuited to a formal report or article written for publication.

Formal: Sales representatives are required to maintain company vehicles at their own expense. (employee manual)

Standard: Salespeople must pay for routine maintenance of their cars. (business letter)

Informal: Remind the reps to change their oil every 3,000 miles. (email)

Slang expressions can be creative and attention getting, but they may be inappropriate and detract from the credibility of formal documents.

Appreciate the Impact of Connotations

Connotations are implied or suggested meanings. Connotations reflect a writer's values, views, and attitudes toward a subject. A resort cabin can be described as a *rustic cottage* or a *seedy shack*. The person who spends little money and shops for bargains can be praised for being *thrifty* or ridiculed for being *cheap*. The design of a skyscraper can be celebrated as being *clean and streamlined* or criticized for appearing *stark and sterile*.

The following pairs of words have the same *denotation* or basic meaning but their connotations create strikingly different impressions:

young	inexperienced
traditional	old-fashioned
brave	ruthless
casual	sloppy
the homeless	bums
unintended landing	plane crash
teenage prank	vandalism
uncompromising	stubborn
strong	dictatorial
free	lawless
interviewed	interrogated
tax break	tax relief
destroy a wetland	clear a swamp
developer	homebuilder
gambling interests	gaming industry
abortionist	abortion provider
lobbyist	activist
public servant	government bureaucrat

CREDITS

Text

Chapter 4. 70: "A Doctor's Dilemma" by James Dillard from NEWSWEEK, June 12, 1995. Copyright © 1995 Newsweek, Inc. All rights reserved. Reprinted by permission. **74:** "Champion of the World" copyright © 1969 and renewed 1997 by Maya Angelou from I KNOW WHY THE CAGED BIRD SINGS by Maya Angelou. Used by permission of Random House, Inc.

Chapter 5. 129: "Letter from Ground Zero: The Power of the Powerful" by Jonathan Schell reprinted with permission from the October 15, 2001 issue of THE NATION. For subscription information, call 1-800-333-8536. Portions of each week's Nation magazine can be accessed at http://www.thenation.com.

Photographs

P3.1	**Pg. 56 (b)** © Bettmann/CORBIS
P3.2	**Pg. 57 (br)** © CORBIS
P3.3	**Pg. 58 (tl)** © Dennis Stock, 1955/MAGNUM
P3.4	**Pg. 59 (t)** AP Photo
P3.5	**Pg. 62 (t)** US Army Signal Corps/Time & Life Pictures/Getty Images
P3.6	**Pg. 63 (tr)** © SuperStock
P3.7	**Pg. 63 (b)** © MAGNUM
P4.1	**Pg. 106 (c)** © Michael Ainsworth /Dallas Morning News/Corbis
P5.1	**Pg. 159 (t)** Mary Ellen Mark
P6.1	**Pg. 211 (t)** © JIM BOURG/Reuters/Corbis

INDEX

absolute statements, avoidance of, 18–19
abstract words, examples of, 119
academic disciplines, writing for, 11–13
ad hominem attacks, avoidance of, 19
Adler, Mortimer, 411–416
age, in perceptual world, 10
alternative interpretations
    in analysis, 303, 344
    ignorance of, 20
Alton Enterprises, 341–342
"American Islam," 142–146
American Psychological Association (APA)
        documentation guidelines,
        A-566–A-569
analysis, 299–349
    blending the modes in, 323, 331, 339
    checklist for, 349
    critical thinking, 302–303
    defined, 299–300
    detailed observation, 301–302
    readings, 305–342
    reading strategies for, 303–304
    student paper example of, 346–349
    subjective and objective, 300–301
    topics for, 345
    of visual images, 343–344
    in writing, 4
    writing strategies for, 344
Angelou, Maya, 82–86
appeals
    effectiveness of, 540
    to hostile readers, 505–506
    persuasive appeals, 502–504
appreciating language
    analysis, 304, 307, 311, 315, 323, 327, 332,
        339, 342
    argument and persuasion, 507, 510–511, 516,
        521, 525, 529, 533, 536, 538
    cause and effect, 462, 464–465, 468, 472, 476,
        480, 484, 486, 491

comparison, 227, 229–230, 233, 236, 240, 245,
    249, 256, 259
definition, 172, 177, 180, 183, 187–188, 191,
    197, 205, 210
description, 122, 124, 128, 131, 136, 140,
    145–146, 153, 155, 158
division and classification, 357, 362, 366, 371,
    376, 381, 387, 392–393, 394
narration, 68–69, 73, 77, 80, 85, 90, 95, 102, 105
process, 410, 415, 420, 424, 427, 431, 435,
    439, 442
argument and persuasion, 501–549
    checklist for, 548–549
    critical thinking for, 506–507
    defined, 501–502
    hostile readers and, 505–506
    persuasive appeals, 502–504
    purpose of, 5, 500
    readings in, 508–538
    reading strategies for, 506–507
    student paper example for, 543–548
    topics for, 541–542
    visual image analysis, 539–540
    writing strategies, 540–541
assertions, qualifying of, 494
associations, causes mistaken for, 461
assumptions
    avoiding errors in, 20
    critical thinking about, 21
audience
    for analysis, 304
    for argument and persuasion, 506
    for comparison and contrast, 226
    for definitions, 171
    for description, 122
    reader as, 7–8
Austin, James, 368–372

background information, in process writing, 406
backup of computer writing, 42

Barrett, Paul M., 142–146
Bayou Printing, 154–155
begging the question, avoidance of, 19
beginning and end, in process writing, 406
Begley, Sharon, 242–245, 275–278
Bell, Gordon, 333–340
Benton, Thomas H. (pseudonym), 377–382
bias
    comparison and contrast, 226
    evaluation in analysis, 302
    visual image analysis and, 64
"Black Men and Public Space," 477–481
"Black Political Leadership," 53–55
blending the modes
    analysis, 323, 331, 339
    argument and persuasion, 510, 516, 520
    cause and effect, 480, 487, 499
    comparison and contrast, 249, 256
    definitions, 177, 187, 197, 205, 210, 218
    description, 136, 145, 152
    division and classification, 362, 372, 387, 392
    narration, 73, 76, 80, 102
    process, 415, 423, 439
Bletter, Diana, 474–476
body language, visual image analysis and, 64
"Bomb, The," 123–125
"Border Story," 129–132
borrowed authority, avoidance of, 19
Braaksma, Andrew, 78–81
brainstorming, guidelines for, 24–25
Brown, Lee P., 485–487
Budish, Armond D., 417–420
Burciaga, José Antonio, 133–136

Capote, Truman, 126–128
Carson, Rachel, 231–233
Castro, Janice, 178–180
categories
    in classification writing, 355–356
    in division writing, 353
Catton, Bruce, 237–241
cause and effect
    checklist for, 499–500
    critical thinking strategies for, 460–462
    deduction and induction, 456–458
    defined, 455–456
    errors involving, 20–21
    establishment of, 458–459
    examples of, 5
    readings in, 463–492
    reading strategies for, 462
    results predictions, 459–460
    student paper example for, 496–499
    in writing, 5
    writing strategies for, 494

"Champion of the World," 82–86
checklists
    analysis, 349
    argument and persuasion, 548–549
    cause and effect, 499–500
    comparison and contrast, 267
    definition, 218–219
    description, 165–166
    division and classification, 404
    internet sources, A-553–A-555
    narration, 114
    process, 453
"Chinese Space, American Space," 228–230
chronology, in narration, 67–68
citations
    APA style for, A-566–A-569
    MLA style for, A-558–A-634
class, in perceptual world, 10
class discussion, preparation for, 50
classification
    checklist for, 404
    critical thinking for, 355
    defined, 351–354
    division vs., 354
    reading strategies for, 356–357
    student paper example for, 401–404
    in writing, 4
    writing strategies for, 398
"Cleaning Battery Terminals," 441–443
clichés, avoidance of, 120
"Closing the Credibility Gap," 324–327
clustering, prewriting with, 25–26
cohesion, in collaborative writing, 43
collaborative writing
    examples of, 1–2
    guidelines for, 42–44
communication
    different styles of, 257–259
    writing as, 7–8
"Communications Styles: United States and
        Taiwan," 257–259
"Company Man, The," 181–183
comparison
    definition through, 170
comparison and contrast, 221–267
    checklist for, 267
    defined, 221–223
    organizing papers using, 223–226
    point-by-point method, 225–226
    purposes of, 222–223
    reading strategies for, 226–227
    student paper as example for, 263–267
    subject-by-subject method, 224–225
    writing strategies for, 261
composing style, creation of, 34

compositions
    final draft, 36–37
    guidelines for writing, 33–41
    planning for, 36
    prewriting phase of, 35–36
    revised draft, instructor's annotations, 37–39
computers
    collaborative writing using, 44
    internet searches on, 45
    writing on, 41–42
conclusions, qualifying of, 494
    in argument and persuasion, 540
connotation
    in descriptions, 120–121
    ethical issues, 121
    visual image analysis, 60–61
context
    argument and persuasion, 541–542
    cause and effect, 495
    definitions in, 170–171, 213–214
    description, 162
    division and classification, 400
    in essay writing, 33
    narration, 109
    process, 446–447
    visual image analysis and, 56–64
    writer's role in, 6–7
    writing and, 2–3, 13
contrast, visual image analysis and, 57–59
Cook, Dan, 178–180
Covenant House, 537–538
"Covenant House Needs Your Help," 537–538
critical reading
    class discussion preparation, 52
    example exercise in, 53–55
    learning by, 49
    strategies for, 49–52
    Sundance Reader method, 55–56
    visual image analysis, 56–64
critical thinking
    analysis, 307, 311,315, 322, 327, 331,
        339, 342
    argument and persuasion, 506, 510, 511, 517,
        520, 524, 529, 533, 536
    cause and effect, 464, 468, 472, 476, 480, 484,
        486, 487, 491, 493
    comparison and contrast, 236, 240, 244, 249,
        255, 259
    definition, 176, 180, 183, 187, 188, 191,197,
        205, 211
    description, 124, 128, 131–132, 140, 145,
        153, 155
    division and classification, 352, 355, 362, 366,
        371, 372, 376, 380, 386, 392, 394
    narration, 72,76, 80, 85, 90, 94, 102, 104

process, 415, 420, 423, 426, 431, 435, 439
    want ad example, 154–155
    writing and, 15–22
cultural definitions, 168–169
cultural issues, visual image analysis and, 62–63

data
    in analysis, 302, 304, 344, 345
    filtering, avoidance of, 303
Declaration of Independence, as collaborative
        writing, 42–43
Declaration of Independence, The, 488–492
deduction, cause and effect writing and,
        456–457
definition, 167–219
    checklist for, 218–219
    context for, 170
    cultural definition, 168–169
    evolving definition, 168
    invented definition, 169
    methods of, 169–170
    personal definition, 169
    purpose of, 170
    qualifying definition, 168
    reading strategies for, 171–172
    regulatory definition, 168
    standard definition, 167–168
    student paper as example for, 215–218
    topics using, 213
    in writing, 3–4
    writing strategies using, 212–213
denotation, in descriptions, 120–121
description, 115–166
    blending the modes, 136, 145, 152
    definitions of, 115–116
    definition through, 169
    denotation and connotation in, 120–121
    examples of, 115–118
    objective description, 116–118
    in process, 407
    readings in, 123–158
    reading strategies for, 122
    resume as, 156–157
    strategies for writing, 160–161
    subjective description, 116–118
    topic suggestions for, 161–162
    verbs in, 120
    want ad as example of, 154–155
    in writing, 3
details
    analysis, 302
    argument and persuasion, 502
    critical thinking about, 16
    description, 115–118
    process, 406–407

Dillard, James, 65–66, 74–77
directions, in process writing, 407–409
disagreements, in collaborative writing, 44
discussion, writer's block management and, 45
"Distracted: The New News World and the Fate of Attention," 512–517
division and classification, 351–404
   checklist for, 404
   critical thinking for, 352–353
   defined, 351–352
   readings in, 358–396
   reading strategies for, 356–357
   student paper example for, 401–404
   topics, 399–400
   writing strategies for, 398
"Doctor's Dilemma, A," 64–65, 74–77
documentation of sources, A-551–A-570
   APA guidelines for, A-566–A-569
   criteria for, A-553
   internet sources checklist, A-553–A-555
   limitations and exceptions to, A-552–A-553
   MLA guidelines for, A-558–A-566
   problem avoidance strategies, A-569–A-570
   sample documented essay, A-564–A-566
dominant impressions, critical thinking about, 16
"Doublespeak," 382–387
drafts
   final drafts, 39–40
   first drafts, 36–39
duplication, visual image analysis, 61
"Dyslexia," 173–177

"East vs. West: One Sees the Big Picture, The Other is Focused," 242–245
editing, in essay writing, 34
education, in perceptual world, 10
effects, causes mistaken for, 461
"Effects of the Telephone, The," 433–435
Einstein, Albert, 1–2
"E-Memory Revolution, The," 333–340
emotion, persuasive appeal and, 503
Encyclopedia of Psychology, 207–208
"End the Demand, End the Supply," 485–487
errors, in critical thinking, 18–21
essays, writing guidelines for, 33–34
ethical issues
   connotation and, 121
   persuasive appeals based on, 503–504
"Evaluating a Job Opportunity," 432–435
evaluating strategy
   analysis, 304, 307, 311, 315, 322–323, 327, 331, 339, 342
   argument and persuasion, 506–507, 510, 516, 520, 524, 529, 533, 536, 538

cause and effect, 462, 464, 468, 472, 476, 480, 484, 487, 491
comparison and contrast, 227, 229, 233, 236, 240, 244, 249, 255–256, 259
definition, 171, 176–177, 180, 183, 187, 191, 197, 205, 210
description, 122, 124, 128, 131, 135–136, 140, 145–146, 152, 155, 157
division and classification, 357, 362, 366, 372, 376, 380–381, 386–387, 392, 394
for essay writing, 34
narration, 68, 72–73, 76, 80, 85, 90, 94, 102, 104
process, 410, 415, 420, 423, 427, 431, 435, 439, 442
in resumes, 156
want ads example, 154
evidence
   in cause and effect writing, 494
   collection and evaluation of, 29–30
   logic and presentation of, 502
evolving definitions, 168
examples
   definition through, 169
   in process, 407
   thesis support from, 29–30
existing definitions, 212
experts
   writing by, 13
   writing for, 13
explanations, in process writing, 405–407
extended definitions, 170
   relevancy of, 212
extended readership, writing for, 8

facts
   critical thinking about, 21–22
   documentation of, A-553
   thesis support from, 29–30
false analogy, avoidance of, 19, 303
false dilemma, avoidance of, 19
"Fender-Bender, The," 87–90
"Fender-Benders: Legal Do's and Dont's," 417–420
figurative language, in description, 120
film
   context in visual analysis of, 59–60
   visual analysis of, 57
filtering of data, avoidance of, 20
final draft, for compositions, 39–41
first drafts
   analysis, 346–347
   argument and persuasion, 543–545
   cause and effect, 496–497

comparison and contrast, 263–265
compositions, 36–39
definition, 215–216
description, 163–164
division and classification, 401–402
narration, 110–112
process, 448–450
first reading, strategies for, 50
focus, in narration, 66–67
"Four Kinds of Chance," 368–372
freewriting
for essays, 35
guidelines for, 23–24
writer's block management using, 45
Friedman, Thomas, 309–312
"Friends, Good Friends—and Such Good Friends,"
358–363

Gansberg, Martin, 91–95
Garcia, Cristina, 178–180
Gatto, John Taylor, 466–469
Gemmel, Jim, 333–340
gender
in perceptual world, 10
visual image analysis and, 62–63
generalizations, avoidance of, 303
"Get Out the Wallets," 313–317
goals
in cause and effect writing, 494
for collaborative writing, 42–43
writer's block management and identification
of, 44
Goodman, Ellen, 181–183
grammar checks, on computers, 42
"Grant and Lee," 237–241
Grinslade, Liz, 432–435
group focus, in collaborative writing, 43

Harris, Marvin, 405–406, 421–424
hasty generalizations, avoidance of, 18
hazards, in process writing, 408
history, cause and effect writing
and, 455
hostile readers, appeals to, 505–506
"How Our Skins Got Their Color," 405–406,
421–424
"How Television Distorts Reality," 300–301,
317–323
"How to Mark a Book," 411–416
"Hyphenated Americans," 531–533

images, in process writing, 409. See also visual
image analysis
In Cold Blood, 126–128
individual readers, writing for, 8

induction, cause and effect writing and,
457–458, 494
inflated phrases, avoidance of, 120
information, in analytical writing, 299
"In Praise of the 'F' Word," 518–521
instructors
annotations from, 37–39
writer's block and discussions with, 45
internet sources, documentation checklist,
A-553–A-555
interpretations, avoidance of slippery
slope, 461
in-text citations
APA guidelines for, A-566–A-569
MLA guidelines for, A-558–A-566
introduction, in argument and persuasion
writing, 540
invented definitions, 169
"I Refuse to Live in Fear," 474–476

Jackson, Maggie, 512–517
Jacques, Martin, 522–525
Jefferson, Thomas, 488–492
Jencks, Christopher, 251–256
"Job Announcement," 154–155
judgments, critical thinking about, 21–22

Kenna, Peggy, 257–259
King, Martin Luther Jr., 364–367

Lacy, Sondra, 257–259
Lamont, Lansing, 123–125
learning
critical reading as tool for, 49
documentation in support of, A-552
legal definitions, 182
"Listening to Madness," 184–188
Literary Digest, 459
locations for writing, writer's block management
and changes in, 46
logic, as persuasive appeal, 502–503
logical fallacies, 302–303
logical stages, in process writing, 406
Lord, Walter, 67, 103–105
Lutz, William, 382–387

Malcolm X, 436–440
Malveaux, Julianne, 534–536
Manhattan Project, 2
manipulation of images, visual image analysis,
61–62
Martin, Andres, 388–393
measurement standards, in classification
writing, 355
meeting guidelines, for collaborative writing, 43

Miller, Russell, 118
mistakes, anticipation in process writing of, 409
Mizell, Louis R. Jr., 301, 328–332
moderators, for collaborative writing, 44
Modern Language Association (MLA)
        documentation, guidelines and examples
        of, A-558–A-566
modes of writing, 3–4
Moskos, Peter, 482–484
Motion Picture Association of America,
        394–396
Mukherjee, Bharati, 246–250
"My Ecumenical Father," 133–136
"My First Conk," 436–440

narration, 65–114
    basic principles of, 65
    checklist for, 114
    chronology in, 67–68
    examples of, 65–66
    focus in, 66–67
    in process writing, 405
    readings in, 69–106
    reading strategies for, 68
    student paper example, 110–114
    topic guidelines for, 108–109
    writer's purpose in, 65–66
    in writing, 3
    writing strategies for, 107–108
"Neat People, Sloppy People," 234–236
"Needs," 189–192
negative instructions, in process, 409
non sequiturs, avoidance of, 19
note cards, writer's block management using, 45
numbered steps, in process, 409
numbers, documentation of, A-553

objective analysis, 270–271
objective description
    examples of, 117, 124, 128, 145
    principles of, 115–116
objective narration, 66
"Once More to the Lake," 147–153
"On Teenagers and Tattoos," 388–393
opinions
    critical thinking about, 21
    facts vs., 302–303
    thesis statements as, 28
opposing viewpoints
    argument and persuasion, 522–530,
        531–536
    cause and effect, 482–487
organization techniques, comparison and contrast,
    223–226

Orwell, George, 96–102
Oswald, Lee Harvey, FBI report on
    description in, 116
"Our Friend the Smear," 373–376
outlines, development guidelines for, 30–33
"Out There," 126–128
oversimplification, avoidance of, 352–353

paraphrases, guidelines for using, A-557
"Parents: Stay Ahead of the Curve!," 394–396
parts of the whole
    in analysis, 303
    avoidance of, 20
    in classification, 355
    inclusion of, 353
past experience, in perceptual world, 9–10
past performance, faulty future predictions based
    on, 461
Pei, Minxin, 526–530
perception, visual image analysis and, 64
perceptual world, in communications research,
    9–11
Pérez, Ramon "Tianguis," 87–90
personal definitions, 169
personal experience, thesis support from, 29
personal observation, thesis support from, 29
perspective, visual image analysis and, 57–59
persuasion
    critical thinking for writing, 506–507
    defined, 5, 501–502
    definitions and, 170
    hostile readers and, 505–506
    persuasive appeals, 502–505
    reading strategies for, 506–507
    in writing, 5
persuasive appeals, 502–505
Philips, Joseph C., 193–198
photographs. See also visual image analysis
    gender and cultural issues in analysis, 62–63
    perspective and contrast in, 57–59
    visual analysis of, 56–64
plagiarism
    avoiding plagiarism, 46–47
    collaborative writing and avoidance of, 44
    source documentation and, A-551–A-552
planning phase of writing, compositions, 36
point-by-point method, comparison and contrast,
    225–226
political connotations, visual image analysis and,
    60–61
post hoc reasoning, errors in, 20
prediction of results, cause and effect and,
    459–460
"Preliminary Security Analysis," 341–342

prewriting
    compositions, 35–36
    guidelines for, 23–27
process, 405–454
    checklist, 453
    critical thinking strategies, 406–407, 408–409
    defined, 405
    explanations, 4, 405–407
    giving directions in, 407–409
    readings, 411–443
    reading strategies, 410
    strategies for, 445
    student paper example for, 448–453
    topics for, 445–447
professional experience, in perceptual world, 10
propaganda, vs. persuasion, 541
purpose
    analysis, 344
    argument and persuasion, 540
    comparison and contrast, 222–223
    definition, 170
    description, 118
    narration, 65–66

qualifying definitions, 168
Quart, Alissa, 184–188
questions
    in analysis, 299
    prewriting using, 26–27
Quindlen, Anna, 478–481
quotations
    documentation of, A-553
    guidelines for using, A-555–A-557

Radford, Benjamin, 317–323
Raudsepp, Eugene, 428–431
readers
    cause and effect and needs of, 462
    hostile reader, appeals to, 505–506
    process, 408
    role in writing of, 7–11
readings. See specific authors and titles
reading strategies
    analysis, 303–304
    argument and persuasion, 506–507
    cause and effect, 462
    comparison and contrast, 226–227
    critical reading, 49–55
    definition, 171–172
    description, 122
    division and classification, 356–357
    narration, 68
    process, 410
Rechy, John, 117

"Reconstructed Logbook of the Titanic, The,"
    103–105
recursive writing process, defined, 34
red herrings, avoidance of, 19
reference groups, in perceptual world, 9
references list, APA guidelines for, A-566–A-569
regulatory definitions, 168
"Reinventing the American Dream," 251–256
research papers, cause and effect writing and, 456
responding to images
    analysis, 343–344
    argument and persuasion, 539–540
    cause and effect, 493
    comparison, 260–261
    definition, 211–212
    description, 159
    division and classification, 397
    narration, 106–107
    process, 444
responsibility, in process writing, 408
resumes, as description, 156–158
"Resumes That Rate a Second Look," 425–427
revisions
    analysis, 347–349
    argument and persuasion, 545–547
    cause and effect, 497–499
    comparison and contrast, 263–267
    definition, 216–218
    description, 164–165
    division and classification, 402–404
    narration, 112–114
    process writing, 451–452
    revised drafts with instructor's annotations,
        36–39
role
    analysis, 300–301
    definition, 212
    description, 160
Roosevelt, Franklin D., 2
Rosenberg, Don D., 209–210
Rosenberg, Scott, 324–327
Rowan, Carl T., 115, 137–141

scope of analysis, 302
Scudder, Samuel, 69–73
second reading, strategies for, 50–52
"Seeing Your Way Past Interview Jitters," 428–431
self-contained directions, in process writing, 408
"Seven Deadly Sins of Students, The," 377–381
Sherry, Mary, 518–521
"Shooting an Elephant," 96–102
"Silent Spring," 231–233
Simpson, Eileen, 173–177
situational needs, definitions and, 212

"slippery slope" interpretations, avoidance of, 461
social roles, in perceptual world, 9–10
software for writing, evaluation of, 41–42
"Some Lessons From the Assembly Line," 78–81
sources
    analysis, 344
    cause and effect and evaluation of, 494
    documentation guidelines for, A-551–A-570
    documentation problems, avoidance of, A-569–A-570
    in sample documented essay, A-564–A-566
Sowell, Thomas, 189–192
"Spanglish," 178–180
specific words, examples of, 119
spell-and-grammar software, writing using, 42
standard definitions, 167–168
standards
    in analysis, 302
    mixing of, 355
    writer's block management and lowering of, 45
Staples, Brent, 477–481
statistics
    documentation of, A-553
    thesis support from, 30
status, in perceptual world, 10–11
"Still Hyphenated Americans," 534–536
Stransky, Tanner, 470–473
student papers
    analysis, 346–348
    argument and persuasion, 543–547
    cause and effect, 496–498
    comparison and contrast, 263–266
    definition, 215–216
    description, 163–164
    division and classification, 401–403
    narration, 110–113
    process, 448–452
    sample documented essay, A-564–A-566
"Stuff is Not Salvation," 508–511
subject-by-subject method, comparison and
    contrast papers, 224–225
subjective analysis, 300
subjective description, 116–118
subjective narration, 65–66
subject limitations, for analysis, 344
Sundance Reader, critical reading using, 55–56
supporting material, for theses, 29–30
synonyms, as definitions, 169
Szilard, Leo, 1–2

"Take This Fish and Look at It," 69–73
tape-recorded thoughts and notes, writer's block
    management using, 45
technical terms, in process, 406

Teller, Edward, 1–2
testimony, thesis support from, 29–30
testing of directions, in process, 409
thesis
    documentation in support of, A-552
    evolution of topic to, 27–28
    support for, 29–30
thesis statement, elements of, 28–29
"Thirty-eight Who Saw Murder and Didn't Call
    the Police," 91–95
thoughts and feelings, critical thinking about, 15
"Three Ways of Meeting Oppression,"
    364–367
timelines, as narrative, 103–104
time relationships
    cause and effect and, 460–461
    errors in, 20
    process and, 407
timing, visual image analysis, 61
"Too Dangerous Not to Regulate," 482–484
topics for writing
    analysis, 345
    argument and persuasion, 541–542
    cause and effect, 494–495
    comparison and contrast, 262
    critical thinking about, 15–17
    definition, 213–214
    description, 161–162
    division and classification, 399–400
    evolution to thesis from, 27–29
    limitations on, 28–29
    narration, 108–109
    process, 445–446
    writer's block and switching of, 45
transitional statements
    in comparison and contrast writing, 261
    in process writing, 407
Treganowan, Lucille, 441–443
"TV Addiction," 199–206
"Two Ways to Belong in America," 246–250

understanding meaning
    analysis, 304, 307, 311, 315, 322, 326, 331,
        339, 342
    argument and persuasion, 506, 510, 515–516,
        520, 524, 529, 532–533, 536, 538
    cause and effect, 462, 464, 468, 472, 475–476,
        479–480, 483–484, 486, 491
    comparison and contrast, 226, 229, 232, 236,
        240, 244, 249, 255, 259
    definition, 171, 176, 180, 182–183, 187, 191,
        196–197, 205, 209–210
    description, 122, 124, 128, 131, 135, 140, 145,
        152, 155, 157

division and classification, 352, 356, 366, 371, 375, 380, 386, 391–392, 394
  narration, 68, 72, 76, 79, 84–85, 90, 94, 101–102, 104
  process, 410, 415, 420, 423, 426, 430, 434, 439, 442
unexpected changes, anticipation of, 409
"Unforgettable Miss Bessie," 115, 137–141
unnecessary words, elimination of, 119–120
Urrea, Luis Alberto, 129–132

values, in perceptual world, 10
variations, in process writing, 406–407
verbs, diluted verbs, avoidance of, 120
video
  context in visual analysis of, 59–60
  visual analysis of, 57
Viorst, Judith, 358–363
visual aids
  in comparison and contrast writing, 261
  documentation of, A-553
visual image analysis
  context, 59
  critical reading and, 56–64
  cultural and political connotations in, 60–61
  gender and cultural issues, 62
  manipulating images, 61
  perception and analysis, 64
  perspective and contrast in, 57–59
  photographs, film, and video, 57
  timing and duplication, 61
  visual connotations, 60–61

want ads, as description, 154–155
Wasik, Bill, 373–376

Weisbord, Anne, 425–427
West, Cornel, 53–55
"What's in a Word?," 305–308
"What's Our Sputnik?," 309–312
"When China Rules the World," 522–525
White, E. B., 147–153
"Who is Black?," 193–198
"Who Killed Miss America?," 470–473
whole representations
  in analytical writing, 303
  avoidance of, 20
"Who's Listening to Your Cell Phone Calls?," 301, 328–332
"Why China Won't Rule the World," 526–530
"Why Schools Don't Educate," 466–469
Williams, Armstrong, 531–533
Winn, Marie, 199–206
words
  precision in use of, 118–119
  specific words, examples of, 119
works cited list, MLA guidelines for, A-557–A-559
writer
  goals and purposes of, 3–4
  role of, 6
writer's block, management strategies for, 44–46
writing
  on computers, 41–42
  process of, 15–47
writing contexts, 13
writing process, 15–47
writing strategies. See specific types of writing

Yi-Fu Tuan, 228–230

Zakaria, Fareed, 313–316